I0833315

1837
ARTES
SCIENTIA
VERITAS
LIBRARY OF THE
UNIVERSITY OF MICHIGAN
E PLURIBUS UNUM
TUEBOR
SI QUÆRIS PENINSULAM AMŒNAM
CIRCUMSPICE

Jewish Education

in

New York City

By

ALEXANDER M. DUSHKIN

Head of Department of Research, Bureau of Jewish Education

PUBLISHED BY

THE BUREAU OF JEWISH EDUCATION

NEW YORK

1918

Oversized Foldout

Jewish Education

in

New York City

By

ALEXANDER M. DUSHKIN

Head of the Department of Research
Bureau of Jewish Education

Submitted in partial fulfillment of the requirements for the degree of Doctor of Philosophy under the Faculty of Philosophy, Columbia University

Published by

The Bureau of Jewish Education
New York

1918

Lipshitz Press
New York

To

My Teacher and Friend

DR. SAMSON BENDERLY

A dauntless pioneer in American Jewish education
this book is dedicated

PREFACE

Whatever affects the education of American children — whether directly through the American public schools or indirectly through voluntary school systems — is of interest to the student of American education. This book, submitted in partial fulfillment of the requirements for the degree of Doctor of Philosophy under the Faculty of Philosophy (Teachers College), Columbia University, treats of the educational activities of the Jews of New York City in the light of their relation to American national aspirations, as the activities of a community that wishes to preserve its group life in this country. Only those educational activities have been included which are undertaken by Jews expressly for the continuance of Jewish ideas and institutions in America through the transmission of the Jewish race heritage to their children. The facts presented bear upon the general problem of America's national organization and development, particularly with respect to the assimilation and adjustment of American ethno-religious groups.

The available material has been studied historically and statistically, for the purpose of an educational survey. Since this is the first attempt to study Jewish educational activities in a comprehensive manner, the aim was rather to cover the whole field than to treat any portion or phase of it exhaustively. My purpose has been to sketch the entire problem, present the available data, and indicate the methods to be pursued in further investigation. Practically all discussion of American Jewish education hitherto has been in the form of opinion and of empiric conviction. What is greatly needed, both by Jews and by non-Jews, is a scientific literature which shall present the facts in Jewish education objectively, and interpret their significance to the Jewish community and to the American Commonwealth of which it is a part. I cherish the hope that this book may prove to be the first contribution toward a scientific literature on American Jewish education.

I desire gratefully to acknowledge my indebtedness to Professors George D. Strayer, E. L. Thorndike, William H. Kilpatrick and Richard Gottheil of Columbia University; to

Professors Israel Friedlaender and M. M. Kaplan of the Jewish Theological Seminary; and to Mr. Julius Drachsler, Secretary of the School for Jewish Communal Work, for their valuable criticism and for their many helpful suggestions. Thanks are also due to Mr. George H. Chatfield and Mr. Louis Siegel of the Board of Education for their courtesy in putting at my disposal the necessary public school records, and to Mr. A. S. Freidus, head of the Jewish Department of the New York Public Library, for his constant cooperation in the preparation of this work. From among my friends and co-workers who have helped me in many ways, I wish particularly to thank: Miss Lotta Levensohn for her generous sacrifice of time and energy and her painstaking care in editing the manuscript and reading the proofs; Miss Leah Klepper for her aid in the work of research; Mr. I. B. Berkson for his criticism of various portions of the book; and Mr. Meir Isaacs for the many hours which he spent unstintingly in cooperating with me in the obtaining of data, in statistical tabulation, and in preparing the index.

Finally, I must express my very deep obligations to Dr. S. Benderly, Director of the Bureau of Jewish Education and Chairman of the Administrative Committee of the School for Jewish Communal Work. Without him this work would not have been possible. His unfailing aid, stimulation and guidance have enabled me to undertake this work and to carry it through. Through the community of interests and aims which Dr. Benderly has created among the men and women whom he has gathered about him, this volume has become the offering not of myself alone, but of a group of workers in American Jewish education.

TABLE OF CONTENTS

PART I

HISTORY OF JEWISH EDUCATION IN NEW YORK CITY

CHAPTER I

THE SOCIAL BASES OF JEWISH EDUCATION IN AMERICA

CHAPTER II

HISTORY OF JEWISH EDUCATION IN NEW YORK BEFORE 1881

Jewish educational activity. Science and democracy.
pp. 129-141

Part II

STATUS OF JEWISH EDUCATION IN NEW YORK CITY IN 1918

Chapter I

EXTENT OF JEWISH EDUCATION IN NEW YORK CITY

Chapter II

JEWISH SCHOOL BUILDINGS AND ACCOMMODATION FOR JEWISH EDUCATION

Chapter III

ORGANIZATION OF JEWISH SCHOOLS
(Variation and Coördination)

Chapter IV

ORGANIZATION OF JEWISH SCHOOLS
(Administrative Control)

CHAPTER V

ORGANIZATION OF JEWISH SCHOOLS
(TIME-SCHEDULES)

CHAPTER VI

SCHOOL FINANCES

CHAPTER VII

SCHOOL MANAGEMENT
(THE PUPILS AND THEIR TREATMENT)

CHAPTER VIII

SCHOOL MANAGEMENT
(ELIMINATION AND RETARDATION)

CHAPTER IX

THE TEACHING STAFF

CHAPTER X

THE CONTENT OF JEWISH EDUCATION
(INTENSIVE CURRICULA)

CHAPTER XI

THE CONTENT OF JEWISH EDUCATION
(EXTENSIVE CURRICULA)

APPENDICES

Bibliography

PART I

The History of Jewish Education in New York City

Chapter I

THE SOCIAL BASES OF JEWISH EDUCATION IN AMERICA

There are over three million Jews in the United States,[1] residing in every state and every territory of the Union. The history of their coming to America extends from 1492, when Jewish sailors accompanied Columbus on his voyage of discovery,[2] to 1918, when war-ridden Jewish families are still making their way to this land, from out of the zone of fighting. In this land the Jews are making a struggle for adjustment to their American environment, an adjustment not only economic, but also social and psychic. Their social reorientation is of importance not only to themselves, but also to the country in which they live. How much of their cultural and religious heritage, how many of their folk ways, how much of their social organization shall they preserve, in order to live complete lives in America? How shall they educate their children so as to make them heirs of their social heritage, and, at the same time, insure their full adjustment as American citizens? These questions are of significance to the future of America and of American education.

To comprehend the educational implications of the Jewish problem of adjustment, it is necessary to know something of the complexity of Jewish life and of Jewish thinking in this country. While it is the intention of this book to describe the educational situation in New York rather than to discuss its principles and philosophy, nevertheless an analysis of the social forces which express themselves in education is essential for a discussion of Jewish education.[3] Such a review is needed particularly because, from the point of view of the American student of education, the modern Jewish school offers a virgin field.

No single analysis, briefly made, can describe the complexity of Jewish social life, in all of its details. As in every heterogeneous

---

[1] American Jewish Year Book, 1914-1915, calculates Jewish population of United States as 2,933,374, on July 1st, 1914.

[2] Kayserling, M. "Christopher Columbus and the participation of the Jews in Spanish and Portuguese Discoveries," 1894 (trans. Gross).

[3] The phrase "Jewish education" is used throughout this book instead of the more technically correct "Jewish training" or "Jewish instruction," because of the sanction of popular usage.

social group, there is no clear distinction between one class of Jews and another; they tend rather to merge into one another gradually. Any classification, by its very nature, must be an analysis of types, or perhaps of extremes, and not of distinct, mutually-exclusive groups. This analysis is made, then, merely for the sake of clearer comprehension of the situation, and not as an actual description of it. Moreover, the great majority of Jews, like other human beings, do not have the highly conscious motives in their living or thinking which the analyst sometimes imputes to them. The masses usually drift, and their lives are shaped largely through imitation or necessity. In the majority of cases, the American Jew does not hold to sharply distinct attitudes. His views are eclectic, and partake of the characteristics of several classes.

(A) Differences of Social Attitude Among Jews

Keeping these qualifying factors in mind, it is possible to proceed to an analysis of the Jewish social situation in America. Such an analysis may be either historical, showing how the differences in social attitude are the results of the different waves of migration of the Jews to this country, and the customs and ways of living which they brought with them, or, it may be an attempt to show a sociological cross-section of present Jewish life. As it will be necessary to trace the historical development later in dealing with the history of the Jewish schools in New York City, the cross-sectional view is here proposed.

The fundamental differences among the Jews of this country arise from the degree and the manner of their affiliation with the Jewish group. This affiliation expresses itself in various forms. It finds embodiment in the preservation of peculiar customs and festivals; in the organization of synagogues and schools; in the support of special Jewish philanthropies; in the formation of special Jewish societies (such as lodges, clubs, mutual benefit societies); in the organization of special representative Jewish bodies (such as the American Jewish Committee, the Jewish Communities [Kehillahs], and the American Jewish Congress); in marriage between Jews only; in the tendency to live together within certain neighborhoods; in the study and use of special languages (Hebrew and Yiddish); in a common interest in Palestine and in other Jewries of the world; in a Jewish press; in a Jewish theatre; in Jewish music, and in other forms of social living. Underlying all of these activities, and at the basis of whatever motives may be actuating those who are doing it, is the feeling that there is closer kinship and greater common responsibility between Jews, than between Jews and non-Jews. While American Jews participate fully and freely in the general social life of America, the great majority of them also join in special forms of social living, which bring them into closer contact with other Jews.

It is but natural to expect a heterogeneity of thought and social attitude in this large group of Jews. Indeed, there are differences among them concerning every phase of their social life in America, its aims, its content, and its methods.

Preservation and Fusion [4]

The most far reaching opposition is between those whose aim is to preserve Jewish group life, and those who wish to amalgamate or fuse with non-Jews in this country. This difference between preservation and fusion is a difference in *aim*, and is for that reason more irreconcilable than any other difference in social attitude among Jews. Whatever differences as to content and method may exist among those who aim to preserve Jewish life, they are united in disagreeing with those who look towards an immediate merging with the "Anglo-Saxon" group, or with those who wish that the Jews in this country shall fuse in the "Melting-Pot."

The most outspoken fusionists are those who consider themselves unaffiliated *individuals*, having no social affiliations as Jews, and desiring none. While they may be ready to admit their immediate Jewish antecedents, and even a theoretic interest in things Jewish, they nevertheless wish to make their adjustment to American life as individuals only. To this group belong not only many whose families have been here for generations, but also some who have but recently arrived. The characteristic attitude of both is their conscious severance of all social bonds

[4] "Fusion" is here used instead of the more customary term "assimilation," because, as will be pointed out later, "assimilation" has a different sociological connotation.

with the Jewish group. They take part in none of the forms of Jewish social life, and consciously or unconsciously allow themselves to fuse as *rapidly* as possible with the non-Jewish community.

But there are also *gradual fusionists,* those who consider themselves Jews temporarily, in the sense that they realize both the impossibility and the undesirability of cutting loose completely from their immediate past, and of abrogating peremptorily the customs and modes of living in which they were trained as children. They believe that *rapid* assimilation would be injurious both to the Jews and to America, and maintain that the method of fusion must be that of slow merging. They consider themselves members of the Jewish group, and are willing to take part in its common life; but they look upon it merely as a temporary modus vivendi, as a means for ultimate complete fusion. For the present, they are willing to support the agencies dealing with the *abnormal phases* of Jewish life: hospitals, immigration bureaus, homes for the aged, institutions for delinquents and orphans, poor relief organizations, and similar institutions. They are anxious to put the Jews in this country on a level at least equal to that of other Americans, in their struggle for existence and for social recognition. They maintain the spirit of the early Jewish immigrants to New Amsterdam, who, in 1654 promised Governor Peter Stuyvesant, "that the poor among them shall not become a burden to the community, but be supported by their own nation."[5] They do not, however, readily support the *normal* phases of Jewish life, particularly those which express themselves in the synagogue and in the religious school. Whenever they do support these institutions, they do so either because their non-Jewish neighbors support institutions of similar character, or as a matter of family custom, or in the spirit of philanthropy. Between these gradual fusionists and those who strive for the preservation of Jewish life in this country, there is naturally no sharply drawn line of demarcation.

In contradistinction to fusion is the attitude which deals with the entire problem of Jewish life as the problem of a community, which wishes to preserve the integrity of its group life. Those

[5] Oppenheim, Samuel: "The Early History of the Jews in New York, 1654-1664"; p. 8.

who hold this attitude believe that the continued conservation of those values which are worth while in Jewish life, can but work for the enrichment of the character of the American Jew, and must therefore redound to the benefit of America. They contend that America will accomplish its destiny to the fullest, only if it will permit complete social expression on the part of all the peoples which come to its shores, provided, of course, such expression is coöperative, and does not militate against the common good. This view seems to be in line with the thinking of many of the modern American social philosophers.[6]

Nation and Religion

Among the Jews who believe in the preservation of their group life, the greatest differences center around the problem of what they should preserve. There are those who look upon the Jews as a *religious body,* and would therefore continue the Jewish religious institutions and customs. The tendency for these is to emphasize the *expressions of life which are connected with the synagogue and with the religious customs of the family and the home.* The extreme followers of this attitude would tend to be almost *denominational* in their outlook, that is, they would classify the Jews as a group, not merely coördinate with Christians and Mohammedans, but coördinate even with sub-groups, such as Catholics and Protestants, and in some cases, with Episcopalians, Presbyterians and Methodists.

But the great majority of Jews make no distinction between religion and nationality. The group which looks upon the Jews as a religious body, greatly overlaps those who maintain that the Jews are a *nation.* The nationalists tend to stress what are commonly called the *cultural elements* of Jewish life: language, literature, historic consciousness, and common group life outside of the synagogue. The extreme nationalists would consider the Jews as a secular ethnic body, similar in every way to any other of the existing nationalities.

---

[6] Dewey, John: "Principles of Nationality" Menorah Journal, Sept. 1917. Adler, Felix: "A Vision of New York as the Democratic Metropolis," 1916. Kallen, H. M.: "Democracy vs. the Melting Pot," The Nation, Feb. 1915. Bourne, R. S.: "Trans-National America"—Atlantic Monthly, July 1916. Menorah Journal, Dec. 1916. Collier, J.: "Give the Immigrant a Chance," Report of People's Institute, Jan. 1914.

It must be emphasized that the demarcation between the religious and the national attitudes is no more distinct and no more real than the geographic line of the equator, or the zone lines.

Orthodox, Conservative and Reform

If now we analyze the group which wishes to preserve the Jews as a religious body, we shall find differences not only as to *how much* of the religious life they want to preserve, but also as to the best *methods* for such preservation. The division is that between the *orthodox*, the *conservative*, and the *reform*. There are really at present, only two parties in religious Jewry: the orthodox and the reform. There is a large class of Jews, however, who are neither orthodox nor reform, and who represent a social attitude rather than any definite party.

Orthodoxy and Reform may of course be defined in many ways. For the purpose of this book it is probably best to deal with them as attitudes toward Jewish social living, and to point out along what lines the conservative attitude tends to differ from both.

The characteristic attitude of the *orthodox* is the wish to preserve unaltered those religious institutions and customs which have been codified into Jewish law, particularly into the code of Rabbinic laws known as the "Shulchan Aruch" ("The Table Set"). This legal code deals with every aspect of life in great detail. It is in the nature of an encyclopedic manual of several volumes. Its purpose is to bring to the ordinary Jew, in an available form, the vast rabbinic legal tradition, which regulates every phase of human life. Prayers, meals, business transactions, marriage, birth, death, recreation, work, all possible human relationships are regulated in accordance with the development of Jewish tradition, which has its origin in the Bible, and continues through the Talmud to the post-Talmudic rabbis. In addition to this code of laws, which was compiled in the 16th century,[7] there have been numerous additions and modifications made by the rabbis of various lands. It is fair, therefore, to call those Jews orthodox, who consciously shape their lives, or attempt

[7] The Shulchan Aruch was compiled by Joseph Caro, ca. 1560. For fuller information see "Caro, Joseph," in Jewish Encyclopedia. H. Lowe: "Der Schulchan Aruch" (German translation) 1896.

to shape them, in accordance with these codified laws, particularly the regulations of the "Shulchan Aruch."

Opposed to this attitude is that of the *Reform Jews,* who are the adherents of the movement beginning in Germany with Moses Mendelssohn, in the latter part of the 18th century. This movement found its highest expression in Germany in the early part of the 19th century, and was at the height of its development in America between 1850 and 1900.[8] The Reform movement abrogated practically all of the laws which arose and were codified after the Talmud, as well as many of the Talmudic regulations, and even some of the biblical injunctions. Its leaders called themselves followers of Prophetic Judaism, meaning thereby that they wished to make the Prophets, rather than the Pentateuch, the guides and authorities for their Jewish social life. Their aim was to interpret the values of Judaism for the modern environment in which the Jews lived, following upon their emancipation in the countries of Western Europe. Their more concrete reforms were in making the Jewish synagogue ritual more simple and more aesthetic. Thus, they shortened the time of the service, introduced prayers and sermons in the vernacular, insisted upon greater decorum among the congregants than prevailed previously in German and Polish synagogues, permitted the Western custom of praying with bare heads, did away with the segregation of the sexes in the seating arrangements of the synagogue, made use of the organ in the services, and instituted other similar reforms. More fundamental was the change in the form of the Messianic ideal of the Jews. This ancient ideal conceived the Messianic age as emanating from Zion, under the leadership of an ideal king or leader, the Messiah. The Reform movement changed this conception into that of the Jews as a Priest-People, scattered throughout the world, and serving mankind wherever they may be, so as "to hasten the millenium." It might be said that this movement changed not only the *forms* of Jewish life, but also an essential element in its *content.* Thus, it abandoned the hope for the restoration to Zion, deleted the prayer for Zion from the Jewish prayer book; abrogated the Jewish dietary laws; and even, in some cases, changed the Sabbath day to Sunday.

---

[8] Philipson, David: "The Reform Movement in Judaism" and The Proceedings of the Central Conference of American Rabbis.

The *conservative* attitude is still in the process of formulation. In its essence it seems to be a determination to preserve the historic continuity of the Jewish people by permitting such changes in religious customs and institutions as appear to be necessary for preserving this continuity. It emphasizes the more permanent and more universal in Jewish law and custom, and tends to neglect intentionally the local and the temporary. Thus, conservative Jews observe the Jewish Sabbath as a day of rest, worship and study, but do not necessarily follow the biblical and rabbinic prohibitions concerning the carrying of objects, or the kindling of lights, on that day. They obey the Jewish dietary laws, but are not very scrupulous in following the many injunctions connected with the complete separation of milk and meat with regard to the use of dishes, etc. They pray in the synagogue on Sabbaths and holidays, but may forego the three daily prayers on some of the week days. This attitude is not merely negative, not a mere compromise. It is the *"evolutionary"* attitude in Judaism. It refuses to *break* with the past, but instead, gradually discards those customs and laws which are felt to be no longer tenable or necessary. It is a *"functional"* conception of Judaism. For, as in the natural evolution of organisms, so also in conservative Judaism, *use* and *disuse,* rather than intellectual recognition, determine the development of new forms or the abrogation of old ones. It is an *"organic"* attitude. It refuses to make the distinction between the spiritual, or the *religious* phases of Jewish life, and the corporate or *national* aspects. It claims that Jewish spirituality has meaning only with reference to Jewish group life. Thus, it may be said, without fear of successful contradiction, that the conservative class, more than either the orthodox, or the reform, looks to the practical upbuilding of a Jewish life in Palestine, as a necessary element in its religious philosophy. It does not consider Jewish religious life as having ceased its development. It seeks new values, new laws, and new customs; but these must be the natural expression of a normal Jewish people living on its own land and developing its group life in accordance with the ideals of its past. As distinguished from the orthodox, who place the codified *law* at the center of Jewish religious life, and from the reform Jews, who emphasize Jewish *ideas* of life as the guide of their religious thinking, the conservative attitude seems to look to the Jewish *people* as the perpetual source of its religious life, and would therefore consider the welfare, continuity and development of the Jewish group as an essential in its *religious* outlook.

From this description of differentiation in religious attitudes, it will be seen that here too it is impossible to draw any sharp lines of separation. In most cases the distinctions would not be extreme difference of attitude, but rather different emphasis upon the particular elements involved.

Indigenous, Centralized and Decentralized Nationalists

Among the nationalists also there is a gradual differentiation, centering around the problem of how and where the Jewish nation can be best preserved. There are those who believe that Jewish national life can be continued only in Palestine. The rest of the world, the diaspora, or the *galuth* (exile), is only the temporary abode of the Jews. As long as Palestine is not yet the "legally secured, publicly assured home-land of the Jews,"[9] it is the duty of the Jews throughout the world to work for the realization of this ideal. When, however, this age-long dream shall have come to pass, those Jews who will migrate to Palestine will continue their national life, and those who will remain in the lands of the diaspora, must sooner or later fuse with the particular nations among whom they live.[10] This attitude might be called *indigenous nationalism*, confining the future of Jewish national life to the soil of Palestine alone. It denies the possibility of continued Jewish life outside of the home land of the Jews, and looks to the establishment of a political state in Palestine as the solution of the Jewish problem.

Very different from this attitude is that of the *decentralized or diaspora nationalists.* They maintain that Palestine is not needed for the preservation of Jewish national life, but that the Jews in every land in which they live in sufficiently large numbers, can maintain their national institutions: their language,

---

[9] From the Zionist "Basel Program." The Zionist program does not, however, stand necessarily for this Palestine-only attitude.

[10] Herzl, Theodore: "Der Judenstaat." In fairness, however, to the founder of the Zionist movement, it should be said that he changed this view later, after his famous book had been written.

their literature and their customs.[11] They would not deny that Palestine too might become the place where Jews should live and develop their national life, but they negate the idea that Palestine is *essential* for the Jewish future. The clearest exponents of this attitude in this country, are the so-called Yiddishist-Radicals, who believe in the maintenance of Yiddish-speaking groups throughout the world, where the Jews reside in sufficient numbers. This group originated in Russia, during the days of the Revolutions of 1905 and 1907. It arose in many instances as a reaction of the Jewish Bundists[12] to the general awakening of Jewish national consciousness at the time. The attitude is limited in this country to a comparatively small group of recent immigrants; and owing to changes in Eastern Europe it has most likely but little chance for growth in America.

Between these two attitudes, and including elements of both, is a great body of nationalists who claim that Jewish life is possible everywhere, throughout the world, but *only if* Palestine becomes the national center of the Jewish people. They agree that complete national development, including the legal, political and economic phases of life, is possible only in Palestine. They maintain, however, that some of the cultural and spiritual phases of Jewish life can be continued by Jews wherever they live. Due to the breaking down of the ghetto walls and the free intermingling of the Jews with the neighboring peoples, it will be impossible for them to preserve their cultural traditions and institutions, *unless* there is a normal, developing national center in Palestine.[13] This center need not be large. It may include only a very small percentage of the Jews of the world. But because there the Jews will be in the majority, and will therefore be able to express their values of life in all human relationships, economic and political, as well as social and cultural, this center will serve as a tangible bond of union between the Jews of the world, and as

[11] Dubnow: "Die Grundlagen des National Judenthums" (trans. I. Friedlaender) 1905; also "Dubnow's Theory of Jewish Nationalism," address by I. Friedlaender, New York, 1905. Zhitlowsky: "Gesammelte Schriften" (Yiddish), especially vols. 2 and 4.

[12] For history of the Bund see "Revolutionary Russia" (Yiddish) published by the Jewish Socialist Federation, New York, 1917; also Burgin: "History of the Jewish Labor Movement" (Yiddish).

[13] Achad Ha'am: "Al Parashat Derachim" (Hebrew), four volumes, or: "Selected Essays," (trans. L. Simon).

a normal source of developing cultural and religious Jewish life. The Jews who live in the various lands outside of Palestine, are to pay political allegiance *not* to Palestine, but to the states in which they reside. They are to consider themselves integral members of the respective nations of the world. They shall participate in the cultural and social life, as well as in the economic and civic activities of the particular territorial nation or state to which they belong. But they are also to pay *cultural and spiritual fealty* to the land of their Jewish past. Their claim is that in the domain of the spirit, in cultural life, more than one allegiance is possible, nay, desirable. Cultures which do not antagonize one another, may actually supplement and enrich one another. The Jew will be a richer personality, of more worth to himself and to America, if besides his complete patriotism for America he also entertains a supplementary loyalty, a spiritual allegiance, to a Jewish center in Palestine. This is the *centralized national* attitude of Jewish life.

The differentiation in the case of the nationalists is, therefore, somewhat more distinct than that which takes place in the religious group; but here also it is very gradual, and is again a difference of emphasis in thought rather than an actual difference in desire. The Declaration of the British Government favoring "the establishment in Palestine of a national home for the Jewish people"[14] has brought all nationalist Jews more closely together in the immediate tasks connected with the Restoration of Palestine, the Redemption, or "Geulah." But it has also brought to the attention of every Jew the need of deciding more definitely which of the several nationalist attitudes he wishes to hold for himself and for his children.

Summary

It is now possible for us to *summarize* briefly the differences in social attitudes among the Jews of this country towards the problem of their adjustment in America.[15] These differences arise from the degree and manner of their affiliation with the Jewish group. The most fundamental difference is that between

---

[14] November 2d, 1917.

[15] For a graphic representation of the variety of Jewish attitudes, and how they overlap one another, see Appendix AA.

fusion and group preservation, as desirable goals of life in this country. The fusionists differentiate along the lines of method, as to whether this process shall be rapid or gradual. Among those who wish to preserve Jewish group life, the largest differences center about the problem of *what* shall be preserved, the *religious* or the *national* elements of Jewish life. Those who wish to conserve the Jews as a religious body merge very markedly with those who look upon the Jews as a nation. The religious group is divided into: (1) the orthodox, who make the codified *law* the center of their religious life; (2) the reform Jews, who emphasize Jewish *ideas* in their religious thinking; (3) the conservative, who see in the Jewish *people* the source and the embodiment of both laws and ideals. The nationalist attitude differentiates itself into: (1) the indigenous nationalists, who hold that Palestine alone is the place where continued Jewish group life is possible; (2) the decentralized nationalists, who maintain that Palestine is not essential for the preservation of Jewish national life; and (3) the centralized nationalists, who believe that with Palestine as a center, Jewish group life, more particularly Jewish cultural life, is possible everywhere.

(B) Variety of Educational Systems Based Upon Differences of Jewish Attitudes

This analysis indicates how complex and heterogeneous are the Jewish social attitudes in this country. It is natural that these differences in social outlook should give rise to a variety of educational institutions among the Jews. Those who consider themselves individuals merely, and believe in *immediate fusion* as the solution of their problem, are naturally not interested in Jewish education. Whenever they deem it necessary to belong to some religious-ethical group, these individual Jews join, in great numbers, the ranks of Christian Science and of Ethical Culture.

The fusionists who maintain that the method of social merging must be *gradual,* are interested to some extent in Jewish education. But their interest arises from three motives: they may support Jewish education in the spirit of philanthropy, believing that it is instrumental in bridging the gap between the immigrant parent and his American child; they may send their children to

Jewish schools, because of family tradition, which enjoins upon every parent to send his child to Sunday School as a matter of family custom; or else, they may favor the Jewish school as a reaction against social anti-semitism, which sometimes refuses to allow the Jewish child to join the Christian Sunday School on an equal footing. This group of Jews does not maintain any schools of its own. Those of them who merge on the religious side with the reform group, send their children to the reform Sunday School; whereas those (particularly of the laboring classes) who merge on the national side with the decentralized nationalists, would be apt to favor the national-radical school.[16]

The Cheder and the Yeshibah

Of the religious group, the *orthodox* resort naturally to the older forms of education, which they used throughout the centuries, especially in the countries of Eastern Europe. There are three types of education which are particularly characteristic of the orthodox: (1) the *Cheder* (lit. room) or the private Hebrew school; (2) private Hebrew tuition by the *Melamed* (teacher), at the home of the child; and (3) the *Yeshibah* (lit. session or sitting), the Jewish parochial school.[17] While it is true that the orthodox have also established in this country Talmud Torahs, or the communal weekday schools, and even Sunday Schools, yet the tendency is for many of them to be dissatisfied with both of these types of schooling, and to look to the Yeshibah (parochial school), as the solution of their educational problem.[18] The two differentiating characteristics of the Yeshibah are: (a) the emphasis laid upon the Talmud as the center of the Jewish curriculum; and (b) the teaching of secular studies.[19]

---

[16] For description of these schools, see below.

[17] The term *Yeshibah* was applied historically only to the Talmudical High School or Academy. In this country, however, it has come to be used as the Hebrew equivalent for the parochial school.

[18] This is more particularly true of the Russian and Polish orthodox Jews, than of the German and Spanish-Portuguese types.

[19] These schools, as well as the following ones, will be described in very much greater detail, in Part II of the book. It will be shown there, that the influence of the Jewish parochial school is very small. The total number of pupils in Jewish elementary and secondary parochial schools in America in May 1917 was less than one thousand (925).

The Sunday School

The reform Jews have laid particular stress upon the *Sunday School.* The children are taught in the vestry rooms of the synagogue on Sunday mornings (rarely also on one or two weekday afternoons), and two or three hours' instruction each week is given to them in Jewish catechism, Jewish history (mostly biblical), ethics, and the rudiments of Hebrew. This type of school is familiar to Americans. Historically it originated as a result of the example set by the American Sunday School Union, organized in Philadelphia, and throughout its development it has fashioned its curriculum and management on the Protestant model.[20]

The Talmud Torah

The educational institution with which the followers of the *conservative* attitude have been identifying themselves is the *Talmud Torah* (lit. Study of the Law), or the *supplementary weekday school.* To these schools they send their children in the afternoons, after public school hours, and on Saturdays and Sundays. While some of them also send their boys to the *Chedarim,* or private one-room schools, it can hardly be doubted that they look to the *Talmud Torah* as the most hopeful educational institution for the preservation of Jewish life in this country. These weekday schools may be *communal,* that is, supported by a group in the community, or *congregational,* connected with some particular congregation. In these schools the Bible, and post-biblical literature, form the center of the curriculum. Jewish history, religion and ethics are important elements in the course of study.

The National Hebrew School

Among the nationalists, we find that the "Palestine-only," or indigenous nationalists, have not built up any school system of their own in this country. The nearest educational expression of their attitude may be found in the *National Hebrew Schools.*

---

[20] The American Sunday School movement may be said to have begun in Philadelphia in 1791. It culminated in the organization of the American Sunday School Union in the same city in 1824. It was in this city also that Rebecca Gratz founded the first Jewish Sunday School, in 1838.

In general, the curriculum of these schools does not differ very much from that of the Talmud Torahs, except in so far as they make the Hebrew *language and literature* the center of their studies, putting particular stress on the linguistic study of Hebrew as a modern language.

THE NATIONAL RADICAL SCHOOL

The *decentralized nationalists* have also not succeeded in building up a system which represents fully their point of view. They have, however, coöperated[21] in the building up of the *National Radical Schools,* or the "Yiddishe Volks-Schulen," where the main subject of the curriculum is the Yiddish language and literature. Religion as a subject is not taught, nor is there any teaching of ethics aside from literature and history. In most of these schools Hebrew is included as a subject of study, though in some cases it is not taught at all. While these schools do not claim to be anti-religious, many of them avow frankly their secular non-religious character.

THE JEWISH SCHOOL CENTER

Finally, the group of *centralized-nationalists,* who believe that cultural Jewish life is possible everywhere, provided Palestine becomes the national center, have shared with the conservative group in the building up of the *Talmud Torahs,* or the supplementary weekday schools, in this country. These schools do not confine themselves to any particular phase of the Jewish heritage, either the religious *or* the national. Whatever is the spiritual product of the Jewish people, from the simplest Jewish folk ditty having human worth, to the loftiest conceptions of God, these schools consider legitimate study for Jewish children. Thus, they include in their curricula, not only the Bible and post-biblical literature, history and religion, but also folk songs, Jewish current events, modern Hebrew literature, Hebrew conversation, and, some of them, also Yiddish. The Talmud Torahs are developing into *Jewish school centers,* with provision not

[21] Among the builders of the National Radical Schools in this country must also be included the Poalei Zion, a Jewish National Labor Party, which considers Palestine an essential element in its program of Jewish life.

only for study, but also for recreation and worship. As will be described later[22] the Jewish school center is attempting to meet all of the social needs of the entire Jewish family, adults and adolescents as well as school children.

There are therefore several distinct types of Jewish educational institutions in America. These different school systems tend to represent the differences of social attitude among the Jews. But here too it must not be assumed that any one school system represents exclusively the social attitude of any one group. While particular groups tend to emphasize particular school systems, the same system may be supported by several groups, and *vice versa,* one group may support several types of schools.[23]

The Jewish schools are the most concrete expressions of the attempt of the Jews to adjust themselves in America. The variety of types in Jewish educational institutions results from a variety in methods of adjustment. This adjustment is of particular significance to America because it affects profoundly its own problem of assimilation.

(C) Effect Upon Problem of Assimilation in America

The term "assimilation" has been loosely used for either one of two ideas: adjustment or fusion. In its essence it is the problem of creating like-mindedness, similarity of thought, feeling and action, among those living on a common soil and participating in common government.[24] Its central problem is the age-long antagonism between the individual's liberty and progress on the one hand, and the social order and stability on the other. How far must the liberties of any one element in the community, whether individual or group, be curtailed, so as to insure the best interests of the entire community?

Amalgamation vs. Co-operation

With relation to the life of distinct groups, there have been two solutions offered for this problem: amalgamation, and co-operation. Each of these two methods of assimilation has been

---

[22] Part II, Chap. 12.

[23] For a graphic representation of the relation of the types of Jewish schools to Jewish social attitudes in America, see Appendix BB.

[24] Giddings, F. H.: "Principles of Sociology."

variously interpreted, giving rise to four theories of American life. One view of amalgamation, as a method of assimilation, is the *"Americanization" theory.* This theory assumes that there is a definite American type, of the Anglo-Saxon variety, to which all incoming peoples should be made to conform as closely as possible.[25] Another interpretation of amalgamation is the *theory of the "Melting-Pot."* This much-used phrase expresses the view that American life is a huge social cauldron, into which various national and religious metals are being poured, so that a new, and totally distinct, alloy may emerge. It has been pointed out that when carried to its logical conclusion, it would seem, that if the melting pot process is to be real, not only the national but also the religious groups must fuse; that America must, to a certain extent, cease being Christian, and evolve a religion of its own.[26]

Coöperation also has been interpreted in two ways. The first view is that of a *Federation of Nationalities,* similar to Switzerland or Austria-Hungary. It is assumed that the various nationalities which are living on American soil tend to congregate within certain areas. These should be given national rights, to shape their laws, and their schools, in accordance with what is supposed to be their national or hereditary genius.[27] Such division, on territorial, residential lines seems neither possible nor wise, chiefly because it is artificial and unduly segregating.

Another conception of coöperation as the method of adjustment, is the *community theory* of American life.[28] In this theory, the various ethnic and religious groups are considered as organic parts of the American commonwealth. Belonging to one body politic, the members of all groups live together and strive together for the common good. But they seek in the particular ethnic or religious community with which they are affiliated, that which the general Commonwealth cannot give them, namely, certain

---

[25] Cubberly, E. C: "Changing Conceptions of Education."

[26] Guthrie, W. N: "Uncle Sam and Old World Conquerors." Coit, Stanton: "The Soul of America." Davidson, Thomas: "American Democracy as a Religion" International Journal of Ethics, 1899.

[27] Kallen, H. M: "Democracy vs. the Melting Pot"—The Nation, Feb. 1915.

[28] This theory is developed in a Ph. D. dissertation, T. C., Columbia University, written by I. B. Berkson. The analysis of the theories of assimilation was taken from this dissertation.

cultural and spiritual aspects of life which they share in common only with those citizens of the commonwealth to whom they are related by means of a common past. The historic community or grouping, which is based upon a sharing of historic experiences, institutions and interests, has a special function to perform for the good of the individual citizen, and is therefore supplementary to the American commonwealth. In this conception the individual citizen, and not the state, is the ultimate consideration, and the *raison d'etre* for any community or grouping consists in the need which individual American citizens have for it, provided it can be satisfied without encroaching upon the rights of other American citizens. In education the community theory of adjustment lays stress upon a system of education which shall not supplant but rather *supplement* the training which the American child receives in the public schools.

From this formulation of the four theories of American life insufficient though it is, it is evident that the Jews may hold to any one of these theories. Many of those who believe in immediate fusion, are willing to follow the Americanization theory, and "Anglo-Saxonize" themselves as rapidly as possible. The "Melting-Pot" theory seems to be shared not only by the gradual fusionists, but also by the indigenous nationalists, who would claim that outside of Palestine the Jews must ultimately become parts of new ethnic bodies, formed by the intermingling of various nationalities.

Concentration vs. Individuation

The decentralized nationalists, perhaps more than any of the others, lean towards the theory of the Federation of Nationalities. They look forward to the *concentration* of Jewish life in this country, so as to preserve a distinct Jewish language, literature and customs.[29] The tendency toward concentration is also true in the case of some of the orthodox.

The centralized nationalists, and practically the entire religious group, more or less consciously, hold to the community view of

[29] Zhitlowsky, Ch: "Die Zukunft vun die Yidden in Amerika," Gesammelte Schriften, vol. 4; also various articles in the "Vorwærts," Jewish daily, New York. There are also some centralized nationalists who believe in this theory; but they do not seem to be typical.

American life. They all tend to believe in *partial* separation, as their method of adjustment in America. They claim that whereas in most phases of life the Jew should mix freely with all the members of the American Commonwealth, he should, at the same time, have special opportunity to come into close contact with the members of his own Jewish group. The difference between orthodox, conservative and reform is merely a difference in the extent and degree of this separation. Practically none of them desires complete separation, but all of them would consider a certain amount of it necessary for forming Jewish individuality. The relationships, which the Jew wishes to share particularly with Jewish members of the American Commonwealth, are those which are connected with the synagogue, the life of the family, and some of the cultural interests.

(D) Possible Contributions of Jewish Group Life to America

The great body of American Jews who believe in the coöperative, community method of adjustment, base their attitude on two fundamental ideas: first, that as individuals they have a *right*, in a democracy, to preserve that culture and those ideals which they consider of great worth to themselves and to their children, unless these values are prone to be detrimental to the interests of the majority; second, that they can be of *greater service* to America by making their adjustment not as individuals, but as socii of a highly conscious group, rich in historic memories and in the imperative of *noblesse oblige*. The contention which bases Jewish group life and Jewish education on the *right* of individuals to follow their own cultural and spiritual life, without interfering with the rights of others, needs hardly any elaboration or proof. It is becoming an ultimate in democratic thinking. But the exercise of this right, especially by a group, is not significant, unless it somehow contributes to the common good. The *contributions* to America which the Jews claim as possible outgrowths of their own effort at adjustment, would proceed along four lines.

1. Better Citizenship

American education for citizenship has been defined in two ways. The first definition is in terms of enrichment of personality.[30] Just as the American public school enriches the personality of its children, by transmitting to them the experiences and spiritual heritage of America and of humanity, so do the Jews wish to *add* to this enrichment, by giving to their children the historic experiences of the Jewish people and the ethical ideals which the Jews have thought worth while struggling for these many centuries. According to this view, the personality of the Jewish citizen of America would be extended in three directions: *in space,* by connecting him with the Jews of the entire world, cutting across territorial limitations; *in time,* by giving him the long historic perspective of his people, making him the immediate scion of centuries of development and of struggle; and *in content,* by giving him an additional culture, another language and literature, the ethical ideals of the prophets and the martyrs of Israel, and the religious attitudes of the "People of the Book."

The second definition of American education for citizenship is in terms of the training for the duties and privileges of democratic life. American educators now agree that the public school has been poorly balanced in its training for citizenship, because it has trained only for the privileges and rights of civic life, but not for its duties. Loyalty as a virtue, and duty as an imperative, have been but little emphasized, and in consequence the outlook of the American child has been improperly focused upon getting what it can out of life, and giving in return as little as possible. To be sure the great war has affected this situation in ways which may be permanent. But in so far as the contention is right, Jewish education can fundamentally contribute to the general scheme for the education of the American Jewish citizen, because it must, of necessity, go to the other extreme and train for duties and for loyalties mostly, and for tangible privileges but little. The Jewish teacher has nothing to offer to the Jewish child in terms of material or social advancement. He must stress values of life other than the tangible ones. He must make the conscious adherence to loyalty and to duty the central attitudes in his teaching. His task is to instruct American Jewish children to be true to their Jewish obligations and responsibilities *because they are obligations and responsibilities.*

---

[30] Dewey, John: "School and Society"; also "The Curriculum and the Child."

2. Religious Education

Immediately arising out of the efforts to enrich personality, is the Jewish contribution to the problem of religious education in America. Catholics, Jews, and Protestants of all denominations, have felt that the public school cannot offer complete education to the American child. Ever since the state asserted the right to the education of its citizens, the problem of religious education has been a very pressing one. The Catholics offer the *parochial school* as a solution to this problem. They maintain that religion, if it is to mean anything, must be at the center of the education of the child, since it is of necessity a reinterpretation of all of life's experiences. The overwhelming majority of Jews in this country oppose this as a solution of their educational problem.[31] They oppose it because of its possible danger to America, since it means practically the complete segregation and indoctrination of the child. In spite of its tempting possibilities for intensifying group life, the Jews have refused to adopt the parochial school on a large scale, because they have considered it harmful to democracy, which in essence implies that the individual must have wide opportunities for choosing his interests and modes of life.

The Protestants have attempted to meet the problem of of religious education through the *Sunday School*. In this they were followed by the Reform Jews of this country. But both Jew and Gentile are now realizing the insufficiency and inefficacy of the Sunday school for religious instruction.[32] Aside from the general fact that the Sunday school makes religious education a Sunday affair only, and limits the personal influence of the religious teacher to two or three hours a week, some thirty times during the year, there is for the Jews the additional difficulty of having to teach a rich curriculum in an absurdly short time.

---

[31] As has already been indicated, the total number of children in Jewish elementary and secondary parochial schools in America is less than one thousand, or less than one-fifth of one per cent. of the total number of Jewish children of school age.

[32] Resolutions adopted at the Mass Meeting of the *Interdenominational Committee on Weekday Religious Instruction*, Nov. 12, 1917. Wenner, Geo. W.: ''Religious Education and the Public School,'' pp. 188-190, being the recommendations of the Special Committee of the Federal Council of Churches of Christ to consider ways and means to promote weekday instruction in religion. Central Conference of American Rabbis, Proceedings, 1916.

For they must impart to their children a complex language, a rich literature, a long history, a highly symbolic ritual, and a comprehensive liturgy.

The distinct Jewish contribution to the problem of religious education in America is in the direction of testing out a *supplementary system of weekday religious education,* in which the children attend the public school for the greater part of the day, and come to the Hebrew school after public school hours, several times during the week.[33] Such a supplementary system of education can be operated in conjunction with almost every plan of public education, under certain conditions.[34] While the Jews are not alone in the belief that weekday religious instruction offers the best solution for the religious educational problem in America, they have nevertheless tried it longest, and on the largest scale, and may be in a position to contribute their experiences to the general problem.

3. More Effective Americanization

The third possible contribution which the Jews claim to be in a position to make in this country, is that of aiding in a more satisfactory Americanization of the Jewish immigrant than has been current hitherto. Usually this phrase is confined to teaching English and Civics to the recently arrived. Its implications, however, are much deeper. The immigrant Jew in many cases has to undergo a transition, during the first few years of his residence in America, which has taken centuries in the history of the human race. His child makes this transition very easily and very readily. For the parent it is a slow and difficult task. The result is that a chasm is created between parents and children. America becomes the unconscious perpetrator of many a family tragedy, arising from the fact that the child despises that which is holy to its father and mother. For the father this makes Americanization doubly difficult. It creates an antagonistic set of mind, which induces him to look upon America as the cause of his family tragedies.

---

[33] In the fifth chapter of Part II of this book will be discussed the various schedules that are now being tried in weekday Jewish schools, so as to get the best results in religious instruction for the American Jewish child.

[34] These conditions will also be discussed in the fifth chapter, Part II.

But the parent is not alone in suffering from the harmful effects of this break. The Americanization of the child, too, is abnormal. There are neurologists who claim that the very rapid transition which the Jewish child must go through in the brief period of his school life, causes the child many mental conflicts and psychic repressions, because of his constant, painful attempt to suppress and hide his home life and his past attitudes. These conflicts tend to express themselves in increased nervosity and even in cases of unbalanced mentality. Moreover, in his search for companionship and leadership, which his home can no longer give him, the Jewish adolescent goes to the opposite extreme, and sometimes imitates the lowest type of "American," who introduces him to the worst phases of the free life. It is claimed that this rapid "Americanization" is the chief cause for the high proportion of Jewish adolescents in psychopathic wards and in penitentiaries.[35]

The Jewish schools can therefore offer signal aid in the process of Americanization, by teaching the child to know and to be interested in some of the things which his father knows and is interested in, and by making the parent feel that Americanism does not necessarily imply opposition to Judaism. If the father can be made to see that his American son may still be interested in some of the things which are dear to him, it will help create in him a proper attitude of mind towards his own process of Americanization. For the child the Jewish school proposes more conscious and more gradual transition. It wishes to aid him in tiding over the periods of his mental conflict. It reinterprets the home and the past of the child, so as to do away with shame and repression, and their psychic consequences in self-depreciation. By exerting this mental therapeutic influence on the child, the Jewish school may prevent many a Jewish American personality from becoming psychically maladjusted.

4. Internationalization

Another possible contribution which may be expected by Jews as a result of their attempt to orientate themselves properly in their American environment, is that dealing with America's

[35] Brill, A. A.: "Mental Adjustment in Jews," the *Jewish Teacher*, May, 1917.

problem of adjusting the ethnic communities which have come to its shores. American education is conceived by our leading educators as being not only a national education, that is, an education for America, but, if it is to be significant, it must also be an international education, an education for humanity.

The history of human development has been in terms of a broadening of the group with which the individual is affiliated. This development reached its climax in the cosmopolitanism of the eighteenth century in which humanity and the world became the group of affiliation for the individual. We realize now, however, that this is an impossible *unit* of organization for human kind, although it should properly form the aim of human organization. The modern nation or national state seems now to be the largest territorial group possible for direct individual allegiance. This territorial unit has its basis in the deepest human impulses and human needs: food, shelter, ownership, gregariousness, etc. It is fostered by common trade, common government, and common education. It seems, therefore, to be the normal and logical unit of organization for human life, and one which must persist. But the inherent difficulty in making any territorial unit the basis for human organization is that the political and economic interests of that unit may be diametrically opposed to the interests of some other territorial unit. War, with all that precedes and follows it, is an expression of this inherent conflict. It is necessary, therefore, for humanity to evolve some method of human organization whereby the national unit shall remain intact, and yet this inherent conflict be overcome.

The suggestion made, as the one which must underlie all peaceful group living in the future, is that of *internationalization.* In its essence, it seems to mean that the individual shall pay political and civic allegiance to the territorial nation of which he is a part, but that he shall also have other allegiances, with groups that cut across political boundaries. These allegiances must not be equal, that is, complete allegiances, but rather partial allegiances. They must deal only with certain phases of human life, namely, the spiritual or cultural phases. Thus it is claimed that an Irishman in America may be a better American, and a better human being, if at the same time that he pays unswerving allegiance politically and civically to America, he yet continues to be interested in Irish culture and art, and aids in the development of Irish life and ideals. The President of the United States in his famous war message,[36] seemed to suggest the possibility of this attitude, even in most trying times, when he pointed out to the American people that while at war with the Kaiser and his government, America had no animosity against the German people. His statement implied that an American citizen may be a political enemy of German political aggression, and may yet continue to cherish German culture and certain of the German values of life. This illustration is perhaps as *extreme* a case as is possible of what is here meant by internationalization.

The Jews as a highly conscious community may prove of value in this world undertaking, if they can but work out for themselves the methods of internationalization, and smooth out the difficulties which it brings in its train. This is particularly the effort of that group of Jews who advocate the centralized or cultural-national method of Jewish affiliation in this country. Their aim is to work out a form of community life in this country, which will enjoin undivided political, civic and cultural allegiance upon every American Jew to America, and yet connect him religiously and culturally with the Jews throughout the world, particularly with the Jewish life in Palestine.

(E) Relation of Jewish Education to American Education

If, then, these contributions to America which the Jews expect as the results of their socialized effort at adjustment are significant, the problem of Jewish religious education may lay large claims to the interest of the American educator. This book is written from the point of view of the American student of education, who is investigating one phase of a complete, comprehensive system of *American* education. It is an attempt to describe and interpret the religious educational activities of the Jews of New York City, not apart from, but as a part of the American educational system, just as public and private education are only parts of this system.

[36] April 5, 1917.

The purpose of the above rather detailed analysis, is therefore, first, to show the significance of Jewish education, as *part of a complete scheme of American education;* and second, to point out that *Jewish education is not religious education, merely in the denominational sense.* The tendency of American educators has been to look upon the Jewish schools as a more or less homogeneous system, teaching the beliefs and doctrines of a Jewish religious sect. The Jews are included in denominational schemes as one of the "denominations." At best the only distinction made is between the orthodox and the reform. Many a non-Jewish educator has for that reason been unable to account for certain of the studies in some of the Jewish schools. From the point of view of the religious-devotional life, it has been difficult to understand why Jewish schools should teach Jewish folk songs, Jewish current events, Hebrew as a modern language, etc. In point of fact, however, the great majority of Jews do not look upon themselves as a religious sect *only;* they include in their heritage many cultural-national elements which do not center about worship. Jewish education is community education; it is a system of religious-national training. It expresses a variety of attitudes towards the problem of socialized Jewish life in America, and prepares the Jewish child to take its place among the Jewish people, both in America and throughout the world.

No single definition of Jewish education will cover the whole field. It may be best, therefore, to define it objectively from various aspects:

(1) *Psychologically,* Jewish education is the process of *enriching* the personality of American Jewish children, by transmitting to them the cultural heritage of the Jews, and by training them to share in the experiences of the Jewish people, both past and present.

(2) *Sociologically,* Jewish education has two meanings:

(a) It is the *transmission* of group consciousness by Jewish fathers to their children, so as to preserve Jewish life.

(b) It is the mental and social *adjustment* of the American Jewish children, so that by preserving the values of their people, they may be able to live the completest, and, at the same time, the most coöperative lives.

(3) *Religiously,* Jewish education may be defined as the training of Jewish children to understand and obey the *will of God* as it has expressed itself in the history, literature and laws of their people.

CHAPTER II

THE HISTORY OF JEWISH EDUCATION IN NEW YORK BEFORE 1881

The history of Jewish education in America, presents a field of study which has received but scant attention from the student of American education. Besides a few stray notes on individual schools, and two or three general historical reviews, the subject has been completely neglected. There is a good deal of available material, but it has never been compiled. In order to trace the history of the Jewish religious schools of New York, it was therefore necessary to have access to original sources: minutes of congregations and schools; proceedings of educational and historical societies; magazine articles and newspaper notices; reports, pamphlets, souvenir books, etc.[1] These sources were supplemented by personal conferences with individuals who have themselves fashioned some of the unwritten history of Jewish educational activities during the last thirty-five years.

In the previous chapter an attempt was made to analyze the differences in social attitudes among the Jews of America which affect their educational endeavors in this country. In order to understand more fully the origin and character of the Jewish educational institutions, it is also necessary to know something of the different migrations of Jews to America, and the attitudes and customs which they brought with them. Before presenting the historical data in chronological sequence, it will be well, therefore, to give a brief account of the coming of the Jews to this country, as a necessary background for the development of the Jewish schools.

American Jewish history is usually divided into three periods: (1) the period of the Spanish-Portuguese Jews, 1654-1848; (2) the period of the German Jews, 1848-1881; and (3) the period of the Eastern European Jews, from 1881 until the present day. These three periods are designated after the Jewish types dominant in each, according to the countries from which they emigrated to America.

---

[1] For material utilized in this study, see Bibliography: "Source material for history of Jewish schools in New York."

Spanish-Portuguese Jews

The Spanish-Portuguese Jews are the descendants of the Jewish refugees who were exiled from Spain in 1492, and came to this country, either by way of South America, whither the Portuguese Inquisition had followed them, or from Holland and England, where many of their ancestors had found shelter. Although there were Jews in South America from the first day that white men landed on the shores of the New World,[2] it was not until 1654 that they began to migrate to North America.

The first party of Jewish immigrants came to New Amsterdam on September 12, 1654, in the bark *Catarina*, which brought twenty-seven refugees from the religious persecution of the Portuguese Inquisition in Brazil. In spite of the opposition of Governor Peter Stuyvesant, "that the deceitful race be not allowed further to infect and trouble this new colony," they were permitted to settle, on condition that "the poor among them shall not become a burthen to the company or the community, but shall be supported by their own nation," and also that they do not become "thereby entitled to a license to exercise or carry on their religion in synagogues or gatherings."[3] For these reasons their religious life as well as their educational activities during the first seventy-five years, were carried on quietly in the privacy of their homes. Even after the coming of the English, the little Jewish community continued to pursue its Jewish life unostentatiously. Sixty years later, in 1729-1730, they built their first synagogue on Mill Street, now South William Street. When the Revolutionary War broke out, the congregation sided whole-heartedly with the patriotic party, and upon the capture of New York by the British, moved in a body to Philadelphia, together with their Hazan (rabbi or praecentor), Gershom Mendes Seixas. From there they returned to New York at the end of hostilities. In 1834 the center of their religious life was removed from the synagogue on Mill Street to Crosby Street; thence in 1860 to Nineteenth Street, and in 1897 to their present building at Seventieth Street and Central Park West.

---

[2] Kayserling, M.: "Christopher Columbus and the Participation of the Jews in Spanish and Portuguese Discoveries," 1894 (trans. Gross).

[3] Oppenheim, Samuel: "The Early History of the Jews in New York, 1654-1664," p. 8.

The number of Spanish-Portuguese Jews was never large.[4] Their ranks were augmented from time to time by new arrivals from England and Holland, but the source of supply in Europe was very limited. Conversions to Christianity, intermarriage with non-Jews, and removal from the centers of Jewish life, depleted their numbers. Their congregation, Shearith Israel (Remnant of Israel), had to be constantly reinforced by the admittance of German and Polish Jews as members.

The Spanish and Portuguese Jews are described as proud, almost haughty, and conscious of the beautiful chapter which they contributed to Jewish history—poets, philosophers and martyrs. "The many sufferings which they had endured for the sake of their faith (at the hands of the Spanish and Portuguese Inquisitions) had made them more than usually self-conscious; they considered themselves a superior class, the nobility of Jewry, and for a long time their co-religionists, on whom they looked down, regarded them as such. This sense of dignity which the Sephardim (Spanish Jews) possessed, manifested itself in their general deportment. Even those among them whose station in life was low, maintained the old Spanish 'grandezza' in spite of their poverty."[5]

The most marked differences between them and the other Jewish immigrants were, and still are, in matters of ritual. They use the so-called Sephardic (Spanish) ritual, whereas the other Jews follow either the German or the Polish forms of the Ashkenazic (German) ritual.[6] Their pronunciation of Hebrew is purer and more correct than the pronunciation prevalent among the German-Polish Jews. All their Jewish life centered about

---

[4] In 1791 the first United States census gives the total number in New York State as 385. But there were probably more than this number, because the method used for computing the number of Jews was fallacious. (See Pub. American Jewish Historical Society, Vol. VI, p. 141.) In 1810 there were estimated to be from 300 to 400 Jews in New York City, there being "about 50 families of Jews in New York, which, with the number of unmarried men, making from 70 to 80 subscribing members to the Congregation Shearith Israel." Pub. Am. Hist. Soc. Vol. VI, p. 141, quoting from the "History of Jews," by Hannah Adams, 1812.

[5] Kayserling, M.: in Jewish Encyclopedia "Sephardim," Vol. XI, p. 197.

[6] These differences in ritual consist primarily in a different arrangement of the prayers, different synagogue procedure, a simpler form of cantillation, and the fact that they use some prayers written by the Spanish-Jewish poets.

the synagogue, not only their religious but also their educational and philanthropic activities.[7]

Of late a new migration of these Sephardic Jews, the so-called "Oriental Jews," has come to this country, from the Turkish Empire and from North Africa. All of the new immigrants are related to the earlier Spanish-Portuguese Jews in matters of ritual, and most of them are also descended from the exiles of the Spanish Inquisition. There are now estimated to be between 15,000 and 20,000 of these Oriental Jews in New York. Some of them speak Greek and Arabic as their native tongues; but most of them speak a Spanish-Jewish language of their own, called *Espagnol* or *Ladino,* which is a Castilian dialect of the 15th century, written in Hebrew script and containing many Hebrew elements. The new arrivals are, of course, much poorer economically than the earlier immigrants, and although they have formed congregations and societies of their own, they receive the patronage and guidance of the Shearith Israel Congregation, both in religious and in educational matters.

German-Jewish Migration

There were probably some German Jews among the earliest settlers of New Amsterdam, the first reference to them being as early as 1756.[8] Prior to 1848 their numbers increased slowly. During this period they came not in mass but as individuals, and their motives for coming were chiefly economic, arising from the distress caused by the Napoleonic wars. For a long time there was very great social aloofness between these poorer immigrant Jews and their more dignified and wealthier Portuguese forerunners. But slowly, as the new settlers gained in wealth and position, these social barriers were removed. The names of many of the most prominent members of the Shearith Israel Congregation indicate their German origin.

By 1824 the German Jews were in the majority in this country. It was in this year that they organized their first

[7] Cf. Chap. 5, Part I, page 140.

[8] A note appended to a letter of the Dutch Company, to Peter Stuyvesant, reads as follows: "The Jews of Ft. Amsterdam are divided into two distinct bodies, viz.: Portuguese and German Jews. The first class is far the wealthier." See Pub. Am. Jew. Hist. Soc. VIII — 75.

congregation in New York. "In 1824 a portion of the Congregation (Shearith Israel), consisting mainly of members of Polish or German birth, separated from the synagogue on Mill Street, and purchasing a church on Elm Street, formed a distinct congregation."[9] The cause for this separation, as stated by the founders, consisted in the fact that "a large portion of our brethren, who had been educated in the German and Polish Minhag (ritual), find it difficult to accustom themselves to what is called the Portuguese Minhag, in consequence of their early impressions and habits." "With the gracious permission of the ancient and respectable congregation Shearith Israel," the new Congregation *B'nai Jeshurun* was organized, to worship "according to the Minhag of the great synagogue in London."[10] Since then German Jewish congregations have multiplied rapidly. By 1850 twelve different congregations were organized in New York.[11]

But the real migration of German Jews did not begin until 1848. The unsettled conditions arising from the revolutionary upheavals in Germany during that period were responsible for this mass migration. The extent of the migration can be seen from the fact that between 1840 and 1877, the number of Jews in the United States increased from 15,000 to over 230,000.[12]

"The greater part of them" (the German immigrants) still continued to be recruited from the "uncouth, illiterate, and poor ......"[13] They had to wage an uphill economic struggle for sustenance and position in the new land. "By the dint of strict frugality, of unceasing activity, of indomitable energy and of considerable innate, if uncultivated abilities, they succeeded in acquiring more or less considerable fortunes, and in raising themselves to positions of honor and trust."[14] These "simple-minded

[9] Daly: "Settlement of Jews in America," p. 57.

[10] Souvenir book, Educational Alliance Fair, 1895, p. 110.

[11] See Appendix C: "German-Polish Congregations prior to 1850."

[12] In 1840 the American Almanac estimates the number of Jews as 15,000. In 1877 the Population Study undertaken by the Union of Am. Hebrew Cong. (Wm. B. Hackenburg) gives the number of Jews as 230,257. See Am. Jew. Yr. Book, 1914-1915, p. 3339. Cf. Appendix J. "Estimates of Jewish Population."

[13] Kohler, M.: "German-Jewish Migrations to America." Pub. Am. Jew. Hist. Soc. Vol IX, p. 90.

[14] Ibid.

but staunch-hearted Jewish immigrants,'' came mostly from the rural communities of Germany and Austria. ''They were strictly orthodox, loyal to the teachings of their ancestral religion and staunch in the observance of its practices. Their educational standards were simple (and traditional), like their conditions of life.''[15]

But there were among the new immigrants many idealists and men of culture. The Period of Enlightenment and the unrest of 1848 deeply affected the life of the Jews in Germany. Their leaders brought with them a new cultural ideal, that of the emancipated Occidental Jew, and a new interpretation of Judaism, that of Reform, whose purpose was to adapt the Jews to their modern environment.[16] In America the new ideals spread rapidly. Reform Judaism was widely accepted. Now, practically every one of the important German Jewish congregations in this country follows the reform ritual.

The signal contribution of the German Jews consisted in taking the philanthropic phases of Jewish life out of the synagogue, and in developing splendid eleemosynary institutions for taking care of their dependents and their needy. In educational matters they followed the same philanthropic ideals. They took *philanthropic* education, that is, the education of the poor, out of the domain of the synagogue, and communalized it, in the form of the Hebrew Free School Association.[17] But *normal* religious education, that is, the education of their own children, they continued under synagogue auspices. At first they organized their religious schools as parochial day schools, which they called Talmud Torahs.[18] Later, they introduced the Jewish Sunday School, which became widely accepted, and is still the predominating religious educational institution of the German Jews.

The German Jews also attempted to bring coördination and centralization into American Jewish life. The Union of American Hebrew Congregations, which was organized in 1873, created two

[15] Friedlaender, I.: ''Problem of Jewish Education in America, and the Bureau of Jewish Education.'' U. S. Bureau of Education, 1913, Vol. I, Ch. XVI.

[16] For a discussion of Reform Judaism, see Chap. I, p. 7.

[17] See below, pp. 46 and 64.

[18] These differed from the modern conception of the Talmud Torah as a *supplementary* religious school.

bodies for the purpose of coördinating the work of the Jewish schools. The first was the Hebrew Union College, founded in 1875, for the training of rabbis and teachers, and the second was the Hebrew Sabbath School Union, organized in 1886, for the sake of providing "a universal system for all the Hebrew Sabbath Schools in the United States."[19] The center of the activities of the German Jews was in Cincinnati, Ohio. It was from there that their schools in New York received guidance. In New York City, the Jewish Theological Seminary, with its Teachers' Institute, is the product of the organizing abilities of German Jews, but its student body and most of its faculty are Jews from Eastern Europe.

Eastern European Jews

By far the greatest migration of Jews to this country is that which came from the countries of Eastern Europe, principally from Russia, but also from the bordering countries of Galicia and Roumania. They form now the largest element of Jews in this country. In New York City over 85 per cent. of the Jewish population consists of those who have themselves come from Eastern Europe, or are descended from those who lived there.[20]

As has already been indicated, there were Eastern European Jews in this country before the days of the Revolution. The well-known Hayim Solomon, who gave his fortune to the cause of the American Revolution, and who suffered imprisonment at the hands of the British, is called "the countryman of Kosciusco." There were several congregations of Polish Jews in this city during the first half of the last century. The first typical Russian Jewish congregation in New York was organized in 1850 as the Beth Hamidrash Hagodol, and has continued till this day (1918). But this earlier migration was hardly typical of the tremendous wave of immigration which began in 1881.

Between 1881 and 1910 there came to this country more than a million and a half Jews, 93 per cent. of whom came from the

[19] Cf. Appendix D. "Hebrew Sabbath School Union."

[20] The Federal Census of 1910 gives the number of Yiddish-speaking Jews in New York City as 861,980. Joseph Jacobs in the Jewish Communal Year Book, of the New York Kehillah, estimates the total number of Jews for 1910 as ca. 900,000. Assuming that this estimate is probably too low, there would still be from 85% - 90% of the Jews who are Yiddish-speaking.

countries of Eastern Europe.[21] The infamous Russian May Laws of 1881, which circumscribed the rights of the Jews in Russia as to domicile, education, occupation, position, and practically every other phase of their life, were the immediate causes for this huge influx. The pogroms, expulsions and blood accusations, perpetrated upon them periodically by the now overthrown tyranny of Russia; the perfidious religious persecutions of Roumania; the poverty of Galicia; all tended to send tens of thousands of Jews yearly to these shores.

At first the new immigrants depended upon their wealthier German forerunners for help and leadership. But they have been gradually establishing a great variety of institutions of their own, are introducing new attitudes and new ideas into American Jewish life, and are assuming leadership in many phases of the work of the American Jewish community.

It is difficult to describe the characteristics of the Eastern European Jews. To one who knows them intimately, they present a wide variation of customs and outlooks. There are four types, however, which are of particular interest. The first of these is the *immigrant orthodox* type. This is the type familiar to visitors of the New York "slums," as the "long bearded, ear-locked patriarch of the East Side." His physical appearance in most cases bespeaks the difficult life he has had to lead. His frame is bent from persecution and poverty, and his eyes are reminiscent of past wrongs. He is minutely observant of the great mass of rabbinic tradition by which he regulates not only his outward quaint appearance, but also the austere morality of his inner life. He is well versed in the literature of the Talmud and the codes, sometimes knowing hundreds of pages of Jewish legal discussion by heart. The customs and the likes which he has brought with him from "home," he preserves with as little deviation as possible in the new land of his adoption. The two concepts which best sum up his ideals, are *Lamdan* (learned), and *Chassid* (pious).[22]

[21] Migration of Jews to America from 1881-1910, total 1,562,800; from Russia, 1,119,059—71.6%; Austria-Hungary, 281,150—17.9%; Roumania, 76,057—4.3%; from Eastern Europe, 1,467,266—93.8%. Cf. "Jewish Immigration to the United States," Samuel Joseph, page 93-94, Ph.D. dissertation, Columbia University, 1914.

[22] For the sake of exactness a distinction should be made between the Chassidic, emotional type, and the Talmudistic, intellectual type, but this distinction is not evident to the outsider.

The second type is familiarly called the "*all-right*" type. By dint of sheer industry and brains, he has fought his way above the level of economic want, and is now materially "all right." The tendency for him is to live his Jewish life on the basis of momentum only, and not to worry greatly over the many problems which confront Jewish life in America. Religion, for him, deals with birth, marriage, and death, but not very much with the life between these important events. He is not antagonistic to Jewish activity or to Jewish education, but is, rather, indifferent to these efforts, and will support them, if properly appealed to. He is an American by imitation, and is inclined to imitate the outer and the cruder values in American life, the energetic bustle, the love of success, bold initiative and grand display.

The third type is that of the *nationalist* Jew, who is the product of two historic movements. The Haskallah (Enlightenment) movement in Russia during the middle of the last century, caused many Jewish students to forsake the Talmudical halls of learning and seek the wider culture of the western world. Instead of poring over the subtle reasoning of the rabbis, young men began to devote their energies to the creation of a new literature in Hebrew, expressive of the facts of modern life and of the new orientation of the Jews in the modern world. The ideal of this movement, the *Maskil* (the enlightened), is one who is acquainted with science, literature and art, and who knows thoroughly the literature of his people, both ancient and modern, even to the extent of being able to contribute to it. With the Haskallah movement another force combined in creating the nationalist Jew. This force was Zionism. Modern Zionism originated in Russia as a "Love of Palestine" movement, and spread throughout the world under the leadership of Dr. Theodore Herzl, the founder of the Zionist world organization. It is simply a modern formulation of the age-long yearning of the Jew for Zion. It looks to the establishment of "a publicly secured, legally assured homeland for the Jews in Palestine," and to the "fostering of Jewish consciousness throughout the world."[23] These two movements, Haskallah and Zionism, are expressive of the Jewish inter-

---

[23] From the Zionist Basel Program. See discussion of Indigenous and Centralized Nationalism, Chap. I, pp. 9-11.

ests of the nationalist Eastern European Jew. He makes up the rank and file of Zionists in this country, and he can be found in every movement which makes for the organization and development of American Jewish life.

The fourth type is the *Radical.* The Russian Jewish radical is the creation of the intense revolutionary efforts in Russia, which finally led to the great Russian Revolution. His is a loud cry for social justice, and he is impatient alike of social convention and of governmental regulations, which may interfere with his sense of justice. He swells the ranks of the radical socialist and labor movements in this country. While he throws off the religious elements of his Jewish life, and in many cases also the national phases, he nevertheless ardently preserves his Jewish affiliation in intensely socialized forms: special Jewish organizations, Jewish labor unions, Jewish newspapers, Jewish schools. etc. He has converted the Jewish intellectual ideal into that of the "free-thinker," one who frees himself from the sanctions of the past, and attempts to live by "cold" intellect alone.

These are but four of the many types that make up the mass of Eastern European Jews. Yet in spite of this evident variation in type, all of them have in common several characteristics, which are of significance to Jewish education. In the first place, they all speak a distinct common language, *Yiddish* or Judeo-German. This is a German dialect of the fifteenth century, written in Hebrew script, and containing many Hebrew words and phrases, as well as many expressions taken from the language of the particular land in which it is spoken. During the last century it has developed an extensive literature of its own, containing belles-lettres, philosophy, humor and poetry.

Another common characteristic of the Eastern European Jews has already been alluded to. It is their high degree of *intellectualism.* Whether these intellectual qualities find expression in Talmudic lore, modern Hebrew literature or radical philosophy, the eager desire for knowledge is common to them all. It has been ascertained that the Russian Jews, in spite of their comparative poverty, send more of their children to the High Schools of this city, and permit them to stay there longer, than any other ethnic group.[24] It is common knowledge that more than three-fourths of the pupils in the College of the City of New York are children of Eastern European Jews. This intellectualism affects also their desire for Jewish education. The educational standard in the Jewish schools of the Eastern European Jews is throughout much higher than that which satisfies their German or their Portuguese fellow-Jews. They lay stress on the literary elements of their cultural heritage. The "Yodea Sefer" (knower of books) is still an essential element in their educational ideal. This ideal accords fully with the historic appellation of Israel as "the People of the Book."

Another common social trait of the Eastern European Jews is their tendency to remove many forms of their socialized life from the domain of the synagogue. Even among the most orthodox, the *tendency* is to make charity and education more and more communal and less and less congregational. In this they have gone further than the German Jews in America. They are encouraging lay instruction and supervision not only for the education of their poor children, *philanthropic* education, but also for the *normal* religious education of *all* of their children. This holds true in almost all of their educational institutions. The Talmud Torah in the sense of a supplementary weekday school; the Cheder, or private school; the Yeshibah as an elementary parochial school; the Yeshibah, as a secondary Talmudical school; the National Hebrew schools; the National Radical schools; all of these educational institutions are controlled and managed by special *educational* societies, outside of the jurisdiction of any particular congregation.

Periods in the History of Jewish Education in New York

With this brief account of the three migrations of Jews to the United States, and the types dominant in each, we may proceed, with greater understanding, to the development of Jewish relig-

[24] Van Denburg: "A Study of Retardation and Elimination in the High Schools of New York City." Ph. D. dissertation, T. C. Columbia University, 1910. In an investigation of the number of Jewish students in the New York City high schools made by Leo J. Linder, and published in the Jewish Daily News (Tageblatt) of Feb. 12, 1918, it is stated that 45,000 out of the 85,000 students in the city high schools are Jews, or 53% of the total enrollment.

ious education in New York City. Chronologically the history of Jewish schools may be divided roughly into the following periods:

1. Prior to 1800.
   The Portuguese Jewish school as a typical colonial school.
2. 1800-1840.
   The Portuguese Jewish school as a part of the Common School System.
3. 1840-1855.
   (a) German Jewish congregational day (parochial) schools.
   (b) Private Jewish boarding schools.
4. 1855-1865.
   Rise of the Jewish Sunday Schools.
5. 1865-1881.
   (a) Spread of Jewish "Mission Schools," particularly the Hebrew Free School Association.
   (b) Efforts to centralize the work of the Jewish Sunday Schools.
6. 1881-1900.
   Rise of the Eastern European Jewish schools;
      (a) Elementary: Yeshibahs and Seminaries.
      (b) Higher: Yeshibahs and Seminaries.
7. 1900-1910.
   Beginning of the nationalist educational movement.
8. 1910-1918.
   (a) Educational activities of groups within community:
      (1) Oriental Jewish schools.
      (2) The Department of Synagogue and School Extension.
      (3) Central Board of Talmud Torahs.
      (4) National Radical Schools.
      (5) Vaad Hayeshiboth (Central Board of Parochial Schools).
      (6) Teachers' Organizations.
      (7) Jewish Teachers' Institute.
   (b) Educational activities of the Bureau of Jewish Education.

A. Portuguese Jewish School as a Typical Colonial School
Prior to 1800

The history of Jewish education in New York, prior to 1840, is the story of one school, that of the Portuguese Jewish congregation, Shearith Israel. Because of the inhospitable treatment which the Jews were accorded in New Amsterdam, their educational activities were carried on during the first seventy-five years of their sojourn in America in the privacy of their own homes. But with the building of the first synagogue on Mill Street, in 1729-1730, the question of the Jewish education of the children became the concern of the entire congregation. We find that one year after the dedication of the synagogue, the first Jewish school in America was established. "On the 21st of Nisan, (first month) the 7th day of Pesach (Passover, (1731) the day of completing the first year of the opening of the synagogue, there was made codez [consecrated] the Yeshibat [school] called *Minhat Areb,* in the name of the following gentlemen, Mosseh, son of Sarah and Yahacob, of Abraham, and of Mosseh Mendez da Costa, for the use of this Congregation Shearith Israel and as a Beth Hamidras [house of study] for the pupils, in conformity with the direction to that effect given by Jahacob Mendez da Costa Signior, residing in London, to Messrs. Mordechay and David Gomez of New York. And may God bestow His blessing upon us. Amen." [25]

In general, the characteristics of this school, the Yeshibat Minhat Areb, from the period of its founding until 1800, were those of the usual American colonial school. It was conducted entirely under religious auspices. The Hazan (praecentor, rabbi, or reader) acted as school teacher, and the Parnassim (trustees) served as school inspectors. At first the curriculum was confined to "the Hebrew Language" or to "the Hebrew." But it soon became a parochial school, in the usual sense of the word, in which both the secular and the religious subjects were taught. In 1755, the Hazan was instructed to teach "the Hebrew, Spanish, English, writting & Arithmetick." [26] In 1762 Spanish was dropped from the curriculum, and the school was called a "publick-school."

The congregation soon became too large for the Hazan to perform both his own duties and the duties of school teacher. There began, therefore, the differentiation between the school teacher ("Ribbi"), and the Hazan, or minister of the congregation. This

---

[25] For references to the Shearith Israel school, see Appendix A: "Extracts from Minutes of Shearith Israel Congregation."

[26] This fact is of particular interest to the student of Jewish education. It contradicts two current notions: first, that the "*Jüdische Freischule*" in Berlin, 1778, was the first modern school which taught not only Jewish, but also secular subjects (Monroe Cyclopedia on "Jewish Education"); and second, that the Rebecca Gratz Sunday School in Philadelphia, 1838, was the first Jewish religious school in this country.

differentiation is first noticed in 1760, when the Parnassim and Elders of the synagogue wrote to England for a teacher.[27] But until 1800 the teacher was still expected to act as Hazan whenever necessary, as well as to perform sundry other duties, such as those of the Shammas (sexton).

The time of instruction was at first left entirely to the teacher, "either the whole morning or the afternoon as he shall think most proper." But in 1755 the Elders stipulated that the children "be strictly kept to their learning from Nine to Twelve Each forenoon, and from Two until Five in the afternoon."

The Yeshibat Minhat Areb was supported partly by the tuition fees of the pupils and partly by the congregation. In accordance with prevailing custom, the tuition fees were paid both in cash and in kind. Thus in 1747, the teacher received "Eight Shillings pr quarter from Each child that comes to Said school, and one Load Wood Yearly from Each child." But the school also made provision for the children of the poor. The teacher was required to "Teach such children Gratis that Cant afford Payment." (1747).

At first the Hazan, as teacher, received no extra remuneration for his school duties beyond that derived from the tuition fees of those pupils who were able to pay the "Eight Shillings pr quarter and one Load Wood Yearly." It then became customary to add to his salary, in order to compensate him for the extra duties of school keeping. The first salary, in 1760, consisted of forty pounds per annum, drawn from the charity funds of the congregation. It was made up by deducting twenty pounds from the Hazan's salary and "the other Twenty Pounds to be Paid out of the Sedaka (charity funds)." But these were not the only sources of the teacher's salary. In 1762, the congregation allowed the rabbi (teacher) "Twenty Pounds pr annum, with the liberty of having offerings made him in Synagogue." He seems also to have received free rental as part of his salary.

In the stormy days of the Revolution, when the entire congregation removed to Philadelphia, the school of the congregation was temporarily discontinued. But with their return to New

[27] As Holland and England were the "homelands" of the early Jewish settlers in America, the sending to England for a teacher, accords fully with the customary colonial dependence for cultural aid upon Europe.

York, the religious education of their children again began to occupy the attention of the Portuguese Jews, and the religious school of the Shearith Israel Congregation was reopened.

B. The Portuguese Jewish School as a Part of the Common School System

1800-1840

At the very beginning of the century, the *Yeshibat Minhat Areb* was reorganized as the *Polonies Talmud Torah,* and has continued under this name up to the present (1918). "In the Common Year 1800, Meyer Polony, a native of Poland died in New York, and bequeathed to the Congregation the Sum of $900; the interest to be applied towards the establishment of a Hebrew School." [28]

This school continued as a parochial school, and considered itself as a regular part of the Common School System. When the New York State legislature, in the beginning of the 19th century, was pursuing the policy of subsidizing existing schools, the school of the Congregation Shearith Israel also made application for funds. On January 3, 1811, a memorial was sent to Mayor DeWitt Clinton, to be presented by him to the legislature, for the purpose of receiving "the same confidence and encouragement which has been exhibited to others." Evidently a similar memorial had been previously sent directly to the legislature, but had not been acted upon. On April 22, 1811, the trustees of the congregation received the communication from the Mayor, enclosing the section of an act which had passed the legislature for their benefit. This act made it "lawful for the Mayor, Alderman and Commonalities of the City of New York, to pay to the trustees of Shearith Israel in the City of New York, the like sum as was paid to the other religious Congregations respectively......" [29] The first amount thus received by the congregation from the state funds, was $1,565.78, "for the purpose of instructing poor children in the most useful branches of common education, in conformity to the

---

[28] Proc. Am. Jew Hist. Soc. Vol. XXVII—215 (1913).

[29] Cf. Minutes of Congregation Shearith Israel (April 22, 1811), in Appendix A. Also Laws of the State of New York, 34th session, April 9, 1811, Volume VI, pp. 333-334.

conjunctions contained in an act directing the certain moneys to be applied for the use of free schools in New York City.'' It is not known whether this grant was repeated during the following years.

Influenced by the receipt of the state funds, the congregation Shearith Israel attempted to reorganize its school so as ''to abolish the present stipulated prices for the admission of scholars, to remove the school to a more central situation, and to admit all applicants of the Jewish persuasion, above 5 years'' (1811).[30] For this purpose the bequest of Meyer Polonies was added to the state subsidy, and the interest arising from these combined funds were to be used in reorganizing the school.[31] But evidently the funds did not suffice for converting the Polonies Talmud Torah into a communal free school, for we find that the charity aspect of the school was soon limited to the ''tuition of 10 free pupils in Hebrew and English, from the age of five until thirteen,'' and that ''the teacher had the privilege to increase the number of scholars not to exceed forty, on terms as he may be able to agree upon with the parents and guardians (1812).''

In the first quarter of the 19th century the school was known as a ''Hebrew and English School'' (1812). The curriculum still consisted of English, reading, writing, arithmetic and Hebrew, taught ''in the usual manner as heretofore by a congregational teacher'' (1812). Later we find that geography is included as a subject in the curriculum. The only reference to special method consisted in stipulating that the ''translation of the Hebrew and the instruction of the service of the synagogue is to be according to the order of the Portuguese Jews'' (1821), which means, in accordance with the Sephardic (Spanish) ritual. As for school equipment, the teacher was ''to provide the necessary stationery and fuel,'' and ''the parents and guardians of the children to provide reading and spelling books'' (1812), since

[30] It is interesting to note that during this period it was agreed that ''the scholars should only be the children of Jews.'' In view of the fact that many of the church schools, in order to make themselves eligible for the school funds were admitting children of all denominations, this conscious limiting of religious education by the Jews to their own children, is significant.

[31] The school fund was later augmented by a bequest of $200 by Miss Pinto, and in 1864 by the magnanimous sum of $13,000 from Juda Turo, the Jewish philanthropist of New Orleans.

the trustees had refused to "furnish scholars with any article of stationery except ink" (1808). One of the interesting duties imposed upon the teacher, was not to permit his scholars "to riot or make a noise in the synagogue yard, or about the premises, or in any manner to disturb the neighbors" (1822).

The practice during this period was to have individual teachers apply for the privilege of keeping school in the vestry rooms of the congregation. But the Polonies Talmud Torah was not particularly successful. It was frequently disbanded and again reorganized. At one time there were only "one paid scholar and five free scholars" (1821). One of the teachers during this time was informed that "no disposition exists on the part of families to send their children to the school under his superintendence" (1821). There were several reasons for this lack of success. Because of the stationary size of the congregation, the religious school was naturally also small. Besides this normal limitation the custom prevailed among the wealthier members of the congregation of sending their children to be educated by private teachers or in the existing Jewish boarding schools.[32] On the whole, this school did not play a significant part in the development of Jewish education.[33]

During the latter part of the period, the financial grants which religious schools had been receiving from the state ceased. In 1825 the Common Council of New York, as a result of the controversy between the Free School Association and the Beth-El Baptist Church, ordered that the Common School Fund be no longer distributed to any religious society. When the Roman Catholic Societies applied again in 1840 for permission to use the school funds "the Hebrew Congregation on Crosby Street" joined in

---

[32] See below, page 49.

[33] The irregularity and the small size of the school are reflected in a statement made somewhat later in the Asmonean, a New York Jewish weekly, in 1850. The editor, in referring to Jewish schools, writes: "It is said that one of the oldest congregations in this city has long had an organization termed an educational fund, which in the accumulation of years, amounts to over $10,000; but of its expenditures for scholastic purposes or of its educational contributions we have no knowledge." Again: "There is one congregation that has a fund purposely gathered for religious education. The congregation is either not using it at all, or using it for other purposes. Many have even forgotten that this congregation has such a fund." Cf: Asmonean, March 15, 1850.

the petition.[34] The petition failed, but the immediate outcome of it was that common school education was taken out of the hands of the "Public School Society," and the Board of Education for New York City was established in 1842.

During this period the slow evolution of the school from its parochial form into that of a supplementary school for religious instruction only, was becoming more and more evident. In the first place, the time of instruction was limited to three times per week, on afternoons only. The agreement with the teacher in 1823 mentioned merely that he shall "teach the Hebrew language, thereby offering the means of acquiring and diffusing a better knowledge of our holy religion and its divine precepts." In 1829 he was required to teach "the Hebrew, and to give the scholars the necessary instruction in relation to their duties as Yehudim" (Jews). An indication of the recognition of the claim of secular schooling is afforded in 1833, when the "Society for the Education of Poor Children and Relief of Indigent Persons of Jewish Persuasion," asked the trustees of the Polonies Talmud Torah, that the teacher "shall teach the orphans under the care of this society; he having refused to teach them on Sundays, unless they attended the other days when the school was opened, and which they were precluded from doing by their English studies." The teacher was ordered to do so. Somewhat later, in 1845, an agreement was worked out with the same society to conduct the school under combined auspices. It is significant that the purpose of the reorganized school was to be "instruction in the Hebrew language only." One of the school rules specified that "children must be six and over, and able to read and write English" (1845). Sessions were conducted on Sundays from 9 to 1 and on Tuesday and Thursday afternoons.

This tendency toward *supplementary* Jewish education can also be seen in the fact that during this period the Ladies' Association of the congregation, whose purpose was "the general instruction of children of the Jewish persuasion," began to conduct their Afternoon-and-Sunday school, (which is now the Columbia Relig-

---

[34] Cf. Palmer: "The New York Public School," page 96. But I have not been able to verify this statement either in the records of the New York Common Council, or in the Reports of the Board of Education, or in the minutes of the Congregation.

ious and Industrial School for Girls). It was not until somewhat later, (1856), however, that the parochial school idea was officially rejected by the Shearith Israel Congregation.

C. German Congregational Day Schools *1840-1855*

While the German Jews began to organize their religious life in this country as early as 1824,[35] it was not until 1842 that the first of their schools was established. In this year the first German-Jewish congregation in New York, the B'nai Jeshurun Congregation on Elm Street, opened a school called "The New York Talmud Torah and Hebrew Institute." The aim of the school was "to give an elementary English education, and formal instruction in Hebrew and religion." [36] It began with only eight pupils, and the curriculum was that of the ordinary parochial school of the time, including both English and Hebrew studies. It was intended for the children of members only, although the expenses were met entirely by the congregation. Following upon the organization of this school, two congregations opened religious schools simultaneously, in 1845. The "Immanuel" congregation (now Temple Emanu-El at 43rd Street and Fifth Avenue, then at 56 Chrystie Street), opened its religious "Elementary" school on June 2, 1845.[37] The school of the "Anshi Chasid" congregation, (now one of the constituent congregations of Temple Beth-El, 76th Street and Fifth Avenue, then at Henry Street), began its sessions on the 7th of July of the same year.[38] Both of these schools were parochial schools. Other congregations followed with the organization of similar Jewish day schools.

The *Talmud Torah and Hebrew Institute* of the B'nai Jeshurun Congregation is typical, and a description of its organization and management is applicable to the other schools as well. In 1850, with the removal of this congregation to Greene Street, the "New York Talmud Torah and Hebrew Institute" was reor-

---

[35] See above, page 32.
[36] Occident, I - 1: 107.
[37] Stern: "History of Temple Emanu-El," p. 20 and 21.
[38] Occident III - 5: 262.

ganized. A committee was appointed "for the purpose of maturing a plan for founding a public school." The committee brought in a comprehensive report,[39] reviewing the Jewish educational situation in New York at the time, and suggesting the formation of a day school for boys, in which "Hebrew, English and the classical languages shall be parts of the curriculum." They also suggested the establishment of a self-supporting school for young ladies. The school was opened in December 1852, and the curriculum included: "(1) Hebrew Studies: reading, writing, grammar, translation, prayers, scriptures and Bible history; (2) English Studies: reading, writing, ciphering, grammar, geography, history, arithmetic, composition and elocution; (3) needlework for girls; (4) (by special arrangement) Spanish, German, algebra, drawing and the Latin classics."[40] The school was designed to be as nearly self-supporting as possible, and a graduated scale of tuition fees was charged to the pupils. During this period the practice of the *confirmation* of Jewish children began in the United States. It was introduced by Dr. Max Lilienthal, at the Anshe Chesed congregation in 1846.[41] "Every boy of twelve and every girl of eleven is to receive religious instruction from the Chief Rabbi himself from Chanukah (Feast of Lights) to Shabuoth (Pentecost). The instruction is to be in religion in general, Jewish creed and revelations, immortality of the soul and the thirteen creeds. On Shabuoth the children are to be publicly examined."[42] The confirmation ceremony was originally not intended to interfere, however, with the traditional rite of Bar Mitzvah.[43]

Practically all of the instruction in the congregational day schools was of an elementary nature. The only reference to secondary instruction during this period occurs in the curriculum of the "Cheder Reshit Hochma" (lit. School for the Beginning

---

[39] Asmonean, Feb. 15, 1850.

[40] Asmonean, Nov. 26, 1852.

[41] Philipson: "Max Lilienthal," page 58-59.

[42] Occident, Feb. 1847.

[43] The Bar Mitzvah ("son of command, man of duty") ceremony is the traditional of initiating the Jewish boy as a full-fledged member of the Jewish community upon his becoming thirteen years of age. The ceremony consists in calling up the boy for the first time to the reading of the Torah, as a newly admitted member of the Jewish community.

of Wisdom) which was the school of the B'nai Israel Congregation. This curriculum included "Chaldean Talmud, and Poskim"[44] (rabbinic commentaries and decisions). To what extent this expressed simply the pious wishes of its founders we do not know. Its teacher, Mr. S. C. Noot, is supposed to have "introduced the actual speaking of Hebrew in his school," as early as 1841.[45]

The adherence of the German Jewish congregations, at this time, to their native German as the language of the school and the pulpit, may be learned from an interesting advertisement printed in German. This advertisement asked for a teacher, and specified that "in Lehrerfache ist die Fähigkeit erforderlich den Unterricht in der Religion, im Hebräischen, in der deutschen Sprache, und im Rechnen, mit Anwendung der englischen Mundart, erteilen zu können."[46] This advertisemen is later repeated in English, as: "Wanted by Emanu-El Congregation, a teacher, competent in English, Hebrew and German."[47] The custom of teaching German continued in some congregations for a long time, although it was soon eliminated as the language of instruction in the classrooms of the most important German Jewish schools.

While most of these early parochial schools were situated in vestry rooms of the congregations, the practice began at this time of erecting special buildings for religious school purposes. The first of these buildings is that of the School of Shaarey Zedek Congregation, which called itself the "National Hebrew School."[48] The dedication of this building is referred to as "the first consecration of a school house by Israelites of this city."[49] It was situated on Henry Street, and is described as "an unpretending but solid building of brick, erected at the cost of $4,000 and being three stories in height; having one long room on the ground floor and four rooms above."

---

[44] Occident, Sept. 1847, Vol. V - 6: 317.

[45] Occident, April, 1852, Vol. X - 1: 157.

[46] Asmonean, March 26, 1852, p. 233.

[47] Asmonean, August 27, 1852.

[48] Asmonean, VI - 22, & VIII - 17.

[49] Asmonean, December 9, 1853.

D. Private Jewish Boarding Schools

Besides the congregational day schools, there also arose during this period a number of private Jewish boarding schools, which were attended especially by children of the wealthier parents. The most famous of these private schools is that organized by Dr. Max Lilienthal, one of the early leaders of Reform Judaism in America.[50] It grew out of his educational efforts during the period when he officiated as rabbi of the three combined German Jewish congregations in New York (Anshe Chesed, Shaarey Shomayim and Rodeph Sholom). His aim was "to establish a union school of the three united synagogues." The school was organized in 1847.[51] After retiring from his position as rabbi of the three congregations in 1850, he devoted his creative energies to the development of this "Day School for Jewish Young Gentlemen." It was known as the Hebrew Union School No. 1, probably intended as the first of a series of similar schools. It was situated at 307 East 10th Street, in "a large handsome house, fronting on Tompkin's Square." The school was very highly praised by many parents.[52] Students came to it from all over the country, even as far as St. Louis and New Orleans. A description of the school at the time of its organization gives an insight into the content and aims of Jewish education during this period.

"The school embraces an extensive system of education, and looks to the establishment of an elementary school divided into two classes, and a mercantile and polytechnic, divided into three, only such classes to be established in the beginning as are absolutely required, and are within the reach of the funds. The principal languages to be taught are the Hebrew and the English, not the German, although nearly all the children likely to be obtained for the present, are either natives of Europe, or children of emigrants. Only in the polytechnic department is German to be a branch of study, by which means the children are at first to be thoroughly grounded in the language of the country, and then

[50] See: Philipson, David: "Max Lilienthal," 1915.

[51] Occident V: 274 (Aug. 1847).

[52] Cf. An open letter written by Judge Mordecai M. Noah, in Occident VIII-8: 424.

to be instructed how to keep up a connexion with the land of their immediate progenitors. The earlier branches of an English education are to be taught, together with religion, Bible and Commentary, Mishna and Talmud. The government is to be as much as possible paternal, and corporal punishment is to be avoided. Children will be admitted into the elementary school at five years, and each class is to last one year and one-half. Girls are to be taught needlework during the hours that they are not engaged in the studies suited for the male sex chiefly. The entire plan comprises a system of thorough education, and reaches in fact a high school of a very comprehensive kind.''[53] French and German were also taught. It is possible that some form of the natural method in teaching languages was used in this school, for ''scholars were requested to converse in English, German and French with their respective teachers.''[54]

A similar school was that of the Misses Pallaches. It began as early as 1841, as a ''School for Young Ladies,'' and was particularly patronized by the Portuguese Congregation, Shearith Israel, which sometimes offered the vestry rooms of the synagogue for the examination of its pupils (1843). A number of other schools of like nature are referred to in the magazine literature of this period.[55]

E. The Rise of the Jewish Sunday School

1855-1865

But the Jewish parochial school, whether conducted under synagogue or under private auspices, was doomed. Beginning with the second half of the 19th century, the day schools were disbanded by one congregation after another. The German Jewish congregations substituted the *Sunday schools* in their stead, and the Portuguese congregation reorganized its school as an afternoon *supplementary weekday* school.

As has already been indicated, the first Jewish Sunday school in the country was that opened in Philadelphia on March 4th,

---

[53] Occident V - 316.

[54] Asmonean XII - 25.

[55] Frequently recurring advertisements of private Jewish teachers indicate that among both the Portuguese and the German Jews, home instruction was usual

1838, in connection with the Mikveh Israel (Hope of Israel) Congregation.[56] It was organized as a "benevolent" school by a Jewish woman, Rebecca Gratz, and was conducted and taught by women. Aided by the influential rabbi of Philadelphia, Rabbi Isaac Leeser, these large-hearted Jewish women extended the Jewish Sunday school movement to other cities of the United States.[57]

The growth of the Jewish Sunday school movement was hastened by two forces. In the first place, it was aided and stimulated by the example of the American Sunday School Union. The American Sunday school movement began in Philadelphia, about 1791, and culminated in that city in the organization of the American Sunday School Union in 1824.[58] It was not by accident, therefore, that fourteen years later, the first Jewish Sunday school was opened in the same city. The Jews were accustomed to the Sunday school as the religious educational institution of their non-Jewish neighbors, and they therefore accepted it readily. The policies and methods employed in the Jewish Sunday schools were in many instances fashioned very consciously after the model of the older Protestant organization.

Another cause for the wide popularity of the Sunday school was the lessened importance of Hebrew in the Reform interpretation of Judaism. As has already been pointed out, Reform laid stress on Jewish ideas rather than on Jewish institutions. The synagogue service of the Reform temple soon changed from a Hebrew to an English service. This change eliminated one of the chief reasons for the study of Hebrew, the most difficult subject in the Jewish school curriculum. The reduction of the time of instruction to Sunday mornings only, did not, therefore, present great obstacles.

The first congregation to establish a Jewish Sunday school in New York, was the Emanu-El congregation. "By dint of great exertion, it [the parochial elementary school] was kept up until 1854, when overcome by insurmountable difficulties, the under-

---

[56] Morais: "Jews of Philadelphia," pages 146-147.

[57] Historically, there is some doubt as to whether the Sunday school in Richmond, Virginia, which was organized at about the same time as the Rebecca Gratz School, was influenced by it, or arose independently of it.

[58] Cf. Brown, M. C.: "Sunday School Movement in the United States," Ph. D. dissertation, Columbia, 1912.

taking had to be abandoned. In its place a religious school was instituted, and the Sabbath and Sunday were set apart as the days devoted to such instruction.''[59] It was practically a decade, however, before other German Jewish congregations began to follow the example of Emanu-El. On January 5, 1862, the B'nai Jeshurun Congregation "opened its Sunday school," and by 1870 practically all the important German Jewish congregations had Sunday schools connected with them.[60]

The Shearith Israel Congregation also abandoned its day school, but did not establish its present Sunday school until almost twenty years later (1874). In 1856, two years after the Emanu-El Sunday school was organized, the congregation decided "that the present organization of the Polonies Talmud Torah school, as related to the instruction both in Hebrew and English, be discontinued, and that it be opened for the instruction (without charge) in Hebrew, to scholars attached to this congregation, on every Wednesday afternoon and every Sunday morning, except on festivals." It thus became practically a Talmud Torah in the modern sense, and has continued as such until the present day (1918).[61]

The work of the Sunday school of this period was divided into three branches: "religion, Hebrew language and vocal music." The instruction was designed for children of members only, but many congregations included "*all* persons of Jewish faith above nine years of age."

The magazine literature of this period, and the period following (1865-1881), is expressive of the sentiment of the community towards the Jewish Sunday schools. At first the general sentiment was that of appreciation and encouragement, but it slowly changed to frequent expressions of dissatisfaction with the work and management of these schools. Two complaints were frequently reiterated. The first was directed against the volunteer system of teaching, which permitted young boys and girls, themselves but recently confirmed, to teach their younger brothers and

---

[59] Stern: "History of Temple Emanu-El."

[60] Some of them also continued their "Talmud Torahs" with sessions on one or two afternoons a week; but these were secondary to the Sunday schools.

[61] It now holds sessions, however, only on Wednesday afternoons, and Sundays.

sisters.[62] The second complaint dealt with the continued diminution of the importance of Hebrew in the curriculum. Owing to the marked decrease in the time of instruction less time and attention could be paid to the study of Hebrew, and the standard in most Sunday schools decreased to the degree of merely requiring sufficient ability to read Hebrew mechanically in order to follow the short synagogue service, and to understand some of the more simple prayers and responsa.

F. Development of Jewish "Mission Schools" *1865-1881*

Besides the religious schools for the children of their own members, the German Jewish congregations were also instrumental in the establishment of Jewish schools for the children of the poor. These schools were called "Mission Schools." Their functions were: (1) "to teach morality, and to exert a refining influence upon the Jewish children on the East Side"[63]; and (2) to counteract the work of the Christian missionaries.

The first of these philanthropic educational societies has already been referred to (1833),[64] as the "Society for the Education of Poor Children and the Relief of Indigent Persons of Jewish Persuasion." Many of the wealthy congregations also established religious schools for the education of poor children. Particularly was this true of the sisterhoods of the congregations and later also of the Council of Jewish Women. But by far the most important of the "mission schools" were those organized by the Hebrew Free School Association.

Hebrew Free School Association

In the spring of 1864 a number of Christian mission schools were opened in neighborhoods where large numbers of poor Jewish families resided. Their children were enticed by gifts of

---

[62] As late as 1876 the general policy was not to pay teachers of Sunday schools, and while the tendency is now for the more important congregations to pay their teachers, the volunteer system still exists in many of the smaller Jewish Sunday schools of the country.

[63] Cf. Paper on "Mission Work Among the Unenlightened Jews," by Mrs. Minnie D. Lewis, delivered before the Jewish Women's Council, Chicago, 1893.

[64] Cf. p. 45.

confectionery and clothing to attend classes ostensibly for instruction in the Hebrew language, but they were in reality "nurseries of Christian teaching."[65] In May of that year, therefore, "an important meeting of presidents and trustees of our city congregations was held at the Clinton Street Synagogue, for the purpose of checking the influence of the mission school which called itself 'Free Hebrew School,' and has an attendance of 200 children. These children attend church regularly, and a few have actually been baptized."[66] The trustees resolved to create an adequate fund for the support of Jewish religious schools, to counteract the activities of these missionaries, and to appoint a Board of Commissioners, one from each congregation, who should have charge of the management of such schools as were to be organized. The first school, located at 42 Avenue C, near 5th Street, was opened in June, 1865, as "a Hebrew and English school." It evidently supplied a much felt need, for in rapid succession other schools were opened, at 6th Avenue near 8th St., Bayard St., Chrystie St., 29th St., 44th St., 5th St., 36th St., 92nd St., and East Broadway. Besides these schools, several congregations offered their vestry rooms for the use of the Hebrew Free School Association.

But while the schools were very popular among the poorer classes for whom they were intended, they were constantly laboring under the difficulty of inadequate support. Aside from the indifference of a part of the Jewish public to the problem which the Hebrew Free Schools were trying to meet, there were also many who objected strenuously to its "sectarian influence," especially to Hebrew Free School No. 1, which was conducted as a parochial school. The charge of conducting parochial schools was made against the Association, in spite of the fact that all its other schools were supplementary afternoon schools. The question of abolishing the parochial arrangement in Hebrew Free School No. 1 was raised again and again,[67] but due to the fact that "the parents of the children wanted them at home after 3:00 o'clock" and also "insisted upon the teaching of German in these schools,"[68] it was not until 1875 that this school too was con-

[65] Souvenir Book, Educational Alliance Fair, 1895, page 42.
[66] Occident XXII - 2: 93, & XXV - 3: 157.
[67] Messenger, XXX - 22.
[68] Messenger, December 11, 1868.

verted into an afternoon school. But the reputation for supporting parochial schools clung to the Hebrew Free School Association for some time, even as late as 1894, after they had publicly insisted that all their pupils must attend the public schools.[69]

Beginning with 1869, the Association received subsidies from the state and from the city, as a charitable institution; for besides religious instruction, many of the children were also provided with food, clothing, and industrial training. Similar grants were repeated in subsequent years.[70] But the financial difficulty still persisted, and the Association had to replenish its treasury frequently by conducting charity balls, benefit theatre performances, and entertainments. The average expense per pupil is variously quoted as from $6.00 to $24.00 per annum. Several times during the history of the Association, some of its schools had to be closed temporarily because of the lack of funds.

The conduct of each school was in the hands of a Discipline Committee. Sessions were conducted daily (except on Fridays and Saturdays) from 4 to 6 p. m., and on Sunday from 9 a. m. to 12 m. The subjects taught were Hebrew (reading, spelling, translation and grammar), religion, and Bible history.[71] Later, singing and sewing were added,[72] and also "composition" in Jewish history.[73] The examinations and confirmation exercises of the Hebrew Free Schools were well advertised, and became important occasions each year. During these exercises a great many prizes were distributed, at one time as many as 50 prizes being mentioned.[74]

At best the education given in these schools was meagre. The difficulty was ascribed to the indifference of the parents who "think that six or twelve months education is more than sufficient, prior to their children going into trade." But the association also made the first attempt to provide secondary

---

[69] American Hebrew, LVI - 8: 248.

[70] In the Report of the Committee on Political Reform of the Union League Club, Feb. 22, 1872, entitled "Sectarian Appropriations of Public Money and Property," p. 13, it is stated that the Association received a total of $2,260.00 from the city in 1869; $5,515.00 in 1870; and $3,892.00 in 1871.

[71] Messenger XXXIV - 23.

[72] American Hebrew VI - 4.

[73] American Hebrew XIII - 5.

[74] Minutes of H. F. S. A., June 3, 1883.

Jewish education. In 1874 the Association formed higher classes for the reading of Hebrew, in which the more advanced pupils were instructed twice a week in Hebrew, Grammar, Pentateuch and Rashi (commentary).[75] These were known as the *Collegiate Classes.* They were later merged with the *Preparatory School* of Temple Emanu-El, conducted by Rabbi Gustav Gottheil for the purpose of training American rabbis and teachers. Some of the graduates were given the opportunity of teaching in the Hebrew Free Schools.

About this time questions of Orthodoxy and Reform began to agitate the deliberations of the Association. The reform members on the Managing Board refused to act with the orthodox members, on the ground that the various synagogues of the city were not equitably represented, and also because old-fashioned teachers and text books were used in the schools. The chief dissenting body was Temple Emanu-El; and its rabbi, Dr. Gottheil, took the leading part in bringing about certain reforms in the management and instruction of the Hebrew Free Schools.[76] A Committee on Grievances was appointed, and an Advisory Board of Ministers was organized, who were to visit the schools regularly, and advise as to changes in curriculum and management. As a direct result of this reorganization, the curriculum was modified; the number of days of attendance was reduced, and wherever possible "gentlemen teachers were replaced by lady teachers."[77] A normal school, known as "the Ladies' Hebrew Seminary," was organized by the Advisory Board, in 1882, and existed for five years. The purpose of this "seminary" was to supply teachers for all the congregational schools in the city.[78]

But the Hebrew Free School Association did not confine itself to religious school work only. It was from the very beginning conceived as a missionary effort on the part of the wealthier Jews to their indigent co-religionists. The pupils were supplied with clothing and other necessities, and were frequently

[75] Compared to the curricula of the schools of the Eastern European Jews, this educational standard was very low.

[76] American Hebrew VI - 10. Minutes of the Hebrew Free School Association, Jan. 27, 1880 & Feb. 18, 1880.

[77] Minutes of H. F. S. A., Feb. 27, 1882.

[78] American Hebrew XXXIII - 6.

taken out on excursions.[79] A number of philanthropic institutions were either organized or supported by the Association. The first of these was an industrial school for girls, opened in 1879, and continued until 1894, when it was transferred to the Educational Alliance. The first Jewish kindergarten was established by the Association on Avenue D, in 1882, under the direction of lady directors connected with the Association. This kindergarten was successful from the start, and another was soon added to it. Besides the actual teaching, a good deal of attention was paid to the physical needs of the kindergarten children, who were supplied with shoes, clothing, "a warm meal daily" and other necessities.

When the Hebrew Technical Institute for Boys was founded in 1884, the Association contributed to its annual support, assisted in its direction, and also encouraged the graduates of its schools to enter the Technical Institute, upon their leaving the Hebrew schools. The Association also conducted, for a number of years, classes for Americanizing Russian Jewish immigrants.

Towards the end of the 80's, the need began to be felt of erecting " a large mission building, in which some of the schools in this Association, together with other kindred charitable and educational institutions might find a suitable home." The suggestion for the construction of such a building was made in 1885, and resulted in 1890 in the construction of the Educational Alliance and Hebrew Institute, East Broadway corner Jefferson Street, now known as the Educational Alliance. This institution was "an *alliance* of the Hebrew Free School Association, the Young Men's Hebrew Association and the Aguilar Free Library." Thereafter, for a period of eight years, the work of the Hebrew Free Schools was conducted in the new building, and in its branch building, at 624 East 5th Street. On May 1st, 1899, an act was passed by the legislature of the State which practically reorganized the Educational Alliance, and effectuated the legal transfer of the assets of the Hebrew Free School Association to the new institution. The work previously carried on by the

---

[79] The expenses for these excursions were at first supplied by the Association, then by the Sanitary Commission of the city, and later by an organization of the pupils themselves, called "Our Own." See American Hebrew XXXIX - 13.

Association now took the form of the religious school of the Educational Alliance.

As an indication of the influence and extent of the work of the Hebrew Free School Association, it may be well to quote the statement of the committee appointed by the Educational Alliance "On the Work Heretofore Done by the Hebrew Free School Association." "From a very small beginning, the Hebrew Free School Association increased to such an extent, that at the time of its amalgamation with the Educational Alliance, there were in its classes nearly 3,500 children, and nearly a thousand children and as many adults were attending the divine services instituted by that Association."[80]

The significance of the Hebrew Free School Association in the history of Jewish education in New York, may be summed up as follows: (1) It was the first organization to try supplementary Jewish education in this country on a large scale; (2) it was the first to experiment with secondary Jewish education, and with the training of Jewish teachers; (3) it opened the first Jewish kindergarten in this city; (4) it popularized Jewish education for girls, among classes which were then averse to the training of their girls, and confined their Jewish schooling to boys;[81] (5) it was the first attempt to communalize Jewish education, by taking it out of the jurisdiction of any particular congregation. It had no lasting influence, however, narrowing down finally to the school at the Educational Alliance.

Other Mission Schools

Besides the schools of the Hebrew Free School Association, there were a good many other "mission schools."[82] Practically every sisterhood of the more important temples, both among the German and the Portuguese Jews, opened mission schools down town. Later the Council of Jewish Women also took part in this work, and attempted to centralize it. These schools were Sabbath and Sunday schools. The curriculum consisted of biblical history, prayers and responsa, and "behavior." Particular stress

---

[80] Annual Report of Educational Alliance, 1899.

[81] During the latter part of its existence, more than half of its pupils were girls. Cf. Educational Alliance Report for 1899.

[82] See Appendix D: "Mission Schools in 1896."

was laid upon the dispensing of charity to the pupils of these schools, and because the hearts of the donors were better than their grasp of the conditions, this phase of their work sometimes led to abuse.[83]

The best known of these schools was the Louis Downtown Sabbath School, organized and conducted by Mrs. Minnie D. Louis, a teacher of Temple Emanu-El. It was opened in 1880, and its original purpose was to hold exercises on Sabbath afternoons, "for attendance at which it was necessary for the children to be tidy looking."[84] The school was partly supported from "a fund contributed every Sunday by the children of Temple Emanu-El Sunday School."[85] The program and spirit of this school are typical of Jewish mission schools. "Instruction in the Sabbath School is given on Saturday afternoons from 1 to 4 p.m., and includes lessons in Bible work, hygiene, behavior, and singing. A meal of bread, butter and milk is furnished, also a bath and clothing for those requiring it."[86] Later, industrial branches were added, and the school developed into what is now the Hebrew Technical School for Girls, situated at Second Avenue and Fifteenth Street. The Albert Lucas Religious Classes, organized later (1899), and still in existence (1918), arose as a similar "missionary" effort.

Somewhat different in organization but of the same character, were the institutional schools of this period. The most important of these were the religious school of the Hebrew Orphan Asylum and the mission school of the United Hebrew Charities. The outstanding figure in this educational work was Mr. Louis Schnabel, for many years the Superintendent of the Hebrew Orphan Asylum, and the editor of *Young Israel,* "an illustrated monthly for young people," (1871-1876).

G. Efforts to Centralize the Work of the Jewish Sunday Schools

In the magazine literature of this period, the wish is frequently expressed that the work of the various Hebrew schools be unified and centralized, and that some coördinating agency be established for this purpose. The first reference to an attempt on the

[83] American Hebrew Vol. XLV: 12 "Annual Meeting of Louis School."
[84] Stern: "History of Temple Emanu-El," p. 71.
[85] American Hebrew, VI - 13.
[86] American Hebrew, Vol. XXXVIII: 4.

part of the Jews of New York to centralize the work of their Jewish schools, was that made by the B'nai Jeshurun Congregation. "In 1846 an effort was made by Jews of New York to establish schools for Jewish children of this city, under the patronage of the community. On March 22, 1846, a conference between the directors of the Emanu-El Congregation and a committee of the Talmud Torah and Hebrew Institute, was held for this purpose. After much deliberation the project was considered impracticable by the directors [of Emanu-El] and they discountenanced it."[87]

Y. M. H. A. Examinations

It was not until 1875 that any serious effort was made to centralize the work of the Jewish religious schools of New York. In that year the Y. M. H. A. of this city struck upon the idea of holding annual competitive examinations, in which the pupils of all the schools of this city should participate.[88] But while some of the institutional schools and mission schools, as well as some of the private schools, took part in these examinations, they did not receive the support of the congregational schools. It was the intention of the committee in charge of these examinations, to exert also some influence upon the method of instruction, "proper grading, selection of text books," etc. The rules to govern these examinations were adopted by the representatives of the schools themselves. The Board of Examiners consisted of five rabbis and teachers, and the examination was in history and in Hebrew.

But after a few years the experiment failed, due to the lack of support from the congregations. This was attributed to the inability of their pupils to meet the educational requirements. "It was not through indifference to the value of these competitive examinations, but rather because their children get practically one day's instruction in Hebrew during the week."[89] At the third competitive examination "no minister or trustee of synagogues was present."[90] The results of the experiment are described as "not very satisfactory, except in so far as they point out some difficulties in Hebrew education in New York."[91]

---

[87] Stern: "History of Temple Emanu-El," p. 23.
[88] Messenger LI - 17.
[89] Messenger XXXVII - 22.
[90] Messenger XLI - 18.
[91] Messenger XLIII - 22.

HEBREW SABBATH SCHOOL UNION

While the effort to introduce competitive examinations as a means of centralizing the work of Jewish schools failed, the agency organized for this purpose by the Union of American Hebrew Congregations, in Cincinnati, was more successful. This union of reform congregations came into existence in 1873, and one of its first concerns was naturally to aid the religious schools of the congregations affiliated with it. At its first General Convention in 1873, a Committee on Sabbath Schools was appointed. On June 29, 1886, the *Hebrew Sabbath School Union* was organized. Its object was "the advancing of common methods and discipline, in Jewish Sabbath schools."[92] The program of the Sabbath School Union was to provide "a universal system for all the Hebrew Sabbath schools, by promulgating a universal course of study, and by training competent teachers." The first of its efforts was to gather information concerning the Jewish Sunday schools throughout the country.[93] It elaborated a detailed course of study for Sunday schools, and published a series of school books and graded lessons.[94] It introduced the leaflet lesson system, issuing every week a pamphlet which contained some lesson either in history or in ethics. These leaflets were distributed widely among the Sabbath schools in the United States. In 1905 the Hebrew Sabbath School Union was merged into the Union of American Hebrew Congregations, as one of its departments.[95]

II. HIGHER EDUCATION

Prior to 1881 there was a good deal of discussion concerning the establishment of higher schools for Jewish learning, but although several interesting attempts were made, no permanent higher educational institution was established in New York City itself. The discussion, begun as early as 1843, by Judge Mordecai M. Noah,[96] led to the establishment of the Maimonides College in Philadelphia in 1867. In 1855 a "Zion Collegiate

[92] Cf. Appendix D: Hebrew Sabbath School Union, (section 1).

[93] Ibid, (section 3).

[94] Ibid, (section 2).

[95] Cf. "Department of Synagogue and School Extension," Chap. III, pp. 92-94.

[96] Occident, Vol. 1 - 5: 303.

Association was organized,[97] and the Zion College was established.'' But its influence was small, and when the Hebrew Union College was opened in 1874 by the Union of American Hebrew Congregations, under the leadership of Dr. Isaac M. Wise, the Zion College ceased to exist. There were also classes for more advanced pupils in some of the schools and congregations of this city. The Collegiate Classes of the Hebrew Free School Association, and the Preparatory School of Temple Emanu-El, conducted by Dr. Gottheil under the auspices of the Emanuel Theological Association,[98] have already been referred to. Similar classes were conducted by Dr. H. Pereira Mendes, rabbi of the Shearith Israel Congregation.[99] But these classes also ceased to exist with the organization of the Hebrew Union College.

Another attempt to establish a higher Jewish school in this city was made in 1876. In May of that year a ''Hebrew college convention'' was held at the Y. M. H. A., and congregations from several cities took part in its deliberations. A Hebrew Seminary Association was organized, whose purposes were: ''(1) to establish classes for Hebrew and German, for those who are already able to translate Pentateuch; (2) to arrange with an improved grammar school or high school to have Hebrew as a part of the regular course; and (3) to make arrangements for complete secular and religious training for pupils of the Hebrew Free Schools, or of the Orphan Asylum, who may show particular abilities.''[100]

But these deliberations bore no practical fruit. It was not until the next period, 1881-1905, that higher schools for Jewish learning were established in New York City.

---

[97] Asmonean, Oct. 5, 1855.

[98] Stern ''History of Temple Emanuel,'' p. 65.

[99] Messenger, Vol. XXXVI - 12.

[100] Messenger, Vols. XXXIX - 21 and XL - 6.

Chapter III

HISTORY OF JEWISH EDUCATION IN NEW YORK SINCE 1881

A. Development of the Eastern European Jewish Schools

1881-1900

The great influx of Jewish immigrants from the countries of Eastern Europe in 1881, brought about an intensification of Jewish life in this country. The new immigrants brought with them a greater knowledge of Jewish literature and law, and a closer feeling of group solidarity, than had been current among the Portuguese or the German Jews. This more intensely Jewish life had its direct expression in the work of the Jewish schools. Previous educational activities had been largely shaped by the American environment, and were the results either of imitation or of necessity. The congregational day schools (though called by the traditional name, Talmud Torahs[1]), the private boarding schools, the Sunday schools, the mission schools, were all influenced to a greater extent by non-Jewish educational institutions in America, than by any Jewish models in England, Holland or Germany. But the new immigrants were zealous concerning the religious education of their children. They brought with them educational institutions to which they had been accustomed for generations, and these traditional schools they determined to transplant in the new country of their adoption. A brief review of the three types of schools which were current at this time among the Jews of Eastern Europe, will help us to appreciate their educational activities in America.

The Three Types of Jewish Schools in Eastern Europe

An elementary Jewish religious education was practically compulsory among the Jews of Eastern Europe. There was no state law compelling the Jewish father to send his child to the Jewish school, but it fared ill, socially, with any Jew who per-

[1] It should be pointed out that the Polonies Talmud Torah was not the same kind of Talmud Torah as will be described in this chapter. Its curriculum was very elementary and it made use of but one afternoon during the week.

mitted his boy to grow up to manhood without having given him sufficient knowledge to enable his participating, with understanding, in the synagogue service. This was true only of the Jewish boy. The schooling of the Jewish girl was practically neglected until the beginning of the present century. Her education consisted of practical training in home and synagogue customs, and of whatever she could imbibe from the intensely Jewish environment about her.

The ordinary school to which the masses of Jews sent their boys for religious instruction, was the *Cheder,* or the private one-room school. It was usually situated in the home of the teacher, called the Rebbi (master) or the Melamed (teacher). Either the living room was used for this purpose, or a separate room was set aside as the school room. The equipment was primitive, consisting of a table or a pulpit, and some backless benches. The text books were standard: the Prayer Book, the Bible, the Talmud and the Codes. Only rarely were secular studies taught in the Chedarim during this period (1880). The pupils were taught eleven to twelve hours daily; from 8 o'clock in the morning until 2 in the afternoon, and from 4 in the afternoon until 9 o'clock at night.[2]

There were three kinds of Chedarim in accordance with the varying ages and capacities of pupils. The first were the *Dardeki Chedarim* (infant schools), in which youngsters below five years of age were taught the rudiments of mechanical Hebrew reading (Ivri), as well as some of the simpler prayers. From these they were transferred to the *Chumash Chedarim,* (Pentateuch Schools) where pupils were kept for a number of years at the study of the Torah, Prophets, Hagiographa, and the Rashi Commentary on the Bible.[3] The study of the Bible began with Leviticus, the third book of Moses, called "The Law of the Priests," on the ground that the pure, innocent child should be introduced to the holiest portion of Jewish literature first. The method employed was that of verbal translation, and consisted in repeating word after word and phrase after phrase, until the language was mastered. From this school, in accordance with the

---

[2] On Fridays and Saturdays this schedule was somewhat modified.

[3] The commentary on the Bible and the Talmud by Rashi (Rabbi Solomon Itzchaki) a French Jewish commentator, 1040 - 1105, is the standard commentary among the Jews.

mental abilities of the particular boy, he was transferred sooner or later to the *Gemarah Cheder* (Talmud School). Here, at the age of eight or nine years, the boy entered upon the study of the Talmud and the commentaries, usually beginning with some easy portion of the civil code. In the Gemarah Cheder he continued studying tractate after tractate, until he left the school to enter some trade, or business occupation, or else went to the Yeshibah (Talmudical High School).

In the Yeshibah the young man continued to study the Talmud with but little assistance from the teacher. The lecture method was used, and the pupils came to the teacher for examinations, and for the solution of difficult problems in reasoning or law. Usually the student left his home and travelled to the nearest Yeshibah while still a young boy, and as he grew older, went from one Yeshibah to another in quest of knowledge. The Yeshibah Bachur (student) was a "toiler in the law" and followed punctiliously "the manner becoming for the study of the Torah." He "ate his morsel of bread with salt"; he "drank water by measure"; he "slept on the ground"; and lived a life of tribulation.[4] The degree of memorized knowledge and of sharp reasoning attained by the students was remarkable. Some young lads of 13 or 14 were able to recite whole tractates and hundreds of passages by heart. There were no class graduations at the Yeshibah. The student lived there until he was married, and sometimes even after his marriage, (if his father-in-law could afford the luxury of a student son-in-law). The most capable of the students were ordained as rabbis, and became the religious heads of the Jewish communities. The less capable became teachers, or turned to more remunerative occupations.[5]

The secondary Jewish education in the Yeshibah was communal; it was free to all pupils. But in the elementary and intermediate schools, from the infant to the Talmud courses, every self-respecting father paid for the tuition of his children. *Sechar Limmud* (tuition fee) was one of the most important items in the family budget, and many a Jewish parent denied himself the conveniences of life in order to pay for the education of his boys.

---

[4] Cf. Sayings of the Fathers, Chap. 5.

[5] But study did not cease after leaving this school system. The Beth Hamidrash (House of Study) was common in every town and in every village. This was a real community center, and here many a busy man of affairs would spend an hour or two daily in quiet study.

For the children of the poor, the community organized charitable educational institutions, the *Talmud Torahs,* or the Institutions for the Study of the Torah. These philanthropic institutions were usually supported by private donations and bequests. In the larger centers they were housed in fairly commodious school buildings. But more usually the Talmud Torah building was a ramshackle structure, situated in the poorest part of the town, and was considered socially on a level with the Hekdesh, or the combined poor-house-lunatic-asylum of the community. The program of study, in most cases was confined to the elementary subjects, most of the children being compelled, because of economic circumstances, to leave school after Bar Mitzvah (confirmation), at the age of thirteen. No self-respecting father sent his child to the Talmud Torah. It was for the poor, and the stigma of poverty was upon it.

These three educational institutions, then, the Cheder, the Talmud Torah and the Yeshibah, the Eastern European Jews brought with them to this country. But here each of them underwent profound modification.

The Cheder

In America the Cheder degenerated. Several causes contributed to this degeneration. In the small communities of Eastern Europe, where every individual and his activities were known, there was a general unofficial control and supervision of the Cheder, exerted by public opinion. Every one knew the qualifications and abilities of each teacher. The teachers were therefore men of knowledge and good character, especially in the higher Pentateuch and Talmud schools. After several years of experience, either as an apprentice to some other teacher, or in his own school, the teacher usually acquired the most essential requisites in the teaching process: patience, devotion, and a pragmatic understanding of the child mind.

But in a large community like New York, it is not possible for public opinion to pay attention to particular efforts of individual teachers. Every person, qualified or unqualified, who wished to supplement his weekly earnings by keeping school, could do so without hindrance. Today, many of the New York Chedarim are taught by men who were formerly teachers in Eastern Europe.

These men came to this country too late in life to make new adjustments, and they therefore continued in the only occupation which they knew in the land of their birth. The lot of these earnest, mediaeval men, zealously trying to impart unwished-for knowledge to the unwilling youngsters of the New World, is a sad one indeed. But there are many other Chedarim kept by those who are less worthy. These are usually ignorant men who spend their mornings in peddling wares or in plying some trade, and who utilize their afternoons and evenings for selling the little Jewish knowledge they have to American children, at so much per session (10c.—25c. per week, for 10 or 15 minutes' instruction daily). The usual procedure is for a group of boys to gather in the home of the self-appointed "Rebbi," and to wait their turn or "next." While one pupil drawls meaninglessly the Hebrew words of the prayer book, the rest play or fight, with the full vivacity of youth.

Another cause for the degeneration of the Cheder lay in the economic condition of the parents. In Eastern Europe their educational standard had been high. But in this country the new immigrants were too much occupied with their daily struggle for existence to be able to devote much of their time to the question of the religious education of their children. The educational standard of many parents consequently decreased, so that elementary Jewish education, on the plane of the Dardekei Cheder, began to suffice. The ideal of many parents came to contain but three elements: (1) fluency in the mechanical reading of Hebrew prayers ("Ivri"); (2) knowledge of the Kiddush or Sabbath Eve benediction, and the Kaddish, or prayer for the dead; (3) ability to read the portion of the Torah assigned at the Bar Mitzvah initiation ceremony, and to deliver a "confirmation speech."

In the towns of Eastern Europe, the Cheder was the only educational model before the child, and therefore its equipment, management and teacher lost nothing by comparison. In New York, the congested life of the tenement made the sanitary conditions of the Cheder much worse than in the communities of Europe. The equipment continued to be as primitive. Many of the Chedarim are still situated in unbelievable places: above stables, at the back of stores, in cellars, in garrets, and in similar well-nigh impossible locations.[6] When the Jewish child compares this school to the highly developed public school, Jewish education suffers greatly by the comparison. There are estimated to be over 500 of these Chedarim in this city.[7] It is not possible to survey or to supervise them. They arise without notice, and usually disappear after a brief existence. Their only announcement is the sign on the front of the house, and in many cases even that is lacking to tell of their whereabouts.

As a direct outgrowth of the conditions which caused the degeneration of the Cheder, came the great number of itinerant Melammedim (teachers). The entire school equipment of the itinerant teacher consists of a worn-out prayer book securely placed under his arm. He goes from house to house, bringing the Cheder *to* the child, for in aim, content and method, the home instruction which he gives, differs in no way from that of the Cheder. There are hundreds of these teachers in New York City. They are either maladjusted individuals, whose earnestness must not be underrated, or mercenary disbursers of Ivri (Hebrew reading), who are an obstacle to the progress of Jewish education in America.

The Talmud Torah

In contradistinction to the degeneration of the Cheder, the Talmud Torah underwent a transformation for the better in this country. It began on the European model, as an institution for the children of the poor. But it came to be housed in special school buildings, which the school laws of the state required to be sanitary and safe. Because of its situation in congested quarters of the city, it reached many pupils, and was therefore capable of developing a system of grading and school management similar to that of the public schools. The necessity for raising communal funds for its maintenance, brought it constantly to the attention of the Jewish public. These reasons caused it to develop into an

---

[6] For a scathing condemnation of the sanitary conditions in these Chedarim, Cf. Weekly bulletin of the Department of Health in New York, Vol. IV - 16, April 17, 1915, page 129. See also, report of the Committee on Education, of the New York Kehillah, in American Hebrew, March 4, 1910.

[7] There are of course some Chedarim that are more modern and taught by younger men. But these arose since the beginning of the century and are the product of a movement which will be described later.

educational institution which shows the greatest promise for the development of Jewish education in this country.

The first of the Eastern European Talmud Torahs was organized in 1862 by Rev. Pesach Rosenthal, and continued for 17 years. In 1879 it was discontinued for lack of funds, but began sessions again in 1881, and two years later, March 3, 1883, it was reorganized as the School of the *Machzike Talmud Torah* (Supporters of Talmud Torah.)[8] The school began in two rented rooms at 101 East Broadway. It then moved to 83 East Broadway, and in 1886 purchased its present building at 227 East Broadway. This building and the adjoining one were remodelled as one school building capable of accommodating 800 pupils. It was for a long time the pride of the Eastern European Jews on the East Side.

At first the language in which the business of the Board of Directors was transacted, as well as the language of instruction in the classroom, was Yiddish. In 1899 English began to replace Yiddish as the language of instruction. This movement towards the Americanization of the Talmud Torah was aided by Mr. Jacob H. Schiff, who promised to give his support to the Talmud Torah, on condition that English be substituted for Yiddish. This was done, and a building fund was started by Mr. Schiff to erect branches of the Machzike Talmud Torah throughout the city. But only one branch was erected, at 68 East 7th Street.

The Machzike Talmud Torah was the first of a series of Talmud Torahs, which were soon established in various parts of the city. In Manhattan the Downtown Talmud Torah, or as it was then known, the First Austrian Talmud Torah, was organized in 1894. It began in a small room on Attorney Street. From there it removed to a dilapidated house at 77 Sheriff Street, and in 1909 to its present building at 394 E. Houston Street. In the same year (1894) the *Montefiore Talmud Torah* was opened at 28 Suffolk Street, and in 1895 removed to its present building at 40 Gouverneur Street. The following year some of the members of the Beth Hamidrash Hagodol (the first Russian Jewish congregation in America), removed to Harlem, and there opened the *Uptown Talmud Torah,* in 1895. It was then situated at 210 E.

[8] American Hebrew XXIX - 10: 152, and Minutes of the Machzike Talmud Torah, March 3, 1883, and July 1, 1883.

104th Street, and in 1909 erected its own building at 132 E. 111th Street. This school is the most capacious Jewish school house in the city, and is capable of accommodating 2,000 pupils.

In Brooklyn the first known Talmud Torah was organized in 1890, at 46 Leonard Street. With its removal in 1900 to 61-65 Meserole Street, it became the present *School of Biblical Instruction.*[9] The *Hebrew Free School,*[10] at 414 Stone Avenue, the largest Jewish school in Brooklyn, was first organized in 1901, and was rebuilt in 1912. In the Bronx there was probably not a single Talmud Torah during this period. The first reference is to the Tremont Hebrew Free School, on East 171st Street, in 1906.

Many other Talmud Torahs were opened during the early part of this century. Besides these institutions, which were built and conducted by special educational societies (Talmud Torah Associations), some of the congregations also organized Talmud Torahs in their vestry rooms. An early illustration of this kind of congregational Talmud Torah is that of the Khal Adath Israel, on 57th Street, which was in existence in 1887.[11]

The Machzike Talmud Torah served as a model for the Talmud Torahs which followed, and is therefore typical of all other such schools prior to 1905. Its object was "to instruct poor children gratis in the Hebrew language and literature, and to give them a religious education."[12] But besides religious education, shoes and clothing were also provided for the children of the poor. A ladies' auxiliary, Malbish Arumim ("clothes for the naked") society, was organized in connection with the Talmud Torah, for this philanthropic purpose. The Talmud Torah was maintained, "firstly, from dues of members who pay from $3.00 and upwards per year, or proportionately monthly, and secondly, from

[9] This school arose in a curious manner. A number of young ladies connected with one of the Brooklyn congregations, raised a certain amount of money for the needs of the congregation. In some miraculous fashion they managed to raise more money than was needed, and as in accordance with Jewish tradition, money raised for holy purposes cannot be devoted to secular purposes, the young ladies organized themselves into a Machzikei (supporters) Talmud Torah Ladies' Society, and opened a Hebrew school. (American Hebrew LXXX - 1: 20).

[10] It had no connection with the Hebrew Free School Association described in chapter 2.

[11] "Jews and Judaism in New York," M. Weinberger, N. Y., 1887. Pages 17 - 25 of this book, written in Hebrew, contain an interesting account of the conditions of Jewish education in New York during this period.

[12] Constitution of Machzike Talmud Torah, 1885, Art. II, Sec. 1.

donations and charity boxes, and such other incomes as the Board of Directors decide upon.''[13] Members and donors had the privilege of admitting two or three free pupils to the school every year. Besides this privilege, special religious solicitation and benefits were given to the members in case of sickness or death.[14]

The Talmud Torah was managed by a Board of Directors. The first Committee on Education of this school was called Mashgichey Ha-Talmud Torah (Inspectors of the Talmud Torah). Each of these Mashgichim (inspectors) was required to visit the school during certain specified days and report back to the Board of Directors upon the conditions of instruction and management.[15] There was also a principal of the school, but aside from helping to plan the course of study, and exercising general disciplinary functions, his influence was insignificant.

The instruction during this period was carried on daily from 4 to 8 o'clock every afternoon of the week except Fridays, also from 2 to 5 on Saturdays, and from 9 a. m. to 3 p. m. on Sundays.[16] Besides the afternoon classes, there were ''day'' classes, from 9 to 12 every morning, for young children below public school age. These classes were for the purpose of teaching young children the elements of Hebrew reading and some of the prayers.[17] In the Machzike Talmud Torah these day classes were abolished in 1902, but they still exist in some of the other Talmud Torahs.[18]

The curriculum of the Talmud Torah during this period was as follows: ''(a) reading of Hebrew, beginning from A B C up to fluent reading, in accordance with the rules of Hebrew grammar; (b) holy Scriptures and grammar; (c) benedictions and prayers, and translation of same; (f) meaning of holidays; (g) reading of the portion of the week (in the Bible) and the Hafto-

---

[13] Cf. Appendix E: ''Extracts from the constitution of the Machzike Talmud Torah Association.''

[14] Some of the pupils of the school were required to recite the Psalms when members or directors fell ill, and to follow their funerals when they died. Cf. Montefiore Talmud Torah pamphlet, 1906, also Appendix F: ''Extracts from the Const. of the Machzike Yeshibath Etz Chayim.''

[15] Minutes of the Machzike T. T., April 29, 1833.

[16] Cf. American Hebrew XXIX - 10: 152. Const. of the Machzike T. T., Art. XIX - Sec. 3, 4 & 5. Minutes of the Machzike T. T., May 20, 1883.

[17] Cf. Dardekei Cheder, p. 65.

[18] Viz. Tifereth Jerusalem T. T., 145 East Broadway.

rah (prophetic portion), according to the accentual marks and notes, also the benedictions pertaining thereto; (h) Shulchan Aruch and Orach Chayim;[19] (i) decrees of the Jewish faith, and Jewish history. If the Board of Education finds it necessary to teach Talmud also, and they have the necessary means, they may open classes for its instruction.''[20]

While the Talmud Torah began as an institution for the education of the poor only, it soon modified this policy. The following year, after its reorganization, the Mashgichim (inspectors) were ordered to determine which children could afford to pay for their tuition. The payment of tuition fees was made weekly or monthly; in a few instances the fees were paid by the season. There was a wide range of prices, and each particular case was decided independently by the Mashgichim or by the secretary of the school. In the course of time, some of the directors of the institution began to send their own children as pupils. The Talmud Torah thus lost its charitable aspect to some extent, and gradually became a communal educational institution, for *all* Jewish children.

The Yeshibah

But the Talmud Torah was not sufficient for the demands of some of the Eastern European Jews, because it failed to make proper provision for the study of the Talmud. Talmud had formed a very important element in their Jewish curriculum, in many cases the only element. It stressed the development of the "intellect," and this intellectual ideal the Jews from Eastern Europe retained here also. Because the shorter time at the disposal of the Talmud Torah made it very difficult to meet this demand for instruction in Talmud, except to a limited extent, the most orthodox of the Eastern European Jews began to turn their attention to the third of their educational institutions, the Yeshibah.

In America the Yeshibah, too, underwent an important transformation. The term began to be used in two senses. It kept the original idea of a higher Talmudical Academy, but it also began to be applied to elementary Jewish parochial schools.

---

[19] Cf. Discussion of Shulchan Aruch in Chap. 1, page 6.

[20] Const. of Machzike T. T., Art. XIX, Sec. 1 and 2. Cf. Appendix E.

There was no institution in this country which corresponded to the Talmud Cheder of Eastern Europe.[21] The Yeshibah was, therefore, made to take its place. It was created for the purpose of giving an intensive Jewish training to the Jewish boy, so as to enable him to reach the study of the Talmud as quickly as possible. Because supplementary weekday instruction did not permit sufficient time for this intensive Talmudical study, the Yeshibah was organized as a parochial school, in which the secular studies were to be in Jewish hands. There was for a time confusion as to which of the two functions the Yeshibah was to perform in America: that of a parochial elementary school, or of a higher Talmudical academy.

Elementary Yeshibah

The first Yeshibah was organized in 1886. On September 15th of that year the Yeshibath Etz Chayim (Tree of Life) was incorporated as the Etz Chayim Talmudical Academy. It was an intermediate Talmud Cheder, rather than an elementary Jewish school, and was fashioned very consciously after its European model. It originated as the result of opposition to the Machzike Talmud Torah, because that institution made no satisfactory provision for the teaching of Talmud. The early days of the institution are well characterized in the words of one of its founders, who is still connected with the institution. "A few of us Jews wanted that the Machzike Talmud Torah should teach Talmud, but they refused to do so. And so we went out into the street and picked up some boys, nine and ten years old, who knew the Bible with Rashi from 'home,' and began to teach them Talmud. We rented a room at 47 East Broadway. But our financial condition was so poor that we had no money with which to buy books. So we bought one Gemarah (Talmud) for 90 cents, and tore it into three parts, giving one part to each of the three Melammedim (teachers). To start our Yeshibah, the directors went about the neighborhood collecting nickels and dimes, which were given to us. In order to maintain the Yeshibah, the directors had to post up boxes in private homes and in synagogues, and then go personally to collect the money which good people deposited in them for our Yeshibah."

[21] Cf. above p. 66.

The aim of the institution was "to give instruction to poor Hebrew children in the Hebrew language and the Jewish religion —Talmud, Bible and Shulchan Aruch, during the whole day from 9:00 in the morning until 4:00 in the afternoon; also from 4:00 in the afternoon two hours shall be devoted to teaching the native language, English, and one hour to teaching Hebrew, Loschon Hakodesh, (holy language), and to read and write Jargon (Yiddish)."[22]

The founders of the institution were zealously orthodox, and possessed a high degree of Jewish knowledge. Any director, teacher or official of the institution who was accused of breaking the slightest regulation of the "Polish-Russian ritual," or of making the slightest innovation, was to be cross-examined and was liable to expulsion.[23] Their minute books were written in Hebrew and are still kept in that language. Because of this intellectualism, no special principal was needed to take charge of the school. "A committee, consisting of six members, who shall be called leaders, Menahalim, shall superintend the course of study in Talmud, Bible and Shulchan Aruch; appoint Hebrew teachers; and also be in a position to discharge a Hebrew teacher, if they have sufficient reason for it."[24]

The new institution was greeted with enthusiasm among the orthodox circles of the Eastern European Jews.[25] For some time it was the only Yeshibah in New York. It was housed in a poor, unsanitary building at 1 Canal Street, from which it removed to 85 Henry Street. It was constantly struggling under the burden of financial deficits. Besides the regular day classes, it later added some supplementary afternoon classes for teaching the Pentateuch with Rashi Commentary. No provision whatever was made by this Yeshibah or by any of the subsequent ones, for the education of Jewish girls. The Talmud Torahs were slowly changing the hoary principle that the Jewish women need no book knowledge, but the Yeshibahs have refused to part with it.

While the Etz Chayim Yeshibah was an intermediate Jewish school, it also made provision for the instruction of some older

---

[22] Const. of the Society Machzike Yeshibah Etz Chayim, Art. II, Sec. 1. Cf. Appendix F. Part 1.

[23] For the resolution to that effect, see Appendix F, part 2.

[24] Constitution, Machzike Yeshibath Etz Chayim, Art. IV - Sec. 3.

[25] Weinberger: "Hayehudim Vahayaduth B' New York," (The Jews and Judaism in New York) 1887, N. Y., p. 17 - 25.

boys, who were pursuing higher Talmudical studies. For this reason it came into conflict with another Yeshibah, the Yeshibath Yitzchak Elchanan, organized in 1897 as a higher Talmudical Institute. The misunderstanding as to the function of the Yeshibah was not obviated until recently, (1915), when the two Yeshibahs combined into the Rabbinical College.[26]

Fifteen years after the founding of the Yeshibah Etz Chayim, another Yeshibah was organized on somewhat different principles. In 1901 a few individuals who wished to give their *own* children an intensive Jewish Talmudical education, engaged one Hebrew teacher and one English teacher, and opened a school under the name Beth Sefer Tifereth Jerusalem (Glory of Jerusalem School).[27]

Two years later the school was taken out of the hands of individuals and made "public property." Its name was changed to the Yeshivas Rabbenu Yaakov Yosef (Rabbi Jacob Joseph School).[28] It was housed at 197 Henry Street, and recently removed, (1913) to its present building, 165 Henry Street. It differed also from the previous Yeshibahs, in that it was an *elementary* parochial school, teaching elementary Jewish studies as well as the Talmud. It is now by far the largest Jewish parochial school in the country, giving Jewish and secular instruction to over 500 pupils.

Several of the schools during this period called themselves Yeshibahs, but they were in reality supplementary afternoon schools, with emphasis upon Talmud in the higher grades. During the next period, three other Yeshibahs were organized, two of which still continue (1918), as parochial schools.

The Rabbi Jacob Joseph School, the largest and the best known of these parochial schools, may serve to show what the Yeshibah is aiming to do in this country. It was organized because "the ordinary Talmud Torah was unable to give a complete mastery of the history, literature and the precepts of our religion," and because "there was no school in which a complete secular education could be given, without reducing the time needed for religious training."[29]

---

[26] Cf. Below p. 97.

[27] Cf. Special Pinkos (chronicle) of the Rabbi Jacob Joseph School.

[28] Named after Rabbi Jacob Joseph, who in 1886 became the chief rabbi of several Russian Jewish congregations in New York.

[29] Pamphlet entitled: "The Rabbi Jacob Joseph School; Its High Aims and Ideals."

The curriculum of the school included Hebrew reading and writing, religion, Bible and the Talmud, which began in the sixth grade for boys of 10 and 11 years old.[30] The secular curriculum was the same as that of the public school, except that certain of the "unnecessary" studies were eliminated.[31] The language of instruction in the Jewish studies is Yiddish, and in the secular studies it is English. The Jewish teachers are not required to know English. The secular teachers are mostly young men who teach in the public schools of this city until 3 p. m. In the mornings, before 3:00 o'clock, the Jewish studies are taught, and the hours from 4 to 7 are devoted to the public school studies. The reasons for putting the Jewish studies in the morning, are, in the first place, so that they might get "the best time of the children,"[32] and in the second place, that public school teachers might be engaged for this work in the afternoons.

Many of the children of the Yeshibah come from a very great distance, and carfare is provided for some of them. Also a kitchen fund, managed by the lady directors of the institution, provides breakfast and luncheon for the children. The great majority of the pupils are immigrant children who previous to their coming to America, received Jewish training in Russia and Poland. The elementary Yeshibah lays emphasis upon Jewish knowledge, and hopes through a thorough grounding in Judaism to keep the boys within the fold. But it wishes also at the same time to give its pupils sufficient secular training to prepare them for life in the American environment.

Higher Yeshibahs

Besides the elementary Yeshibah, the Eastern European Jews also brought with them the original idea of the Yeshibah, as a higher Talmudical academy. In 1897 "arose" the Yeshibath Yitzchak Elchanan, the Rabbi Isaac Elchanan Theological Seminary.[33] The term "arose" is used advisedly because this school

---

[30] At first the course of study was designed to include also the higher Talmudical studies, for boys between 14 and 16. With the organization of the Rabbinical College in 1915, this policy was changed, and the graduates of the Rabbi Jacob Joseph School are now sent to that college.

[31] For a detailed discussion of the elementary Yeshibah, see Part II, Chaps. 5 and 10.

[32] Quoting the words of a principal of one of the Yeshibahs.

was not "organized" until much later (1908). The manner in which the school originated is very significant of the social psychology of the immigrant orthodox Jew from Eastern Europe. "Some pious Jews found out that there were a few young men who would like to devote their entire time to sit and study (the Talmud) if someone would provide them with food. These Jews, therefore, (themselves by no means opulent)" collected among themselves $5.00 every week, and gave two of these young men $2.50 per week each, if they would sit and study. Gradually the number of young men increased, and a school "arose."[34] Apart from the "good deed" of encouraging young men "to study the Torah for its own sake," it was also hoped that the students would prepare themselves to act as rabbis. Practically no teachers were required, since these young men had previous Talmudical training. No school house was needed, a room for this purpose being set aside in the building of the Yeshibath Etz Chayim. No supervision was necessary, except that of the lay Mashgiach (overseer), who made sure that the young men earned their "two and a half per week," by constant application.

But as the students became more Americanized, they realized that Talmudical study alone was not sufficient preparation for even the most orthodox rabbi in this country. They began to demand that secular studies also be provided for them. Another cause for dissatisfaction arose from the fact that the directors opened several classes for younger boys. There was misunderstanding in this institution also, as to whether its aim should be to prepare well-versed immigrant young men for the American rabbinate, or to give Talmudic training to younger children.[35] The dissatisfaction expressed itself again and again, and culminated in a "strike" of the students in 1906. An appeal was sent by them to the Jews of New York, demanding "(1) that they learn systematically the right thing at the right time; (2) that they be given permission to learn the Hebrew language, Jewish culture, (i. e. not only Talmud) and Jewish history; (3) that the program of studies include the English language, history, and the general sciences; (4) that they be taught oratory

---

[33] Named after the famous Rabbi of Kovno, Isaac Elchanan Spektor.

[34] Jewish Morning Journal, May 15, 1908.

[35] Jewish Morning Journal, May 6, 1908.

and public speaking; and (5) that their material support be so arranged as not to make it necessary for them to make special requests for every little thing needed.''[36] This quaint appeal was signed by ''all the pupils of the Yeshibah.'' The students threatened to leave the institution in a body, and actually carried out the threat. They removed for a short time to a little ''Klaus'' (private synagogue of a ''chevra'' or society). But an agreement was finally reached. The Yeshibath Yitzchak Elchanan was limited to higher Talmudical studies, and the Yeshibath Etz Chayim was to be only an elementary Yeshibah. The other demands of the pupils were also met. Upon the new basis the Yeshibah was ''organized'' in 1908. At this time it was housed at 156 Henry Street. Recently, in 1915, it combined with the Yeshibath Etz Chayim, as the Rabbinical College of America.[37]

Jewish Theological Seminary of America

Ten years before the founding of the Yeshibath Yitzchak Elchanan for rabbinical students of the immigrant orthodox type, a seminary for the training of conservative rabbis was established in this city. In 1886, a conference of conservative Jewish ministers was held in the 19th Street Synagogue (Shearith Israel) for the purpose of organizing a seminary ''to train teachers of the future generations in sympathy with the spirit of conservative Judaism.'' The Hebrew Union College, established in Cincinnati in 1874, taught the tenets of Reform Judaism, and its graduates could therefore not be acceptable to orthodox or conservative Jews. In January 1887, the Jewish Theological Seminary was opened in New York, and in the same year a branch was organized in Philadelphia.[38] Dr. Sabato Morais was chosen president of the seminary, and the institution was managed by an advisory board of ten ministers, some of whom also constituted the faculty.

The course of study, as outlined in 1886 in an open letter addressed to the Jews of America, was divided into three parts: preparatory, junior and senior. It provided instruction for both rabbis and teachers. ''The students will be subjected to practical

---

[36] Jewish Morning Journal, Jan. 27, 1906.

[37] Cf. Below p. 96.

[38] The opening of the Seminary properly comes within this period of the development of the Eastern European Jewish schools, because whereas its founders and organizers were mostly Portuguese and German Jews, the faculty and students were predominantly Eastern European.

exercises, according to their intention of becoming teachers. readers or preachers.''[39] At first classes were conducted in the vestry rooms of the 19th Street Synagogue, and the initial enrollment consisted of ten pupils. Rooms were later procured in the Cooper Union Institute; from there the Seminary migrated to 736 Lexington Ave., and in 1902 it removed to its present quarters at 531 West 123rd Street. Reciprocal academic privileges were arranged with Columbia University, so that students of the Seminary could pursue post-graduate studies at that institution.

Upon the death of Dr. Morais in 1897, the Seminary continued under the general management of the Board of Trustees until 1902. In that year Dr. Solomon Schechter was invited from England to become its president, and the institution was reorganized as the Jewish Theological Seminary of America. Under the leadership of Dr. Schechter, the Seminary grew to be one of the most important schools of Jewish learning in this country. Dr. Schechter continued at its head until his death in 1915, when Dr. Cyrus Adler, of Dropsie College, Philadelphia, was called to be its acting president.

In 1903 special classes were opened for the purpose of training teachers for Jewish Schools. But these classes were inadequate to meet the growing demand for Jewish teachers. Six years later, in 1909, the Teachers' Institute of the Jewish Theological Seminary was organized.[40]

Jewish Chautauqua Society

An educational society of a very different nature was the Jewish Chautauqua Society, which began its activities in 1893, with Dr. Henry Berkowitz of Philadelphia as Chancellor.[41] It was fashioned after the secular Chautauqua Literary and Scientific Circle. Its purpose was to assign books and courses for young people and adults ''who have neither school nor teacher at hand.''[42] It wished also to ''create courses for teachers in relig-

---

[39] ''The Jewish Theological Seminary,'' an open letter to the Jews and Jewish Congregations of America, Nov. 1886.

[40] Cf. below p. 97.

[41] It should be mentioned that this organization was the work of German and not of Eastern European Jews.

[42] Proc. of Fifth Annual Session of the Jewish Chautauqua Society, 1901, p. 15.

ious schools."[43] In accordance with these aims it issued reading and study courses in Bible, Jewish history, literature and Hebrew. It conducted annual summer assemblies as literary institutes. In the assembly of 1900, it started a "School of Practice" for Sunday school teachers, for the purpose of offering them some opportunity of discussing the theoretic and practical phases of their work. In October 1911, a Correspondence School for Teachers was organized, with Dr. William Rosenau of Baltimore as corresponding director. The influence of the Chautauqua Society is difficult to estimate, though it probably has not been significant for the development of Jewish education in New York.

Jewish Religious School Union

About 1897 the Jewish teachers of this city were organized into the Jewish Religious Union of New York, under the combined auspices of the Board of Ministers, the Hebrew Free School Association, and the New York Section of the National Council of Jewish Women. The objects of the Union were: "to awaken the community to the need of more efficient religious education for the young; to establish systematic courses of study for religious teachers, and those interested in the moral training of the young; to provide manuals for teachers and class books for scholars, and such other pedagogical aids as may be deemed desirable; to improve methods of instruction and suggest changes in the courses of study; to establish a standard of qualifications for teachers; to open mission schools; and to organize a Teachers' Union for the discussion of religious and pedagogic themes, and with a view of fostering a spirit of fellowship among the Jewish religious school teachers."[44]

The Union was active for a few years in conducting lecture courses for teachers on the subjects of the Sunday School curriculum for the purpose of helping the Sunday school teachers in their work. Dr. Kaufman Kohler and Miss Julia Richman

---

[43] Ibid, p. 20.

[44] From Constitution (typewritten), in possession of the New York Public Library.

were among the prominent figures connected with the Union. After a brief existence, however, the Union ceased its activity.[45]

B. The Growth of the Nationalist Educational Movement *1900-1910*

During the last years of the preceding century, new movements and new ideals began to affect Jewish life, particularly in Eastern Europe. The two movements which produced the Nationalist Jew, Haskallah and Zionism, modified profoundly the content and methods of Jewish education. Jews had begun to migrate to Palestine and to build up agricultural colonies in the land of their fathers. The modern Jewish life in Palestine was emphasizing Hebrew as a spoken living language, and Palestinian schoolmen were introducing the natural method of teaching that language. Jewish intellectual energies began to turn to the creation of a new Hebrew literature. Educators commenced to write text books for teaching the reborn Hebrew language and the newly created modern Hebrew literature. The contact with western culture also had its effects upon the Cheder. The pedagogic principles of Western Europe began to infiltrate into the Jewish schools and the Cheder Methukan (improved school) arose as the result. The aim of the new type of school was nationalistic, and its spirit and management were in fuller accordance with modern life and conditions, than were the earlier schools.

National Hebrew Schools

The nationalist Jewish movement first found concrete educational expression in our country toward the end of the last century. The first Jewish school fashioned in the spirit of the new nationalism was established in this city as a private Hebrew school, on October 10th, 1893, by S. H. Neumann, a Russian-Jewish teacher. It was called the *Shaarey Zion School,* and was situated at 40 Leonard Street, Brooklyn. In the circular announcing its opening it was proclaimed as "a model school for the better youth," in which "Hebrew in all classes is taught

[45] The Jewish Religious School Union organized in 1913 (see p. 97) had no connection with this organization.

as a living language . . . so that children six or seven years old speak Hebrew wonderfully.'' The pupils were carefully chosen, and more pupils applied to the school for admission than could be accepted. ''Most gladly'' the circular continues, ''are small children, (beginners) admitted, before their education becomes corrupted.''[46]

The school was divided into three grades. The *Elementary School* for beginners, the *Middle School,* and the *High School.* The Elementary School was for a number of years conducted as a parochial primary school. Sessions were held from 9 A. M. to 3 or 4 P. M., and not only was the usual Jewish instruction given in the rudiments of Hebrew (conversational method) and in the beginnings of Pentateuch, but English and Arithmetic were also taught. The purpose of teaching the secular subjects was to keep the children as long as possible under Jewish influences, so as to give them a good start in the study of the Hebrew language. ''No extra charge was made for teaching English and Arithmetic.'' But after a few years of futile effort in this direction, the Elementary School discontinued its morning classes and was joined to the two other grades of the Hebrew School: the Middle and the High Schools, which were regular ''afternoon'' schools. Sessions were held after public school hours, from 4 to 7 or 8 P. M., and the instruction comprised the Hebrew language (conversation, reading, writing and grammar), Bible and Commentary, Jewish History, Talmud, ''and other subjects, taught according to the best methods, mostly original.''

The first years were years of struggle, not only against an untoward environment, but also against the unsympathetic parents of the pupils. The teaching of Hebrew as a living language was then considered an unwelcome ''fad,'' and several ''secret'' meetings were held by the parents of the school children to make Mr. Neumann stop his ''vagaries'' and get down to the good old-fashioned teaching of ''prayers and translation.'' But undaunted, Mr. Neumann persisted in his educational pathfinding. He wrote his own ''textbooks,'' and devised his own ''methods.'' The novel results which he was successful in obtaining, assured the success and the good name of his school.

---

[46] For copy of circular see Appendix G.

FIRST NATIONAL HEBREW SCHOOL IN NEW YORK CITY

HEBREW AND GERMAN SCHOOL IN 8 CLASSES. (Established October 10, 1893.)

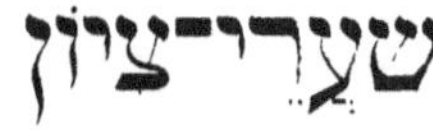

מוסטער־שולע פיר דיא בעססערע יוגענד אין 8 קלאַססען.

זאָן א״ב ביז גמרא, תנ״ך, דקדוק, יידישע היסטאריע, א. ז. ו. העברעאיש אלס איינע לעבענדע שפראכע · שרייבען אונד שפרעכען אויך דייטש אונד יידיש שרייבען, ענגליש אונד רעכנען (פיר קליינע)

40 לעאנארד סטרי

צווישען מק־קיבבען אינד סינ

ז. ה. נ

The school is still in existence (1918) as the Neumann Hebrew School, 210 Stockton Street, Brooklyn, New York.

The second nationalist educational institution was organized much later, in 1905. It also originated in Brooklyn, being situated at 156 Graham Avenue. It began as a private school, and proposed to teach Jewish girls to read and write Yiddish, as well as to read Hebrew prayers (Ivri). It was one of many similar institutions in this country, fashioned after the Jewish private teacher of girls in Eastern Europe, whose chief function was to teach young ladies to write a letter.

But in the same year its character changed radically. Several young men imbued with the new spirit of Jewish nationalism, under the leadership of Mr. Ephraim Kaplan, took hold of the institution, and organized it as a *National Hebrew School* for girls. In this institution also was Hebrew taught by the natural method, Ivrith be Ivrith, (Hebrew in Hebrew), and emphasis was laid upon modern Hebrew literature, as well as upon Hebrew conversation. The school was confined to the teaching of girls, for two reasons: first, because it was easier to get Jewish parents to permit the teaching of these modern "fads" to girls than to boys, and second, because the nationalist movement made the education of Jewish women an essential part of its program. The institution flourished, and soon several branches were established in Brooklyn.

Five years later. in 1910, a similar school was organized in Manhattan, also called "The National Hebrew School for Girls," or "Die Yiddische Volks-Schule." It arose as an offspring of the Hebrew Kindergarten and Day Nursery. The Young People's Auxiliary of that institution had interested themselves in the curriculum of the kindergarten and in its methods. They demanded from the Board of Directors that one of their members be placed on the Board, and when this demand was refused, they left the institution and organized the new school. At first situated at 302 Madison Street, the school was for a number of years located at 183 Madison Street. The "Madison Street School" has come to be the best known of the Nationalist schools. Its curriculum includes a very intensive course of readings in Hebrew literature, biblical and post-biblical. The language of the school, both in and outside of the classroom, is Hebrew, and the children are encouraged to do much collateral reading in juvenile Hebrew literature. Recently, 1918, it has removed to more commodious quarters at 206 East Broadway where it is continuing its work under its indefatigable and zealous founder and principal, Mr. A. H. Friedland.

The Modern Private Hebrew School

A new type of Cheder developed during this period. This was the modern private Hebrew school, conducted by one or two men, on a business basis, but educationally superior to the previously existing Chedarim. There are now a number of these schools in the city. They fashion their work after the model of the Cheder Methukan (improved school) of Eastern Europe. The best of these schools resemble the National Hebrew schools, or the modern Talmud Torahs, many of which also became nationalist in spirit during this time.

Hebrew Kindergarten

In May, 1905, the first *Hebrew Kindergarten* was founded at 87 East Broadway. The immediate cause for its organization was the attempt to counteract the work of the missionary kindergartens, of which there were many on the East Side. But the founder and superintendent, J. H. Luria, and those who were working with him, were imbued with the new spirit of Jewish nationalism, and the kindergarten proposed to introduce children below public school age to Hebrew as a spoken language, and to Jewish customs and ceremonies. It was modelled very consciously after the Hebrew kindergartens in Palestine, which were then receiving the enthusiastic admiration of Jews throughout the world. Palestinian kindergarten teachers were engaged. The curriculum and methods were those of the regular Froebel kindergarten, except that the games and songs were in Hebrew, and the language of the teacher was Hebrew. It is now the only institution of its kind in New York City. Several attempts have been made to organize kindergartens on the same model, but they have not succeeded.

Owing to the difficulty of obtaining sufficient financial support, another function was added to this institution. It became a day nursery, making it possible for poor Jewish mothers to earn their living without thereby endangering and neglecting their children. The name of the institution was changed to the Hebrew Kindergarten and Day Nursery. In 1914 it erected its present building at 35 Montgomery Street, and most of the children are kept in the building all day, because of this added function of the institution. But this is not an essential part of the Hebrew Kindergarten idea.

Zionist Education

Zionism, with its romantic promise of national rebirth, began to stir the imagination of the American Jewish youth in the early years of the present century. Zionist ideas and Zionist ambitions were at first studied and fostered in spontaneously organized self-governing clubs and societies rather than in regularly constituted Jewish schools. The Intercollegiate Zionist Association, the Hatikvah Movement, Young Judea and the School of Zionism, are the various forms through which the search of eager students for "the New Judaism" found educational expression.

The first students' Zionist society,[46a] was organized by college students in 1903 at the College of the City of New York. It was called the "City College of New York Students' Zionist Society" and its purpose was to spread the study of Zionism and of Zionist ideals in the American colleges. Similar societies were organized in other colleges of the city, and in 1906 these organizations combined into the "Collegiate Zionist League." For a number of years the League exerted marked influence on the colleges of New York City. It organized lectures for college students, issued a yearly booklet "The Collegiate Zionist" (1910), conducted a speakers' bureau and engaged in similar educational and propaganda activities. Later, however, it became "a society of graduates," and its place in the colleges was taken by the Intercollegiate Zionist Association, formed in 1915. The "I. Z. A." with its headquarters in Baltimore, has now (1918) over twenty-five constituent societies in colleges and universities throughout the country. In 1918 it issued its first Annual "Kadimah," and in the same year the Association was made

[46a] Kadimah, p. 193.

part of the Educational Department of the Zionist Organization of America, under the directorship of Miss Henrietta Szold.

From the City College of New York sprang also the movement for Zionist study among high school students. In 1912 the students of the academic, or High School Department of the City College (called Townsend Harris Hall) organized into the first Hatikvah (Hope) Society for the study of Zionism and of Jewish problems. It was a variant from the usual High School Debating and Literary Society, with a specific instead of a general "program." Rapidly the movement spread until there is now (1918) a Hatikvah Society in almost every important High School of New York City.

More extensive in influence and better known than either of the above student organizations has been the club movement outside of colleges and schools, known as "Young Judea."

In 1905 there were in existence several Zionist clubs of boys and girls in various sections of the country. A committee on Junior Organization was appointed by the Federation of American Zionists to coördinate the work of these clubs and to spread the nationalistic attitude among Jewish children and adolescents.[47] In 1909 this work was reorganized as "Young Judea," with Prof. Israel Friedlaender as its first president, and David Schneeberg as its secretary.

The aim of Young Judea is to "popularize Jewish study, to arouse enthusiasm for learning Jewish history, Jewish literature and Hebrew, to secure respect for Jewish tradition and observance, and to instil loyalty for the Jewish race and devotion for Palestine as the Jewish homeland."[48] It is "a distinctly educational program of Zionist endeavor."[49] The means employed to carry out its aims are: club work, mass celebration of festivals, and the distribution of Zionist literature. In 1910 it began the publication of a monthly magazine in English, "The Young Judean," and in 1917 the first issue of its Hebrew publication "Yizreel," appeared.

---

[47] Similar organizations existed at this time in other parts of the country. In Baltimore, the organization known as "Herzl's Children," was directed by Dr. S. Benderly, and in Chicago the "Junior Knights of Zion" was organized by D. P. Pollack.

[48] Cf. Young Judea Annual, 1917, p. 19, "History of Young Judea."

[49] Ibid.

One of the most serious problems in the work of Young Judea has been that of securing well trained volunteers to lead the Young Judea clubs. As in most educational movements depending upon volunteers, it was found that "those who could serve would not, and those who would, could not." Several attempts were therefore made to establish Training Schools for Young Judea Leaders. The most interesting of these endeavors was that of Miss Jessie Sampter in organizing the School of Zionism in 1914. The School held sessions at the Young Women's Hebrew Association, 31 West 110th Street, several evenings a week, and in its classes instruction was given in Zionism, Jewish History, Hebrew, Public Speaking and Club Leadership to young women who desired to obtain the information necessary for Zionist work. This school, as well as the entire Young Judea movement, became part of the Zionist Education Department in 1918.

The fortunes of the War have profoundly affected and quickened the hopes of American Zionists. The possibility of realizing "The Third Jewish Commonwealth" "quickly, in our own day," has increased the responsibility of the Zionist organization to spread the love of the "old-new land" among American Jews. The scattered, overlapping and loosely organized Zionist educational endeavors were not sufficient for the effective carrying out of that responsibility. In 1918 all of these educational movements were therefore united into an Educational Department under Miss Henrietta Szold, the recognized leader of Zionist women in America. This Department has set for itself the task of teaching Palestine and Jewish nationalism to all ages and to all classes of American Jewry.

The Menorah Movement [49a]

Growing out of the modern Jewish renaissance, which had its particular expression in Zionism, another movement arose in Jewish self-education among American college students. The Menorah Movement originated at Harvard University in 1906 with the organization of the Harvard Menorah Society.[49b] The

---

[49a] See: "The Menorah Movement," Ann Arbor, Mich. 1914. "The Menorah Journal," 1914 to date.

[49b] A Society of Jewish students existed at the University of Minnesota in 1903, but it was not the original "Menorah" society.

roots of this movement lay in the yearning of young men and women for the "New Judaism," and most of its leading spirits were ardent Zionists. In Harvard itself the first Menorah society was preceded and influenced by the Harvard Zionist Club, organized during the previous year (1905). "The Zionist Club, however, was practically confined to those students who were Zionists. The members themselves felt that, in addition to their partisan organization, there was room at the university, and need, for a non-partisan organization, devoted to the study of Jewish history, literature, religion, philosophy, jurisprudence, art, manners, in a word, Jewish culture, and to the academic discussion of Jewish problems.

"The motives of the founders of the Menorah Society at Harvard were: to win for the field of Jewish history and culture its rightful place in the university; to show the authorities that there did exist an interest in that field and to feed that interest among the student body; to provide, meanwhile, in lieu of regular courses, and later, it was hoped, in addition to the regular courses, an informal opportunity for all the students to get more adequately acquainted with Jewish life and thought and thereby become the more cultivated and less prejudiced men; above all, to dispel the ignorance and to raise the *morale* of the Jewish students."[49c] In brief, the object of the Harvard Menorah Society, and of the Menorah Societies which followed it, was "to study and to promote the culture and ideals of the Jewish people."

With infectious rapidity the Menorah Movement spread through the colleges and universities, so that by this time (1917) there is a Menorah society in practically every American institution of higher learning where Jewish students are taught. There are throughout the United States and Canada about 65 Menorah societies with a student membership of over 3,500, exerting Jewish educational influence over ten thousand students.[49d] In New York City the first Menorah societies were organized in 1909, at the College of the City of New York and at Columbia University. There are (1917) six Menorah societies in this

---

[49c] "The Menorah Movement" pp. 1 and 4.

[49d] For figures see Menorah Bulletin, February and March 1918.

city,[49e] with a membership of 1,250 young men and women; and from two to three thousand students come within its sphere of influence.

The work of these societies is conducted through meetings, lectures, and special study circles in the "Jewish humanities." The Menorah Societies are not religious organizations. "Indeed they are not sectarian in any sense, since the membership is open to Jews and non-Jews of all beliefs. Nor are the Menorah Societies Zionistic. Zionism is naturally one of the subjects of discussion and study by the societies, but no Zionistic propaganda can be carried on by them. Not only are the Menorah Societies non-sectarian, but they are non-partisian on all Jewish questions as well as on all political and religious movements." [49f]

In 1912 the various Menorah societies of the country were federated into the Intercollegiate Menorah Association, with Mr. Henry Hurwitz as its Chancellor, and its headquarters at 600 Madison Avenue, New York. The Intercollegiate Menorah Association helps its constituent Menorah Societies by providing for an exchange of information and ideas between them, and by giving them suggestions and advice. It provides lectures for them; furnishes them with plans and syllabi of courses of study; and supplies them with Menorah libraries of Jewish books and periodicals. The Intercollegiate also conducts intervarsity prize competitions as stimuli to study and research. It has been carrying on efforts aiming toward the establishment of regular courses of study in the curriculum and the founding of chairs of Jewish history, literature, etc. Lastly, it publishes the Menorah Journal, a review of Jewish life and thought which has proven of the highest interest not only to Menorah members, but to all cultivated men and women who wish to approach Jewish history and ideals and modern Jewish questions from an intellectual and non-partisan point of view.

The influence of the Menorah movement upon the Jewish college students has been marked. It has promoted the sense of *noblesse oblige* among Jewish university men and women through more intelligent appreciation of their heritage and

---

[49e] Besides the two above institutions there are societies at the following colleges: Adelphi, Hunter, New York University (Heights) and New York University (Square).

[49f] See circular: "What is the Menorah?"

ideals, and it has brought about a deeper understanding and respect for them on the part of non-Jews. It has facilitated mutual understanding and coöperation between various groups of Jewish students by providing them with a common organization and a common ideal. Students and graduates have been stimulated not only to study Jewish problems, but to participate in Jewish life. The Menorah Movement has provided non-partisan forums both within the universities and without, for the broader comprehension of Jewish issues and problems, especially in their relations to the general questions of the day. Finally, it has introduced a much greater interest in Jewish studies and in Jewish humanities at American colleges and universities.

C. Centralizing Educational Activities of Groups Within the Community
1910-1918

The year 1910 marks the beginning of a new era in Jewish education in New York City. The eight years which followed were more productive in the creation of new schools, and in the improvement and coördination of old ones, than any previous period in the Jewish educational history of New York. The educational activities during this period may be divided into two parts: (1) the activities of groups within the community, and (2) the educational activities of the organized Jewish Community (Kehillah) through the Bureau of Jewish Education. From the point of view of the student of education, the second is the more important, and deserves a separate chapter, because of the many significant educational changes which it has brought about in New York during the past eight years.[50]

The whole period is characterized by a growing consciousness of the need of Jewish education, and the realization that it is not a matter for individuals, but that combined effort is needed for solving the various problems connected with it. All of the Jewish immigrant groups, Portuguese, German and Eastern European, have been active in the creation of schools during these eight years.

---

[50] Cf. Chapter IV: "Educational Activities of the Bureau of Jewish Education."

Oriental Jewish Schools

About the year 1908, there began to come to this country a group of "Oriental" Jews. All of the newcomers are related to the Spanish-Portuguese Jews in matters of religious procedure, since they also follow the Sephardic (Spanish) ritual.[51] Most of them are also descendants of the exiles from the Spanish Inquisition, who fled from ungrateful Spain to the domains of the Turkish Empire. The first of their schools was that of the Congregation Ahavat Ve-Achavat Yanina, (Love and Brotherliness of Janina), established in 1910, at Allen and Grand Streets. It was an afternoon Hebrew school, for Greek-speaking children only. Hebrew was taught in Greek, and for a time, Greek was the ordinary language of conversation in the classroom.

When the Federation of Oriental Jews was organized in 1911, it took charge of the Janina school and enlarged it. A branch school was opened in the basement rooms of the Uptown Talmud Torah, 132 East 111th Street, and was maintained by small monthly contributions. But the Federation of Oriental Jews was unable to support these schools, and in 1913 they were taken over by the Congregation Shearith Israel. Both schools were made free schools, none of the pupils paying tuition fees. Recently a committee of Oriental Jews was appointed, for the purpose of raising funds and elaborating plans for more systematic instruction of their children.

Department of Synagogue and School Extension

The Hebrew Sabbath School Union, which had been organized in Cincinnati in 1883 for the purpose of unifying and systematizing the work of the Jewish Sunday schools throughout the country, was combined in 1905 with the religious circuit work of the Union of American Hebrew Congregations. It was reorganized as the Department of Synagogue and School Extension, with Rabbi G. Zeppin as its director. Besides the work previously carried on by the Hebrew Sabbath School Union,[52] the purpose of the new Department was also to provide educational facilities for religiously neglected communities and for isolated

---

[51] Cf., p. 31.

[52] Cf. above, p. 61.

groups, such as farming communities, summer colonies, etc. Much of its work is carried on by correspondence or by circuit visiting.

While some of the larger Jewish Sunday schools in this city had been affiliated with the Department since its inception, it was not until 1911 that the Department turned its attention specifically to the problem of New York City. In that year a new congregation was organized, (Sinai Congregation of the Bronx) under the special auspices of the Department of Synagogue and School Extension.[53] Aside from establishing a religious school of its own, the new synagogue took steps "to support a series of branch religious schools in various parts of the Bronx, under the auspices of the Sinai Congregation."[54] The tendency toward weekday supplementary instruction had become sufficiently strong, so that the new school was organized from the very beginning as a supplementary school, meeting three times a week. By 1914 there were two other schools affiliated with this organization, reaching altogether about 400 pupils. A New York Board of Managers was appointed, to whom was delegated the task of increasing the religious educational facilities in this city. In 1916 a survey of the Jewish educational conditions of the Bronx was made under the auspices of this Board. This survey showed that of the 50,000 Jewish children in the Bronx, only 5,000 were receiving any religious education.[55] In the same year, the Board opened a Hebrew school in a building leased for that purpose. The new school, the Ezra Hebrew School, at 1729 Washington Avenue, was organized on the regular model of the Talmud Torah, with attendance three times a week, on afternoons and Sundays. It soon became the largest school in the Bronx, instructing over 500 pupils.[56] Of late, however, its influence has been constantly decreasing.

---

[53] The spirit of this synagogue, and the schools which were established later by the Department, was akin to that of the "Mission Schools" described in the previous chapter. "It was our object to demonstrate that a synagogue adopting modernized methods would find a host of adherents in this section of the city that was considered exceedingly orthodox in theory, and hopelessly irreligious in practice." ((1917 Report, U. A. H. C., p. 8042).

[54] 1913 report of U. A. H. C., p. 1003 - 7004.

[55] Cf. Survey of Religious Education in the Bronx, 1916.

[56] This school attempted to co-operate with the public schools in the vicinity which had been testing the "Gary Plan" of instruction, but without success.

Central Board of Talmud Torahs

In 1909 several gentlemen interested in Jewish education issued a call to some of the larger Talmud Torahs of this city to send their representatives to a meeting at which was to be discussed the plan of organizing a central authority for the guidance of these institutions in matters of a purely educational character.[57] After a number of sessions, this effort resulted in the formation of a "Central Board of Jewish Education." Dr. Joseph I. Bluestone was its chairman and leading spirit. The Board consisted of delegates selected by the Talmud Torahs, one for every two hundred pupils enrolled. It intended to devote itself largely to developing a uniform curriculum for the various Talmud Torahs of the city, so that a pupil moving from one part of the city to another should not have to "start all over." But its efforts to centralize the work of the Talmud Torahs were not successful, and shortly after the organization of the Bureau of Education of the Kehillah, it ceased to exist.[58]

National Radical Schools

Another new type of school, with new aims and new content, appeared during this period. Among the labor elements of the Jewish immigrants from Eastern Europe, socialist tendencies were becoming prevalent. Labor organizations were being created, not only for collective bargaining, but also for spreading socialist ideals among the masses of Jewish workingmen. The first of these was the Arbeiter Ring, or the Workmen's Circle. Its outlook was cosmopolitan. While it was anxious to maintain the class spirit among Jewish workingmen, it was openly in favor of fusing with the non-Jewish workers, and antagonized the efforts to preserve Jewish life in this country. In opposition to the Arbeiter Ring, the Nazionaler Arbeiter Verband, or the Jewish National Workers' Alliance of America, was organized in 1910. In its economic outlook it too was socialistic, but nation-

---

[57] The attempt to centralize the work of the Talmud Torahs had begun somewhat earlier, 1906, but bore no fruit until three years later. Cf. Jewish Daily News.

[58] Recently, 1917, a Federation of Talmud Torahs was organized, including some of the smaller Talmud Torahs of the city. But it has been inactive and does not seem to be significant.

ally and culturally it considered itself a part of the Jewish people, and was anxious to maintain its group life. Whereas the Arbeiter Ring opened socialist Jewish Sunday schools for teaching socialism to Jewish children, the Verband favored the opening of Jewish schools which would teach not only socialist doctrines, but also Jewish history and Jewish culture, both Yiddish and Hebrew. With the Verband, two other associations of workingmen united,—the Poalei Zion (Workers of Zion), and the Socialist Territorialist Party.

Toward the end of 1911, the first of their schools was organized, under the name of the *National Radical School*, at 183 Madison Street. It was a Sabbath and Sunday school, but taught no religion. Its curriculum consisted of the Yiddish language and literature, the rudiments of Hebrew, and Jewish history. The language of instruction was Yiddish. The Jewish festivals were celebrated not as religious festivals, but purely as national festivals. The majority of the founders were Jewish journalists, and the first teachers were also journalists. They had no pedagogic experience, but were imbued with the spirit of creating a new institution. Later a teachers' council was formed, which took charge of the pedagogic management of the schools.

The following year a conflict arose as to the place of Hebrew in the radical school curriculum. The Yiddishists, particularly the Socialist Territorialists, objected strenuously to any teaching of Hebrew. The contention was, that Hebrew as the language of prayer and religion, and as a "dead" language, had no place in the curriculum of the radical nationalist Jewish school.[59] The center of the agitation was in Chicago. For a long time the two sections of the National Radical party separated, each maintaining its own schools. An agreement was finally reached, in 1915, whereby Hebrew was to be included in the curriculum of the National Radical School, but each school was to be autonomous in deciding in what grade the instruction of Hebrew was to begin, and the method to be pursued in teaching it.

Through the agency of the societies affiliated with the Jewish National Workers' Alliance, the National Radical School movement spread throughout the country, so that there are now some

---

[59] These are the extreme decentralized nationalists, who wish to maintain Yiddish-speaking groups all over the world, wherever Jews are found in sufficient numbers. Cf. Chapter I, p. 9.

thirty-five such schools in the various cities of the United States. Four of these are situated in New York. The first of these schools is now located at 188 Ludlow Street, and in 1916 was converted into a regular weekday supplementary school. A similar afternoon school was organized in the Bronx, at 1387 Washington Avenue. The two other schools in this city were until recently continued on the Sabbath and Sunday program. One of these is located in Harlem, and the other in Brownsville.[60] In 1917, the Brownsville School was also turned into a weekday school.

The great majority of the pupils of these schools are girls, most of whom come from conservative and orthodox homes. There are two *social* reasons for this rather strange fact. In the first place, Jewish parents in Eastern Europe have become accustomed to the idea of teaching Yiddish to their girls, for practical reasons. Secondly, those radical parents who are interested in giving their boys a Jewish education, prefer to send them to the Talmud Torahs or Chedarim.[61]

Central Board of Parochial Schools

The Yeshibah (parochial school) movement also grew somewhat during this period. Efforts were made to centralize and spread the work of the various Yeshibahs. A number of new Yeshibahs were organized in New York, and some of the other large cities. In 1908 the Yeshibah of Harlem was organized, and in 1912 the Chayim Berlin Yeshibah was opened in Brooklyn. Both of these institutions are parochial schools. There are at present, therefore, four Jewish parochial schools in New York.

The biggest event in the history of the Yeshibahs occurred in 1915, when the Etz Chayim Talmudical Academy, the first American Yeshibah, combined with the Rabbi Isaac Elchanan Theological Seminary, and the two were reorganized as the Rabbinical College of America. A new building was erected for the combined institutions, at 9-11 Montgomery Street, and Dr. B. Revel was appointed Rosh Ha-Yeshiboth (Head of the Yeshi-

---

[60] For fuller discussion of these schools, Cf. Part II, Chap. II. As this book goes to press the name of the National Radical Schools has been changed to "Yiddishe Volks-Schulen," and the Arbeiter Ring has begun to establish similar schools.

[61] This statement is made on the authority of the superintendent of one of the National Radical Schools.

bahs). This institution combines an elementary parochial school with a parochial high school, and a seminary for the training of orthodox rabbis. It acts also as the central institution to which the various parochial schools in this city send their graduates.

The efforts to centralize the work of the various Jewish parochial schools of this city crystallized in 1917, in the formation of a Central Board of Parochial Schools (Vaad Ha-Yeshiboth). "At a meeting of the representatives of all the Jewish parochial schools in New York City, it was decided to form a joint committee of these schools, for mutual encouragement, and for the solution of problems that come up in connection with parochial schools. It was decided to start an active campaign for the promotion of the idea of Jewish parochial schools, and to encourage the study of the Talmud and higher Jewish learning, in the different Talmud Torahs of this city."[62] Dr. B. Revel is the chairman of this Board (1917).

Teachers' Organizations

Another interesting phenomenon during this period was the growing consciousness among Jewish teachers as a professional body. The first of the teachers' associations was organized as the *Agudath Hamorim,* United Hebrew Teachers of Greater New York and Vicinity. It consists entirely of teachers of the nationalist Jewish type, who came to this country from Eastern Europe as adults. While many of these have thorough Jewish knowledge and have also had pedagogic experience in the countries of Eastern Europe, their knowledge of the English language is limited, and most of them have no professional training. The Agudath Hamorim held its first "congress" on January 1, 1913. This organization has edited two educational magazines: (1) Hed Hamoreh (Echo of the Teacher), a pedagogic journal which appeared monthly for about a year; and (2) He-Abib (Spring), a weekly Hebrew paper for children. Both publications have been discontinued. Recently, (1917) the Agudath Hamorim conducted a strike for higher salaries, with partial success.

In 1913 the Sunday school teachers of this city organized themselves into the Jewish Religious School Union. This union of Reform Sunday school teachers is under the auspices of the

[62] From an announcement issued by the Vaad Hayeshiboth.

Eastern Council of Reform Rabbis, and its work has confined itself to lectures and institutes for Sunday school teachers.[63]

The following year, 1914, another society of teachers was organized, the Jewish Teachers' Association of New York. The founders were directly connected with the Bureau of Education of the Jewish Community (Kehillah), and its members are college and university men and women, most of whom are teaching in the schools affiliated with the Bureau. The members are professionally trained Jewish teachers, who have been taught in the Teachers' Institute of the Jewish Theological Seminary, and are engaged in Jewish teaching as a profession. In January 1916 they began to issue their publication, "The Jewish Teacher," which is a semi-annual educational journal in English, devoted to the interests of the Jewish school. It is the first Jewish educational journal in America written in the English language.

Jewish Teachers' Institutes

The movement toward professionalizing Jewish teaching was aided by the establishment of a training school for Jewish teachers. The previous courses for teachers, which had been offered in the Jewish Theological Seminary since 1903, proved inadequate to meet the demand of the Jewish schools. It was realized that a special training school was needed, with a special teaching staff, and under adequate supervision. In 1909, Mr. Jacob H. Schiff donated to the Seminary a fund of $50,000, the income of which was to go toward the maintenance of a school for the training of Jewish teachers, to be conducted under the auspices of the Seminary. Rabbi Mordecai M. Kaplan was appointed principal of the new school. Its classes were at first taught in the rooms of the Uptown and Downtown Talmud Torahs, but it is now located in quarters of its own, in the building of the Hebrew Technical Institute, 34 Stuyvesant Street.

Since 1910 two other teachers' training schools have been established in New York. In 1917 the Mizrachi Association of America,—which is the American branch of an international organization of orthodox Jewish nationalists,—opened a Teach-

---

[63] For previous organization of Sunday school teachers see p. 80.

ers' Institute at 86 Orchard Street, with Dr. M. Waxman as principal. At about the same time (1918) the Federation of National Radical Schools (Yiddishe Volks-Schulen) established its Lehrer-Seminar under Mr. Judah Kaufman at 293 East Broadway.[64]

School for Jewish Communal Work

As the scope of Jewish education has been broadening, the aim of those who are directing Jewish education in this country has been more and more clearly manifesting itself in terms of *Community Service.* Not only imparting knowledge of the Jewish past, but also direct preparation for participating in the affairs of the Jewish community is considered to be the function of a Jewish educational system in America. The most specific communal need in this direction has been that of training of proper leadership for Jewish communal institutions. Very few of the workers in the Jewish social service institutions of this country have been trained professionally for their work. With the view of supplying this necessary training, the *School for Jewish Communal Work* was organized, under the stimulus of the Jewish Community (Kehillah), by the executive heads of some of the largest Jewish institutions of New York.

This school is national in its scope and its purpose is to train workers for all Jewish institutions in the United States. Its first summer course was held in the summer of 1915, but it was not until the fall of 1916 that it was fully organized and began its regular sessions. It offers three types of courses. The first consists of general lectures for the purpose of acquainting various Jewish groups with the many phases of Jewish communal work. The second is in the form of institutes for those who are actually engaged in the work of Jewish social service institutions, and are designed to give these workers a background for the work which they are doing. The most advanced course consists in professional study for graduate students, who are training themselves to head various Jewish communal institutions. These students are given part-time positions in the particular field

[64] For full discussion of curricula and conduct of these teachers' training schools, see Part II, Chap. 9, pp. 285-287.

which they have selected, so that they may combine practical work with theoretic study. The School coöperates with the various colleges and universities of New York, particularly with Columbia University, and its courses are included in the Extension Courses of that University.

Chapter IV

THE ACTIVITIES OF THE BUREAU OF JEWISH EDUCATION

Since 1875 efforts had been made to centralize and coördinate the work of the Jewish schools of New York. But prior to 1910 none of these efforts had any appreciable effect, or any lasting influence. The educational efforts were individualized; each school was laboring under the burden of its own local problems. Even those educational agencies which were created by groups of Jews within the community since 1910, have been dealing only with special types of Jewish schools, and view the problem from the angle of some one party. The Department of Synagogue and School Extension, for example, is concerned chiefly with the Sunday schools of the reform congregations.[1] The now extinct Central Board of Talmud Torahs attempted unsuccessfully to deal with the problem of the orthodox Talmud Torahs. The Federation of National Radical Schools has been trying to centralize the work of the radical schools. The Central Board of Parochial Schools has been aiming to coördinate the work of the orthodox Yeshibahs. All of these agencies look at the problem from the view point of orthodoxy or reform, or of nationalism. Besides being limited in scope, these agencies are also limited in extent of influence, for the number of children reached by all of them is small, compared with the great mass of the unschooled.

An agency was needed to represent the *entire* Jewish community of New York, and to deal with the problem as a nonpartisan, *Jewish* problem. It was necessary to coördinate the work of all the Jewish schools. It was equally necessary to organize new schools, and to promote religious education for all Jewish children in a systematic communal manner. The creation of such a central agency, and the work which it has set in motion, is to the student of education, the most significant chapter in the history of Jewish education in New York.

The story of the Bureau of Jewish Education is the story of rousing a people to realize the chaos prevailing in the education

[1] Its "mission" work in establishing weekday schools in the Bronx, and its correspondence work have been mentioned, but these are of secondary importance, its main field being that of the Sunday school.

of its children, and of bringing some program and order into this chaos. It is the uncompleted story of a handful of men, under the guidance of a masterful leader, who in spite of the prevailing chaos, relied upon sheer love for their people, and upon mere faith in its future, in their determination to grapple with this fundamental problem of Jewish life in America. To increase the demand for Jewish education; to organize this demand; to raise funds; to train men and women; to publish books in order to supply the demand; to experiment with curricula, methods and management so as to determine along what lines the forces in Jewish education should be utilized most effectively; and lastly to coördinate all efforts made by individuals or by groups in carrying on the common work—this was the task which the Bureau set for itself from the very first day of its organization.

The educational activities of all the Jews could not be stimulated or coördinated, as long as all their other communal activities remained uncoördinated. Unless the various Jewish groups were organized into a Community, it was not possible to deal systematically with the problem of Jewish education. The organization of such a Community in New York has been an unusually difficult task. The Jewish community of New York is the largest settlement of Jews, not only of the present time, but of all times.[2] The fact that the great majority came to this country within the last 35 years, makes New York Jewry particularly complex and heterogeneous.[3] Moreover, the new democratic conditions in America required a new form of communal organization for the Jews.[4] In other words, the largest and most

[2] There are estimated to be in Greater New York more than 1,500,000 Jews. (Cf. Jewish Communal Register, of the New York Kehillah, 1918, p. 75, "The Jewish Population of New York," by A. M. Dushkin.)

[3] For a comparison of the size of New York Jewry with the Jewish population of the countries of Western Europe and of the largest cities in the world, see Appendix I. For the extraordinary growth of the Jewish population in New York, see Appendix J.

[4] The two previous forms of communal organization in the history of the Jews were: (1) the mediaeval Kahal, or self-governing community, with taxing, legislative and police powers, and (2) the modern ecclesiastical community (Kultus Gemeinde, Consistory, or Gemina). Neither of these was applicable to conditions in New York, because: the Jewish community can not levy taxes; the heterogeneity of New York Jewry makes organization along purely religious lines very difficult; and also because the new conditions of American Democracy necessitate a new form of communal adaptation.

heterogeneous Jewish settlement in the world's history must be organized under conditions which permit no imitation of precedent. This gives some indication of the difficulties in the task of organizing a Jewish Community in New York.

But in spite of these difficulties, it has long been felt that centralized community organization is imperative for the preservation of Jewish life in this country. Two occurrences helped to bring it about in New York. The Kishineff pogroms and massacres, in 1905-1907, banded the Jews of New York together for the common purpose of relieving and defending the massacred Jews of Russia. While this work bore no immediate fruit in creating a permanent central organization for the Jews of this city,[5] it nevertheless unified the Jews of all parties, for the first time, in a common task. The immediate incentive to communal organization came in 1909, when General Bingham, Police Commissioner of New York at that time, charged the Jews with supplying 50 per cent. of the criminals of New York. The falsity of the accusations aroused a great wave of indignation. It was felt that "a representative, permanent and authoritative organization" should be formed, which would "dare to speak for the Jewish people."[6] In 1909 the Kehillah (Jewish Community) of New York was organized as such a permanent representative body, with Dr. Judah L. Magnes as its executive chairman. Its function was to organize and coördinate Jewish life in this city.[7]

From its very beginning, the Kehillah considered the problem of Jewish education as one of its most important functions.[8] At its constituent convention in 1909, it was felt rather vaguely that the Kehillah must aid in centralizing the work of the Jewish schools. "What the community might do, for example, is to help such a movement as is now beginning to develop, that of forming a Board of Jewish Education, and of employing a Superintendent of Instruction."[9]

---

[5] As its direct outcome, the American Jewish Committee was formed, which is a national body, with New York as its main district.

[6] "The Jewish Community" 1909, address by J. L. Magnes, delivered before the Constituent Convention of the Kehillah.

[7] For a summary of the work of the Kehillah, see pamphlet called: "What the Kehillah Has Given New York Jewry," 1917, by J. L. Magnes.

[8] Cf. Appendix H: "Extract from Act of Incorporation" of the Kehillah.

[9] "The Jewish Community," 1909, address by J. L. Magnes, before Constituent Convention of the Kehillah.

One of the first tasks of the Kehillah was to appoint a Committee on Education, for the purpose of surveying the conditions of Jewish education in New York. The chairman of this committee was Rabbi M. M. Kaplan, and the investigation was carried out under the supervision of Dr. Bernard Cronson, a New York public school principal.[10]

The committee made a street-to-street canvass and reported its findings at the first convention of the Kehillah in 1910. The report startled the Jewish community. It stated that of the 170,000 Jewish children estimated to be in New York City at that time, fully two-thirds received no religious education whatever. Most of the Jewish schools were unsatisfactory and inefficient. Many of them, especially the Chedarim and the smaller Talmud Torahs, were stated to be a liability rather than an asset in the attempt to preserve Jewish life in this country.

As a first step to remedy these conditions, Mr. Jacob H. Schiff donated $50,000 for a period of five years, and later $25,000 were added to this sum by the New York Foundation. Dr. Samson Benderly, who was conducting the school of the Hebrew Education Society in Baltimore, was asked how this fund should be used, so as to obtain the best results. Dr. Benderly advised that instead of spending this money for creating new schools, much more significant results could be obtained by using it as "a lever" for the purposes of study, experimentation and coördination. He suggested the organization of a Bureau of Education with the following objects:

"1. To study sympathetically and at close range all the Jewish educational forces in New York City, including alike those that restrict themselves to religious instruction, and those that look primarily to the Americanization of our youth, with a view to cooperation and the elimination of waste and overlapping.

2. To become intimately acquainted with the best teachers and workers who are the mainstay of these institutions, and organize them for both their material and their spiritual advancement.

3. To make propaganda through the Jewish press and otherwise, in order to acquaint parents with the problem before them and with the means for solving it.

---

[10] For report of the committee, Cf. American Hebrew, March 4, 1910, Vol. LXXXVI-18: 458.

4. To operate one or two model schools for elementary pupils, for the purpose of working out the various phases of primary education, these schools to act also as concrete examples and guides to now existing Hebrew schools, which will undoubtedly avail themselves of the text books, methods, appliances, etc., worked out in the model schools, as soon as public opinion shall have ripened. These model schools, while devoting themselves to the solution of the problem of primary Jewish education, might also act as preparatory schools, that is, as feeders to the Teachers' Institute founded last year.''[11]

Accordingly ''The Bureau of Education of the Jewish Community of New York'' was opened on Oct. 1, 1910, and Dr. S. Benderly was appointed its Director.[12] The Bureau expanded rapidly and its central offices at first located at 356 Second Avenue were removed later (1918) to 114 Fifth Avenue. The history of the Bureau of Education may be divided into four periods: (1) the period of study, 1910-1911; (2) the period of initiation, 1911-1912; (3) the period of administration and execution, 1912-1916; and (4) the period of reconstruction, 1916-1918.

A. 1910-1911 (Period of Study)

In carrying out the purposes for which it was organized, the first undertaking of the Bureau of Education was to make a more careful survey of the Jewish educational situation in New York City. The financial as well as the pedagogic aspects of the problem were studied, and the results were embodied in three publications: ''A Survey of the Financial Status of the Jewish Religious Schools of New York City,'' ''The Problem of Jewish Education in New York,'' and the ''Aims and Activities of the Bureau of Education.''[13] The survey showed that of the 200,000 Jewish children estimated to be in New York City, only 41,000

---

[11] Cf. ''The Bureau of Education,'' Bulletin No. 1 of the Jewish Community of New York.

[12] An interesting fact in connection with the personnel of the Bureau indicates in how far it was really *communal* effort. The donor, Mr. Schiff, was born in Germany; the executive chairman of the Kehillah, and the prime mover in the organization of the Bureau, Dr. Magnes, was born in California; Prof. I. Friedlaender, Chairman of the Trustees of the Bureau of Education, was born in Russian Poland; and the Director, Dr. Benderly, is a native of Palestine.

[13] For other publications of the Bureau, see Bibliography on ''Source Material for the History of Jewish Education, in New York.''

were receiving any sort of religious instruction, that is, more than three Jewish children out of every four were without any religious training whatever. Of those who were attending some sort of Jewish school, 14,000, *i.e.*, more than one-third, were frequenting Chedarim conducted by men whose sole purpose was to eke out some kind of livelihood, which they failed to obtain by any other means. But even the best and the largest of the Talmud Torahs were laboring under great financial and pedagogic difficulties. A large part of their contributions came from the poorer classes of Jews. The cost of collecting these contributions, as well as that of collecting the tuition fees from the pupils, was high. The teachers were underpaid, the average salary being about $38 per month. There was no uniformity in the programs of studies. No satisfactory text books were available. The constant "dropping out" of pupils from the schools was discouraging, and in general each school was oppressed by the weight of its own problems.

Conference of Principals and Uniform Program

Under the auspices of the Central Board of Talmud Torahs, the Director of the Bureau of Education met with the principals of the various Talmud Torahs of New York, for the purpose of remedying this condition of affairs for the Talmud Torahs. A series of conferences was held, and a uniform program was elaborated for these schools.[14] This program discusses the aim, content and methods of Jewish education. The paragraph concerning the parochial school is of sufficient significance to be quoted in full:

"Par. 3: As the isolation of our children in parochial schools, though undoubtedly effective from a purely Jewish point of view, might injuriously affect our political and social status in this country, and would, in addition, demand financial sacrifices at present beyond our reach, and as, on the other hand, the giving of religious instruction at the public schools would contradict the basic American principle of eliminating religion from our state institutions, it follows that the present system of teaching our children in Hebrew schools after public school hours is the most desirable under existing circumstances."

---

[14] See "A Brief Survey of Thirty-one Conferences held by Talmud Torah Principals in New York City," published by Bureau of Education, 1912.

The program adopted by the principals outlined a graded course of study for seven years. The subjects included were: Hebrew; Bible; selections from the Mishna[15] and the Midrashim;[16] portions of the Talmud and of mediaeval Jewish poetry; Jewish history; and Jewish religious observances. The natural method of teaching the Hebrew language was adopted.

The program thus agreed to formed the basis for unifying the work of the various Talmud Torahs. Each of the principals consented to carry out the program in his own school as far as possible. This was the first opportunity for the principals of the Talmud Torahs of this city to come together for a common purpose, and in order to insure coöperation between them, they were organized into an *Association of Hebrew Principals.* For the purpose of superintending the execution of the program, the Executive Committee of the Kehillah appointed a *General Board of Talmud Torahs,* consisting of two representatives from each of the larger Talmud Torahs of Manhattan.

While the Bureau aided in the elaboration of this uniform program, it was not sponsor for it. The program expressed the attitude of one type of Jewish schools and of one group of Jews. Changes and modifications were to be brought about, not by the Bureau, but by the principals themselves, together with the General Board of Talmud Torahs.[17] Besides the Talmud Torahs, the Bureau also began to coöperate, during this period, with some of the institutional schools. The Hebrew Orphan Asylum and the Educational Alliance were the first of the institutions to cooperate with the Bureau of Education.

Text Books

But mere acceptance of a program was not sufficient for the proper use of the curriculum which was adopted. Text books were needed which would embody the principles agreed upon. Most of the text books available at that time were written for children in Eastern Europe, and contained, therefore, many foreign elements not understood by the American child. Moreover,

---

[15] The Talmud consists of two parts: the Mishna, or the statement of the law, and the Gemarah, the discussion of it.

[16] The Midrashim are ancient interpretative commentaries on the Bible.

[17] Cf. A Brief Survey of Thirty-one Conferences held by Talmud Torah Principals in New York City, p. 14.

the physical appearance and the pedagogic organization of these books were far from satisfactory. The books were not graded, so that the Jewish schools could not use them systematically one after another. New text books were needed which would overcome these difficulties. For this purpose a text book fund of $10,000 was obtained. An editorial board of text books was organized, which first turned its attention to the editing of school books in Hebrew. A graded series of twenty-eight text books began to be issued, four books for each of the seven years of the elementary Jewish school curriculum.[18]

Hebrew Preparatory Schools

Besides text books, actual demonstration was needed to point the way in the instruction and management of Jewish schools. During the first year of the Bureau's existence, two model schools were organized, known as the *Hebrew Preparatory Schools*. The first of these schools was situated in the building of the Y. M. H. A., 92d Street and Lexington Avenue, and the second at 307 Henry Street. These schools had a double purpose. Besides serving as educational laboratories in which schedules, curricula, and methods, were to be tested, they were also to be training schools for Jewish teachers, and "prepare" the material for the Teachers' Institute of the Jewish Theological Seminary. At first the schools were intended for both boys and girls. The first school accordingly enrolled pupils of both sexes. But soon it was felt that these schools should confine themselves to the teaching of girls only, first, because the coöperation of the Talmud Torahs, particularly that of the Downtown Talmud Torah, 394 East Houston Street, made special schools for boys unnecessary, and secondly, because owing to the traditional neglect of the education of Jewish girls, it was considered of particular importance to emphasize their education now.

B. 1911-1912 (Period of Initiation)

The following year was the storm and stress period of the Bureau of Education. It was a year of much achievement, but also of opposition from various groups in the community. For

[18] Sixteen of the series have already been published (1918).

better or for worse, new educational forces began to make themselves felt, and the community was trying to make up its mind what attitude it should take toward these forces. Commendation and condemnation, sincere and otherwise, now fell to the lot of the Bureau. This was inevitable, and, on the whole, desirable. For in the very nature of the undertaking it was necessary that, at least for a time, the searchlight of public opinion be turned upon the Bureau, its personnel and its activities.

The storm of criticism aroused at this time cannot be understood, however, except in the light of the fact that the Bureau was putting forth every effort to accomplish, as rapidly as possible, the aims which it had set for itself. Its achievements during this period serve, therefore, as a necessary background for the expression of public opinion by the community.

Education Fund

The most important accomplishments of the year were connected with the improvement of the financial status of the Jewish schools. Previous study had shown that progress in the conduct of the Jewish schools would be impossible unless their financial status were improved and stabilized. A fund of $250,000 was therefore raised, which was known as the Education Fund, for the purpose of standardizing the Jewish schools. Because this fund was limited, financial grants were to be given only to such of the larger Talmud Torahs as would themselves offer to affiliate with the Bureau of Education.[19] The grants were made in the form of scholarships for children who could not pay for their tuition. One dollar and twenty-five cents per month (estimated per capita cost) was to be given "for every child taught in the Talmud Torah free of charge, provided the number of such children does not exceed one-third of the total attendance."[20] There were six conditions attached to this grant:

"1. The teachers shall at once receive a salary of not less than $60 per month, which shall be increased at the rate of $5.00 per month every year, until it reaches the sum of $80 a month.

[19] Cf. "Aims and Activities of the Bureau of Education," by S. Benderly, pp. 13-15.

[20] "Aims and Activities of the Bureau of Education," page 16.

2. No teacher shall be employed in the school who does not possess a temporary certificate issued by the Board of License of the Bureau of Education.[21]

3. The curriculum shall be the one worked out by the principals during the past year and approved by the chairmen of the Boards of Education of the largest Talmud Torahs. All changes in this curriculum shall be made only by a two-thirds majority of the General Board of the Talmud Torahs, together with the Principals' Association.

4. The pupils already in the schools, and the new pupils prior to their admission, are to be investigated by the Bureau of Education, to determine whether they can pay the full tuition fee, or half of the tuition fee, or are to be taken free of charge.

5. The tuition fees are to be collected by a collector in monthly installments at the homes of the children. The collection of the tuition fees shall be in the hands of the Bureau of Education for a period of three to six months, until the route has been firmly established.[22]

6. The Bureau of Education is entitled to gather any statistics it may need for the purpose of studying the financial and educational status of the institutions.''[23]

It was evident that with the funds available, it was not possible to include all the Talmud Torahs in the new arrangement. Key positions were needed to control the situation, and these had to be provided for first. Accordingly, four of the largest Talmud Torahs affiliated themselves with the Bureau in agreement with the above conditions of the grant. These were the Downtown Talmud Torah, 394 East Houston Street; the School of Biblical Instruction, 61 Meserole Street, Brooklyn; the Uptown Talmud Torah, 132 East 111th Street; and the Rabbi Israel Salanter Talmud Torah, 74 East 118th Street. Other Talmud Torahs were included later.

Department of Investigation, Collection and Attendance

The two points in the agreement, dealing with the collection of tuition fees and the certification of teachers, necessitated the organization of two new departments in the Bureau of Education.

---

[21] See below, p. 111.

[22] With the consent of the schools, the collection of tuition fees is still (1918) done through the central agency of the Bureau.

[23] ''Aims and Activities of the Bureau of Education,'' pages 16-18.

The first of these was the Department of Investigation, Collection and Attendance.

In an educational system which cannot be based upon taxation, the question of collecting the tuition fees of children is an important one. The American Talmud Torah teaches not only the children of the poor, but also those who are in a position to pay for their tuition. There were two methods current in collecting these fees. According to the first of these methods, the teacher was to collect the tuition fees in the classroom. The teacher stopped his lesson and asked the children to bring their tuition fees to him. He would hand them receipts for this money, and address a daily reminder to the delinquent children who did not bring their fees. At the end of the week or the month, the teacher turned over the money to the secretary of the school. The second method was that of assembling the children in the office of the secretary, where they would pay their tuition fees directly to him. Both of these methods were debasing, for the teacher and for the pupil. The money had to go through the hands of the children, and many cases occurred where it was either spent or lost on the way to school. The children who did not pay for their tuition were intentionally or unintentionally singled out from their fellows. The method was expensive, not only because it wasted the time of the teacher and the principal, but also because in the larger schools a special secretary had to be engaged for this work. There was a wide range of prices. Some of the children who could afford to pay, did not do so, whereas children of the poor would sometimes be forced to bring their pittance.[24]

For these reasons the Bureau of Education determined that the collection of tuition fees must be taken out altogether from the hands of the teacher and the child, and must be made a transaction only between the parent and the principal or the secretary of the school. A systematic gradation of tuition fees was introduced, and a corps of college students were engaged to act as investigators and collectors. These young men investigate the financial condition of each child who applies for admission to the Jewish schools, and visit monthly the homes of those children who can afford to pay, in order to collect the tuition fees from

---

[24] For a fuller description of the methods of collecting tuition fees employed by the Jewish schools, see "Aims and Activities of the Bureau of Education," pp. 17-18.

their parents. They also act as a connecting link between the home and the school, for on the one hand, they bring to the parents a monthly report of their children's progress and attendance, and on the other, they report to the school any complaint which the parents may have. The Collection Department also follows up the attendance of irregular pupils, and thereby attempts to reduce the number of pupils who leave the Jewish schools prematurely.

Another function exercised by the department is that of canvassing for new pupils. Such canvassing is needed to persuade the parents of the neighborhood to send their children to the Jewish school and to be willing to pay for their religious instruction. It is needed also to compete with the degrading influence of the Cheder. Moreover, since there is no compulsory requirement to send children to the Jewish schools at a definite age, the number of applicants varies from year to year. This variation makes proper grading and classification, especially in the higher grades, very difficult. Therefore, to obtain a stable base for the Jewish school population, the department canvasses the neighborhood every term for new pupils, so that a full quota of applicants may be obtained for each new class.

Board of License

Another department created by the Bureau during this time dealt with the certification of teachers. The certification of Jewish teachers had long been felt to be a very real need. In 1910, there were very few thoroughly equipped Jewish teachers. Aside from the older teachers, or "Melamedim," there were two types of teachers in the Jewish schools. On the one hand, there were immigrant young men who came to this country as adults, and who, though possessed of a thorough knowledge of the Hebrew language and of Jewish literature, were not sufficiently acquainted with the English language and with secular culture. On the other hand, there were college students who were willing to teach in the Jewish schools, but had not the requisite Jewish knowledge. In order to create a standard for Jewish teaching, the Bureau of Education organized a Board of License. On this Board were represented schoolmen and rabbis. It issued educational certificates to Jewish teachers, on the condition that they prepare themselves more fully for their work.[25] In order to aid them in such preparation, two kinds of courses were offered to them. For the un-Americanized, morning courses were conducted in English, history and pedagogy. For the college students, courses were given in the Hebrew language and Jewish literature. These courses were later taken over by the Teachers' Institute of the Jewish Theological Seminary.

Extension Schools

During this period the school work of the Bureau was also extended and new types of schools were created. Besides opening another Hebrew Preparatory School in the Hebrew Free School building, 414 Stone Avenue, Brooklyn, the Bureau extended its educational experimentation along two lines. It attempted to reach children, both below and above the age of its "preparatory school" pupils, who were from eleven to fourteen years old.

The Bureau clearly realized that it would be impossible to create sufficient school facilities in the immediate future for the 150,000 Jewish children who were outside of the Jewish schools. Such new buildings as could normally be erected, would hardly suffice to accommodate the annual increase of Jewish children, an increase estimated at that time to be 7,000 every year. To reach the great number of unschooled, therefore, an extensive, rather than an intensive form of education was needed, and a method had to be devised whereby many children could be reached easily and at little cost.

In order to deal with this problem, the Bureau of Education saw that Extension work must be organized, as an educational *movement,* with as wide a scope as possible, and that novel methods both of instruction and of management must be utilized to make such work count in the lives of great numbers of children. The celebration of festivals and the social phases of Jewish life, rather than any book instruction were, from the first, conceived as the central element in this work. The task of Jewish Extension Education was to bring together as many children as possible as frequently as conditions permitted, in order to have them

[25] The Board of License was discontinued after a brief period of activity because conditions were not yet ripe for the certification of Jewish teachers.

acquire the essentials for their life as American Jews, without necessitating the use of regular classroom machinery. It took a good deal of experimentation to discover how this task was to be accomplished.

At first the Bureau of Education organized several "Extension Centers." These centers were situated mostly in the vacant auditoria of Jewish institutions, which were obtained free of charge. Several Extension groups were located in one Center, each group coming once or twice during the week. A group consisted of from three to four hundred children, eight to ten years old, who gathered either on Sundays or during afternoons, for the purpose of mass instruction. The center was open to all the children in the neighborhood, practically free of charge. At first only Jewish melodies and biblical history were taught, but at the urgent request of the parents for Hebrew, that subject was included and a small tuition fee was charged.[26] Besides the celebration of festivals and the explanation of customs and ceremonies, the curriculum consisted of the elements of Hebrew, Jewish Bible stories and Jewish singing. All of the instruction was done with the aid of stereopticon slides; and very elaborate devices were worked out, whereby the natural method of language teaching was combined with a series of phonetic drills.[27] One teacher taught the entire group, and an assistant operated the stereopticon machine. To aid in the management of these schools, and to introduce the very much needed personal contact with the pupils, the entire school was divided into groups of thirty. At first some public school teachers volunteered to take charge of these groups during the sessions. Later, Jewish high school girls were made the "leaders" of these groups, and the training for the work of "leader" was made part of their own Jewish training. The Extension Centers were situated at the Odeon Theatre, on Clinton Street; at the Educational Alliance; at the Uptown Talmud Torah; and later at the Hebrew Free School, Brooklyn. But, as will be pointed out later, this proved to be only the first step in developing an Extension system of Jewish education.

---

[26] In the course of time the fee was made three dollars per year.

[27] For a somewhat fuller description of these methods, see Fourth Annual Report of the Kehillah, 1913, p. 35.

Jewish High School Girls' Association

The other direction along which the educational experimentation of the Bureau of Education expanded, was that dealing with the problem of the adolescent. How was the Bureau to reach the great numbers of Jewish boys and girls between the ages of fourteen and twenty-one years, for whom no provision whatever had thus far been made in Jewish education? During the most formative periods of their lives these young people were being permitted to drift away from all Jewish influences. Here was another important field for the Extension work of the Bureau. The problem was essentially the same as in the case of the younger unschooled children, except that the very different psychology of the adolescent required different methods of treatment.

The first step consisted in the organization of classes for high school girls for the purpose of training them as teachers, in preparation to their entering the Teachers' Institute. Later, the courses were made more general and more diversified in their scope. A number of clubs for working girls were organized, so as to extend to them also the influence of Jewish education, and all of these girls were combined into a self-governing "Association of Jewish High School Girls."

Opposition to the Bureau

These constructive efforts of the Bureau of Education did not go unchallenged. Opposition was aroused in various quarters and the year 1911-1912, so rich in initiation and organization, also saw the culmination of this opposition. From one group came the complaint that the Bureau of Education dealt with the educational problems of the orthodox only, that it was trying to make Hebrew the spoken language of the Jews of America, and that it was fostering the segregation of American Jews. This complaint came chiefly from those, who, consciously or unconsciously, believed in the fusion and ultimate disappearance of the Jews in this country. On the other hand, a number of people claiming to speak for the orthodox group complained that the Bureau was not sufficiently orthodox, that it was trying to impose a non-orthodox curriculum and a reform point of view upon the Talmud Torahs, and also that it was autocratic and arbitrary. The opposition on this score came from the Central Board of

Talmud Torahs, the Morgen Journal (a Jewish daily), and the Union of Hebrew Teachers (Agudath Hamorim).

The following quotation in answer to these charges is self-explanatory:

"As a Kehillah Bureau, we feel we must be above all parties in Judaism. The children of the so-called Reformed Jew must be as dear to us as the children of the Orthodox Jew, and the children of the Jew without any religion at all are also dear to us. We do not conceive it to be the function of the Bureau to emphasize this kind or that kind of Judaism. The trustees of the Bureau have their individual views, and doubtless the work of the Bureau is colored by these views. But our chief aim is purely technical: to devise methods of instruction, to prepare text books, to work out a system of financing schools and similar matters of school machinery. We find at hand a mass of material called Judaism. We find schools desirous of teaching this to children. We come to them with expert advice as to what appears to us to be the best way of imparting this instruction. We say: if you want to teach Hebrew, we think that such and such a method with such and such books, during such and such hours, and under such and such conditions, is the way to do it; or history, or ethics, or religion, or singing. It becomes the function, as it should be the chief privilege, of each individual school to put its own religious stamp upon its teaching, to give its own purpose to the methods we recommend and to the material we offer. Moreover, it is rank ignorance of our purpose to say we want to make Hebrew the language of daily speech to the detriment of English. We recommend the method of teaching the Hebrew language as a living language in the first place because it is so; and in the second place because we believe that any language, from a pedagogic point of view, should be taught in this way."[28]

The opposition culminated in a long debate on the floor of the Third Annual Convention of the Kehillah in 1912. But only a small minority was in the opposition; the majority was appreciative of the significance and non-partisanship of the work of the Bureau of Education. A resolution was passed by the convention, expressing "unbounded admiration for the work thus far accomplished by the Bureau of Education, and confidence in its leaders."[29]

---

[28] Third Annual Report of the Kehillah, 1912, pp. 10-11. Address of Chairman.

[29] Third Annual Report of the Kehillah, 1912, p. 56.

C. 1912-1916 (Period of Execution and Administration)

During the following four years, the policies outlined by the Bureau of Education, and the movements and institutions which it initiated, were carried out and extended.

A survey of schools outside of New York was undertaken, and two trips were made by a representative of the Bureau, for the purpose of learning the status of Jewish education in the United States. The first trip (1913) covered sections of the Middle West, and the second trip (1914) was through the New England and the Middle Atlantic States. A *Department of Information* was organized for the purpose of keeping in touch with the schools thus surveyed, and of rendering to them aid and guidance in their work.

Besides the Talmud Torahs and institutional schools, the Bureau began to coöperate with other types of Jewish schools, particularly the Sunday schools. A special Hebrew curriculum was outlined, and in some of the larger Sunday schools, Hebrew teachers were specially assigned for the purpose of testing this curriculum.

The Text Book Department of the Bureau also expanded its activities. Besides the editing of Hebrew school books, it began the publication of correlative reading material. Two juvenile periodicals were issued. "The Jewish Child," a weekly paper in English for children between the ages of nine and sixteen, was started in 1912, and "Shachruth," (The Jewish Youth), a Hebrew monthly for older boys and girls, began its appearance in 1916. A series of illustrated history folders, together with a history album, were published during this time.[30]

The schools of the Bureau were enlarged. Two new preparatory schools were opened: School No. 4, at the Young Women's Hebrew Association, 31 West 110th Street, and School No. 5, in 1916 at the Hebrew Technical School for Boys, 34 Stuyvesant Street. Besides the selected pupils who were being trained for the Teachers' Institute, regular classes were established for girls between the ages of eleven and fourteen. The pupils who were graduated from the Extension Centers entered the Preparatory Schools, and the graduates of the Preparatory Schools continued

---

[30] These books and educational material can be obtained from the Bureau of Jewish Education, 114 Fifth Ave., New York.

their studies in the High School Classes, so that a graded system of girls' education began to appear.

In extension education these four years were spent in testing the curricula and methods in the Extension Schools. On the whole, it was a period of intensive elaboration rather than of extensive effort to reach large numbers of children, and as will be seen later, was a transitional stage in the developing of extension education. In the work with adolescents the Association of Jewish High School Girls reached out to include adolescent girls from all walks of life. High school boys were also organized for similar purposes into an association of their own, the "Association of High School Boys." But this too was a transitional stage, preparatory to a more comprehensive form of educational organization.

The functions of the Bureau of Education during this period of administration, 1912-1916, may be summarized under three headings. In the first place it served as a *Jewish Educational Foundation*, similar to non-Jewish Educational Foundations. It studied the field scientifically, and obtained statistical information; it worked out text books and suggested curricula; it elaborated standard record forms and methods of management in the Jewish schools; it disseminated information and gave advice to Jewish schools in New York and in other parts of the country.

The second function of the Bureau of Education was that of a *Department of Education of the Jewish Community*. Its work was in this respect similar to that of any State Board of Education. It granted financial aid to Jewish schools, with a view to their standardization; it sent general and special supervisors to the schools, in order to aid the principals in their work; it took charge directly of central educational activities, such as investigation of truancy, and the collection of tuition fees; it certificated teachers, at least temporarily; it coördinated the work of the principals of the various schools through the Principals' Association; and it influenced indirectly the attitude and work of the Jewish teachers through the Jewish Teachers' Association, and through the Teachers' Institute of the Jewish Theological Seminary.

The third function of the Bureau was that of a *Board of Experimental Schools*. It conducted ten Extension Schools; five Preparatory Schools for Girls, offering both special and regular

FUNCTIONS OF THE BUREAU OF EDUCATION
1912 — 1916

- Executive Committee of Jewish Community
  - Board of Trustees
    - Director
      - 1. JEWISH EDUCATION FOUNDATION
        - Dept. of Study and Appraisal → Surveys of schools, special studies, preparation of budgets.
        - Dept. of Information → Correspondence with schools in New York and out of town. Sending of material and of information.
        - Dept. of Text Books and Curricula → Editing Hebrew text books. Publication of English and Hebrew juvenile periodicals, history folders, reading cards, etc. Making stereopticon slides and illustrative material.
      - 2. BOARD OF EDUCATION OF JEWISH COMMUNITY
        - Div. of School Aid → Granting of financial aid to schools, and standardization.
        - Dept. of Collection, Investigation, and Attendance → Canvassing of new pupils. Investigation of irregular attendance and of pupils who left school. Collection of Tuition Fees.
        - Div. of Supervision → Special supervisors and teachers, for Talmud Torahs, Sunday Schools and Experimental Schools.
        - Board of Licence → Certification of teachers (temporary)
        - Assocs. of Principals and Teachers → Aid and direction of Association of Hebrew Principals, and Jewish Teachers' Association.
      - 3. BOARD OF EXPERIMENTAL SCHOOLS
        - Girls Schools
          - Supervisor
            - Extension Schools → Mass instruction for girls between 8 and 11 years old.
          - Supervisor
            - Preparatory Schools → Regular courses for girls, ages 11-14. Special Preparatory classes for selected girls.
            - High School Classes Girls → Classes for specially selected High School girls.
          - Supervisor
            - High School Clubs Girls → Self-governing clubs for High School and working girls.
        - High School Assoc.
          - Supervisor
            - High School Clubs Girls
          - Supervisor
            - High School Clubs Boys → Self-governing clubs for High School and working boys.
          - Supervisor
            - High School Classes Boys → Secondary classes for boys; graduates of weekday schools.

courses; and two Associations of High School Students. Through these educational activities it reached *directly* from four to five thousand Jewish boys and girls.[33]

D. 1916-1918 (Period of Reconstruction)

The following years, beginning with 1916 and continuing to the present time (1918), may be called the period of reconstruction. Some of the policies of the Bureau underwent profound modification, and the scope of its work was very much enlarged.

Separation of the Bureau from the Kehillah

The Bureau of Education realized that its educational endeavors could not be very much ahead of the Jewish community itself, and that unless it began to reach beyond the walls of the classroom into the activities of the community, its own work would be impeded and circumscribed. But as the Bureau of Education began to interest itself in the work of the community, the problem of its own existence and its relation to the general Jewish community formulated itself more clearly. The Kehillah was organized as a democratic body. The Bureau of Education is an expert professional agency, supported not by the general public, but by a few individuals. The possibility therefore presented itself, in the changing fortunes of a democratic institution like the Kehillah, that the party temporarily in power might vote to undo all that had cost years of labor. Moreover, many felt that the Kehillah as an organization of a heterogeneous Jewry ought not to undertake directly the work of educational experimentation and of school administration. The educational functions of the Kehillah were conceived to be those of supervision, rather than of direct participation.

At the Eighth Annual Convention of the Kehillah (1917), therefore, the Bureau of Education was made independent, and a Committee on Education was appointed to execute the supervisory functions of the Kehillah. The work of this Committee

---

[33] For the extent of the Bureau's influence, cf. pamphlet "Some of the Activities of the Bureau of Education," 1915: "The Bureau directs, supervises or cöoperates with 179 schools, 521 teachers and 31,700 pupils" (ibid).

consists in interesting the Jewish Community to aid and enlarge Jewish religious educational activities, and to condemn and disapprove any attempt which may be considered harmful to the education of Jewish children. The Bureau of Education on the other hand continues its work as an independent educational agency under the name of the "Bureau of Jewish Education."

The Board of Jewish School Aid

Another very important work of reconstruction dealt with the granting of financial aid to the schools. The Bureau of Education had long felt that the subsidizing and standardizing of Jewish schools should be done not by a specialized educational agency, controlled by a few individuals, but rather by a democratically selected body within the community. This communal body should undertake the task of raising the necessary funds, and bear the responsibility for their distribution. The Bureau wished to organize a "Board of Jewish School Aid" which should exercise this double function, connected with the standardization of the Jewish schools. With the organization of the Federation for the Support of Jewish Philanthropic Institutions, in 1916, the establishment of this Board was quickened, in the following manner.

The Talmud Torahs, and all other weekday Jewish schools, have become communal institutions, for the children of rich and poor alike. They represent, not alone the philanthropic, community-supported, Talmud Torah of Eastern Europe, but also the self-supporting Cheder. The financial basis for their maintenance must therefore be *self-support,* in the traditional sense of self-support, which obliges the parents to pay for the tuition of their own children, and the community at large to bear the financial responsibility for teaching the children of the poor. The Jewish schools have been striving to obtain this condition of self-support. Parents were gradually being accustomed to pay for the Jewish instruction of their children, and many fathers and mothers denied themselves some of the conveniences of life in order to live up to this dignified spirit of the Jewish tradition.

But it was estimated that from 25 to 30 children out of every hundred could not afford to pay for their Jewish instruction. In the congested districts of the city the proportion was even higher. For these children, the schools came to the community at large, and raised the necessary funds in the form of membership dues, donations, special entertainments, bazaars, benefit theatre performances, raffles, and similar unreliable sources of income. These methods were wasteful. They wasted a great deal of the time of the directors of the schools, and much of the community's money, because of the high cost of collection. On account of the indefiniteness and instability of these sources of income, the financial condition of the schools was precarious. A demoralizing state of affairs existed, which permitted any one, who could but give some of his leisure time to gathering money, to become a director of a Jewish school, and control educational policies, irrespective of his other qualifications. The salaries of principals and teachers were paid irregularly, and the work of the school was kept on the level of "lowest possible cost."

When the Federation for the Support of Jewish Philanthropic Institutions was organized in New York, it coördinated the finances of the Jewish charitable institutions, so that contributions came through this one central agency, instead of being scattered among the individual institutions. But at first the Federation did not include the Jewish schools among its affiliated societies, on the ground that it did not wish to deal with the complex problem of religious education. Many of the previous members of the Jewish schools gave their entire contributions to the Federation. The schools were therefore confronted by a critical situation: they were not able to meet their current expenses nor pay their teachers' salaries; much less could they plan for the future.

To meet this situation, the directors of the largest Jewish educational institutions were organized by the Bureau of Jewish Education into a temporary Committee of Twenty-five, for the purpose of bringing the matter to the attention of the Federation. The Federation finally agreed to admit the Jewish schools, and in order to protect itself against any possible charge of meddling in the religious affairs of the community, it specified that it would "have nothing to do whatever with curricula or religious beliefs."[34]

[34] Report of Special Committee of Seven (Federation for the Support of Jewish Philanthropic Institutions) May, 1917, p. 11.

One of the conditions of the agreement was, that since the budget submitted by the Jewish educational institutions amounted to more than had been subscribed for them by the members of these institutions who now became members of the Federation, the schools were themselves to raise the additional money for the Federation. The Board of School Aid was now organized, with the immediate purpose of conducting the campaign necessary to raise this money. It consists at present of twenty-five members, most of whom are representatives of Jewish educational institutions or are interested in the general problem of Jewish education. Besides raising the funds which will enable the Federation to assume communal responsibility for the education of the children of the poor, the Board also hopes to be able to enlarge the scope of Jewish education, to erect new school buildings, and to create better facilities for Jewish education.

Graded System of Jewish Religious Schools: Elementary, Intermediate and High

The educational activities of the Bureau of Education itself also underwent reconstruction during this period. This is particularly true of the Bureau's work in extension education. The Extension Schools, while reaching some 2,000 Jewish children, were not satisfactory from the point of view of the purpose for which they were created. It was found to be hardly possible by means of these schools to reach quickly, and at little cost, the great mass of unschooled Jewish children. The per capita cost of the schools alone, while as low as three dollars per year, was sufficient to limit the number of children reached. Nor were the Extension Schools, as organized, a satisfactory basis for a regular Jewish school system. While mass instruction was found to be a good mode of procedure for the teaching of certain subjects, such as singing and Bible stories, it did not produce satisfactory results in the teaching of Hebrew. Moreover, in spite of the many devices employed for introducing personal contact with the child, classroom instruction was needed to enable the teacher to exert more intimate influence over her pupils.

The girls' school system was therefore organized. The Extension Schools became *Elementary Schools,* with instruction both in the classroom, and in the auditorium.[35] The name of the Preparatory schools was changed to *Intermediate Schools,* with preparatory courses for the special pupils to be trained as teachers, and regular courses for the average child. Above these schools were the *High School* classes, not only for girls, but also for boys who had finished their course of study in the Talmud Torahs.[35a]

Circle of Jewish Children

To deal more effectively with the problem of giving an extensive Jewish training to the great number of unschooled, a new educational institution was created, the *Circle of Jewish Children of America.* The central idea of Jewish Extension Education was again brought to the foreground. The Circle emphasizes the social life of the Jewish schools, their festivities, clubs, and entertainments. It makes this work a means for attracting all the unschooled children in the neighborhood to the regular school. The entire neighborhood is districted, and children are appointed as "leaders," whose duty it is to visit each child in the vicinity, for the purpose of enrolling him or her as a member of the Circle of Jewish Children. The members of the Circle are organized into groups. They receive special Children's Bulletins, they read the "Jewish Child,"[36] and they are regularly invited several times during the year to educational festivities and holiday celebrations. A nominal fee of five cents per year is charged to members, and a special Jewish Child button forms the badge of membership. Within the first two years of its existence, the Circle enrolled a membership of over 30,000 Jewish children, including both the children who attend Jewish schools, and those who do not. As an educational movement, the Circle of Jewish children is national in scope, although its activities are at present confined to New York.

The League of the Jewish Youth

Similarly, in the work with adolescents, it was found that the attempt to combine the school work with extension activities, in

[35] For a discussion of time schedules, cf. Part II, Chap. 5.

[35a] The preparatory classes for girls (both intermediate and high) are called the *Florence Marshall Classes,* and are supported by an endowment fund established by Mr. Louis Marshall in memory of his wife.

[36] See above, p. 116.

the form of the Jewish High School Association, was not productive of the desired results. The high school classes were therefore made a part of the regular school system, and the Jewish High School Association was reorganized into the *League of the Jewish Youth of America.* This League has been attempting to deal with the problem of the adolescent through a new method of approach.

The problem of the adolescent has always been a difficult one for the teacher, and especially for the religious teacher. The problem is primarily a psychological one. The adolescent can not be reached through the same measures as the child. To most young people, prescribed studies are distasteful. The self of the adolescent reaches out vaguely beyond itself, to a hazy wanting of something bigger than itself. There is a revolt against restriction and authority, and an uneasy desire for self-activity. It is the period of expanding selfhood, of vague, new desires, of "storm and stress."

Realizing the difficulty of educating the adolescent, and realizing also the fact that it is impossible to provide school facilities, in the near future, for the 200,000 Jewish young men and women between the ages of fourteen and twenty-one, the Bureau organized the League of the Jewish Youth. The central idea of this League is to create a *Community of Adolescents,* which will bind the individual young man and young woman to all the other Jewish young men and young women in America. It utilizes the impulse of the adolescent self to expand, by having him pledge allegiance to a cause greater than himself, that of "the age-long past, the world-wide present, and the idealistic future" of the Jewish people.

The organization of the League is modelled after the organization of Jewish life in Palestine during biblical times. The entire city is divided into Districts (*Galil*), and each district is divided into twelve Tribes. Each Tribe is subdivided into Camps bearing names of places in Palestine. A Camp consists of ten Households named after some personage in Jewish history. At the head of each Household is an "Organizer," a young man or young woman, whose function consists in visiting each boy or girl in the particular territory of the Household (usually several city blocks), and in influencing him or her to affiliate with the

League. Directing each camp is an "Elder," who is an adult person, devoting to this work one evening a week as a volunteer. Willingness to affiliate with the League, and the payment of nominal dues (10c. per year), constitute membership in the League.

The educative content of the League comes from several sources. The organization is itself a source of Jewish influence. Through it Jewish boys and girls are brought together as Jews, for common purposes, and by means of this social bond, are brought nearer to Judaism and to the Jewish people. An elaborate series of Initiation Ceremonies is being developed, for which the youth must prepare by learning some of the literature and customs of the Jews. There are three stages in this initiation. The Junior Initiation at the ages of thirteen and fourteen deals with symbols of biblical times; the Intermediate Initiation for boys and girls of sixteen and seventeen years, is centered about the symbols of the prophetic and rabbinic periods, and the Senior Initiation for young men and young women, eighteen to twenty-one years old, symbolizes their entrance into the modern Jewish community.

Besides the Initiation Ceremonies, Jewish festivals are celebrated, special bulletins are distributed, and annual mass meetings are held at which the members of the League are addressed by their own Elders, and by leaders of the Jewish community. The members are also encouraged to form themselves into clubs for recreational, social or educational purposes, and the League tries to obtain for them rooms and leaders from the existing social service institutions (Y. M. H. A.'s, Jewish Settlements, etc.).

Another source of educative influence is somewhat more indefinite, depending entirely upon the Jewish community itself. As a community of adolescents, the League is not partisan, that is, it does not represent any one attitude in American Judaism. All Jewish groups and Jewish agencies, whether Zionist, orthodox or reform, are through it able to send their message more readily to the Jewish youth. The League acts as the means through which the various educational agencies and social service institutions may the more easily distribute literature and books, and organize classes and clubs for Jewish young men and young women. The League is at present confined to New York, and has an enrolled membership of nine thousand.

The Jewish Parents' Association

Reaching beyond the young men and the young women into adult life, and basic for all educational efforts with school children, is the work of organizing Jewish parents. Particularly important is this work in Jewish education, because to a much larger extent than public education does it intimately depend upon the understanding and the good will of the individual parent. There is no law to compel attendance at, or financial support of Jewish schools, and no governmental authority to prescribe studies and methods. Indeed *all* of Jewish education depends upon the intelligence and devotion of Jewish parents. The Jewish home can aid or mar profoundly the work of the Jewish school. For a long time, therefore, the Bureau of Jewish Education encouraged the formation of Parents' Associations in the various schools coöperating with it. These separate school associations were, in 1917, formed into a central "Jewish Parents' Association (Eltern's Verband) of New York." The Central Association was organized with the aid of the Association of Hebrew Principals, and now (1918) includes the parents of the pupils of the eight largest Jewish schools in the city. The aims of the Association are: "(1) To bring into closer union the homes of the children with the schools in which they receive Jewish instruction; (2) to help morally the Jewish educational institutions and their holy work; and (3) to agitate for Jewish education so as to awaken Jewish public opinion concerning the problems of Jewish education."[37] Toward attaining these aims a number of committees were organized, the names of which suggest their functions, such as committees on Synagogue, School Books, Library, Social Life, Class Visiting, Friendly Groups, Children's Clubs, Malbish Arumim ("clothes for the naked"), etc. The central authority of the Association is vested in an Executive Committee consisting of representatives from the various Parents' Associations affiliated, the Hebrew Principals' Association, and the Board of Jewish School Aid. The Parents' Associa-

---

[37] Monthly Bulletin (Yiddish) of the Jewish Parents' Association, July, 1918, Vol. 1, No. 1.

tion is still (1918) in its infancy, and its possibilities for usefulness are limited only by the vision and the determination of its leaders.

CONTRIBUTIONS OF THE BUREAU OF JEWISH EDUCATION

In summarizing the work of the Bureau, it is hardly possible as yet to evaluate its contributions to Jewish education.[38] Some of the forces which it has set in motion have already achieved concrete results, but much of its work still consists in building for the future. It is the first agency created by the Jews of America to deal with the problem of Jewish education in a comprehensive, nonpartisan way.[39] It has emphasized the *scientific professional study* of the field, and has worked out a systematic program based upon actual conditions. It has gathered about it a group of professionally trained young men and young women who are willing to devote themselves to the profession of Jewish education. It has encouraged and aided professional institutions like the Teachers' Institute of the Jewish Theological Seminary. It has *stimulated* at least a part of the Jewish community to realize the vast problem confronting it with regard to the education of its children, and the danger of neglecting this problem. It has *coördinated* the work of the hitherto separate Talmud Torahs of this city, and has stabilized and improved their work. It has organized the directors, principals and teachers of the schools for their common interests. It has brought some order and system into the *finances* of the schools. It has issued text books and periodical literature for Jewish children and adolescents. It has created for the first time a *graded system of schools* for Jewish girls, beginning with the child of eight, and providing instruction up to the age of twenty-one. It has attempted to deal with the great mass of *the unschooled*, both children and adolescents, aiming to provide religious educative influence for every Jewish boy and girl between the ages of seven and twenty-one, no matter what his or her occupation or previous training may have been.

---

[38] For a concise summary of its work, see Jewish Communal Register, New York, 1918, pp. 1143-1146.

[39] "The future of Judaism in America belongs to no one party, and the problem of Jewish education will not be solved along party lines." Dr. S. Benderly in "Jewish Teacher," Vol 1,—1:27; Jan., 1917.

But the Bureau of Jewish Education itself conceives its achievements as significant only in the light of the larger unsolved problem: the indifference and ignorance still prevailing; the great majority of Jewish children who are still unschooled; the bungling, waste, and inefficiency still reigning supreme in the work of Jewish schools; the blind, narrowly selfish activities of various groups still working at cross purposes; the demoralizing carelessness, and the smug disregard of the situation and its significance still indulged in by the Jewish community at large. While yet this problem remains, the story of the Bureau of Jewish Education is an unfinished story. It has brought to Jewish education in America a little tested knowledge, a few devoted personalities, and some basic principles for future effort. But above all, it has brought with it the determination to make the whole community realize that quickly, in our own day, must the chaos and the dearth of resources in Jewish education be eliminated, and that order, purpose, and plenty must be introduced into the Jewish education of our children, if the Jewish people is to continue to live as a self-perpetuating community in America.

Chapter V

TENDENCIES IN JEWISH EDUCATION

(Historic Summary)

The history of Jewish education is a specific example of how the Jews are trying to adjust themselves in this country so as to preserve their power of spiritual self-perpetuation. It is the resultant of two interplaying forces: the conditions of American life, and the traditions which the Jews brought with them from the various lands in which they sojourned, prior to casting their lot with America. The character of their schools during the different stages of development depended, on the one hand, upon the standard prevailing in American education in general, and on the other, upon the strength of the educational heritage which they carried with them. The weaker and the less distinct their own traditions of Jewish educational organization and methods the more likely were they to *imitate* implicitly the examples set by their neighbors. The stronger and the more definite their educational heritage, the better were they able to *adapt* their own educational ideas and institutions to American conditions, without at the same time losing the continuity and the momentum of these institutions.

The earliest Jewish settlers, the Spanish-Portuguese Jews, opened the first Jewish school in New York in 1731. This school, the *Yeshibat Minhat Areb,* was a typical American colonial school, under ecclesiastical auspices. After the American Revolution, it was reorganized as the *Polonies Talmud Torah,* and for a time it was one of those schools conducted by religious bodies in New York which formed an integral part of the Common School System and were subsidized from public funds. For half a century it was conducted as a typical parochial school. But with the growth of American sentiment against parochial education, toward the middle of the last century, the Polonies Talmud Torah was changed slowly into an afternoon weekday school, supplemented by a Sunday school.

The German Jews began to organize their schools in this country in the 40's. Within one decade a number of *congregational day schools* and *private boarding schools* arose. They were parochial schools, in that they taught both secular and religious subjects. Neither in curriculum nor in management did they differ much from the typical American school of that time. This was in the period just before the states made the education of all children their rightful domain. Congregational and private education was still the order of the day. But no sooner did public opinion crystallize in favor of State Education, than in rapid succession these German-Jewish parochial schools were either disbanded or reorganized. Their place was taken by *Sunday schools* and *Mission schools,* modelled wholly after the experiences and example of their non-Jewish neighbors. Each congregation conducted a Sunday school for the religious instruction of its own children, and the more important congregations combined in supporting the schools of the *Hebrew Free School Association*, where besides receiving the rudiments of a Jewish education, the children of the "ignorant poor" were taught good behavior and were furnished with "shoes, clothing, and bath." The German Jews made several attempts to coördinate their educational activities. But while, in accordance with their genius for philanthropic organization, they succeeded to some extent in centralizing the education of the poor through the Hebrew Free School Association, they were less successful in coördinating the work of their own congregational schools. Whatever centralizing influences there were, came from Cincinnati rather than from New York.

The Eastern European Jews brought with them more definite educational traditions than did their forerunners. They came at a time when American educational policy was definitely committed to State education. What they did, therefore, was to keep their educational institutions intact, but to change their character in such a manner as to fit them into the new conditions. The *Talmud Torah,* the *Yeshibah,* and the *Cheder,* all underwent profound modifications in this country. Beginning with the first European Talmud Torah, the forerunner of the present *Machzike Talmud Torah* (1860), and extending to our own day (1918), the Talmud Torahs have been gradually transformed from charitable institutions for the education of poor children only, to democratic communal institutions for the education of all children. The Cheder, on the other hand, degenerated in this country, from the normal self-respecting school of the Eastern European Jews, to the level of the worst unorganized and unsanitary one-room country schools (though they are situated in the midst of congested city districts). The character of the Yeshibah has also been changed from the earlier conception of a Talmudical Academy to that of a regular parochial school, with both elementary and secondary grades. On the whole, the Eastern European Jews have committed themselves definitely to supplementary Jewish education, in the Talmud Torahs. Some of the orthodox Jews, however, are trying anew the plan of parochial education, prompted by their intense desire to perpetuate in this country Jewish scholarship and learning, as well as the strictly orthodox practices. Their influence, at least numerically, is very small, their four parochial schools in New York reaching fewer than one thousand children. In higher Jewish education, this desire for Jewish scholarship, greater among the Eastern European Jews than among either the German or the Spanish-Portuguese Jews, was productive of the establishment of several institutions for higher Jewish learning in this city: the Jewish Theological Seminary, the Rabbinical College, and the three Institutes for Jewish teachers.

With the beginning of the present century new forces began to make themselves felt in Jewish education. First came the wave of "Jewish nationalism," which swept over the Jewish world and expressed itself in this country educationally in *National Hebrew Schools, Hebrew Kindergartens, National Radical Schools.* Simultaneously a number of self-governing club organizations of young people, such as *Young Judea,* the *Intercollegiate Zionist Association,* and the *Intercollegiate Menorah Association,* began the "study of Jewish ideas and ideals," stimulated in most cases by the romance of Zionism.

Since 1910 the most fruitful educational force has been that of centralization and coördination of activities, either on the part of groups within the community, or by the community as a whole. The now extinct *Central Board of Jewish Education,* the *Vaad HaYeshiboth* (Central Board of Yeshibahs), the *Federation of National Radical Schools,* are all expressive of the efforts made to centralize the work of particular types of schools. Jewish teachers have banded themselves into several organizations, the

Agudath Hamorim (Union of Hebrew Teachers), the *Jewish Teachers' Association*, the *Jewish Religious School Union*, and the *Moriah*. The principals of Jewish schools have formed the *Hebrew Principals' Association;* the parents are organized into a *Jewish Parents' Association;* and the leading trustees of the schools are brought together in the *Board of Jewish School Aid*.

All of these are specialized centralizing organizations, dealing either with a specific group or with a specific educational problem. *The Bureau of Jewish Education* was created for the purpose of dealing with *all* types of Jewish schools and with *all* phases of the Jewish educational problem. Its work during the past eight years of its existence (1910-1918) has been in the direction of *study and research* to learn scientifically the facts in Jewish education; of *experimentation and initiation* to undertake those tasks which are greatly needed in Jewish education but which the community does not know how to do, or else is not yet willing to undertake; and lastly, of *coördination and guidance* to utilize and to direct to the best advantage all Jewish educational forces, no matter in what group in Jewry they originate or for what type of school they are intended.

In this review of the history of Jewish education in New York, several significant tendencies have become apparent. The most important of these tendencies are: (1) That the standard of Jewish education has risen considerably, both in pedagogic management and in the degree of knowledge required; (2) that the Jews have, since the beginning of their history in this country, been struggling away from the parochial school idea, in spite of its seeming advantages for intensive Jewish education; and (3) that Jewish educational activity in America has been steadily leaving the domain of the individual synagogue or group, and is being communalized, that is, undertaken and supported by the entire community.

The Rising Standard of Jewish Education

The standard of Jewish education has risen both in general methods of instruction and of management, as well as in the educational requirements in terms of Jewish knowledge. While it is true that Jewish teachers still have to be warned not to per-

IZED O ED BY	TYPE OF SCHOOL	DATE ORGANIZED	DATE OF CURRICULUM	SECULAR STUDIES	JEWISH STUDIES	SOUR CURR
hearith el	Parochial	1731	1755	Spanish, English, writing and arithmetic	"The Hebrew"	Mi
hearith el	Parochial	1800	1812	English, reading, writing arithmetic, geography	"The Hebrew language"	Mi
	Afternoon	1856	1845		"Hebrew and the necessary information as Yehudim"	Mi
Bnai run	Parochial	1842	1852	English, reading, writing, ciphering, Grammar, geography, history, arithmetic, composition, elocution, needlework. Special: Spanish, German, French, Latin, drawing	Hebrew: reading, writing, grammar translation prayers, Scriptures, Bible History	Peri
ations: Chesed Sholom Shorim	Parochial	1845	1845	Elementary: English, history, geography. Higher: U. S. history, English, arithmetic, algebra, geometry, bookkeeping, French, German. (Girls: Fancy needlework.)	Elementary: Catechism, Bible, Hebrew, grammar, prayers Higher: Catechism, Hebrew, whole Bible, Jewish History, Orach Chayim	Peri
nuel	Parochial	1845	1845	English, German	Hebrew	Per
gation	Sunday	1854	1857		Religion, Hebrew language, vocal music	Per
Bnai ael	Afternoon	1847	1848		Hebrew, Chaldean Talmud, Possekim	Per
Max nthal	Private Boarding	1847	1847	English, German, classic languages, bookkeeping, French, U. S. history, universal history. Classic and Polytechnic courses.	Hebrew, Religion, Bible and Commentaries Mishna, Talmud	Per
Free ool iation	Afternoon	1864	1870 ca.	Sewing and industrial arts	Hebrew, reading and spelling, translation and grammar, religion, Bible, history, singing, composition (in Jewish history), Rashi (for advanced pupils.)	Per
H. A.		1875	1876		4th Grade (12 yrs.): Reading of Prayer Book and simple rules of pronunciation. 3rd Grade (14 yrs.): Translation from Pentateuch, grammar. 2nd Grade (16 yrs.): Translation from Joel, Amos, Obadiah, with grammar and analysis. 1st Grade (16 yrs.): Translation from Mishna with grammar and analysis.	Per
innie D. uis	Sabbath	1880	1888	Industrial arts (later)	Bible, hygiene, behavior, and singing	Pe
American w Congations innati)	Sunday	1873 1886	1886		*a.* Principles of Judaism; *b.* Bible in translation; *c.* Hebrew language: Prayers and portions of Bible; *d.* Jewish history: Biblical and Post-Biblical; *e.* Music, in preparation for services.	U. I
hzike d Torah ssoc.	Afternoon	1883	1885		Hebrew, reading, Scriptures and grammar, writing, construction of Hebrew sentences, benedictions and prayers (with translation) meaning of holidays, reading portion of week and Haphtora (with accents and benedictions) Shulchan Aruch, Orach Chayim, Jewish creed, Jewish history, and Talmud.	Co
i Jacob Society	Parochial	1905	1907 ca.	Public school curriculum	Hebrew: Reading, writing, spelling, grammar, composition, and (conversation), prayers, benedictions, synagogue responses, meaning of holidays, Bible (complete and review); portion of week with Rashi; Talmud (seven tractates) Shulchan Aruch, Jewish history, Yiddish newspapers.	Co
tional w School ssoc.	Afternoon	1910	1910		(1) Hebrew: Speaking, reading, writing, grammar, composition and rhetoric; (2) Bible (complete); (3) Geography of Palestine; (4) Legends from Talmud and Midrash; (5) Talmud; (6) Jewish history (complete); (7) Jewish life in different countries; (8) Hebrew literature: mediaeval (poetry, philosophy and codes); modern Haskallah period and contemporaneous. *Special:* (9) Development of Jewish national thought; (10)	I

mit their pupils "to riot or make a noise in the yard or about the premises, or in any manner to disturb the neighbors,"[1] yet there is no doubt that the modern Jewish school is much nearer to the standards of public education than were its predecessors. To be sure many Jewish schools are still mediaeval in equipment and in management; but there are in various parts of the city Jewish schools which, in every respect, compare very favorably with the best of the city's public schools. Good school buildings, thoughtful programming, careful grading and classification, the introduction of modern methods of teaching, and the emphasis upon the social life of the school children (clubs, dramatics, festival gatherings, etc.) have made the modern Jewish school far more attractive than were the schools in which our fathers were taught. In this improvement of educational management the general standards prevailing in American education were operative, rather than the historic traditions in Jewish education. Indeed, it is remarkable how rapid was the process of transformation of the Jewish schools from mediaeval to modern standards, from the Cheder or Talmud Torah of Eastern Europe, to the American Jewish School Center.

More dependent upon the educational traditions of the Jews was the rising standard of requirements in terms of Jewish knowledge. With the growth of the Jewish community of New York, there was an intensification of Jewish life, and a consequent increase in the demands made upon Jewish education. The accompanying chart[2] shows clearly two tendencies: on one hand, the secular studies were steadily eliminated during the successive periods, and on the other hand, the Jewish curricula of the schools kept increasing both in their scope and in the amount of knowledge required. This is particularly true of the last thirty-five years.

It is difficult to ascertain what standard prevailed in teaching "the Hebrew" in the early Shearith Israel School. But from the minutes of the congregation, it may be assumed that the standard was very low. The curricula of the German Jewish schools are more specific. The standard of instruction in their earlier schools, particularly in the day schools, was somewhat higher

---

[1] Minutes of Cong. Shearith Israel (1822); cf. Appendix B.

[2] Opposite p. 134.

than in the Spanish-Portuguese school. More advanced subjects are mentioned in their curricula, and provision was made occasionally for more advanced pupils. But with the introduction of the Sunday schools, the standard of Jewish education again decreased considerably, not only in the Sunday schools themselves, but in the afternoon schools as well. Attempts to establish schools of higher Jewish learning in New York, prior to 1881, were not successful.

The Eastern European Jewish immigrants were better versed in Jewish lore than their predecessors, and they naturally raised the standard of Jewish educational requirements. They demanded more knowledge, not only intensively, by requiring from their children more thorough knowledge of such subjects as Hebrew, the Bible, and religious customs, but they also enlarged the curriculum extensively by laying stress upon the study of the Talmud, Shulchan Aruch and Commentaries, and by introducing new subjects, such as modern Hebrew (language and literature), folk music, and current Jewish history. For this curriculum the Sunday school was insufficient. The Eastern European Jews have, therefore, continued the system of weekday religious instruction. The indications are that the Sunday school experiment in Jewish history, lasting some sixty years, has not been successful, and that it will be replaced once more by weekday schools. Historic evidence seems to point to the fact that the Sunday school is not the normal educational institution of the Jews in America, although for a long time it will still persist, at least as a substitute, in those places where conditions make weekday instruction difficult of practical achievement.

Connected with the rising standards in Jewish education are the recent efforts to create a complete *system* of Jewish schools in New York, so that educational provision may be made for all Jewish boys and girls, no matter what their age or occupation. The attempt is made to differentiate Jewish education, so as to reach young and old, student and worker. The accompanying chart[3] shows how such a system is being developed. Prior to 1910 Jewish elementary schools were confined almost wholly to the education of boys. In these schools the same studies were

[3] P. 135. The arrows show the progress of children through the school system.

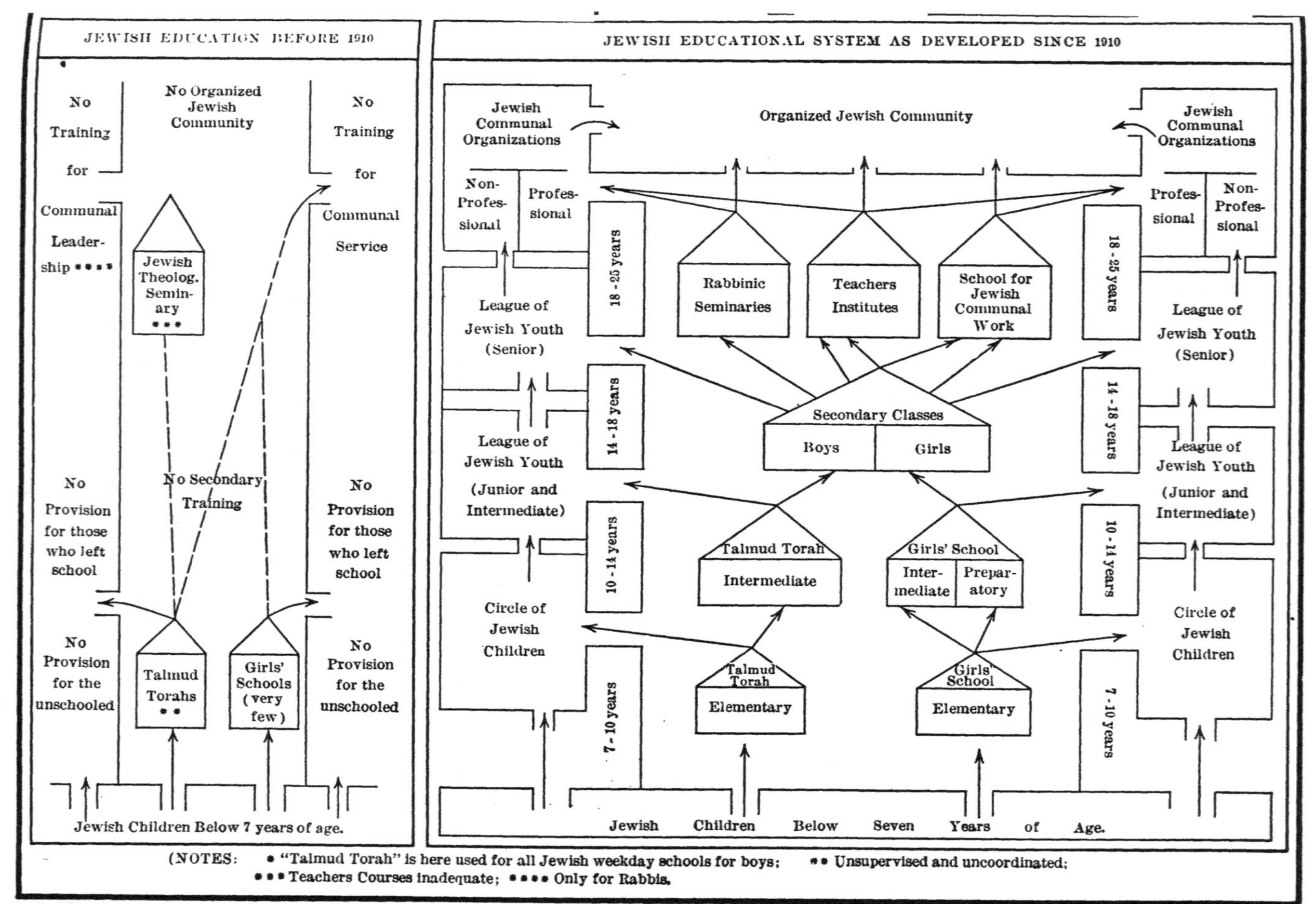

(NOTES: * "Talmud Torah" is here used for all Jewish weekday schools for boys; ** Unsupervised and uncoordinated; *** Teachers Courses inadequate; **** Only for Rabbis.

taught to all pupils of school age, without regard to their mental abilities or their aptitudes. For those children who were not receiving regular classroom instruction, no provision whatever was made. Boys who finished the course of studies in the elementary Jewish schools, could receive no secondary instruction, and only the very few who wished to become rabbis, managed to find their way into the Jewish Theological Seminary.

Since 1910 conditions have changed considerably, chiefly through the instrumentality of the Bureau of Jewish Education. Now Jewish children first enter the Elementary Talmud Torahs for Boys, or the Schools for Girls. Those who do not go to the regular schools, find some educational provision made for them in the Circle of Jewish Children. From the Elementary Schools the pupils either proceed to the Intermediate Schools, or else, if they leave school, they continue to be reached by the Circle of Jewish Children. In the Intermediate Schools for Girls further differentiation is made for those who wish to prepare themselves to become Jewish teachers, by means of the "preparatory" classes. From the Intermediate Schools the boys and girls go on to the Secondary Classes (for High School Boys and High School Girls); or else, if they leave the Jewish school, they join the League of the Jewish Youth as junior members. Beyond the Secondary Classes they may continue their education in professional schools: the Rabbinic Seminaries, the Teachers' Institutes, or the School for Jewish Communal Work. Here they are trained for the "Jewish profession." If they go into business or into other professions, they may still be affiliated with the League of the Jewish Youth as senior members, until, as adults, they join the Jewish community. Thus, the attempt is being made to develop a differentiated system of Jewish education, which in adapting itself to existing conditions, will be able to exert an influence over all boys and girls throughout the years of their growth.

3. The Struggle Away from the Parochial School

Closely bound up with the demand for more intensive Jewish education, is the problem of the parochial school. From our review of the history of Jewish education it is clear that every group of Jews that came to this country tried the parochial school as the readiest solution to the problem of intensive religious instruction for their children. The Portuguese and the German Jews abandoned it toward the middle of the last century, one group substituting the Sunday school, and the other, weekday religious instruction. Some of the Eastern European Jews are still trying out the parochial school, though the great majority have declared themselves unequivocally in favor of *supplementary* Jewish instruction.

There is one fundamental difference, however, between the earlier Jewish parochial schools, and those that are in existence today. The Portuguese and German Jewish parochial schools existed at a time when the parochial idea was current, and their schools were largely influenced by imitation. Shortly after the establishment of the public school system (1842-1853), these schools ceased to exist. But the present Jewish parochial schools were organized at a time when the parochial school was no longer the normal educational institution for the American child. They arose because of the dissatisfaction of some of the "consistently orthodox" with the educational standard of the weekday school, especially in the instruction of the Talmud. They are based, therefore, not upon imitation, but upon conscious purpose. Like the Catholic parochial schools, they want to make "sure" of the child. Unlike the Catholic schools, however, they are conducted by laymen, and not by the clergy.

There is no doubt that the Jewish parochial school is the easiest and most alluring method of preserving Jewish religious life in this country, or at least a certain type of orthodox Jewish life. To subject the Jewish child completely to Jewish influences, and not to permit the "give and take" process between him and his non-Jewish neighbors, may be a temporarily effective way of making "sure" of the child. But it is fraught with danger for America and for the American Jew. The Jews of this country have realized that they cannot plan for the education of their children, without taking into account the whole problem of their adjustment in America. Aside from general considerations of America's welfare, the Jews realize that they are in the minority, and that "sectarianism" may undermine the spirit of tolerance which is among America's proudest claims. Jewish educators have felt that they must develop schools which will preserve Jewish life in this country, without interfering with America's cherished plan of a system of common schools, for "all the children of all the people." "The public school system is the rock bottom upon which this country is rearing its institutions, and we Jews must evolve here a system of Jewish education that shall be complementary to and harmonious with the public school system."[4] From the historic evidence, as well as from a survey of the parochial schools themselves,[5] it is clear that after a brief period of growth, the modern Jewish parochial schools will also have to be re-organized or at least, greatly modified.

Communalization of Jewish Educational Activity

As already pointed out, the earliest Jewish religious schools in New York, the Yeshibat Minhat Areb and the Polonies Talmud Torah, were the synagogue schools of one congregation. The early German Jewish day schools, as well as the Sunday schools which followed them, were conducted entirely under synagogue auspices. The private Jewish boarding schools were owned and conducted by individuals. But in the 60's, philanthropic religious education, in the form of Mission schools, began to be communalized, particularly through the schools of the Hebrew Free School Association, which was a communal organization not affiliated with any single congregation, and received both its pupils and its support from the community at large. The Hebrew Technical Institutes, both for Boys and for Girls, and the Hebrew Orphan Asylum, organized during this period, also show the tendency to communalize philanthropic education.

With the coming of the Eastern European Jews, the communalizing tendency was accelerated. Their earliest schools, the Machzike Talmud Torah and the Yeshibath Etz Chayim, were not connected with any congregation, but were organized and managed by special Educational Societies and were supported by the community at large. Most of the larger Talmud Torahs and Yeshibahs which came later, also partook of this com-

---

[4] "Bureau of Education," Bulletin No. 1, of Kehillah, pamphlet by Dr. S. Benderly.

[5] See Part II of this book, especially Chapters 5, 6 and 10.

munal nature. Not only philanthropic education for the children of the poor, but *all* religious education was separated from the control of the individual synagogue.[6] Even Jewish parochial education is now conducted by educational societies without being connected with any particular congregation. More recently, a number of agencies arose, particularly the Bureau of Jewish Education, which have attempted to cöordinate the work of many schools, and to extend the scope of Jewish education beyond the existing schools.

Among the congregational schools it is interesting to note a significant difference with regard to the tendency toward communalization. The schools conducted by "German-Jewish" congregations are true "congregational" schools, that is, the purpose of each school is, in large measure, to continue that particular congregation. The school privileges are therefore practically limited to the children of members of that congregation. This is not true of the schools connected with the congregations of Eastern European Jews. These schools, although conducted in synagogue buildings and under congregational auspices, are in reality communal schools. Any child in the vicinity of the synagogue may be enrolled in the school, and the school's management does not differ in fundamentals from that of the Talmud Torah or the Hebrew School.

The indications are, that this tendency to take Jewish education out of the control of individuals or of particular congregations, will continue in the future. It is a most interesting commentary on the Jewish conception of religion and of religious education. It illustrates the idea that religion among Jews is non-ecclesiastical, that it is not confined to the synagogue, but that it is as broad as the life of the people itself. It makes clear the conception that the *Congregation of Israel (Knesseth Israel)* in its largest sense, is synonymous with the *Community of Israel (Zibbur, or Kahal)*. Jewish education is, therefore, not denominational education, but communal education. The teachers in Jewish schools, and most of the directors and organizers of Jewish education, are not rabbis, but laymen. The devotional

---

[6] There are synagogues connected with some of the Talmud Torahs (cf. Appendix F), but they are incidental, and are not congregations in the ordinary sense.

element in Jewish religious education is but one phase of the curriculum of the Jewish school; the literary, the historic, and the cultural elements are at least of equal importance. Community education, and not denominational religious education, is the keynote to the school endeavors of the Jews in this country.

Science and Democracy

The tendencies in Jewish education can be best understood in the light of the two universal ideas which have profoundly affected all of our modern life, namely, Science as a Method, and Democracy as an Aim. These two ideas have left their lasting impress upon Jewish education. The rising standard of Jewish education has been possible only through the introduction of scientific theory and practice into the domain of the Jewish school. True it is that the Jewish school has as yet much to learn from the growing science of education. But men and women are now bringing the training which they receive in American universities to their constructive tasks as Jewish teachers and as educational leaders. The scientific tendency in Jewish education has as yet only begun, but it is bound to become, in ever increasing measure, the method of work of the Jewish schools of tomorrow.

Democracy has affected the aims of Jewish education just as Science has affected its methods. The historic struggle away from the parochial school has been made inevitable by the fundamental need of a democratic state: that of permitting each of its individual citizens to share his interests and experiences with other citizens, outside of his particular group or class, so as to make possible broad and free choice of individual development. The communalization of Jewish educational endeavor means the reorganization of Jewish schools on a democratic basis. The transformation of the Talmud Torah from an institution for the poor only. to the democratic school for all Jewish children, is an illustration of the effects of American Democracy. The gradual broadening of educational interest and of school control from individuals to the whole community, is similarly the result of the new democratic environment.

The American Jew has accepted both the scientific method and the modern conceptions of Democracy for his educational endeavors in this country, because it was essential that he do so, if he would preserve his power of spiritual self-perpetuation. He has given up nothing which fundamentally affects his desire for traditional continuity. He is endeavoring to continue the best in his educational traditions with the best of modern American education, and the result, as it is developing in his system of weekday supplementary instruction, will, in all probability, be a distinct contribution to American education.

PART II

The Status of Jewish Education in New York in 1918

(Educational Survey)

Chapter I

THE EXTENT OF JEWISH EDUCATION IN NEW YORK CITY

Introductory Statement

During the past two decades, the educational profession has been developing a scientific technique of study. The attention of leaders of American education is no longer occupied with general discussions of methods and principles, but rather with detailed, and in so far as possible, objective methods of analysis. Statistical studies of various aspects of school management; objective scales for measuring the educational achievements of pupils; score cards for evaluating the efficiency of the teaching staff and the worth of school buildings; scientific experiments to determine the merits of particular methods of instruction; standardized minimum curricula in the various school subjects; uniform records and reports—these are some of the forms thus far assumed by the modern methods of educational study.

The educational *survey,* which has been extensively employed in American schools within recent years, offers a good opportunity for utilizing these modes of scientific educational study. It focuses the methods of the statistician, the psychologist, the sociologist, and the business man upon a practical school situation. It is true that opinion, as expressed by the educational specialist, continues to predominate, and is the controlling factor in these surveys. But the suggestions and the criticisms which surveyors offer, are now more largely based upon facts presented objectively. During the past decade, numerous such surveys have been made in almost every part of the Union. These educational surveys include whole state systems, cities, counties, and rural communities. American educators do not doubt the salutary effect of these surveys in improving the public school system.[1]

A similar survey needs to be made of the present status of Jewish education in New York City, which will utilize the methods of educational study and analysis thus far developed.

[1] Koos, L. V. "The Fruits of School Surveys," School and Society, Jan. 13, 1917, (V 107:35).

With the possible exception of one or two pamphlets,[2] the writer knows of no instance where Jewish education has been treated in terms of modern objective methods. Discussion in Jewish education is still in the realm of opinion and theory. There has been no effort to resort to a scientific analysis of actual conditions, in order to determine what validity these opinions and theories have in point of fact. Even the few efforts in this direction which have been made hitherto, are fragmentary. There is no verifiable body of fact from which the layman, or the student of education, may obtain an unprejudiced view of the situation. Yet it is essential for the development of Jewish education in this country, that the method of study which has proven of so much worth in general American education, be applied also to the work of the Jewish school.

What is urgently needed for the future development of Jewish education in this country is a scientific educational literature, which shall stimulate the student of the field to further research and enable him to take up the thread where it has been left off. Only the faintest beginnings of such a literature have thus far appeared. If this book is to contribute anything in that direction, it must therefore be, in a large measure, pioneer effort. The aim of this book will be to study every phase of the Jewish educational problem, with the object of supplying a verifiable body of fact, and to interpret it impartially. School accommodation and organization, financial and educational management, the teaching staff, the curricula and methods of instruction, the social life of the Jewish schools, are the several phases of the problem which will be treated.

The Number and Location of Jewish Children of School Age

The first question which naturally presents itself to us in a study of Jewish education in this city, is the extent of the problem. How many Jewish children are there of school age? What provision have the Jews of this city made for their

[2] "Financial Survey of Jewish Religious Schools," published by the Bureau of Education of the Jewish Community of New York, 1911. "Surveys of the Jewish Religious Schools of the Bronx," published by the Department of Synagogue and School Extension, 1916, also educational articles in the "Jewish Communal Register," New York, 1918.

religious training?[3] How adequate are the educational provisions thus made?

The question concerning the number of Jewish school children cannot be answered directly. The United States Census has judiciously refrained from gathering detailed statistics concerning religious belief.[4] The public school has been jealously guarded against any possible differentiation along religious lines. A direct house-to-house canvass, carried on by any non-governmental organization,[5] is necessarily very costly, and inaccurate. In consequence, indirect methods must be used in determining the number of Jewish school children.

In the past, estimates of Jewish school population were based upon corresponding estimates of the entire Jewish population, the assumption being that the same proportions hold true between Jewish adults and Jewish school children, as in the general community.[6] Thus, if there were a million Jews in New York City, there would be approximately 200,000 Jewish children of school age. Two difficulties, however, impair the value of these estimates.

In the first place, there has been no accurate basis for determining the total Jewish population. Such estimates were based upon the opinions of social workers, journalists and others.[7] These personal judgments were supplemented, or "checked," in various ways: by means of Jewish immigration figures, calculations of estimated death and birth rates, cemetery statistics, and approximations based upon the proportion of inhabitants with certain Jewish names, such as Cohen and Levy.[8] In consequence

---

[3] It should be remembered that the term "religious" will be used throughout this dissertation, in the sense of "religious-national."

[4] The data gathered in the 1910 Federal Census concerning the Yiddish-speaking population are inadequate for determining the entire Jewish population because the Yiddish-speaking Jews, although in the majority, do not represent the entire Jewish population of New York.

[5] Cf. Sociological Canvass made by the Federation of Churches, New York, 1912, under Dr. Walter Laidlaw.

[6] For illustration of such an estimate, cf. "Aims and Activities of the Bureau of Education," p. 8.

[7] Appendix J shows the estimates of Jewish population from early American history to the present time. In cases where questionnaires were used, the result is simply the sum of many such personal estimates made by individuals in various communities of the United States.

[8] For examples of studies of this nature to determine the Jewish population, cf. American Jewish Year Book, 1914-1915, pp. 339-358. Also Directory of the Jewish Community of New York, 1912, pp. 3-14; also "The Jews of New York," by Prof. W. Chalmers, in American Journal of Statistics, July 1913.

of these imperfect means of calculation, there was wide difference of opinion concerning the number of Jews in New York City.[9]

But besides their inadequacy due to the fact that the original judgments were inaccurate, these estimates present another difficulty which is of great importance to the practical Jewish schoolman. It may be well for the sake of general information, and for propaganda purposes, to state that there are so many Jewish children in New York City, but the question which concerns the practical educator is: *where* are these children located, and how much provision is made for them? These questions cannot be answered by general estimates. It was felt, therefore, that another, a more accurate, and a more detailed method, must be found for estimating the number of Jewish school children in New York, before any real study of the problem would be possible.

Estimate Based Upon Attendance in Public Schools

There was one factor in the life of the Jews which gave a clue to the possibility of obtaining a better estimate of the Jewish school population. The Jews of this country, with practical unanimity, observe the Jewish High Holidays (the New Year and the Day of Atonement). On these days, Jewish children stay away from public school. If, then, the percentage of absence in the public schools on these days could be compared with the percentage of absence on normal days, it would give a fairly accurate basis for estimating the proportion of Jewish school children in the public schools. With the permission of the New York public school authorities, this information was obtained.[10] A study was made of the proportion of children who attend public school in the various districts of the city, on the two days of the Jewish New Year, and on a normal day of the year 1913; and also, on the two days of the Jewish New Year, on the Day

---

[9] Cf. Appendix J—particularly for the years 1897 and 1912.

[10] The attendance figures for the public schools of New York are kept only in monthly summaries in the central offices of the Board of Education. Special questionnaires were therefore sent to the school principals to furnish the desired data from their own daily records.

of Atonement, and on a normal day of the year 1914.[11] From this study *it appears that 40.5% of the children in public schools of New York are abnormally absent on Jewish holidays.*[12]

For practical purposes we may assume that this abnormal absence on Jewish holidays is due entirely to the Jewish children. There are two sources of error in this calculation, however, which though they tend to balance each other, are nevertheless probably not equal, and must therefore be given further consideration. The first consists in the fact that not *all* of the Jewish children are absent on these holidays from public school. No doubt a number of Jewish children attend school on one or all of the Jewish holidays. This source of error would tend to make the actual proportion of Jewish children in the public schools higher than 40.5%. But this source of error is probably not large.

The other source of error is more important. It is certain that there are a goodly number of *non-Jewish* children who are abnormally absent on the Jewish holidays. Because of the large number of Jewish pupils absent in some of the districts, excuses for absence are readily granted, and non-Jewish children take advantage of the general "holiday." This factor has a real effect upon the situation, tending to make the actual proportion of Jewish children lower than 40.5%. In view of the results obtained by another method of estimating, which will be described

---

[11] Cf. Table I. No figures could be obtained for the years 1915 and 1916, because in 1915 the Jewish holidays came during registration week of the public schools, and in 1916 the epidemic of infantile paralysis made the attendance figures of the schools worthless for the purpose of study. The per cent. of abnormal absence was calculated as follows: The average per cent. attendance on the Jewish holidays was divided by the per cent. attendance on normal days, in order to correct for the per cent. of children who were *normally* absent on the Jewish holidays. The two corrected per cents of attendance were then averaged. In order to obtain the *abnormal* absence, the average was deducted from 100% of the register.

[12] Cf. last column Table I. In Manhattan the proportion reaches to more than one-half, or 51.2% of the register, in the Bronx it is 42.3%, in Brooklyn 38.0%, in Queens 7.3% and in Richmond 5.8%. The amount of abnormal absence varies from 4.3% in district 41 Queens, to 99.1% in district 5 Manhattan. The median district has 23.1% abnormal absence. The lower quartile is 9.5% and the upper is 59.0%; the average is 36.9%. It may be seen that all of these points are comparatively low when compared to the total proportion of abnormal absence, 40.5%. This is due to the fact that the density of the Jewish population tends to vary directly with the density of the total population of the district. In other words, the large congested districts have a higher proportion of Jews than the more sparsely settled smaller districts.

presently, the proportion of Jewish children in the public schools was reduced to 38%.[13] By boroughs the proportion estimated is as follows: Manhattan 48%, Bronx 40%, Brooklyn 38%, Queens 7%, and Richmond 5%.[14] Since the total register in the public schools, 1915-1916, was 730,756, it would seem that there were in that year 277,687 Jewish children in the eight grades of the New York public schools. Of these 131,724 were in Manhattan, 39,800 in the Bronx, 106,207 in Brooklyn, 4,337 in Queens, and 717 in Richmond.[15]

Judgment of Jewish Names in the School Census

In order to corroborate the proportion of Jewish children of school age obtained in our study of school attendance on the Jewish holidays, another method of estimation was resorted to.[16] The Bureau of Attendance of the New York Board of Education keeps a continuous school census of the population of New York. Some million and a half cards are filed in the census

[13] It was found that in the judgment of names in the School Census (see below) 33% of *all* children, whether in public, parochial or private schools were Jews. This sets for us the limits within which we must put the proportion of Jewish children in the public schools: it is not lower than 33% nor higher than 40.5%. Twelve competent judges acquainted with the factors that affect the situation, were asked to judge what was probably the true proportion. Their average (median) judgment was 38%. This proportion was then applied in reducing the proportions in each school district. Cf. Table III.

[14] Cf. Table III. A check on our estimate is furnished by the data obtained in the investigation of the United States Congress Immigration Commission of 1910. The method used by the Congressional Commission consisted in questioning children of the public schools concerning the nationality of their fathers. The per cent. of children designating their fathers as of Hebrew nativity was 46.1% in Manhattan, 20.2% in the Bronx, 29.9% in Brooklyn, 3.5% in Queens and 2.8% in Richmond. Considering the fact that the figures of the Immigration Commission do not include the per cent. of the Jewish children who designated their fathers as of American, Russian, German or other races, the similarity is significant. The largest discrepancy between these figures and those of our estimate is in the Bronx. But it is a matter of common knowledge that there has been a very large influx of Jews into the Bronx within the past seven years. Cf. Appendix K.

[15] For estimates by districts and for full data, cf. Table III. It is assumed in that table that the same proportions of Jewish to non-Jewish children held true in 1916 as in 1914. While slight error may be caused by this assumption in particular districts of the city, the total proportion would not be affected.

[16] It is necessary to caution the reader from the very outset, that this method is not intended as a basis for the estimate itself, but merely as a check on the school attendance method.

PROPORTION OF JEWISH CHILDREN
in the
ELEMENTARY PUBLIC SCHOOLS OF NEW YORK

Average 38%

Borough	Proportion
Manhattan	48%
Bronx	40%
Brooklyn	38%
Queens	7%
Richmond	5%

division of the Bureau, each of which represents a complete family, parents and children. From these cards, 4,215 families were selected at random, representing a total of 10,332 children of school age. The names on these cards were judged as to whether they were Jewish or non-Jewish.[17] About one-third, 33%, of all the children of school age, in the public, parochial, and private schools of this city were judged to be Jews.[18]

Agreement Between the Two Methods

The results obtained by the method of judging the names in the school census, are in close agreement with those obtained in the study of school attendance on Jewish holidays. Since the 33% of the census names represents not only the public school children, but also the children in private and parochial

---

[17] The method of selection and judgment was as follows: At intervals of about 350 cards, two cards were selected, the first cards forming set I, and the second cards forming set II. The names were then judged by a graduate student of Columbia University and by myself, as to whether they were Jewish or non-Jewish. In order to insure careful judgment, five categories were used: "Jewish; non-Jewish; doubtful-Jewish; doubtful-non-Jewish; doubtful." In these judgments we were greatly aided by the information upon the cards, which gave the first names of the father and mother and of all the children, the nativity of the parents and of the children, the length of their stay in America, the year of their immigration, the country of their emigration, and the occupation of the father. It will be readily seen that these data furnish good clues for judging whether the family is Jewish or not. In most cases there was no doubt whatever in the judgment. In the case of German names, such as Bamberger, or Anglicized names, such as Brown, these data, while not equally certain, were also effective. Thus, if a child attended a Catholic parochial school, it would certainly be safe to assume the family non-Jewish. If in an immigrant family the son's first name was the same as his father's, it would be reasonable to assume the family non-Jewish, because it is not customary among Eastern European Jews to name their children after living relatives, especially after the father. The data, furnished by the cards themselves, were so helpful in deciding the judgments, that only 196 cases, or 4.6% of cases, were included in *any* of the doubtful categories. To guard against the temptation to call doubtful cases Jewish, *all doubtful cases were counted as non-Jewish.* The *census* districts of the New York Board of Education do not coincide with the *school* districts. But as the cards are arranged geographically, (by city blocks) each block or set of blocks was judged individually, and formed into the corresponding school district. There is a slight overlapping of some of the school districts, due to the fact that several of the intermediate schools (6B—8B) draw their pupils from neighboring districts. But a study of this factor convinced the writer that its net results are negligible.

[18] Cf. "the average of the two sets of judgments" in Table II (last column). In Manhattan the proportion was 38%, in the Bronx 32%, in Brooklyn 37%, in Queens 5% and in Richmond 3%. The proportion judged to be Jews in the total population, is about the same.

schools, it is necessary to add to the 730,756 (elementary public school register 1915-1916), the 200,000 children estimated to be in the elementary parochial and private schools.[19] This would make a total of 930,756 children of school age in New York, between the ages of 5 and 14, of whom 307,149 were Jewish children.

By the school attendance method we computed that there were 277,687 Jewish school children in the elementary public schools of New York (1915-1916).[20] To this number should be added approximately 20,000 Jewish children in the private and parochial schools,[21] making a total of 297,687 children of elementary school age. The difference between the two methods is therefore about 9,450, or a difference of 3.0%. Considering the fact that not all of the Jewish children between the ages of 5 and 14 are at school,[22] the agreement between the two methods is very striking.[23]

Corrected Estimates

In accordance with these computations, we are forced to the conclusion that the number of Jewish children of elementary school age (*i.e.* 5 to 14 years), in this city, is nearly 300,000.

[19] Estimate of the Statistical Division of the Department of Education, New York State.

[20] See above, p. 150.

[21] This estimate was derived as follows: The State authorities give the number of children in the private schools of New York as about 75,000. The City authorities place it nearer 90,000. More accurate figures are not available. Since the Jewish school population is about 33% of the total school population (Cf. Table II), the number of Jewish children in private schools would be from 25,000 to 30,000. While the majority of New York Jews are recent arrivals, who do not send their children to private schools, there is on the other hand a well-known predilection among the richer Jews for such schools. It is safe therefore to assume that there are 20,000 Jewish children in the private schools of New York.

[22] Some obtain their working certificates at the age of 13, and others are out of school temporarily. The per cent. of children between 10-14 in New York State who attend school, is given as 94.4% (Federal Census 1910, Population Vol. III, p. 214).

[23] Another indication of the close agreement between these two methods of estimating the number of Jewish children, is shown by the coefficient of correlation which is calculated in Table IIa, and is shown to be .955, or almost perfect correlation. This means that whenever a district was estimated to be above the average in its proportion of Jewish population by the School Attendance Method, it was also judged to be equally above the average by the Census Judgment Method. Thus, if in District 5, Manhattan, the proportion of Jewish population is judged to be highest by one method, it is also judged to be highest by the other method.

Startling as this figure may appear, it is fully warranted by a consideration of the facts. To safeguard against the possibility of exaggeration, however, we shall discard our estimate of the Jewish children in the private and parochial schools, and make use of the public school figures only. We shall certainly be safe in placing the total number of Jewish children of elementary school age (5-14) as low as 275,000.[24]

This figure, with its subdivisions by school districts, is probably as true an estimate of the number of Jewish children of elementary school age in New York City, as can be made under present conditions, without resorting to an actual government census.

Proportion of Jewish Children Receiving Jewish Instruction

With this estimate of the number of Jewish children of elementary school age as a basis, the first significant question which confronts us is: In how far do the Jews provide Jewish training for the 275,000 Jewish school children of New York? In order to answer this question adequately, a survey of the Jewish schools of this city was undertaken.[25] The survey extended from January to August, 1917, and reached all Jewish schools which are conducted under the auspices of educational societies, congregations, and institutions, and in which instruction is given to groups, (classes, etc.) and not to individual children. Private schools employing two or more teachers were

---

[24] There are probably in 1917-1918, at least 300,000 Jewish school children. No allowance was made for the Jewish children who attend private schools, nor for those Jewish boys and girls who attend public school on one or more of the Jewish holidays. Then, too, 275,000, the estimated number of Jewish children, is based on the school register of 1916, and not upon the register of 1917-1918.

[25] Three methods were employed: First, the writer himself visited, at least once, every important Jewish school in the city. To some of the larger schools, as many as a dozen visits were made, in order to obtain adequate information. The second method used consisted in the sending of questionnaires to all Jewish schools not visited personally by the writer. These questionnaires asked for information concerning enrollment, management, curriculum and teachers. Thirdly, under the personal supervision of the writer, a number of investigators, (college men) made a street-to-street canvass of the entire city, and obtained specific information from every school which they located. For questionnaires see Appendix L.

also included. There are therefore excluded from this study only the small, unorganized one-teacher schools, or "Chedarim." [26]

The survey included 181 Jewish schools, which give instruction to 41,403 children, as follows:[27]

Borough	Number of Schools	Number of Pupils	Proportion of Total Number of Jewish Children in the Borough
Manhattan	89	22,413	17.5%
Bronx	30	5,360	13.4%
Brooklyn	55	13,002	12.6% [28]
Queens	6	578	11.3%
Richmond	1	50	6.4%
Total	181	41,403	14.9%

In order to include all of the Jewish children receiving Jewish instruction, we must add to this number the children who are taught individually in the small unorganized schools, not reached by the survey, as well as those who are taught at home by private Jewish teachers. Concerning these forms of education no accurate information is possible. It is estimated that 10,000 children are taught by private teachers,[29] and that 14,000 more are provided for in the Chedarim.[30]. The total number of Jewish children receiving some form of Jewish training in New

[26] The schools surveyed are listed in Appendix M and are located on map facing frontispiece. *The date of the school registers is approximately June 1, 1917.*

[27] Cf. Table IV.

[28] This proportion, of course, only holds true of Brooklyn as a whole. In certain parts of Brooklyn the proportion is much higher.

[29] It is the average opinion of eight competent judges that there are about 1,000 Jewish private teachers in New York City. Since it is estimated that the average teacher instructs 10 pupils, it is liberal to put the number of children thus taught at 10,000.

[30] A survey of these schools made by the Bureau of Jewish Education in 1912, credits them with teaching 13,952 children. (Cf. A Survey of the Financial Status of the Jewish Religious Schools, p. 6). As some of the larger of these schools have been included in our survey, and as the number of children taught in Chedarim probably has not increased since 1912, owing to the growth of organized Jewish schools, the same figure is kept.

York City is, therefore, 65,400.[31] *This is less than 24% of the estimated number of Jewish children of elementary school age.*

With regard to secondary Jewish instruction, the proportion is even smaller. Of the 40,000 Jewish boys and girls estimated to be in the public high schools of New York,[32] only about 400 receive secondary Jewish training. The following institutions are the only ones which offer courses for high school boys and girls which might be dignified with the name of secondary Jewish instruction:[33]

	Boys	Girls
Bureau of Jewish Education	132	123
Rabbinical College	50	—
National Hebrew School (Man.)	—	50
Uptown Talmud Torah	40	—
Total	222	173

The total number of high school pupils taught by these institutions is, therefore, 395, or *hardly one per cent. of the entire number of Jewish boys and girls in the public high schools of this city.*

Necessity of Increasing Facilities for Jewish Education

These facts are striking. They do not, however, fully represent the situation with regard to the amount of religious education among the Jews of this city. Two qualifying factors must be taken into consideration before we can compare the proportion of Jewish children receiving Jewish training with the proportion of non-Jewish children receiving Christian training. In the

[31] The children reached by the Extension activities of the Bureau of Jewish Education, and in the club work of Young Judea, are not here included, because this work is not regular instruction.

[32] A study made by the Hatikvah Society (society of Jewish high school students), under L. J. Linder, Feb. 12, 1918, places the number of Jewish students in the New York City high schools at 45,000. Cf. Jewish Daily News of that date (English section).

[33] Some of the synagogues have post-graduate classes, but these are not here included, because the instruction in them is of an elementary nature, and the course of study unorganized. The Teachers' Training schools, of which there are three in New York, are also not included, even though they are in reality secondary schools, because their aim is professional training.

PROPORTION OF JEWISH CHILDREN RECEIVING JEWISH INSTRUCTION in 1917

first place, most of the 65,000 Jewish children receive *weekday* religious instruction, several periods during the week. Of the Jewish children taught in Jewish schools, 12% are instructed in Sunday and Sabbath schools, and 88% are given the more intensive weekday training, from two to six periods during the week. Of the Christian children taught in New York, from 60% to 70% receive religious instruction only one period during the week, on Sundays.[34] It is evident, therefore, that such religious education as *is* provided, is, on the whole, likely to be more intensive among the Jews.[35]

Another factor to be considered is, that although only 24% of the Jewish children are now receiving religious training, this figure does not represent all of the Jewish children who receive instruction during some period in their life. One of the striking phenomena in Jewish school management is the very large amount of premature "leaving" and readmission, which keeps many children out of school for some time. This is due primarily to two causes: (1) Jewish parents must pay for the religious education of their children, which influences some parents to limit the number of years of instruction, and (2) there is no systematic transfer of pupils to care for the frequent removals from one part of the city to another.[36] Children are, therefore, withdrawn from school for weeks and months at a time, to be later admitted into some other school. Moreover, it has been the practice among many Jews to give their children some form of intensive Jewish training for a short period,

[34] It is not possible to estimate satisfactorily the proportion of Christian children receiving weekday religious instruction, because it is not possible to get accurate data. In a pamphlet issued by the Interdenominational Committee, estimates are given which may be used as a basis. The writer attempted to verify these estimates by personal interviews with the heads of the various denominational school systems. The Protestants report 225,000 children in their religious schools, which are practically all Sunday Schools; the Roman Catholics report about 100,000 in their Sunday Schools and 8,000 in their weekday supplementary schools. There are probably 150,000 children in Christian parochial schools in New York. This would make the total number of Christian children taught about 483,000. Of this number no more than 160,000 or 33%, receive weekday (i. e. supplementary *and* parochial) instruction.

[35] With the exception of the training given in the parochial schools (Catholic and Lutheran), which, as regards religious training, are probably more intensive than the supplementary weekday schools among the Jews.

[36] For fuller discussion and confirming evidence, cf. Part II, Chapter eight.

usually from one to two years prior to their Bar Mitzvah or confirmation.[37]

But while these considerations should be borne in mind, in order to interpret properly the figures cited above, the fact nevertheless remains that, at any one time, educational provision is made for only 24% of the Jewish children of elementary school age. In other words, only one child out of four is given some form of Jewish training at any one time. This includes all forms of Jewish instruction. If we exclude the individual instruction given by private teachers, or in the Chedarim, only 14.9%, or approximately *one out of every seven* Jewish children is taught in some Jewish school.

These are significant figures. They indicate concretely the problem which confronts the Jews in their attempt to preserve their religious and cultural life in this country. No group can hope to maintain its spiritual life successfully, if it provides schools for only one-seventh of its children. The necessity for giving education to all of its children is so essential to the continuation of any community or group, that it is accepted as a truism. If the Jews, therefore, are to continue their life as Jews in this country, they must realize that their fundamental problem is to increase the facilities for Jewish education, so as to include a greater proportion of Jewish children than are now reached.

Difficulty of Providing Adequately for Jewish Education

Several conditions make this task a difficult one. The most fundamental of the difficulties inherent in any attempt to create an adequate system of Jewish education are: (1) the lack of power to levy taxes for religious education, and (2) the inability to compel attendance at the Jewish school. The reasons for this legal powerlessness are evident, and are in full accord with American principles of government. The Jewish school is backed neither by mandatory government, nor by a centralized powerful church.[38] There can therefore be no *compulsion* in Jewish edu-

---

[37] Allowing for these factors, it is estimated that of the Jewish boys, about two-thirds receive some form of Jewish training before they reach their thirteenth year. Cf. p. 253.

[38] Cf. Part II, Chapter 3, p. 188.

cation, either legal or clerical. It must be based entirely upon *persuasion,* and upon the conscious desire of parents. The powerlessness of the Jewish school is the fundamental difficulty; from it arise all the practical phases of the problem.

The most important of the practical obstacles are: (a) the economic burden placed upon the Jewish masses; (b) the satisfying conditions of the new environment, and the consequent indifference which it engenders to the historic religion and culture; and (c) the inadequate organization of the Jewish community with regard to its educational problem.

As has already been suggested, in a system of education which has not the support of the state, and which is not conducted by a strongly centralized church, (as among the Catholics) *the parents themselves must bear the major part of the financial burden of education.* For many centuries the Jews have paid for the religious education of their children. Only for the poorest children was education provided by the community.[39] In this country the self-supporting tradition of the Jewish school has continued, so that normally Jewish parents pay for the tuition of their children. But the cost of maintaining Jewish schools in America is higher than it was in Eastern Europe, and the economic struggle is intense. A large proportion of the Jews of New York are immigrants. The conflict for the necessities and comforts of life, and for social position, is therefore very keen, and deters parents from spending liberally for the Jewish education of their children. Many satisfy themselves therefore with what they regard as the *minimum* of religious instruction. When we remember how difficult it has been in American public education to get the majority of parents to spend any money directly upon the training of their children, even in such small sums as are involved in the cost of text books, we can realize the difficulty presented in inducing parents to pay a sum of $15 to $25 annually for the religious instruction of each of their children.[40] Indeed, it is surprising to find that the Jewish masses of this city have been willing to spend yearly over a *million dollars* for Jewish

---

[39] Cf. Part I, Chapter 3, p. 67.

[40] This is the annual per capita cost in the larger weekday Jewish schools for boys. For fuller discussion, see Part II, Chapter 6, pp. 220 and 229.

religious education in *direct payments of tuition fees.*[41] This fact would seem to indicate that there is a conscious desire on the part of the Jewish masses to give their children Jewish training. Only the force of age-long tradition, which is behind the self-supporting Jewish school, can explain how the Jews have been able to overcome even partially the economic difficulty inherent in American Jewish education.

But the obstacles presented by the economic necessity for maintaining the schools, are not so great as are the difficulties arising from *the non-Jewish influence of the American environment.* The new culture and the new conditions of life are in themselves satisfying. In consequence, even those who do not wish to lose their historic culture and their social group life, drift away because of indifference. The rewards of general education are tangible. They can be measured in terms of livelihood, of position and of social approval. The rewards of Jewish education are not tangible. They cannot be measured in terms which the people can easily understand and appreciate. The contradiction is therefore the more glaring. Public education, whose rewards are direct and easily understood, is offered "free"; Jewish education, which offers no such tangible, compelling rewards, must be paid for. This contrast makes the task of the Jewish school doubly difficult.

To counteract the natural tendency to indifference, which is stimulated by the satisfying conditions of the environment, there seems to be only one effective means, namely, that of *purposeful organization.* What is needed is a strongly centralized community organization, which is to represent the religious and cultural efforts of all the Jews of this city. This organization of all the Jews is to consider the work of the Jewish schools as a communal function, and not as individual isolated effort. It should teach the need of Jewish education to the Jewish parents of this city; it should stimulate the establishment of new schools, and should help the schools already in existence to attain higher educational usefulness. Such an attempt has been made, within the past eight years, by the Kehillah (Jewish Community) of New York.[42] But thus far, this attempt has proven wholly in-

[41] For corroborating evidence, cf. Part II, Chapter 6, p. 228.

[42] Cf. Part I, Chapter 4.

adequate. It has not yet been able to unite all the Jews of this city for organized common activities, because of the extraordinary size and heterogeneity of the Jewish community of New York. There are no Jewish schools directly connected with it. The Bureau of Jewish Education, which it created, has now been separated from it, and the work of the Bureau itself is as yet far from being all-inclusive. Other organizations which have attempted to supervise the work of *special types* of schools, such as the Jewish parochial schools, or the national radical schools, have dealt with only a part of the problem. Centralized coördinated effort has not yet been achieved, and the work of the Jewish schools of New York is practically completely decentralized. We need but turn to the history of American education to realize how difficult it is for any decentralized educational system to enlarge its influence, and to make progress.[43]

To recapitulate, these are the three main practical obstacles to increasing the facilities for Jewish education: (a) the financial burden upon the masses; (b) the indifference caused by the non-Jewish environment; and (c) the inadequate organization of the Jewish community. Underlying them is the legal powerlessness of the Jewish school in this country.

Efforts to Solve the Problem

The specific attempts made to enlarge the facilities for Jewish education, are directed along several lines. Efforts on the part of various groups are being put forth directly or indirectly: (1) to provide for more accommodation, by the building of new Jewish school buildings; (2) to supplement the work of the regular Jewish schools by an extension scheme of Jewish education, which will not be costly nor require much additional accommodation; (3) to change the present management of Jewish schools, so as to increase the number of children who can avail themselves of the present school accommodation; (4) to improve the content and the methods of instruction in the Jewish schools, in order to make them more attractive to Jewish parents and to their children; and (5) to carry on an organized educational

[43] The effects of this decentralized system will be discussed in Part II, Chapter 3, pp. 183-188.

campaign among Jewish parents and in the Jewish community at large for more and for better Jewish instruction than is now provided. The subsequent pages of this book discuss these efforts to solve the problem of Jewish education in New York City.

Chapter II

JEWISH SCHOOL BUILDINGS AND ACCOMMODATION FOR JEWISH EDUCATION

With the growth of modern ideas in education, there has come the recognition of the importance of the physical environment in school work. The construction of school houses, the physical equipment of the school plant, and the provision for proper sanitary conditions, have been among the important concerns of the modern schoolman. Recently attempts have been made to standardize the construction of public school buildings by setting up definite, measurable standards in school architecture.[1] Rapid progress is being made toward making American school houses among the finest educational structures in the world.

But in Jewish education the question of housing has, until recently, received but very little consideration. With but a few notable exceptions, Jewish schools offer their pupils cheerless, unsanitary quarters amidst unattractive surroundings. Any effort to extend and to improve Jewish education in the future must naturally depend upon the construction of more Jewish school buildings, built in the spirit of modern school architecture. In how far this is a fundamental need in Jewish education, may be seen from a consideration of the four types of school accommodation in vogue among the Jews of this city, for the Jewish instruction of their children.

A. The first type is that of the *special school building*, constructed specifically as a Jewish school house. The tendency has been to utilize in the construction of these buildings, the experience of American school house architecture, so that a few of the modern Jewish school buildings in New York are fine educational structures, having well designed classrooms, auditoriums, gymnasiums and other facilities.[2]

B. The second type of Jewish school is located in *institutional buildings*, whose main purpose is other than that of Jewish religious education. These schools are found in the Hebrew

---

[1] Cf. "Strayer Score Card for School Buildings," published by Teachers' College, Columbia University, New York, 1918.

[2] Cf. Illustrations.

JEWISH SCHOOL BUILDING

Type A

CENTRAL JEWISH INSTITUTE
125 East 85th Street

(1916)

JEWISH SCHOOL BUILDING

Type A

JESHIBATH RABBI JACOB JOSEPH
165 Henry Street
(1914)

JEWISH SCHOOL BUILDING

Type A

DOWNTOWN TALMUD TORAH
394 East Houston Street
(1911)

JEWISH SCHOOL IN INSTITUTIONAL BUILDING
Type B

BUILDING OF EDUCATIONAL ALLIANCE
East Broadway and Jefferson Street
(1890)

JEWISH SCHOOL IN INSTITUTIONAL BUILDING

Type B

BUILDING OF Y. W. H. A.
31 West 110th Street

(1914)

JEWISH SCHOOL IN INSTITUTIONAL BUILDING

Type B

MAIN BUILDING AND ANNEX
HEBREW NATIONAL ORPHAN HOUSE
57 Seventh Street, 52 St. Marks Place

JEWISH SCHOOLS IN REMODELLED BUILDING

Type C

MACHZIKEI TALMUD TORAH
225 East Broadway

JEWISH SCHOOLS IN REMODELLED BUILDINGS

Type C

TIFERETH JERUSALEM TALMUD TORAH
147 East Broadway

NATIONAL HEBREW SCHOOL
183 Madison Street

(Now abandoned)

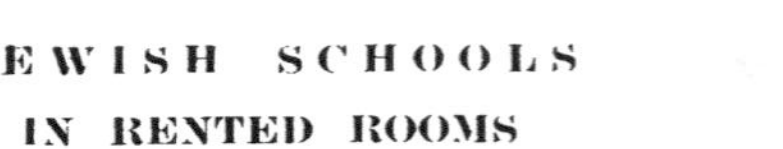

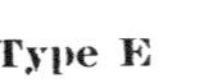

JEWISH SCHOOLS IN RENTED ROOMS

Type E

(Worst Type of Jewish School)

JEWISH SCHOOLS IN RENTED ROOMS

Type E

Reproduced through the courtesy of the Department of Synagog and School Extension, Hebrew Union College.

Orphan Asylums, the Educational Alliance, Y. M. H. A.'s, and Jewish social settlements. The worth of these rooms naturally varies with the particular institution. In the larger institutions, adequate provision is made, while in some of the smaller ones, conditions are no better than those found in the poorer types of Jewish school buildings.

C. A third type of Jewish school accommodation is that of the *building remodelled* for school purposes. Dwelling houses, churches, meeting halls, and other buildings have been remodelled for just such purposes. In point of educational merit, these buildings range from ill-lighted, non-fireproof, poorly equipped private houses, in which only a few of the most necessary alterations were made, to buildings in which merely the outer structure was kept, and the inner architecture was completely changed to meet school needs. But even the best of these buildings do not approach the modern standards of school architecture. In most of them, sanitary conditions are poor. Not one of them provides for gymnasium and similar facilities, and they all bear the marks of poor adaptation.[3]

D. Another type of Jewish school accommodation, and the one most frequently found, consists of *synagogue vestries,* or other parts of synagogue buildings. These rooms are usually located in the basement of the synagogue, below the main hall. With few exceptions, they too are ill-lighted and poorly ventilated. In the smaller congregations it is difficult to keep the vestries as clean and sanitary as desirable, and the consequent effect is, that they are unattractive and detrimental to the health of the children and to the welfare of the school. The tendency in recent years has been for the new synagogues to provide classrooms above the main halls of the synagogue, or else to build separate school buildings.[4] This provision will make it possible for the congregational classrooms to approach some of the modern standards in school construction, and the tendency is much to be commended.

E. Lastly, there is the *rented room* as a place for the impart-

---

[3] Cf. Illustrations.

[4] These buildings, as well as those described in Type A, are constructed as community centers, for the purposes of social service. Cf. Part II, Chap. 12.

ing of Jewish instruction. Societies, congregations and individuals rent one or more rooms in vacant houses, in tenements, or in other buildings, for the purpose of accommodating their children. It may be said without hesitation that this is the worst type of Jewish school accommodation. While some of the better schools situated in rented rooms provide facilities equal to those of the remodelled dwelling, or of the synagogue vestry, many are found in such places as stores, basements, back rooms, meeting halls and similar undesirable places. The majority of the schools so situated are of the Cheder type, that is, they are unorganized one-teacher schools.[5]

From a study of the number of Jewish schools under each of the above types of accommodation, and of the number of children who are so accommodated, in each borough,[6] it appears that only 12.7%, or one-eighth of the 65,000 children who are given Jewish instruction at all, are accommodated in school buildings. By far the largest proportion are taught in rented rooms, in the vestries of synagogues, or in the homes of the pupils, as follows:

	Number of Schools	Number of Pupils	Proportion of all children receiving any Jewish instruction
In Rented Rooms........	530 [7]	17,460	26.8%
In Vestries of Synagogues.	85	15,247	23.5%
In Private Homes........	—	10,000	15.5%
In Remodelled B'ldgs.....	32	8,967	13.8%
In Special School B'ldgs...	10	8,265	12.7%
In Institutional B'ldgs....	16	5,011	7.7%
Total	673	64,950 [8]	100.0%

In the city of New York, having a Jewish population of 1,500,000, there are only *ten specially constructed Jewish school buildings.* In the well populated borough of the Bronx, there is not a single Jewish school building constructed for the purposes

[5] In the accompanying illustrations are shown some of the places rented as Jewish classrooms.

[6] See Table V.

[7] The Chedarim are here included, since practically all of them are in rented rooms.

[8] For discrepancy, see Table V.

JEWISH SCHOOL ACCOMMODATION

Showing Porportion of Jewish Children Taught in Each Type of Accommodation

of Jewish education, nor a single institutional building conducting Jewish class instruction.[9] The same is true of the boroughs of Queens and Richmond.

Present School Accommodation Inadequate

In addition, therefore, to the fact that three-fourths of the Jewish children of school age in New York are not provided with religious instruction at all, those children who are given Jewish training are very improperly accommodated. *Only one-eighth of the children taught are in school buildings worthy of the name.*[10] The remodelled buildings are ill adapted for school purposes, and even under the best circumstances make a poor showing when compared with the demands of modern school architecture. Institutional buildings are not *school* buildings; they make it difficult for the teachers and children to foster a distinct "school atmosphere," so necessary in school work. The classrooms are part of a large plant, devoted to other purposes, and the school is but one of many activities of the institution. This difficulty is particularly great where the head of the institution is not very enthusiastic about the work of the school.

Synagogue vestry rooms, when situated in the basement, are an abomination. Even the best of them have a dark, dank, subterranean atmosphere, which chills enthusiasm and is detrimental to the welfare of both teachers and pupils. The rented rooms are usually even worse than are the synagogue vestries. The best of them are no better than the classrooms found in the poorer remodelled school buildings. The worst of these rented rooms should not be tolerated by the Health Depart-

---

[9] Cf. Table V.

[10] In order to represent adequately conditions existing in all of these types of Jewish school accommodation, it would have been desirable to measure them by some objective test, such as the Strayer Building Score Card. But the task of doing this was too large and too difficult. Only two buildings, the best of Type A and the best of Type B, were therefore measured, in order to set the standard for Jewish school architecture, and to indicate what may be done in the direction of measuring the worth of Jewish school buildings. The results of this measurement are shown in Appendix N. It shows that one of the best of the remodelled dwellings is a very poor type of school building, receiving a rating of only 413 out of a possible 1,000 points. The school of Type A, on the other hand, is a worthy structure with a rating of 743 (Cf. Appendix N).

ment, and the community should do its utmost to aid the city authorities in condemning these "filthy fire traps."[11]

Some Essentials in the Construction of Jewish School Buildings

Evidently one of the basic needs of Jewish education is the erection of more school buildings, and better buildings than have been constructed hitherto. As the Jews of New York become better organized, and as their efforts are more centralized, it will be increasingly possible for them to construct special school buildings, for the purposes of Jewish education. Of the ten special school buildings in New York,[12] eight have been constructed since 1910. The latest of these buildings, the Central Jewish Institute, erected in 1916,[13] shows a marked improvement in the standard of Jewish school house construction.

It has been previously stated, that a great deal of progress has been made in school architecture within recent years. School men have aided architects in the building of effective school houses.[15] Every Jewish school administrator who is interested in the erection of Jewish school buildings must, therefore, acquaint himself thoroughly with the standards thus far developed, and must be capable of adapting these standards to the peculiar needs of his own school. School house construction is a technical matter, and while there are certain general principles operative, the Jewish schoolman must bring to it detailed technical knowledge, if he wishes to make his building help his school work and not hamper it.

The best type of modern Jewish school buildings should be designed as a community center, with facilities for reaching the entire family, and not alone the child of school age. Provision should be made for wide use of the school plant by the neighborhood. In designing classrooms it should be kept in mind, therefore, that all, or most of them, will be used for purposes of club meetings and similar activities. A large assembly hall should

[11] See New York Health Department Bulletin, Vol. IV—16, p. 129.

[12] Cf. Table V.

[13] See illustrations opposite page 164; also Appendix M.

[15] See "American School Houses" by F. Dresslar, in U. S. Bureau of Education, Bulletin 1910 No. 5.

be provided, conveniently situated near the street entrance, which could be converted into a synagogue on Saturdays and holidays, and into a hall for lectures or moving pictures during weekdays. On some of the floors, at least, it should be possible to convert several classrooms into a small assembly room for similar purposes of mass gathering for children, when the large hall is in use. Social rooms should be provided which could be frequently used by the neighborhood for social functions, art exhibits, family celebrations, etc. A gymnasium, a library, and an open-air playground are necessary features in the modern Jewish school building. A large room should be set aside for kindergarten purposes during the day time, as a game room on afternoons and evenings and, when occasion requires it, as a dancing floor for small parties. To aid in the attempt of the Jewish school center to reach the entire family, some of the modern Jewish school centers have provided kitchenettes in the buildings, through which kosher dinners and luncheons can be arranged. These are some of the features that should go into the consideration of modern Jewish school centers. To them should be added the many requirements of modern school architecture with regard to lighting, heating, ventilation, fire-protection, sanitary facilities, etc.[16]

Impossibility of Providing School Buildings for All Jewish Children

How many such new school buildings should the Jews of New York build in order to care properly for the religious instruction of their children? It is evident that it will be impossible to provide school buildings for *all* the Jewish school children of New York, at least in the near future. If to all the school accommodation, in all of the schools surveyed, be added all the *unused* available accommodation in these schools, there would be place for only 54,636 children.[17] There would, then, still remain 221,512 children unaccommodated. Even if from three to four children use the same seat, in shifts,[18] 55,378 classroom seats

[16] Bruce William G. "School Architecture: a handy manual for use of architects and school authorities." 1910. Strayer G. D. "A Score Card for School Buildings." 1916.

[17] Excluding, of course, Chedarim and private tuition.

[18] See Part II, Ch. 5 for schedule which makes this possible.

would be needed for these children, or a total of 1847 classrooms,[19] as follows:[20]

Borough	No. of Jewish Children of School Age	No. for whom any Accommodation Available	No. of Children Not in Jewish Schools	No. of Rooms Needed 1917
Manhattan	128,206	30,594	97,612	814
Bronx	39,857	6,297	33,560	280
Brooklyn	103,098	17,217	85,881	716
Queens	4,207	478	3,729	31
Richmond	780	50	730	6
Total	276,148	54,636	221,512	1,847

The building of these 1800 rooms would cost approximately $13,500,000[21] and would require a staff of at least 1800 teachers more than are now available. The mere statement of the need is sufficient to show the impossibility of expecting the Jews of New York to provide, at present, regular classroom instruction for all of their children. As an indication of the rate at which the Jews have been constructing new buildings, within the past seven years, the following is presented:

New Rooms Built 1910-1917	A. Rooms in Special School Buildings	B. Rooms in Institutional Buildings	C. Rooms in Remodelled Buildings	Total
Manhattan	64	10	25	99
Bronx	0	0	19	19
Brooklyn	40	0	32	72
Total	104	10	76	190

In the seven years, 1910-1917, therefore, 190 additional rooms have been provided, excluding vestries of synagogues and rented rooms. In other words, the Jews have been adding to the school

[19] Calculated at 30 seats per classroom. While it is possible to put more than 30 seats into the average school room, the maximum number of children who would be using it, would certainly not be more than 120 (30 x 4).

[20] The complete data from which this and the following table were compiled, can be found in the files of the Bureau of Jewish Education, 114 Fifth Avenue.

[21] Calculated at $7,500 per classroom, see below, page 173.

accommodation of their children approximately *27 additional rooms each year.* Even if to this number be added the rooms provided in the vestries of synagogues, unsatisfactory as they are, it would still be evident how impossible a task it is for the Jews at present to construct the one hundred or more additional buildings, containing the 1,800 rooms, needed to seat all of their unschooled children.

Minimum Additional Accommodation Needed Immediately

And yet there is a minimum number of new rooms which the Jews *must* provide for their children now, if the problem of enlarging the facilities for Jewish education is to be met at all. At least those children who now receive some kind of Jewish instruction should be adequately accommodated. At least this fourth of the total Jewish school population should be provided with seats in decent school buildings.

Upon this basis, twelve new buildings are needed,[22] containing 182 classrooms. Of these buildings, three should be erected in Manhattan, two in the Bronx, and seven in Brooklyn, as follows:[23]

Borough	Number of Rooms Needed in 1917	Number and Size of Buildings Needed		
		8-room	12-room	16-room
Manhattan	62	1	2	–
Bronx	31	1	–	1
Brooklyn	84	1	6	–
Queens	4	–	–	–
Richmond	1	–	–	–
Total	182	3	8	1

Cost of Buildings Immediately Needed

The cost of constructing these twelve buildings would amount to *over a million dollars.* In American public schools, the cost

[22] For full data Cf. Table VI.

[23] Cf. Table VI for data by school districts. See also map (frontispiece) for location of needed school buildings.

of construction per classroom ranges from $5,000 to $10,000.[24] The Jewish school buildings constructed during the past seven years, have cost on the average about $6,500 per classroom.[25] The tendency toward making the Jewish school buildings more widely useful to the community, offering facilities not only for children, but for all the people in the neighborhood, must necessarily increase the cost of construction per classroom. Upon a conservative basis of $7,500 per room, therefore, an eight-room building would cost $60,000; a twelve-room building would cost $90,000, and a sixteen-room building $120,000. The construction of the twelve buildings needed immediately, in order to accommodate properly one-fourth of all the Jewish children of school age, would amount to $1,020,000.

This is the *minimum* sum which the Jews of New York must now spend upon school buildings, in order to seat one-fourth of their elementary school children in Jewish schools. To this should be added some provision for secondary Jewish instruction. It is certainly not extravagant to demand that at least 10% of those Jewish adolescents who go to the public high schools should receive secondary Jewish instruction. To meet this minimum requirement, the Jews of this city would have to provide accommodation for 4,000 Jewish boys and girls. Because these classes must be smaller than in the elementary schools, no more than 80 pupils could possibly be accommodated per classroom, (four classes per teacher, alternately). It will therefore be necessary to provide 40 classrooms for this purpose. Assuming that one-half of these young people can be taught in the evening, 20 additional classrooms, or a minimum outlay of $150,000 must be added for this purpose in any community building program, making the minimum financial expenditure for additional accommodation, for elementary and secondary instruction, $1,170,000.

Jewish Extension Education

But it must be borne in mind that the erection of the twelve new buildings would provide instruction for only one-fourth of

---

[24] Cf. Cleveland School Survey. School Buildings and Equipment. L. P. Ayres. 1916.

[25] Based upon the cost of the six largest special school buildings constructed since 1908, cf. Table VII.

the children of New York. Besides the inability to furnish sufficient seating accommodation, it has been pointed out that there are other difficulties which make it impossible to provide classroom instruction for all of the unschooled Jewish children. The problem of teachers needs but to be mentioned. In order to teach those children who are not now in Jewish schools, at least 1,800 additional full-time teachers would be needed. The total teaching staff in all of the Jewish schools of New York is at present hardly half that number. It is evident, therefore, that some other educational arrangement is needed which should care for the great numbers of children outside of the Jewish schools. This arrangement, whatever it be, can only be a substitute. It can never take the place of regular classroom instruction. But that it is essential, in the present situation, the 76% of the Jewish children who receive no Jewish instruction testify.

The proposal made by the Bureau of Jewish Education, as well as by the Zionist organization, Young Judea, is that a supplementary system of extensive education be conducted parallel to the regular intensive school work. Young Judea conducts its activities primarily in the form of clubs. It reaches[30] 1,700 children of elementary school age in New York City, and 1,200 Jewish adolescents. These are organized into 94 clubs for children, and 77 clubs for adolescents. Besides the club work, it has also in the past conducted mass celebrations of Jewish holidays. Its aim is chiefly to teach Zionism to Jewish children and adolescents, both to the schooled and to the unschooled.[31]

The extension activities of the Bureau of Jewish Education are more general in scope. These activities have already been discussed.[32] They are conducted in the form of the Circle of Jewish Children for boys and girls of elementary school age, and as the League of the Jewish Youth for adolescents. The primary purpose of the Circle is to extend the facilities of the school to the many children in the neighborhood who are not reached through direct classroom instruction. There are at present three "districts" of the Circle: one in Harlem, another on the lower East

[30] In 1917.

[31] Cf. Part I, Chapter 3, p. 87.

[32] Cf. Part I, Chapter 4, pp. 124-127.

Side, and the third in Brownsville. In these three districts, the Circle reaches[33] about 20,000 boys and girls of elementary school age, who are not taught in Jewish schools, as well as 11,000 children who are taught in the larger schools of the respective districts. The work is organized as follows: The district is subdivided into small territorial units. Boys or girls from the schools or outside of the schools, are made the "leaders" of each of these territorial units. Each "leader" is at the head of a group of twenty children. It is the function of the leaders, in the first place, to make a house-to-house canvass, in order to enlist the interest of other boys and girls, their playmates and neighbors, who live in the particular territory allotted to them. Willingness to belong to the Circle is practically the only requisite for membership. The leaders then become the intermediaries between the twenty members of the Circle in their particular groups, and the Circle itself. Thus, the boy and girl leaders distribute Jewish literature, such as the juvenile magazine called "The Jewish Child," holiday bulletins, history pamphlets, etc. They also distribute tickets and invitations to mass celebrations of Jewish holidays and to other mass functions, such as outdoor pageants, outings, etc. As already stated, the pupils of the school are also part of the Circle. All of the social activities of the school, its club work, its festival celebrations and similar social activities are carried on under the auspices of the Circle.[34]

Different in spirit, though similar in organization, is the League of the Jewish Youth, whose central purpose is to provide a means of social-religious education for adolescents, without utilizing regular classroom machinery. The Jewish school is not the center of the League as it is in the Circle, although the High School boys and girls who are taught in the secondary Jewish classes are members of it. The League conducts its work in five "centers": Bronx, Harlem, Yorkville, East Side, and Brownsville. It has an enrollment[35] of 3,270 young men and 5,300 young women, a total of about 8,500 young people between the ages of 14 and 21. These are divided into three "ranks": *junior,* between the ages of 14 and 16; *intermediate,* between 16 and 18;

---

[33] In 1918.

[34] Cf. also Part II, Chapter 11.

[35] In September 1917.

and *senior,* young men and women between 18 and 21 years of age.[36]

The organization of the League is very similar to that of the Circle, except that the boys and girls are given much more freedom of self-government. The division of the city into Districts (Galils), Tribes, Camps and Households has already been described.[37] Thus, a boy may belong to the Household of David, Camp Bethlehem, Tribe of Judah, in the Harlem District. The functions of the "organizer," who is head of the Household, are similar to those of the "leader" in the Circle. The "organizer" acts as the agent of the League for the members of his or her household: distributes literature, invites the members to mass meetings, festival celebrations, League conventions, initiation ceremonies. The heads of the Households and Camps are combined into the Tribe Council, led by the District Secretary, who is a paid official of the Bureau of Jewish Education, and the executive head of the Center. The Tribe Councils send representatives to the Central City Council.[38]

Accommodation Needed for Extension Education

In order that any such system of extension education as is being developed by the Bureau of Jewish Education, may have its effect in enlarging the proportion of children who should be receiving Jewish instruction, at least another fourth of the total number of Jewish children should be added to those for whom instruction is to be provided in Jewish schools. In other words, 65,000 boys and girls more should be included in a system of Extension Education. It can be readily seen that the accommodation required for bringing these children under the influence of extension education is very much more limited than that which would be necessary for providing sufficient school seats for them. Nevertheless, the Jews of New York must be ready to add sufficient accommodation for this purpose to their community building program. The Circle of Jewish Children needs one room[39]

---

[36] There were (September 1917) 3,985 juniors, 2,835 intermediates, and 1,750 seniors enrolled in the League.

[37] Cf. Part I, Chapter IV.

[38] Cf. also the following chapters, particularly Chaps. 11 and 12.

[39] As a Circle office or meeting room for the leaders.

and an auditorium to provide extension education through mass activity, for the unschooled Jewish boys and girls in any one district. It also needs meeting rooms for club work, requiring for this purpose a total of 53 rooms, at an approximate cost of $400,000.[40] This must be added to the community building program, in order to provide for Jewish extension education effectively. For the League of the Jewish Youth no additional accommodation is needed, because its activities are carried on in the evenings, and it can therefore utilize the regular school rooms.

A Community Building Program

The additional accommodation needed for extension education would bring the complete sum which the Jews of New York should spend now upon new school buildings to $1,570,000, or approximately *a million and a half dollars.* This sum would provide accommodation for elementary school work for 25% of the Jewish children in the public schools, secondary instruction for 10% of the Jewish boys and girls in the high schools, and Jewish extension education for 25% of the boys and girls of school age.

Besides the sums needed *at present* for the building of schools, a constructive community program must also provide for new buildings annually, to care for the natural increase in the Jewish child population. It is estimated that the increase in the number of Jewish elementary children is from 7,500 to 10,000 children yearly.[41] To accommodate these boys and girls alone four or

---

[40] It is the aim of the Circle to provide regular club work for one-fourth of its members. Club room accommodation will therefore have to be furnished for 16,000 Jewish boys and girls. The maximum use that can be made of one room for this work, would be 12 clubs per week, at two hours per meeting. If each club is to consist of 25 children, one room would thus be able to provide club meeting facilities for 300 children. In other words, 53 additional rooms will be needed for this work.

[41] The American Jewish Year Book (1918-1919, p. 44) gives the percentage of increase in Jewish population (births over deaths), as 2% to 2.5% per year. At this rate the annual increase in the Jewish population of New York would be from 30,000 to 37,500. The proportion of children between 5 and 14 years in the native population of the country is given in the U. S. Census of 1910 (Vol. III, p. 220) as 26%. This proportion is certainly not smaller among the Jews. On the contrary, the proportion of children to "normal" Jewish population *(i. e., exclusive of "unattached" immigrants)*, is probably greater. From a study of over 4,000 families, selected at random from the Census cards in the Bureau of Attendance of the New York Board of Education, it was found that the average Jewish

five new school buildings are needed,[42] necessitating a yearly expenditure of $400,000 to $500,000.

How shall this money be obtained, and what program is there for the construction of these buildings? Some of the difficulties which have militated in the past against the erection of adequate Jewish school buildings, have already been suggested. The decentralized condition of the Jewish community has made it necessary for each group of Jews that has wished to construct a school building for its children, to raise a large part of the money immediately, because it was found difficult to obtain the necessary mortgages on the school buildings. Moreover, individuals were discouraged from undertaking the responsibility of erecting Jewish school buildings, because the financial burden of managing and administering the schools weighed heavily upon them, since much of the income of the schools was in the form of uncertain and insufficient donations and membership dues.[43] Two conditions are therefore prerequisite in any program which will attempt to provide new Jewish school buildings on any large scale: (1) the advancing of sufficient funds in the form of *mortgages;* (2) *reorganization of the financial management* of the Jewish schools, so as to relieve their sponsors from constant financial uncertainty and debt.[44]

The Board of Jewish School Aid,[45] or some similar agency representing the Jewish community, should undertake to stimulate and aid the Jews of this city to provide for the school buildings that are immediately necessary. Their program, in brief, should be as follows:[46] Whenever any local community or society of Jews is willing to erect a school building, and can

family has 2.5 children at school, whereas the average non-Jewish family has only 2.35 children at school. At present, owing to the large number of immigrants in the Jewish population, the proportion of school children is smaller (about 18%); but in calculating future increases the proportion of children can be taken to be at least as great as in the native population. Assuming that the proportion of Jewish school children would be about 25%, the annual increase in school children would be from 7,500 to 9,375.

[42] A community school building (12 to 16 classrooms) can provide regular and extensive Jewish education for approximately 2,000 boys and girls of elementary school age (exclusive of adolescents and adults). Cf. ch. 12, p. 377.

[43] Cf. Part II, Chapter 6, p. 225.

[44] For a detailed discussion of the reorganization of Jewish school finances, cf. Part II, Chapter 6.

[45] Cf. Part I, Chapter 4, p. 121.

[46] This program is based upon a plan now under consideration.

raise 25% of the necessary costs, the Board of School Aid should arrange to advance 50% of the cost, as first mortgage on the building. This loan is to be underwritten by the Board of Jewish School Aid. The necessary additional 25% of the cost will then be advanced by the Board of Jewish School Aid, as second mortgage. Funds with which to make second mortgage loans, could be raised by the Board in the form of building shares of $100 and more. Should the Board of Jewish School Aid be successful in carrying such a program into execution, it will undoubtedly stimulate the erection of many new Jewish school buildings, since there are probably a number of groups of responsible Jews in this city who would eagerly avail themselves of such coöperation.

A minimum building program for New York would require that the community raise in equity and second mortgages three quarters of a million dollars for present needs, and about a quarter of a million dollars annually thereafter. To require of the Jews of New York that they raise three-fourths of a million dollars immediately for the erection of Jewish school buildings, may appear a large demand. Yet, this is the minimum needed for the creation of a Jewish school system which would be at all adequate to provide for the continuation of Jewish life in this city. It has been estimated that the Jews of New York spend annually six to eight times that sum upon organized charity.[47] The budget of the Federation for the Support of Jewish Philanthropic Societies alone is now four times this sum. The community of New York is the wealthiest Jewish community in the world. The difficulty has been, that Jewish education has not been placed in the center of Jewish social work, but has been considered as one of its less important aspects. A building fund, such as has been shown to be essential, will be forthcoming only if the importance of providing adequate Jewish school accommodation will be sufficiently understood by the great number of Jews in this city who are able to contribute the necessary outlay for these buildings, and if the Jewish community will provide for the adequate financing and proper administration of these schools.

---

[47] In the Jewish Communal Register, New York, 1918, p. 103, it is estimated that four million dollars are spent annually on philanthropic-correctional work and about one million for semi-philanthropic institutions.

The Jewish educational system does not differ from any other educational system in its dependence upon concrete institutions, in the form of *school buildings.* No "methods" or "plans" can take the place of the *building* as a center of potential energy. Let the Jews provide sufficient school buildings, and all else—programs, curricula, plans of management, teachers, textbooks, etc.—will inevitably follow.

Chapter III

ORGANIZATION OF JEWISH SCHOOLS

(Variation and Co-ordination)

A community program in Jewish education, whether it be for the purpose of erecting new school buildings, or for the improvement of school work, must consider in large measure the organization of the existing Jewish schools. To the extent to which there is coöperation and a minimum of uniformity among the present schools will it be easy or difficult to bring about community action on behalf of Jewish education.

Variety of Organization—Types of Control and Time Schedules

It has been pointed out[1] that the Jews of New York are a complex, heterogeneous group, varying in their educational traditions, as well as in their outlook concerning the adjustment of Jewish life in this country. It is to be expected that this variation in aims should express itself in a variety of forms in educational organization. These concern: firstly, the *type of control;* and, secondly, the relation to the public school system, as shown in the *time schedules* of the schools.

As regards control, Jewish schools are (1) *communal,* conducted by an educational society, and supported by the community at large; (2) *congregational,* under the auspices of a particular congregation; (3) *institutional,* as part of the activities of some Jewish institution, (such as the Educational Alliance, or the Hebrew Orphan Asylum); and, lastly, (4) *private,* owned and controlled by an individual. Exclusive of the 500 or more Chedarim and private schools, there are in New York City 71 communal schools, 87 congregational schools, and 14 institutional schools. Among the congregational schools a distinction should be made between those which confine their teaching to the children of members only, and those which teach all children in their vicinity. The former, usually connected with the reform congregations of the earlier settlers, are truly

[1] Cf. Part I, Chapters 1 and 2.

congregational schools, in that their aim is to preserve the continuity of the congregation; the latter, common among the congregations of Eastern European Jews, are in reality communal schools, though housed in synagogue buildings. Most of the Eastern European congregational schools are Talmud Torahs, differing in but few respects from the communal Talmud Torahs.[2]

The relation of Jewish schools to the public schools is seen in their time schedules. They are (1) *parochial,* or all-day schools, *substituting* the public school and taking its place; (2) *weekday* schools, in which the instruction is given outside of public school hours, (on afternoons, Sabbaths and Sundays), and which *supplement* the public schools; or (3) *Sabbath* or *Sunday* schools which are *unrelated* to the public school, since their time schedules in no way depend upon the time schedule of the public school. Not counting the Chedarim and private schools, there are in New York 127 weekday supplementary schools, 41 Sabbath or Sunday schools, and 4 parochial schools. Of the 127 weekday schools, 67 are communal, 50 are congregational and 10 are institutional schools. Of the 41 Sabbath and Sunday schools, 37 are congregational and 4 institutional. *Not one of the Sunday schools is under communal control, most of them being connected with the reform congregations. On the other hand, most of the weekday schools are communal, practically all of them being directly controlled by Eastern European Jews, with the aid of various elements in the community. All of the parochial schools are communal schools, established by orthodox Eastern European Jews. All of the Jewish private schools are weekday schools.*

With regard to the number of pupils, it is found that: of all the Jewish children receiving Jewish instruction, 21,109 pupils (32.5%) are in the communal schools, 15,354 pupils (23.6%) are in congregational schools, 3,710 pupils (5.7%) in institutional schools, and the rest (38.2%) are in Chedarim or are taught at home.[3] *In other words, less than one-fourth of the children are under direct synagogue control, about one-third are taught in schools managed by special educational societies, while almost*

---

[2] For the difference in outlook suggested by this fact, see Part I, Chapter 5, p. 140.

[3] Cf. Table IX.

two-fifths receive their instruction at the hands of private teachers.

With reference to time schedules, there are: 31,237 pupils in the weekday supplementary schools which are included in the survey; 7,951 are in Sabbath or Sunday schools; and 985 in parochial schools. *This means, that of the 65,000 children in New York who receive religious instruction, 56,000*[4] *or 86% are given some form of weekday religious training, 12% are in Sunday schools, and only 1.5% in parochial schools.*[5]

These figures furnish interesting proof of the attitude of the Jews in this country with respect to the religious education of their children. In the first place, religious education among the Jews is not necessarily synagogue education. It is religious-national training, which is just as likely (or more likely) to be in the hands of laymen, as in the hands of the Jewish ministry. In the second place, the normal form in which this religious-national instruction is given to Jewish children, is that of the supplementary weekday school, conducted outside of public school hours. The great majority of Jews do not favor the parochial school, and are not satisfied with the Sunday school.

Jewish Education A Decentralized System

The above facts concerning the differences in type of control and in relation to the public schools, indicate how varied are the forms of Jewish educational organization in New York, and how difficult must be any attempt to coördinate or unify the work of all the schools. Indeed, there is no unity or coöperation among the existing Jewish schools of New York. They form a completely decentralized system. The 181 Jewish schools surveyed are practically so many distinct and separate institutions. There are in New York City only eight organizations which conduct more than one school. These are:

The Federation of Jewish National Radical Schools	4	schools,	725	pupils
The National Hebrew Schools, Brooklyn	3	"	695	"
The Machzike Talmud Torah	2	"	1,197	"

[4] To the 31,237 children were added 1,230 in the private schools included in our survey, and the 24,000 children in Chedarim who are taught at home after public school hours.

[5] Cf. Table IX.

ORGANIZATION OF JEWISH SCHOOLS
Showing Proportion according to

A. Time Schedule (Weekday, Sunday, Parochial)
B. Type of Control (Communal, Congregational, Private)

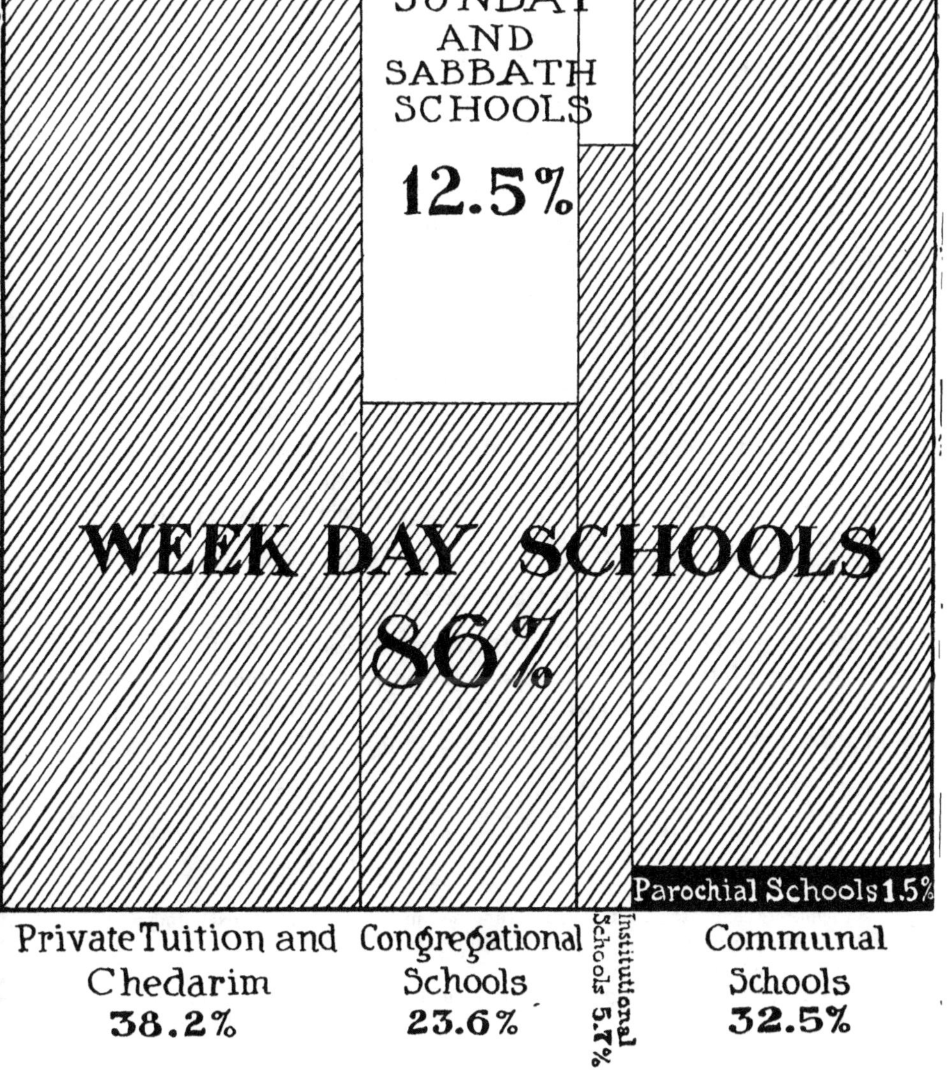

The Bureau of Jewish Education........	5 schools,	2,911	pupils[6]
The Free Synagogue....................	4 "	977	" [7]
Department of Synagogue and School Extension (Union of Am. Heb. Congs.)..	2 "	938	"
Shearith Israel Congregation...........	2 "	317	"
Ohab Zedek Congregation..............	2 "	195	" [8]

Aside from these 25 schools, several of which are conducted under the same auspices, each individual Jewish school is managed by its own Board of Directors, without relation to any other school. It has its own program, its own methods of instruction and management, and attempts to meet its financial problems in its own way. The only educational organization which exerts any coördinating or centralizing influence upon the Jewish schools of New York is the Bureau of Jewish Education, which supervises and guides the work of the larger Jewish weekday schools. But its influence, too, is limited, reaching only the largest schools. Such other centralizing organizations[9] as the Vaad HaYeshiboth, the Federation of National Radical Schools and the Department of Synagogue and School Extension, confine their interest to a small number of schools of a particular type. The great majority of Jewish schools are, therefore, wholly unrelated institutions, and their work is not coördinated in any manner whatever.

Results of Decentralization

The most immediate result of this decentralization is reflected in the size of the Jewish schools. One-half of the schools surveyed have registers of less than 160 pupils, and three-quarters of them have registers of less than 300 pupils, as follows:[10]

40 schools	enrolling less than	100:	Total 2,592	pupils	6.3%
67 "	"	100— 200:	" 9,291	"	22.4%
30 "	"	200— 300:	" 6,934	"	16.7%
16 "	"	300— 400:	" 5,420	"	13.1%

[6] Including elementary, intermediate and secondary grades, and excluding its Extension activities, which enroll 40,000 children and adolescents.

[7] Sunday and Sabbath schools only.

[8] There are a few congregations that conduct sisterhood schools, but the number of children whom they reach is insignificant from the standpoint of systematic instruction.

[9] Cf. Part I, Chapter 3, pp. 91-97.

[10] Cf. Table VIII.

8 schools enrolling	400— 500:	Total	3,829	pupils	8.5%
9 " "	500— 600:	"	4,303	"	11.5%
4 " "	600— 700:	"	2,438	"	5.9%
2 " "	700— 800:	"	1,442	"	3.5%
2 " "	800— 900:	"	1,688	"	4.0%
1 " "	900—1000:	"	950	"	2.3%
2	1000 and over:	"	2,516	"	5.9%
Total 181			31,403	pupils	100.0%

It appears, therefore, that even if the great number of one-teacher schools or (Chedarim) be excluded, *three-fourths of the Jewish schools of New York (enrolling 45.4% of the children), are small schools having less than 300 pupils on their registers.* In a large city like New York, it is not possible to provide schools which teach fewer than 300 pupils with proper school quarters or adequate grading.[11] Small schools, unless supported by some central agency, or charging very high tuition fees, are in no position to employ a competent principal or efficient teachers. In American education, the small decentralized district school has been condemned in the strongest terms.[12] It is now supplanted in large communities by the city school, and in the smaller communities it is being replaced by the consolidated county school. It is folly to conduct small schools, analogous to the now disappearing American district schools, in densely populated communities, such as those of the Jews on the East Side of Manhattan or in Harlem.[13]

Another immediate result of the prevailing decentralization is the paucity of proper Jewish school accommodation. It has been pointed out [14] that there are only ten schools which are housed in special Jewish school buildings. All of the others are

[11] Assuming even as low an average as 30 pupils per class, and assuming a course of studies extending over at least five years, a minimum of 300 pupils (30 x 5 x 2) would be needed to have a graded school.

[12] Cf. Webster, Wm. C: "Recent Centralizing Tendencies in State Educational Administration"—Columbia University, 1897. Bard, H. E: "The City School District"—Teachers' College, N. Y., 1909. Dutton & Snedden: "Administration of Public Education in United States," 1912, Chapters VI and VII. Cubberly, E. P: "Public School Administration," 1916, Chapter V. Also "Educational Administration and Supervision," March, 1918.

[13] It would have been desirable to gather more detailed and accurate information concerning the finances and management of these small schools, but no records are kept which would make possible any objective study.

[14] Cf. previous chapter, p. 166.

SIZE OF JEWISH SCHOOLS

(Showing Number of Schools with Given Registers)

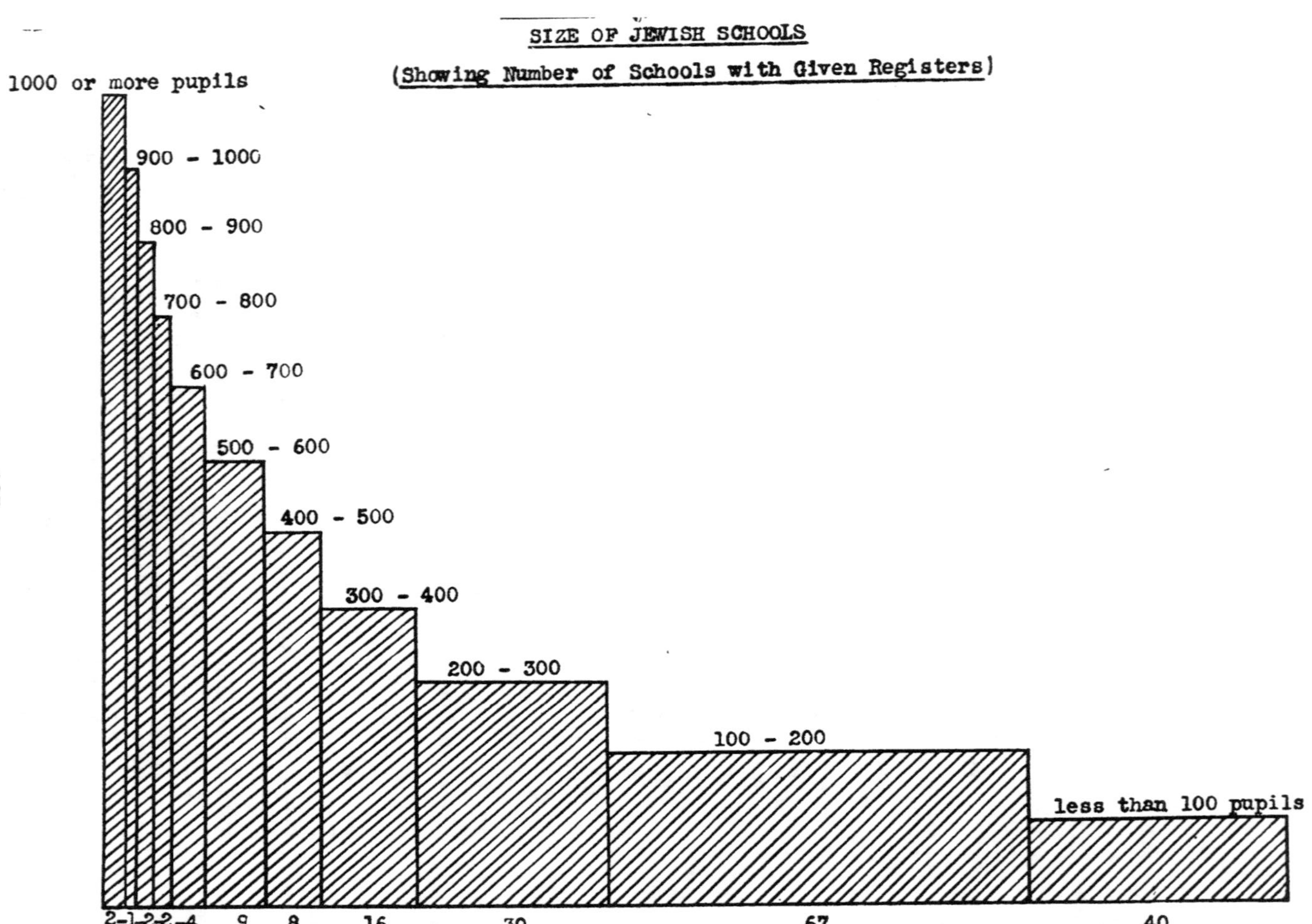

found in remodelled dwellings, in vestries of synagogues, in institutional buildings, or in rented rooms. Only in these ten instances, was there sufficient centralized effort among the Jews of New York to erect proper school structures.

This, then, is the "system" of Jewish education in New York City: about two hundred Jewish schools, most of them small independent institutions, incapable of proper accommodation or management; divided among themselves as to aims and methods into weekday, parochial and Sunday schools; controlled by a variety of independent organizations, communal, congregational and institutional and reaching only a small portion of the Jewish children of school age.

An analysis of the causes of the present decentralization will show, however, that this condition is not wholly to be condemned. It is the result of many deep-seated forces:

(1) *Lack of legal or clerical power.* There is no agency among the Jews which has the power to levy taxes for school purposes, or to compel parents to send their children to the Jewish schools. Nor is there centralized clerical authority among the Jews, as there is among the Catholics. While the Jewish synagogues group themselves into orthodox, reform, conservative, etc., each congregation is at the same time completely independent in its policies and management. There is no power which can *compel* centralization of educational effort.

(2) *Differences of Aim.* We are living at present in a great transitional period of Jewish history. The Jews of America are learning how to adjust their Jewish life in this country. Many and various theories and plans of adjustment are being tried. Orthodoxy, conservatism and reform; different conceptions of nationalism and of Americanism; preservation and assimilation[16] —each has its own theory of Jewish life and wishes to impart it to the next generation. It is to be expected therefore that each group should maintain its own schools and decide all questions concerning the content of Jewish education independently.

(3) *Traditional strength of the Jewish private school.* Another factor militating against centralization has been the traditional

---

[16] In the first chapter of the book, in which these theories are discussed at length, the more correct term "fusion" is used instead of "assimilation."

custom among Jews, over a period of many centuries, of sending their children to the school of some private teacher. For generations, only the poor went to the communal school, or Talmud Torah. In spite of the example set by the common secular state school in this country, many Jewish parents still feel uncomfortable about sending their children to the communal Talmud Torah. This fact has had its undoubted effect in weakening the development of large communal schools.

(4) *Social grouping on the basis of immigration.* An interesting social phenomenon which has decentralized Jewish life in New York, is the strong tendency among Jewish immigrants to organize themselves on the basis of the locality in Europe from which they emigrated. A group of "landsleit," fellow-townsmen, form themselves into a Chevrah, or society, which cares not only for their religious and social needs, but also for the religious education of their children. Thus, there are Suwalker, Tarnopoler, Podolsker, and similar societies of Jews.[17] Many of these societies insist on conducting small, independent Jewish schools, chiefly for the children of their own members.

Complete Centralization Undesirable

Some of the causes of decentralization will disappear in time. Jewish parents will come to understand that the private school has no future in America, and that it does not offer the best type of training for their children. The social organization on the basis of "Landsmannschaft," (country of emigration), will also be greatly weakened when Jewish mass immigration ceases, as it most probably will, after the war. But the other causes will not disappear. Jewish education can never be centralized on the basis of legal or even clerical power. Nor will the differences in educational aims disappear for a long time to come. Each group will continue to test its theories of life in terms of Jewish education; it will insist that its children be imbued with the principles and attitudes which it considers right. As the American Jewish community becomes more homogeneous, there

[17] A recent study made by the Kehillah (Jewish Community) revealed that out of a total of some 3,600 organizations, there are about one thousand synagogues and societies in New York which call themselves by the name of some locality in Eastern Europe.

may gradually evolve an *American Jewish school,* which will preserve the best of that which the various groups wish to contribute, and at the same time fully reckon with conditions in this country. But for the present, there must continue to be different types of Jewish schooling. Jewish parents must continue to have the opportunity of deciding whether their children shall be taught in weekday schools, parochial schools, or Sunday schools; whether the education of their boys and girls shall be in the hands of their own congregations or in the hands of the community.

Complete centralization of the Jewish schools in this city, is, therefore, neither desirable nor possible. For a long time to come, the Jewish schools of New York will have to be decentralized, at least to the extent of safeguarding their individuality and independence. It is well that this is so. No one is at present wise enough, or daring enough, to say just what type of Jewish school shall dominate exclusively the training of Jewish children. The schools representing the various groups cannot combine, nor should they be uniform, except in administrative matters. Centralization and coördination may be possible with regard to buildings, organization, finances, management, social activities, and even special methods. But questions affecting content and program will continue to be decided by each group independently.

Centralizing Forces

But while complete centralization is not possible nor wise, a minimum of centralization is indispensable to the progress of Jewish education in New York. By the side of so highly centralized a system as the New York public schools, a decentralized system is not able to obtain the interest of either parent or child, nor is it able to do any really effective work. It cannot cope successfully with the problem of increasing facilities for Jewish instruction, nor can it raise the standard of such instruction as is now being given to Jewish children. If not all of the Jewish schools, at least the larger ones should coöperate, and if not in all phases of their work, at least in their administrative problems.

There are several centralizing forces at work in Jewish education in New York City. The Board of Jewish School Aid; the Hebrew Principals' Association; the various Teachers' Associations (Agudath Hamorim, Jewish Teachers' Association, Jewish Religious School Union, and Moriah) and the Jewish Parents' Association, are bodies organized for the purpose of centralizing the work of the Jewish schools, by uniting trustees, principals, teachers or parents for common aims. The Federation for the Support of Jewish Philanthropic Societies[19] has begun to exert a strong centralizing influence with regard to school finances and business management. The Bureau of Jewish Education, as an expert educational agency, is continuing to bring about minimum uniformity, at least in the administrative essentials, among the Jewish schools of New York City.

Each of these agencies has a distinct and necessary function to perform in a scheme of non-compulsory coördination, such as must be developed for unifying the work of the Jewish schools of New York. Coördination in Jewish education cannot be brought about by "impersonal" law or decree; and any agency, no matter how powerful, attempting to force centralization, would therefore meet with insurmountable opposition and distrust. Coördination of Jewish schools must be developed by means of understanding and persuasion, by unifying for their own benefit the various *personal* elements which control the destiny of Jewish education: the parents, the teachers, the principals, the trustees, the contributors and the community as a whole. Each of these elements approaches the problem of Jewish education from a somewhat different angle, and all of them must be included in any plan of non-compulsory coördination. Every agency previously mentioned arose to meet the needs of some one of these elements.

1. *The Central Jewish Parents' Association* was formed by uniting the parents' associations existing in some of the larger Jewish Weekday schools. While there are as yet many parents' associations which are not affiliated with this Central Association, and while in very many of the schools the parents are not yet organized at all, it should be possible, in the course of time, to unite in this manner the parents of all the children attending communal weekday schools, and perhaps also, many of the congregational weekday schools. It will hardly be possible, however,

---

[19] Cf. Part I, Chapter 4, pp. 122-123.

for the present, to include the parents of children attending the Sunday schools, because of the wide variation in interests.

The function of the Central Parents' Association should be twofold. It should, in the first place, *stimulate the desire for Jewish education* among Jewish parents, their friends and their neighbors, by making each parent who is affiliated, an agent for propagating among his or her acquaintances the need of Jewish training for Jewish children. In this phase of the work the underlying fundamental idea should be that every parent must be interested not only in his own children, but also in all other children with whom his children associate; because, if the boys and girls who are attending the Jewish schools are to derive any benefit from their instruction, they must not be placed in an environment of scoffing indifference to things Jewish. The parents can safeguard the Jewish interests of their children only by safeguarding the environment of the children. This environment includes not only the "street" and the playground, but also the *home*. The Association is the best agency for fostering the much desired sympathy and coöperation between the Home and the School in the training of Jewish children.

In the second place, the Association of Parents has before it the delicate but essential task of working toward *uniform desires and demands* in the conduct of the Jewish schools. The Association should be utilized by principals, teachers and others, as the medium for explaining to Jewish parents the methods of teaching, the subjects of study, and the methods of educational management in Jewish schools. The meetings of the Association, and such literature as it may be able to distribute among the parents, should have this purpose pre-eminently in mind. The guiding aim of the Parents' Association should be, that all of the parents shall want Jewish education for their children, and that they shall want the best kind of Jewish education.

2. There are several *Teachers' Organizations* that are trying to unite the Jewish teachers of New York. The "Agudath Hamorim" works with the Jewish teachers of the Talmud Torahs and private schools; the "Jewish Teachers' Association" unites the younger American-bred teachers of the Jewish Schools (chiefly of the communal weekday schools); the "Moriah" reaches teachers of private and parochial schools; and the

"Jewish Religious School Union" represents the Sunday school teachers. The functions of these organizations are: (1) *to promote a professional spirit* and attitude among Jewish teachers; (2) *to safeguard the professional interest* of the teachers and to work toward the improvement of their status, both economic and social; and (3) *to foster uniform methods* in teaching and class management, in accordance with the best pedagogic practice of the time. These functions cannot be performed effectively, however, until (1) the principals, parents and trustees are properly organized, so that the teachers will have responsible organized bodies to deal with, and to influence; and until (2) the various organizations are united into a central *Teachers' Council* representing all of the Jewish teachers of New York. With sufficient tact and persistency, it should not be too difficult a task to organize such a central Council to represent at least the first three organizations. While the average teacher in the Agudath Hamorim and the Moriah differs very widely from the average member of the Jewish Teachers' Association, the best and most intelligent representatives from the one group do not differ as widely from the best members of the other group. To include the Religious School Union as a constituent body in this Council will probably be, for the present, an unwise undertaking, because the Sunday School teachers are not "professional" Jewish teachers, the Jewish school being a "side issue" with them.

3. The Teachers' Council should be closely connected with the *Hebrew Principals' Association.* This Association includes at present (1918) representatives from 12 of the largest Jewish weekday schools, and has corresponding members throughout the United States. Its function is to standardize the educational and administrative policies of the schools by interchanging experiences and suggesting improvements. All questions of school management and all matters relating to program and methods, are properly within the scope of this Association. With the growth of the Association to include all the important Jewish weekday schools, and with the gradual introduction into its midst of well trained modern men, this body should be in a position to exercise a strong influence upon the conduct of Jewish education not only in this city, but throughout the country.

4. *The Federation for the Support of Jewish Philanthropic Societies* safeguards the interests of the *contributors* to Jewish education. Its primary interest should be to insure that the schools have adequate financial support from the community, and that these funds are spent effectively by the Jewish schools, with as little waste as possible. The standardization of all matters that can be measured in terms of money, should be in its hands. It cannot, however, attempt to direct educational programs or methods of work, any more than the contributors themselves should be in a position to control the detailed school policy or methods.

5. *The Board of Jewish School Aid* is the organization that is endeavoring to speak in the name of the *trustees* of the Jewish schools. It should be in close contact with the Principals' Association on the one hand, and with the Federation for the Support of Philanthropic Societies on the other. Intimately in touch with the needs of Jewish education, it should represent these needs before the Federation, and before the community at large. It should act as the agent of the Federation in the elimination of waste in the schools. It should coöperate with the principals in bringing about the necessary uniformity in the conduct of the Jewish schools of New York. But it should also perform the grand task of bringing before the community the inadequacy of present educational facilities and of doing everything in its power to extend these facilities by aiding in the erection of new buildings and in the undertaking of similar activities.

6. In the last analysis it is the *Jewish Community* itself that must be the coördinating influence in Jewish education. True it is that in the organization of Jewish life in New York no organization that speaks for the whole community will be able to exert any direct control over the Jewish schools. The interests of New York Jewry are too complex and its attitudes toward education too varied, to make this possible. What it can do, however, is to afford an opportunity for those of its constituent organizations that are coördinating the work of the Jewish schools to bring Jewish education before the *entire* community, and enlist its interest and support in any undertaking in which these organizations may wish to engage. The *Kehillah* (Community) of New York is attempting to act as just such a common platform.

It aims to make of the entire community the *audience* for the agencies that are controlling the destiny of Jewish education in New York. A number of agencies are at present striving directly or indirectly to become the "Kehillah," the Jewish Community of New York. But whether the attempt at unified communal organization through the present Kehillah be successful, or the Zionist Organization broaden its activities to include all matters of communal interest beside Palestine, or the Federation for the Support of Philanthropic Societies come to represent the community, one thing seems reasonably certain: whatever body will represent the Jewish community of New York will have to take an active part in promoting Jewish education. Through a *Community Board of Education* or simply through a *Committee on Education* it should strive to aid the various educational agencies in reaching all elements of the community. It should act as the medium between the whole community and the coördinating organizations previously mentioned.

7. But no real coördination is possible unless it is based upon specialized educational knowledge, and unless it is guided by expert opinion and advice. All of the bodies which attempt to control Jewish education in any manner, must have at their disposal professional men and women who are specializing in Jewish education. To attach such a staff of specialists to each of the agencies mentioned above, would be wastefully expensive and would invite overlapping and friction. One expert educational agency is needed which should coöperate with all the coördinating organizations, the Parents' Association, the Teachers' Council, the Principals' Association, the Federation, the Board of School Aid, and the Community Committee on Education. Such an agency is the *Bureau of Jewish Education.* Its primary interests, from this point of view, should be to gather about it a corps of adequately trained men and women who should be capable of ascertaining the facts concerning Jewish education in New York and elsewhere; of proposing new plans in accordance with the needs of the situation; of testing plans for extending educational facilities; of experimenting with methods of teaching and of management as applied to the Jewish school; of measuring the effectiveness of various programs and courses of studies; and of guiding the actual daily work of the various

coördinating agencies. It should bring specialized knowledge and broad-minded interest to bear upon the plan of centralizing Jewish education in New York City on the "personal" basis.

Such coördination, as here outlined, seems complex and difficult to carry out. In point of fact, however, the plan is nothing more than a projection of the centralizing forces that are now at work. It is the normal development of the agencies that are performing just such functions as have been suggested for them. But even if the plan be complex, there is no reason for distrusting it, in view of the actual situation. All plans that involve voluntary coöperation, unaided by compulsion, are complex and difficult. The organization of Jewish life in America can not be simple. The *raison d'etre* for the Jewish group in this country is complex and many-sided, and their school organization must necessarily reflect this complexity of their life. The Jews of New York must be ready to try involved and difficult plans of educational organization, if they are to continue their group life.

Chapter IV

ORGANIZATION OF JEWISH SCHOOLS:

(Administrative Control)

In a decentralized educational system, such as is formed by the Jewish schools of New York, the inner organization of the individual school determines very largely the quality of that school's work. Each school must look to its own trustees and executive officers for direction, with but little assistance from outside agencies. The efficiency with which the school administration is organized, is therefore of very great importance in the conduct of Jewish education. The administrative organization of Jewish schools is most characteristically represented by the communal type of school, which usually goes under the name of Talmud Torah.

The communal school (Talmud Torah) is established because of the desire of a group of men, organized into a society, to give Jewish training to their own children, and to the children of their neighbors. They thereupon open a small school, usually employing at first only one or two teachers. Men and women in the community are asked to become members of the school, so as to aid in its financial maintenance.[1] The membership dues range from three dollars to a hundred dollars per year.

Board of Directors

The organizers of the school usually constitute themselves the Board of Directors. An annual meeting is called of all the members to elect these directors from year to year. The election is only nominal, however, for in reality the Board of Directors both nominates and elects its own successors, so that the same men continue at the head of the institution for many years.[2]

One of the most striking facts about the organization of the Jewish schools is the large number of members on their Boards

[1] For some of the large weekday schools this has been changed recently, due to the Federation for the Support of Jewish Philanthropic Societies.

[2] There are directors in some of the existing Jewish schools who have acted in this capacity for more than 25 years.

of Directors. The following is the number of members on each of the managing boards of the largest Jewish educational institutions in New York:[3]

SCHOOL	NUMBER DIRECTORS	NO. TEACHERS [1] EMPLOYED
Uptown Talmud Torah	48	24
Rabbi Jacob Joseph School	64	30
Salanter Talmud Torah	12	7
Machzike Talmud Torah	31	10
Central Jewish Institute	35	6
Downtown Talmud Torah	31	8
Bureau of Education	5	35
TOTAL	226	120

Excluding the Bureau of Jewish Education, *these schools have from two to five directors for each teacher employed.* It is probably too mild to call such a situation abnormal. The opinion of American educators is overwhelmingly in favor of the small Board of Education of seven or nine members, even for the largest cities.[4] Two successive commissions condemned the previous Board of Education of New York City because of its large size, (45 members for the 20,000 teachers employed).[5] By recent legislation,[6] New York City reduced the size of its board from 45 to 7 members. The situation in the Jewish schools, therefore, is certainly to be condemned. It is impossible to manage efficiently any school which has thirty or more directors.

The reasons which gave rise to the unwieldy Boards in the Jewish schools are easily understood. The necessity for obtaining sufficient funds was the chief stimulus for increasing the membership of the Board. In order to influence men to contribute liberally to the support of these institutions, it was necessary to

[3] Institutional schools, like the Educational Alliance, are not included here.

[4] Cf. Theisen W.: "The City Superintendent and the Board of Education"; Teachers' College, Columbia University, 1917.

[5] Goodnow and Howe Report: on the Organization, Status and Procedure of the Dept. of Education of New York City, 1912-1918. Hanus Report: "School Efficiency. A Constructive Study Applied to N. Y. C." 1913, Chap. VIII.

[6] New York State Laws, Chap. 786, Article 33A, Section 865-868, enacted June 8, 1917.

make them feel in a measure responsible for the management of the schools, and membership on the Board of Directors has been the usual means of creating such a sense of responsibility. Moreover, the high esteem in which religious education is held among Jews, has also contributed toward increasing the size of school boards. "The Study of the Law" is considered the greatest of "good deeds" (Mitzvoth). Pious Jews therefore are anxious not only to send their children to the religious school, but also to get the opportunity of doing something personally on behalf of Talmud Torah (Study of the Law). Thus, most boards contain three types of directors: (1) the active, responsible officers and heads of the institution; (2) inactive but influential members; (3) active pious members who have little influence.

The large Board gives rise to many evils. In the first place, not all of the members of the Board attend the meetings, or are in any way interested in the management of the school. Each school has a small group of active men, usually the officers of the institution, who bear the burden of responsibility alone. Busy men of affairs, whose direct coöperation would be very much desired, find no incentive to join a Board which has from 30 to 60 members. In the second place, owing to the fact that there are so many members, the need arises for supplying them all with work. Many committees are appointed to execute every detail of the work of the school, and these committees interfere with the employed executives, the principal, the secretary and their staffs. The following standing committees are usual in Jewish schools: Executive or Administrative, Finance, Building, Education, House, Membership, Publicity or Propaganda, and Synagogue. Besides these, there are any number of special committees. A study of the minutes of four of the largest Jewish schools[7] showed that of all the matters discussed, more than one-fifth consisted merely in the appointment of committees and hearing their formal reports.

There is no distinction made between the legislative, or the controlling functions of the Board, and its executive or administrative functions. The boards busy themselves with minutiae of management, and spend much time upon details which should

[7] Minutes of the Uptown Talmud Torah, Downtown Talmud Torah, Salanter Talmud Torah, and the Hebrew Free School, for the year 1915-1916.

be left to their executive officers. Such items as minor repairs of the building; details of arrangement for annual meetings, graduations, and "benefits"; acknowledgment of small donations; and similar details, are found to occupy the attention of the entire Board.[8] Meetings are held frequently, but the usual attendance is small. Much time is spent in random discussion of a social or "personal" nature. The business of the school is of secondary importance.

The poor management of many Jewish schools can be traced directly to the abnormal size of the Board. In American education, the best practice favors the *Board of seven or nine members, which legislates and controls, but which entrusts the administrative aspects of school work to its appointed officers.*[9] Some of the larger Jewish schools have felt the need of decreasing the size of their Boards. But the general practice in Jewish schools is, as yet, far from being in accord with this principle of efficient management.

The accompanying chart shows the relation of the Board of Directors to its executive officers. These officers are: the principal, the secretary, and also the janitor.[11] In many schools these executive officers are coördinate, and are responsible directly to special committees of the Board: the Principal is responsible to the Education Committee, the Secretary to the Finance, Executive and other Committees, and the Janitor to the House Committee.[12] In some cases there is also a special Supervisor of Social Work (evening clubs, etc.), who is coördinate with the other officers. He is responsible either to a special committee, or else, directly to the Board.[13]

---

[8] Minutes of the Uptown Talmud Torah; Downtown Talmud Torah, Salanter Talmud Torah, and the Hebrew Free School, for the year 1915-1916.

[9] Cf. Theisen, W.: "The City Superintendent and the Board of Education," Teachers' College, Columbia University, 1917.

[11] Other officers, such as the Rabbi and the Sexton, who are connected with some of the Jewish educational institutions, are not included, because they do not deal directly with the school work.

[12] The duties of the janitor are those usually performed by the school janitor, but his powers in some instances are truly "tyrannical."

[13] This was more particularly true until recently; but the practice has been discouraged, and the tendency is now for the principal (or the director) himself to supervise the evening work.

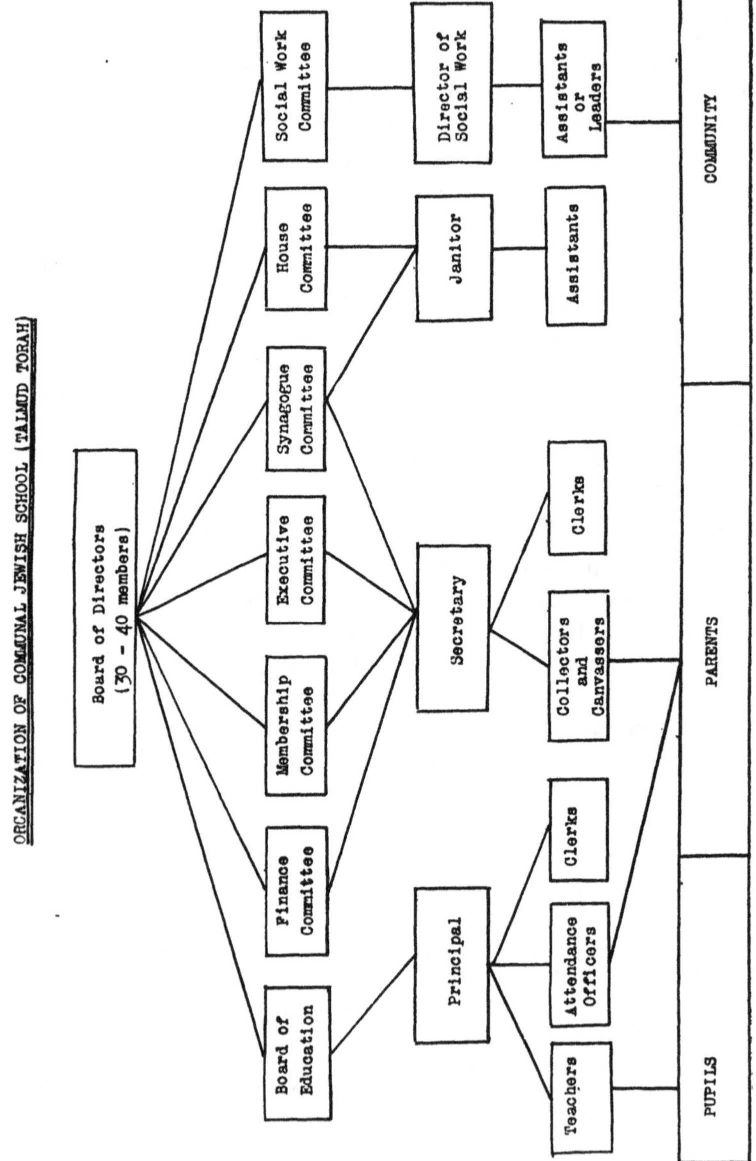
ORGANIZATION OF COMMUNAL JEWISH SCHOOL (TALMUD TORAH)
Board of Directors (30 - 40 members)
Board of Education
Finance Committee
Membership Committee
Executive Committee
Synagogue Committee
House Committee
Social Work Committee
Principal
Secretary
Janitor
Director of Social Work
Teachers
Attendance Officers
Clerks
Collectors and Canvassers
Clerks
Assistants
Assistants or Leaders
PUPILS
PARENTS
COMMUNITY

The Principal

To understand the status of the Jewish school principal it is necessary to know that he has comparatively greater and more varied responsibility than the principal of the American Public School. In Jewish schools the principal must perform the functions not only of the ordinary school principal, but also those of the supervisor and of the superintendent. He must not only manage the school, but must also attend to many financial and communal matters, must guide the policy of his school, and must take the initiative in its enlargement and in the improvement of its work.

To execute these functions properly, his powers ought to be commensurately large. He should be made the chief executive with regard to the administrative phases of the school work. He should be given freedom to plan and to develop the curriculum and methods of instruction; should submit an annual budget for the school; should propose and, with the approval of the Board, execute changes in the policy of the school; and should have full supervision of all the officers employed by the Board. He should act not only as the manager of the school, but also as the adviser and guide of his Board, and of all the other executive officers.

In actual practice, however, the status of many of the present school principals with relation to their Boards, does not satisfy these requirements. The Jewish school principal is still in the stage of an employee entrusted with carrying out certain administrative details. The Boards themselves perform many of the functions which properly belong to the principal. The principal does not guide the policy of the school; he merely obeys. In many schools he has not even the power of appointing his own teachers, but must work with teachers who are elected by his Board without consulting him. In very few of the schools does he have anything to do with the financial aspects of the school work. He has no control of the expenditure of school moneys, and all the records of the school are kept by the secretary, without any supervision or assistance from him. Not only the secretary, but the janitor as well, is "independent" of his control.

This condition is to be ascribed in part to the Board of Directors. The school boards managing the Jewish schools suffer from the same lack of appreciation of expert service, and from the same inefficient methods as still prevail in many American cities.[14] But, in part, the fault also lies with the principals themselves.

To make full use of his responsibility, the Jewish school principal must be properly equipped. He should possess not only a thorough knowledge of Jewish literature, history, and customs, but should also be pedagogically trained, and acquainted with the best practice in modern education. Besides being a teacher, he should also be a man of affairs, understanding fully the business phases as well as the social aspects of his school work. Only a few of the Jewish school principals are thus properly equipped for the work which they are doing. The following data concerning the age, nativity, training and experience of the principals who are conducting the ten largest Jewish schools in the city, are indicative of the situation:

Name	Age	Salary 13a	Nativity	Jewish Training 15)	Ability to Speak English 16)	Secular Training 17)	Special Pedagogical Training
A	26	$2,400	America	B	A	A	Yes
B	55	2,250	E. Europe	A	A	C	No
C	30	2,000	America	B	A	A	Yes
D	39	1,800	E. Europe	A	B	C	No
E	35	1,500	"	A	B	B	No
F	40	1,350	"	A	B	C	No
G	60	1,200	"	A	B	C	No
H	45	1,200	"	A	B	C	No
I	38	1,200	"	A	C	C	No
J	50	900	"	A	C	C	No

Two interesting facts are here presented. In the first place, there are a large number of principals in Jewish schools, whose secular training is not sufficient for the proper management

[13a] These salaries were for 1917. Some salaries have been increased since then due to the war conditions.

[14] Cf. Theisen, W.: "The City Superintendent and the Board of Education," Teachers' College, New York, 1917.

[15] *A*—Education in Yeshiboth and schools of Europe; *B*—Education in American Rabbinical Seminary or equivalent.

[16] *A*—Ability to speak English in public; *B*—Ability to speak English in private conversation; *C*—Inability to speak English.

[17] *A*—Higher degree (above B.A.); *B*—B.A. degree or equivalent; *C*—No college degree or equivalent.

of the American Jewish school. In the second place, it is evident that *the Jews of this city are willing to compensate men for such training*. Of the three men receiving salaries of $2,000 and more, all have a good knowledge of the English language, and two are college graduates who received pedagogic training in American universities.[18]

Upon the basis of these facts the typical Jewish school principal may be described as follows: He is about forty years of age, was born in Eastern Europe, and came to this country when already a mature man. He has a thorough knowledge of Judaism and Jewish literature, and long classroom experience as a Jewish teacher. His secular education is insufficient, and he has received no professional educational training whatever. His salary is about $1,200 per year,[19] and his work consists in admitting new pupils, caring for the discipline of the school, supervising the collection of tuition fees, conferring with the Committee on Education concerning the curricula and some of the policies of the school, and in carrying out these policies.

The work of supervising the classroom work of the teachers, which is one of the most important functions of the school principal, is, in most cases, sadly neglected. Such supervision as exists is practically all of the "inspecting" kind. The principal visits the classrooms a few minutes daily, primarily for the purpose of "checking up" the teacher, and not for the purpose of improving his work. But even of this form of inspection there is little to be found in the average Jewish school. In very few cases is there a genuine attempt to criticise the work of the teacher constructively, that is, not merely to point out faults, but also to indicate good qualities in teaching, as well as to suggest new attitudes or new methods of work. Teachers' meetings are held in some of the larger schools; but these are of an administrative nature, dealing with the details of school management, rather than with the educational problems concerning the educational work of the school. Many of the matters that consume the time of these meetings are of a trivial nature, and could better be transacted by a written order or note sent from the principal

[18] Teachers' College of Columbia University.

[19] This was true in 1917; it is about $1,500 now (1918).

to the teachers. Few of the principals realize the possibilities which these meetings have for stimulating interest and initiative, and for promoting the educational growth of the teachers. In some of the schools, attempts are made to utilize other means of supervision, such as demonstration lessons, teachers' institutes, and observation by weaker teachers of the work done by the more capable ones. But as a general rule, these means of supervision are as yet unknown in the Jewish schools of New York.

Strong tendencies are making themselves felt, however, which are destined to change this condition of affairs. The information previously presented concerning Jewish school principals, indicates that American Jews are beginning to attract younger men as principals of their schools, and are willing to compensate them properly for this work. These men are given large powers, and are made the sole executives of their school. They have control and supervision, not only of the educational aspects, but also of all other aspects of the school work. Moreover, under the guidance and stimulus of such organizations as the Hebrew Principals' Association, the principals of the larger Jewish schools are exchanging experiences, and planning their programs and policies in common. A professional spirit is slowly developing among them, which has significant possibilities for the future.

The Secretary

The powers of the secretary vary in the different schools, from those of virtual superintendent to those of bookkeeper or clerk. In most cases the secretary is an elderly man who has been connected with the institution for many years. He keeps the minutes of the Board of Directors, (usually in Yiddish), and takes care of such books and financial transactions as the school may have. He is responsible to the president of the Board of Directors, or to the finance committee. In only a few instances is he directly responsible to the principal. With rare exceptions, the books of the schools are not well kept,[20] and the methods employed are not systematic or businesslike. While the salaries of the secretaries are not high,[21] yet any efficient clerk acting

[20] For corroborating evidence, cf. Appendix O.

[21] The average salary of the secretary in the ten largest Jewish communal schools is about $850 per year (1917).

both as a bookkeeper and as general clerical assistant to the principal, under the guidance of a public accountant, could perform the secretarial functions in a far more efficient manner than is done by many of the present incumbents.

The present practice is not to require, and in some instances not to permit, the school principal to supervise any of the financial records of his school. This work is entrusted entirely to the secretary, under the auspices of the finance committee. This is an obnoxious custom. One of the American superintendents of education pointed out the folly of this practice in American education, showing how inconsistent it is for Boards to appoint two distinct executive officers, one to be responsible for the educational work, and the other for finances. "Imagine" he said, "a shoe manufacturer who engages an expert in the production of shoes, but does not require of him to know anything of the cost of production, and on the other hand employs a specialist in business methods, but does not wish him to know anything of the processes involved in the production of shoes."[22] Yet this is exactly the situation in practically all of the Jewish schools. The principal is supposed to take care of the educational product, but is not required to know anything of what it costs to produce the desired results. On the other hand, the secretary is paid for guarding carefully the finances of the school, but is totally ignorant of the educational significance of the financial expenditure.

Reorganization Needed

A more effective plan of organization is needed than now prevails in Jewish schools. The most significant changes which should be made, are: (1) reduction of the size of the Board to seven or nine members, making of it a business board of control rather than an administrative body; (2) elimination of all standing committees, the Board itself acting as a committee of the whole; (3) centralization of executive power in the hands of the principal or director of the school; the secretary, the janitor and all other executive officers, as well as the teaching staff, to be

[22] "Applied Scientific Management" by Supt. Spaulding in N. E. A. Proceedings, 1913, pp. 259.

subordinate to him. The accompanying chart shows how these changes would affect the organization of the school.

What is true of the organization of the communal Jewish school (Talmud Torah), applies also to the organization of the congregational and the institutional schools. The following differences should be noted: The rabbi of the congregation, or the superintendent of the institution, has general supervision of the work of the school. The management of the school is in the hands of a specially appointed committee on education (sometimes called school committee, or religious school committee). In most of the congregational and institutional schools, the rabbi or superintendent also acts as the principal of the school. This is decidedly an unwise policy. While it is true that under present conditions many of the rabbis or superintendents are as capable (or incapable) of managing the Jewish schools as some of the Jewish school principals are, yet this cannot serve as a criterion. Unless the rabbi or superintendent himself has received special professional training in education, he should entrust the actual management of the school to one who has had such training, and should reserve for himself only supervisory control as regards the content of instruction and the general management. In the larger schools, where it is possible to engage an efficient school principal, the rabbi or superintendent should have the power, jointly with the trustees of the school, to appoint the school principal; but after his appointment, everything pertaining to the school should be put into the hands of the principal.

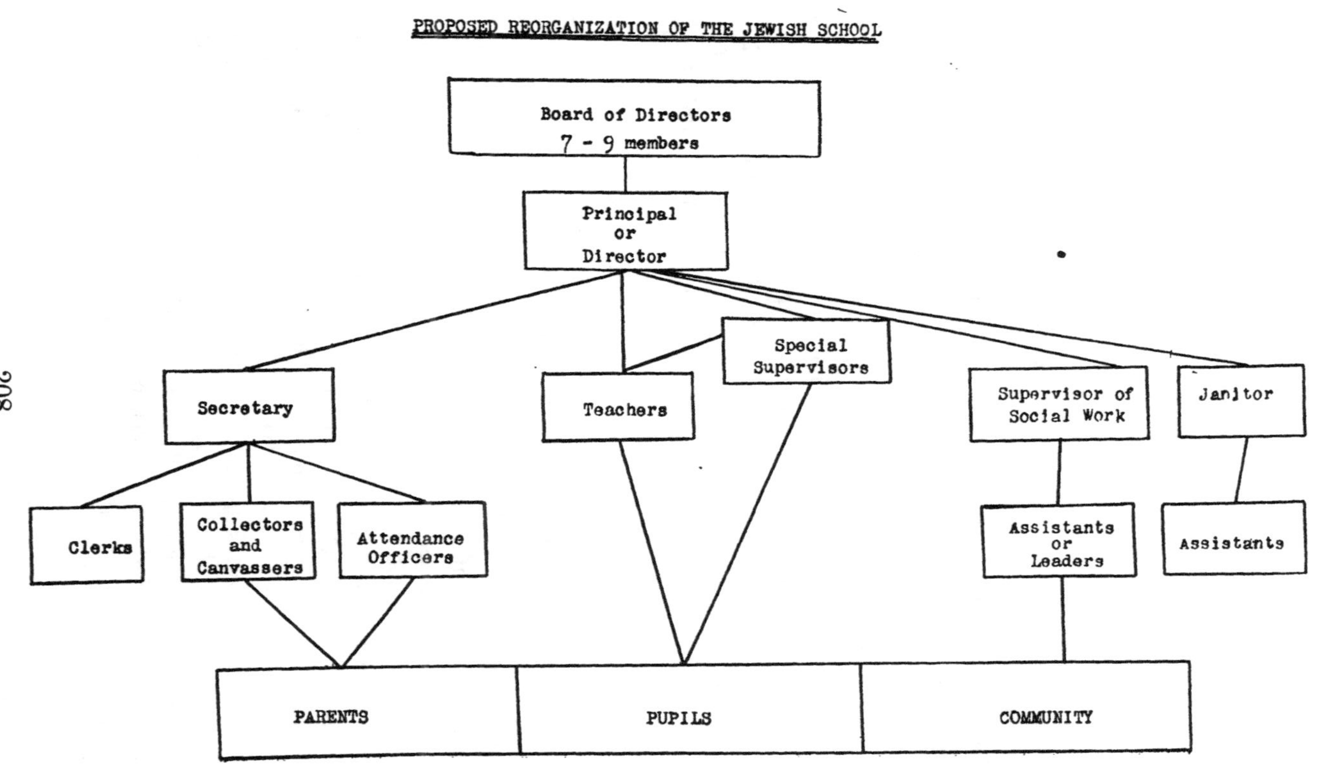
PROPOSED REORGANIZATION OF THE JEWISH SCHOOL
Board of Directors
7 - 9 members
Principal
or
Director
Secretary
Teachers
Special Supervisors
Supervisor of Social Work
Janitor
Clerks
Collectors
and
Canvassers
Attendance Officers
Assistants
or
Leaders
Assistants
PARENTS
PUPILS
COMMUNITY

Chapter V

ORGANIZATION OF JEWISH SCHOOLS:

(Time Schedules)

One of the most evident differences in organization among the Jewish schools, is in the matter of time schedules. The Jews of New York make use of all the three forms of religious instruction found in this country: weekday, parochial and Sunday school instruction. These time schedules express, on the one hand, the relation of the Jewish school to public education; and, on the other hand, they indicate the intensiveness of training as it can be measured in terms of hours of work. The data previously presented [1] show that the great majority of the Jews of New York have committed themselves to the supplementary weekday school. Out of every 100 children taught, about 86 are given weekday instruction, 12 are in Sunday schools, and only one in parochial schools.

Sunday or Sabbath School Schedule
(One session during the week)

The schedules used in Jewish Sabbath schools are practically all alike. The pupils attend from one to three hours either on Sunday mornings, or on Saturday mornings or afternoons. Each teacher teaches one class. Part of the time is devoted to a general assembly, usually in the nature of a children's service, and the rest of the period is given over to classroom instruction. The graduating or confirmation classes also come one afternoon during the week for special instruction by the rabbi of the congregation. The Jewish Sunday or Sabbath schools are of two kinds: (1) *congregational* schools for the children of the members of the congregation; and (2) "*mission*" schools conducted for the poor children of the neighborhood. These mission schools are usually conducted by the sisterhoods of the wealthier congregations.

---

[1] Cf. above pp. 181-183.

Weekday Schedules

(From two to five sessions during the week)

The educational organization of the Jewish weekday schools is far more complicated than that of the Sunday schools, and the time schedules are more varied. While weekday religious instruction among the Jews is of very long duration, yet the particular adaptation of it to American conditions is still in the experimental stages. Several types of schedules and methods of classification are therefore found in these schools. In order to understand the significance of this variation, it is necessary to remember; (1) that the cost of Jewish instruction must be as low as possible and yet permit sufficient time for adequate training; and (2) that the Jewish child must be given a minimum of "free" time for recreation, home work, music and other studies.

In practically all of the Jewish weekday schools, several classes are instructed by each teacher, the children coming in "shifts" at alternating hours. The following table shows at a glance the arrangement of a Jewish teacher's classes on the several days of the week, in accordance with the various schedules used in the Jewish schools of New York:

Schedule	Mon.	Tues.	Wed.	Thurs.	Fri.	Sat.	Sun.
A	1 2 3	1 2 3	1 2 3	1 2 3	.. .. ..	.. .. ..	1 2 3
B	1 2	3 4	1 2	3 4	.. ..	1 2 3 4	4 3 2 1
C	.. 1	.. 2	.. 3	.. 4	.. ..	1 2 3 4	4 3 2 1
D	.. 1 2 ..	.. 3 4 ..	.. 5 6 ..	.. 7 8 ..	.. ..	1 2 3 4	5 6 7 8

Schedule A (five-times-a-week) is, with slight local variations, the most commonly found time schedule in Jewish weekday schools. It provides for instruction on every weekday afternoon except Friday, and also on Sunday morning. On every one of these days three classes come in alternating shifts, from 4 to 8 p. m.[2] No instruction is given on Fridays or Saturdays.[3] Each class is taught from 1 hour and 20 minutes to 2 hours per day, making a total of from 6 hours and 40 minutes to 10 hours per week. The approximate cost of instruction for each child is $22 per year.[4] Usually the younger children are taught less time and the older children are given more time.

Schedule B (four-times-a-week), is not so commonly found in Jewish schools as the previous schedule. It differs from the more customary schedule in four respects: (1) It makes use of Saturday as a day for regular Jewish instruction; (2) it reduces the cost of instruction by giving each teacher four classes instead of three; (3) it does away with late hours of teaching, only two classes coming on each of the weekdays, and (4) it gives the children more "free" time during the public school days. This schedule provides instruction for each child on two afternoons during the week, and on both Saturday and Sunday mornings and afternoons. During weekdays two classes are taught from 4 to 7 p. m., each class being taught 1 hour and 30 minutes.[5] On Saturdays and Sundays two classes come in the morning (9 a. m. to 12 m.) and two in the afternoon (1 to 4 p. m.). On these days, which are "non-public school days," two hours of instruction are given to each class, one hour being devoted to mass instruction in the form of history lectures or children's services, and the other hour to classroom instruction.[6] The total teaching time per class according to this schedule is 7 hours per week. Each teacher teaches four classes, and the cost of instruction is from $15 to $18 per year.[7] Where the cost is not a very

[2] During the summer vacation, sessions are held in the morning between 9 A. M. and 1 P. M.

[3] In many of these schools, however, the pupils come for prayers or for special instruction on Saturdays.

[4] Cf. next chapter.

[5] The session can be reduced to 6:30 P. M., by giving the younger pupils *one* hour instruction during weekdays, instead of one hour and a half.

[6] Classes are combined for assembly, services and history lectures.

[7] Cf. next chapter.

important factor the schedule can be modified, with better results, by giving only two classes to a teacher.

Schedule C (three-times-a-week) is the one employed in the Intermediate Girls' Schools of the Bureau of Jewish Education. It is like the previous schedule (B) except that it still further increases the "free" time of the child on public school days, and limits the hours of instruction to not later than 6 p. m. The pupils attend three days during the week: one weekday afternoon, (Monday, or Tuesday, or Wednesday, or Thursday), and on Saturday and Sunday. During each of these days they receive two hours' instruction, making a total of 6 hours per week. Each teacher instructs four classes, and the cost of instruction is approximately $12.00[8] per year.

Schedule D (twice-a-week): This schedule is the one requiring the least time of the child, and the least expenditure of money. It provides for three to four hours' instruction for each child during the week. The pupil comes to school twice; once on a weekday afternoon, and once on Saturday or Sunday.[9] Each teacher, (whose full time of service is twenty hours per week) is enabled to teach *eight classes* during the week, giving each class three hours of instruction. This schedule is chiefly employed for younger children in the Elementary Girls' Schools of the Bureau of Jewish Education. The cost of instruction for each child, according to this schedule, is approximately $6.00 per year.

The Parochial School Schedule

The Parochial school schedule differs from the weekday schedules, both in intensity and in organization. The mornings are devoted to the Jewish studies, and the afternoons are given over to the subjects of the public school curriculum.[10] Jewish in-

---

[8] This includes, however, only the cost of teaching and supervision. These schools have no buildings of their own and have no expenses for rent or maintenance. The total per capita cost, if all items be included, would be about $18.00 annually per child.

[9] On Saturdays and Sundays, classes are combined for services and lectures.

[10] When this book went to press, (June 1918) the New York State Commissioner of Education demanded from the Jewish parochial schools that they change their time schedule so as to give to the public school subjects the regular public school hours. This order, if carried out, will greatly affect the future of the Jewish parochial schools. The material presented here was kept, however, as a description of conditions existing hitherto.

struction is given every day of the week, with the exception of Saturday, from 9:00 a. m. until 12:00 m., and from 1:00 p. m. until 3:00 p. m. Each class thus receives during the week 30 hours of Jewish training. On five afternoons during the week (excluding Fridays and Saturdays), instruction is given in the secular public school subjects, from 4:00 p. m. until 7 p. m., making a total of fifteen hours' instruction per week in the public school branches. Every parochial school pupil attends school, therefore, 45 hours every week, and is taught by two teachers, a Hebrew teacher in the morning, and an English teacher in the afternoon.

While the Jewish parochial schools are like the Catholic and Lutheran parochial schools, in that they take the place of the public schools, teaching both religious and secular subjects, yet they differ from the Christian schools in certain fundamental respects. In the first place, as has already been pointed out,[11] the Jewish parochial schools are not synagogue schools. They are managed by special educational societies and not by congregations. They are, therefore, not parish schools in the Catholic sense, but rather communal schools. In the second place, the cost of Jewish parochial education is far greater than it is among the Catholics. The per capita cost in Jewish parochial schools is from $65 to $70 per year.[12] *It costs the Jews practically eight to ten times as much per child for their parochial education, as it does the Catholics.*[13] The reasons are evident: There is no class of trained *volunteer* teachers among the Jews, such as the Catholic teaching orders of priests and nuns, nor are Jewish parochial school buildings endowed, as are many of the Catholic schools. Remembering that no system of Jewish education can have the support of either government or of centralized church, the high cost of instruction of $65 to $70 for each child per year, indicates how impossible it would be to support Jewish parochial schools on a large scale.

---

[11] See above p. 182.

[12] Cf. next chapter (Part II, Chapter IV), p. 221.

[13] The cost of Catholic Parochial Education is given as $7.00 to $8.00 per annum per child. Cf. Burns: "Growth and Development of the Catholic School System in United States," pp. 292-293.

THE RELATIVE WORTH OF TIME SCHEDULES

Neither the parochial school schedule nor the Sunday school schedule seem to be satisfactory as a basis for the development of Jewish education in this country. While the Sunday school schedule is not costly, and permits sufficient free time for the child, the training which it provides is grossly inadequate. There is probably not one responsible schoolman or minister, whether Jew or Gentile, who is satisfied with the product of the Sunday School. On the other hand, while the training given by the parochial school is certainly sufficiently intensive, its cost is prohibitive and it monopolizes the time of the child. The boy who leaves the Jewish parochial school at seven o'clock in the evening, after ten hours' attendance, (of which eight are spent in actual study), is not able to care properly for his physical and recreational needs. Nor is he in a position to provide for his general cultural education: the study of music, general reading, etc. Moreover, many Jewish parents, especially among the poorer classes, need some help from their children, either in their stores or at home. A Jewish school schedule which monopolizes the time of the child is therefore incapable of extensive use. Some form of the supplementary weekday schedule seems to be essential to meet the needs of Jewish education in this country.

Which of the weekday schedules enumerated above is best suited to the needs of Jewish education in this country? It is, of course, not possible to pass judgment without knowing the particular conditions in each community or neighborhood, and the specific needs which it has in Jewish education. In general, however, there are three criteria, previously suggested, which should be kept in mind in judging the relative worth of any time schedule: (1) Does it insure *adequate training* for Jewish boys and girls; (2) does it allow for enough "free" *time* for the child, so that the child can properly care for its recreational needs, as well as for its other, non-Jewish studies; and (3) are the majority of the Jewish parents *capable of paying* the necessary tuition fees, so that the Jewish school will be able to maintain itself?

---

[14] "Utilize it and standardize it as you may, the Sunday session will not furnish an adequate religious education for our people." Athearn C. W.: "Religious Education and American Democracy," 1917.

These are the basic considerations, and the weight given to each of them will determine the time schedule to be used in each case.

In a community program of Jewish education it will not be possible to adhere solely and exclusively to any one time schedule. In the case of the majority of the children the elements of cost and of time seem to be of greater importance than the element of intensive training. General Jewish education must therefore be organized so that the parents themselves are the chief source of maintenance, and the Jewish schools must arrange their time of instruction so that attending Jewish school shall not prove an unbearable burden upon the average public school child. But, at the same time, the community must insure that a selected capable minority shall obtain as intensive a training as possible, irrespective of cost or sacrifice of time.

The most practical policy for the community to pursue, therefore, seems to be that of making a distinction between *elementary education*, which should extend over a period of three or four years, for all children between the ages of seven to ten or eleven; and *intermediate education*, in which the pupils should be separated according to their ability and interest into (1) intensive Hebrew classes, (2) general classes conducted in the vernacular; and (3) extension groups (clubs, etc.). The community should aim to organize its system of *elementary schools for all children* upon a basis which will permit financial "self-support,"[15] in the sense that the average parent should be able to pay for the "instruction costs" of his child. The time schedule used in these elementary schools should make it possible for the pupils to have "free" time during the week for recreation, study and other activities. From the several weekday schedules previously presented, it seems that the *four-times-a-week schedule* (Schedule B) is best suited for this purpose. Its cost is not prohibitive, it provides sufficient time for instruction, and it does not demand too great a sacrifice of time on the part of the child.[16] The curriculum employed should be a "basic" curriculum, that is, it should be designed to teach the essentials that *every* American

---

[15] For a fuller discussion of this important question, cf. next chapter.

[16] The chief difficulty in this schedule consists in the fact that it compels the Jewish teacher to teach also on Saturdays. This is undoubtedly a hardship. But religious education on Saturdays is traditional among the Jews, and Jewish teachers must be taught the value of teaching on that day.

Jew should know in order that he may be an intelligent, loyal member of the Jewish community.[17]

In the intermediate schools, at least two different time schedules should be used: one for the pupils who are to pursue an intensive Hebrew course, because they show themselves capable of such intensive linguistic and literary study; and the other for those who are to be given the general "vernacular" training, in which the same subjects (Bible, Hebrew, History, etc.) are taught in English. For the Hebrew course *a five-or six-times-per-week* schedule should be introduced following the same arrangements as the previous schedule except that two classes are taught by each teacher, the pupils coming to school every day but Friday. This would of course raise the cost of instruction, making it practically twice as much as in the four-class-per-teacher schedule. The community must be ready to support these classes fully, since they will contain the small minority of children who will be the future spiritual leaders of American Jewry. For the intermediate classes, on the other hand, the *four-times-a-week schedule* would still be quite sufficient, and would reckon with the needs of the average American child.

This then seems to be the plan of organization which the community should strive to achieve in course of time. It is not intended, of course, that all of the Jewish schools should or could be immediately reorganized on that basis. Present conditions involve a number of factors which will make all kinds of deviation from this plan necessary as a matter of practical conduct. The wishes of parents, the personal desires of teachers and principals, the problem of obtaining adequate community funds, the traditions brought from Eastern Europe,—all of these will doubtless make Jewish schools try out a variety of time schedules. The leaders of the community, however, should have some such plan, as here outlined, before them, in order to guide intelligently the development of Jewish education.[18]

Public School Co-operation Necessary

But while the Jewish school should not overburden the average child, it is essential that the public school, in its turn, also should

[17] Cf. Chapter X "Content of Jewish Education."

[18] Further discussion of the plan will be found in the following chapters.

not monopolize the time of the child. "The schools and the colleges are not the only educational agencies in the country. The churches, the art schools, the private teachers of music, domestic and fine arts, etc., are all educative agencies.... It is well for the public school to recognize that it is not the only educative agency in the community and limit the amount of its claims upon the child."[19] *Sufficient time* must be allowed for Jewish instruction on weekdays. The less time the public school permits for this purpose, the stronger becomes the position of the parochial school, whose sole *raison d'etre* among the Jews seems to be the desire to provide sufficient time for Jewish training. Just how much time the public school shall leave free, to be utilized by other educational agencies, such as religious schools, is still a mooted question.[20] For the purposes of the Jewish school, any public school plan which grants several free hours each day to large numbers of children, would satisfy the minimum needs of Jewish education in New York.

---

[19] Athearn, C. W.: "Religious Education and American Democracy."

[20] It is not within the scope of this book to analyze at length the suggestion for adjustment made by the promoters of the "work-study-and-play" schedule known as the Gary Plan. The matter has been fully discussed elsewhere (cf. particularly, Athearn: "Religious Education and American Democracy," 1917; also "Jewish Teacher," Vol. I, Nos. 1 and 2). The sentiment of Jewish educators has been very strongly against it. Whatever attempts have been made at coöperation between the "Gary" schools (in the Bronx) and the neighboring Jewish school, Ezra Hebrew School, 1739 Washington Avenue, have been a failure. From the viewpoint of the administrator of Jewish education, the following are some of the main difficulties: (1) difficulty of adjusting the "free" time of the child to meet the needs of any particular religious group, owing to the many other demands made upon the "flexibility" of the Gary schedule; (2) lack of uniformity in time distribution among the schedules of the several public schools within any one neighborhood; (3) uncertainty as to how long a particular arrangement will be adhered to by the public school principal, who is anxious to keep adjusting his schedule for the best interests of his own school; (4) impossibility of grading the instruction in the religious school, unless a certain number of children of the same grade are given their "free" time at the same time; and (5) the additional per capita cost of Jewish instruction necessitated by the smaller classes and longer hours of work for each teacher, since Jewish teachers would have to spend practically all day in the Jewish schools, from morning until evening. Besides these difficulties, there exists the danger of a division in the American public school along religious lines, even if the division takes place not within the classrooms, but on the street in front of the school house. The Gary schedule, as usually understood, (that is, the eight-hour-school-day schedule) is detrimental to the development of Jewish education.

Chapter VI

SCHOOL FINANCES

From whatever angle we view the development of systematic Jewish education in this country, we shall find the problem of finances fundamental. It is evident that the possibility of increasing the educational facilities depends very closely upon obtaining proper financial support. Equally dependent is any attempt which may be made to reorganize the existing Jewish schools, either as regards their administrative or their educational functions.

Jewish education is a voluntary system, which can be based upon no other power than that of the free choice of each individual parent. Because of this inability to exert the legal compulsion of the State, or the clerical pressure of a centralized Church, the problem of financial maintenance must necessarily be very difficult. The support of the Jewish schools is more *uncertain* than that of the public schools, because it cannot be met through taxation. It is more *complicated* than in the case of the Catholic parochial schools, because it is not backed by a powerful church, utilizing large clerical orders of well-trained volunteer teachers. It is more *urgent* than in the Protestant Sunday Schools, because the Jewish weekday schools give more time to the child and must therefore be more costly. For the progress of Jewish education it is essential, therefore, that some answer be obtained to the following questions: (1) *What is the cost of Jewish education?* (2) *How are the Jewish schools maintained?* (3) *What are the purposes for which the money is spent?* and (4) *How wisely does the community spend its money for Jewish education?*

Inadequacy of Financial Records

Any one who attempts to study the finances of the Jewish schools is confronted, at the very outset, with the difficulty of inadequate and inaccurate records. This is but another effect of the decentralized condition of Jewish education. Even the largest

[1] The information here presented was obtained from a detailed examination of the financial records of fifteen of the larger Jewish schools, and from the questionnaires sent to all of the other schools.

and best organized of the Jewish schools do not keep their records in such a way as to make possible the accurate consideration of such elemental questions as: the cost per pupil; the cost for each department of activity; the net income from each source (school, synagogue, etc.); and similar questions, without which the proper financial management of the schools would seem quite impossible. Not only are the records grossly inadequate for educational purposes, but in most schools even such records as are kept are seldom audited and published.[2]

One of the prime necessities, therefore, in regulating the finances of Jewish schools, is the reorganization of their systems of financial accounting. It should be among the important duties of organizations like the Bureau of Jewish Education, the Board of Jewish School Aid, and the Federation for the Support of Jewish Philanthropic Societies, to bring about an adequate, uniform system of financial accounting in the Jewish schools.[3]

Per Capita Cost of Jewish Education

Inadequate though the existing records are, it is nevertheless essential that some definite knowledge be obtained from them concerning the cost of Jewish education. Particularly important is it to know the cost of instruction *per pupil* in each of the various forms of Jewish education: weekday, Sunday, and parochial. The information which is here presented needs to be supplemented by further study, but it is amply indicative of the actual conditions.

A. Sunday School Costs

In the Jewish Sunday Schools of New York,[4] the cost per pupil ranges from as low as 45 cents per year to as high as $29.55 per

[2] Of the 14 largest Jewish schools in this city, 6 have published no reports at all during the last five years; 6 published reports irregularly during this period, and only one, a philanthropic-educational institution, issued reports every year.

[3] In *Appendix O* the conditions prevailing in the present financial records of Jewish schools are discussed, and a uniform system of financial accounting is outlined, giving record forms to be used.

[4] In the questionnaires sent to all the schools, information was asked concerning the amount of money spent during the last fiscal year. The reported sum was divided by their reported registers. In most schools only one register could be obtained. Only in the larger schools was it possible to get some sort of *average register*. Of the Sunday schools, 22 reported out of the 41 in this city.

year. An examination of the data[5] reveals an interesting situation which explains this wide variation of cost:

There are two types of Sunday schools: in one type the average cost is about $2.00 to $2.50 per child annually, and in the other it is from $10.00 to $15.00 per child annually. The first group consists of Sunday schools in which all or most of the teaching is done by unpaid *volunteer teachers.* In the second group the teaching staff is composed of regularly *paid teachers.*[6] The per capita costs of about $2.00 in the Sunday schools with unpaid teaching staffs, and of about $14.00 in Sunday schools with paid teaching staffs, furnish 60 hours of instruction per year (30 weeks at two hours per week). Jewish Sunday school instruction costs, therefore, about *3.8 cents per hour for each pupil* in "non-paying" Sunday schools, and about *24 cents per hour for each pupil* in "paying" Sunday schools. This cost represents only the cost of *instruction* (teachers' salaries and school supplies). All other costs (such as maintenance, administration, etc.) are not charged to the school but to the congregational budget directly.[7]

B. Weekday School Costs

The average cost of Jewish weekday instruction is $22.75 annually per child.[8] Here, too, there is a wide variation of cost, ranging from $7.85 in the lowest school to $43.33 in the highest. These are the *gross* per capita costs, including *all* forms of expenditure: (instruction, supplies, maintenance and operation, administration and supervision, collection, etc.). The indications are, therefore, that the per capita cost in the communal weekday

[5] Cf. Table X. This table shows a gradual distribution of per capita cost from 45c. to $3.52 per child annually; then there is a sudden jump to $6.87, after which the per capita cost increases rapidly, until in one Sunday school it is as high as $29.55 per child.

[6] It is probable that if we had more cases in the second class, the distribution would also be as gradual as it is in the first.

[7] This is surprisingly high as compared with the cost per hour in Jewish weekday schools. Cf. below p. 225.

[8] Cf. Table XI, which shows the distribution of per capita costs reported by 34 out of the 67 communal Jewish weekday schools in the city. There are some congregations in this city which conduct both Sunday and Weekday schools. These have not been included, however, because of the large variation among them as to the amount of time devoted to weekday instruction, and because many of their items of expenditure are charged to the congregation or institution, and not to the school. Only communal weekday schools are therefore included in Table XI.

schools is about $22.00 per year.[9] The schools vary, however, very widely, the cost depending upon: the particular time schedule,[10] the salaries paid to teachers, the cost of maintenance of the building, the number of extra-classroom activities (festivals, clubs, etc.), and similar factors.

C. Parochial Education

With regard to parochial education among Jews, the following data are presented from three out of the four parochial schools:[11]

School A spent	$35,700	annually for	525	pupils, at	$68.00 per pupil
School B spent	15,000	annually for	200	pupils, at	75.00 per pupil
School C spent	8,000	annually for	100	pupils, at	80.00 per pupil
Total........	$58,700	annually for	825	pupils, at	$71.15 per pupil

It appears, therefore, that the gross cost of Jewish parochial education is over $70 per child annually.[12] The pupils, most of whom are the children of recent immigrants, can pay but a very small part of this cost. In fact, in some of the parochial schools there is no charge for tuition. Practically all of the $70 per child annually must, therefore, be supplied by the Jewish community, in the form of voluntary contributions.

Purposes of Expenditure in Jewish Schools

What are the purposes for which these sums of money are expended? Particularly is it important to determine this in the case of the weekday instruction, which affects the majority of Jewish children. For what items are the $22.00 annual cost per child spent in the weekday schools? An examination of the

[9] As a check upon these figures, the writer made a *detailed* examination of the records of eleven schools, and found that the gross cost per child annually is from $20.00 to $23.00. This was true in 1917, but owing to the marked increase in the cost of living and its immediate effect in increasing school expenses, the per capita cost in 1918 was probably nearly $25.00.

[10] Cf. previous chapter.

[11] The fourth school gives high school and collegiate as well as elementary instruction, and its costs cannot therefore be included in this study. It costs about $200.00 per pupil annually.

[12] The average per capita cost for Catholic parochial schools is calculated at $7-$8 per year. Cf. Burns "Growth and Development of the Catholic School System in U. S.," pp. 287-293.

detailed financial statements [13] of representative Jewish weekday schools shows the following facts concerning the distribution of expenditure:

For every dollar that is spent in Jewish weekday schools:

19 cents are for payment of debt service and fixed charges; (mortgages, interest, etc.).
15 cents are for expenses of operation and maintenance; (heat, light, janitorial service, etc.)
9 cents for administration; (chiefly secretarial service and office supplies)
46 cents for instruction and supervision; (salaries of teachers and principals, books and supplies)
and
11 cents are spent in obtaining the dollar.[14] (in the form of collection and similar costs)

Sources of Income

Who pays for this instruction? Since neither taxes nor church fees can be depended upon for defraying the expenses, what are the sources of income of Jewish weekday schools? From a detailed analysis of the financial statements of these schools [15] it appears that for every dollar of income:

33 cents come from the pupils; (chiefly in the form of tuition fees)
10 cents come from the synagogue and building rents; and
56 cents come from the community. (in a variety of forms: membership dues, subscriptions, donations and bequests, charity boxes and collections, charity entertainments, communal funds, etc.)[16]

About one-half of the income in Jewish schools is obtained, therefore, from "self-paying" sources, (tuition fees, synagogue, building rents, etc.), and the other half comes through a variety

[13] For the itemized distribution of expenses in ten Jewish weekday schools, cf. Table XII. Cf. also Summary Table XIII.

[14] Cf. Table XIII.

[15] Cf. Table XIV for itemized income of the same schools whose expenditures were itemized in Table XII. Cf. also Table XV for Summary of Income.

[16] Cf. Table XV.

PURPOSES FOR WHICH THE DOLLAR
IN JEWISH EDUCATION
IS SPENT

SOURCES FROM WHICH THE DOLLAR IN JEWISH EDUCATION IS OBTAINED

of uncertain and costly channels. The attention of the Boards of Directors of most Jewish schools is occupied almost wholly with the task of obtaining this second half of their income. Some of the evils which grow out of this condition have already been mentioned. The inordinately large size of the Boards, the dependence of the principal, the low salaries of the teaching staffs, and the general lack of stability in school organization, can in a large measure be traced directly to the necessity of obtaining more than one-half of the school's income from many and varied "charitable" sources.

Comparison of Costs

How costly is Jewish weekday instruction? The above analysis of expenditure makes it possible to compare the cost of Jewish weekday instruction with the cost of public education on the one hand, and with the cost of Jewish Sunday school instruction on the other. Since in public education there is no cost of "collection and similar outlay" (11%), and since the "cost of the building" (19%: mortgages, interest, etc.) is not usually reckoned into the per capita cost of public education, it is necessary to compare only the cost of "instruction, supervision, administration, operation and maintenance." In the Jewish weekday schools, these costs amount to about $15.50 per child for about 400 hours of instruction during the year,[18] or 3.9 cents for each hour. In the public schools of New York the same items of cost amount to $43.00 per child [19] for about 950 hours of instruction during the year,[20] or 4.5 cents for each hour. It seems, therefore, that Jewish weekday religious instruction costs somewhat less per pupil per hour than public education. Similarly, weekday instruction is less costly than Sunday school instruction,

---

[18] 48 weeks at 6½ to 10 hours per week (312-480 hours); 70% of $22.00.

[19] In the 1915-1916 Report of the Superintendent of Education (New York), (page 393) the annual cost per pupil is given as $35.94. This includes only sums spent from the *General Fund* (i. e. salaries of principal and teaching staff). To this should be added the sums spent from the *Special Fund* (operation, maintenance, administration and supplies) which amount to over $8.00 per child ($8.45), making a total of about $43.00 per child. (No later figures are available at present: May, 1918).

[20] Cf. 1915-1916 Report of Superintendent of Schools, New York City, p. 18.

which in Jewish schools with paid teaching staffs, costs 24 cents per pupil per hour.[21]

Sums Spent Annually on Jewish Education

Even more significant than a comparison of costs is the need of determining how much the Jewish community of New York spends annually upon Jewish education, and whether these sums could not be spent to better advantage than at present. On the basis of the above per capita costs, the total amount which the Jews of this city spend every year upon the religious instruction of their children can be estimated with a fair degree of accuracy.[22] In accordance with the number of children receiving the various forms of Jewish instruction, the estimate is as follows:

Type of Instruction		Number Pupils	Per Capita Cost	Total Annual Expenditure
Weekday	Communal	20,124	$22.00	$442,728
	Congregational and Institutional.......	11,113	15.00	166,695
	Private	25,230	25.00	630,750
Sunday and Sabbath............		7,951	6.00	47,706
Parochial		985	70.00	68,950
Total..................		65,403	.....	$1,356,829

[21] Cf. above p. 220. This is due to the fact that in Sunday schools the teacher instructs only one class, whereas in weekday schools he teaches several classes, in alternating shifts. The smaller size of the Sunday school class is another factor in this high per capita cost. Cf. also Table XVII.

[22] The per capita costs used in this estimate are: Communal weekday schools $22.00; Congregational weekday schools $15.00; (due to the fact that many of these schools have only partial weekday instruction, that is, two sessions during the week); Parochial schools $70.00; Sunday schools $6.00 (two-thirds at $2.00 and one-third at $14.00, cf. Table X); and Private instruction $25.00. (The cost of private instruction is certainly above that of the communal weekday schools).

AMOUNT OF MONEY SPENT ANNUALLY UPON JEWISH EDUCATION IN NEW YORK CITY

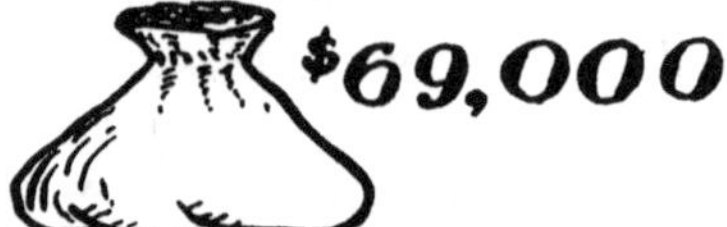

Parochial Education

Week Day Instruction

To these sums should be added the cost of extension education[23] which amounts (1918) to about $35,000; and of higher education, amounting to about $75,000. The Jews of New York, therefore, spend annually *about a million and a half dollars for Jewish education, of which about a million and a quarter are spent on elementary weekday religious instruction.* This is a large sum of money to be spent voluntarily upon religious education for less than one-fourth of the Jewish children of New York; and while it is small in comparison with the sums which the Jews of this city *ought* to spend for the instruction of all of their children, it nevertheless does prove that the masses of the Jews want to perpetuate their Jewish life in this country, and are willing to support a system of supplementary Jewish schools which shall make this possible. Including all forms of instruction, about one million dollars, or two-thirds of the entire annual expenditure of Jewish education, are furnished in the form of direct payment of tuition fees by the parents of the children, and one-third, is contributed by the community.[24]

Community Program for the Support of Jewish Education

Is the community spending these sums most effectively? Leaving out of consideration the Sunday school instruction and the education given in Jewish parochial schools, which may be intended to serve particular purposes, do the $1,240,000 spent on weekday instruction yield the most promising returns?

The bulk of this money is spent upon giving all pupils practically the same sort of training.[25] No differentiation is made between the capable and the less capable; almost no distinction is drawn with regard to the age of the children who begin their Jewish studies; and no provision is made for the particular interests or aptitudes of pupils. All are put through the same grinding, costly, educational routine. The five-times-a-week

---

[23] See below p. 235.

[24] The community contributes about 60% of the cost of communal weekday schools; 50% of congregational and institutional weekday school costs; none of the costs of private instruction, nor of the Sunday schools; 80% of the parochial schools costs, and the entire cost of extension and professional education.

[25] This training stresses the linguistic element, especially Hebrew reading, to the detriment of all other elements in the Jewish curriculum. Cf. Part II, ch. X, "Content of Jewish Education."

schedule (schedule A) used in most Jewish schools,[26] costs at least $22.00 to $25.00 per child annually, in schools which are modern in equipment and staff. This cost is only partly paid by the parents of the pupils themselves. Out of every 100 pupils in Jewish weekday schools, 19 are taught "free" of charge, and 18 are "delinquent payers," that is, they are supposed to pay, but do not.[27] The remaining 63 pupils pay from 65 cents to $1.25 per month, with an average of about $1.00 per month or $12.00 per year.[27] In other words, the community pays an additional $1,444.00 for every 100 pupils in weekday schools,[28] without questioning whether all of these children should be getting the same kind of intensive training or not.

As a matter of fact, the experience of educators, both Jewish and non-Jewish,[29] has shown that it is extremely unwise to force the same kind of curriculum upon all children alike, without regard to their abilities or interests. In Jewish education it has been found that less than a third of the pupils remain in school beyond the third grade, and less than a sixth stay beyond the fourth grade.[30] Most children leave the Jewish school after they receive merely the rudiments of Jewish training. And yet all Jewish children are taught as if they were to remain in the Jewish school until the end of the course of study, and a great deal of time and money is devoted to teaching subjects which are merely "preparatory."[31] Would it not be a matter of wise economy, therefore, for the community to face these facts, and to realize that a distinction must be made between the majority of children for whom a basic curriculum must suffice and the capable minority who should be given as intensive a training as conditions will permit?[32] The community should seek to organize its *general* elementary and intermediate schools upon as nearly a "self-paying" basis as possible, at the same time sparing no expense in the instruction of its *special* intermediate classes.

---

[26] Cf. previous chapter, pp. 210-211.

[27] Cf. Table XVI.

[28] 37 pupils x $22.00 and 63 x $10.00.

[29] Cf. Ayres, L. P.: "Laggards in Our Schools."

[30] Cf. Chapter VIII. p. 253.

[31] Cf. Chapter X "Content of Jewish Education," pp. 312-313.

[32] These curricula are suggested in detail in Ch. X.

(A) "Self-Supporting" Elementary Schools

The question of self-pay or "self-support" has occupied much of the attention of leaders in Jewish education. "Self-support" means the organization of the Jewish schools so as to make it possible for the average parent to pay for the Jewish education of his children. The principle involved is, that as long as there are Jewish children who do not receive any Jewish instruction, and as long as there are those who cannot afford to pay for their Jewish schooling, the community has no right to spend its money upon those children who are in Jewish schools and who can afford to pay for their tuition themselves. Whatever funds the community has available for Jewish education should be spent upon teaching the children of the poor, and upon increasing the educational facilities so as to reach the children who do not receive any Jewish schooling whatever. The average Jewish parent should be encouraged and urged to pay for the religious tuition of his boys and girls. This principle has the sanction of centuries of dignified Jewish tradition behind it.[33]

The reorganization of Jewish elementary schools upon the basis of the four-times-a-week schedule,[34] would bring Jewish education nearer to this ideal of "self-support." At the same time, this schedule suffices for the needs of the average American Jewish child both in point of adequacy of training and in the matter of "free" time. By utilizing this schedule each teacher is enabled to teach four classes (in shifts) instead of two or three classes, as at present. The number of pupils per teacher would thereby be increased from 70 pupils[35] to about 100 pupils, and the cost per pupil would be proportionally reduced to 7/10 of the present cost, or from $22.00 to about $15.50 per year.[36]

---

[33] Cf. Part I, Chapter III, pp. 64-67.

[34] Cf. Schedule B, previous chapter, p. 211.

[35] Cf. Table XVII.

[36] This cost would be further reduced by letting some central communal agency, such as the Federation for the Support of Jewish Philanthropic Societies collect the community funds for Jewish education. Such centralization of community funds would eliminate much of the 24% of the cost which is at present spent on "collection, administration, interest on loans, etc.," (see Table XIII) necessitated by the costly and uncertain methods of obtaining funds from the community. In point of fact, the Federation for the Support of Jewish Philanthropic Societies has already set a precedent in this direction. It now (1918) collects funds from the community for some of the largest Jewish schools in this city, and gives to

But the present (1917-1918) costs of Jewish school work cannot serve as the sole criterion for organizing the finances of Jewish education. These costs are constantly rising; first, because of the general, rapid increase in all items of expenditure; and second, because the salaries prevailing in Jewish schools are grossly inadequate and are being constantly increased. The following is an analysis of the cost of each classroom in the Jewish weekday schools, as it is at present (1917-1918) and as it should be increased on the basis of rising costs:[37]

Item	Present (1917) Classroom Accommodating 70-75 Pupils	Proposed Classroom Accommodating 100-120 Pupils
Debt Service and Fixed Charges (Mortgage, Interest, etc.).......	$300	$375 (a)
Operation and Maintenance (Heat, Light, Repairs and Janitors)....	225	300
Teaching	750	900 (b)
Supervision	75	150 (c)
Administration (Secretarial Service, and General Supplies)...........	130	125 (d)
Collection and Sundry Outlay......	170	150 (e)
TOTAL	$1,650	$2,000

The total annual cost of a modern Jewish classroom, accommodating four classes with an enrollment of 100 to 120 pupils,

---

these schools the amount which they need to meet their budgetary obligations, beyond that which the schools themselves collect from tuition fees and other "self-paying" sources. In 1918 the sums which the Manhattan and Brooklyn Federations thus distributed to the Jewish schools amounted to over $150,000. The Federations will be able in the course of time to extend this phase of their work so as to include all the important Jewish schools in New York City. For fuller discussion, cf. Part I, Chapter 4; also "Jewish Teacher," May, 1917.

[37] (a) The cost of building a modern classroom is about $7,500. This at 5% interest would be $375. (b) For teachers' salaries cf. chapter IX, pp. 292-295. (c) The salaries paid to principals and school directors are being rapidly increased. The minimum for principals of small schools (500 pupils) should be $1,500 per year with a per pupil increase for larger schools. (d) The decrease in this item is due to the proposed elimination of much of the clerical and secretarial service due to elaborate and wasteful methods of collecting the community funds. (e) The cost of collecting tuition fees is about 10%. Of the 120 pupils per classroom, only 75 would pay, and the total income from this source would be $1,000 per room, costing $100 in collection.

would be $2,000, or $18 to $20 per pupil annually. Who is to pay for this instruction? Excluding the cost of "debt service and fixed charges," (that is, interest paid on mortgages)[38] the cost of instruction, supervision, etc., per pupil would be from $14 to $15. The present tuition fees paid by Jewish parents in the larger Jewish weekday schools, (the full fee amounting to $15 per year), would therefore suffice to pay for the instruction *of their own children.* The community would have to pay (1) for the interest on building mortgages; (2) for the "delinquent" payers who do not pay regularly; (3) for children who can pay only a partial sum; and (4) for those who are too poor to pay at all.

It was shown previously[39] that 37% of the pupils do not pay for themselves, and that the remaining 63% pay an average of $12.00 per year. In the future the community will probably have to provide for the tuition of forty pupils out of every hundred.[40] Assuming that present tuition fees are not to be increased,[41] the cost of instruction for every 100 pupils, which on the basis of four classes per teacher amounts to about $1,800, would be paid for as follows:

$720 (40%) obtained in tuition fees;
(from 60 pupils at an average of $12.00 per year)
$180 (10%) from other self-supporting sources;[42]
(synagogue, building rents, etc.), and
$900 (50%) contributed from central community funds.

---

[38] This cost, together with "operation and maintenance," should be charged to all activities of the school building, and not to the school alone.

[39] Cf. above p. 229, also Table XVII.

[40] That is, 25% of the pupils who are too poor to pay for themselves, and about 15% will continue as "delinquent payers." The present proportion of "free" cases is about 20%; but because of the difficulty of financial maintenance, many of the schools have been particularly "strict" in this matter, excluding some children who should have been admitted. Cf. Table XVI, also next Chapter, p. 242.

[41] The present range of tuition fees is from 50 cents to $1.50 per month, most of the larger schools having but two fees, 65 cents and $1.25 per month. In view of the increased costs of instruction and maintenance, it should be possible, however, to increase these fees to 75 cents and $1.50 per month.

[42] The present proportion of income from these sources is 10% (cf. Table XV). This proportion should continue about the same, because while the number of pupils will increase from 70 to 100, the cost per pupil will decrease from about $25 to $18 as follows: $\frac{10}{7} \times \frac{18}{25} = 1.02$

In other words, it should be possible to operate a community system of elementary Jewish schools, on a large scale, so that about half of the cost would come from "self-paying" sources, and the other half from central community funds. This would preserve the traditional Jewish spirit of "self-pay" in education, and yet permit the necessary Jewish schools to be organized on a stable financial basis.

(B) Intermediate Schools

Upon being graduated from the elementary schools, those pupils who remain in the Jewish school should be divided into two groups: (1) those who are to continue their training through a general vernacular curriculum; and (2) those who are to receive intensive Jewish training, with Hebrew as the medium. The first group should continue their schooling on the same four-times-a-week schedule as was suggested for the elementary schools, with approximately the same costs per pupil, and the same financial organization. The second group, consisting of pupils especially selected because of their abilities and interests, should be urged to come to Jewish school almost every day in the week, possibly five or six times during the week, for one and a half-hours' instruction each session.[43] Only two classes of these children should be given to a teacher, and they should be assigned to teachers who are specially equipped for this purpose. The cost of such instruction would be twice as much as for the other group, or about $35.00 per pupil annually. Assuming that the same amount could be obtained from tuition fees and other "self-paying" sources as in the elementary school, it would mean that the cost of 100 pupils in these intensive Hebrew classes, amounting annually to about $3,500.00 would be paid for as follows:

$720 (20%) from tuition fees;
(60 pupils at $12 per year average)
$180 (5%) from synagogue, etc; and
$2,600 (75%) from central community funds.

The Jewish community should be ready to spend willingly the sums needed for the education of this minority of capable chil-

[43] On Saturdays this schedule might be modified.

dren. In the last analysis, it is this "prophetic tenth" upon whom the task must fall of preserving Jewish culture in this country, and of continuing the Jews' conception of themselves as the "People of the Book."

(C) Secondary and Higher Education

It should be the aim of the Jewish community to prolong the religious education of its children beyond the elementary and intermediate school periods. At present but very, very little is done for Jewish adolescents.[44] Nevertheless, the Jews of New York are beginning to realize how important it is that they should keep the interest of their young men and young women. It should be a part of the community's program to provide regular instruction for at least 10% of the Jewish boys and girls who are studying in the public high schools of the city. Here, too, the distinction must be maintained between the special and the general courses. Because of the smaller classes which are made necessary in secondary education, the general courses would probably cost about $25 per pupil, and the intensive Hebrew courses about $50 per pupil annually. These sums must be supplied entirely by the community. The Jewish tradition of "self-pay" applies only to elementary education; secondary instruction was always supported by the community.

The same provisions hold true with regard to higher Jewish learning. Here the intensive Hebrew courses are represented by the *Rabbinic Seminaries* and the *Teachers' Institutes,* and the non-Hebrew courses are continued through the *School for Jewish Communal Work.* The present (1918) budget of all of the institutions for professional training amounts to less than $100,000 annually, but the community should be ready to contribute liberally to the development of these professional training schools for the future leaders of American Jewry.

(D) Extension Jewish Education

But while the community should put forth most earnest efforts toward building up such a system of Jewish schools, it must not be forgotten that the majority of Jewish children are not reached

---

[44] Cf. Part II, Chapter I. p. 156.

by the schools, and probably can not be reached in the near future. The indifference of parents, the sacrifice which Jewish education entails both of the time of the child and of the family budget, the lack of adequate school facilities, are all potent in keeping Jewish children out of the Jewish school. But is the community ready to say that the 75% of the Jewish children in New York who are unschooled shall have no share in the future of American Israel? Will even that instruction which is given to the children who attend Jewish schools be effective, if these children are surrounded by a much greater number who are not under the influence of Jewish education? The Jewish community of New York must, therefore, provide for the 225,000 children who are now out of the Jewish schools, and "extension," non-classroom education is the means proposed to meet this problem in part.[45]

The parents cannot be expected to pay for this form of training, and the community must therefore be ready to give it free of charge. Designed as it is to reach large numbers of children, its per capita cost must be as low as possible. The experiences of the Bureau of Jewish Education indicate that extension education, on a large scale, can be given to elementary school children (Circle of Jewish Children) and to adolescents (League of the Jewish Youth), at a cost of one dollar per pupil per year. If the community is to reach, through this form of education, one-fourth of its children, or 65,000 of the unschooled, and also 50,000 adolescents, it must be ready to spend over $115,000 annually for Jewish Extension Education.

Connected with extension education are the many activities which every modern Jewish school center conducts in the form of "neighborhood work." Club work, gymnasium, dancing and other recreational facilities, lectures and neighborhood meetings, special classes for adults, the celebration of festivals, both Jewish and American, are some of the activities through which Jewish school centers in New York attempt to reach both young and old in their vicinity. These activities cannot pay for themselves and the community must be ready to support them. It has been estimated [47] that in well conducted centers about one-fifth of the

---

[45] Cf. Part I, Chapter IV; also Part II, Chapters II and XI.

[47] From the experiences of such school centers as the Central Jewish Institute.

total budget should be spent on these neighborhood or "social service" activities.[48]

There are other forms of Jewish extension education, such as Zionist education and the Menorah movement,[49] which offer non-classroom Jewish education to large numbers of the Jewish youth. These and similar forms of Jewish extension education should receive the liberal support of the community, because whatever their merits may be pedagogically, they are creating a Jewish cultural environment without which the continuation of religious-national cultural life in this country is possible.

(E) Community Budget

It is difficult to propose a community budget for Jewish education in New York. But a comprehensive budget is essential, if the leaders of the community are to direct wisely the development of Jewish weekday education during the next decade.[50] Whatever its inadequacies may be, therefore, a community budget is here proposed on the basis of the above discussion:

Type	Pupils	Cost		Community Contribution	
		Per Pupil	Total	%	Amount
Elementary Schools	40,000	$18	$720,000	50	$360,000
Intermediate-Non-Hebrew	15,000	18	270,000	50	135,000
Intermediate-Hebrew	5,000	35	175,000	75	130,000
Secondary-Non-Hebrew	3,000	25	75,000	100	75,000
Secondary-Hebrew	1,000	50	50,000	100	50,000
Higher Education	400	250	100,000	100	100,000
Extension Education	115,000	1	115,000	100	115,000
Social Service Activities	......	...	245,000	...	245,000
Total	179,400	...	$1,750,000	69%	$1,210,000

This budget proposes that the community spend not much more money than it does at present upon Jewish education, but

[48] That is, a school center whose annual budget is $25,000 should spend about $5,000 for social service activities.

[49] Cf. Part I, Chapter III, pp. 86-91.

[50] Sunday schools are not included because they are supported by the particular congregations to which they are attached.

that the funds should be apportioned more effectively. Instead of spending a million and a quarter dollars almost wholly upon the uniform, wasteful training given to the 56,000 children at present receiving elementary weekday instruction, this money could be redistributed so as to provide elementary, intermediate and secondary weekday instruction to almost 65,000 children and adolescents, in accordance with a systematic, differentiated program. The million and a half dollars, which at present provide for eighty or ninety thousand children and youth through all forms of Jewish training, both intensive and extensive, could be redistributed so as to provide for *more than twice that number.* Toward this community budget about 70%, or a million and a quarter dollars, would have to be contributed from central community funds.

Of course, this budget looks at present (1918), like a "paper" scheme, far removed from the actualities in Jewish education. A decade of earnest effort will probably have to pass before the New York community will realize the need, and achieve the means for organizing its educational funds in such a fashion. And yet a beginning can be made in this direction now, by the Board of Jewish School Aid. The Board represents educational institutions controlling about $300,000 annually. These institutions give weekday instruction to 9,000 children and extension training to 30,000. The Board should aim toward a more judicious distribution of its funds, as follows:[51]

To Elementary Schools........	48%	$144,000	8,000 pupils
To Intermediate General Classes	15	45,000	2,500 "
To Intermediate Hebrew Classes	12	35,000	1,000 "
To Secondary General Classes	2	6,000	250 "
To Secondary Hebrew Classes.	3	10,000	200 "
To Extension Education.......	13	40,000	40,000 "
To Social Service Activities...	7	20,000	——
TOTAL....................	100%	$300,000	51,950 pupils

[51] This calculation is based upon the previous budget, but has been modified to meet present conditions.

For the Board of School Aid to attempt to force such reorganization upon its schools would be out of the question; for it would meet with most obstinate opposition. But the needs of the environment on the one hand, and the pressure of financial economy on the other, will, in the course of time, bring the Jews of New York to realize that some such budget as here proposed is the most economical and most effective distribution of Jewish educational funds.

Chapter VII

SCHOOL MANAGEMENT

(The Pupils and Their Treatment)

Perhaps the most significant change of attitude which distinguishes modern education from mediaeval education is the transfer of attention from the school *curriculum* to the *child* as the center of all educational activity. The child's needs and child nature are determining in ever increasing measure both the methods and the content of education. The modern teacher and the modern principal no longer treat the child as a "vessel" into which certain stored knowledge is to be poured; they are beginning to treat it rather as an individual, with needs of its own, and with distinctive traits of character, which must form both the starting point and the material for all educational effort. To this change of attitude both Democracy and Science have contributed: Democracy by insisting upon the rights of the individual, and Science by pointing out the necessity of studying individuals instead of discussing generalizations. "School management" as a subject deserving earnest attention and demanding a definite theory and technique, is the direct result of the growing recognition that the individual child is of paramount importance in education.

In the Jewish schools the change from mediaeval to modern attitudes has proceeded with abnormal rapidity. Several centuries of development separate the American Jewish school center from the Talmud Torah or the Cheder of Eastern Europe. This transformation took place within the life time of one generation, nay rather, within a dozen years, and so rapidly did it proceed, that both the modern school center and the mediaeval "house of child torture" exist side by side among the Jews of New York. To be sure, in some of the better Jewish schools, elaborate means have been developed for keeping in touch with the pupils as individuals; but the great majority of Jewish school principals still focus their attention upon the subject matter rather than upon the child.

School Population

Who are the pupils in the Jewish schools of New York? What is their economic and social status? What are their ages? In what proportions are the sexes represented? What are the relations of the pupils to the Jewish schools and what are the attitudes of the principals and the teachers towards them? How long do they stay in the Jewish school, and how do they progress through the grades? These are questions which have most important significance for the management of the schools, and need to be answered. Only fragmentary data are available, however, bearing upon these questions.

(A) Proportion of the Sexes

A number of interesting facts are revealed by a consideration of the following proportions of boys and girls in the Jewish schools of New York:[1]

In the Sunday schools 55% of the pupils are girls
In the Weekday schools 27% of the pupils are girls
In the Parochial schools 0% of the pupils are girls
In Private Instruction 15-20% of the pupils are girls[2]

It appears, therefore, that of 65,000 Jewish children who receive religious instruction, one-fourth are girls.[3] While this proportion may seem low, it is nevertheless a remarkable proof of the positive effects of the modern American environment upon Jewish education. Tradition confined the education of Jewish girls to the home. A knowledge of the customs and laws applying to the life of the family, familiarity with Jewish folk lore and folk song, and training as virtuous, industrious and loyal wives and mothers—these were the standards of female education among the Jews for many centuries. Of school learning there was none for the Jewish girl. It is a matter of common knowledge that while in the countries of Eastern Europe illiteracy was very low among Jewish men, it was very high among Jewish women. The rising status of woman in general, however, was bound to have its effect in changing this age-long tradition. Beginning with the twentieth century efforts were made in the various countries of Europe to provide some formal education

---

[1] Cf. Table XVIII.

[2] Estimated.

[3] Obtained by multiplying the proportions given, by the number of pupils in each type of instruction.

for Jewish girls. In this country, the increasing equalization of opportunity for American women, the American public school, economic conditions prevailing in the American city, (throwing as they do the responsibility upon the mother for supervising the education of her children), the spread of Jewish nationalism with the changes of attitude which it brought with it—have all been factors in aiding the Jews of New York to overcome, at least partially, the traditional neglect of the schooling of Jewish girls. The time is probably not far off when girls will be receiving Jewish religious instruction in equal proportion with boys. The present proportion of 25% is an encouraging indication in that direction.

There is marked differentiation, however, in the proportion of girls in the various types of Jewish schooling. In the Sunday schools more than half of the pupils are girls; in the Weekday schools they are about one-fourth of the register; but there is not one girl in the parochial schools. The fact that 55% of the pupils in the Sunday schools are girls can be accounted for by two causes: (1) the instruction given in the Sunday schools does not seem to attract boys so much as girls; it is proverbially "goody-goody" and "namby-pamby"; and (2) some Jewish parents are willing to send their girls to Sunday schools but insist upon more intensive training for their boys. At the opposite extreme from the Sunday Schools are the Jewish parochial schools, which have adhered unyieldingly to the traditional custom with regard to female education. Unlike the Catholic parochial schools, they have thus far made no allowance whatever for the schooling of girls. The weekday schools, pursuing a middle course, are constantly providing more and more facilities for girls' education.[4]

(B) Economic and Social Status

The general opinion is that the wealthier classes of Jews, especially among the earlier German-Jewish and Portuguese-Jewish settlers, do not provide Jewish religious instruction for

---

[4] It may be pointed out in passing, that strange as it may appear, some of the most orthodox weekday schools permit coeducation. There are several schools in New York in which boys and girls are taught together. In most cases, however, it was brought about by the financial necessity of having large enough classes rather than by any pedagogic consideration.

their children as readily as do the middle and poorer classes of Jews in this city. This opinion is probably correct, although there is no evidence to prove it. On a previous occasion, it was pointed out[5] that the earlier Jewish settlers send their children to the Sunday schools, while the later arrivals from Eastern Europe support the weekday schools for the instruction of their children. The Sunday schools are themselves of two kinds. In the Congregational Sunday schools are found the children of the wealthier Jews who are members of the Reform temples; and in the "mission" Sabbath schools are taught the children of the poor.

The modern Talmud Torah has been gradually becoming a democratic institution, attended by the children of all classes. The economic status of the pupils depends of course upon the neighborhood in which the particular school is situated. On the average, it appears that four-fifths of the pupils in the Jewish Weekday Communal Schools (Talmud Torahs) are able to pay for themselves, either in full or in part, and about one-fifth are too poor to pay for themselves.[5a] A study of a thousand of these poor "free" cases[6] was made to determine the economic status of the families of these pupils. The typical family of the "free" child is composed of six to seven persons, of whom four are children under 16 years of age, that is, non-contributing. The yearly income of the family is $700 or about $2.25 a week for each person. The family pays $14.50 a month for rent, living in three or four small rooms. About 20% of these families are recipients of charity. These children come, therefore, from the homes of the really poor.[7] The proportion of "poor" in the Jewish schools is probably much higher than in the general Jewish population, and points to the fact that either because the stigma of charity still clings to the Talmud Torah, or because of considerations of convenience and "privacy," the middle classes and the wealthier Jews do not send their children to the weekday schools in the same proportions as do the poor. If they

---

[5] Cf. above p. 140, and p. 182.

[5a] Cf. Table XVI but also note 40 on p. 232.

[6] Selected at random from the Pupils' Record Cards, filed with the Bureau of Jewish Education.

[7] In the 1,000 families studied there were 99 persons incapacitated through illness, and 212 widows, that is, one family in every five was fatherless.

wish to give their children weekday religious training, they prefer the Cheder or employ private teachers.

This preference must be an important consideration in any community program for Jewish education. For a long time to come many children from well-to-do homes will continue to be instructed by private teachers. Instead of decrying this situation as wasteful and undemocratic, the community should develop a system of *supervised private teaching.* A central educational agency, such as the Board of Jewish School Aid, should maintain a corps of well trained private teachers, and should assign them to particular pupils. Jewish parents would in the course of time come to look to this agency for teachers, and would pay the tuition fees to it, instead of to the teachers directly. Supervisors should be appointed to help in planning and standardizing the work, and regular reports should be submitted by the teachers for that purpose. In this manner much of the present waste and chaos existing in Jewish private tutoring could be eliminated.

School Records

It would be very desirable to have more information concerning the economic and social status of the pupils than is now available. The difficulty lies in the fact that most Jewish schools in New York do not keep adequate records. This was found to be the case in school finances, and it applies equally to all the other questions pertaining to school management. Indeed the average Jewish school is still in the position of the small shopkeeper or tradesman, who does not need any "bookkeeping," because he keeps all his accounts in his head, or on a convenient scrap of paper. For, in reality, school records are educational bookkeeping with the school and the child as debtor and creditor. This conception is very different from the notion entertained by most teachers and school principals that school records are merely for the purpose of "statistics," to be in no way connected with the practical work of the classroom. It is no more possible for the school to meet its educational obligations properly without well-kept school records, than for the business establishment to conduct its affairs without an adequate set of books.

Important as records are in public education, they are even more necessary in Jewish schools. Jewish education is a voluntary system, and the interest and welfare of each child should be of even greater weight in it than in a system of compulsory attendance. "The price" of Jewish education is "eternal vigilance" on the part of the teachers and principals. Then, too, the fact that in the Jewish school the teacher must instruct more than one class, makes the attitude of the small shopkeeper particularly dangerous. There are too many "customers" to trust to memory. A simple yet adequate system of school records, covering all the significant questions, is therefore absolutely essential.

(A) Individual Records

Based upon the experience of the schools affiliated with the Bureau of Jewish Education, a uniform set of records is here proposed.[8] It outlines only the more permanent records and does not attempt to include the many intermediary and temporary records which every school principal must develop for himself in accordance with his peculiar needs.

The starting point in all school records is naturally the "*Teachers' Record Book*" (or Roll Book).[8a] With it as a basis, two sets of records should be kept: (1) individual records for keeping in touch with the individual pupils, and (2) general school or class records to obtain a "bird's-eye view" of the status of each class or of the school as a whole.

For records of individual pupils, the teacher should report at the end of each month on the "*Teachers' Monthly Class Report,*" the summary of information contained in his Record Book concerning attendance, progress, etc. This Report gives at a glance each pupil's standing for an entire term. From it the information should be copied at the end of each term, upon the "*Cumulative Pupil's Record Card.*" On this card, too, should be recorded the subjects of study in which the child either excels or is deficient, and also any extra-classroom activities in which it may have engaged. This is the child's permanent record, which, if properly kept, can give adequate information

[8] Cf. Appendix P; forms 1—6.

[8a] For forms see Appendix P.

concerning its entire life in the Jewish school. In the case of removal, this card should, if possible, be transferred with the child to the new school, so that the new principal need not start over again without knowledge of the child.[9]

(B) General Records—Attendance and Elimination

Besides the individual records, it is necessary that the principal be kept informed regularly concerning the status of his school as a whole. The two most significant indications of the wellbeing of the school are : (1) the regularity of attendance, and (2) the proportion of children who are "eliminated" or leave school. In order that the principal may watch closely these two "indicators," the teacher should fill out at the end of each week the *"Teachers' Weekly Attendance Report"* for each of his classes. From this Report the principal can summarize the daily attendance on the *"Principal's Daily Attendance Summary"* and also make out his *"Principal's Monthly Report,"* showing the regularity of attendance and the proportion of elimination for each class.

These are all of the essential records needed in the educational management of Jewish schools. Particular efforts should be made by such organizations as the Board of Jewish School Aid, the Hebrew Principals' Association, and the Bureau of Jewish Education, to make these records uniform for all the Jewish schools of New York. Some of the better schools are now using all or most of these records, and whatever information is available concerning the problems of attendance, elimination, etc., can be obtained only from these schools.

The problem of elimination or "leaving" is so serious in the Jewish schools that the whole of the next chapter will be devoted to it. As regards regularity of attendance, it is found that in the communal weekday schools the proportion of those present daily is 82% of the register.[11] Excluding the summer months, in which the attendance is very irregular, the proportion of attendance is as high as 86%. Considering that the Jews have no compulsory attendance system which can follow up truants, this figure compares favorably with that of the public schools of

[9] The "Cumulative Record Card" does not take the place of the "Pupil's Report Card," which most schools give to the pupils as a report to the parents.

[11] Cf. Table XIX.

New York, in which 91% of the register are reported present daily.[12]

The reasons for this comparatively regular attendance in the Jewish schools may be accounted for by the fact that those parents who pay for their children's tuition, insist upon their regular attendance in the school, whereas those who are taught gratis attend regularly lest they be deprived of this privilege. Moreover, just because attendance in the Jewish school is non-compulsory, those children who are likely to be truants, and would thereby lower the regularity of attendance, leave school altogether, and swell the ranks of the rapidly eliminated.

Some of the Jewish schools attempt to follow up truancy. The schools affiliated with the Bureau of Jewish Education, for example, require the teachers to report regularly whenever a pupil is absent twice in succession. The home of the pupil is visited the following day by a special investigator to notify the parents, and to determine the causes of absence. In this way many an incipient case of "lack of interest" or of "misunderstanding" is treated when it is still possible to deal with it adequately. There are few faults of management which so disorganize a school as failure to keep constant watch over the regularity of attendance.

School Discipline

The problem of attendance is but one of the many problems of school discipline. In its narrower sense, school discipline means the obeying of certain school regulations necessary for carrying on the work of the school. In its broader sense, however, it means the treatment of the pupils, the attitudes that are engendered in them, and the traits of character that are developed. Whatever may be our attitude toward the efficacy of formal ethical instruction, no amount of ethical teaching is so potent in developing child character as the proper treatment of pupils in the everyday school activities. More than the subjects taught, do the relations of teachers and principals to their pupils bear fruit in affiliating the children with the Jewish people, and in implant-

[12] Cf. Annual Report of Superintendent of Schools, N. Y., 1915, p. 22. In the N. Y. Evening Elementary Schools, the per cent. of average attendance is 71 per cent.

ing in them love and loyalty to its aspirations and to its ideals of life.

In the Jewish schools the problem of discipline is in one way made easier than in public education, by the fact that the "incorrigibles" either leave, or may be dismissed. But it is rendered far more difficult than in the public schools by many circumstances. It is a voluntary system, unable to exercise compulsion, having neither the prestige nor the power of the public school. The teachers in many of the Jewish schools are "strangers" in the eyes of the American children. They are different in manner and in attitude, and have not even received the little training in classroom management which public school teachers usually are given. The principals are often no better fitted to impress the pupils. In too many schools the children are still treated as the "enemy" who must be controlled. The problem is further aggravated by the late afternoon hours which are left for Jewish instruction, when the children come tired and restless from the public schools, bringing with them the remnants of their energy and interest. The fact that each day there are several shifts of pupils adds to the tenseness and to the possibility of noise and confusion.

Discipline in the Jewish schools must therefore be based on love and interest, or else it becomes a veritable bug-bear. In the well-regulated schools there is an attachment between pupils and teachers, and a devotion to the school, which often surpass the conditions found in the ordinary public school. The treatment of the pupils is free and easy. There is but little of the "lock-step" order, and the children are encouraged to come into intimate contact with their teachers and principal. But where the basis is not that of love and interest, "discipline" is the all dominating problem, and the teacher's merit is judged very largely in terms of his "disciplinary" ability.

The most helpful attitude in school discipline is very much like that of the physician in treating the health of his patients. Discipline in the school, like health in the body, is at its best when it offers no conscious problems. Whenever anything goes wrong with the discipline of the school, it should be treated as "disease," needing careful diagnosis and specific treatment. Poor discipline may arise because of disorders in any one of the factors involved in the educational process. The *teacher* may be weak, unpleasant, impatient, tactless, irascible, unsympathetic, or uninterested in his work. His dress may be slovenly, or his manners provoking. He may not know his subject well, or may not take the trouble or time to prepare his work properly before coming to his class. The *pupil* may have defective eyesight or hearing, or decayed teeth; he may be suffering from a diseased throat or nose, or from nascent nervous disorders, or from general anaemia and malnutrition. The *course of study* may not be properly graded or well organized. It may be ill adapted to the age of the child; it may be monotonous, or unrelated to the child's interests. The *methods of teaching* may be at fault. They may not provide for sufficient self-activity on the part of the child; they may not have proper motivation, or they may lack concreteness. The *principal* of the school may be careless or inefficient, and the child may be accustomed to a low standard of behavior in the school outside of the classroom. The principal may be weak, and unable to deal properly with the child when appealed to by the teacher. The *school room* may be poorly lighted, heated or ventilated. The seats may be uncomfortable, the general appearance of the room untidy and inviting disrespect. The books and other school material may be cheap and unattractive. The child may hear the Jewish teacher and Jewish school disrespectfully spoken of by his *parents and friends*. He may have been made to feel that his Jewish school work is but of temporary and minor importance.

These are but a few of the elements involved in poor discipline. Who shall say that all of these causes can be treated alike? In every case of disciplinary trouble, any combination of these elements may be involved. Thus, a child may have defective eyesight, the teacher may be tactless and impatient, the principal weak, the home unsympathetic, the work too difficult, the methods uninteresting, and the school seats uncomfortable. Each case of "discipline" is a distinct variety of educational ailment. School discipline must therefore be approached from the professional viewpoint, and teachers and principals must realize that each case may be a combination of a great many educational disorders, some of them lying in the teachers or principals themselves, others outside of them. They must become educational diagnosticians. They must in the first place acquire the professional attitude of carefully diagnosing each case as to the particular educational ailments involved. Then, with constant, determined application, they may learn what particular remedies are best for particular combinations of misbehavior.

There is no royal road to good school discipline. Books on discipline will be helpful when read as general discussions rather than as special guides.[13] But the responsibility rests particularly upon each principal to create that atmosphere in his school, and to engender those attitudes which will attract the children and hold them to the Jewish school, and in consequence to Jewish life, on the basis of understanding and of love.

---

[13] Cf. Morehouse, F. M.: "Discipline of the School."

Perry, C. A.: "Management of a City School," also "Discipline as a School Problem."

Bagley, W.: "Classroom Management."

CHAPTER VIII

SCHOOL MANAGEMENT

(ELIMINATION AND RETARDATION)

The elementary schools of any nation, church or community, express the minimum cultural standards, the lowest educational requirements of that group. No community is able to maintain its cultural level and transmit its spiritual heritage to future generations, unless it is successful in giving at least a large proportion of its children that which it considers to be an elementary course of instruction. From this viewpoint it is of the utmost significance to know how effective are the Jewish schools of New York in giving their pupils the training represented by the elementary course of study. What proportion of the children who receive Jewish instruction complete the Jewish elementary curriculum? Unless the children stay long enough in the Jewish schools, and progress normally through the grades, they cannot ordinarily attain even this minimum. Here, then, are two ready measures of the effectiveness of the Jewish educational system in New York: the "holding" power of the schools, and the progress of the children through the grades.

The terms in education which technically apply to these two problems are *Elimination* and *Retardation.* "Eliminated" pupils are those who leave school before completing the prescribed course of study. "Retarded" children are those who are too old for their grade. The data available on elimination and retardation are insufficient,[1] but they shed some light upon two of the acutest problems in the management of the Jewish schools.

ELIMINATION

In the public schools of this country it has been estimated [2] that only 40% of the pupils complete the eight grades of the elementary schools, and that out of every 100 children who begin school, 30 leave before reaching their fourteenth birthday. If

[1] What is needed in this connection is a careful study of several thousand individual pupils, selected at random and watched over a period of several years, to learn why and at what point, Jewish children become retarded or leave the Jewish school. This it is not possible to do unless adequate Pupils' Cumulative Records are kept (cf. previous chapter).

[2] E. L. Thorndike, in the U. S. Bureau of Education, 1907, Bulletin No. 4, whole No. 379.

in the public schools, which exercise the right of compulsory attendance and provide adequate school facilities, the problem of the pupil who leaves before graduation is so aggravated, how much more must it be true of a system of education which is non-compulsory and inadequately organized! We should therefore expect that a very large proportion of pupils leave the Jewish schools before completing the elementary course of study.

This is actually the case.[3] For every

100 pupils in the first grade (year)
64 are in the second grade (year)
44 are in the third grade (year)
30 are in the fourth grade (year)
16 are in the fifth grade (year)
9 are in the sixth grade (year)
3 are in the seventh grade (year)

In other words, for every hundred children who begin their studies in the Jewish schools, the indications are that only *30% succeed in reaching the fourth grade and only 3% the last or seventh grade.*[4] Most of the children enter school when they are seven to ten years old, and the largest "drops" occur when the children are 12 and 13 years old.[5]

These figures are suggestive. They indicate to what extent the Jews of New York have been able to provide for the religious instruction of their children. It was shown previously that out of the 275,000 Jewish children of school age in New York City,

---

[3] Cf. Table XX—A.

[4] Care should be taken against assuming this statement as a definite conclusion. While the difference in the numbers of pupils in the various grades is due chiefly to *elimination* and *retardation*, another factor should also be considered, technically known as the factor of *population*. (Cf. Ayres: "Laggards in Our Schools"). The number of children who enter the Jewish schools is not the same each year, and consequently it would be more accurate to compare the register of the seventh grade with the register of the first grade *seven years ago*, than with the register of the *present* first grade. But in the Jewish schools it is not possible to determine or even to estimate this difference, because the basis used in estimating the "entering group" in public education does not apply to Jewish education, since only a small proportion of all Jewish children are reached by the Jewish schools. Accurately speaking, the figures quoted above indicate only grade population.

[5] Cf. Table XX—B. These statements are based upon information obtained from five of the largest weekday schools. In the smaller Jewish schools the elimination must be considerably larger.

ELIMINATION OF PUPILS FROM THE JEWISH SCHOOLS
(Showing Comparison with the Public Schools)

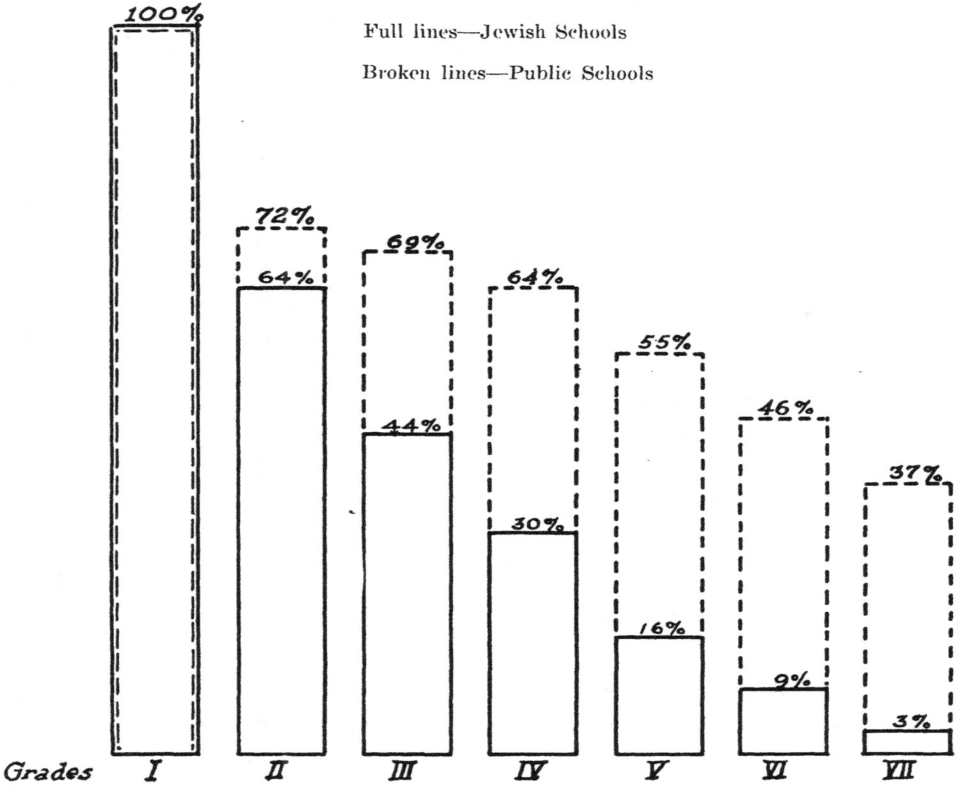

Full lines—Jewish Schools

Broken lines—Public Schools

100%
72%
64%
69%
44%
64%
30%
55%
16%
46%
9%
37%
3%

Grades I II III IV V VI VII

65,000, or about 24%, receive Jewish instruction *at any one time.* But evidently a much larger proportion of the 275,000 children receive instruction during *some* period of their lives. Since the average pupil stays in the Jewish school system about three years,[6] it is estimated that about 125,000 of the Jewish children now of school age (1918) have received or will, at some time or other, receive Jewish instruction.[7] In other words, almost one-half (45%) of all the Jewish children of school age receive Jewish instruction at some period. More than two-thirds of the Jewish boys (68%) and about one-fifth of the Jewish girls (21%) are at some time or other given Jewish instruction.[8] This instruction lasts about three years, and the training given is equivalent to the work of first two grades in the Jewish school.

Two to three years of schooling, given after public school hours, a few hours each week, is certainly not a sufficient educational basis for preserving the cultural heritage of a people. And yet, if at least this minimum of education were properly organized, and if the facilities in Jewish education were made more attractive and more adequate, the present desire for instruction evinced by Jewish parents, particularly in the education of their boys, could form the beginning of a comprehensive and potent Jewish educational system in this city. The difficulty, however, is that the Jewish community as a whole is doing very little to stimulate the individual Jewish parents in their desire for Jewish instruction. Further consideration of the problem of elimination shows that disorganization and lack of educational facilities are in large measure responsible for the brevity of the stay of pupils in the Jewish schools.

---

[6] Only 44% complete the second grade or the second year's work. But as there is doubtless a good deal of "repeating" in the first grade of the Jewish schools, due to removals and other causes, the average pupil probably stays in the Jewish school about three years.

[7] This estimate is based upon the assumption that the normal school life of the child is from 6 to 7 years. Since the average Jewish pupil spends only three of these years in the Jewish school, the present facilities in Jewish education actually reach during the six school years twice the number of children whom they accommodate at any one time. In other words, out of the 275,000 children, twice 65,000, or 130,000, have received or will receive Jewish instruction at some time or other.

[8] Of the 125,000 children taught, one-fourth, or about 30,000, are girls, (Cf. previous chapter, p. 240) and about 95,000 are boys. Assuming that of the 275,000 children of school age one-half or about 138,000 are boys, and one-half are girls, the proportion of girls who receive some form of Jewish instruction would be 21%, and the proportion of boys 68%.

Shifting School Population

Much of the apparent elimination, or "leaving" in the Jewish schools of New York City, is due to change of residence. Many pupils leave school not because they desire to discontinue their studies, but because they move out of the neighborhood of that school. Owing to the present decentralized and uncoördinated condition of Jewish education in this city, no transfer system exists among the Jewish schools, so that it is not possible to tell whether the pupil who leaves one school attends another, near his new residence, or not. In many instances the child is compelled to discontinue his studies because there is no suitable Jewish school nearby.

To learn the extent of this shifting of the school population, a study was made of the attendance reports of ten Jewish weekday schools over a period of two years (July 1916-1918).[9] It appears that during these two years the larger Jewish schools lost about 6.3% of their register every month, that is to say, that 65%-70% of the registers in these Jewish schools change every year.[10] In other words, if the schools start with 100 pupils, they must admit 70 pupils more during the year, in order that there may be 100 pupils left at the end of the year.[11] Some of the 70 pupils who leave, enter other schools, but many discontinue their studies entirely.

This process of "admission and leaving" is a constant one. New pupils are enrolled and old pupils leave practically every day of the school year. The admission of pupils is somewhat

---

[9] Cf. Table XXI. The monthly attendance reports were obtained from 5 boys' schools, 4 girls' schools and 1 mixed school, situated in various parts of the city. These monthly reports are sent regularly to the Bureau of Jewish Education, and because they are needed for purposes of collecting tuition fees, are as reliable as any that can be obtained. To the initial register of each month were added those who were admitted during that month, and the monthly proportion of children who left was calculated upon this *total* register.

[10] Allowance is made for the fact that the first year (1916-1917) included some of the months during which the epidemic of infantile paralysis raged in New York. This factor was probably not so great as one would expect, however, because pupils who left during the period of the epidemic were counted as "*temporarily discontinued*" and not as "*left.*"

[11] Under *ideal* conditions pupils would leave only through graduation, and a school having seven grades would lose approximately one-seventh, 14%, of its register each year.

more periodic than the elimination, two months being particularly set aside for the purpose of admitting new pupils; the months of May and November. But as regards elimination, the "exodus" is unceasing. It is particularly aggravated during the summer months, when the pupils leave school "temporarily," for their summer vacation; and, once gone, many of them never return.

The extent to which the school population shifts yearly varies among the different schools from as low as 40% to over 100% of the register during the year.[12] The prestige of each school and the number of years it has operated in its particular neighborhood, seem to affect the rate of elimination. The sex of the pupils also has a marked effect upon the rate of leaving, the proportion being considerably higher among girls than it is among boys.[13] But there are doubtless many other factors of school management which determine the proportion of elimination. Some of these will be discussed presently.

Length of Stay of Pupils

Before analyzing the causes of elimination, however, one more fact must be considered in order that the seriousness of the situation be appreciated. If the pupils who leave the Jewish schools were to do so only after staying in the school for a number of years, then the large proportion of yearly elimination would not necessarily mean the lack of educative influence upon those children. In other words, if the 70 pupils out of every hundred who disappear yearly, were to leave after several years of attendance, the school would still be in a position to give them a certain amount of definite training. The significant question is, therefore, how long do the pupils stay in each school before they leave?

[12] Cf. Table XXII. The figures in that table are for a period of one year.

[13] This is probably due to the fact pointed out in the previous chapter, namely, that Jewish parents still do not pay so much attention to the education of their girls as they do to that of their boys. But it is in part also due to the fact that the particular girls' schools studied had been undergoing more reorganization during the past two years than did the boys' schools. The greater elimination in the case of girls is just the opposite of the conditions prevailing in the public schools, where the proportion of elimination is larger among the boys than among the girls. Cf. Ayres: "Laggards in Our Schools," pp. 150-158.

From a study of the pupils who left ten Jewish weekday schools during the year 1916-1917,[14] it appears that the *average length of stay of pupils in any one Jewish school, is 8 months. Three-fifths of the pupils, or 61.5%, stay less than one year; and 90.3% stay less than three years.* In other words, out of the 70% of the children who leave the Jewish schools each year:

42 stayed in that school less than one year,
14 stayed from one to two years,
7 stayed from two to three years,
4 stayed from three to four years,
2 stayed from four to five years, and
1 stayed more than five years.

This does not mean that these children do not get instruction elsewhere, after they leave the particular school which they are attending. But it does indicate that the shifting of population in the Jewish schools is enormous. Coupled with the low proportion of pupils in the higher grades,[15] these facts show what havoc the large proportion of elimination plays in the instruction and management of the Jewish schools.

Causes of Elimination

What are the causes of this distressing "exodus" which goes on in Jewish schools continuously? The fundamental causes are (1) the lack of power to compel attendance, as in the case of the public schools, (2) the decentralization and chaos prevailing in Jewish education, and (3) insufficiency in school facilities for those who desire Jewish training for their children. What are the more *specific causes* which prompt children to leave the schools? The task of determining these causes is a very elusive one, and the difficulties in making an accurate study of this sort are manifold. Chief among these difficulties is the evident fact

[14] Cf. Table XXIII. The facts were obtained from the duplicate copies of the Pupils' Record Cards which are kept in the office of the Bureau of Jewish Education. They represent the conditions in 5 boys' schools, 4 girls' schools and 1 mixed school, including 2866 cases. The length of time was calculated from the date of the child's admission to the school to the date of its final leaving. Of the 2866 cases studied, there were 264, or 9.2%, who left school and were readmitted, and then left again. In these cases, the date of final leaving was taken.

[15] Cf. above p. 251.

ELIMINATION OF PUPILS FROM THE JEWISH SCHOOLS

(Showing the Annual Change of School Register)

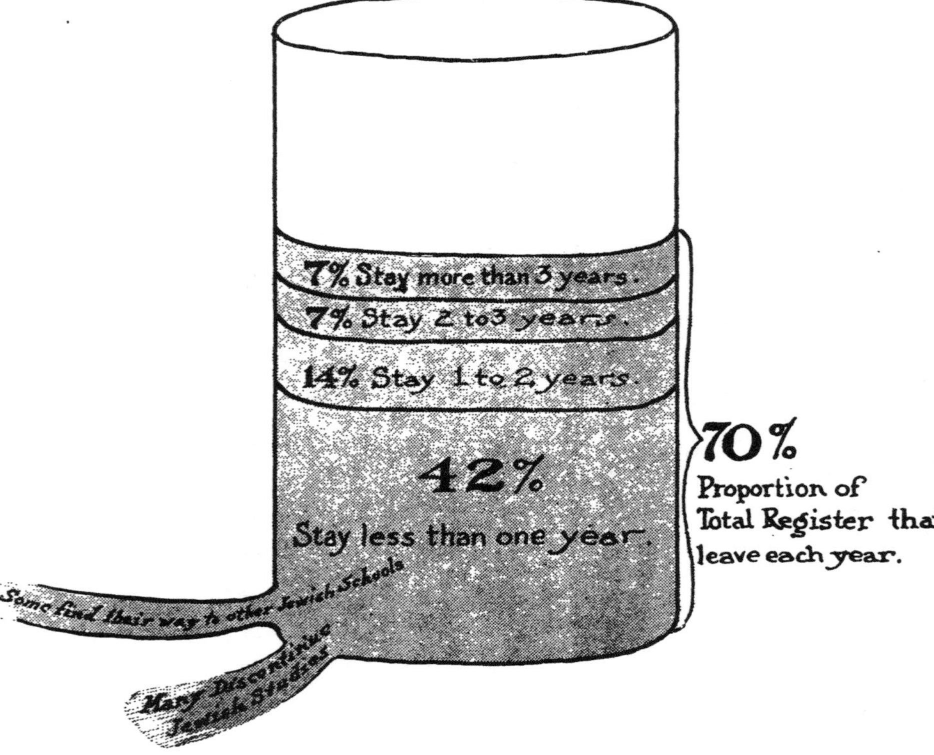

that the *reported* causes are not always *real* causes. Yet some definite information concerning causes for elimination is needed, and in spite of the elusiveness of the undertaking, an analysis was made of 1,140 cases of children [16] who were eliminated in four Jewish weekday schools (two schools in Harlem and two on the East Side). Only the *apparent* causes of elimination are given, that is, the causes as reported by parents and investigators.

The chief apparent causes of elimination in the Jewish school are: (1) *inability or unwillingness to pay tuition fees,* reported in the case of 22.9% of the children who leave; (2) *removal without transfer,* accounting for 21.4%; and (3) *lack of follow-up methods* [17] representing 16.2% of the cases and (4) the various statements of *"dissatisfaction":* with methods, subjects, progress, class, grade or teacher, account for 16.1% of the elimination. These four reasons: inability to pay tuition fees, removal without transfer, lack of "following up," and dissatisfaction with the school, account for over 76% of the children who leave the Jewish schools. It is probable that if the real reasons were known, these four causes would account for even a larger proportion of the elimination in the Jewish schools.[18] Any attempt, therefore, to reduce the amount of elimination in the Jewish schools must deal directly with these four causes.

Retardation

The solution of the problem of elimination is so intimately connected with that of retardation that they cannot be considered apart from each other. The constant shifting of school population has a very discouraging effect upon the progress of the pupils. Slow progress or "retardation" in the public schools is usually caused by one of two factors. A child may be retarded

[16] Cf. Table XXI. These cases were selected at random from the records of the Bureau of Jewish Education. When a pupil is reported as "left" by one of the schools affiliated with the Bureau, either the collector who collects the tuition fees, or a special investigator, is sent to determine as accurately as possible the reason for the child's leaving the school. This reason is then reported by the investigator on the "collection slip" of the child, and put on file.

[17] As indicated by those who "left temporarily and did not return."

[18] "Indifference" of parents, or of children; "Receiving other instruction"; and similar reported reasons, could in all probability be traced back to one of the above four causes.

either because it entered school late, or else because it failed to be promoted from one grade to another. Since the public schools of New York have a uniform curriculum and an adequate transfer system, the shifting of school population is but a minor factor as regards the progress of pupils in these schools. The Jewish schools, however, have neither a transfer system nor a uniform course of study, so that change of residence plays veritable havoc in retarding the progress of Jewish school children. Over and over again they must start, practically every time they move out of the neighborhood of one school to enter another. The facts available show to what extent this condition hampers the progress of children in the Jewish schools:

A study of the ages and grades of the pupils in five of the largest weekday schools[19] revealed the fact that there exists a very wide *variability* of ages in the grades of the Jewish schools. The pupils doing the work of the same grade are sometimes as much as seven or eight years apart in age. Particularly is this true in the first grade, where children who are five years old, and lads of twelve or thirteen years, are found doing beginners' work together. There are but few special ungraded classes for older pupils, so that children many years apart in age are sometimes taught together. This situation is not much better in the higher grades; and if it is true in the largest schools, how much

---

[19] Cf. "*Age-Grade Table*" (Table XXIV). All of the schools studied were Boys' Schools. The table shows the age and grade distribution of over three thousand pupils. The grades are here given in terms of years, because in some of the schools there are *two* "terms" to the years, and in some three. The Age Grade Table should be read as follows: The schools report that in Grade 1, there are 4 pupils who are between 5 and 6 years old, 118 pupils who are between 6 and 7 years old, etc. The horizontal lines show from what age to what age the children are of "normal age," or "under age" and "over age" for that grade. Thus in Grade II there are 4 children under age, 440 of normal age, and 335 over age.

The "normal age" in Jewish schools is based on the assumption that a child should finish the seven-year curriculum of the Jewish weekday school before it is fifteen years old, and should not enter the first grade of the school until it is at least six years old. The normal range of ages is, therefore, three years in each grade. Thus, any child who is six, seven or eight years old and is doing the first year's work, is considered normal; similarly, a child who is seven, eight or nine years old in the second grade (or year), etc. A pupil who is below six years of age in the first grade is considered "under age," and if nine years of age or older is considered "over age" for the first grade. While not in all of the communal weekday schools do Grades I, II, etc., mean exactly the same in point of studies, they are nevertheless sufficiently similar to make the comparison valuable.

more must it be true of the many small Jewish schools where adequate grading is really not possible.

With regard to the children who are too old for their grades, the following figures are indicative:

Year (Grade)	Proportion of Pupils		
	Over-Age	Normal	Under-Age
I	.3%	61.4%	38.3%
II	.5	56.8	42.7
III	1.8	58.6	39.6
IV	2.8	54.9	42.3
V	1.5	72.3	26.2
VI	15.8	75.8	8.4
VII	31.3	68.7	....
Average	1.8%	60.3%	37.9%

It appears that *out of every hundred pupils, 60 are of normal age,* which means that they are in their proper grades, and that if they stay in school until they are 15 years of age, they will be able to finish the elementary school curriculum by normal progress through the grades. Of the remaining forty children, two are too young for their grades, and *38, or almost two-fifths, of all the children are too old for the grades in which they are at present,* that is, they will in all probability not be able to complete the elementary school curriculum, unless by special effort.[20]

Upon closer examination it is found that there is more retardation in the lower grades than in the higher ones. Whereas the average proportion of "over-age" children in the first four years of the Jewish school is 40%, it is less than 12% in the last three years. The reverse is true of the "under-age" children, their proportion increasing in the higher grades. This must mean either that the "over-age" children "skip" or make up grades, or else that they leave school. Since "skipping" or double promotion is not a large factor in the Jewish schools, it

[20] These figures are in remarkably close agreement with the figures reported for the public schools of the country, in which 57% of the boys and 60% of the girls are of normal age; and 38% of the boys and 32% of the girls are over age. Cf. Strayer, G. D.: "Age and Grade Census of Schools and Colleges," pp. 102-103.

RETARDATION IN JEWISH SCHOOLS
Showing Proportion of Retarded, Normal, and Accelerated Pupils in Each Grade

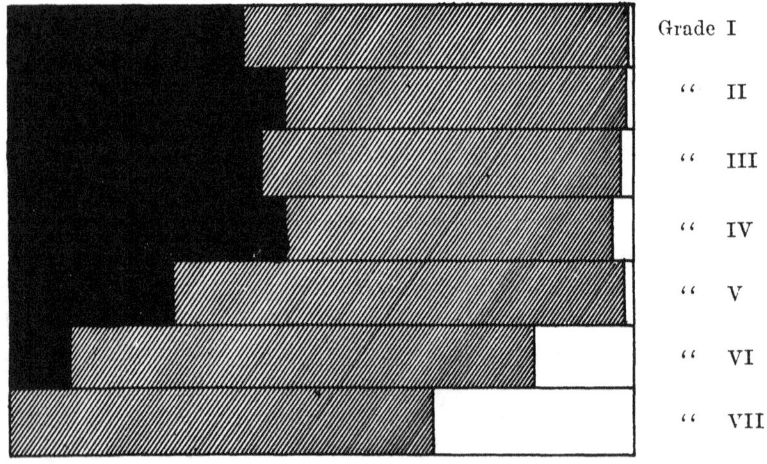

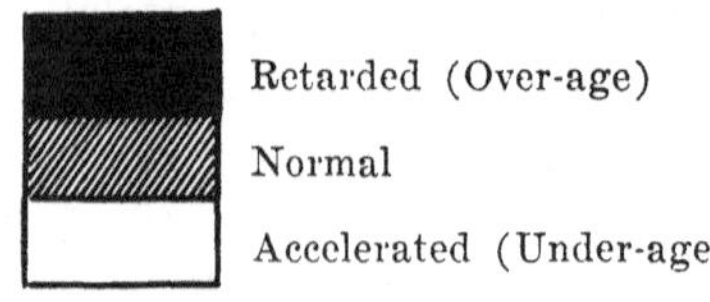

seems *that the children who are "over-age" do not continue in the schools so long as the normal and bright children do.*

Within the past decade the public school world has been greatly agitated by the fact that educators have found 33% of the children in the public schools to be over-age.[21] Coupled with the fact that many children do not complete the elementary course of study, this discovery of retarded children has led to significant educational reforms. Many of the recent efforts to reorganize the public schools, such as the movement on behalf of the junior high school, the introduction of vocational and prevocational training, the differentiation of the courses of study for the benefit of pupils of varied abilities, the introduction of more flexible grading systems, and similar efforts, were directly or indirectly stimulated by these facts of maladjustment of pupils in the public schools.

The figures cited above indicate that a similar state of affairs exists in the Jewish schools. That almost two-fifths (37.9%) of the children are too old for their grades, is evidence that the Jewish schools are not properly adjusted to the needs of many of the children. The over-age pupil is a problem not only to the school and to the teacher, but to the other children as well. He swells the ranks of those who leave the school early, and of those who cause many of the instructional and disciplinary problems. He becomes habituated to failure and self-depreciation, and carries these attitudes with him out of the school into whatever occupation he undertakes later. In a system which is not compulsory, as is the case with Jewish education, it is a reasonable inference that the boy who is too old for his grade, and who is consequently taught with others younger than himself, will not stay long in school; he is not so much interested in Jewish studies, and probably does not derive so much benefit from them, as does the normal child.

It is important, therefore, that the Jewish schools take cog-

[21] For a discussion of Retardation and Elimination, see especially: Ayres, L. P.: "Laggards in Our Schools," 1909; Thorndike, E. L.: "Elimination of Pupils from School," 1907; U. S. Bureau of Education, Bulletin No. 4, whole No. 379; Reports of Supt. of Schools of New York, 1905, and later reports; Keyes, C. H.: "Progress Through the Grades of the City Schools," 1911; Strayer, G. D.: "Age and Grade Census of Schools and Colleges," 1911, U. S. Bureau of Education, Bulletin No. 5, whole No. 451.

nizance of their obligations to the large proportion of retarded children in their classes. Special provisions should be made: (1) for the child who enters school at a later age than the average; (2) for the "slow" or dull child; and (3) for the exceptionally bright, "super-normal" pupil, whose retardation cannot be shown in terms of years, but who nevertheless is "kept back" in his studies by the mediocre average of the class.

Summary of Data on Retardation and Elimination

It may be well at this point to summarize briefly the tentative conclusions reached concerning retardation and elimination in the Jewish schools:

1. The pupils in any one grade of the Jewish schools *vary* greatly in their ages. In some of the grades there is a difference of seven or eight years between the youngest and the oldest pupils. This is much in excess of the normal range of ages, which in the Jewish schools should be not more than two or three years for any one grade.

2. Out of every 100 children in the Jewish schools, *38 are too old for their grades*, and will not in all probability be able to complete the elementary curriculum except by special effort.

3. The proportion of over-age children is much larger in the lower grades than in the higher ones, and the proportion of under-age children, much smaller. *The over-age children do not stay in school so long as the normal or under-age children.*

4. For every 100 pupils in Grade I, 44 children are in Grade III; 30 in Grade IV; and only 3 in Grade VII. *The great majority of Jewish children leave before completing the third grade in the elementary Jewish weekday school.*

5. *Out of 100 children on the register of the Jewish school, 70 are lost every year.* This elimination is continuous, and there is constant enrollment of new pupils to make up for those who leave.

6. Of the 70% of the children who leave each year, 42 stay less than one year in the particular school which they leave, 14 from one to two years, 7 from two to three years, and only 7 more than three years. *The average length of stay in any one school is 8 months.*

7. The chief causes for elimination in the Jewish schools are: (1) *unwillingness or inability to pay tuition fees,* (2) *removal without transfer,* (3) *failure to follow up the pupils who leave,* and (4) *dissatisfaction with the school.* These four causes account for over 76% of the children who leave the Jewish schools.

Some Suggestions for Reorganization

The striking conditions revealed by these facts have been aptly summarized by one of the Jewish school principals. "Our schools," he said, "are like street cars. They are always full, but never with the same people." The havoc caused by the constant disappearing of pupils after a short stay in one school, and the consequent necessity of enrolling new pupils to take their places, does more than anything else to disorganize the management of the Jewish schools. The constant "starting over again," the continuous combination of classes diminished in size, the necessity of devoting the best energies of the principal to obtaining new pupils,—all of these "patch-work" activities tend to demoralize the work of the principal and of the teachers. The large proportion of over-age children makes the task of classroom management particularly difficult. The work must necessarily remain on a low rudimentary level, because the great bulk of the children do not stay long enough to be taught more advanced studies. From the point of view of school management there are no problems more acute or more difficult than the problems of retardation and elimination. How shall the schools attempt to cope with these problems?

It must be repeated that the Jewish schools cannot exercise the power of compulsory attendance, and that even the public schools, which do exercise such power, have been called upon to deal with the problem of the retarded and the eliminated child. It is probably inherent in a voluntary educational system, such as Jewish education in this country, that there should be a certain amount of retardation and elimination. The Jewish parents cannot be compelled to send their children to the Jewish schools at a definite age, or to keep them there a definite number of years. For this reason the Jewish schools cannot do away entirely with these conditions. But they should exert themselves to the utmost to reduce their evil effects.

Naturally no ready remedy nor comprehensive panacea can be applied. For the treatment of elimination, the Jewish schools may be considered as a series of unconnected vessels containing a precious liquid which is constantly and almost inevitably leaking out. The leaks must be made as small as possible; piping must be provided so that the liquid from one vessel may flow into another instead of into the barren sands; and lastly, enough vessels must be constructed to make the piping effective. In terms of actual situation, this metaphoric approach translates itself into a number of concrete suggestions.

1. *Transfer System.* First and foremost in any attempt to cope with the problem of elimination must be the coördination of the existing Jewish schools so as to introduce a system of transferring pupils from one school to another upon change of residence. At present children leave school, when removing from one neighborhood to another, without being directed to any other school, and without even knowing what school in the new neighborhood it is possible for them to attend. While for a long time to come no transfer system will be able to reach the smaller Jewish schools, there should be no great obstacles in the way of organizing a transfer system among the larger weekday schools. The agencies upon which this task devolves are the Board of Jewish School Aid and the Hebrew Principals' Association. Some central agency, such as the Bureau of Jewish Education, should be in a position to do the necessary administrative work. This central agency should receive reports from every important Jewish school in the city as soon as one of the pupils moves out of the district of that school. In cases when the principal is notified of the child's removal before the child leaves the school, he should issue a *transfer card* addressed to the principal of the new school, requesting that the child be admitted. At the same time the new school should be notified of the expected arrival. Together with the child should be sent its Cumulative Record Card [22] from its old school. In cases where the child moves without notifying the school, the Bureau of Jewish Education should, upon receiving the report of removal, send an investigator to determine, if possible, the child's new residence and notify the nearest school in that vicinity of the new arrival. The school so

[22] See previous chapter, pp. 244-245.

notified should send one of its representatives, (one of the teachers or the principal's assistant), inviting the parent to send the child to the school.

Such a procedure would not only help greatly in removing one of the chief causes of elimination in the Jewish school, but it would also make it possible to determine more accurately how many children really discontinue their studies upon leaving any one Jewish school in the city. The number of removals in New York City yearly is very great. The New York public schools issue every year over 200,000 transfers to their pupils,[23] which means that one out of every three or four pupils changes his residence during the year. Among the Jewish pupils the rate of removal must be even greater than that; for as some one facetiously said: "If the general population of New York moves once in three years, then the Jews of New York must move three times in one year." Among the pupils in Jewish weekday schools, there must be from fifteen to twenty-five thousand removals yearly. This figure indicates how large and how urgent is the task of creating a transfer system for the Jewish schools. Besides helping to ameliorate the ill effects of elimination, an adequate transfer system would also bring about one of the very desirable forms of coördination among the Jewish schools of New York.

2. *More School Buildings.* A really effective transfer system is impossible, however, without an adequate number of Jewish school buildings situated where Jewish children are in most need of them. At present there are only ten Jewish buildings in New York, expressly built for school purposes.[24] It has been pointed out that at least twelve new school buildings are immediately needed, three in Manhattan, two in the Bronx and seven in Brooklyn. Every year several more buildings should be erected, if the Jews of the city are to deal successfully with the problem of providing adequate facilities for the large number of unschooled children and for those who change their residence.

3. *Differentiation between Elementary and Intermediate Instruction.* In the internal organization of the schools themselves a number of changes should be brought about in order to limit

---

[23] In 1914-1915 the New York elementary public schools issued 197,337 transfers. Cf. Report of Director of Bureau of Attendance, 1914-1915.

[24] Cf. p. 166.

the evil effects of elimination. The most fundamental of these changes is that of dividing the school into two departments: elementary and intermediate. More than two-thirds of the pupils discontinue their Jewish studies before completing the work of the third grade. The schools must face these facts squarely, and realize that they should reorganize their course of studies so that the majority of children, who receive only three years' instruction, shall be taught a basic curriculum, consisting of those things which are considered fundamental needs for preparing the children to live as intelligent and loyal American Jews. At present a great deal of time is devoted to the study of the Hebrew language, in the nature of "preparation" for more advanced studies. But since the more advanced literary or "content" studies [25] are never reached by the majority of Jewish children, the hours devoted to this "preparation" are for all practical purposes useless.

The Hebrew Principals' Association should work out a *minimum* curriculum for a three-year period of instruction, and advocate its use for the elementary departments of the weekday schools. This curriculum should contain the elements of Hebrew, History and Religion, which the Association considers to be essential.[26] Beyond this minimum curriculum there should be a differentiation of studies. Doubtless many pupils find the usual Hebrew course of studies, with its center of gravity in the study of a difficult and strange language, very irksome. In public education it has been suggested that much of the elimination and retardation is due to similar conditions of maladjustment of curriculum. Many of the children are not fitted for the mental grind which the Hebrew course of study imposes upon them. The Principals' Association should therefore outline two curricula for the *intermediate* department, both of them continuing the work beyond the elementary curriculum but differentiating between the majority, for whom a general course should be provided with English as the medium of instruction, and the capable minority, who should receive an intensive training in the sources of Judaism in the original.

4. *Ungraded Classes.* Another differentiation which is very

[25] Cf, Chapter X: "Content of Jewish Education."

[26] A tentative minimum curriculum is outlined in Chapter X.

much needed is that of providing for the pupils who cannot proceed with their regular classes. These pupils may be: (1) those who entered school at a later age than the average and are consequently too old for their grades; (2) those who are "backward" and lag behind the class after the first few weeks of the term; (3) those who left school temporarily because of illness or similar reasons, and consequently find it difficult to catch up with the work of the class. These "exceptional" pupils [27] should be put into small ungraded classes where they can be given a good deal of individual attention by specially capable teachers. The ungraded classes should be in the nature of "make up" classes, to enable these pupils to get back as quickly as possible to the classes to which they probably belong.

5. *Division of the School Year into Three Terms.* The beginning of the summer vacation in July necessitates a radical change in the management of the Jewish schools. Not only are the time-schedules changed, the children coming in the morning instead of in the afternoon, but at this time a number of children leave school temporarily for their summer vacations. Many of them never return,[28] either because of lack of adequate "follow up" methods by the principals, or because the temporary leave of absence from school causes a change of heart and a diminution of interest. Those who return find their class far ahead of them, and unless they are exceptionally capable, must lose a complete half year in their progress,—an event which is by no means helpful in keeping their interest or in stimulating them to remain in the Jewish school.

At present the school year is divided into two terms: a summer term lasting from March (Feast of Passover) to October (Feast of Succoth). This is the traditional custom in Jewish education. It seems, however, that American conditions demand a modification of this tradition, so that the Jewish school year may coincide more closely with the public school year. The entire year should be divided into three terms: a *winter* term, from the middle of

---

[27] Cf. Van Sickle, J. H.: "Provision for Exceptional Children in Public Schools," United States Bureau of Education, Bulletin No. 14, 1911.

[28] Cf. Table XXV. The fact that the summer months do not show a particularly high proportion of elimination is misleading because the children who leave for the summer vacation are reported as "temporarily discontinued" and not as "left."

September to the beginning of February (approximately 20 weeks); a spring term from the beginning of February to the end of June (approximately 20 weeks)[29] and a short summer term, from the middle of July to the middle of September (approximately 8 weeks). The summer vacation (two weeks) would then fall at the beginning of the summer term and the Succoth holiday at the end of it.[30]

The course of studies during the summer term should be organized to meet two requirements. It should, in the first place, permit of constant readjustment, through "make up" classes, "review" classes, and "rapid advance" classes. The purpose of these classes during the eight weeks should be to encourage each child to proceed at its own pace, so as to adjust it more advantageously to its proper grade. The second purpose of the summer term should be to organize special "vacation" classes for children who are not willing to do intensive work during the hot days of the summer, or who do not attend the Jewish school during the rest of the year, because of lack of time or for other reasons. These vacation classes should be taught the rudiments of Hebrew and Religion; but particular stress should be laid on stories, songs, and play. It should also be the time when Jewish "arts and crafts"[31] can be taught to boys and girls who have more time than they know how to spend profitably. Summer should be a busy time in the Jewish schools, because a great variety of activities can then be undertaken for which there is no time during the regular school year.

6. *Interest as a Basis of Instruction and School Management.* The differentiation of curricula, the introduction of ungraded classes, and the provision for a special summer term, are closely connected with the general problem of *interest,* which is even more pressing in the Jewish schools than in public education. The lack of interest has undoubtedly much to do with elimination

---

[29] In this term would be included a week's or ten days' vacation during the Feast of Passover.

[30] The chief difficulty in the execution of this plan would be the fact that once every three or four years the Jewish High Holidays fall late in September, which would necessitate rearranging the summer schedule for the week or two between opening of the public schools and the Jewish holidays (the Succoth vacation).

[31] Cf. Chapter XI, p. 346.

and retardation. Especially in a voluntary system of instruction is the interest of each individual pupil prerequisite for all efforts. Aside from the evident, fundamental need of interest in all education, there is the added necessity of obtaining the interest of the child in order to *keep it* within the Jewish school. All considerations of methods of instruction, of courses of study, and of questions of school management must be very largely affected by the need of keeping the interest of the pupils. Not that interest necessarily means "ease," and "sugar-coating." On the contrary, all worth-while interest is synonymous with effort.[32] But irksomeness, inattention, irregularity of attendance and poor progress on the part of the pupils, should be "danger signals" to be carefully watched by both teacher and principal. Extra-class activities (such as clubs, festivals, dramatizations) are sometimes very helpful in keeping the interest of pupils who find the regular class routine tiring. But these cannot and should not form the teacher's sole appeal to the child.

7. *Extension Education.* Through various extra-class activities the school can continue its influence even after the pupil has discontinued its regular studies. By organizing these non-classroom means of education into "Extension" educational organizations, such as the Circle of Jewish Children, the eliminated pupils can be kept close to the school environment and, in some instances, can be brought back to their regular studies. The school's obligations do not cease when the child, because of lack of interest or for other reasons, leaves the Jewish classroom. Extension education can be made to play an influential role in continuing the Jewish education of children who leave the Jewish schools.

8. *"Follow Up" Methods.* There is ample evidence to show that the Jewish school principals must bear at least part of the blame for the large proportion of elimination in their schools. The average principal deals not with individual children but with classes. He has no appreciation of the importance of details in regulating the daily welfare and progress of his pupils. The lack of adequate school records makes such "personal" treatment impossible in large schools. A full set of individual and

---

[32] Cf. Dewey, John: "Interest and Effort."

general records, as has been pointed out,[33] is therefore essential in any effort which the principal may make to lessen the evils of elimination in his school.

But records are only a means for work. They must be examined regularly, and the facts obtained from them should be used as a basis for communicating with parents, children and teachers. The principal should develop a system of regular correspondence, consisting of a series of "follow-up letters," which he should use freely. These letters should be used, even after the child officially leaves the school. Personal interviews should be encouraged on the part of parents and children. Home visiting should be frequent, not only by truancy investigators and collectors, who act as intermediary agents between the Home and the School, but as far as possible teachers too should be urged to visit the homes of their pupils. Only detailed personal attention to each pupil by means of a variety of such methods as here suggested, can cope with the baffling problem of elimination in Jewish schools.

9. *Parents' Associations.* Essential to the effective treatment of the individual pupils is the intelligent coöperation of the parents. The indifference of parents is probably the most difficult element in the problem of elimination. It expresses itself in "dissatisfaction" with the school, in "unwillingness to pay tuition fees," and it is most likely also a contributing factor in all other causes of elimination. It affects every effort to reorganize the work of the Jewish schools. The insistence of parents upon the teaching of "Ivri" (mechanical reading of prayers), their demand for long hours of instruction, their desire for the same methods of teaching as those by which they themselves were taught, are in a large measure at the root of the conditions which retard the development of Jewish education in this city. *Parent-Teacher Associations,* including not only the parents, but also the teachers, and if possible, the collectors of the schools, may do much to create good will and understanding on the part of the parents. The meetings held under the auspices of such an Association should encourage the discussion of matters of school routine by both parents and teachers. Wherever possible,

---

[33] pp. 243-245.

a *Visiting Committee of Parents* should be appointed to pay neighborly visits to the homes of the pupils who are irregular in attendance, or who have left the school. The attitude of such a Committee should be that every parent must be interested not only in his or her own children, but in all other children of the neighborhood, since the actions of one child influence the actions of its friends and playmates. These visits to the homes of their neighbors should therefore be undertaken by the parents because they indirectly affect the welfare of their own children. While the Visiting Committee cannot, of course, reach the homes of all the irregularly attending pupils, it can serve a very useful purpose, if wisely directed by the school principal.

10. *Community Coöperation.* The Parents' Associations of the various Jewish schools, banded together into a Central Parents' Association, should aim to bring to the attention of the entire community the problem of interesting indifferent parents. With the coöperation of the Board of Jewish School Aid a comprehensive campaign should be undertaken to interest Jewish parents in the Jewish schools. By means of pamphlets and lectures held under the auspices of the Parents' Association, by means of articles in the Jewish press, and through sermons from the pulpits, the message of Jewish education should be sent repeatedly and forcefully to all Jewish fathers and mothers who have children of school age.

There is no more important task before the Jews of this generation than to habituate Jewish parents to send their children to Jewish schools. The Jews of New York, by providing some form of Jewish instruction for almost one-half of their children (two-thirds of their boys), without any compulsion from the outside, and by spending upon such instruction voluntarily a million and a half dollars every year, have given proof of the strength of their desire to continue the religious-cultural heritage of their fathers. But this desire is expressed in a chaotic and uncoördinated manner. The community takes but little part in aiding and stimulating the impulses for Jewish education which prompt the individual father and mother. On the contrary, their desires are thwarted and made difficult of fulfillment because of lack of school buildings or systematic organization. The striking proportions of elimination and retardation in the Jewish schools are the expression of desire run amuck, of unguided impulses. Ours is the generation in which the centuries'-old desire for Jewish education among the Jewish masses must be harnessed and organized, for unless the leaders of the community are willing to undertake this work of coördination and systematization, the traditional desire may spend itself in a series of futile efforts.

Chapter IX

THE TEACHING STAFF

Jewish tradition endowed the position of the teacher with reverence. From Talmudic times until the recent present the title of teacher, master, or "rabbi," was the most honored title in the Jewish community. The sages of the Talmud placed the honor of the teacher above that of the father, even though "honor thy father and thy mother" constitutes one of the Ten Commandments. For, said they, "while the father is responsible for a man's present life, the teacher enables him to secure the life of eternity." Many Talmudic injunctions serve to illustrate the deep respect in which the teacher or rabbi was held in Jewish life. The fear of one's teacher was considered like the fear of God, and to show disrespect to the teacher was like blaspheming the Almighty. In the presence of his teacher, the pupil had to sit upright as if in the presence of a king; he was not to sit in his teacher's chair, nor was he to sit or to rise until his teacher's permission had been granted. The teachers were called the "town's guardians," the "Lights of Israel," the "Princes of the People." The traditional exaltation of the Jewish teacher persisted throughout the centuries.

But while reverence was copiously accorded to the teacher of adults and of advanced students, the elementary teacher did not share a like exalted social position. The occupation of the "Melamed Dardeke," or teacher of young children, was by no means an enviable one among the Jews. The reasons are evident. In a community where almost every male was literate, and at a time when special training in psychology and in the scientific treatment of child life was not required, no great respect was due to one who was qualified to teach the fundamentals only. Any married man of good character could become a teacher of young children. The elementary teacher had nothing to offer which the average Jew could not accomplish himself, if he but wished to do so. In consequence, the remuneration of the teacher of the elementary school, in terms both of social position and of material compensation, was very meagre. His status remained low from Talmudic times down to our own day, and many elementary Jewish teachers in the countries of Eastern Europe had to supplement their poor earnings by gifts of charity from the community funds or from private benefactors.

Changing Attitude Toward the Jewish Teacher

In America, the position of the elementary Jewish teacher is undergoing transition, just as are all other phases of Jewish life. The number of Jews qualified from the viewpoint of knowledge to teach even the elementary grades, is much smaller than it was in the countries of Europe. Moreover, there is general recognition of the need for special training in the work of the teacher. Modern standards in education have accustomed people to require of the teacher specialized knowledge of pedagogy and of child psychology and definite experience in classroom procedure. These factors tend to raise the status of the elementary Jewish teacher. On the other hand, the baneful indifference to Jewish life, prevalent in the new environment, places the position of the Jewish teacher low in the scale of professional attainment or of social recognition.

The position of the Jewish teacher in this country is, in a measure, an index to American Jewish life in general. No single occupation is so much of a touchstone to the progress which the Jews of America are making in the adjustment of their group life as is that of the Jewish teacher, whether he teaches young children, advanced students, or adults. The extent to which the Jews of America are willing to raise the dignity of the teaching occupation and are ready to make real efforts to enlist their ablest young men and young women as Jewish teachers, to that extent are they safeguarding the future of Jewish life in this country. Thus far the position of the Jewish teacher has not been such as to attract a sufficient number of able American Jewish young men and young women, because it has not been offering adequate rewards either economically or socially.

Number, Age and Sex of Persons Engaged in Jewish Teaching

There are in New York City from 1800 to 2000 persons occupied with Jewish teaching, as follows:[1]

500 teachers in the Chedarim and Private Schools
450 teachers in the Weekday Schools
400 teachers in the Sunday Schools
50 teachers in the Parochial Schools
500-750 Private Tutors.

Excluding the Sunday school teachers, for whom Jewish teaching is not a "profession," and excluding also a number of men and women, particularly among the private tutors, who have other vocations besides that of Jewish teaching, there are from 1,000-1,200 persons in New York whose profession is that of teaching Jewish children.

Most of the Jewish teachers are men. In fact the woman teacher is a comparatively recent phenomenon among the Jews. In some of the early Jewish private schools for girls in New York, women were found as teachers.[2] The Sunday schools, following the example of the Protestant Sunday schools, also freely employed women teachers. But in the weekday schools, particularly in the schools of the Eastern European Jews, there were no women teachers until within the last decade. The growing economic independence of women, the example of the American public school, and the spread of Jewish nationalism, have brought about a continuous increase in the proportion of

---

[1] Out of the 181 schools surveyed, definite information concerning the teaching staff was received from 135. In these 135 schools there were 795 teachers, of whom 263 were in Communal Weekday Schools; 141 in Congregational Weekday Schools; 20 in Institutional Weekday Schools; 54 in Parochial Schools; 302 in Congregational Sunday Schools; and 15 in Institutional Sunday Schools. The 46 schools concerning which no reliable information could be obtained on this point, are among the smallest of the schools surveyed. Estimating from 2 to 3 teachers as the average for these schools, we may say that there would be approximately 900 teachers in the Jewish schools of New York. To this number should be added 500 men who teach in the Chedarim of New York City, and from 500 to 700 individuals who are engaged in private Jewish tuition, in the homes of the children. These last figures were estimated upon the average judgments of six persons thoroughly acquainted with the situation in New York: (three school principals, and three workers in the Bureau of Jewish Education).

[2] Cf. Part I, p. 50.

women teachers in the Jewish weekday schools. The fact that in general women do not enter the Jewish teaching profession as a "life work," and in consequence have been drawing lower salaries than men, has also aided considerably in the introduction of women teachers.

At present 33% of the teaching staffs in the schools are women:[3]

In the Weekday schools 23% are women.
In the Sunday schools 55% are women.
In the Parochial schools 0% are women.

If, however, the Chedarim and private tutors be added, the proportion of women teachers in New York City is only 20%.[4] In other words only about one-fifth of the Jewish teachers are women. Compared to the public schools in which over 85% of the teaching staff is composed of women,[5] the difference is very striking. Yet it is wholly explicable in light of the traditional neglect of formal education for Jewish girls. On the contrary, it must have been a remarkably rapid transformation in the Jewish attitude toward the education of girls, which has made it possible for even the most orthodox schools in this city to employ, by this time, women teachers for their younger pupils. To be sure, the proportion of women teachers is as yet not even so large as the proportion of girl pupils in the Jewish schools;[6] but there seems hardly any doubt that the next decade will witness a large and desirable increase in the number of Jewish women as teachers of Jewish children.

Another very interesting change in the traditional attitude toward Jewish teachers concerns the *age* of the teacher. The

---

[3] Cf. Table XXVII.

[4] To the 257 women teaching in the 125 schools which reported on this item, another 50 should be added for those schools which did not report. There would thus be about 300 women teaching in the Jewish schools of New York. In practically none of the Chedarim are there women teachers; and it is estimated that there are only from 25 to 50 women engaged in private tuition, making a total of about 350 Jewish women in New York City who are engaged in religious instruction. In other words, approximately 20% of the persons engaged in Jewish teaching are women. But if Sunday school teachers be not included, only about 100, or 10% of the professional Jewish teachers are women.

[5] Cf. Annual Report City Supt. of Schools, N. Y. 1915-1916, pp. 28 and 30.

[6] Cf. Part II, Chap. 7, pp. 240-241.

average age of teachers in the Jewish schools of New York is from 20 to 25 years.[7] The average male teacher, both in the weekday schools and in the Sunday schools, is 24 years old, and the average female teacher in the weekday schools is 21 years old, while in the Sunday schools she is 22 years old. Most teachers in the Jewish schools are, therefore, young men and young women in the twenties.

Jewish tradition expected the teacher to be a staid and settled head of a family.[7a] He was required to be "married, and not young." The average Jewish teacher of the past, (like practically all the teachers in the present Chedarim), was doubtless much older than 24 years. In this country the example of the public school system, aided by the fact that many Jewish teachers use teaching as a "stepping stone" to other occupations, has caused *young* men and *young* women to be the teachers of American Jewish children.

The Work of the Jewish Teacher

The daily task of the Jewish teacher is a difficult one.[8] The average Jewish teacher teaches from 20 to 22 hours each week for 48 weeks during the year.[9] He must meet every day from two to three different classes and has in his charge from 70 to 75 pupils. He teaches his pupils in the afternoons and early evenings, after they have spent a long day in the public schools. He instructs them in subjects for which many of them see no immediate practical value outside of the Jewish school. The range of his program includes the Hebrew language, reading, writing and conversation; Jewish literature, especially the Bible; Jewish history; Jewish customs and institutions; and Jewish music.

---

[7] Over 200 teachers filled out the personal questionnaires sent to them (cf. appendix L). These teachers represent 41 of the most important schools of New York, of which 25 are weekday schools, 15 are Sunday schools, and 1 parochial school. The information contained in these questionnaires concerning the age and sex of the teachers, is tabulated in Table XXVIII. To be sure the questionnaires represent only a small proportion of the Jewish schools, but the fact here presented is probably typical, because while in many of the schools not reporting, the teachers are older than the median age, a good many smaller schools, (especially where the teaching is either voluntary or poorly paid) employ young men and young women in their 'teens.

[7a] Except perhaps in the case of teachers who instructed beginners or "alphabet" classes.

[8] Cf. Table XXIX.

[9] Some of them as many as 30 to 32 hours per week.

Compared with the work of the public school teacher, that of the Jewish teacher is certainly not the less difficult. In the first place, he has more children to teach; for while the average Jewish teacher instructs from 70 to 75 children daily, the average public school teacher instructs only 41 children.[10] Instead of meeting his children in one group, he has to adjust himself every day to two or three "shifts" of pupils. The children whom he meets have already given the best of their energies to the public school, and are consequently tired and less easily interested in school work. The subjects which he teaches, although not quite so varied as those of the public school, require an equal amount of preparation and an equal, if not greater, skill in presentation, for much of the time in the weekday school must be spent in teaching a strange and difficult language, Hebrew.

Aside from these daily duties, many of the Jewish teachers are expected by their principals to render a certain amount of volunteer service, such as conducting children's services, leading clubs, preparing for school entertainments and festival celebrations, coaching backward children, helping those who need special instruction for the Bar Mitzvaḥ (Initiation) ceremony, etc. Some of the teachers also engage in extra-school activities. These are either voluntary, or they are undertaken to supplement the insufficient salaries which the teachers receive from the schools.[11] Only a small proportion of the teachers in the Jewish weekday

[10] Cf. p. 22 of the 1915 report of the Superintendent of the New York City Board of Education.

[11] The questionnaires submitted to the Jewish teachers asked whether they had any other occupation besides that of Jewish school teaching. Of the 134 weekday teachers who filled out these questionnaires, the following reported as occupying themselves with extra-school work: (The others reported as having no other occupation, or else left this question unanswered).

REMUNERATIVE	VOLUNTARY
7 Private Tutors	24 Club Work
3 Public School Teachers	5 Other Social Service Work
2 Kindergarten Teachers	6 Students
1 High School Teachers	2 Literary Work
1 Teacher of Music	1 Sabbath School Teacher
4 Club Leaders	—
2 Cantors	38
1 Manager Hebrew Weekly Magazine	
1 Secretary of Several Societies	
1 Literary Work	
1 Technical Work	
1 Absentee Investigation Work	
—	
25	

schools, however, have any other *remunerative* occupation besides that of Jewish teaching. The great majority depend for their livelihood wholly upon the compensation which they receive from these schools.

Salaries of Jewish Teachers

What salaries are paid to Jewish teachers for the work they do? Of late the American public, both Jewish and non-Jewish, has awakened to the simple proposition that teaching is affected by the same economic laws of supply and demand that regulate all other forms of productive labor, and that in order to attract the best type of young men and women to the teaching profession, the schools must offer them a living wage commensurate with the salaries paid in other fields of endeavor. The public school teaching staffs have been depleted of young men, because the more ambitious and more able college graduates are not satisfied with the economic rewards offered to them by the schools. What is true of the tax-supported public schools, is true in even greater measure, of the Jewish schools of New York.[12]

The typical Jewish weekday school pays from $600 to $900 per year to its teachers.[13] The Sunday schools either have volunteer teaching, or else compensate their teachers at an average rate of $2 to $4 per session.[14]

a. Sunday School Salaries

More than two-fifths of the Jewish Sunday Schools of New York depend upon volunteer teachers for the instruction of their pupils. In some of these schools a few of the teachers are paid, while in others the *entire* teaching staff is composed of volunteers. Most of these volunteers are boys and girls in their 'teens, themselves but recent graduates of the Sunday Shools. They have neither the knowledge, maturity nor training required for teaching school children.

---

[12] It has not been possible to obtain complete and accurate data on the problem of salaries. Such data as are here presented are derived from: (1) Personal interviews with principals; (2) An examination of financial records; (3) Teachers' questionnaires; and (4) School questionnaires.

[13] Cf. Table XXX.

[14] Out of 37 Congregational Sunday schools in this city, 30 reported on this item. Of these, 17 have paid staffs and 13 depend upon volunteer teaching.

Whatever may be the merits or the demerits of volunteer teaching in the Protestant Sunday Schools, it must be recognized that the curriculum of the Jewish Sunday School, which is more difficult and more elaborate than that of the Protestant Sunday Schools, requires trained teachers. Individual cases there may be of high-minded men and women who are willing first to undertake an adequate course of training and then to offer their services on Sunday mornings gratis. But as a general rule such training must be rewarded, even for ideally minded young men and young women. Only in very rare instances can really effective and responsible work be expected from unpaid teachers. Many are deluded by the fact that the Sunday School teaching staffs are largely recruited from public school teachers, the assumption being that these are *ipso facto* equipped for Sunday School work. But this is obviously a very erroneous idea, for what is needed is not merely training in general pedagogy and in the treatment of children. The Jewish teacher must also be saturated with Jewish knowledge, and must be able to consecrate his or her main energies to the difficult work of preparing children for Jewish life in the American environment.

The volunteer teacher is the greatest drawback to the efforts that are being made toward establishing Jewish teaching as a socially respected profession. The volunteer can give but little, and the schools dare not ask him for more. The Jewish schools must definitely choose between *unpaid* teachers who are *untrained*, and the ones who are paid and trained. The better Sunday Schools of the city have definitely abandoned the plan of depending upon volunteer teaching. They pay from as little as one dollar to as much as $7.50 for each Sunday morning. The usual sum paid is from $2 to $3 per Sunday. Small as these stipends are, they should nevertheless suffice to require from the Jewish Sunday School teacher a minimum amount of definite training before permitting him or her to teach.[15]

B. Weekday School Salaries

But since Sunday School teaching must, in its very nature, be an avocation and not a profession, the consideration of salaries paid to Sunday School teachers is but of minor importance as

[15] See below p. 298.

compared with the question of salaries paid to the "professional" teachers in the weekday schools. How adequate is the compensation offered to the teachers in the Jewish weekday schools of New York? In 1917 the average Jewish weekday school paid from $600 to $900 per year to its teachers. During the past year (1917-1918), these salaries increased somewhat, so that the range of salaries in the typical school is now (1918) from $600 to about $1,000. The average teacher [16] in 1917 received $750 per year, or about $16 per week for 20 to 22 hours of service,[17] and while due to war conditions the salaries of teachers have been increased generally, the pre-war (1917) salaries serve as an index to the economic status of the Jewish teacher.

Upon the above salaries Jewish teachers were expected to live and to support those who depended upon them. One need not know very much concerning comparative scales of wages to realize that under constantly increasing costs of living, an average salary of $750 per year was bound to drive ambitious young men and young women away from Jewish teaching as an occupation. Miserably low as were the salaries in the public schools of this city, they were generous in comparison with the wages scale prevailing in Jewish schools. For every teaching hour the average Jewish teacher received a compensation of 75 cents, whereas the average teacher in the elementary grades of the public schools received (1915) approximately $1.15 per hour, or more than one and one-half times as much.[18] The

[16] The modal or most frequently found salary is here meant. Cf. Table XXXI. This table reduces the salaries of 151 teachers in 21 communal weekday schools, to a basis of "monthly salary per teaching hour," that is, the salary paid monthly for every teaching hour per week. Thus Table XXXI should be read as follows: One teacher teaches 5 hours per week and his monthly salary is $10, or $2 for each teaching hour; three teachers work 32 hours per week and receive $75 per month or $2.34 per teaching hour, etc.

[17] There has been an increase in 1918 of the average teacher's salary to probably $850 per year. But the difference between the 1917 and 1918 figures is not great, and the more accurate data of 1917 are therefore kept as the basis of discussion.

[18] Only the teachers of grades 1A to 6B were taken for comparison since they are more nearly similar to the grades of the elementary Jewish school. In the 1917-1918 budget of the Board of Education of New York City, it is stated that during the year 1916-1917, $12,939,535 were spent in paying the salaries of 11,605 grade teachers (1A through 6B). This means that the average school teacher in these grades receives annually about $1,115. The public school teacher in New York works 190 days during the year (cf. p.

lowest paid public school teacher received (1916-1917) $720 per year for about 950 hours of service, whereas the *average* Jewish teacher received $750 for about 1000 hours of service.[19] In other words, *the average Jewish teacher was paid no more per hour for his work than the lowest paid public school teacher in New York City.* The outcry raised in recent years against the insufficiency of the salaries paid in the public schools, brings out the more clearly how inadequate was the "laborer's hire" paid to Jewish teachers.

One of the fundamental needs in any program for the development of Jewish education in this country is therefore an adequate wage compensation for Jewish teachers. While, to be sure, Jewish teaching will never be able to attract on the score of tangible rewards alone, as compared to the possible openings in other professional and business fields, nevertheless Jewish teachers, idealistic though they may be expected to be, must be provided with a graded living wage, sufficient to satisfy their daily needs and the needs of those dependent upon them. Unless this is done it seems hardly possible to attract young men and young women to Jewish teaching as a profession.[19a]

The Training and Equipment of Jewish Teachers

The question of tangible compensation is so closely related to the professional equipment of the teacher that the two must be considered together. The economic law of prices holds true also in Jewish teaching: the more adequate the training the higher is likely to be the salary, and similarly, the better the salary the higher is the standard of professional preparation which it can command. There are various types of Jewish teachers and they differ widely in their professional equipment.

18, Report of Supt. of Schools, New York City, for 1915), five hours each day, or a total of 950 hours. At this rate, therefore, the average public school teacher receives as a compensation, approximately $1.17 for each hour of work. This difference is only partly due to the fact that the public school system has many teachers who have been in the system for a long time and are now receiving their maximum salary.

[19] 48 weeks at 20 to 22 hours per week.

[19a] A standard wage scale for teachers is discussed below, under "Program for raising the standard of Jewish teaching."

A. Types of Jewish Teachers

In general, there are three types of teachers in the Jewish schools of New York. The first type is the *"old fashioned" teacher or "melamed."* His education was obtained in a Yeshibah in Eastern Europe, where he was given an intensive training in the Talmud and the Codes. His knowledge of modern Hebrew literature, of Jewish history, and of general Jewish knowledge (the so-called "Science of Judaism"), is very meagre. He has had practically no general secular education, and his pedagogy is based wholly upon a long and bitter experience.

The second type is also an Eastern European product. It represents *the "maskil"* (enlightened) class, which arose in Eastern Europe, under the Haskallah (enlightenment) influences.[20] The typical teacher of this class came to this country in late adolescence or during early manhood. He knows Hebrew literature intimately, and is familiar with Talmudic literature, though not so thoroughly as is the teacher of the first type. His secular knowledge he obtained in a European school, or else by means of private study. In this country he strives hard to acquire more secular education, and to adjust himself to the American environment. His center of interest is in the revival of the Hebrew language and Hebrew literature.

The third type consists of younger men and women, who were *born or trained in this country,* and who received their secular training in the American public school system.[21] Most of them are high school graduates, many are college graduates, and some of them pursue post-graduate studies in the universities of the city. But while they are culturally well equipped, their Jewish knowledge is in most instances inadequate. The fundamentals of Jewish training they received in the Talmud Torahs or Hebrew schools, and this rudimentary training they attempted later to supplement by private study or by attending some higher Jewish school of learning, most frequently the Teachers' Institute of the Jewish Theological Seminary. A number of teachers of this type are students at the Rabbinic Seminaries, and they teach in Jewish schools partly as a means of gaining

---

[20] Cf. Part I. Chapter 2, pp. 36-37.

[21] Cf. Appendix Q: "Data on the Equipment of Jewish Teachers."

their livelihood and partly as valuable experience in preparation for their congregational duties.

These fully Americanized young men and young women have the advantage of knowing the American environment, and of being able to interpret it properly to the American Jewish child. They are the forerunners of the generations of Jewish teachers which American Jewry must raise from its own midst. Until recently the great waves of migration from Eastern Europe brought with them many Jewish teachers. But with the supply from Eastern Europe greatly diminished, much of the hope for continued Jewish life in this country rests upon the training of *American* young men and young women to undertake Jewish teaching as a profession. It is of great interest therefore to determine what are the institutions for the training of such Jewish teachers in this city.

B. Training Schools for Jewish Teachers

There are in New York City three training schools for Jewish teachers. By far the most important of these is the *Teachers' Institute of the Jewish Theological Seminary,* situated at 34 Stuyvesant Street, and headed by Professor M. M. Kaplan. Organized in 1909, it offers (1918) a three years' course to 125 young men and young women.[22] Prior to 1918 it graduated six classes, granting a total of 114 teachers' diplomas.

The requirements for admission to the Teachers' Institute are: (1) A high school diploma or equivalent; and (2) "a knowledge of Jewish subject matter equivalent to that obtained in a two years' course supplementary to the regular training given in the various Talmud Torah schools of this city." [23] Until recently, even these "minimum" requirements could not be strictly adhered to because of the lack of preparation on the part of those who applied for admission. The Institute has had to supplement the knowledge of its applicants by rather elementary courses in Hebrew, History, Religion, etc. It was thus a Jewish secondary school rather than a professional training school for teachers. Applicants were admitted either through entrance

[22] 52 young men and 73 young women.

[23] Cf. Register of the Teachers' Institute of the Jewish Theological Seminary 1917, p. 13.

examination, or else through certification from accredited Jewish schools. Of late the standard of its applicants has been rising perceptibly, as a result of the Secondary or High School Classes for boys and girls conducted by the Bureau of Jewish Education. These classes have been supplying the Institute with better equipped applicants than had come previously. Young men and young women, between the ages of 18 and 21, now enter the Institute after a five to seven-year course in the Talmud Torahs and Hebrew schools, supplemented by four years of instruction in the Jewish secondary classes.

The course of study at the Teachers' Institute extends over three years. Sessions are conducted evenings and Sundays, from eight to ten hours each week. Instruction during the first year is given in the *Hebrew language,* (grammar, reading and composition); in the *Bible; in History* and in *Religion.* In the second year the work in these subjects is continued, and *Modern Hebrew Literature* and *Pedagogy* are added. The work in Pedagogy consists of (1) "Methods of Teaching the various subjects of the curriculum, (Bible, Aggadah, Literary Selections, Grammar and Vocabulary)," and (2) "Visits to Classes."[24] In the last year an additional course in *Jewish Philosophy and Institutions* is offered. Special opportunities are afforded for the study of Rabbinic Literature and of Aramaic Grammar. No provision is made for *Practice Teaching,* since most of the students have full or part-time positions as teachers. The Teachers' Institute also provides instruction for a small group of men and women who are engaged in supervisory or administrative educational work. These more advanced students pursue special studies, selected by themselves, under the guidance of the principal and the faculty.

Mizrachi Institute: In 1917 another Teachers' Institute was opened by the Mizrachi Association of America. The *Mizrachi Institute,* under Dr. M. Waxman, is situated at 86 Orchard Street, and has (1918) an enrollment of thirty pupils. The pupils are all young boys ranging in age from thirteen to sixteen years. A four years' course of intensive training in Hebrew language and literature, (classic, mediaeval and modern) is to be provided for them. The aim of the new Institute is to train

---

[24] From manuscript curriculum of the Teachers' Institute.

teachers who: (1) shall have a thorough knowledge of literary and conversational Hebrew, (2) be familiar with the literary sources of Judaism in the original, and (3) combine the nationalist with the orthodox attitudes in Jewish life.

Yiddish Teachers' Institute (Lehrer-Seminar): A third training school for Jewish teachers was opened in 1918 by the Federation of Yiddishe Volks-Schulen (National Radical Schools), with Mr. Judah Kaufman as principal. It is situated at 293 East Broadway and is designed to prepare teachers for the Yiddishe Volks-Schulen (of which there are four in the city and about forty throughout the country). It offers (1918) a two years' course of instruction to about twenty-five Jewish working men and working women, who have a speaking and reading knowledge of Hebrew and of Yiddish and are conversant with the literatures of these two languages. Sessions are conducted in the evenings, and the subjects of instruction include: Natural Science, Social Sciences and General History, Pedagogy, Advanced Hebrew, Bible Criticism, Mishna, the History of Hebrew and of Yiddish Literature, Hebrew and Yiddish Philology, and Jewish Folk Songs. It is planned to extend the course in the future over a period of three or four years, so as to make it possible for the graduates of the Elementary Yiddishe Volks-Schulen to enter the "Lehrer-Seminar."

C.—Training of Teachers in Service

These training schools prepare the teachers for the Jewish schools of New York. Their yearly output of teachers is as yet far from satisfying the growing needs of the community, and the training which they impart does not suffice for meeting the difficult pedagogic tasks of teaching in a non-compulsory school system. But even such training as they do give is not standardized nor "followed up."

In the first place, there is no certification of Jewish teachers. No standard is set for the training which a teacher must have acquired before being permitted to instruct Jewish children. Every school follows its own sweet will in deciding upon what qualifications it shall require of its teaching staff. The Bureau of Jewish Education attempted to certify Jewish teachers,[25] but the effort was premature and was suspended after a brief trial.

Secondly, no provision is made for continuing the growth of Jewish teachers after graduation from the training schools. It is evident that the teacher who ceases to grow in knowledge and in educational outlook, must soon fall a victim to the spirit of inertia, the great bane of the teaching profession, which works to the detriment both of the pupils and of the educational system.

The most important and most practical method of stimulating the growth of classroom teachers is that of direct *supervision* and guidance by the school principals. But the help which most Jewish teachers now receive from their principals in terms of growth is negligible. Even those principals who take the trouble of visiting their classes more or less periodically, do so perfunctorily, as "inspectors," to check up the teachers' work. They do not consider it necessary to criticise their teachers for the purpose of increasing their efficiency, and no attempt is made to analyze the work observed. The only "criticism" given is in the nature of reprimand. The most important consideration is "discipline," and if the discipline is satisfactory all else is forgiven. This lack of intelligent supervision must be expected under present conditions, because the pedagogic training of most of the principals themselves is grossly inadequate.[26]

Besides the infrequent tours of inspection by the principal, the only other means of supervision used at present by Jewish school principals consists of *teachers' meetings.* These conferences are mostly of an administrative nature, dealing with the details of school routine. In but few instances are they devoted to anything but the submitting of attendance reports, assignment of schedules, explanation of records, etc. Only rarely is use made of the opportunity afforded by these gatherings to discuss more general and more vital problems—questions dealing with the curriculum, with methods of teaching and of school management, with the relation of the school to the home and to the community, and similar topics.

---

[25] Cf. Part I, Chapter 4, pp. 112-113.

[26] Cf. Part II, Chapter 4, pp. 202-205.

Nor are any of the other recognized aids to the growth of teachers available.[27] There is no provision for exchange of visits to classrooms; no "reading circles"; but little demonstration teaching; and no provision for teachers' participation in the making of the curriculum. No Sabbatical years or leaves of absence are granted to Jewish teachers for purposes of travel, education and self-improvement. With the exception of one or two general meetings conducted by the Hebrew Principals' Association and by the Agudath Hamorim, there have been no "institutes" of Jewish teachers in this city such as "the county teachers' institutes" in public education, which last from one day to two weeks and bring all the teachers in the vicinity together for purposes of discussion, study, inspiration and exchange of experiences. These various means of improving the teachers in service are essential for the development of the Jewish teaching profession, but they can come only with the greater systematization and co-ordination of the work of the Jewish schools.

D.—Teachers' Associations

The first spontaneous attempts to improve the professional status of Jewish teachers, economically and socially, have been in the nature of Teachers' Associations. There are (1918) four of these associations in New York City. The oldest of them, the *Hebrew Teachers' Union of Greater New York and Vicinity,* or as it is better known, the *"Agudath Hamorim,"* is composed of teachers of the Eastern European types,[28] and has an enrollment of 160 members. Its activities have been in the nature of a workers' union primarily to improve the economic condition of the Jewish teachers. It called together a convention of Jewish teachers, in 1912, and for a short time published an educational journal in Hebrew, the "Hed Hamoreh" (Echo of the Teacher). But its best known achievement is that of the fairly successful teachers' strike for higher wages, which it conducted in 1917. This strike resulted in the raising of the salaries in some of the larger weekday schools, and in setting a higher standard of teachers' salaries in general.

---

[27] Cf. Ruediger W. C.: "Agencies for Improvement of Teachers in Service."

[28] Cf. above p. 284.

The *Jewish Teachers' Association of New York* is composed of 75 members of the American type of teacher. It is a professional organization chiefly for study and self-improvement, and co-operates both with the Bureau of Jewish Education and with the Teachers' Institute of the Jewish Theological Seminary. It has been issuing, since 1916, the only Jewish educational journal published in English, "The Jewish Teacher."

The Sunday school teachers of the city were for a number of years banded together in the *Jewish Religious School Union.* This Union was organized and managed by the Eastern Council of Reform Rabbis. It brought together the teachers of the various Sunday schools of New York, at more or less regular intervals, to listen to lectures on Jewish History, the Bible, etc., and to observe "model lessons." Of late (1918) this organization has been inactive.

Very recently (1917) another teachers' association was formed known as *"Hamoriah."* It is connected with the Mizrachi organization and is composed in part of elements who were dissatisfied with the Hebrew Teachers' Union. It claims to represent the "national-orthodox" teachers, but its place and function, as a distinct organization, have not yet been fully determined. The "Hamoriah," too, is largely a workers' union, and its first public effort was to help the teachers in one of the Talmud Torahs of the city in their demand for better wages.

All of these teachers' associations carry on their work without any co-operation or understanding among them. There has been no attempt to hold general conferences of Jewish teachers or to combine efforts on any matter of general interest to the Jewish teachers of New York, either for economic, social, or professional purposes. The difference in training and experience has thus far proven an impassable barrier between the various types of teachers.

Program for Raising the Standard of Jewish Teaching

The problem of raising the standard of Jewish teaching and of improving the status of Jewish teachers, is a community problem. The teachers must not be alone in their efforts to uphold the dignity and increase the effectiveness of the Jewish teaching profession. There is a tendency among Jewish teachers, as there is among public school teachers, to organize themselves in the form of labor unions to demand their just dues. But the community cannot afford to look calmly upon the struggles which this tendency must bring in its train. It must meet the teachers more than half way, because to attract new teachers and to provide adequately for those who are now in the service, is among the most important communal tasks.

In the Jewish weekday schools of New York, from 75 to 100 teachers are needed every year, to replace those who leave, and to take care of new schools and new classes.[29] The Jewish training schools of the city have, in the past, been providing new teachers at the rate of nineteen teachers each year.[30] At best all the three training schools in New York can be expected at present to furnish only from 30 to 40 new teachers annually. The diminution in the supply of teachers from Eastern Europe makes these schools practically the only sources for obtaining Jewish teachers, not only for New York City, but in a measure, for the entire country as well.[31] With the increase in school facilities which will inevitably have to be made in the next decade, the Jews of New York face a grave, an almost paralyzing shortage of teachers. Even now appeals for teachers are sent to New York from Jewish communities throughout the country, stating that it is not possible to provide for the instruction of their children, because no Jewish teachers can be found to teach them. The Jewish community of New York is called upon to deal with this problem in a large way.

---

[29] There are no data available from which an accurate estimate can be made. In the New York Public Schools the annual "turn over," as indicated by the "nominations of new teachers," is 5%—10% of the entire staff each year. In the Jewish schools it is undoubtedly larger, because the length of service of the average teacher is a good deal less than in the public schools, and also because there is a constant removal of Jewish teachers to smaller towns in various parts of the country. The annual "turn over" in the Jewish schools is therefore probably at least from 15% to 20%.

[30] The only training school which has thus far (1918) graduated Jewish teachers, is the Teachers' Institute of the Jewish Theological Seminary.

[31] There are only three Jewish training schools outside of New York. These are Gratz College, Philadelphia, the Teachers' Institute of the Hebrew Union College of Cincinnati, and the Teachers' Institute in Boston. These schools can graduate no more than twenty to thirty teachers each year. The students of the Rabbinic Seminaries should be included, but they merely replace the student teachers who leave, and at best provide for only 15-20 teaching positions in the city.

A.—Standard Wage Scale for Teachers

The first requirement is to increase considerably the economic and social rewards of Jewish teaching. A scale of wages is needed for Jewish teachers, which should be standarized by the community and agreed to by all the important Jewish schools of New York. The young teacher should know at the outset what the economic prospects are upon which he may reckon when he enters the profession. Such a standard scale of wages must take into consideration a number of factors:

(1) The regulation of salaries in Jewish education depends upon the standard of salaries prevailing in similar professions. The profession most similar to that of the Jewish teacher is that of the *public school* teacher, and the wages prevailing in the Jewish schools will depend closely upon the salary schedule in vogue in the public schools.[32] Furthermore, both the public schools and the Jewish schools must compete with the commercial and professional fields for the services of young men and women; and while teaching must necessarily offer inducements other than financial, Jewish teachers must nevertheless be provided with a comfortable *living wage* for themselves and their families.

(2) A standardized salary scale should distinguish between *temporary and permanent* Jewish teachers. It has long been recognized that teaching, especially in the large American cities, is used by "ambitious" young men as a "stepping stone" to other professions. Particularly is this true of Jewish teaching. A considerable proportion of the men now teaching in the Jewish schools of New York are *preparing* for the rabbinate, medicine, dentistry, law, engineering, etc. These are not professional Jewish teachers and should be distinguished from those who are ready to devote their lives to Jewish teaching. Some of the young teachers are undergraduate *students* at college, who teach in the Jewish schools during afternoons and on Sundays, outside of their college hours. These student teachers are willing to teach at a comparatively low salary because it is one of the few possible occupations which permit them at the same time to continue their studies. Even after graduation from college, a

[32] At present (1918) the question of salaries in the public schools of New York is still unsettled, and any salary scale proposed for the Jewish schools must therefore be tentative.

period of trial extending over several years should be required to determine which teachers look to Jewish education as their permanent profession and which ones consider it as a temporary occupation, their attention and best energies being directed elsewhere. *Temporary* teaching licenses should be granted by a Community Board of Licenses[33] for the first three years at teaching beyond graduation from the training schools, and *permanent* licenses after this period of trial should be given to those who are willing to make Jewish teaching their profession.

(3) Another distinction which should be made in salaries is between the teachers of the elementary and of the intermediate grades. Particularly in the intensive Hebrew classes of the intermediate school is it necessary to have specially trained teachers who possess a thorough knowledge of the Hebrew language and of the literary sources of Judaism in the original. For such special training, special financial rewards should be offered. The salaries of elementary teachers can be kept within the limits of "self support," as previously explained:[34] but the salaries of intermediate teachers cannot be determined by this financial criterion.

With these considerations in mind the following schedule of salaries is proposed for the Jewish weekday schools of New York:[35]

A. Student Teachers (college undergraduates): $720 per year
B. Temporary License Teachers (3 years' trial): $900 per year
C. Permanent License Teachers:

Elementary: $1000 to $1300 per year in annual increases of $60.

Intermediate: $1200 to $1800 per year in annual increases of $100.

Such a graduated salary scale should be put into effect in the larger weekday schools by the Board of Jewish School Aid, with the co-operation of the Principals' Association and the various

[33] See below p. 295.

[34] See above pp. 230-232.

[35] This schedule is suggested of course on the present (1918) basis of the cost of living. Economic changes after the war may call for considerable changes in salaries.

Teachers' organizations.[36] In general, it provides for about 33 per cent. increase in the salaries of Jewish teachers,[37] regulated so as to bring about economic security and reward for special training and effort.

To ensure the maximum benefit from this standardized wage scale provision should be made for additional financial reward for special merit. While the proposed increase in teachers' salaries is on the basis of number of years of service, care should be taken against lack of stimulus. Able teachers should be stimulated to advance more rapidly than the regular yearly increase allotted to them. It is important that each principal be able to evaluate the efficiency of the work of his teachers, and reward special merit or marked improvement. The dangers of such a proposition lie in the possibility of prejudice on the part of the principal, and of a consequent sense of "injustice" on the part of the teachers. Yet such evaluation and reward take place constantly in the professional and the business worlds, and should prove possible also in the Jewish schools. To minimize the dangers inherent in personal evaluation, it is necessary, wherever possible, to substitute objective analysis for général opinion.[38]

The more ambitious men and women who would still deem the regular teaching salary insufficient, should find opportunity for additional service in the "neighborhood activities" conducted by modern school centers in the evenings, or else they will seek supervisory and administrative positions. One of the natural results in the carrying out of a standardized wage scale would be that more and more women would be introduced as teachers of the elementary grades in the Jewish schools. Very few Jewish women stay in the teaching service for many years, and reasons of economy would compel Jewish school principals to recruit the teaching staffs for the *elementary grades* from women and from young men. Such a tendency is highly desirable.

---

[36] As this book goes to press, the teachers and principals of the New York Talmud Torahs have undertaken the first step toward a uniform wage scale in conjunction with the Board of Jewish School Aid, without providing, however, for graduated annual increases or for distinction between elementary and intermediate teachers.

[37] The salary of the average elementary teachers would be raised from $720 to approximately $960 per year.

[38] For fuller discussion see below pp. 299-300, also Appendix R.

B. Teachers' Pensions and Insurance

If the Jewish community of New York is to deal justly with its teachers, it must go one step beyond the standard wage scale in assuring them economic security and consequent peace of mind. While the salaries proposed in the standard salary scale are much higher than those which are doled out to teachers at present, they cannot enable the teachers to save money so as to provide against chance misfortune for themselves or their families. The terrors of sickness and of old age are considerable factors in determining the attitude of the teacher toward his work, and in keeping many discreet young men from entering the teaching profession. To stabilize the financial income of Jewish teachers, a *pension system* should be established, based on *co-operative insurance*.[39] The pension system should provide for participation by the teachers on the one hand, and for contribution by the community on the other. The schools whose teachers are to be in the system, should set aside regularly a small fraction of the teachers' salaries for pension purposes. To this should be added considerably larger sums contributed by the community, and the administration of the combined funds should be in the hands of a *Committee on Pensions and Insurance* selected by the Board of Jewish School Aid together with the Hebrew Principals' Association and the Teachers' Organizations.

C. Certification of Teachers

The standardization of teachers' salaries will make it possible also to standardize the training and qualifications required from teachers before the community will permit them to teach its children. At present any one who deigns to undertake the work of Jewish teaching may do so, and because of the disorganized state of Jewish education is quite sure to find opportunity to shape the lives of Jewish children for good or for evil. It will hardly be possible to guarantee the effectiveness of Jewish teaching, however, or to raise the social status of Jewish teachers, unless the community finds some method of giving public recognition to those whom it deems qualified to teach in Jewish schools,

---

[39] For full discussion of teachers' pensions in public education, cf. Prosser, C. A.: "The Teacher and Old Age," and also the Seventh and Ninth Annual Reports of the Carnegie Foundation for the Advancement of Teaching.

and of publicly disapproving those whom it considers incompetent and unqualified. For the sake of the profession it is also necessary that the community distinguish between those who use Jewish teaching as a ''stepping stone'' and those who are ready to consecrate their lives to the service of the Jewish schools.

For the effective administration of the standard salary scale outlined above, it is necessary that a *Board of Certification* be organized to grant licenses to Jewish teachers. Before this Board should come the graduates of the Teachers' Training Schools. The Board should determine the standards of knowledge, pedagogic training, age and character qualifications which it wishes to demand from those who apply for licenses as teachers. It should grant *temporary licenses* to applicants who begin their careers in the profession of Jewish education and to those who wish to engage in Jewish teaching as an avocation or as a temporary means of gaining a livelihood. At the end of a period of trial those who wish to enter the teaching profession should again come before the Board for permanent licenses either as *elementary* teachers, *intermediate* teachers, *secondary* or high school teachers, *supervisors* of special subjects, or *administrators* (principals, etc.). For each of these grades of license special requirements in knowledge, experience and training should be made by the Board of Licenses.

A Board of Licenses to be successful must be acceptable to three bodies, namely, the trustees of the schools, the principals and the teachers. It should receive their full co-operation and be ready to consider their demands. This Board should, therefore, have representatives from the Board of Jewish School Aid, the Hebrew Principals' Association, and the Teachers' organizations. It should confer with an advisory committee, selected by the Teachers' Training Schools, the Bureau of Jewish Education, the rabbinical seminaries and similar agencies. The task of organizing and managing a Board of Licenses in New York is not an easy one.[40] But if successfully accomplished, it can become the most effective agency in regulating and standardizing the profession of Jewish education.

---

[40] The Bureau of Jewish Education took the first step toward organizing a Board of License in 1912, but its efforts at that time were premature. Cf. above pp. 112-113.

D. Differentiated Training of Teachers

Following upon the standardization of salaries and the granting of graded licenses to teachers, and coming indeed as a necessary counterpart to these undertakings, is the improvement in the *training* of teachers. The fundamental difficulty under which the Jewish teachers' training schools in New York seem to be laboring, is that the pupils who apply for admission to them are not adequately prepared, and the schools must, therefore, serve as secondary schools for teaching Hebrew, history, etc., instead of devoting themselves to the more truly professional aspects of their work: the interpretation of Jewish literature, history and religion from the teacher's view point; the psychology of Jewish children and Jewish parents; the organization of American Jewish life and the aims of Jewish education in this country; the technique of teaching the various subjects of the curriculum; methods in classroom and school management, and kindred studies. The only way to make the training schools truly professional schools, is to have them draw their applicants from a well organized system of secondary Jewish schools which should give a three or four years' intensive course of training to the most capable graduates of the Jewish weekday schools. The secondary classes of such organizations as the Bureau of Jewish Education and the National Hebrew School are a promising beginning in this direction.

To these more adequately prepared applicants the Teachers' Institutes should offer a differentiated course of study. A minimum of three years' basic training should be required for qualifying to teach the elementary grades of the Jewish schools. Beyond this period students should be stimulated to continue their studies in order to qualify for teaching the intermediate and secondary classes, or for supervising some particular branch of the curriculum. The more ambitious should be encouraged to undertake a special course of training to prepare themselves for the higher administrative positions. The Jewish teachers' training schools, when fully developed, should be in a position to offer three grades of certificates or diplomas: (1) the Elementary Diploma, (2) the Intermediate or Supervisor's Diploma, and (3) the Administrator's or Director's Diploma, which last should be of the same rank, in point of training and of achievement as the degree of Doctor of Philosophy granted by the best American universities.[41]

These graded certificates apply to teachers in weekday schools. The Sunday school teachers should also be required to undergo a period of training before being permitted to teach. The most likely agency to undertake this work for New York seems to be the Teachers' Institute of the Jewish Theological Seminary. The course should be in charge of a supervisor selected by the Eastern Council of Reform Rabbis, since most of the teachers whom this course would serve will teach in Reform Sunday Schools. In conjunction with the Director of the Institute, the supervisor should select from among the students of the secondary Jewish classes or the graduates of the elementary weekday schools,[42] young people who do not want to make a profession of Jewish teaching, but who would gladly serve on Sundays. These students should be offered a course of studies in the evenings, extending over two or three years. The course should be designed to supplement their knowledge of history and religion, and to teach them the essentials of psychology and of classroom practice. Those who complete this course satisfactorily should be granted special certificates as Sunday School Teachers and their minimum compensation should be $20 per month, or from four to five dollars for each Sunday morning.

There is another important direction in which the Teachers' Institutes should extend their activities. There are many immigrant men and women in the city who are thoroughly grounded in Hebrew and in Jewish literature, but whose ignorance of American conditions and of English makes them unfit to teach in American Jewish schools. These are potential Jewish teachers, but they require a distinct type of training. Courses should be provided for them in the English language and literature, in American history and civics, in psychology and classroom practice, in American Jewish history and institutions, and visits of

[41] Such a plan of graded certificates is actually contemplated by the Teachers' Institute of the Jewish Theological Seminary. It is hoping to introduce three degrees: Bachelor, Master, and Doctor of Jewish Education. As cultural prerequisites for these degrees in Jewish Education, it will require, in time, the Bachelor of Arts, Master of Arts and Doctor of Philosophy, respectively.

[42] Either from the Hebrew or the vernacular courses; see below, Chapter 10.

observation should be arranged for them to the American public schools. In 1912-13 such courses were conducted for a short time by the Bureau of Jewish Education, with the co-operation of the Teachers' Institute of the Jewish Theological Seminary. These courses should be continued and extended, for they tap a rich, though perhaps temporary, source of teachers for the American Jewish schools.

E. Improvement of Teachers in Service

But, as has been previously pointed out, the growth of the teacher does not end with graduation from the training school. The classroom work day by day should be a source of broader knowledge and of deeper insight into the difficult task of shaping the lives of children. After the first few years of teaching, the novelty of the task wears off, and a deadening, stultifying classroom "routine" sets in, harmful to teacher and to pupils alike. Opportunity should then be afforded for gaining fresh stimuli and new points of view.

The chief agent for encouraging and guiding the daily growth of teachers is naturally the principal, and his chief method should be that of constructive criticism. But the average school principal (whether Jewish or non-Jewish) is not capable of fulfilling this most delicate and most important of his duties. He has neither sufficient powers of critical analysis nor sufficiently definite standards to enable him to teach his teachers. While nothing can take the place of this lack of native ability or of broad training on the part of the principals, yet two methods may be suggested to aid earnest principals in this phase of their work. The first is the use of a *Teacher's Score Card,* and the second is the employment of *Special Supervisors.*

A "*Teacher's Score Card*" consists of a standard analysis of the various elements that make up teaching, arranged in such a way as to permit the principal to judge the strength of the teacher in each particular element of his work.[43] A score card for Jewish teachers is here presented showing how one teacher in a Jewish school was marked. The scientific basis for this

[43] For a good discussion of this problem, cf. 14th Year Book of the National Society for the Study of Education, Part II, 1915: "Methods of Measuring Teachers' Efficiency," by A. C. Boyce, Chicago, Ill.

score card and how it is to be used, is explained fully elsewhere.[44] School principals should be trained to use this score card and, if properly used, they will find it very helpful in their work of supervision. By means of it both the principal and the teacher can single out the particular points of weakness and devote their attention to them. In this manner the growth of the teacher can be watched from term to term. The emphasis should not be upon the present efficiency of the teacher, but rather upon his capacity for improvement. The score card is the diagnosis, and when compared to the standards set up for each item,[45] it should prove helpful in suggesting the remedy.

The second suggestion as an aid in supervision is that, wherever possible the principal should engage specialists in the various school branches to help him. As yet there are in Jewish education very few *"special supervisors,"* that is, those who specialize in the teaching of Hebrew, or History, or Customs and Ceremonies, or Music, or any of the other Jewish school branches. The work of the Bureau of Jewish Education in this direction is of great value. It has been training special supervisors (particularly in Hebrew, History, and Music) who confer constantly with the teachers in the Jewish schools, helping them plan their work and offering them constructive criticism. These supervisors teach in the Teachers' Institute of the Jewish Theological Seminary, so that they may be in a better position to help the young graduate teachers in their actual classroom teaching. Special supervision is a new venture in Jewish education, and will offer an interesting and constructive field of service in aiding the growth and in increasing the effectiveness of Jewish teachers.

The actual management of the school offers the principal many other opportunities for providing his teachers with new points of contact in their work.[46] "Routinized" teachers should be given additional work (with pay) in the form of investigation of truancy, examination of complaints, drawing up reports for the principal, engaging in special studies (such as regularity of attendance, proportion of elimination), coaching for festival

---

[44] Appendix R.

[45] Appendix R; pp. 528-538.

[46] For a good discussion of this entire question, see Ruediger, W. C. "Improvement of Teachers in Service."

I. PERSONALITY: (Standard Value = 205)

5. A. Physique 85*
- Appearance (features, stature, dress)
- Voice (pitch and force) X
- Speech (rate and distinctness) X
- Sight X
- Hearing
- Health

2 B. Character 120*
- Temperament
  - Reverence
  - Loyalty
  - Cheerfulness
  - Persistence
  - Self Control
  - Sense of Humor X
- Bearing
  - Dignity and Refinement
  - Confidence X
  - Enthusiasm X
- Relation to Principal
  - Cooperation and Friendliness
  - Frankness and Courage X
- Relation to Pupils
  - Patience X
  - Tact X
  - Fairness
  - Sympathy
  - Understanding and Sincerity X
- Relation to Work
  - Devotion and Sincerity
  - Reliability and Responsibility
  - Initiative and Progressiveness
  - Thoroughness and Industry
  - System and Neatness X
  - Professional Attitude

II. TRAINING: (Value 235)

.0 A. Knowledge 85*
- Secular Education
- Jewish
  - Specific (subject teaching) X
  - General
    - Literature X
    - History X
    - Religion X
    - Music X

.5 B. Professional Training 70* (Accredited pedagogic instruction)

.3 C. Pedagogic Experience 45*
- Kind (supervised or unsupervised) X
- Length (in years)

.5 D. Professional Growth 35*
- Study (engaged in at present) X
- Extra School Interests (civic or Jewish)

III. TEACHING ABILITY: (Value 325)

.5 A. Preparation 70*
- Knowledge of subject matter
- Plan (adherence and adaptability)
- Use of illustrative material

.3 B. Technique 90*
- Skill in motivation
- Presentation of New Work
  - Use of apperceptive mass
  - Organization of lesson (aim and sequence)
  - Emphasis and sense of values
- Teaching Process
  - Variation in use of teaching types
  - Skill in use of Teaching types
    - Questioning
    - Narration or exposition
    - Recitation
    - Review and examination
    - Assignment and study

.3 C. Interest and Attention 75*
- Amount (continuity and concentration)
- Kind (spontaneity)

.5 D. Participation of Pupils 90*
- Provision for expression
- Provision for Initiative
- Provision for cooperation

IV. CLASS MANAGEMENT: (Value 175)

.6 A. Discipline 70*
- Class spirit (order, quiet, activity)
- Corrective Discipline
  - Attitude of teacher (persistence and sympathy)
  - Adequacy (suitability of punishment)

.7 B. Class Routine 23*
- Movements in classroom (order, system, speed)
- Distribution of materials, etc. (mechanization)

.8 C. Daily Program 22*
- Scope and Adherence
- Arrangement (distribution for maximum interest)
- Recess (provision for relaxation) X

.0 D. Control of Hygienic conditions of study 60*
- Posture
- Eye and ear strain
- Ventilation
- Temperature
- Sanitation (cleanliness and neatness) X

V. SERVICE: (Value 60)

.5 A. Attendance 30*
- Regularity
- Punctuality

.0 B. Volunteer Service (School activities) 30*
- Amount of time
- Efficiency

celebrations, helping in special cases of discipline or of backwardness, etc. All of these *extra-classroom activities* offer fresh problems, and from them teachers may bring new inspiration and insight into their regular classroom work. The principal should be free to teach a class himself occasionally, so as to enable a particularly weak teacher either to observe him or to visit some other teacher who is strong in the particular elements of teaching in which that teacher is deficient. The teachers' conferences, which should be held regularly, could be made more significant than they are at present, if instead of discussing matters of school routine they be made the means for discussing school policy, and if from time to time some outsiders, possibly the principals of other schools, be invited to confer with the teachers on given problems in school work.

The principal should not be alone in his work of keeping his teachers fit for their task. The community should offer stimuli for broadening their knowledge and their attitudes. In public education many school systems offer their teachers sabbatical years of absence, every seven or ten years, permitting them to engage in travel or study, on full pay. With the upbuilding of Palestine and with the growing importance of Palestinian Jewish life for Jewish life throughout the world, it would be most advantageous if the Jews of New York, through the Board of Jewish School Aid or through the Zionist Organization of America, could offer every year to two or three of the Jewish teachers in the city, *free trips to Palestine* and sufficient funds to keep them there for six months. This would be a fine method of showing the appreciation of the community for the service which its ablest teachers are rendering, and the teachers returning from Palestine every year would infuse new zest and ardor into the entire teaching profession.

The community should also offer every year leave of absence to one or more specially qualified teachers or principals, to engage in specific *studies on some problem in Jewish education*. The problem to be studied should be set by the community and the person chosen to make the study should be afforded opportunity of free tuition at some university, or of travel to some particular school system, in America or in Europe, in accordance with the demands of the problem studied.

F. Teachers' Council

Another very important means for stimulating the interest of teachers in their work and for promoting their growth, consists in the participation of teachers in the affairs of their own profession. Among the first signs of a profession is organization. The spontaneous organizations of teachers which sprang up in this city represent their first public declaration as a profession. Unfortunately, the various organizations of teachers are completely separated from one another, and their power is limited. The Agudath Hamorim, the Moriah, and the Jewish Teachers' Association share nothing in common and carry on their activities independently.[47] It is natural that this should be so since these organizations represent different points of view in Jewish education, and to a large degree, different processes of training and different environments. For the present at least, the various teachers' organizations should continue to be independent. But for the sake of the teaching profession, and for the sake of the economic and social welfare of the teachers, it is necessary that their activities be co-ordinated in order that they may be able to put forth their combined energies in matters of common interest. A *Jewish Teachers' Council* should be organized, representing the three organizations, in whose hands should be entrusted the co-ordination of all professional activities.

The Teachers' Council should be able to serve in many capacities. It should act like the Bar Association upon all questions of professional etiquette. It should serve as the executive committee of a Teachers' Union in regulating the wages paid to Jewish teachers. It should organize and conduct conventions and conferences for all Jewish teachers. It should stimulate the formation of study circles and of lecture courses among the teachers. It should represent the Jewish teachers before the press and before the community at large, and should be represented on the Board of Licenses and on the Committee on Teachers' Pensions. In fine, it should strive to bring back with constancy and far-sightedness something of the traditional Jewish reverence for the teacher.

---

[47] The Jewish Religious School Union is not considered in this discussion because it is now (1918) inactive.

CHAPTER X.

THE CONTENT OF JEWISH EDUCATION

(INTENSIVE CURRICULA)

What do the Jews of this country teach their children? Education is spiritual reproduction, and the content of the Jewish educational curriculum is, therefore, an index to the nature of the life of the Jewish group itself. The subjects of study in the Jewish schools express the culture and the institutions which the Jews of America desire to preserve and to transmit to their children. The aim of the Jewish schools is to *reproduce* American Jewry, that is, to make a new generation of Jews out of the present Jewish children.

But the schools must do more than merely reproduce; they should also create and produce. America is a new land for the majority of Jews who live here, and rapid and profound are the changes which the new environment is causing in the character of Jewish institutions and in the organization of Jewish life. Does the work of the Jewish schools keep pace with these changes? Are the schools teaching stereotyped subjects by stereotyped methods handed down from a previous condition of life, or are they consciously trying to fit their pupils to the new life which will confront them? Are the schools merely aiming to reproduce that which has passed, or are they striving, on the basis of the past heritage, to produce a generation which shall be capable of developing a new link in the historic chain of Jewish life—American Judaism?

These questions are of vital importance to the Jews. To answer them in a thorough and satisfactory manner it would be necessary to analyze the social forces in America that affect the life of the Jews, to determine the essentials which the majority of thinking Jews consider as necessary to teach their children in order to prepare them for the changed conditions of life in this country, and then to measure scientifically the achievement of the pupils in the various branches of study, in order to learn in how far the schools actually accomplish this purpose. At present it is not possible to answer the questions in this manner. Scientific measurement of school work, which has just begun to develop in public education,[1] is as yet practically unknown in the Jewish schools. Jewish teachers must still rely upon individual opinion and upon personal bias for judging the effectiveness of their school work.[2] Moreover, the adjustment of Jewish life is going on so rapidly that it would be meaningless to inquire what the Jews consider to be the minimum essentials in the education of their children, as it is possible to inquire in public education, for instance.[3] For the clearest expression of the essentials in Jewish education, it is therefore necessary at the present time to resort to the schools themselves, to the curricula of the various types of Jewish education: weekday, parochial and Sunday. These curricula show the desires of the principals and the teachers, rather than the achievement of the pupils. The time allotted to each subject of study is significant of the emphasis placed upon it, and of the degree of knowledge that it is possible for the pupils to acquire.

There are two general types of curriculum for the education of Jewish children: (1) the *Intensive* curriculum, based upon the desire to impart a maximum amount of knowledge, and embodied in Talmud Torahs, Hebrew Schools, Yiddische Volksschulen, Parochial Schools, and Institutions for Secondary and Higher Education; and (2) the *Extensive* curriculum, based upon the necessity of giving many boys and girls a minimum of instruction, and expressed in Sunday Schools, in Extension Educational Organizations such as those of the Bureau of Jewish Education and of the Zionist Organization; in the Intercollegiate Menorah Association; and in much of the prevailing private tutoring.

A. Curriculum of the Talmud Torah or Hebrew School

The usual Talmud Torah curriculum provides for six years of study.[4] These schools are in session 48 weeks during the

---

[1] For a summary of what has been done in public education toward the objective measurement of pupils' achievements, cf. Chapman and Rush: "Scientific Measurement of Classroom Products," 1918.

[2] In Appendix S: "Measuring the Achievement of Pupils." This important question is discussed more fully, and an account is given of an attempt to construct a scale for measuring pupil achievement in the mechanics of Hebrew reading (Ivri).

[3] Cf. "Minimum Essentials in Elementary School Subjects," Fourteenth Year Book of the National Society for the Study of Education, 1915.

[4] The questionnaires sent to the various schools of the city, asked for

year,[5] the pupils being granted two weeks' holiday for the Succoth and Pesach festivals (Tabernacles and Passover), and two weeks' vacation during the summer months. The number of hours of instruction during each week varies with the grade, and ranges from an average of six and a half hours of instruction per week in the lowest grade to nine and a half hours in the highest grade.[6] The total time of instruction provided for the Jewish child in the 6-7 year curriculum is therefore about 2,600 hours.[7]

The hours of instruction are distributed by the larger Talmud Torahs and Hebrew schools of New York in the following manner.[8]

SUBJECT (Grade)	I	II	III	IV	V	VI	VII	TOTAL HOURS
Hebrew Language........	238	188	97	74	51	42	60	750
Bible and Jewish Literature.............	...	42	153	208	265	281	342	1,291
History..................	26	40	39	30	41	29	...	205
Religion (Prayers, Customs and Ceremonies).	36	46	45	54	27	28	24	260
Music..................	9	9	8	9	6	4	24	69
Geography of Palestine..	...	...	...	...	2	3	12	17
Total.................	309	325	342	375	392	387	462	2,592

About 35% of the time is given to the study of the Hebrew

the curricula at present in vogue. Among these, 14 weekday schools gave their complete courses of study, together with the time allotment for each subject. All of the 14 schools reported a course of study for the first three grades, (years 1, 2 and 3); 13 reported a course for 4 grades; 10 for 5 grades; 8 for 6 grades; and 2 for 7 grades.

[5] Ranging from 44 to 50 weeks.

[6] The distribution is as follows: Grade (year) I - 6.4 hours per week (average); II - 6.7 hrs.; III - 7.1 hrs.; IV - 7.8 hrs.; V - 8.1 hrs.; VI - 8.1 hrs.; VII - 9.6 hrs.

[7] This is equal to the amount of time provided in *two and a half years of the public school course* (40 weeks per year at 25 hours per week). Since the average Jewish child stays only about three years in Jewish school (cf. Chapter VIII), the total amount of time available for its instruction is equal to about a year and a quarter of the public school course.

[8] This table show the average number of hours reported by the 14 largest Talmud Torahs and Hebrew Schools in New York, for each subject of study and for each year.

language,[9] 42% of the time to the Bible and Jewish Literature (Commentaries, Mishna, Aggadah, Talmud and Modern Literature, of which 30% is given to the Bible itself); 9% of the time is devoted to History; 12% to Religion (prayers, customs, ceremonies); and 2% to Music.[10] The Talmud Torah curriculum is therefore a *literary* curriculum with the main emphasis on the Hebrew language and Jewish literature, and with the center of attention upon the Bible. Evidently the "Yodea Sefer" (one who knows books) is still among the ideals of Jewish education.

In general terms the typical curriculum of the modern New York Talmud Torah or Hebrew School may be described as follows:

HEBREW LANGUAGE

FIRST YEAR (five hours per week)

Mechanics of Hebrew *Reading* (by the Alphabetic or the Natural Methods).

First lessons in Hebrew *Conversation* (in many schools linked with reading by the Natural Method of teaching languages).

Mechanics of *Writing* (Hebrew Alphabet).

SECOND YEAR (four hours per week)

Mechanics of Hebrew *Reading* (Ivri) continued throughout the course to the point of acquiring rapidity in reading the prayers.

Hebrew *Conversation*, centering around the Bible stories, taught during this year and subsequent years.

Hebrew *Writing*, and the rudiments of Hebrew *Grammar*.

FROM THIRD YEAR THROUGH SEVENTH YEAR (one to two hours per week)

Same subjects continued with the addition of *supplementary Hebrew Reading* at home, and of *Hebrew Composition* from the fourth year to the end of the course.

---

[9] In this is included, however, the mechanical reading of prayers (Ivri) whose purpose is "religious" rather than linguistic.

[10] The "geography of Palestine" receives less than one per cent. of the time.

BIBLE AND JEWISH LITERATURE

SECOND YEAR (one hour per week)

Pentateuch (usually through Genesis and Exodus).

THIRD YEAR (three to four hours per week)

Pentateuch, continued.

Rashi Commentary.

Early Prophets.

FOURTH YEAR (four to five hours per week)

Pentateuch (in some schools continued throughout the course as study of Biblical portion of the Week (Sedrah).

Prophets and Hagiographa.

Rashi Commentary.

Mishnah.

Aggadah (usually selections from Bialik's Sefer Ha-aggadah).

Selections from *Modern Hebrew Literature.*

FIFTH, SIXTH AND SEVENTH YEARS (five to seven hours per week)

Same studies continued with the addition of *Talmud;* there being a constant decrease in the time allotted to the Bible and a corresponding increase in emphasis upon Talmud, as well as upon Modern Hebrew Literature.

HISTORY (half hour to one hour per week)

During the first and second years Jewish history is taught in the form of Bible stories, usually told with the aid of stereopticon views of the biblical scenes. In the third, fourth and fifth years, history lectures are given by the teachers to their classes on post-biblical history. These lectures seldom succeed in reaching beyond the period of the destruction of the Jewish state (either 70 or 135 C. E.). In the last years of the course, history disappears altogether as a distinct subject, some historical study being afforded, however, through the study of Jewish Literature.

RELIGION (half hour to one hour per week)

The Jewish weekday schools teach "Religion" under several headings. From the first year on, all of the Talmud Torahs teach "blessings" or benedictions for various acts and occasions; and also the meaning of the Jewish feasts and fasts and the ceremonies connected with them. As soon as the pupils can read, instruction is given in the translation of the daily, Sabbath and holiday prayers and also in the "order of the prayers." From the second or third year on, the pupils are taught to participate in special "Children's Sabbath Services" conducted entirely by the pupils of the school under the guidance of the teachers. In the fourth year the teaching of *Jewish law* (ritual and other) is introduced, the abridged *Shulchan Aruch* being in many instances used as the text book. In very few of the schools are formal talks given on "Ethics" or "Religion" or "Judaism."

MUSIC (fifteen minutes per week)

The teaching of Jewish music usually includes the synagogue chants and responsa, folk melodies (Yiddish), modern nationalist songs, "home" melodies (Kiddush, Zmiroth, etc.) and the special chants connected with the reading of the Torah. During the second and third years specially selected children are given additional musical instruction as members of the school choir, which officiates at the Sabbath Services and performs at festival celebrations of the school. Learning to chant the Torah benedictions and the Haftorah (prophetic portion) constitutes an important part in preparing the Jewish boy for his Bar Mitzvah Initiation, when he is officially accepted into the Jewish community upon becoming thirteen years of age.

Teaching the Jewish Present

The typical Talmud Torah curriculum, as here outlined, confines itself almost exclusively to teaching the Jewish Past and the religious-cultural creations of that Past. Classic literature (chiefly the Bible), Liturgy, and ancient history form the predominant bulk of the spiritual food given to the Jewish children. The relation which these studies have to the child's present, is in the form of the Jewish feasts and fasts and of synagogue ritual which the child as it grows older may or may not be enabled to make part of its daily life. Very little, if any, attention is paid to the Jewish Present and to that which the Present is creating. To be sure, some of the schools provide for a general interest in Palestine, in Jewish current events and in Modern Hebrew Literature; but the time devoted to these studies is in most cases unorganized and insignificant.[11]

Nobody can claim for an instant that the Jewish Past is not of the utmost importance in teaching the American Jewish child. The finest in present day Jewish institutions and life is based on

[11] Only one school, for example, out of the fourteen of the city's best schools, has Palestine as a definite subject in its curriculum.

that Past. The Jewish will-to-live as a group and the hopes for a Jewish future must be explained largely in terms of that Past. The Bible, and the classic literature, the liturgy, the laws, and the history of the Jews are absolutely indispensable for the education of the American Jewish child. But in a rapidly changing, "dynamic" society, such as ours, these studies *alone* cannot suffice for preparing the growing Jewish child for its life in this country. The *Immediate Past,* the *Living Present* and the *Approaching Future* must be included with the more *Remote Past* in any worth-while scheme of American Jewish education.

In so far as it is possible to foresee the future, the American Jew of the next generation will live in an organized American Jewry which will be energetically seeking to create institutions to perpetuate Jewish life in this country and which, in company with other Jewries throughout the world, will at the same time be intensely interested in building up Jewish national life in Palestine, and in defending the civil rights of the Jews wherever they live. It is for this life that the Jewish schools of today prepare their pupils. There are therefore three elements in the Jewish Present which should be included as parts of the curricula of American Jewish schools, namely: America, Palestine, and Israel among the Nations.

America: The American Jew is a member of the general American community as well as of the Jewish community, and the school's obligation is to prepare the child for its position in both of these communities. The American public school exerts, without willing it, a strong anti-Jewish influence upon its Jewish pupils, not because of what it does, but because of what necessarily it fails to do. In all of the history and the literature which the public schools teach, among all the heroes whom they set up for the children to emulate, there is no mention of the Jew. The child comes to the subconscious conclusion that the role of the Jew is an insignificant one, that the Jew has no share in the rich treasure house of the world, beyond having given the Bible to the world long ago, in the dim, uncertain past.

The public schools, in most communities, can hardly be expected to do otherwise. Except in a limited sense, in communities that are predominantly foreign-born, the American public schools are compelled to ignore the particular national or religious background of their pupils. But whereas the public schools cannot interpret life from any one religious-national viewpoint, the Jewish schools can and should undertake this task for Jewish children. How much richer and more intimate would be the child's appreciation of *American history* if it were also taught the *history of the Jews in America;* if, for example, alongside of the life of the dashing pioneer with his gun and his hatchet, were portrayed the life of the Jewish trading pioneer with his pack of civilization's goods; if besides the glorified heroes of America, the Jewish child were told of the unsung Jewish American heroes like Asser Levi, Hayim Solomon, Mordecai M. Noah, Judah P. Benjamin and others, down to the Jews who are helping to make American history in our own day; if the story of the Puritans and of the early institutions of our country were retold in relation to their acknowledged dependence upon the Hebraic spirit and literature! How much deeper would be the child's insight, and how much more balanced his views, if the motives that actuated the great events in American history and the principles that underlie the American Constitution and Government were compared with the motives behind the great crises in Jewish history and the principles of government and life expressed in the Bible and in Jewish law; if questions of Immigration, of Separation of State and Church, of Sunday Laws, etc., were discussed with regard to their effect upon the Jews; if, in short, *American civics* were interpreted from a Jewish viewpoint! Or take *General History,* how different, and more true, would be the Jewish child's attitude towards the Roman Emperors, the Church, the Crusades, the role of Isabella of Spain, of Cromwell, of Napoleon, etc., if their effects upon Jewish history were pointed out! In *Literature,* why should it not be the Jewish teacher who selects for reading with his pupils those classic gems of the English poets and essayists that deal with Jewish themes and are replete with references to Hebrew literature and to Jewish history! In *Biography,* why should the Jewish child grow up a stranger to the life stories of the great Jewish philosophers, poets, statesmen, artists and scientists who have contributed to the world's progress? In short, the interpretation and supplementation of the general curriculum of the public schools, offers a rich field of instruction for fitting the American Jewish child to the general American community in which it is to live.

Equally necessary is it to give the growing Jewish boys and girls some knowledge of the nature and functions of various distinctly Jewish organizations in America, religious, philanthropic, economic and communal; to let them know of the existence of the Jewish press, the Jewish theatre, Jewish music and art; to tell them something of the personalities who are active in all of these endeavors; and to stimulate in them a participating interest in the affairs of the Jewish community of America. It is in this connection that the study of *Yiddish* should prove a valuable asset in the education of the Jewish children of this generation. As long as there is a large part of the Jewish community that speaks and reads Yiddish, and as long as there is in this country a living Yiddish literature and art, it would be depriving the child of contact with that portion of the community, and in most instances of understanding the daily life of its own parents and relatives, if the Jewish school failed to offer it the opportunity of learning to read and to write Yiddish. For pupils who know Hebrew and can speak Yiddish, this is no difficult task, and it will help them greatly in appreciating the life of the Jewish community.

Palestine: To the American Jew the most important "foreign" land will be Palestine. Whatever may be the attitude of the Jewish school toward Zionism as party doctrine, there seems hardly any doubt that Palestine and the upbuilding of Palestine will play a most important role in the life of American Jews. The ceaseless yearning of the Jews for a reconstituted Palestine is in our day approaching fulfillment, and the meaning and potency of that fulfillment will depend upon the devotion and the understanding with which this generation and the next will participate in the "Restoration." For any Jewish school to fail to give Palestine, its history, its geography and its institutions an adequate place in the curriculum, seems to be a clear neglect of duty towards the pupils. It is not sufficient that a vague sentimental love for Palestine be inculcated in the children. Nor should the schools depend upon chance references to Palestine in Hebrew literature and Jewish history alone. Palestine should become a definite study in the Jewish curriculum and specified time should be set aside for teaching its resources and possibilities, its social, economic and religious problems, and the efforts that are being made for its rehabilitation as the center of Jewish organized life in the world.

Israel Among the Nations: Besides instruction concerning the American community and concerning Palestine as the center of Jewish life, Jewish children should be given some information concerning the life of the Jews in the other countries of the world, particularly in Europe. Opportunity should be found, some time before the boy and the girl are graduated from the Jewish school, to acquaint them with the status of the Jews in the various countries, with the character of their communal organization, and with their leading personalities. To this should be added *Jewish Current Events,* in America, Palestine, and elsewhere; and the reading and discussion of current events should form a regular part of the weekly school program. The child's Jewish interests should be broadened so as to reach out to all places where Jews live; it should be made to feel that it is part of a great International Brotherhood which has its center in Palestine.

Differentiated Curricula

To teach these phases of the Jewish Present would necessitate a reorganization of the existing curricula. It would require also special text books, which are yet to be written, and adequately prepared teachers, such as are yet to be trained. Much of the time of the child is at present wasted in the Jewish schools not only because of faulty methods and management, but also because the educational viewpoint is wrong. The schools still hold the East European educational standards before them, and assume that every boy is capable of becoming a learned Jew. Consequently strenuous efforts are made to give him as much instruction in Hebrew as possible to prepare him for the study of the Bible and the Talmud. Thus, during the first three years of the Jewish school curriculum, three-fourths of the time is devoted to the study of Hebrew as a language, chiefly in the form of mechanical reading (Ivri) and laborious translation of words in the difficult language of the Bible.[13] But

[13] Cf. Table on p. 305.

in point of fact, most children will not be "learned" Jews, and the pressure brought to bear upon them in the study of Hebrew is not only displeasing, but also wasteful. It is a desideratum that *all* Jewish children in America should know Hebrew. Indeed, Hebrew must be an essential study in every Jewish school. But one-half of the children never reach beyond the second grade of the Jewish school.[14] Why should *these* children be compelled to spend so much of the little precious time which they give to Jewish education in the study of Hebrew as a "preparatory" subject, preparing them for the study of Jewish literature in which they will never engage? Only a small minority stay long enough to derive any benefit from the study of the Bible and of post-biblical literature. Would it not be common sense educational management to distinguish, in such a manner as has been previously suggested, between the mediocre majority and this capable minority?

The Jewish school curriculum of six or seven years should be divided into three parts. *A basic elementary course of studies* should be given to all children for the first three years of their stay in school. Thereafter *two* intermediate curricula should be offered: an *intensive Hebrew course* to the specially selected pupils who show promise of benefiting from such a course, and a *less intensive general course in English* to the average child who remains in the school, but cannot or will not undertake the more intensive course.

The basic elementary curriculum cannot be the creation of any one mind. The Hebrew Principals' Association should devote its best energies to develop such a curriculum, and years of careful experimentation will be required to determine what can and should be taught during these first three telling years of the child's school life. The following is tentatively suggested as the outline of a basic elementary three-year curriculum. It should provide for teaching:

1. The Mechanics of *Hebrew Reading*—sufficient to enable the child to participate in the life of the synagogue.
2. The Rudiments of *Hebrew as a Modern Language*, organized so as to familiarize the child with a Hebrew

[14] Cf. Chapter 8, pp. 251-252.

vocabulary containing the many familiar Hebrew words in conversation among Jews, to enable it to read very simple Hebrew prose and to "desire" to know Hebrew.

3. *Bible Stories.*

4. Stories of *Jewish Historical Events and Personalities,* selected from the entire range of Jewish history.

5. The meaning of all Jewish *festivals* and the most important *customs and ceremonies.*

6. *Singing* of synagogue responsa and Jewish folk melodies.

7. Talks on the Jewish Present: America, Palestine and Israel among the Nations.

8. Sabbath Services.

The distribution of time among these subjects on the basis of 20-minute periods, assuming a course of study lasting three years, 48 weeks per year and five hours of study per week, would be somewhat as follows:

Subject	Per Week	For Entire Course
Mechanics of Hebrew Reading....	4 periods: 80 minutes	about 200 hours
Elements of Hebrew Language....	4 " 80 "	" 200 "
Bible Stories and Jewish History...	2 " 40 "	" 100 "
Talks on the Jewish Present.......	2 " 40 "	" 100 "
Festivals and Customs[15]..........	2 " 40 "	" 100 "
Synagogue and Folk Music........	1 " 20 "	" 50 "

With this basic curriculum for all children as a foundation, the two intermediate curricula should be developed. The intensive Hebrew curriculum[16] should provide for the study of:

[15] During the third year the time devoted to "Festivals and Customs" and to Music can be given over to juvenile Sabbath Services.

[16] Providing 8 to 10 hours of study during the week.

Subject	Per Week[17] (Average)	For Entire Course (4 years)
1. The Bible	3 hours	575 hours
2. Rashi Commentary	30 minutes	100 "
3. Mishna, Aggadah and selections from Mediæval Hebrew Literature	45 "	150 "
4. Talmud	45 "	150 "
5. Shulchan Aruch and Laws	20 "	65 "
6. Modern Hebrew Literature and Supplementary Home Reading	45 "	150 "
7. Jewish history	30 "	100 "
8. Palestine	20 "	65 "
9. Interpretation of American History and Civics	20 "	65 "
10. Jewish Current Events	15 "	50 "
11. Jewish Music	15 "	50 "
12. Yiddish	15 "	50 "
13. Sabbath Services	1-2 hours	

This intensive Hebrew curriculum should be designed to prepare specially selected children for secondary and higher Jewish instruction. It should in so far as possible be conducted in Hebrew, and the language of instruction, in all subjects permitting it, should be Hebrew. In the general intermediate curriculum, on the other hand, but little Hebrew should be taught, both the texts and the language of instruction being in the vernacular. Jewish teachers generally do not realize that in their zeal to teach the Bible in Hebrew to all children, they prevent the majority of Jewish children from knowing the Bible in any language, whether English or Hebrew. And yet if the Bible is to have any real influence upon the life of American Jews, it should form in its American translation, an important part in the education of the many Jewish children who cannot be expected to know the Bible in the original. The proposed

[17] It is understood of course that "average" for the entire four-year course does not mean necessarily that the subject is to be taught throughout the entire course. Thus "Bible" will be taught for five hours during the first two or three years of the course, and only an hour or two during the last years; "Talmud" will be taught two or more hours per week only during the last year or two, instead of forty-five minutes throughout the four years. The same holds true of some of the other subjects.

"general" curriculum [18] would follow the above more intensive Hebrew curriculum in many of the subjects of study, but would teach them in the English translation:

Subject	Per Week (Average)	Entire Course (four years)
1. Bible (in translation)...............	40 minutes	130 hours
2. Readings (translation) from the Midrash, and from Jewish Literature (mediæval and modern)...........	20 "	65 "
3. Jewish History	40 "	130 "
4. Liturgy (translation of prayers).....	30 "	100 "
5. Yiddish	20 "	65 "
6. Palestine	20 "	65 "
7. Interpretation of American History and Civics, and selections from English Literature (Jewish themes).	20 "	65 "
8. Jewish Current Events..............	15 "	50 "
9. Customs and Institutions...........	20 "	65 "
10. Jewish Music......................	15 "	50 "
11. Sabbath Services..................	1 hour	

In this curriculum Hebrew is continued only in the form of a study of Liturgy as a practical means for enabling the children to participate in and appreciate the life of the synagogue. Yiddish is also taught as a means for enabling the children, (particularly those who speak Yiddish) to understand more intimately the life of their parents and of the Jewish masses in New York. All other subjects are taught in English.

In the actual carrying out of the non-Hebrew curriculum it will of course be possible to combine and to correlate some of the subjects enumerated. Thus for example, "Translations from Jewish Literature," "Jewish History" and "Customs and Institutions" may be very closely correlated; the same may be done for "Liturgy," "Jewish Music" and "Sabbath Services." The subjects proposed are merely elements which should go into the teaching of Judaism to children who cannot undertake an intensive study of Hebrew. The nearest approach to a general intermediate curriculum, as is here suggested, is to be found in

[18] On the basis of the four-times-per-week schedule (cf. p. 211) providing five hours of schooling during the week.

the work of the Regular Girls' Schools [19] conducted by the Bureau of Jewish Education. In these schools text books and methods are being developed which will make the vernacular course practical of realization.[20]

Text Books and Methods

The change of educational viewpoint which the reorganization of the curricula should try to express, is the shifting of the center of attention from the *subject matter* to be taught, as handed down through the generations, to the great body of American Jewish *children*, whose needs are the ultimate guide of the schools. Instead of teaching Hebrew or Bible or Prayers or Talmud, the Jewish schools should teach Jewish children, and for this purpose the selections from the religious-national treasure house of the Jewish people should be such as will best prepare these children for their life as American Jews. There is really but one subject of instruction in the Jewish schools, namely *Judaism;* and while in accordance with modern educational usage, it is divided into language, history, religion, etc., it must be kept in mind that these are merely pedagogic devices. A new environment, and changed conditions of life, demand that new phases of Judaism be developed, in the instruction of Jewish children, besides the old ones; that there be changed emphasis, and, where necessary, educational reorganization. This change of attitude is a fundamental one, and while conditions have already made it a subconscious force in the Jewish schools, much time and effort will be required before it can be realized in the actual work of the classroom. It will affect not only the curricula and the general educational management, but will also bring considerable changes in methods of teaching and in the text books used.

No exhaustive treatment of the textbooks and methods prevailing in the Talmud Torahs and Hebrew School can be undertaken at this point. In the final analysis, that method is best which achieves the best results, and the lack of scientific means

[19] To be sharply distinguished from the intensive Hebrew Preparatory Classes for Girls conducted by the Bureau of Education, see Part I, pp. 117 and 124.

[20] These schools are now experimenting upon a 3½-hour per week basis, instead of a 5-hour basis as here suggested.

of measuring the achievement of pupils [21] warrants us only in giving rough judgments as to the worth of particular methods of teaching the various Jewish school subjects. But there have been certain significant tendencies in teaching the major subjects of the Hebrew school curriculum which it is worth noting.

Hebrew: During the last decade the teaching of the Hebrew language in the Jewish schools has been struggling toward (1) *modernization,* through the introduction of modern methods of language teaching, and (2) *Americanization,* through the emancipation of Jewish schools from the textbooks written in Eastern Europe and the substitution of books written and published in this country.

The controversy concerning the *Natural Method* of teaching Hebrew, or "Ivrith b'Ivrith," was at its height during the years 1910-1914. Its introduction into the Jewish schools was stimulated by two factors: on the one hand, was the recognition on the part of modern educators that this is the method to be pursued in the teaching of all languages, and on the other hand came the revival of Hebrew as the living language of daily intercourse among the Jews of Palestine. The method therefore had not only a pedagogic significance, but also a sociological one; it became identified with the whole striving for the rebirth of Palestine and of the Jewish nation. In language teaching the Natural Method proposes conversation instead of translation; in the teaching of reading it advocates the synthetic-analytic method starting with the whole word as opposed to the phonetic method starting with the isolated letter and syllable. The most popular argument against it was that it failed to teach Ivri or the mechanical reading of the prayers. In so far as to learn to read the prayers fluently is a necessary part in preparing the child to participate in the life of the synagogue (even if the meaning of the prayers must be obtained from the English translation on the opposite side of the prayer-book), and in so far as the teaching of Ivri is a persistent and legitimate demand of Jewish parents, the Jewish schools must provide for it. But under the proper conditions it is just as possible for the pupils to acquire the knowledge of reading Ivri by the Natural Method as by any other method. Many of the Talmud Torahs com-

[21] Cf. Appendix S.

promise to the extent of teaching Ivri by the phonetic method at the same time that they teach the language and the Bible by the Natural Method. A more important difficulty arose from the fact that there were not a sufficient number of teachers properly prepared to teach the language in this more pedagogic manner. But while the controversy has not yet been fully settled, every modern Jewish school has adopted the Natural Method of teaching Hebrew, in some form or other.

In the earlier Jewish schools the only textbooks used for teaching Hebrew were the traditional classics themselves: the Prayer Book (Siddur) and the Bible in the original. But the controversy concerning "method" naturally expressed itself also in a text book literature. For the phonetic teaching of Hebrew reading the most popular current school book was, and still is, "*Reshith Daath*" (ראשית דעת) by *M. Krynski*, published in Russia. The two most widely used books for teaching the language through translation are "*Hamechin*" (המכין) *by I. H. Tawjew,* published in Russia and retranslated in this country into English, and more recently, "*Ibrith*" (עברית) for the First, Second and Third Years, by *Goldin-Silk,* written and published in America. Contrasted with these books are the textbooks based on the Natural Method of teaching, the most popular of which are: for beginners, "*Safah Chayia*" (שפה חיה) by *Fischmann-Liebermann* (Russia) and "*Sefath Yeladim*" (שפת ילדים) two parts, by *Bercus-Bergmann* (Russia); for older pupils, "*Perakim Rishonim*" (פרקים ראשונים) two parts, by *Fischmann* (Russia) and "*Ha-dibur Ha-ivri*" (הדבור העברי) three parts, by *M. Krinsky.*

Almost all of these books have three shortcomings, which make them ill-adapted for use in American Jewish schools: (1) they were written for Russian Jewish children and many of the expressions, names and places are strange to the life of the American Jewish child; (2) they are not properly graded: the words and sentences are "formal" and isolated, and many of the lessons are unrelated and lead to no particular goal; (3) their technical make-up is aesthetically not such as to attract the American Jewish child who is accustomed to the finest product of modern textbook publishers in the public schools. In consequence the Bureau of Jewish Education has set about to write and publish a series of graded American Jewish textbooks for teaching the Hebrew language and literature. It proposes to issue twenty-eight Hebrew readers, beginning with the rudiments and taking the child through the entire range of Jewish literature. Sixteen of these books have already been published. In some instances its first effort has not proven wholly satisfactory, and as it continues to publish the later books it is also revising and improving the earlier readers. Besides these books the Bureau of Jewish Education has been publishing the juvenile Hebrew monthly magazine, "Shacharuth" (שחרות) and has begun to issue a graded series of story pamphlets in Hebrew for supplementary readings at home.

Since the outbreak of the War (1914) the supply of Hebrew textbooks from Russia has been greatly diminished, and to satisfy the demand a number of other American Jewish textbooks have appeared. The best known of these are: *"Shacharith"* (שחרית) by *Hirsch-Tomarow*; *"Ha-zeman"* (הזמן) three parts, by *H. Goldin* (contains English translation); and *"Ben Yisroel"* (בן ישראל) by *Z. Scharfstein.* Hebrew textbook writers have thus far but partially succeeded in embodying in their books the modern principles of pedagogic organization and presentation.

Bible: What has been said concerning the teaching of Hebrew applies also, in large measure, to the teaching of the Bible. Among the earliest attempts in this country of introducing the Bible into the Jewish schools in any other form than the traditional one, was the *"Chumash l'Batei Sefer ve-la-Am"* (חומש לבתי ספר ולעם) by *J. Magilnitzky.* It is an interlinear Bible with the English translation underneath each word. The *"Beth Ha-Sefer"* (בית הספר) by *M. B. Schneider* (Russia) divided the Bible into lessons and had vocabularies and grammatical exercises in connection with each lesson. The most well-known "Ivrith b' Ivrith" Bible readers, besides those published by the Bureau of Jewish Education, are the *"Sippurei Hamikrah"* (ספורי המקרא) edited by the famous Hebrew poet, *N. Bialik.* Because of the shortage of these readers since 1914, the *"Sippurei Hachumash"* (ספורי החומש) by *H. Malachowsky* have been published in this country and are extensively used.

The Talmud Torahs and Hebrew Schools do not teach the

Bible in English to any of their pupils, and there have been consequently no English Bible readers for the use of Hebrew schools. The *Junior Bible* series by Lehman-Kent has been used only by Sunday Schools, and its leaflets have not been found entirely satisfactory as practical Bible readers.[22] It is doubtful whether even those American Jews who do know the Bible in Hebrew should not also know it in English, since the references to it in conversation and in general reading are in English. But there can hardly be any doubt that those Jews who do not know the Bible in its original should know it at least in its English translation. The same holds true of the rest of Hebrew literature. For this purpose the Bureau of Jewish Education has begun to publish a graded series of well-illustrated and annotated *Jewish Literature Readers* for children, in English, giving not only the Bible text, but also selections from the entire range of Jewish literature.

Talmud and Aggadah: In teaching the Talmud to American Jewish children, it has been generally realized that wide changes from the traditional method must be made. On the one hand, only the most superficial knowledge of the voluminous "Sea of the Talmud" can be expected from the average Jew in this country. Intensive study of it must be relegated to the selected scholars in the Rabbinical Seminaries. On the other hand, the child should be instructed in the meaning of the Talmud, its history and development, its leading personalities, its significance in Jewish life; and it should be taught to appreciate its beauties. For these reasons special school editions of the Talmud have begun to appear, such as the "*Gemara Lematchilim*" (גמרא למתחילים) by *J. Goldman, and the "Mebo Hatalmud*" (מבוא התלמוד) by *N. Levin.* Then, too, instead of emphasizing the *Halacha* or the legal portions of the Talmud, the Talmud Torahs and Hebrew Schools have been emphasizing the *Aggadah,* or its narrative and interpretative portions. The book for this purpose most used and most loved in the Jewish schools is "*Sefer Ha-Aggadah*" ספר האגדה by *Bialik-Rawnitzky,* and "*Kol Agadoth Yisrael*" (כל אגדות ישראל) by *I. B. Lewner.* An anthology of much worth in teaching the literature of the rabbinic period to advanced students is the "*Ozar Safruth Yisrael*" (אוצר ספרות ישראל) by *I. L. Baruch.*

[22] See below, p. 347.

History: History as a definite subject in the curriculum is of recent origin in Jewish weekday schools. The fact that Jewish literature covered so much of Jewish history, together with the general lack of "historic sense" among all peoples until the comparatively recent present, accounts for the neglect of History in the Jewish school. But the effect of the historians and of Herbart was also felt by modern Jewish teachers. Particularly was it realized that the Jewish people, living so largely on its Past and glorying in it, must teach history to its children. Several history text books in Hebrew appeared for the use of Talmud Torahs and Hebrew Schools. The books having the widest use before 1914 were: *"Dibre Ha-Yamim le-Am Yisrael"* (דברי הימים לעם ישראל) by *W. Jawitz*: *"Toledoth Yeshurun"* (תולדות ישורון) by *D. A. Friedman* (contains English translation); *"Koroth Ha-Ibrim"* (קורות העברים) three parts by *S. Dubnow;* and *"Toledoth Am Yisrael"* (תולדות עם ישראל) by *A. S. Rabinowitz.* Since 1914 there has appeared the most popular of these books, *"Historiah la-Yeladim"* (הסטוריה לילדים) by *Z. Scharfstein.* Some of the Hebrew schools have also been using History textbooks in English; but as these are much more extensively used in the Sunday schools, they will be discussed later.[23]

The method of teaching Jewish history is that of a chronological recital of tales, starting from "Creation," following the Bible stories with little discrimination as to their historical importance, and finishing, at best, at some point near the modern period. This is particularly true in the schools in which Jewish history is taught in English (instead of in Hebrew). The Bible stories are told as authentic history without discriminating between the historic value of one story and that of another. It has been very difficult for progressive Jewish teachers to know how to tell the Bible stories without, on the one hand, stating them as unadorned fact, and without, on the other hand, relating them as mere myth and fiction. What the Jewish schools need in this regard is a manual and a textbook for teaching the Bible stories which would be written from the viewpoint of social psychology and which would restate the Bible stories so as to emphasize the nucleus of truth that is in them, instead of em-

---

[23] See p. 344.

phasizing, as at present, their plentiful clothing of fiction.[24] The same stories would be told, and the same devices of vivid narration, dramatization and stereopticon views would be used in telling them as are now used in the best Jewish schools, but the emphasis would be different. There should be a separation between the history and the literature of the Bible; and the literature, whether legend, folk tale or allegory, should be told as the tales of the Jewish people concerning its own origin, destiny and ideals of life.

The same general mistakes of lack of selection, poor organization and inadequate presentation, hold true in teaching Jewish history beyond the biblical period. Very few of the history textbooks have any large central ideas which guide them in the choice of material and in the organization of the mass of historic fact. Most of them are satisfied with retelling in the simplest language at their command, the most well-known or most "interesting" of the Jewish events. There is no point of contact between the child's normal interests and the persons or events they describe, and no reason or motive is given to the child for learning about these particular persons or events. The stories are told once, as exhaustively, and as exhaustingly, as possible, and once told they are never referred to again; as if there were some real psychologic reason for teaching young children the events of antiquity and keeping the more recent events for older pupils!

Because of these facts several Jewish teachers, under the guidance of the Bureau of Jewish Education, have begun to experiment with better pedagogic methods of teaching history. The most promising of these methods seems to be the *concentric method* of teaching. It proposes to teach Jewish history in *cycles*, covering it three or four times during the entire course. For the lowest grades, it selects a series of popular folk tales gathered from the whole range of Jewish history. To the pupils of the middle grades it teaches Jewish history in the form of a

---

[24] The best attempt thus far in this direction is the *Manual for Teaching Biblical History* by *Eugene Kohn;* but this book seems to be inadequate because instead of erring, like the books used in the Sunday Schools, in the direction of using the Bible stories as a pretext for preaching entirely unrelated "morals" for everyday conduct, it makes the mistake of using these stories as an excuse for inculcating observance of Jewish customs and ceremonies. In most cases both are equally foreign "interpretations" or "moralizing" of the Bible stories.

series of *biographic sketches* or hero tales, connected chronologically. In the higher grades, it proposes to make the *Jewish people* itself the hero of Jewish history, and to teach its kaleidoscopic story around some central theme, such as "the struggle for group preservation," or any other central idea. For the adolescent, the concentric method proposes a review of Jewish history in terms of the antecedent causes to existing *movements* and *institutions* in Jewish life.[25]

A series of graded textbooks and a teacher's manual are needed to show how to teach Jewish history more meaningfully by the concentric method than is done at present. In the actual process of teaching, all devices which help to make the events and persons concrete to the children, such as pictures, stereopticon views, maps and models, are of course very valuable. It has been felt for some time that a series of motion pictures is greatly needed which should portray serially the important events in Jewish history. Far more than any other pedagogic device such a series of motion pictures would aid the child in *living through* the Jewish past, and in fixing its main features in mind. To produce an adequate series of pictures of this kind would involve a great deal of money and effort; but it is not unreasonable to hope that the Jews of America will find it possible to produce motion pictures for their children and adolescents, dealing not only with Jewish history, but also with present Jewish life in Palestine and elsewhere.[26]

Religion and Other Subjects: Because of the weakening of Jewish home and synagogue influences in this country, the Jewish schools have been compelled to make "religion" a distinct subject of instruction. Up until very recently the conception of religion as something apart from literature, history and the acts of everyday life was quite foreign to the Jew. The child in Eastern Europe learned the prayers and the meaning of the various customs and institutions quite unconsciously as a result of daily participation in the life of its elders. In this country the Jewish child spends most of the day in a non-Jewish environment, and

[25] For a full discussion of this method, see "The Teaching of Jewish History," by Leo L. Honor, in "Jewish Teacher"; series of articles beginning with Vol. I, No. 2.

[26] There is at present extant, one set of motion pictures of Palestinian Jewish life, which was adapted and modified by the Bureau of Jewish Education for school purposes.

consequently the teaching of prayers, customs and ritual laws becomes an important function of the school. The Talmud Torahs and Hebrew schools still have no special textbooks for teaching "religion," and quite properly abstain from giving formal ethical instruction. The *Prayer Book* (Siddur) and the *Shulchan Aruch,* either in its traditional abridged form, or in the special children's edition by *I. B. Lewner,* are the textbooks used. The Sunday schools on the other hand, use a variety of special textbooks for this purpose.[27] In practically all of the Jewish schools the instruction in "religion" is formal, a matter almost of rote repetition. The Jewish classroom practice is still poor in devices for making this work interesting. Recently the Bureau of Jewish Education has begun to develop "*Jewish Arts and Crafts*" for children, which includes teaching the pupils to construct (out of paper, leather, etc.) various objects connected with the teaching of Jewish customs and festivals.[28]

Music as a subject of study in Hebrew schools has become very popular since the spread of the Jewish nationalist movement. Folk melodies were resuscitated and special nationalist songs written. The changed American environment has also influenced this movement, and besides the folk melodies and national songs, the Hebrew schools now teach their pupils synagogue and holiday chants which they once learned at home and in the synagogue. The faint beginnings of an American Jewish song literature, consisting of Jewish popular or national songs in English (not hymns), have also made their appearance, and should be encouraged. While a number of song "collections" have appeared, there have so far been but few music textbooks. The most current song collections are *Ha-zomir* (הזמיר) ; the *Sefer Hashirim* (ספר השירים) by *Idelson;* the "*Jewish Songster*" and "*Friday Evening Melodies,*" by *S. and I. Goldfarb.* These collections of songs consist in the main, either of liturgic responsa or of national-folk songs. A comprehensive music textbook for schools (ספר השירים) containing both liturgic and folk melodies, is published by the Bureau of Jewish Education. In some of the larger schools, the teaching of music is done by a special music teacher, but the better practice is, wherever possible, to train the regular classroom teacher to teach music also.

---

[27] See next chapter, p. 346.

[28] Discussed more fully p. 346.

Jewish Current Events has very recently been introduced into the curriculum by a few of the most modern Talmud Torahs and Hebrew Schools. "*The Jewish Child,*" a weekly juvenile publication, issued by the Bureau of Jewish Education and "*The Young Judean,*" a monthly magazine issued by the Zionist Organization, are used as the basis of reading and discussion. In some schools the discussion of current events is carried on by special children's clubs, outside of the regular sessions.

For teaching the other phases of the *Jewish Present* there are of course no textbooks as yet. To make Palestine, America, Jewish History, the Interpretation of American History and Civics, and the Status of Israel Among the Nations, parts of the Jewish school curriculum would require several carefully graded textbooks and elaborate manuals and teachers' aids. But there is no reason why progressive teachers should wait until these textbooks are written. There are sufficient books and materials at hand which, if used intelligently, can form the basis for instruction in these subjects. Here is a broad field for initiative and for creative work!

B. Curriculum of the Parochial School (Yeshibah)

Much of what has been said with regard to the curriculum, methods and textbooks of the Talmud Torah and Hebrew Schools applies equally to the Jewish Parochial School, or Yeshibah. The chief differences consist in (1) greater intensiveness of study and more time devoted to Jewish instruction, and (2) teaching the secular (public school) subjects under the auspices of the Jewish school.

The Jewish Parochial School [29] is in session 50 weeks during the year for the teaching of Jewish studies, and 40 weeks of the year for the teaching of the public school curriculum. Sessions begin daily at 8:45 in the morning, and until 3:15 in the afternoon the Jewish curriculum is taught, with one hour's recess for lunch. At 4:00 o'clock the public school work commences and lasts until 7:00 o'clock in the evening. The Jewish studies are taught six days of the week, and the public school studies

[29] The data presented here are based upon a personal study of the four Jewish parochial schools in New York, and upon detailed records furnished by the largest and probably the best of these schools.

five days. Recently (1918) the State Commissioner of Education ruled that all schools, including parochial schools, shall teach the public school curriculum during the regular public school hours. This ruling will doubtless affect the conduct of the Jewish Parochial Schools. The following analysis is based on the present (1918) status of these schools.

Jewish Studies

The elementary curriculum of the Jewish Parochial School provides for about 11,500 hours of Jewish studies and for 4,800 hours of secular studies. The time of the Jewish curriculum is distributed as follows:

Subject (Grade)	I	II	III	IV	V	VI	VII	Total	%
Hebrew Language...	1,025	650	750	250	350	300	300	3,625	31.4
Bible...............	......	650	600	1,200	700	650	300	4,100	35.5
Talmud.............	......	......	......	......	600	600	950	2,150	18.6
History.............	......	......	......	......	......	100	100	200	1.7
Religion............	625	350	300	200	......	......	......	1,475	12.7
Total (hours).....	1,650	1,650	1,650	1,650	1,650	1,650	1,650	11,550	100.0%

It is evident that the Yeshibah (Parochial School) curriculum is very much more intensive than the curriculum of the Talmud Torah, providing for more than four times as many hours of instruction. The greatest difference is in the emphasis upon the Talmud, which takes almost one-fifth of the time of the parochial curriculum, whereas in the Talmud Torah it receives but 4% of the child's time. Almost as many hours of instruction are devoted to the study of the Talmud in the Yeshibah as are given to all the subjects in the seven years of the Talmud Torah curriculum. Other evident differences are: (1) there is no teaching of Modern Hebrew Literature; (2) Jewish Music is not taught, except as the cantillation of the Torah, (included under Religion); and (3) History is taught only during the last two years.

In general the instruction in Hebrew, Bible and Religion follows along the same lines as in the Talmud Torahs, but with certain significant differences. First, greater intensity and thoroughness are possible because of the much greater amount of time devoted. Second, there is very much more limited use of modern methods in teaching, such as the Natural Method of teaching Hebrew, or stereopticon views as aids in teaching history. Third, the language of instruction and translation is not Hebrew or English, but Yiddish, chiefly because of the fact that the teachers whom the Yeshibahs employ for teaching the Jewish studies are elderly men who came to this country late in life and who consequently cannot speak English adequately. Fourth, there are practically no special textbooks beyond the first year, the classic books being used in their original form: the Siddur (prayer book), the Bible, the Talmud, and the Shulchan Aruch (abridged).

Secular Studies

What the Jewish Parochial School gains in intensity as regards Jewish studies, it apparently loses in its general cultural curriculum. The total time given to the general studies over an eight-year period is 4,800 hours, distributed as follows:

Subject (Grade)	I	II	III	IV	V	VI	VII	VIII	Total
English	300	333	333	284	250	250	260	250	2,260
Mathematics	100	100	100	100	100	100	100	100	800
Penmanship	67	67	67	50	40	40	30	30	391
Geography	...	...	...	83	80	80	80	80	403
History	...	...	...	...	60	60	60	70	250
Drawing	...	...	...	...	30	30	30	30	120
Physical Training, Recess and Organized Games	133	100	100	83	40	40	40	40	576
Total (hours)	600	600	600	600	600	600	600	600	4,800

The Jewish Parochial School therefore gives 60% as much time to the public school studies as do the public schools themselves. A comparison of the time allotment to each subject of study in the New York Public Schools [30] shows that the Yeshibah gives only 66% as much time as the *minimum* required by these schools.[31] When compared with the average time allotment in American cities, the proportion is even lower than 64%.[32] In only two subjects do the Parochial Schools give as much or more time than is required by the minimum of the New York public

[31] Based on: Elementary School Circular No. 1, 1913-1914, issued June 25, 1915, by the Department of Education of the City of New York.

[32] Cf. Minimum Essentials in Elementary School Subjects, in the Fourteenth Year Book of the National Society for the Study of Education, Part I, 1915, p. 25. See also Table XXXI.

schools, namely: Geography and Penmanship. There is no instruction whatever in the following subjects: Nature Study, Science, Constructive work, Shopwork and Music; and there is very little instruction in Drawing.

These facts seem to suggest that *the Jewish Parochial School does not provide sufficient secular training for its pupils.* This does not mean that the Jewish Parochial Schools of New York have not met the requirements of the New York State Board of Regents. On the contrary, their graduates are admitted into the public high schools on an equal footing with the graduates of the public elementary schools. The reason for this probably lies in the fact that the Jewish Parochial Schools have drawn on a selected group of children, consisting of bright, intellectually keen, immigrant youngsters. They have therefore been able to accomplish as much in the "staple" or "book" subjects with their pupils as the public schools are able to do with the average child in more time.

But the fact remains that such subjects as elementary science, nature study, manual training, music, physiology and hygiene are not taught to these children. Are they necessary? American educators, by including these studies in the public school curriculum, seem to be convinced that they are necessary. Unless the parochial schools extend the amount of time which they allow for secular training, they cannot teach these subjects to their pupils. Moreover, supposing even that the Yeshibahs are able to prepare their pupils for the Regents' Examinations in the "staple" subjects (English, Arithmetic, etc.), are the Jews to be satisfied with giving these bright children a cultural training barely meeting the demands of mediocrity? If the Yeshibahs are to train the future leaders of Jewry, are not these exceptional pupils entitled to a cultural education above the bare average?

If the Jewish parochial schools are to continue in this country, on the ground that they are to act as the special institutions for training the exceptional, highly selected children, who are to be equipped as the teachers and spiritual leaders of American Jewry, they must be thoroughly reorganized. They must, in the first place, do away with the artificial division between the Jewish and the secular studies, between Yiddish-speaking Jewish teachers and English-speaking secular teachers, between the long hours of the morning for the Jewish curriculum and the short hours of the afternoon for the secular curriculum. These schools should take the 16,000 hours at their disposal and divide them approximately into two equal parts, giving 8,000 hours to the public school curriculum (the New York minimum is 7,200 hours), and 8,000 hours to the Jewish studies (more than three times as much as the Talmud Torah curriculum provides). If the law will permit it, the entire course of study should be rearranged, so as to have Jewish and secular subjects alternate for the best interests of the pupils. The attempt should be made by the schools to find teachers who will be able to give instruction in both the Jewish and the secular branches. In the higher grades, where it may not be possible to obtain teachers adequately trained to teach both branches, it should be possible to institute departmental teaching, with special teachers for the various subjects. Modern textbooks and methods of teaching should be introduced to increase the effectiveness of the Jewish parochial schools, so that they may bring to the Jewish community adequate returns for their high cost in money and in time. Much greater stress should be laid by the parochial schools upon the teaching of *Hebrew as a living language* than they do at present. Instead of spending an inordinately large amouut of time upon the study of the Talmud, they should emphasize the study of the Hebrew language, thought, and literature—biblical, Talmudic, mediaeval and modern. Indeed, the Jewish parochial schools should become *Hebrew* parochial schools, centers of radiating energy for the Hebrew spirit and civilization.

Another fundamental objection to the Jewish parochial schools, as they are constituted at present, is that they are not really trying to accomplish their supposed purpose. Even those who believe in Jewish parochial schools do not suppose that it is possible to multiply them on any large scale and to make them the basis of a Jewish school system. But they do claim that the exceptional Jewish children should get an exceptional education; that they should be taken away from the regular Public School-Hebrew School System and put wholly under Jewish auspices for intensive instruction, preparing them to be the Jewish leaders of the next generation of American Jews.

But the difficulty is that the pupils of the parochial schools are not selected on the basis of merit or ability, but upon the basis of proximity of residence and of parents' desires. The Yeshibahs recruit their pupils from the children of the neighborhood, or from homes where the parents are particularly desirous to give their boys an intensive Jewish training. The average pupil of the Yeshibah is mentally and morally hardly better than the average pupil of the Talmud Torah. But in order to accomplish its purpose as a training school for exceptional children, the Yeshibah should not take in all children who apply, but should select very carefully for mental capacity, for diligence and grasp.

Such selection is not possible when the children first begin to attend school; it can take place only after the abilities of the pupils are watched over a period of years. The first three grades of the elementary parochial school should therefore be abolished, and the intermediate grades recruited from the ablest pupils of the lower grades of the Talmud Torahs. It may be possible for the Vaad Ha-Yeshiboth (Central Board of Parochial Schools) to persuade the Board of Jewish School Aid (representing the Talmud Torahs and Hebrew Schools) that some of the very brightest and most promising pupils from each Talmud Torah should be sent to the nearest Yeshibah for free intensive Jewish training. Carfares and lunches should be provided for these exceptional children, wherever it is necessary for them to travel, and the parents should be interested personally in the experiment which the Jewish community is making in the training of their children.

Upon this basis the Jews of America can plainly say that 99% of their children will go to the public schools and will receive their Jewish instruction in supplementary Jewish schools; but one per cent. of their children will be specially selected for the periods of intermediate and secondary schooling to be trained as the "priest class," as the centers of energy for intensive Jewish life.[33] For the education of this

---

[33] One per cent. of the 65,000 children receiving some form of Jewish instruction in New York would give the parochial schools 650 pupils. In point of fact, if the first three elementary grades be excluded, there are less than that number at present in the Jewish parochial schools of New York.

small "tenth of a tenth" of the Jewish children, the Jewish community should be willing to spend a great deal of money and of energy.

C. Curriculum of the Yiddishe Volks-Schule (National Radical School)[34]

One form of Jewish weekday school which differs in viewpoint and content of education, both from the Yeshibah and from the Hebrew School, is the Yiddishe Volks-Schule, or the National Radical School. Its course of study is somewhat shorter than that of the Talmud Torah, being designed for five to six years of instruction, and the number of hours of study averages from 5 to 10 hours per week. These schools differ from the Hebrew schools in two very significant points:

First, instead of Hebrew, the Yiddishe Volks-Schulen make Yiddish the most important subject of study and the center of their curriculum. The Yiddish language and literature receive in these schools approximately the same proportion of time as do Hebrew and Hebrew Literature in the Talmud Torah. In some schools even the Bible is taught in its Yiddish translation. The language of instruction and of school management is Yiddish and all the relations of teachers and pupils, of principals and parents, are carried on in that language. A number of Yiddish textbooks have appeared, some of them imported from Russia, others written and published in this country. The most popular of these textbooks in use among the Yiddishe Volks-Schulen are: *"Die Neie Yiddishe Schul"* (די נייע אידישע שול) by *J. Levin; "Die Yiddishe Schprach"* (די אידישע שפראך) by *Leon Elbe,* and *"Vun dem Yiddishen Qual"* (פון דעם אידישען קוואל) by *Enteen-Elbe.* For more advanced pupils selections from the works of modern Yiddish prose writers and poets are read: Mendele Mocher Sforim, Sholom Aleichem, Peretz, Asch, Rosenfeld, Reisen, and others. Jewish history is taught in Yiddish, though Hebrew is taught by the Natural Method, much in the same way as it is taught in the first years of the Hebrew school.

The second point of departure from the usual Talmud Torah

---

[34] The name "National Radical School" has been recently (1918) officially abandoned by these schools, but it is kept here for better identification.

curriculum lies in the fact that these schools do not teach "Religion." The meaning of Jewish festivals and holidays they do teach, but as national events only, without giving their religious significance. Prayers, customs and ceremonial law they do not teach at all. While they in no way antagonize or teach "against" the observance of Jewish religious customs, they nevertheless do not consider it either as necessary or desirable for the education of the modern Jewish child.

The principles underlying the work of these schools are significant. In the first place, the Yiddishe Volks-Schulen arose because Yiddish was supposed to be the Jewish mother tongue of the children, and was therefore the "natural" medium for transmitting Jewish knowledge to them. Second, it is the language of the Jewish masses and of the parents of the children; it is the language of the Jewish press, and of the Jewish theatre; and in its literature are deposited the customs, institutions and social psychology of the Jewish life in Eastern Europe during the past century. The third, and most far reaching argument advanced on behalf of these schools, is that they are the basis of a distinct Jewish national life in this country, with Yiddish as the national language of daily intercourse.

An examination of these principles discloses first, that the argument based on the supposition that Yiddish is the children's mother tongue is not tenable in this country. The average American Jewish boy and girl born in this country do *not* know Yiddish as their "natural" means of communication, and only children of immigrant parents know it well enough to use it for purposes of daily intercourse. Some of the teachers of the Yiddishe Volks-Schulen quite naively complain that they cannot make their pupils talk Yiddish regularly, and that as soon as their backs are turned the children lapse into "street" English. Every year sees a smaller and smaller proportion of children whose "natural" mother tongue is Yiddish, and with the break in the onrushing waves of immigration, this proportion will continue to decrease.

It is true, however, that Yiddish is still the language of the Jewish masses in this country, and that Jewish children, especially those who come from Yiddish-speaking homes, should have some means for communicating with their parents and the Jewish masses. But for this purpose it is not necessary to have distinct Yiddish schools. Some instruction in the reading and writing of Yiddish can and should be provided for children who know Hebrew, in the Talmud Torahs and Hebrew Schools, particularly in Yiddish-speaking sections; though there is no reason why, on this score, it should be made the center of the curriculum to the detriment of Hebrew and of Hebrew Literature.

The argument on the ground of distinct language-nationality is hardly feasible in this country. The United States is not divided along linguistic-territorial lines, nor has it any large bodies of aboriginal populations conquered by force, as is the case in Austria-Hungary. The foreign language-speaking peoples who came to America during the last century mingled pretty freely as regards choice of residence, so that there are many language-nationalities on the same common territory. Their common language of economic, social and civic life is bound to be English. Only as a means for keeping in contact with the cultures and institutions of their national centers will they be able to preserve their language in this country, particularly where the national culture has risen to the height of religious force and sanction. For this purpose not Yiddish but Hebrew will be the cultural-religious-national language of American Jews, because the heart of Jewry will be not Poland but Palestine, and Hebrew has again become the national living language of modern Palestine. It is probable that the next generation of American Jews will have very few Yiddish elements in their environment, no matter what artificial means be used for keeping Yiddish alive in this country.

D. Secondary Instruction for Jewish Adolescents

Beyond the elementary schools the Jews of New York make but very little provision for continuing the Jewish training of their children. Less than one per cent. of the children who receive some form of elementary Jewish instruction continue their studies into the adolescent period. Such secondary training as is now afforded by the Jews of New York is very recent, practically dating from the advent of the Bureau of Jewish Education. The secondary classes for Jewish high school boys and high school girls, conducted by the Bureau of Jewish

Education, are for selected pupils who were graduated from the Talmud Torahs and Hebrew Schools. These adolescents are taught from 5 to 6 hours during the week over a period of 3 to 4 years. The subjects of instruction are Hebrew (composition and grammar), Bible and Hebrew Literature, Talmud and Jewish History. The instruction in all subjects (excepting History) is conducted in Hebrew, and a great deal of stress is laid upon an adequate knowledge of the language and literature. The secondary classes of such schools as the National Hebrew School do not differ greatly either in content or method from the classes of the Bureau of Jewish Education. While in all of these classes some instruction is given concerning Palestine, their curricula in general are subject to the same criticism in that they fail to pay sufficient attention to the Jewish Present (America, Palestine and other lands), as is true of the elementary schools.[36]

The Yeshibahs, or Jewish parochial Schools, afford their pupils the opportunity of continuing under the same educational régime during the adolescent period, through the Jewish parochial high school conducted by the Yeshibath Etz Chaim. This is a regular Parochial Secondary School, the Jewish studies being pursued in the morning and the secular studies in the afternoon. Like the elementary parochial schools, the high school is under the supervision of the State Board of Regents, and sufficient instruction in the "staple" high school subjects is given to satisfy the demands of the state examinations.

It has been pointed out [37] that the basis upon which American education is organized permits parochial education in the high school period far more readily than it does in the elementary school period. In so far as this is true, the Jews should utilize this fact in providing Jewish High School education for specially selected adolescents, giving them both the Jewish and the general instruction under Jewish auspices. This will be possible however only for a small number of the Jewish high school boys and girls, first because of the very high cost of high school education,[37a] and second because of the competition of the state sup-

---

[36] See pp. 308-312.

[37] Cf. Levin S. "In Milchomo Zeiten" (In War Times), pp. 290-291.

[37a] The per capita cost in the New York City high schools is about $100 annually, Cf. Annual Report of the Superintendent of Schools 1914-15, pp. 393-4.

ported general and technical high schools. It should be both possible and desirable, however, for one Jewish High School to be established in each of the very largest Jewish centers, to act as "vocational" preparatory schools for the training of rabbis and other Jewish leaders.

For the Jewish adolescents who are not fortunate enough to possess linguistic ability, there is no provision for secondary instruction. These children are unable to take part in the existing secondary classes, where attention is almost entirely devoted to the intensive study of the Hebrew language and of Jewish literature. Their Jewish instruction must, therefore, cease when they leave the elementary or intermediate schools. The lack of provision for the interests and abilities of these pupils is unfair to a large proportion of Jewish school children. Vernacular Secondary Classes should be provided for the graduates of the Vernacular Intermediate Classes and for those graduates of the Hebrew classes of the Talmud Torahs who cannot or will not continue intensive Hebrew studies. About four hours of instruction per week should be given to these adolescents. The subjects of instruction should continue to be Jewish Literature (in English translation), and Jewish History and Institutions; but emphasis should be laid on the Jewish Present, providing praticularly for an intimate study of the communal activities and organization of American Jewry: philanthropy, education, industry, recreation, control of vice and crime, and defense against discrimination. Just as the Secondary Hebrew classes have as their specific aim to prepare their pupils to enter the Teachers' Institutes or the Rabbinical Seminaries where they are to be trained as teachers and rabbis, so the Secondary Vernacular classes should aim specifically to prepare their pupils for the School for Jewish Communal Work, there to be trained as the social and communal workers of the Jewish community.

E. Institutions for Higher Jewish Learning

Three types of educational institution form the apex of the intensive Jewish school system in New York. These are the Teachers' Institutes, the Rabbinical Seminaries, and the School for Jewish Communal Work. They constitute, in a certain sense, a loosely organized, uncoördinated "Jewish University" in

New York, with Jewish education, the Ministry, and social or communal work as the professional branches of study.

The three Jewish *Teachers' Institutes* of New York have already been described and their work discussed.[38] One of them forms part of a Rabbinical Seminary; the other two are independent institutions.

There are in New York two *Theological Seminaries* for the training of rabbis. The Jewish Theological Seminary of America, situated at 531 West 123rd Street, of which Dr. Solomon Schechter was formerly president, is now headed by Dr. Cyrus Adler as acting president. About forty young men from various parts of the country are given four years of training in Bible, Biblical Criticism, Talmud, Midrashim, Codes, History, Homiletics (theory and practice of preaching), History of Jewish Literature, Jewish Philosophy, Theology, Liturgy, Hazanuth, Synagogue Practices, and Public Speaking. The work is conducted in the form of lectures and research. Applicants are required to have been graduated from some recognized college. Besides the regular courses leading to the degree of Rabbi, there are special opportunities for advanced work leading to the degrees of Doctor of Hebrew Literature and Doctor of Divinity. A junior department is also conducted for students who wish to prepare themselves to enter the Seminary For them courses are offered in Hebrew, Bible and Talmud. Courses in Pedagogy leading to the diploma as Jewish Teachers are given in the Teachers' Institute of the Seminary.[39]

The Rabbi Isaac Elchanan Theological Seminary, also called the Rabbinical College of America, is situated at 9-11 Montgomery Street, and is under the leadership of Dr. Bernard Revel. The course of instruction leads to ordination or "Semicha" as Rabbi. The subjects taught are much the same as in the Jewish Theological Seminary, namely: Talmud, Codes, Homiletics, Pedagogy, Hebrew and Aramaic Philology, Bible and Jewish History. The general differences between the two institutions are that the Rabbinical College (1) does not make graduation from some college a prerequisite, either for entrance or for ordination; (2) it lays greater stress on the study of Talmud

[38] See pp. 285-287.

[39] See p. 285.

and Codes; and (3) it requires more rigid standards of orthodox attitude and practice on the part of its pupils.

The School for Jewish Communal Work, with headquarters at 125 East 85th Street, is managed by an Administrative Committee of which Dr. S. Benderly is chairman. Its function is to train professional workers for the social and communal work carried on by the Jews of this country. It offers a three years' course of instruction to college graduates, which is divided into Basic Studies and Group Studies. The Basic Courses include: Immigration, Problems of Modern Industry, Child Caring, Correctional Work, Religious Education, Work in Y. M. H. and Kindred Associations, Social Legislation, Public Health, Management and Administration of Communal Agencies, Religion and Modern Life, and the Position of the Jew in America. The Group Courses consist of specialized study in some one phase of Jewish communal work and its related fields of activity. The School also provides opportunity for extension study, in the form of Institutes, for active workers in the various fields of communal activity, who are not able to pursue the more advanced professional courses.

The Rabbinic Seminaries have in the past provided no training in social or communal work for their students. Their graduates, therefore, found themselves at a loss in many of the important duties as rabbis outside of the pulpit, and had to learn the problems of their communities and the means for solving these problems by the costly process of trial and error. Many young rabbis are "good but impractical" persons because the world of Jewish life and activity is different and more complex than was given them to see in their Seminary training. Some of the most significant interests of the American rabbi lie outside of the pulpit, and for these interests and tasks the rabbinical students should be prepared. As a first hopeful step in this direction the Jewish Theological Seminary is co-operating with the School for Jewish Communal Work in giving its students a knowledge of the basic problems of the Jewish community.

The but recently organized (1915) School for Jewish Communal Work, on the other hand, has been suffering because of the lack of adequately prepared applicants. As a graduate professional school, it is not in a position to give to its students the background in knowledge of Jewish history, literature and social psychology, of Hebrew and Yiddish, which are necessary for effective, purposive Jewish communal work. At present all too large a proportion of Jewish social workers are ignorant of the people for whom they are working, and neglectful of its past, its problems and its yearnings. They treat their work from the philanthropic or "human" view point, and in many instances, are hardly better qualified for their Jewish work than well-disposed non-Jews would be. There is no Jewish purpose or intimate group consciousness in their work, and they fail to utilize the deepest impulses of the persons with whom they are dealing. To prepare *Jewish* communal workers, with deep Jewish knowledge and broad human sympathies, is the task of the School for Jewish Communal Work. This task it cannot accomplish, however, unless it is based on a secondary school system with courses designed to prepare the students for professional Jewish work.[40]

One of the problems which has affected the work of all the Institutions for higher Jewish learning, is the need of the students to earn a livelihood while they are pursuing their studies. Instead of concentrating their attention upon their studies, the students are often compelled to undertake meaningless routine work as "pot-boilers" to eke out a living for themselves and their dependents. It is, perhaps, unfortunate that "from the children of the poor must come forth the Law," but it is a fact with which the schools have been trying to grapple. The Rabbinic Seminaries have been giving stipends to their needy pupils. The School for Jewish Communal Work has provided its graduate students with paid part-time work in some communal institution carrying on activities in which the students are particularly interested. Some of the Teachers' Institutes have been seeking to obtain scholarships for their most deserving, but needy pupils, requiring from them a definite amount of study in return for the scholarship. This is an unsolved problem, for no one of the above solutions seems to be sufficient. Several elements of aid are needed. All of the students (particularly the older ones) should be provided with a limited

[40] See Vernacular Secondary courses, pp. 336-337.

amount of paid part-time work connected with their special interests. Thus, for teachers, provision should be made for paid practice teaching or school clerkship; rabbinical students should be employed as junior assistants to rabbis, or as Jewish school teachers; for communal students, work should be found with institutions of particular interest. The amount of time which the students are to give to such part-time work should be carefully regulated. To those students whose financial needs are larger than the part-time salaries which they would receive, scholarships should be offered for which definite return in study and achievement should be required.

The various professional schools constituting the uncoordinated "Jewish University" of New York, are naturally independent institutions under the auspices of distinct and separate bodies. They should and most probably will continue to be distinct and separate schools. But where several schools are doing interrelated work with tangential, if not similar purposes, there is bound to be unnecessary waste and overlapping. It is not beyond reason to hope that some co-ordination is possible among them. Perhaps an Academy of Jewish Learning, or simply a Committee on Jewish Professional Schools could be organized, representing the various schools, in order to avoid wasted energy through unnecessary duplication of work, and to stimulate such activities as the exchange of lecturers, for example. Without attempting to interfere in the curricula, spirit or management of the respective institutions, the Committee could yet be very useful in promoting Jewish professional training.

It seems that for the "Jewish University" of New York, a "Finishing School" will develop, and that school will be Palestine. To indulge in prophecy, it appears that the time is not far distant, when no serious Jewish professional worker, whether rabbi, teacher or communal worker, will consider his training complete before visiting the Land of the Fathers, there to drink deep of the reawakened fountain of Jewish life, and to bring back new inspiration and redoubled zeal for his work in this country.[41]

To be sure, if American Jewry is to continue as an integral

---

[41] There has been much discussion among the Jews concerning the founding of a "Hebrew University" in this country, conducted along the general lines of one of the existing Catholic Universities. Aside from the

progressive unit of international Jewry, it must produce leaders from its own midst. American young men and women, trained in American institutions, must be depended upon to fashion American Jewish life. But the American training schools for professional Jewish workers are situated in the midst of an indifferent non-Jewish environment, and consequently find it very difficult to inculcate in their students the living Jewish spirit and the group will which the professional worker must embody. In ever increasing measure, therefore, will Jewish teachers, communal workers and rabbis, make pilgrimages to the Hebrew University in Jerusalem for the purpose of "finishing" their training before beginning their life work in America. And through teaching the teachers of International Jewry, the Hebrew University can become a unifying cultural force in universal Israel.

---

doubtful feasibility of the plan, and its possible undesirability, the establishment of a parochial university in America has certainly become even less urgent than heretofore, in view of the founding of the Hebrew University in Jerusalem, which could and should act as the pinnacle of the Jewish educational system throughout the world.

Chapter XI.

THE CONTENT OF JEWISH EDUCATION

(Extensive Curricula)

Besides the intensive system of schooling (elementary, intermediate, secondary and high), which should form the backbone and center of the Jewish educational activities in this country, there is needed, and for a long time to come there will be needed, provision for the extensive education of the great numbers of Jewish children who cannot be accommodated in the regular weekday schools. It has been pointed out above[1] that at any one time less than one-seventh of the Jewish children of school age are found in all of the intensive Jewish schools (Talmud Torahs, Hebrew Schools, Yiddishe Volks-Schulen and Yeshibahs).[2] The great majority who are outside of Jewish weekday schools consists of (1) those who do not desire any Jewish instruction, (2) those who wish but a minimum of such training, and (3) those whose desires for Jewish education cannot be satisfied because of inadequate school facilities.

To deal effectively with this great army of Jewish children who are not in weekday Jewish schools, and to provide for at least a minimum of educational influence to prepare them for their life as American Jews, is one of the great problems of Jewish educators and of communal leaders. The failure to educate these children affects not only the unschooled, but those who *are* in the schools as well, because to teach a small minority successfully when these children are surrounded by friends, acquaintances and playmates who are not taught and not interested, is a very difficult task. Some one has pithily said: "It is like trying to boil water at the North Pole." Unless a proper Jewish atmosphere envelops the children who are given intensive Jewish training, they cannot be expected to keep "warm" for any length of time. It is in this large task of providing Jewish education for the children who either do not desire or cannot obtain the intensive training of the regular weekday school, that the Jewish Sunday Schools, the extension educational activities

---

[1] See p. 159.

[2] Including the Chedarim, the proportion of children who could be taught at any one time in intensive Jewish schools is about one-sixth (17%).

of the Bureau of Jewish Education and of the Zionists, the Menorah Movement, and much of the prevailing private tuition, play a significant role.

A. Curriculum of Sunday Schools

The course of study of the typical Jewish Sunday School extends over four or five years,[3] 34 weeks during each year,[4] and two and a half hours each week.[5] Sessions are held on Sunday mornings from 9 or 9:30 to 12 o'clock. The total time of instruction during the Sunday School course of five years is about 420 hours, distributed among the various subjects of study as follows:

	(Grade) I	II	III	IV	V	Total	
						Hours	%
Hebrew	21	29	29	25	25	129	30.7
History	45	40	38	38	40	201	47.8
Religion and Ethics	14	16	16	18	20	84	20.0
Bible	..	..	2	4	..	6	1.5
Total (hours)	80	85	85	85	85	420	100.0%

The largest proportion of time (almost one-half) is devoted to *Jewish History;* almost one-third of the total time is given over to teaching the rudiments of *Hebrew;* and the rest of the time of instruction is given to *Religion and Ethics.* The *Bible* as a distinct subject of study is practically not taught at all!

In most of the larger Sunday Schools an Assembly, or Children's Service, is held either before or after the classroom instruction. The Assembly lasts from fifteen minutes to half an hour, and usually includes the singing of hymns, recitations of biblical "memory gems," and a "sermonette" by the rabbi.

[3] Ten of the larger Jewish Sunday Schools of New York gave their complete courses of study, together with the time-allotment for each subject. All of the 10 schools reported curricula for three grades; 8 reported for four grades; 5 reported for five grades, and 4 for six grades.

[4] Two schools reported 30 weeks; three reported 32 weeks; one 35 weeks; three 36 weeks and one 40 weeks.

[5] The first grade receives somewhat less time.

Some of the Sunday Schools also conduct so-called "post-confirmation" classes. But practically none of these classes in New York has a definitely organized course of study; the subjects and methods in each case depending upon the knowledge of the teacher, the whims of the pupils, and the particular "conditions." In the better schools the time is spent in talks and discussions on Reform Judaism, Jewish History and Current Topics.

Methods and Text Books

History: Just as the curriculum of the Talmud Torahs and Hebrew Schools is a *literary* curriculum, so that of the Sunday schools is a *history* curriculum. Although *history* does not receive any more (gross) time than in the Hebrew schools (200 hours), it nevertheless occupies the center of attention in the Sunday Schools. The most popular history textbooks used in these schools are the series of books by *M. H. Harris*: *"The People of the Book"* (three parts), *"A Thousand Years of Jewish History," "History of Mediaeval Jews"* and *"Modern Jewish History"*; and the *"Outline of Jewish History"* by *Lady Magnus*. Besides the poor organization and the purposelessness which characterize the present teaching of history in most of the Jewish schools,[6] the Sunday School teachers also commit the pedagogic "crime" of exhausting a "moral" from every history lesson which they teach. No tale, no historical character or event, but was intended by Almighty God as a moral lesson for "you children." Moreover, the children cannot be relied upon to draw the moral themselves, the teacher must make sure that they "know" it, that is, that they can repeat it in the particular words in which she wants them to retain it. Every lesson is fully "exhausted" until the pupils know it "once for all." Consequently, it is but natural to find very few Sunday School graduates who really know anything beyond the "Destruction." Much of the namby-pamby, goody atmosphere of the Sunday Schools, with its glib lip worship and its blissful lack of understanding, is due to this constant pressing of the "moral" out of every good tale or thrilling historical narrative. To far better advantage would it be for the Sunday Schools to select about

[6] See pp. 322-324.

100 to 150 good tales, including a cycle of folk tales, (biblical and other), and a cycle of biographic sketches,[7] gathered from the whole of Jewish history, and to tell these tales simply as good stories, vividly and with all the aids at the disposal of the modern teacher: stereopticon views, pictures, maps, models, dramatization, etc. This change of method would help clear the "moral" atmosphere of the school, and would leave more lasting and worth-while impressions than are left at present.

Religion and Ethics: The spirit of "moralizing" prevails even to a greater extent in the teaching of Religion. As ordinarily understood, the subject of Religion contains a number of elements, among them: conduct, institutions and customs, worship and theology. Very little of conduct can be taught abstractly and, to children, even less of theology. Educators have long debated the possibilities and value of teaching ethics formally.[8] Scientific opinion seems to favor strongly the idea that ethics, or principles of conduct, can be taught only in relation to actual life situations. The time which the child *lives* in the Sunday School is so short, and the situations so different from ordinary life, that conduct can be taught only to a limited degree in the Sunday Schools by the *natural* method. In most cases it would be better to do away entirely with the teaching of "formal ethics." It may prevent the Sunday Schools from deluding themselves with regard to the amount of influence which they can exert upon the daily life of their pupils.

If the Sunday Schools do wish to teach formal ethics let them at least do so through inspiring stories, from the Bible and elsewhere, organized around traits of character, and selected to illustrate various phases and expressions of particular traits of character.[9] The inferences derived from such stories should be the children's inferences, and if these do not agree with the expectations of the teacher, she must select another story that will illustrate her meaning more clearly. Certainly, biblical dicta or phrases, and meaninglessly "good" poems for children,

---

[7] Cf. Discussion of "Concentric Method," p. 324.

[8] Dewey, J.: "Moral Principles in Education." Gould, F. J.: "Moral Instruction." Adler, Felix: "Moral Instruction of Children."

[9] Gould, F. J.: "Children's Book of Moral Lessons" (four vols.); "Stories for Moral Instruction"; and also "Syllabus of Moral and Civic Instruction."

are not particularly related to the life of the pupils, do not elicit enthusiastic interest, and cannot form the basis for teaching conduct. A number of manuals on teaching the Jewish Religion are used in the Sunday Schools, which attempt the impossible task of talking ethics into children.

Jewish customs and institutions, on the other hand, can be more hopefully taught. Most of the pupils in the Sunday Schools come from homes where but few of the Jewish customs are observed. Consequently these "bits of life" are strange to the children, and the teacher's task is the more difficult because of it. The current textbooks for teaching the Jewish customs and institutions used by the Sunday Schools are: *"Religion of Israel"* by *J. H. Greenstone; "Sabbath School Companion"* by *A. Guttmacher; "The Jewish Religion"* by *H. P. Mendes;* and, for older pupils, *"Judaism as Creed and Life,"* by *M. Joseph.*

In teaching Jewish Customs and Institutions to Sunday School children, the two important considerations are: *concreteness,* and provision for some form of participation or *activity.* School collections of ceremonial objects, the celebration of Jewish festivals within the school, pictures, illustrations and stereopticon views of Jewish institutions, are of great aid in this direction. *The Jewish Arts and Crafts,* developed by the Bureau of Jewish Education, should also prove very helpful to the teacher in eliciting the active interest of the pupils. This work thus far consists of (1) paper cutting and constructing of toy ceremonial objects connected with all of the festivals (Succah, Purim Mask, Gift Box, etc.), for which purpose printed designs and instructions are supplied to the pupils; (2) leather work and designing in leather, in which Jewish objects and figures are used as the designs; (3) sewing and crocheting of such Jewish "home" objects as the Chalah Cover, Matzoh Cover, Mizrach Decoration, etc.; and (4) "Illuminating," that is, "printing" and coloring of Hebrew texts.

Throughout the Sunday School course the attempt is made to teach the Jewish "creed" or the principles of the Jewish faith. Particular stress is laid on this phase of the work during the year before the pupils are confirmed, when they are required to come an extra session during the week for special religious instruction by the rabbi. On the whole, however, the method of *catechism* is but little employed in modern Jewish Sunday Schools. This neglect of catechism is very much to be commended, for it is more important for Jewish teachers to make sure that their pupils really understand the great perennial *questions* of religion, than to give them glib, stereotyped and partially-true *answers*.

Bible: It is striking to find that the Jewish Sunday Schools do not teach the Bible. They teach *about* the Bible; but not the Bible itself. In a few schools the "*Junior Bible for Jewish Children*" by *Lehman-Kent,* consisting of 95 leaflets, is being used. But this series, necessitating continuous buying of leaflets and binding them together, has not been found wholly practical. The leaflets are not sufficiently illustrated (one picture for the leaflet), and the questions at the end of the leaflet smack strongly of the usual moralizing. The series of *Bible folders* issued by the Bureau of Jewish Education (10 folders through the Five Books of Moses) are better illustrated, but they are not in the language of the Bible, and whatever may be their worth in aiding the teacher to tell the Bible stories, they cannot be used as texts for teaching the Bible itself. The same criticism holds true of the "Junior Bible Stories," a series of leaflets issued by the Department of Synagogue and School Extension, (Cincinnati), and of other Bible story books.

American Jewish children are not taught to read the Bible in English. They are given biblical memory gems, proverbs, psalms, etc., which they commit to memory; they are told the stories of the Bible; but they are not taught to read the Bible itself. This is an indictment against the Jewish Sunday Schools. It may be that the Bible language is somewhat too difficult for the children. Perhaps better juvenile Bible readers are needed than those now available. But the fact remains that the Sunday Schools are not teaching the Bible text to their pupils.

Hebrew: One-third of the time of the Sunday School is given over to the teaching of Hebrew. The textbooks in current use for this purpose are the "*Union Hebrew Readers*" by *Krauskopf-Berkowitz,* and the "*Chautauqua System*" of teaching Hebrew, by *Gerson B. Levi.* Some of the largest Sunday Schools in New York have begun to teach Hebrew by the natural method, and have introduced the "*Sefer Hatalmid*" (first year), issued by the Bureau of Jewish Education.

The aim of the schools is to enable the children to read the Hebrew prayers sufficiently well to follow the synagogue service and to understand the meaning of some of the most important synagogue responses (Shma, etc.). But modest as this aim is, it is very seldom accomplished. Probably less than 10% of the Sunday School graduates are able to read the Hebrew prayers of the Union Prayer Book well enough to take part in the services. The reason for this failure to teach even the rudiments of Hebrew reading is not far to seek. The total amount of time which the Sunday Schools are in a position to devote to Hebrew during the entire five-year course, is about 130 hours, equaling approximately the first half year of the Talmud Torah curriculum. In other words, the maximum achievement in Hebrew which it is possible for Sunday Schools to attain is equal to the first half year of the Talmud Torah work. Subtract from this, teachers who are incompetent to teach Hebrew and are indifferent to it, subtract also six days of forgetting between each lesson and three months of vacation between each of the five school years, and the result is pretty nearly an utter waste of effort.

The Sunday Schools have clung to the minimum of Hebrew which they teach, because of the "sacredness" of the language, because its very presence in the school supplies a certain amount of "Jewish" atmosphere, and because they hope to accomplish the desired results of teaching their pupils to read the Hebrew prayers. If it were possible to achieve tangible, worth-while results by devoting to the study of Hebrew the limited time at the disposal of the Sunday School, Hebrew should by all means be taught. But the facts indicate that it is wiser to *eliminate* Hebrew entirely from the Sunday morning curriculum. The time now devoted to it can be given over to more teachable subjects, and special efforts should be made to teach Hebrew during the *weekdays* to those children who can be interested in its study.

Some congregations have realized the futility of teaching Hebrew on Sunday mornings only, and have changed to weekday schools, with instruction two or three afternoons during the week. In many congregations, however, it is not possible to make this desirable change. The parents are satisfied with a minimum of Jewish instruction, and the limits of that minimum are set by what can be accomplished on Sunday mornings. In these congregations, the rabbi should make strenuous efforts to persuade individual parents to teach their children Hebrew during the week. Small "private" classes, of five or six pupils per class, can be organized for this purpose. These private classes should be taught in the homes of the pupils by special Hebrew teachers, who should report regularly to the Rabbi and act under his general supervision. Each Hebrew teacher would be in a position to teach several such groups during the week. The tuition may be paid by the parents as tuition fees, or as special congregation dues, and the fees in each case will vary with the amount of instruction and with the size of the group.

In this manner many children of the congregation, and many homes, may be interested in learning Hebrew. Those children whose parents cannot be induced to make the additional sacrifice or to show the necessary interest to enable them to learn Hebrew, are not really reached by the present Sunday morning "dose" of Hebrew either. The time saved from the teaching of Hebrew could be utilized to far better advantage in the study of the Bible, in its American-Jewish translation, and in giving the pupils some information concerning the various aspects of the Jewish Present.[10]

As long as the Sunday School curriculum is confined to Sunday mornings only, it must necessarily be a "minimum" curriculum. It cannot form the basis of a Jewish educational system in this country. For the regular Jewish instruction of their children, the Jews of New York are looking to the intensive weekday school system. But alongside of elementary and intermediate weekday schools, the Sunday Schools can serve a useful purpose in exerting some educational influence over the children of those parents whose Jewish educational desires are limited to Sunday mornings.

Private Tutoring

Very different from the Sunday School curriculum, and yet actuated by like motives of "minimum essentials" in Jewish instruction, is much of the Jewish private teaching in New York. Not that all parents who teach their children at home wish to give them only a minimum of Jewish training. On the contrary,

---

[10] Cf. above pp. 308-312.

many Jewish parents employ private teachers for the Jewish instruction of their children because they wish to give them *more* intensive training than they believe can be obtained in the available schools. They spare no effort or money to offer their children the best that they can obtain for them in Jewish instruction. If the results in most instances are meagre, and below the achievements of the modern Hebrew School, it is because there are no more adequate school facilities to attract those children.

On the other hand, many Jewish parents resort to private tutors because they are baffled by the problem of giving their children adequate Jewish instruction in this country. The natural tendency for the average parents is to express the traditional impulse through the traditional channels, and if it is not the "good, old-fashioned" Cheder, then it is the *Melamed,* or itinerant teacher. In despair, these parents say: "In this country our children will not be rabbis anyhow, let them at least know that which they must know as Jews." Because of the lack of adequate school facilities, therefore, and because of the ignorance of parents as to the best means of providing for the Jewish interests of their children, much of the private tutoring by Melamedim or in the poorer Chedarim, resolves itself into an extensive curriculum for teaching what the parents consider to be the minimum essentials.

The amount of time which is devoted to private instruction at home [11] averages from two to three hours per week.[12] The subjects of instruction are: *Ivri* (mechanical reading of Hebrew prayers), which takes up most of the time; some *Chumash* (Pentateuch); *Berachoth* (benedictions); the *Kiddush* (Friday Eve Benediction); the reading of the *Haftorah* (Prophetic Portion); and a *Confirmation Speech* for Bar-Mitzvah (Confirmation). Many of the children thus taught are of course not able to complete the entire "curriculum," and their training is limited to the laborious reading of Ivri. The instruction is conducted in the homes of the individual pupils, and is carried

---

[11] What is said of private instruction at home by Melamedim, applies also, in large measure, to much of the Cheder instruction. There are of course Chedarim and private Jewish teachers whose work approximates that of the regular Talmud Torah. But these are not the general rule.

[12] From 20 to 30 minutes, five times during the week.

on in Yiddish, or (where the children cannot speak Yiddish) in a "patois" English. The Melamed (teacher) is an elderly immigrant, who was either a Hebrew teacher in "the old country," a sexton or some other "religious official," or else, a petty tradesman who supplements his meagre earnings in this fashion. The methods used by these itinerant teachers consist of alphabetic and syllabic Hebrew reading taught by rote repetition, and of word for word translation of the Pentateuch. Their textbooks are: The *Siddur* (Prayer Book) and the *Pentateuch*, and but infrequently do any of these teachers use special textbooks for teaching Hebrew.[13] The result of their teaching in most instances is that the children learn to read Hebrew a little, and dislike Jewish study and Judaism very much.

And yet, under present conditions, the private teacher, or the Melamed system, which reaches ten to twenty thousand Jewish children [14] in New York, is not an unmixed evil. As long as the Jewish community of New York is not able to supply adequate Jewish school buildings and modern school facilities for all its school children, the traditional impulse for Jewish education must find some expression, unfortunate as that expression may be. Viewed from the standpoint of Jewish extension education, it is better that the "unschooled" children be taught something, than that they be not taught at all. It is the fault of the community that the "something" is given to Jewish children in so wasteful and repugnant a fashion. The desire is there, created by the long educational tradition of the Jews; it is the community's responsibility to house that desire in modern school buildings and to teach Jewish parents that the American environment demands new educational content and other educational methods than those to which they were accustomed in Eastern Europe.

There will probably always be parents who, for various reasons, will be either unable or unwilling to send their children to regularly constituted Jewish schools. For these children some communal agency, like the Board of Jewish School Aid, should organize a modern system of supervised private instruction, as

[13] See previous chapter, pp. 318-320.

[14] Ten thousand at any one time, and more than twice as many during the entire school age period. See Chapter VIII, p. 253.

already described.[15] A corps of well-trained Jewish teachers should be organized who are to teach children individually or in small groups at their own homes. Tuition fees should be paid not to the individual teachers, but to the central agency, the teachers to be required to report regularly to special supervisors appointed for the management of this work. The intensiveness of the instruction and the amount of time devoted to it may vary with the particular children or group, and several graded curricula should be planned for that purpose. These curricula would follow along the lines of either the basic elementary course,[16] the intensive Hebrew course, or the vernacular course. If organized along these lines, private tutoring may become an organized asset to a Jewish educational system, instead of being a wasteful, meaningless chaos.

Extension Activities of the Bureau of Jewish Education

Even before any scientific study was made of the Jewish educational situation in New York, it was realized that neither the Sunday Schools nor private teaching, are taking care of the great number of boys and girls who are not in Jewish weekday schools. Every investigation has brought out the fact that a large majority of the Jewish children of school age are not under any Jewish educational influence. To accommodate all Jewish school children at the present time, at least 137 new school buildings would be needed, and about 1,800 new teachers,[17] clearly an impossible task for the immediate future. In order to deal immediately with the great army of the unschooled, a plan of educational organization is therefore needed which does not require regular school facilities (classrooms, teachers, etc.), but which should nevertheless be capable of exerting Jewish influence over large numbers of children. The Bureau of Jewish Education has for the past eight years been experimenting to find the means for accomplishing this purpose of reaching quickly and with little cost the masses of unschooled Jewish children in New York.[18] Its efforts have crystallized in the

[15] See Chapter VIII, p. 243.

[16] See previous Chapter, pp. 312-317.

[17] Cf. Part II, Chapter II, p. 171.

[18] For the history and development of these activities, see Part I, Chapter 4.

Circle of Jewish Children for boys and girls of elementary school age, and in the *League of the Jewish Youth* for adolescents.

The lowest minimum of Jewish educational content which must be imparted to Jewish children in this country is the sense of *affiliation* or "belonging to" the Jewish people. All intensive Jewish education is simply the elaboration and enrichment of this sense of "belonging to" the Jewish people, by teaching its content and significance. It was felt, therefore, that the irreducible minimum and basic aim of extension Jewish education must be the inculcating of this sense of "belonging to." This minimum educational content the Circle of Jewish Children transmits, first, by making its children members of a definite Jewish organization, an organization of the Children of the Jewish People; second, by encouraging them to participate in the social phases of Jewish life, particularly in the celebration of Jewish festivals; and third, by putting into their hands readable material concerning the Jews of today and the Jews of the past.

The Circle of Jewish Children is organized as a "movement," that is, it considers the very act of "belonging" as educative, and strives to make this act as conscious as possible. It therefore distributes special Circle Buttons to its members, teaches them special Circle Songs, and has them make special Circle pledges. The boy and girl "*leaders*" of the various groups [19] are especially imbued with the sense of Circle loyalty. They meet frequently, are told inspirational stories from Jewish history, and in various ways are made to feel that the responsibility of making the Circle meaningful in the lives of their friends and playmates, rests upon them. Special pamphlets explaining the meaning and the work of the Circle are distributed among the children, and other devices are employed designed to make the act of belonging to the Circle conscious and pleasing.

In view of the fact that it is clearly impossible to teach the *literary* or the *historical* phases of Judaism without adequate school facilities, the Circle emphasizes the *social* phases of Jewish life, the holidays, customs and institutions. It invites its mem-

[19] The general plan of organization of the Circle and the League is explained in Part I, Chapter 4, pp. 124-126; and in Part II, Chapter 2, pp. 175-176.

bers to attend celebrations of many of the historic Jewish festivals (Pesach, Shabuoth, Succoth, Chanuckah, Purim, Tisha be'Av, Lag b'Omer, Chamisha Asar b'Shevat); the commemoration of such national American holidays as the Fourth of July, Thanksgiving Day, and the Birthdays of Washington and Lincoln; the celebration of some of the modern Jewish national holidays, such as the Palestine Flower Day and the Jewish Flag Day. There are thus a dozen or more occasions during the year which offer opportunities for assembly and celebration. Around these festival celebrations, the actual "teaching" of the Circle is organized. The story of the festival is told, usually with the aid of stereopticon views, and the meaning of the customs connected with it is explained to the children. The children themselves participate in the festival songs, and prepare an appropriate "entertainment," consisting of dramatization, recitation, dancing and singing. To prepare for these entertainments "festival clubs" are organized composed of Circle members who are especially able or interested. There are a variety of festival clubs: *choir clubs* to learn the folk and festival melodies; *dramatic clubs* for preparing plays, sketches, tableaux and recitations dealing with the festivals; *dancing clubs* to learn folk dances and interpretative dancing; and *"arts and crafts" clubs* to make out of paper, leather, etc., artistic objects and designs for these festivals.[20] The work is planned for a cycle of three years, and every year a different aspect of the festival is emphasized.

To aid in affiliating the children with the Jews all over the world and with the Jewish Past, reading material is distributed periodically, particularly *"The Jewish Child."* This is a juvenile weekly containing the most important Jewish news of the day, short stories, poems, illustrations and explanations of customs and institutions. In some cases "Jewish Child Clubs" or "Current Events Clubs" are organized for discussing the content of *The Jewish Child* magazine. Besides this magazine, festival pamphlets are distributed giving the historic background of the Jewish festivals.

It is evident that the Circle program of activities can be of benefit not only to the unschooled children, but to those who

---

[20] For discussion of "Jewish arts and crafts," see above p. 346.

attend Jewish schools as well. Indeed, it is the aim of the Circle to associate the unschooled with those who are in school, and to stimulate in them the desire to attend school also. For this reason the Circle is organized about existing Jewish schools, some of the pupils of the schools often acting as "leaders" of groups of unschooled friends and playmates. It is the aim of the Circle of Jewish Children to encourage the organization of branches in connection with every Jewish school.

If a system of extension education is important for children of school age, it is even more greatly needed for adolescents. The Jewish community makes far less provision for the education of its young men and young women than it does for its school children, and the traditional educational impulse which actuates Jewish parents is not so potent beyond the elementary school period, as it is during that period. But if the Jews are to preserve their group life in this country, it is essential that they do not lose hold of their young during the most impressionable period of their life—adolescence. The League of the Jewish Youth was organized for this purpose of providing Jewish affiliation and interests for the adolescent. The educational philosophy of the League is similar to that of the Circle. Its central ideas are: (1) affiliation with the Jewish People through belonging to an organization composed of the Youth of that People; (2) participation in the social phases of Jewish life; (3) acquaintance with the current life and problems of the Jews; and (4) service to the Jewish community.

Besides the various devices for affiliation used in the Circle (special pins, songs, etc.), the League also proposes an elaborate series of Initiation Ceremonies, to mark the difference in the life of the adolescent and its correspondent ranks in the League. At 13 or 14 years of age the boys and girls are received into the League as Junior members, through a formal ceremony based upon the customs and institutions of the biblical period of Jewish history. At 16 years of age the Juniors are promoted to the rank of Intermediates, and the ceremony for that occasion is taken from the life of the Jews during the rabbinic period. At 18 years of age the young men and women become Senior members formally, going through an initiation fashioned in accordance with the events and institutions of modern Jewish history. Lastly, when they reach the age of maturity, they are officially to be received into the adult Jewish community by its foremost men and women.

The division of the League into "tribes, camps and households" on the biblical plan, is a means not only for increasing the sense of affiliation, but is also used to acquaint the members with the historic background of their particular units. Thus a member of the "household of Hillel, camp Bethel, in the tribe of Judah" is required to know something concerning Hillel, Bethel and Judah. Similarly, the young men and women are stimulated to acquaint themselves with the meaning of friendly or rival "tribes, camps and households," and for this purpose "Leaflets on Names and Places" are to be published for distribution in the League. In particular are the "organizers" or heads of the households and camps, expected to know the meaning of these names and places, and special courses are being developed for instructing them in Jewish history and in current Jewish life.

The celebration of festivals is carried out by the League much in the same way as it is done by the Circle, with the additions and differences which are necessary because of the difference in the age of the participants. Even to a larger extent than in the Circle does the preparation for the festivals lie in the hands of the various "festival clubs" of the young people themselves. Friday evening services have also been instituted in various localities, which are largely managed by the members of the League and are open to all League members and their friends.

The study of current Jewish life, and its relation to the past, is as yet but poorly developed in the work of the League. A periodical magazine for adolescents, similar to The Jewish Child, is needed. Series of Mass Lectures on topics of current Jewish interest can be arranged for the members, and Open Debates might be conducted at regular intervals through which the young men and women should be given the opportunity of expressing their views on current problems. Pamphlets, syllabi and bibliographies, dealing with particular phases of the history and institutions of the Jews, are to be distributed among them. Some of these activities are now being carried on by the League. It were well that these activities be extended and arranged to cover the entire period of adolescence. •

Like the Circle, the League is organized about Jewish institutions; it includes, however, not only schools, but also social settlements, synagogues and other Jewish centers. The aim is to help in affiliating the young people with these centers and to interest them in some specific phases of their work: literary, athletic, religious, etc. The League is in this respect a supplementary agency to every Jewish institution that works with adolescents.

The link that unites the League, as a community of adolescents, to the adult Jewish community, is *service.* The motto of the League is: "Torah, Avodah u-Gemiluth Chasadim" (תורה עבודה וגמילת חסדים) translated as: "Study, Reverence and Service." It is through participating in actual tasks on behalf of the community in which they live, that young men and women can find their best preparation for their communal activities as adults. The League, therefore, has begun to undertake such tasks in the service of the Jewish community as those dealing with community organization, charities, Palestine propaganda, war relief, national war work, etc. If the significance of these activities can be constantly brought home to the young men and women who participate, the habituation to service on behalf of the community should prove a very important element in adolescent Jewish education.

Intercollegiate Menorah Association

For a special class of young men and women, namely the college students, another agency is doing work in Jewish extension education. The Intercollegiate Menorah Association, of which Mr. Henry Hurwitz is Chancellor, has Menorah branches in practically every important college and university in this country. In New York there are Menorah societies in Columbia University, New York University, the College of the City of New York, Hunter College, and Adelphi College. These societies, together with some sixty others throughout the country, are united into the Intercollegiate Menorah Association, and their work in this city is co-ordinated by an Intervarsity Menorah Council of Greater New York.

The Menorah societies are constituted as self-governing clubs "for the study of Jewish ideas and the pursuit of Jewish ideals." They aim to do for the American colleges and universities, what the Jewish elementary schools wish to do for the American public schools, namely to *supplement* them, by giving to the Jewish students their cultural heritage as Jews. This they do: (1) through *lectures* on a great variety of topics: Jewish history, literature and art, modern Jewish life and its problems, the meaning of Judaism and of Jewish ideals; (2) through *reading and study circles* in Hebrew, history, literature, etc.; (3) through *concerts* of Jewish music and exhibits of Jewish art; and (4) through the distribution of the *Menorah Journal,* which is issued bi-monthly by the Intercollegiate Menorah Association, and is among the finest Jewish periodicals in the English language. Recently, the Menorah societies have also begun to interest themselves in current communal problems. With the co-operation of the School for Jewish Communal Work, the various aspects of the communal work of New York Jewry have been presented to the college students. Of particular interest should be the study of community problems to the graduate Menorah Society in New York, which has been attempting to continue the general Menorah program beyond college graduation.

As a movement for the study of Jewish ideas and for the spread of Jewish knowledge, the Menorah movement has been reaching out beyond the undergraduate college societies to all the intellectual classes of the community, both Jewish and non-Jewish. The Menorah Conference on Education, organized in December, 1918, consists of professors and instructors in various American universities and in schools for higher Jewish learning, and is the most recent step taken by the Menorah organization toward becoming a general intellectual Jewish movement in America.

The Menorah Movement has contributed considerably to changing the attitude of Jewish college students toward their affiliation as Jews. It has made "Jewish culture" a goal worthy to be striven for, and has injected Jewish consciousness and pride into the mass of indifferent college students. It created a "movement" which swept many Jewish young men and women back into the Jewish fold. The work of the Menorah societies, however, is from the pedagogic point of view not adequately organized. Although the "Central office" strives valiantly each year to help the various Menorah societies through lectures and syllabi, each society practically determines its own activities, and each generation of students begins the groping process of trial and error anew. If the Menorah movement is to be in reality what it purports to be, namely an "Extension Jewish University," it would seem to require a definite curriculum, consisting of optional courses of study, with accompanying syllabi and aids to study, and designed to cover the entire collegiate period of four years. The entering Freshman should know what opportunities are offered in Jewish studies just as he or she knows the opportunities offered in general studies. The important task of the Intercollegiate Association would then be to help various societies in obtaining lecturers for these *definite courses* and in providing them with textbooks, syllabi, bibliographies, and reading material. From this viewpoint the Menorah societies in New York can form the extension department of the "Jewish University,"[22] consisting of the various Jewish professional schools in New York.

Educational Activities of American Zionists

The work of the Zionist Organization of America on behalf of Jewish children and youth is carried on through *Young Judea* and through the *Intercollegiate Zionist Association.* These activities were at first carried on independently, but have recently (1918) become integral parts of the Zionist organization, and are now managed by the Secretary for Education, Miss Henrietta Szold.

Young Judea is organized in the form of self-governing clubs for children and adolescents, between the ages of 10 and 20 years. These clubs usually meet once each week, thirty or forty times during the year, and half an hour to an hour during each meeting is devoted to talks, discussions and readings in Jewish history, Palestinian geography, and Zionism. The clubs are led by volunteer leaders who are not always sufficiently equipped either in Jewish knowledge or in leadership, to direct effectively the education of those in their charge. In some

[22] Cf. previous chapter, pp. 337 and 340.

phases of the work syllabi have been prepared as aids to the leaders; but, these are hardly sufficient to overcome the lack of training. Leaders' Training Courses have therefore been organized, extending over a period of two years, and designed to equip those men and women who wish to lead Zionist clubs with a general knowledge of Jewish history and institutions, of the geography, resources and problems of Palestine, and of the history and principles of Zionism and present day Zionist activities. A juvenile monthly magazine, "The Young Judean," is published for the Young Judea clubs, and is used by the leaders as a basis for reading and discussion with the members of their clubs. For similar purposes several pamphlets, song collections, and festival folders have been issued by Young Judea. Some of the Jewish festivals are celebrated by Young Judea through mass celebrations, much in the same way as is done by the Circle of Jewish Children.

The general criticism of the conduct of these activities is that they do not seem to have taken thus far full advantage of the educational resources of the Jewish community. Zionism is not merely a body of new facts in Jewish life—it is viewed essentially as a reinterpretation and reorganization of *all* of Jewish life. For the proper understanding of Zionism, therefore, some knowledge of Jewish history, literature and ideals, is prerequisite. And yet in the past, Young Judea has devoted its energies primarily to children who do not necessarily attend Jewish schools, and are ignorant of the prerequisite Jewish knowledge. Consequently, most of the work of the Young Judea clubs consists in teaching the rudiments of Jewish history and institutions; and it is evident that because of the very short time at their disposal, the educational achievement of the clubs (outside of affiliating the children with Zionism) amounts to very little. Only in isolated instances has Young Judea consciously tried to organize the pupils and graduates of existing Hebrew schools for instruction in Zionism.

To be sure, in many communities and in many sections, Young Judea is compelled to deal with unschooled children, since there is not a sufficient number of modern Hebrew schools; and groups of unschooled children and adolescents, organized spontaneously as Zionist clubs, turn to Young Judea for guidance. In New

York City, however, it would seem wisest for Young Judea to concentrate its main energies in *supplementing* existing Jewish schools and extension educational organizations, instead of trying to create an independent educational system. It should seek to organize Zionist clubs and classes from among the older pupils and the graduates of the existing Jewish schools, and when possible, to interest the teachers in those schools to become the club leaders. Similarly, it should foster among the members of the League of the Jewish Youth, the Y. M. H. A.'s the Y. W. H. A.'s, Young Folks' Societies, and similar organizations, efforts to organize themselves into Zionist study groups, and then supply these groups with the necessary leaders and study material. The Zionist Education Department can also contribute to the actual classroom work of the Jewish schools by co-operating with such agencies as the Bureau of Jewish Education in editing textbooks on modern Palestine and Palestinian life.

The Intercollegiate Zionist Association would seem to stand in the same relation to the "Jewish University" of New York, that is, to the Jewish professional schools and to the Menorah Movement, as Young Judea stands with relation to the elementary and intermediate Jewish schools. It should *supplement* these educational institutions by spreading Zionist information among their students. It should seek to make certain that every student of the Rabbinical Seminaries, of the Teachers' Institutes, and of the School for Jewish Communal Work, and every member of the Menorah societies, shall organize his or her studies, and plan his or her life work in proper perspective toward the Restoration in Palestine. The Intercollegiate Zionist Association is but a young organization (reorganized 1917);[23] its program cannot therefore be fully determined. It has thus far conducted a course of lectures on Zionism and has issued a collection of Zionist essays "Kadimah." It would seem practical and wise for both the Intercollegiate Zionist Association and for Young Judea to concentrate their main efforts upon making "Zionists" out of "Jews," instead

[23] For history see Part I, Chapter 3.

of engaging upon the difficult and very costly task of creating an independent educational system for making Jews out of those who are ignorant or indifferent.[23a]

Besides these educational organizations for the youth, the Zionist Organization has also taken over various educational activities for adults, which were formerly conducted by Hadassah (an organization of Zionist women) and by the Histadruth Ibrith (Society for the Promotion of Hebrew).[23b] Should the Zionists succeed in developing the organization of their various community districts throughout the country and in establishing local Education Committees for each district, they will be in a position to wield much influence over the future course of Jewish education in this country.

THE JEWISH KINDERGARTEN

Several attempts have been made to establish *Jewish Kindergartens* in New York, but none of these has as yet crystallized into a definite model to be followed on a large scale. The most successful of the kindergartens is the *Hebrew Kindergarten and Day Nursery,* under H. Luria, at 35 Montgomery Street. This institution is modeled partly after the modern Palestinian kindergartens. The language of instruction is Hebrew and the young children are taught Hebrew conversation, Hebrew songs and games. But the work of this Hebrew Kindergarten, piquant though it may be, is not such as to form the basis of a wide Jewish kindergarten movement in this country. In the first place, it is connected with a day nursery, and the children are left in the charge of the institution throughout the entire day,—a situation which is evidently different from the normal kindergarten in which the children would come for only a few hours during the day. Secondly, its insistence upon Hebrew has compelled it to "overwork" the precocious, linguistically inclined children who are encouraged "to show what the class can do" on every occasion. The organization is certainly very different from the conception of the modern kindergarten, as an institution for "child culture."

[23a] This statement applies to the educational work of the Zionist organization. Should the Zionists, however, in the course of time come to control the affairs of the New York Jewish Community, all that has been said of "Kehillah" would apply to their work. See p. 195.

[23b] Organized in 1916. President, Reuben Brainin.

Many Jewish parents in New York have felt that they would like to send their young children, between the ages of three and six years to a Jewish kindergarten, because in this manner they would be able to attach the child more closely to the Jewish home and the family. There is a good deal of strength in this idea. The very young child belongs psychologically to the home far more than the older child. Its dependence upon the home is greater, and its chief teacher is the mother. The kindergarten is by modern teachers considered as a prolongation of home training.

Much of the work of the modern Froebelian and post-Froebelian Kindergarten can be organized around Jewish life and institutions. The stories can consist of biblical stories and Jewish folk tales; the morning talks and the nature talks can be developed about the Jewish calendar; many of the "occupations" can have Jewish designs or motives; the songs and games may be Jewish, both in Hebrew and in English; the festivals celebrated can be the Jewish ones; and the general atmosphere can as far as possible reproduce the Jewish home and represent the Jewish mother. It seems that in this country it is hardly feasible to establish the Jewish kindergarten upon a Hebrew-speaking basis. At present, however, it is possible only to surmise. It is highly worth while for the Jews of America to experiment with the education of very young children, in order to learn upon what principles American Jewish kindergartens should be conducted.

Range of Jewish Education in New York

The discussion of various methods of intensive and extensive education reveals how elaborate and variegated are the educational activities of the Jews of New York, even though at the same time they are unco-ordinated and unsystematized. Ranging in age from the elementary schools to the professional schools, and in intensity from the parochial schools to extension education, the Jews of New York have been trying in a haphazard manner to create a complete educational system. Put in tabular form, their educational influence at any one time is somewhat as follows:

INTENSIVE EDUCATION

Hebrew Schools, Talmud Torahs and Modern Private Schools	35,000 pupils[24]
Parochial Schools	1,000 "
Yiddishe Volks-Schulen	750 "
Secondary Education	400 "
Professional Schools	300 "

EXTENSIVE EDUCATION[25]

Sunday Schools	8,000 "
Chedarim and Private Teachers	20,000 "
Extension Activities of the Bureau of Jewish Education	40,000 "
Menorah Societies (members and auditors)	3,000 " [26]
Zionist Educational Activities (children and adolescents)	3,500 "

In a fully developed system of Jewish training varied opportunities for instruction must be offered. The kindergarten is to be the first step in the schooling of the Jewish child. Thereafter the intensiveness of its instruction, and the kind of educational content which will be given to it, will depend, first, upon its own abilities; second, upon the Jewish desires and attitudes of its parents; and lastly, upon the degree to which the community provides for its education. The central educational problem of the community is to establish adequate facilities for intensive Jewish training, sufficient to care for all those who desire and can profit from such training. But it must at the same time not neglect the great body of children who for various reasons are not in a position to receive intensive schooling. For them various forms of extensive education must be provided, so that the Jewish schools may send forth their pupils into a sympathetic and appreciative Jewish environment. The Jewish educational system has been likened to a tree, with its central core, its rings of wood and its outer bark. Educational sap must flow through all of these layers, no matter how near they are to the exposure of wind and sun; but it can flow through them only in varying degrees.

[24] Only approximate or round figures are given.

[25] There is much overlapping in pupils between extensive education and intensive education, some children and adolescents being reached by both.

[26] Approximation.

Chapter XII.

THE JEWISH SCHOOL AS A COMMUNITY CENTER

Throughout the ages the Jews sought to "see life sanely and see it whole." Their communal life, from earliest times until the recent past, was envisaged as an organic unit. In direct contrast to the Greeks and the Romans, who separated sharply their political and civic interests from their religious life, the Jews made no distinction between the religious and the other aspects of their community life. Among the Greeks, for example, the political forums and assemblies were institutions distinct from the temples, and the instruction in the gymnasia and music schools was given outside of the temple walls. The Jewish senate, or Sanhedrin, on the other hand, met within one of the chambers of the Temple at Jerusalem. The synagogue was from the earliest time not merely the place of worship, but the institution of study, both for old and young.

This contrast reveals one of the most deep-lying antitheses between the Hellenic and the Hebraic outlook on life. The Greeks saw the diversity in existence; the Hebrews felt the unity that runs through it. The Greek philosopher divided the world into categories, so that the forces of nature were expressed in a host of deities, and for the same reason, human society was divided into classes, (the philosopher, the soldier, the merchant and the laborer; the intellectual and the non-intellectual; the owner and the slave). The Hebrew prophet brooked no such distinctions. He refused to divide the world artificially into classes, whether of gods or of men. One of the deepest traits of the Jewish group is made manifest in this intuitive emphasis upon the essential unity of life.

As the Jew participated increasingly in the life of the Western World, and as the complexity of this life necessitated more and more specialization, a division of functions took place within communal Jewish organization. The synagogue tended to lose its rather inclusive character and to become limited to the single function of a place of worship. The school, or at least the elementary school, became a distinct and separate institution. The other communal Jewish problems, such as relief of the poor, aid to the sick, control of the delinquent, were also taken out of the synagogue and given over to special institutions. Distinct agencies were thus created to deal with almost every aspect of Jewish life.

But tendencies are already making themselves felt for a reintegration of Jewish communal life. More and more are the Jews of America coming to feel that they must try to place all of the activities of their communal life under the roofs of unifying institutions. The recent movement toward community centers in America has greatly stimulated this tendency towards reintegration. A new unit, an American Jewish unit of social life, is needed to fulfill the various communal needs of the American Jew. This institutional unit must be synonymous with the unit of Jewish life, which is the family. The family as a whole, with all of its problems and its needs, forms the basis of the Jewish community.

Agencies Aiming Toward Reintegration

There are at present three agencies which aim by broadening their activities, to become the unit of organized Jewish life. These are the Synagogue, the Settlement and the School. The Synagogue, which is primarily the institution of the *adult*, is extending its scope in order to reach more effectively both adolescents and children. It is becoming the *Institutional Synagogue* in attempting to provide activities for all the members of the Jewish family. Many of the younger rabbis are beginning to emphasize this phase of their work. They are devoting more attention to organizing clubs, classes, and similar activities for recreation and for study, so as to reach all the members of the congregation, from childhood to old age. In general, this work is similar to that carried on in many progressive Christian churches.

The Jewish *Settlement*, especially the Young Men's and Young Women's Hebrew Associations, originally created as institutions for the *adolescent*, also tend in this direction. Through the introduction of the Hebrew school, they are attempting to reach downward to the child; and through the religious services, lectures and forums, they are trying to reach upward to the adult. The leaders of these institutions have realized the futility of attempting really to influence adolescents without controlling their street and home environment. They have found that it may often be too late to start with the young men and young women, and that, therefore, it is necessary to begin further back, when they are still boys and girls. By extending their activities, the settlements are on the one hand, going *back* to influence the child before adolescence; and on the other, they are broadening out to include its parents and adult neighbors as well as its adolescent friends.

Similarly, the modern Jewish *School,* as it developed, found that it could not confine itself to the *child* alone. If the education it offers is to be effective, it must reach the child's home, its parents, its brothers, its sisters, its friends and neighbors. Especially in a voluntary system of education, such as Jewish school work, it is essential for the school to have the understanding, good will and coöperation of the parents and the neighbors of its pupils. The Jewish school cannot progress more rapidly than the community wishes it to progress. The parents and adult neighbors need therefore to be brought into actual contact with the work of the school.

From the purely educative viewpoint, it is also important to broaden the scope of the school's activities. If education is "*the direction of personality,*" the few hours which the child spends in the classroom are not sufficient. The school must reach the child's many phases of personal growth, its play activities and various social relations, as well as its more serious hours of study. Particularly in the religious school is this reaching-out to interpret and direct the child's life important. The Jewish child is to be taught not merely a special body of facts called Jewish knowledge, but even more essentially is it the function of the Jewish school to lead the child to interpret *all* of its acts and relationships from the viewpoint of the group to which it belongs, that is, to give *Jewish reasons* for the various acts of its life. Besides these general educational considerations, there is an added incentive for broadening the work of the Jewish school. There are no distinct Jewish high schools, Jewish evening schools, or Jewish popular lecture systems. Under the present conditions of American life, the Jewish school building is in a position to include all of these institutions. It can serve not only as a primary school for children, but also as an educational agency for adolescents and adults as well.

These three agencies, therefore, the Synagogue, the Settlement, and the School, are aiming at the same thing, namely, to become the unit of Jewish communal organization. It is well that there are these various methods of approach. In the present transitional stage of American Jewish life, it would be most unwise for anyone to attempt to say definitely just how American Jewry should be organized. All of the forces now at work ought to be stimulated to express themselves, in order to promote the best interests of American Jewry. In the end, it will probably make but little difference from what origin the Community Centers develop, provided they suffice for the various needs of all the members of the community.

The difference between the three agencies is one of method or of approach. The school seems to have several advantages in this striving to become the unit of Jewish organization. In the first place, its approach offers the broadest appeal, that of *child welfare and education.* The instinctive interest of the parents in their children, especially during the age when the children are still dependent upon them, can be utilized as a strong motive force to create the necessary interest in the various activities of the school center. Secondly, the school is in a position to cut across many of the distinctions which have arisen in Jewish life: distinctions of wealth and social status, and even distinctions of belief and attitude. The rich and the poor, the orthodox, the conservative and the liberal, the educated and the uneducated, can all participate on a common footing in certain phases of the Jewish education of their children.

The Community School Center—Its Aims and Methods

Along what lines are the Jewish schools of New York working to become the units of organization in Jewish communal life? Five or six of the larger schools are developing in this direction, though none of them has as yet succeeded in fully becoming a real Community School Center. The Central Jewish Institute, under Mr. I. B. Berkson, at 125 East 85th Street, is the clearest indication of the efforts that are being made along these lines.

and its program of activities[1] illustrates some of the general principles which guide those who are developing the American Jewish school center.

The most important of the *aims* of the Community School Center are: first, to make the school center a neighborhood house; second, wherever possible, to make it a central community house; third, to emphasize Jewish knowledge and Jewish educational activities in the life of all of its members; and lastly, to help the children, the adolescents and the adults to determine their relationship as Jews to the general American community. Its most effective *methods of work* are those by which it tries to reach the unaffiliated through those already affiliated (parents through children, brothers through brothers, friends through friends, etc.); and in that it endeavors, as far as possible, to make its management self-governing rather than philanthropic.

The Jewish School As a Neighborhood House

It is proverbial that people have fewer neighbors in a large city than in a village community. "City loneliness" is particularly hard to bear for those who have been accustomed to the intimate neighborly relations of smaller communities. A large proportion of the Jews of New York came to this country from small towns and villages in Eastern Europe, and their congestion into special districts, or "immigrant colonies," is certainly due, in part, to their desire for neighborliness. If wisely directed, the normal desire for neighbors who are "like-minded" may be a powerful motive for organizing Jewish life in America.

The Jewish school ought to become the center of the neighborhood, and as a neighborhood house, make all possible provisions for the bringing together and common meeting of all of its Jewish neighbors. It is therefore more than a school. It is

---

[1] Cf. Appendix T: "Program of the Central Jewish Institute." Among the best examples of Jewish *settlements* that are developing into community centers are: the *Educational Alliance*, 197 East Broadway, and the *Young Women's Hebrew Association*, 31 West 110th St. A number of modern synagogues (e. g. *Congregation Anshe Chesed*, 114th Street and Seventh Avenue) illustrate the tendency to broaden the synagogue into the community center. *The Jewish Center* at 131 West 86th Street, under Rabbi M. M. Kaplan, is an interesting attempt to create a model community center with a synagogue as its nucleus.

a *recreation center,* providing facilities for physical exercise and mental relaxation. It is a *forum and lecture hall* for discussing topics and problems of interest to the neighborhood, such as clean streets, housing conditions, anti-Jewish influences, etc. Its rooms provide a *meeting place* for spontaneously organized clubs, societies and lodges in the neighborhood that need to be housed. It may also act as the *charities headquarters* of the neighborhood, for, at the same time that it strives to satisfy the needs of its normal neighbors, it will also render philanthropic aid to its "subnormal" neighbors; the poor, the delinquent, and the sick. Lastly, the school center can be the *neighborhood synagogue* to be used for worship in common, and for the performance of the various religious functions and ceremonies.

The family and not the individual is the unit with which the community school house works. The "Familiensinn," or sense of family loyalty, which psychologists tell us is strongly developed among the Jews, should find adequate provision for expression. Children and parents, brothers and sisters, friends and relatives, should be encouraged to participate in the common activities of the center. Festival celebrations, school exhibitions and class graduations are some of the forms in which Jewish school centers gather whole families for purposes of common recreation and instruction.

The Jewish School As a Jewish Community House

The local community in the neighborhood of the school center is but one unit, inseparable from the larger Jewish community of the city. Besides acting, therefore, as a gathering place for neighbors, the Jewish school building in some instances, also serves as a central meeting house for city-wide Jewish organizations, such as Jewish professional societies, Zionist organizations, lodges, labor unions, etc. Various Jewish communal organizations in New York are encouraged to hold conventions and mass meetings in its auditorium, and to conduct classes in its rooms. In a well-organized Community or Kehillah, many of the school centers would serve as the Kehillah centers (for information, meeting, etc.) for their neighborhood. In general, the fully developed community school center strives to gather into itself as much as possible of the life of the whole Jewish community.

The Jewish School As an American Civic Center

Beyond the Jewish community is the general American community of which the Jews, in turn, are an inseparable part. The Jewish school center endeavors to help the individual Jew to understand more intensely the life and ideals of America, and to define more clearly his position as an American Jew. Not only does the School Center offer opportunity for discussing sanitary ordinances, social legislation and civic movements, but it also can arrange for the community celebration of American holidays (Fourth of July, Thanksgiving Day, Lincoln's Birthday, etc.) Whenever possible, the legislation discussed and the festivals celebrated should be interpreted from the Jewish point of view, giving to the modern American life the rich background of Jewish history and experience. Thus, Lincoln becomes an American Jewish figure, part of the complete past of the American Jews, and his personality is discussed in the light of Jewish ideals of personality. In like manner the Jewish school center offers its accommodations willingly to civic bodies, like the Board of Education, the Department of Health, the War Work Committees, and similar organizations, in order that these may come into closer contact with the various elements of the American Jewish community.

Emphasis Upon Jewish Education

The Jewish school center differs both from the settlement and from the synagogue, in its emphasis upon the element of *study*, rather than upon *recreation*, or *worship;* although to be sure, it provides for these activities also. Learning or study was the universal occupation of the Jews throughout the centuries. The most cherished tradition of the Jews was that they were the "Am Ha-Sefer," the People of the Book. The student class was the privileged class, and daily study was a religious injunction. It is essential that this intellectual tradition of the Jew should continue, for only through the fullness of knowledge is it possible to maintain a religious-national culture without the usual bonds of government and of political allegiance. For this reason the elementary Hebrew school, secondary classes for high school boys and girls, branches of the Circle of Jewish Children, of the League of the Jewish Youth, and of Young Judea for the unschooled, and special evening classes and study groups for adults, form the heart of the Jewish School Center.

With Jewish education as the nucleus of its activities, it follows that the spirit of the institution becomes pervadingly Jewish. Not only the regular classroom study, but every other phase of its work suggests aspects of Jewish culture, of the Jewish past, and of Jewish aspirations. The decoration of the building, the management of the social functions, the library, the club programs, the common celebration of festivals, are all rich in Jewish educative suggestion and influence.

Methods of Affiliation

Through all of these activities the Jewish school center attempts to become the inclusive unit of organized Jewish life. Since the elementary Hebrew school is organized as a "family unit," the children serve as the natural means through which all the members of the family are affiliated. And, if the Jewish elementary school is well organized, it can be made into an effective instrument for reaching the entire neighborhood. The unschooled children of the neighborhood are attracted through the pupils of the school; the adolescents through the students of the secondary classes; and the adult neighbors through the parents of the school children.

As an illustration there is the branch of the Circle of Jewish Children. The pupils of the school invite their friends and playmates to become members of the Circle. No dues or class attendance is required, so that membership in the Circle is made as easy as possible. The entire neighborhood is divided into blocks or area units. From the children in the school and the Circle are selected the most active boys and girls, who are made "leaders," and whose primary function it is to enlist new members from their particular blocks, and to keep in touch with them: that is, to distribute juvenile Jewish literature among them, and to invite them to take part in the various activities of the Circle.

Similarly, the *adolescents* can be reached through the *League of the Jewish Youth;* they are invited to become members of the League either through their younger brothers and sisters in the school or in the Circle, or through their friends in the secondary

Jewish classes or in the League itself. The general principle of the organization is the same as that of the Circle. The neighborhood is divided into area units, and the members of the League are organized into "households," consisting of ten boys or girls who live in the same area. The "households" are then combined into "camps" and the "camps" into "tribes." To the members of the League the school center offers a variety of activities: literary, debating, athletic and dramatic clubs; arts and crafts clubs; music circles; gymnasium classes; and kindred activities. For the studious, classes in Hebrew, history, customs and institutions, and other subjects are offered. All of these activities are conducted under the guidance of a special League Supervisor. As far as possible, the League is self-governing, its affairs being entrusted to various councils and committees of the members themselves.

In the work of the school center with *adults*, the parents are those who are the most easily reached. They are organized into a *Parents' Association.*[4] Into this association are enrolled every father and mother of the pupils of the school and of the members of the Circle and the League. Regular monthly or bi-monthly meetings are held, at which the parents discuss not only the educational activities on behalf of their own children, but also the affairs of the center as a whole. The parents also participate in all of the festival celebrations, graduations and gatherings of the school, the Circle and the League.

Through the parents it should also be possible to reach the other adult neighbors, namely, the unmarried young men and women, and married people who have no children of school age. With the Parents' Association as a nucleus, there can be organized a *Community Center Association,* consisting of all the adult men and women of the neighborhood. Into the hands of the Association should be entrusted much of the general management of the school center. The members of the Association should pay a nominal annual fee (about one dollar), and may be divided into a *Men's League* and a *Women's League.* All the social service work of the center should be carried on by this Association. It should help the needy and visit the sick neighbors. It should interest its members in the neighborhood's social

[4] For the activities of these associations and of the City Parents' Association, cf. p. 192.

problems, such as the eradication of vice and crime, the improvement of living conditions, the enforcement of city ordinances, discussion of civic issues, etc. It should also conduct the synagogue of the community school center for common worship by all the neighbors and for the celebration of many of the vital occasions of their family life: births, confirmations, weddings, etc.

Self-Government vs. Philanthropy

The members of the Community Center Association and of the Parents' Association should themselves be responsible for the government of the Community School Center. In the past this would have been quite impossible. The Jewish institutions depended completely upon the gifts and efforts of a few individual "benefactors," who themselves received no "benefit" from the institution and were consequently its all-powerful directors. But with the organization of the Federation for the Support of Jewish Philanthropic Societies, which has made of philanthropy a communal undertaking rather than a system of isolated, individual contributions, it is becoming more and more possible to take the direction of these community school centers out of the hands of the "benefactors" and place it into the hands of the "beneficiaries." To facilitate such a change in management, the activities of the community school center should be conducted, wherever possible, on a "self-paying" basis; and the members of the Community Center Association should be stimulated to contribute annually, in accordance with their means, to the general philanthropic funds of the community.

The following plan of organization is proposed for the self-governing, fully developed Jewish community school center. The Board of Directors should consist of nine members, three of whom should be elected to represent the Parents' Association, three to represent the Community Center Association, and three to represent the community at large. The three directors representing the community at large, may be either elected by the members of the Community Center Association, or else they may be appointed by the trustees of the communal funds which contribute to the maintenance of the institution. The Board of

Directors so constituted should appoint a *Principal* or *Executive Director,* who is to have complete charge of the activities of the center. Assisting him there should be an *Assistant Principal* in charge of the school; a *Supervisor of Extension Activities* in charge of the Circle and the League; an *Assistant Director of Community Activities* who should act as secretary of the Parents' Association, and of the Community Center Association, and who should also be in charge of the evening activities (classes and clubs); and, lastly, an *Administrator* who should have supervision over the janitors, clerks and collectors, and be responsible for the physical administration of the plant.[5] (See accompanying chart.) Where the Director is not himself an ordained rabbi, a rabbi should be engaged to care for the religious life of the community center.

Community School Buildings

In order to make the establishment of community school centers possible, the Jews of New York are gradually assuming a new attitude toward the erection of Jewish school buildings. Jewish school architecture, like recent public school architecture, is attempting to provide for the needs not only of children but of adolescents and adults as well, and not only for study but also for recreation.[6] A well constructed school building, fit for community center purposes, would cost from $100,000 to $125,000 (upon a 12 to 16-classroom basis).[7] The cost of conducting such a school center would be from $30,000 to $40,000 per year.[8]

Each school center would then be in a position to give regular elementary and intermediate Jewish instruction to 1,000 boys and girls; special intensive Hebrew training to 150 or 200 advanced pupils of intermediate and secondary grades; extension education to 2,000 children and adolescents; and social-

---

[5] Such a general plan of organization applies to large centers, and will naturally be modified in accordance with particular conditions. In small school centers, for example, the Executive Director will, himself, perform the functions here assigned to some of his assistants.

[6] Cf. "The City School as a Community Center," Tenth Year Book of the National Society for the Study of Education, 1911. Also Ward, E. J.: "The Social Center," 1913.

[7] Cf. p. 173.

[8] At $2,500 per room per year. Cf. above, pp. 231 and 235.

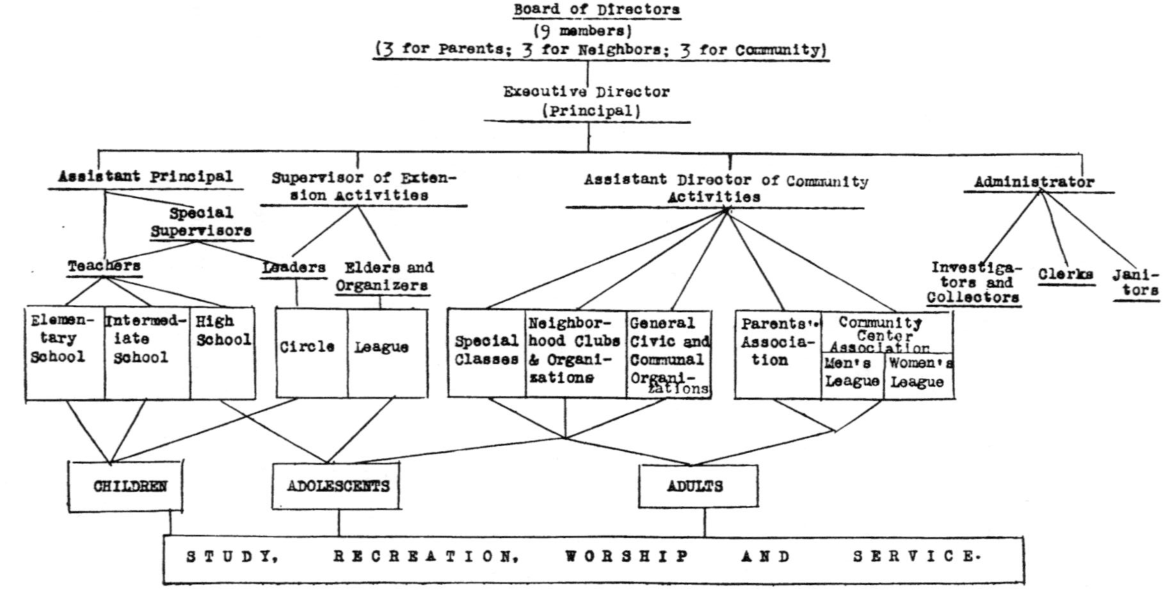
PLAN OF ORGANIZATION
FOR THE
JEWISH COMMUNITY SCHOOL CENTER
Board of Directors
(9 members)
(3 for Parents; 3 for Neighbors; 3 for Community)
Executive Director
(Principal)
Assistant Principal
Special Supervisors
Teachers
Elementary School
Intermediate School
High School
Supervisor of Extension Activities
Leaders
Elders and Organizers
Circle
League
Assistant Director of Community Activities
Special Classes
Neighborhood Clubs & Organizations
General Civic and Communal Organizations
Parents' Association
Community Center Association
Men's League
Women's League
Administrator
Investigators and Collectors
Clerks
Janitors
CHILDREN
ADOLESCENTS
ADULTS
STUDY, RECREATION, WORSHIP AND SERVICE.

educational activities to all the members of the neighboring Jewish families. If the Jews of New York were to construct a chain of twenty-five to fifty such school centers throughout the city, they would be laying the securest foundation for the upbuilding of a healthy, constructive Jewish community life. In this direction lie the most sanguine hopes for American Jewish education.

Chapter XIII.

THE OUTLOOK IN JEWISH EDUCATION

(SUMMARY)

Jewish education is the clearest expression of the will of the Jewish people to continue as an integral community in America. No other activity is so sure an index to the problematic future of Jewish life in this country as is the work of the Jewish schools. Shall American Jews transmit to their children the heritage which is embodied in their literature and their institutions, or shall they withhold this heritage from their children and permit the process of assimilation to lead to the disappearance of Jewish institutions and of Jewish life in this land? Of what significance to themselves and to others is the desire of the Jews for the continuity of their group, and what are the possibilities for maintaining such continuity through education? These are the "root problems" of American Jewish life; all other problems, no matter how complex or how important, grow out of them.

The Significance of Jewish Education

No period in Jewish history has been more fruitful or more epoch-making than our own. The revolution in Russia, the breaking up of the "established" order in the other autocracies of Europe, and the wonderful possibilities for rebirth of Jewish national life in Palestine, have completely changed the status of the Jews in the world. American Jewry will have to play a very important part in the Reconstruction and in the New Order. To the tender sensitive plant of Jewish national life in Palestine and to the uprooted Jewries of Europe, the American Jewish community will have to stand, in a measure, both as gardener and as guardian. Without the full coöperation and sympathy of American Jews, the Jewish national center in Palestine will battle against very great odds. Generations of American Jews must be taught to work for and with the Jews of Palestine, and upon the wisdom and the zeal of the American Jewish teacher much of the future development of Palestine will depend.

To the Jews in other lands, the continuance of a strong Jewish community life in America is also important. It is hardly more than a century since the Jews have been admitted to citizenship in the western nations. Through long ages they learned to persist in spite of persecution. Can they also continue their community life under conditions of freedom? Nowhere have the Jews a fairer opportunity to answer this question than in democratic America. In Germany, under the old régime, the teaching of religion was compulsory, and the state prescribed both the content and the form of Jewish instruction. The amount of Jewish training and its line of development were therefore in a large measure *determined* for the Jews of Germany by the German Government. In England, the struggle between the aristocratic Anglican church and secular democracy for control of the schools is still undecided, and the present arrangement of partial control and subsidy is by no means satisfactory to the Jews of England. In the new republics that are rising out of the old empires of Russia, Germany and Austria-Hungary, it is not possible to foretell with any degree of assurance what the conditions will be, and how they will affect Jewish life in these lands. In America alone have the Jews the opportunity of developing Jewish education by the side of a stable democratic system of public education which in no way proposes to affect or to control the teaching of religion. The answer to the challenge of freedom which American Jews will make in the course of the next century through the education of their children and through the organization of their communal life, will be of profound importance to the Jews of all lands.

In the life of American Jewry itself education has come to be all-important. During the past thirty-five years, the continuous waves of immigration from the Jewish centers of Eastern Europe hid the havoc that was being wrought in American Jewish ranks through ignorance and indifference. It seems hardly likely that Jewish immigration to the United States will be on the same large scale as hitherto, and with the decrease in immigration, American Jewry will have to fall back on itself, and rear its own generations of Jews. Hitherto *charity* could serve as the basis of organization in American Jewish life. Affiliation with some Jewish charitable institution was the criterion of interest in Jewish communal affairs. But with the economic adjustment of the masses of Jewish immigrants, and with the gradual assumption by the State of its duties toward the needy, the sick and the defective, *charity* can no longer serve as the main basis of Jewish organization. Nor is *religion,* in the ordinary sense, the binding concern of all the Jews of America. Clefts have been created along lines of religious difference, which seem well-nigh irreparable. In recent years *Palestine* has loomed large as a vivifying influence uniting the Jews everywhere; most of the Jews of the world are interested in Palestine in one way or another. But Palestine alone cannot suffice as a basis for upbuilding American Jewry. It must form part of a larger program of education in which, besides Palestine, the Jewish Past, the Jewish Present the world over, and the life of American Jewry, are essential elements. Education, in its widest meaning of "transmission of group consciousness and of common civilization from one to another," seems to be that bond of union among American Jews that has the greatest promise for the continuity of Jewish life. The desire to transmit the common heritage of their children is in the final analysis the surest touchstone for separating those who desire to remain Jews from those who do not.

Education is the spiritual procreative power of a people—its guarantee for the future. Every civilized people recognizes the dependence of its national welfare upon education. This interdependence of group welfare and the education of the young is possibly even more binding in the case of the Jews than among other peoples. "Normal" peoples may depend for cohesiveness upon the social forces and impulses which express themselves in their daily social and civic life, in language, in laws, and in essential institutions. But the desire of the Jews to remain an international entity is not a "normal" desire, and requires for its fulfillment more conscious purpose, more "ideal" motive, than do desires that are "normal." The Jews have therefore found it necessary in the past to direct their energies into the particular channel of *study.* For this reason learning, study, was the universal occupation of the Jews throughout the centuries. Even now when it is beginning to be possible for them to turn their energies into more normal channels—by sharing more freely in their own communal life and in the civic life of the country in which they live, as well as by directing their energies toward the creation of a "normal" Jewish environment in Palestine—even now the necessity still exists for maintaining Jewish self-consciousness through fullness of knowledge. The Jews must make up for the lack of "normal" social forces by a degree of self-consciousness, a clearness of purpose and of ideal beyond that of other peoples. Self-consciousness is the price which the Jews must pay for living an international life, and this price can be paid only through education. The very nature of American Jewish communal life, whose aims are not civic-political, but rather international-religious, makes education—meaning transmission, habit formation, enrichment of experience, adjustment, direction of personality—the sole dependable force in the problematic Jewish struggle for communal integrity in this country.

As regards America, the experiments which the Jews are making in the religious-national education of their children, affect two of its most vital problems; namely, the relation of the racial or ethnic communities to the entire American nation, and the relation between the State and the Church.

The problem of how to assimilate its immigrants, without at the same time obliterating all that is worth while in the national heritage they bring with them, has been recognized by American philosophers to be intimately bound up with the future welfare of America. Whether the immigrant comes from the northwest of Europe, or from the southeast of Europe, or from the Balkans, or from Asia, or from any other part of the world, he brings with him cultural values in terms of language, literature, history, institutions and ideas, which if he can preserve at the same time that he acquires the cultural values of his new home, will enlarge his own interests and those of his children, and will make them more intelligent citizens of the American democracy. The solution of this problem of proper "Americanization" is a pressing one, and although the course of future immigration is uncertain, the problem of the adjustment of the immigrant will probably be present with America for a long time to come.

The Jews, as a highly self-conscious community, with a long

tradition of adjustment behind them, are in a position to try experiments aiming toward the solution of this problem for America. The method of solution which they propose is that of *community organization*. They would bring all the citizens of the American commonwealth together in most of life's relationships. But they would also permit the members of any one national or religious community to develop distinct organizations and institutions to deal with matters of peculiar interest to themselves, except in so far as such activity would curtail the rights of other American citizens. The clearest example of the community method of adjustment is found in the weekday Jewish school, which requires Jewish children to mingle with non-Jewish American boys and girls in the public schools, and yet gathers them together for specifically Jewish instruction during the time when they are free from their public school duties.[2]

The Jews of this country are opposed to the parochial idea in education. Of the sixty-five thousand children who receive Jewish training in New York City, for example, less than one thousand are taught in Jewish parochial schools. The separation between State and Church is a basic concept in American national organization. To entrust the education of American children to the church alone, may mean the ultimate division of American life along lines of historic creed, just as to entrust the education of American children to racial or ethnic groups alone may mean the artificial division of America along lines of historic national affiliation. And yet American educators realize that by depriving the public school of the possibilities of teaching religion and historic folk *mores,* the government fails to provide in full for the interests of the American child. In fairness to the religious groups of this country, America sees the need of somehow permitting them to influence their children religiously. Along what lines may this problem be solved?

The parochial school, whether religious or national, if conducted on a large scale, seems to be dangerous both to the American polity and to the common welfare of the groups within it. The Sunday school has proven to be insufficient for the

---

[2] The Jewish Welfare Board, as part of the American War Organization, is another fine illustration of this method of adjustment.

needs of the Catholics, of the Jews, and even of the Protestants. The Jews have committed themselves to weekday religious instruction. In New York City, seven-eighths of the Jewish boys and girls who receive Jewish instruction are taught in weekday schools, after public school hours. This Jewish system of weekday religious-national instruction is of large import for the ultimate satisfactory adjustment between the State and the Church in America, and between the various ethnic groups and the American Commonwealth. The Jewish educational solution would appear to be that any national or religious group which is highly conscious of its culture and civilization, and desires to perpetuate it in this country, shall have the opportunity of doing so by means of instruction supplementary to the public school system.

In this endeavor the Jewish group is somewhat unique, in that it partakes of the characteristics of both nation and religious sect. The Jewish training which is offered in New York City cannot be characterized as "religious" instruction in the ordinary denominational sense of the term. It is rather religious-national, or "community" instruction, in that it strives to satisfy all the religious-cultural-national interests of the American Jews. Of the thousand or more Jewish teachers in New York, the overwhelming majority are not rabbis or rabbinical students, but laymen. Fewer than one-fourth of the children who receive Jewish instruction are taught in synagogue buildings or under congregational auspices; the other three-fourths are taught by special educational societies or by individuals. The emphasis laid upon the formal "religious" aspects of the Jewish curriculum varies from the ultra-orthodox pious Yeshibahs to the non-religious Yiddishe Volks-Schulen; and the attention given to the nationalist elements in education, ranges from the anti-nationalist Sunday schools to the training provided by the Zionist organizations. The Jewish school system of New York is the educational expression of the Jewish *community* of New York, and exists for the purpose of preparing its children for life adjusted to all of the varied aspects of community living, in the synagogue and out of it. The most tangible expression of this community attitude in education is to be found in the erection and organization of modern Jewish school buildings as Community Centers.

It is through these Community school centers that American Jews are endeavoring to solve for themselves, and perhaps indirectly also for their neighbors, the problem of fitting their interests and needs as a religio-ethnic community into their needs and interests as citizens of the American Commonwealth.

The work of the Jewish schools is thus an integral part of American education and both public educators and Jewish educators must come to regard it not as something extraneous to American life, but as part and parcel of it, vital to its welfare. It seems short-sighted policy for public educators to regard the educational work of the Jewish community as completely out of their sphere of interest. The concern of the public educator is the *entire* American child, and everything which affects its growth and education should be of interest to him. The public school system is but a part of American education, and not the whole of it. Doubtless it is the most important part; but even so, it must be willing to coöperate with that part of American education which is entrusted to the religious school. The education of the American Jew is the common task of both public and Jewish education. And while officially the State cannot, and for practical reasons should not, have any control of the religious schools, or any other non-public schools supported by special groups within the Commonwealth, the work of the Jewish educational institutions should be recognized as a necessary element in a complete scheme of American education.

Closely allied with the significance of Jewish education for America, is its import for Democracy. Everywhere the hope is for a free, flexible, democratic world, no matter what the particular form of government or of organization may be. The experiments in democratic living that are made in any part of the globe are of universal interest. The apparently isolated and "sectarian" educational efforts of American Jews, when interpreted broadly, are in their own way related to the great world's quest for democracy.

First, the measure of progress in a democracy is individual progress, and the enrichment of individual personality. The individual human being in his social relationships is the primary concern of the democratic state. Any process which enriches his personality, widening his interests and deepening his emotions, is helpful to democracy. Jewish education aims to do this for the Jewish citizens of America. The function of the Jewish schools is to transmit to American Jewish children a range of interest and to inculcate in them a group of emotions which are outside of the realm of the American public school. Jewish education wishes to *enrich the personality* of the American Jew in *content,* by giving him an additional culture, another language and literature, the ethical ideals of the prophets and martyrs of Israel, and the religious attitudes of the "People of the Book." It wishes to enlarge his personality in *space,* by connecting his interests with those of the Jews of the entire world. It desires to extend his outlook in *time,* by giving him the long historic perspective of the Jewish people, making him the immediate scion of centuries of struggle and development.

Second, the motives of action in a democracy must come from within. Inner desire rather than outer compulsion is a fundamental test of democratic living. The State has properly found it necessary to safeguard the interests of the majority of its citizens by compelling parents to send their children to the public schools. But it is to the interest of democracy that as many opportunities for education as possible be provided which are not compulsory, but *voluntary.* In persuading the individual American Jew to send his children to the Jewish school *voluntarily,* Jewish education is essentially democratic. It is making some of the citizens of American base one of their social acts upon ideal voluntary motives even to the extent of sacrifice. It is significant that over two-thirds of the Jewish boys in New York receive some form of Jewish training, at some time during their elementary school period. It is certainly worthy of note that the Jews of New York are spending, *without compulsion,* a million and a half dollars annually for instruction which is not designed to be useful to their children in terms of material or financial compensation, and that two-thirds of this sum are paid by the parents themselves in the form of tuition fees.

These voluntary sacrifices are prompted by a sense of loyalty to the duty of "thou shalt teach them to thy children," [2a] aided mightily by the momentum of Jewish tradition. At this time American educators are pointing out the moral weakness of the

[2a] Deuteronomy VI: 7.

public school system in its over-emphasis upon utilitarian training, its constant preparation of its pupils for *privilege* only, and its lack of provision for training in the proper performance of *duty*. Democracy demands loyalty to duty as an ideal. The continuance of the Jewish educational tradition, whatever its contribution, is thus in the service of democracy. It means the voluntary assumption of a social responsibility because it is a responsibility.

There is another standpoint from which the relations of American Jewish education to democracy may be viewed. Democracy implies that the individual shall not be confined within any artificial barrier, whether the barrier be economic, social or national. Democracy implies inter-class and inter-group relationships. It extends even beyond the limits of our own nation. It connotes *internationality*. The truly democratic individual has many spiritual affiliations. That the citizens of any land shall know only one culture, or one religion, or one language, is essentially tyranny. In political and civic life, multiple affiliation is neither possible nor desirable. It is not possible for the individual to obey more than one set of political and civic laws, since these are potentially conflicting and mutually exclusive. Multiple *political* affiliation is a contradiction, as harmful to the individual as to the country in which he lives. In his political and civic life, therefore, the individual must necessarily have a single affiliation. But it *is* possible for one individual to know many languages, to be acquainted with many literatures, and to be imbued with the ideals of many groups. Democracy not only permits such multiple spiritual affiliations, but encourages them to the utmost. Jewish education, in giving to American Jews another spiritual affiliation beyond those they find in their general American life, is fundamentally democratic. It seeks to create an Internationality with its "citizens" in Palestine, and with religious-national affiliations wherever Jews live.

To American Jews, therefore, whether as members of international Jewry or as citizens of America, or as individuals in a Democratic Order, the preservation of Jewish communal life in America through the training of Jewish children, is of the greatest significance. Are the Jews of America aware of the importance of Jewish education? Are they coping with the problem which American life presents in the training of their children? In this book the facts have been presented concerning the educational activities of New York Jews which must determine the answer to these vital questions. These facts are of interest not only to the Jews of New York, but in the degree in which they are typical of the conditions prevailing in Jewish education in this country, they are also of significance to other American communities. New York, containing about one half of the American Jews, is not *typical* of the Jewish community in America, but it is *pivotal,* and its educational activities will have large import for all American Jews.

The Desire for Jewish Education

The Jews of New York are just beginning to organize their communal life. For the past half century the New York community has been growing too rapidly to be able to turn its attention to the inner spiritual problems of its existence as an integral group within the American commonwealth. From a settlement of some sixty thousand in 1877, New York Jewry has grown in one generation to a huge conglomeration of over one million and a half souls, whose various parties and organizations differ widely among themselves both in tradition and in outlook. As a community, the Jews have been preoccupied until now with the immediate problems of immigration and charity. It is only within recent years that the successful economic adjustment of the masses of Jewish immigrants, aided by the decrease in Jewish immigration, has enabled the Jews of New York, as a community, to turn their attention to the more perennial problems of education and of community organization.

But despite the pressure of economic adjustment in the new land, despite also the more concrete and immediate claims of immigration and charity, the Jews of New York have not lost sight of the imperative imposed upon them by "the push of their past and the pull of their future"—the imperative of "thou shalt teach them to thy children." In the midst of a new and baffling environment, without the aid of authoritative government or of powerful church, depending solely upon the momentum of Jewish tradition and upon inner forces, the Jews have succeeded in establishing the beginnings of an American Jewish educational system.

A great variety of educational forms, transplanted from the old "homes" or else created anew in this country, is being developed for the training of Jewish children. The "system" of Jewish schools in New York reaches from the kindergarten through the professional schools. It includes a variety of elementary and intermediate schools; makes some provision for secondary Jewish instruction; and finds its apex in an uncoordinated "Jewish University," with pedagogy, the ministry and communal work as the professional branches of study. The regular intensive school system consists of Talmud Torahs, Hebrew Schools, Yiddishe Volksschulen, Yeshibahs, high school classes, and professional schools. Alongside of this intensive school system there is also an intensive system of Jewish education, consisting of Sunday schools, private tutoring (at home and in Chedarim), the Circle of Jewish Children, the League of the Jewish Youth, the Menorah movement, and Zionist education. These forms of extensive education attempt to provide instruction for the children and adolescents who, for various reasons, are not reached by the regular intensive Jewish schools.

About one-half of the three hundred thousand Jewish children of elementary school age in New York City are given some instruction, however meagre, in the religious-cultural heritage of their people during some period of their "school life." Most of these boys and girls receive weekday instruction after public school hours, and only a small minority are taught in Sunday schools. The Hebrew language, Jewish literature (biblical and post-biblical), Jewish history, Jewish customs and institutions, and Jewish music, comprise the curriculum offered to the pupils of the modern Hebrew schools and Talmud Torahs of New York. Large sums of money are expended annually by Jewish parents in order that in accordance with the behest of Jewish tradition they may teach their children the Torah, "the best merchandise." Neither their supposed materialism, nor the "practical" example of their neighbors, nor the complex demands of the new environment, has thus far been able to extinguish the desire in the hearts of the Jewish masses to transmit to their children the learning and the life of Israel.

Indeed, new forces have begun to express themselves in Jewish education in this country, which bear much promise for the future. Parties and classes in New York Jewry have begun to interest themselves in the Jewish training of their children which have hitherto been indifferent or antagonistic to it.[3] Then, too, the influence of the American environment has not been all on the side of making Jewish education difficult in this country. The example of the public schools has caused marked improvement in the equipment and management of the better Jewish schools of New York. Modern men and women have begun to utilize the principles and the technique of American education for the upbuilding of an effective Jewish school system. The democratic spirit of the country has also affected the Jewish schools. The Talmud Torahs are becoming more and more the educational institutions for all children, instead of charity schools for poor children only. Particularly in the education of Jewish girls has the spirit of modernity found striking expression. It has caused the Jews to cease their unwarranted and utter neglect of the schooling of their daughters, the future "mothers in Israel," so that now some of the finest Jewish schools in New York are schools for girls. And while it is true that as yet only one-fifth of the Jewish girls of elementary school age in New York receive Jewish instruction, (as compared to two-thirds of the boys), nevertheless the tendency is undoubtedly toward an equalization of the sexes in Jewish education.

Present Jewish Education Inadequate and Ineffective

The facts presented indicate that the desire for Jewish education exists, at least among the Jewish masses of New York. But the means for achieving it are very ineffective and inadequate. Indeed, it could hardly be otherwise. The assimilative forces of the new environment have had their undoubted effect in weaking the desire for Jewish life. There is no "reason," no

[3] Witness the tendency to broaden the scope of instruction in the Reform Sunday schools, and in the National Radical Schools (Yiddishe Volks-Schulen. As this book goes to press, the Workingmen's Circle (Arbeiter Ring) a large organization of Jewish workingmen, which has hitherto been "international," and opposed to everything distinctively Jewish, has begun to establish a number of Jewish schools for teaching Yiddish, Hebrew, Jewish history and Jewish customs.

compelling motive for Jewish education, either in terms of economic reward or of social recognition. Many of the ablest and most forceful personalities in New York Jewry are interested in the broad human problems, and pay but little heed to fostering and guiding the desire of the Jewish masses for the continuity of their Jewish life. Most of the Jewish parents (immigrants of the first or second generation) have been accustomed to the mediaeval forms of schooling existing in Eastern Europe. These forms they brought with them to the new land with but little modification. To be sure, the American environment has caused profound changes in the character of the Talmud Torah, the Cheder and Yeshibah, but it has not yet been able to do away with all the methods of mediaeval education in the Jewish schools. The modern and the mediaeval exist side by side in the teaching of Jewish children in New York. In one tenement house of New York can be found children who attend a modern Jewish school center, while some of their playmates are still afflicted in that mediaeval institution for child torture, the Cheder, and others are taught at home by equally mediaeval itinerant teachers. Such school facilities as exist in New York City are grossly inadequate. The schools are not effectively organized or administered, and the instruction given does not reckon sufficiently with the needs of the modern American Jewish environment.

Jewish school facilities are provided for less than one-fourth of the Jewish children of elementary school age of New York City. Of the three hundred thousand Jewish children of elementary school age only sixty-five thousand can find any sort of accommodation and instruction at any one time. Exclusive of the Chedarim and the private tutoring, only one-seventh of the children are accommodated in Jewish schools. The provision for adolescent Jewish education is even less adequate; for less than one per cent. of the Jewish boys and girls in the public schools are facilities provided for secondary Jewish training.

Of the children who do receive some instruction, the great majority are miserably accommodated. Only a small minority are taught in school buildings constructed especially for educational purposes. The great majority are taught in rented rooms, (many of them unfit for habitation), in dark vestry rooms, in private homes, or in remodelled dwelling houses. In the City of New York, with its million and a half Jews, there are only *ten* specially constructed Jewish school buildings. In the well populated borough of the Bronx, there is not a single Jewish school building constructed for the specific purpose of Jewish education, nor a single institutional building where Jewish class instruction is given. Whereas the Jewish child population increases every year at the rate of 7,500 to 10,000 children, the Jews of New York have been building at the rate of only twenty-seven classrooms per year, capable of accommodating at the utmost from 2,000 to 3,000 pupils. The Jewish community has therefore failed thus far not only to provide proper school accommodation for the majority of its children whose parents are desirous of giving them Jewish training, but it has also failed to make provision for taking care of the annual increase in the number of Jewish children.

Among the Jewish schools themselves there is no unity or coöperation. The two hundred schools of New York are practically so many distinct and separate institutions. Each school is under its own management, and has practically no relation to any other school. The schools form a completely decentralized system in which each institution is fully "autonomous." The result is that there are very few large Jewish schools even in the densely populated sections of the city. Even if the great number of one-teacher schools (Chedarim) be excluded, three-fourths of the Jewish schools of New York are small schools, having less than three hundred pupils on their registers. In a large city like New York it is almost inevitable that these small schools should offer inadequate facilities both in accommodation and in instruction.

No agreement exists among the schools as regards curricula, methods of instruction or grading. There is no uniform system of records and reports, nor is there a transfer system for transferring the pupils who remove from the vicinity of one school to that of another. The utter lack of uniformity in content and management increases greatly the proportion of children who are "eliminated" or drop out yearly from the Jewish schools. This process of "elimination" is a constant one. The pupils who leave either discontinue their studies altogether, or else enter some other school without transfer or guidance, and must find their place in the new school as best they can. The average child stays about three years in the school system, reaching only second grade work. More than two-thirds of the pupils leave before they reach the work of the fourth grade, which means that two-thirds of the pupils do not achieve more than the rudiments of Jewish knowledge.

The inner organization and administration of the schools also are not effective. The schools are managed by large boards of directors, and in some of the larger Jewish schools there are as many as four or five directors for every teacher employed. The "top-heavy" size of the Jewish school boards is the source of much inefficient management. The principals are looked upon, in most instances, as executive clerks, and have but little supervision of the other school officers (such as the secretary and the janitor), or of any of the financial or communal affairs of the school outside of the work in the classrooms. The financial management of the schools is wasteful and insecure, and the accounting is very inadequate and unsystematic. Much of the income is obtained in the form of individual contributions from the community, and except in the case of the larger schools, affiliated with the Federations of Jewish Charities, this source of income is uncertain and wasteful.

Only one costly and undifferentiated course of study is provided for all pupils, irrespective of their abilities or aptitudes. Having brought with them the educational ideal of the "learned man" from Eastern Europe, the Jews are forcing practically all their children through the same traditional "literary" curriculum designed to produce learned men, without realizing that in this country the great majority of American Jews will not be "learned." Much time is wasted in preparing the pupils for the study of biblical and post-biblical literature, in which the majority never engage, since they leave the school system in the meantime. The course of study in the Jewish schools deals almost entirely therefore with the Jewish Past and with the spiritual creations of that Past. Very little time or attention is given to the Jewish Present, its modern institutions and its problems. No attempt is made to interpret for the children that which they learn in the public schools, or to relate their Jewish life with their life as citizens of America. Concerning Palestine, its resources, and its modern Jewish life but little definite instruction is given; and even less is taught concerning the status and the problems of the Jews in the other countries of the world.

The same lack of proper adjustment to the needs of American life is evident in the textbooks used and in the teachers employed. Most of the textbooks current until very recently in the Jewish weekday schools, were written by Russian Jewish authors for Russian Jewish children. Only within the past few years have Jewish teachers realized the inadequacy of these books for Jewish children in New York, with their very different environment and experiences. Besides, most of the Jewish teachers and principals are themselves products of Eastern European training, and consequently many of them are unable to understand the interests and the needs of the American Jewish child. A large proportion (over one-third) of the children who receive instruction are taught in Chedarim and by private itinerant tutors, under conditions which are glaringly unattractive, and incomparably inferior to those prevailing in the public schools. In but a minority of the Jewish schools are the teaching staffs composed of American-trained men and women supervised by American-bred school principals.

Community Program of Jewish Education for New York

These failings are not inherent in American Jewish education. While, to be sure, it is more difficult to improve and systematize a voluntary scheme of education, than it is to affect an educational system which is based upon legal compulsion or the force of centralized clerical authority, there are nevertheless many evidences that point to the awakening of the Jewish community to its educational problems. The first steps have already been made towards the treatment of these problems. There has been more discussion of education and more educational activity among the Jews during the past eight years than during their entire previous history in this country. Modern Jewish school buildings are now being built that are comparable with the best in American school arcitecture. American college-trained young men and women are being attracted to the profession of Jewish education, and good textbooks are being written that reckon with the needs of the American Jewish child. Educational bodies composed of communally-minded men have also been organized to deal with the problems of Jewish education from the viewpoint of community welfare.

What is primarily needed is that the Jewish community of New York place education at the *center* of its various activities. Until now, *charity* has been at the center. To help needy fellow-Jews was the activity around which American Jews rallied; and to belong to some Jewish philanthropic institutions was the sign of interest in Jewish communal affairs. But charity is not reproductive. It does not guarantee in any way that the children of the Jewish philanthropists will continue to support or to be interested in Jewish charities. On the other hand, education *is* essentially reproductive, for it means the transmission of interests to the next generation. With education at the center of communal life, charity and all other communal activities, inevitably *follow*. With charity at the center of communal life, not even the continuation of Jewish charity is assured.

Just as in American education the development of schools and of educational facilities lagged until the State took education into its hands; so Jewish education is bound to lag and remain chaotic until the community as a whole turns its attention towards it. A broad *community program* is needed, based upon an accurate knowledge of the situation, and *community will* is necessary to achieve that program and to adjust it from time to time to meet new needs and changing conditions. A full community program in Jewish education can result only from the coöperation of many minds, and will require much careful experimentation and scrutiny. On the basis of the prevailing conditions, however, certain outstanding elements in such a program become evident.

Community School Buildings. To provide adequate school accommodation in New York even for the present small proportion of Jewish school children who receive some sort of Jewish instruction, at least *twelve* modern Jewish school buildings are needed immediately. Of these, three should be situated in Manhattan, two in the Bronx, and seven in various parts of Brooklyn. (See frontispiece map.) Besides these buildings, which are needed now, the Jews of New York should build at the rate of at least three or four school buildings each year. Modern school buildings cost about $7,500 per classroom. A sum of $1,500,000 should therefore be available at present for building needs; and hereafter, about half a million dollars annually. Assuming that one-half of the necessary sums could be borrowed as first mortgages, $750,000 are needed for building purposes immediately and about $250,000 every year thereafter. Of these sums, one-half should be raised by various groups or organizations in the community as equity, and the other half should be obtained by some central communal organization, in the form of second mortgages. Modern Jewish school buildings should be constructed not only for classroom purposes, but also to serve the various needs of the community school center. They should include auditoria, gymnasia, reading and study rooms, kindergarten rooms, and playgrounds; and they should conform to modern standards in school architecture.

Jewish Extension Education. For a long time to come, however, there will be great numbers of Jewish children of school age for whom there will be no place in regular classrooms. To attempt to provide school seating facilities for *all* children in New York, would require at least 137 new school buildings immediately, with a staff of over 1,800 teachers—evidently an impossible proposition. Nor is it necessary to plan for such a building program. There are many Jewish parents, who, though desirous of giving their children some Jewish instruction, do not wish to send them through the regular intensive Hebrew school. For these children, as well as for the large numbers who cannot be accommodated, extensive forms of Jewish education are indispensable. The Sunday schools and private tutoring can take care of but a small fraction of these Jewish boys and girls. A method of extension education is needed, such as is being developed by the Bureau of Jewish Education through the Circle of Jewish Children and the League of the Jewish Youth, or by the Zionist Organization through Young Judea, which will not require regular classroom facilities for teaching large numbers of children. This form of education should not be considered an adequate *basis* for an American Jewish school system; but it can serve several essential purposes: in the first place, it does give some Jewish knowledge and Jewish affiliation to children who could not be reached otherwise; secondly, it contributes to general Jewish education by emphasizing the social phases of Jewish life (festival celebrations, clubs, etc.) in the education of Jewish children; and lastly, it helps to create a wholesome Jewish atmosphere or environment, so that the pupils of the regular schools are surrounded by sympathetic and appreciative friends and playmates. The Jewish community should make it possible for at least one-fourth of its children and adolescents (seventy-five thousand children and fifty thousand adolescents) to be reached by such extensive education.

Community School Centers. The regular Jewish weekday schools should be organized as community school centers, aiming to meet all the communal needs of the Jewish children, adolescents and adults in their neighborhoods. The boards of directors should be small legislative and controlling bodies with no direct administrative functions. They should consist of seven or nine members elected to represent the parents and members of the center as well as the central community funds. At the head of the school center should be a Director or Principal, who should bear all executive responsibility.

The activities of the community school center should include those of a regular *Jewish school* for children and adolescents, a *neighborhood house* and *synagogue* for uniting all the Jewish residents in the vicinity, a *community house* for bringing its members into direct relation with the entire Jewish community of New York, and a *civic center* for interpreting American life and ideals to American Jews. The entire family should be the unit of operation. The children can be reached through the kindergarten, the elementary and intermediate schools, and the Circle of Jewish Children. The adolescents can be influenced through the secondary or high school classes, the League of the Jewish Youth and the various club activities. The adults should be affiliated through the Parents' Association and the Community Center Association, into whose hands should be entrusted the general management of the social and religious activities of the center.

The cost of conducting the various educational and social activities in each of these community school centers will be from thirty to forty thousand dollars yearly.[4] From 50% to 70% of these costs will have to be contributed from central community funds, such as those of the Federation for the Support of Jewish Philanthropic Societies, and the rest of the costs will come from "self-paying" sources (tuition fees, club dues, etc.). In order that the centers might be organized on this financial basis, as many of the activities of the center should be as "self-paying" as possible. Particularly would the basic education given to the Jewish children in the elementary Hebrew schools have to be conducted on a "self-supporting" basis, permitting each father to pay for the "instruction costs" of his own children, and requiring the community to pay for those who cannot or do not pay for themselves. Such a school organization, "self-supporting" in accord with the proudest Jewish tradition, is possible for elementary schools in New York at an annual cost of $18 per pupil, or about $2,000 per classroom, provided a *four-class-per-teacher schedule* is introduced into the elementary schools. This schedule, which utilizes both Saturday and Sunday for instruction and requires the pupils to come to the Jewish school four times during the week, is economical both in cost and in time, and is sufficient for the needs of the majority of Jewish children.

Community Coördination. The school centers must not be isolated institutions. Their activities should be related and coördinated. To coördinate the work of the present Jewish schools and of those still to be built, is among the most delicate, and at the same time, among the most important tasks of the community. It is very undesirable to try to bring about complete and rigid centralization of the Jewish schools; and yet combination of effort and to a certain extent uniformity in essentials is absolutely necessary. Such uniformity cannot be brought about in modern Jewish life by impersonal law or by imposed authority. It can only result from understanding, persuasion, and the coöperation of the various *personal* elements that control Jewish education in New York: the parents, the teachers, the principals, the trustees, the contributors of funds, and the community as a whole. The Jewish Parents' Association to unite the parents, the Hebrew Principals' Association to coördinate the work of the principals, a Teachers' Council to

[4] For centers having from twelve to sixteen classrooms.

represent the various organizations of Jewish teachers, the Board of Jewish School Aid to act as a Community Board of School Trustees, the Federation for the Support of Jewish Philanthropic Societies to protect the interests of the contributors to the schools against inefficiency and waste, and the Kehillah (Jewish Community) to bring Jewish educational activities before the court of Jewish public opinion—these are the agencies upon which devolves the task of uniting the various "personal" elements for mutual understanding and common effort. Working with all these bodies there should be an expert educational agency like the Bureau of Jewish Education, in order to bring to them the benefit of specialized educational knowledge.

The lines along which uniformity is most to be desired in Jewish schools at present are: the installation of uniform records and reports, both in financial and in educational accounting; the creation of a transfer system among the various schools, so as to encourage pupils who leave one Jewish school to enter another near their new homes; and the fostering of sufficient agreement in matters of grading, curricula and methods of instruction, to make it possible for the pupils of one school to enter another, upon removal, without having to lose standing or to "start over again."

Differentiation of Jewish Instruction. Agreement upon curricula and grading does not mean, however, that there should be only one kind of curriculum. On the contrary, in so far as the Hebrew schools at present follow the traditional curriculum aiming at the traditional educational product, the "learned" man, the instruction is too much alike and too undifferentiated. In reckoning with the needs of the American environment, it is imperative that a distinction be made in Jewish education between the large majority of children who will not be "learned" Jews and who cannot profit from intensive instruction in the literary sources of Judaism, and that capable minority which is able to profit by such instruction. It must be recognized that the *child* and not the *curriculum* is the center of Jewish education, and that the preparation of the child for completely adjusted life as an American Jew is the aim of the Jewish schools in this country.

A number of varied curricula should therefore be developed, in accordance with the needs and aptitudes of various classes of children. A basic elementary course of study, extending over a period of three years, four sessions during each week, should be provided for all boys and girls. This curriculum should lay stress on Hebrew, from both the linguistic and the religious aspects, and it should also include instruction in all other elements of Jewish knowledge which are essential for the American Jew. Beyond the basic elementary curriculum, differentiation should be provided in the intermediate schools. The capable minority, consisting probably of about one-fourth of all those who complete the basic elementary course of study, should be given intensive Hebrew instruction, five or six sessions per week, with emphasis upon the Bible and Jewish literature in the original. For a specially selected one per cent, composed of the very brightest pupils, it may prove wise to furnish the still more intensive parochial education, to prepare them for Jewish scholarship and leadership. For the "average" majority, however, a vernacular curriculum, four sessions per week, would seem to be satisfactory and highly desirable. In this curriculum Hebrew would still have its place, but the Bible and Jewish literature would be studied in the English *translation*, and the emphasis would be laid upon Jewish history, and upon America, Palestine and the other aspects of the Jewish Present.

Community Budget. Such a differentiation in the character of the Jewish instruction given to children would make possible a far more effective and economical distribution of funds spent on Jewish education than takes place at present. Upon the teaching of the traditional curriculum, transplanted with but little modification from Eastern Europe, the Jews of New York spend large sums of money annually. Without much increase in the sums now spent, the Jews of New York could obtain very much better educational results if they would *regulate* their expenditure in Jewish education. Instead of spending over a million dollars almost wholly upon the uniform, wasteful training given to the children at present receiving elementary weekday instruction, this money could be redistributed so as to give elementary, intermediate and secondary weekday instruction to sixty-five thousand children and adolescents, in accordance with a systematic, differentiated program, and provide also for higher education, (ministry, pedagogy and communal work); for the extension education of over one hundred thousand children and adolescents; and for social service activities to reach all Jews residing within the neighborhood of Jewish schools.

Under ideal conditions, a "community budget" of about a million and a half dollars would enable the community to conduct *fifty school centers* with an annual expenditure of thirty to forty thousand dollars per center. Each school center would be in a position to give regular elementary and intermediate Jewish instruction to over a thousand boys and girls; special intensive Hebrew training to about two hundred advanced pupils of intermediate and higher standing; extensive education to some two thousand children and adolescents; and social-educational activities for all the members of the neighboring Jewish families. Fifty such school centers in New York could form the backbone of Jewish communal life.

The Profession of Jewish Education. To carry on the work of these fifty school centers about a thousand modern teachers, supervisors and educational leaders are needed. To obtain such a staff is perhaps the one most essential element in a community program for Jewish education. Very little can be hoped for in the way of progressive development unless the community can attract from among its very best men and women those who are to be the teachers, principals and supervisors of the Jewish schools. The community should take hold of this problem in a broad-minded, practical manner. While in the last analysis the ranks of Jewish education must be recruited from those who passionately desire the existence of the Jewish people because they are stirred by the epic romance of Jewish history and of Jewish aspirations, it is not possible to draw enough American young men and women to the Jewish teaching profession on the basis of interest alone; the work of the Jewish teacher must be made more attractive economically and socially than it is at present.

The salaries of Jewish teachers should be standardized by the community, and the average salary raised so as to make possible a graduated living wage for teachers, supervisors and principals. A pension system should be developed, based upon the principles of coöperative insurance, and administered by a committee representing the trustees, the principals and the teachers. The beginning of such standardization of teachers' salaries should be made by the schools connected with the Board of Jewish School Aid.

A Board of Certification of Teachers' Licenses should be organized for the purpose of granting a variety of temporary and permanent licenses: to elementary teachers, to intermediate and secondary teachers, to supervisors, and to principals. The Jewish Teachers' Institutes of New York should offer several courses of study in order to train their students for these various graded certificates. Training courses should also be provided for Sunday school teachers and for the workers in extension education. Nor should the immigrant Jewish teachers be forgotten, who need special training to prepare them to teach in American Jewish schools.

For the advancement of common professional interests the activities of the various organizations of teachers and principals should be coördinated through a Teachers' Council, or an Educational Council. In conjunction with this Council, the community should reward educational merit by making it possible for capable Jewish teachers to visit Palestine, or to undertake special research work in some field of Jewish education at the American universities. Such investment of community funds would bring manifold returns in that knowledge and zeal which are most essential for the preservation and development of Jewish life; for upon the teachers and the "breath of the children" in their charge, rests the future of the Jewish world.

These are the broad outlines, the framework, of an educational program for the Jewish community of New York. New York Jews are far from being ready for such a community program. They seem to have neither the combined will, nor the power, nor the persons needed to make this program a reality in the immediate future. Perhaps the most fundamental difficulty in effecting a common educational program is the divergence of New York Jews with regard to their communal outlook. Besides the "fusionists,"[5] who are opposed or indifferent to Jewish education, there are the orthodox and the reform; the conserva-

[5] A full discussion of the variety of Jewish communal attitudes is presented in Part I, chapter 1 of this book.

tive and the radical; the Zionists and the anti-Zionists; the nationalists who consider Palestine as the *only* place for the development of Jewish life, and the nationalists who believe in *international* Jewry, with Palestine as the center. Practically each of these parties has its own educational program, and strives to effect its own educational organization. And yet, in spite of these differences and difficulties, it is the part of wisdom for the community's leaders to hold a broad educational program before them. Some such program as here outlined is needed to guide the future educational efforts of the Jews of New York, in order that slowly, in the course of years, a unified American Jewry may arise from the now stridently "independent" Jewish parties.

Educational Programs for other American Jewish Communities

Educational programs, similar to that proposed for New York, are needed for all other Jewish communities in America. In no community, of course, will the program outlined be applicable in its totality. Many factors must be taken into consideration in adapting the program to the local needs. The size of the community and the nature of its composition—the proportion of first generation immigrants, the countries of their emigration, and the strength of the various Jewish parties—will affect profoundly the particular program. In general, it seems that the smaller and the more compact the Jewish population, and the more homogeneous its composition, the easier will be the solution of its educational problem.[6] The degree to which the rest of Jewish communal life in the community is organized, will also have its direct effect upon the educational program. Where the Jewish charities are federated, or where the synagogues are

[6] Reports from small American Jewish communities, for example, state that the proportion of Jewish children who are given Jewish instruction in the small towns is considerably greater than in the large cities. But this is only broadly true. In the very small communities the problem is very difficult and is apt to be neglected just because of lack of volume: there are not enough families in these communities to enable them to give their children more than the barest rudiments of Jewish instruction. Some day the student of Jewish education will be able to tell us what is the ideal size of the Jewish community in America, and what the ideal conditions would be for a really effective and progressive American Jewish educational system.

united, the educational problems are more definite and more readily solved than in communities whose entire communal life is disorganized. Lastly, each community must inevitably shape its educational program in accordance with its existing educational resources, both in men and institutions.

While these determining factors must be given their proper place in modifying the educational program outlined in New York, before it can be applicable to other American communities, certain elements in that program are of general interest and validity. The leaders of every Jewish community should have definite detailed knowledge concerning the educational activities in their community. In the larger communities a continuous *educational survey* is necessary to obtain reliable detailed information. On the basis of such information a *community budget* should be drawn up, which though impossible of immediate or near-future execution, should guide the efforts of the leaders toward a wise distribution of the educational funds. A very important part of the program must be the provision for sufficient school facilities. School buildings should be constructed so as to serve as *community centers,* combining the functions of the school, the synagogue and the social settlement. Where the synagogue forms the main feature of the building, classrooms should be built on the floors above or adjoining to it, but never in the basement rooms underneath. The Jewish instruction given in these community school centers should be differentiated, provision being made for a *basic* Hebrew curriculum for all elementary school children, and for two curricula in the intermediate grades: an *intensive Hebrew* course for specially selected capable pupils, and a general *vernacular* course for average children. Not only the Hebrew language and the Jewish Past (history, literature, customs, etc.) but also the Jewish Present, in its many aspects, should be taught to American Jewish children everywhere. In all communities some provision should be made besides the regular instruction for the *Extension Education* of children and adolescents, (if not because of lack of classroom space, then for the sake of introducing into the schools the social elements, the "movement" idea, of such organizations as the Circle of Jewish Children and of Young Judea). In the large towns it should be possible to organize

Jewish instruction for the majority of the school children on a *"self-supporting" basis,* so that the average parent may be able to pay for the "instruction costs" of his children. The costs of the schools beyond the income from tuition fees should be defrayed from central *community funds,* and where this is possible a *Community Board of Jewish Education* may be organized to act as the trustees for these funds. The function of this board should be to eliminate waste and to introduce necessary uniformity in matters of records, transfers and grading, without interfering with the independence or initiative of the individual schools. For real coördination, however, all Jewish school systems in this country will have to depend not upon any scheme of organization but rather upon the voluntary coöperation of parents, teachers, principals, trustees, contributors and all other "personal" elements that control Jewish education.

None except the large Jewish communities will be able to train their own teachers, supervisors and principals. The smaller communities will necessarily depend upon the larger centers for their professional workers in Jewish education. Because of the lack of adequate supervision and of educational leadership, the smaller cities and towns will find it very difficult to maintain professional standards in Jewish education and to infuse professional interest among their teachers, unless a large national organization be effected in the professional interests of American Jewish education. Indeed, such an organization is as important for the teachers and principals in the large cities as it is for those in the small towns. An *American Association for Jewish Education* is needed, organized along the lines of the National Education Association, and other American professional societies. To it should be invited Jewish teachers, supervisors, principals, and all others professionally engaged in Jewish education, for the purpose of hearing reports concerning the educational work done in various parts of the country and for discussing their problems and suggestions with one another. All the different kinds of Jewish educational endeavor should be included: Talmud Torahs, Hebrew Schools, Sunday Schools, Yeshibahs, Yiddishe Volksschulen, organizations for extension education, Zionist educational organizations, institutions for higher Jewish learning, teachers' associations and training schools, principals' associations, boards of education, etc. Besides the general conferences and discussions, the Association should provide for sectional meetings in accordance with particular educational interests (principals, Sunday Schools, etc.). A National American Association for Jewish Education, holding its convention once every year, and attracting to it teachers and principals throughout the country for interchange of views and experiences, could do very much for the development of American Jewish education and for infusing hopefulness and professional interest among its workers in all the Jewish communities of this country.

Outlook Problematic but Hopeful

The outlook, though problematic, is distinctly hopeful. American Jewry is in a great transitional period. The old order and the old ideas of organization and of communal life are discredited and are rapidly losing their hold. New ideas and new forces have appeared whose potency and influence are as yet vague and uncertain. With the old yearning for Zion within reach of practical realization, with the lashing compelling power of persecution happily (though too slowly) disappearing, the Jews of the world are facing the most delicate and most difficult problem of adjustment in their long and checkered history. It is hazardous to foretell how successfully this adjustment will be made.

As in the past, it is largely a matter of will. From the days of Isaiah the belief in the "indestructibility of Zion" and of the Jewish people, has been a mystic conviction among the Jews down to our own day. The miracle of Jewish existence through the ages, in different environments and under varying conditions, is accounted for, in no small measure, by the desire and the capacity of the Jews to adjust their group life to the country in which they live. Their history has shown that in the past they have had the insight and the will required in re-arranging their modes of life, so as to conform to the habits and cultures of the surrounding peoples, without losing any of the fundamental values of life which they consider to be their own.

In America too, this process of adjustment is under way. Jewish education has not yet found itself in the midst of the new American environment, and many difficult problems confront Jewish educators in this country. But the Jews of America are capable of making the necessary adjustment, and the beginnings have already been made. The educational system which American Jews are developing is designed to make of their children fully adjusted individuals, combining in themselves both the American and the Jewish values of life.

TABLE I.

ATTENDANCE IN NEW YORK PUBLIC SCHOOLS ON JEWISH HOLIDAYS

Districts		1913										
		Oct. 2		Oct. 3		Average			Oct. 9 Normal			Corrected % Attendance
		Reg.	Att.	Reg.	Att.	Reg.	Att.	%	Reg.	Att.	%	
Manhattan	1	13,715	11,634	13,678	11,160	13,696	11,397	83.2	13,663	12,657	92.6	**89.8**
	2	8,456	521	8,406	494	8,431	507	6.0	8,342	7,976	95.6	**6.2**
	3	11,827	235	11,828	229	11,827	232	1.9	11,782	11,106	94.2	**2.0**
	4	14,186	395	14,183	386	14,184	390	2.7	14,061	13,256	94.2	**2.8**
	5	10,388	95	10,387	122	10,388	109	1.0	10,277	9,794	95.3	**1.0**
	6	13,519	2,881	13,431	2,456	13,475	2,669	19.7	13,381	12,734	95.4	**20.6**
	7	18,813	1,326	18,790	1,245	18,802	1,286	6.8	18,675	17,690	94.7	**7.1**
	8	12,023	7,340	11,940	7,372	11,981	7,356	61.3	11,902	10,856	91.2	**67.2**
	9	11,573	9,806	11,550	9,911	11,561	9,858	85.2	11,568	10,690	92.3	**92.3**
	10	6,388	4,772	6,421	4,866	6,405	4,819	75.2	6,391	5,717	89.4	**84.1**
	11	7,785	6,022	7,754	6,071	7,769	6,046	77.8	7,664	6,952	90.7	**85.7**
	12	9,194	6,695	9,195	6,811	9,195	6,753	73.4	9,168	8,428	91.8	**79.9**
	13	7,817	5,489	7,799	5,535	7,808	5,512	70.5	7,756	7,259	93.6	**75.3**
	14	7,842	6,140	7,823	6,335	7,832	6,238	79.6	7,751	6,855	88.4	**90.0**
	15	13,410	7,815	13,354	8,087	13,382	7,951	59.4	13,281	12,524	94.3	**63.0**
	16	14,232	5,420	14,139	5,464	14,185	5,442	38.3	13,990	12,838	91.7	**41.7**
	17	18,534	6,950	18,479	6,958	18,506	6,954	37.5	18,327	17,043	92.9	**40.3**
	18	8,871	5,656	8,817	6,501	8,844	6,079	68.7	8,789	7,715	87.7	**78.3**
	19	15,673	5,342	15,629	5,728	15,651	5,535	35.3	15,633	14,639	93.7	**37.6**
	20	14,069	6,661	13,936	6,673	14,003	6,667	47.6	13,829	12,942	93.6	**50.9**
	21	12,763	8,068	12,693	8,431	12,728	8,249	64.8	12,667	11,010	86.9	**74.3**
	22	14,339	8,068	14,326	10,219	14,333	9,144	63.7	14,314	13,168	91.9	**69.4**
Total		**265,417**	**117,331**	**264,558**	**121,054**	**264,987**	**119,193**	**44.9**	**263,211**	**243,849**	**92.5**	**48.6**
Bronx	23	18,223	11,189	19,164	11,454	18,194	11,322	62.3	17,976	16,648	92.6	**67.2**
	24	23,217	9,470	23,106	9,919	23,162	9,694	41.9	23,008	21,404	93.0	**45.0**
	25	28,432	11,403	28,388	11,919	28,410	11,661	41.0	28,294	26,310	92.9	**44.1**
	26	18,670	15,545	18,613	16,036	18,642	15,790	84.5	18,564	17,093	92.0	**91.8**
Total		**88,542**	**47,607**	**88,271**	**49,328**	**88,408**	**48,467**	**54.7**	**87,842**	**81,455**	**52.7**	**59.0**
Brooklyn	27	14,056	11,443	14,098	11,782	14,077	11,613	82.4	14,068	12,825	91.1	**90.4**
	28	13,072	11,391	13,017	11,351	13,084	11,371	86.7	13,155	12,293	93.4	**92.9**
	29	15,808	11,741	15,774	12,010	15,791	11,875	75.2	15,752	14,269	90.5	**83.2**
	30	19,163	15,868	19,136	16,144	19,149	16,006	83.9	19,137	17,763	92.8	**89.9**
	31	16,175	6,068	16,093	6,120	16,134	6,094	37.7	16,038	15,003	93.6	**40.2**
	32	25,512	9,574	25,483	10,375	25,498	9,974	39.1	25,366	23,695	93.5	**41.9**
	33	16,207	3,730	16,158	3,643	16,183	3,687	22.4	16,159	15,375	90.0	**23.5**
	34	14,504	11,367	14,468	11,549	14,486	11,458	79.3	14,465	13,300	92.2	**86.0**
	35	16,490	10,587	16,433	10,704	16,462	10,646	64.7	16,405	15,438	94.1	**68.6**
	36	16,292	13,148	16,244	13,105	16,268	13,126	80.7	16,338	15,375	94.0	**85.9**
	37	23,180	16,041	23,094	16,416	23,137	16,228	69.9	22,967	20,998	91.6	**76.3**
	38	20,608	15,538	20,535	16,266	20,572	15,902	77.6	20,380	18,498	90.7	**85.5**
	39	24,888	1,953	24,782	2,009	24,835	1,981	7.9	24,518	21,029	85.6	**9.4**
	40	25,228	10,263	25,154	10,464	25,191	10,364	41.4	25,065	23,225	92.7	**44.3**
Total		**261,133**	**148,712**	**260,569**	**151,938**	**260,877**	**150,325**	**57.7**	**259,813**	**239,176**	**92.1**	**62.6**
Queens	41	9,736	8,136	9,709	8,385	9,723	8,260	85.2	9,694	8,818	91.0	**93.7**
	42	15,354	12,465	15,241	13,054	15,297	12,759	83.5	15,250	13,992	91.5	**91.3**
	43	11,884	9,805	11,882	9,928	11,883	9,867	83.2	11,818	10,571	89.4	**93.0**
	44	19,458	15,920	19,372	16,566	19,415	16,243	83.6	19,210	17,521	91.3	**91.6**
Total		**56,432**	**46,326**	**56,204**	**47,933**	**56,318**	**47,129**	**83.4**	**55,972**	**50,902**	**91.0**	**91.6**
Richmond	45	7,971	6,619	7,966	6,897	7,968	6,758	85.1	7,948	7,321	92.3	**92.2**
	46	6,326	5,112	6,325	5,470	6,326	5,291	83.6	6,330	5,727	90.4	**92.4**
Total		**14,297**	**11,731**	**14,291**	**12,367**	**14,294**	**12,049**	**84.4**	**14,278**	**13,048**	**91.5**	**92.2**
Grand Total		**685,871**	**371,707**	**683,893**	**382,620**	**684,884**	**377,163**	**55.0**	**681,116**	**628,430**	**92.1**	**59.8**

ABLE I—Continued

ATTENDANCE IN NEW YORK PUBLIC SCHOOLS ON JEWISH HOLIDAYS

	Districts	1914												Corrected % Attendance	Average Corrected % Attendance	Abnormal Absence
		Sept. 21		Sept. 22		Sept. 30		Average			Oct. 1 Normal					
		Reg.	Att.	Reg.	Att.	Reg.	Att.	Reg.	Att.	%	Reg.	Att.	%			
Manhattan	1	14,474	11,871	14,425	12,008	14,068	11,960	14,322	11,946	83.3	14,014	12,755	90.9	**91.6**	90.7	**9.3**
	2	8,662	645	8,627	583	8,306	652	8,532	626	7.3	8,308	7,745	93.3	**7.9**	7.0	**83.0**
	3	12,153	183	12,153	179	11,908	134	12,071	165	1.3	12,021	11,338	94.3	**1.3**	1.7	**98.3**
	4	15,551	281	15,541	271	15,272	299	15,455	284	1.8	15,191	14,520	95.7	**1.8**	2.3	**97.7**
	5	10,854	101	10,818	104	10,294	49	10,655	85	.8	10,288	9,716	94.4	**.8**	.9	**99.1**
	6	14,300	2,825	14,277	2,740	13,791	2,668	14,123	2,744	19.4	13,712	12,608	91.9	**21.1**	20.8	**79.2**
	7	20,299	1,480	20,229	1,370	19,770	1,644	20,099	1,498	7.4	19,742	18,724	94.8	**7.8**	7.5	**82.5**
	8	13,095	8,383	13,076	8,622	12,438	8,613	12,869	8,539	66.4	12,656	11,332	89.6	**74.0**	70.0	**30.5**
	9	12,297	10,308	12,311	10,439	12,075	10,616	12,228	10,454	85.3	12,003	11,085	92.2	**92.5**	92.4	**7.6**
	10	6,621	4,933	6,557	5,016	6,353	5,077	6,510	5,009	76.9	6,339	5,776	91.1	**84.4**	84.3	**15.7**
	11	8,106	6,092	8,103	6,157	9,892	6,251	8,700	6,167	70.8	7,887	6,852	87.0	**81.3**	83.5	**16.5**
	12	9,551	7,108	9,524	7,165	9,260	7,295	9,445	7,189	76.2	9,285	8,552	92.2	**82.0**	81.2	**18.8**
	13	8,736	5,977	8,711	6,369	8,535	6,287	8,660	6,211	71.7	8,430	7,889	93.4	**76.7**	76.0	**24.0**
	14	8,193	5,899	8,128	6,488	7,938	6,596	8,086	6,328	78.4	7,937	7,084	89.3	**87.7**	88.8	**11.2**
	15	14,143	8,493	14,015	8,845	13,535	8,428	13,898	8,589	61.8	13,501	12,653	93.6	**66.0**	64.5	**35.5**
	16	15,140	5,656	15,046	5,704	14,473	5,380	14,886	5,580	37.5	14,507	13,545	93.3	**40.2**	41.0	**59.0**
	17	19,790	6,838	19,694	6,789	18,951	6,863	19,478	6,830	35.1	18,962	17,698	93.2	**37.7**	39.0	**61.0**
	18	9,432	5,915	9,391	6,735	9,185	6,087	9,336	6,246	66.8	9,225	8,054	87.3	**76.4**	77.4	**22.6**
	19	16,328	5,891	16,225	6,302	15,878	5,960	16,144	6,051	37.5	16,011	14,778	92.0	**40.7**	39.2	**60.8**
	20	15,731	7,180	15,628	7,196	15,764	7,596	15,708	7,324	46.6	15,187	13,918	92.0	**50.7**	50.8	**49.2**
	21	13,775	9,297	13,745	9,508	13,416	9,644	13,645	9,483	69.4	13,425	11,991	89.2	**77.8**	76.0	**23.0**
	22	16,252	8,779	16,261	10,998	15,824	8,916	16,112	9,564	59.3	15,884	14,417	91.0	**65.3**	67.3	**32.7**
Total		**283,483**	**124,135**	**282,485**	**129,588**	**276,925**	**127,015**	**280,962**	**126,912**	**45.1**	**274,475**	**253,030**	**92.2**	**49.0**	**48.8**	**51.2**
Bronx	23	19,084	11,350	18,904	11,568	18,097	10,817	18,695	11,245	60.3	18,104	16,817	92.8	**64.9**	66.0	**34.0**
	24	26,141	9,185	25,930	9,628	24,675	9,245	25,582	9,353	36.8	24,777	22,973	92.8	**39.6**	42.3	**57.7**
	25	33,443	13,128	33,894	13,505	32,811	13,178	33,383	13,270	39.9	33,047	30,332	91.7	**43.5**	43.8	**56.2**
	26	20,702	17,306	20,726	17,578	20,189	17,440	20,539	17,441	85.1	20,084	18,845	94.0	**90.5**	91.2	**8.8**
Total		**99,370**	**50,969**	**99,454**	**52,279**	**95,772**	**50,680**	**98,199**	**51,309**	**52.2**	**96,012**	**88,967**	**92.5**	**56.4**	**57.7**	**42.3**
Brooklyn	27	15,248	12,528	15,234	12,697	14,928	13,111	15,137	12,779	84.3	14,909	13,722	92.2	**91.4**	90.9	**9.1**
	28	14,218	12,099	14,153	12,051	14,040	12,118	14,137	12,089	85.4	13,988	13,008	93.3	**91.5**	92.2	**7.8**
	29	16,539	12,087	16,488	12,331	16,274	12,692	16,434	12,370	75.1	16,290	14,897	91.5	**82.2**	82.7	**17.3**
	30	19,990	16,557	19,952	16,756	19,693	16,631	19,878	16,648	83.7	19,612	18,061	92.0	**91.1**	90.5	**9:5**
	31	17,678	6,348	17,598	6,415	17,081	6,394	17,452	6,386	36.5	17,172	16,111	94.0	**38.9**	39.6	**60.4**
	32	28,226	9,456	28,210	10,320	27,590	9,457	28,008	9,744	34.6	27,568	25,575	92.6	**37.4**	39.6	**60.4**
	33	16,922	3,755	16,864	3,760	16,481	3,918	16,755	3,811	22.7	16,541	15,525	94.0	**24.1**	23.8	**76.2**
	34	15,099	12,141	15,076	12,274	14,903	12,378	15,026	12,264	81.4	14,909	13,820	92.6	**87.9**	87.0	**13.0**
	35	17,285	11,078	17,356	11,403	16,897	11,247	17,179	11,243	65.6	16,912	15,833	93.5	**70.2**	69.4	**30.6**
	36	16,994	13,184	16,880	13,278	16,472	13,202	16,782	13,221	78.9	16,525	15,616	94.5	**83.4**	84.7	**15.3**
	37	25,081	17,597	25,052	17,707	24,575	17,586	24,903	17,630	70.8	24,617	22,498	91.2	**77.5**	76.9	**23.1**
	38	22,021	16,718	21,912	17,454	21,629	17,414	21,854	17,195	78.5	21,623	19,963	92.1	**85.2**	85.4	**14.6**
	39	27,406	2,091	27,370	1,940	26,626	1,926	27,134	1,986	7.3	26,603	25,108	94.5	**7.7**	8.5	**91.5**
	40	27,228	10,555	27,061	10,607	26,269	10,751	26,886	10,638	39.5	26,373	24,321	92.4	**42.8**	43.6	**56.4**
Total		**279,935**	**156,194**	**279.206**	**158,993**	**273,558**	**158,825**	**277,565**	**158,004**	**57.0**	**273,642**	**254,058**	**93,0**	**61.3**	**62.0**	**38.0**
Queens	41	10,184	9,110	10,180	9,204	9,984	9,093	10,116	9,136	90.4	10,036	9,293	92.5	**97.7**	95.7	**4.3**
	42	16,452	14,200	16,480	14,240	16,183	14,295	16,372	14,245	87.0	16,205	15,182	93.6	**92.8**	92.0	**8.0**
	43	13,072	10,901	12,989	11,023	12,727	10,946	12,929	10,957	84.6	12,713	11,573	90.8	**93.3**	93.2	**6.8**
	44	20,565	17,167	20,475	17,553	20,080	17,214	20,373	17,311	85.2	20,010	18,367	91.6	**93.0**	92.3	**7.7**
Total		**60,273**	**51,378**	**60,124**	**52,020**	**58,974**	**51,548**	**59,790**	**51,649**	**86.4**	**58,96**	**54,415**	**92.2**	**93.7**	**92.7**	**7.3**
mond	45	8,327	7,438	8,346	7,474	8,283	7,466	8,319	7,459	89.6	8,271	7,784	94.0	**95.3**	93.8	**6.2**
	46	6,760	6,078	6,753	6,071	6,696	6,075	6,736	6,075	90.4	6,698	6,216	93.0	**97.2**	94.8	**5.2**
Total		**15,087**	**13,516**	**15,099**	**13,545**	**14,979**	**13,541**	**15,055**	**13,534**	**90.0**	**14,969**	**14,000**	**93.5**	**96.2**	**94.2**	**5.8**
Grand Total		**738,148**	**396,192**	**736,368**	**406,425**	**720,208**	**401,609**	**731,571**	**401,408**	**55.0**	**718,062**	**664,470**	**92.6**	**59.2**	**59.5**	**40.5**

TABLE II.

TABLE SHOWING PROPORTION JUDGED TO BE JEWS IN SCHOOL CENSUS CARDS NEW YORK CITY

	District	Total Population							Children of School Age						
		Set I			Set II				Set I			Set II			
		Jews	Total	%	Jews	Total	%	Average %	Jews	Total	%	Jews	Total	%	Average %
Manhattan	1	..	115	..	2	106	2	**1**	0	66	0	1	66	2	**1**
	2	39	61	64	31	54	57	**60**	18	31	58	19	32	60	**59**
	3	71	71	100	75	75	100	**100**	38	38	100	37	37	100	**100**
	4	72	100	72	83	100	83	**78**	38	52	73	57	65	88	**81**
	5	65	65	100	73	74	99	**99**	32	32	100	43	44	97	**98**
	6	68	101	67	59	87	67	**67**	37	62	60	32	52	61	**61**
	7	88	145	60	113	178	63	**62**	43	74	58	67	108	62	**60**
	8	19	56	34	8	64	12	**23**	9	31	29	6	36	16	**22**
	9	0	107	0	0	100	0	**0**	0	63	0	0	53	0	**0**
	10	6	67	9	2	54	4	**7**	4	32	12	2	34	5	**8**
	11	22	100	22	2	72	3	**13**	14	54	26	2	35	5	**16**
	12	13	91	14	17	109	15	**15**	5	41	12	11	56	19	**16**
	13	15	83	18	19	91	21	**20**	7	51	14	7	52	13	**13**
	14	2	50	4	0	64	0	**2**	1	22	5	0	44	0	**3**
	15	17	77	22	20	80	25	**23**	9	38	23	11	38	29	**26**
	16	53	129	41	56	116	48	**45**	28	76	37	33	67	49	**43**
	17	99	212	51	76	174	43	**48**	59	121	48	43	99	43	**46**
	18	18	72	25	22	79	28	**26**	11	47	23	10	31	32	**23**
	19	49	127	38	52	102	51	**45**	28	76	37	26	53	49	**43**
	20	58	169	35	35	141	25	**30**	39	105	37	20	76	26	**32**
	21	34	100	34	39	105	37	**36**	19	55	35	18	68	26	**30**
	22	42	95	44	39	117	33	**38**	25	58	43	22	67	33	**38**
Total		**851**	**2,197**	**39**	**811**	**2,138**	**38**	**39**	**464**	**1,225**	**38**	**467**	**1,214**	**38**	**38**
Bronx	23	40	118	34	23	105	22	**28**	25	72	35	17	64	26	**30**
	24	83	203	41	77	213	36	**40**	37	110	33	51	136	37	**35**
	25	89	187	47	74	180	41	**44**	53	103	51	45	110	41	**46**
	26	8	128	6	3	109	3	**5**	6	77	8	1	57	2	**5**
Total		**220**	**636**	**34**	**177**	**607**	**29**	**32**	**121**	**362**	**33**	**114**	**367**	**31**	**32**
Brooklyn	27	12	129	9	8	119	7	**8**	8	70	11	4	65	6	**9**
	28	21	179	12	19	164	12	**12**	9	111	8	13	105	12	**10**
	29	33	153	22	30	126	24	**23**	22	98	22	16	65	24	**23**
	30	20	143	14	18	130	14	**14**	11	90	12	8	65	12	**12**
	31	87	192	45	78	160	49	**47**	55	112	49	40	82	49	**49**
	32	90	140	64	99	141	70	**67**	54	79	68	55	80	69	**69**
	33	46	71	65	50	81	62	**64**	23	29	77	21	39	54	**67**
	34	9	44	20	5	55	9	**15**	7	29	25	4	32	13	**19**
	35	21	112	18	23	100	23	**20**	11	62	18	11	49	23	**21**
	36	49	130	38	34	119	28	**33**	29	75	38	19	69	27	**33**
	37	40	211	19	35	195	18	**19**	19	128	15	23	113	20	**18**
	38	29	188	15	42	157	27	**21**	19	118	16	27	95	28	**22**
	39	204	261	78	202	273	74	**76**	127	166	76	121	163	74	**75**
	40	92	172	54	94	192	49	**52**	50	101	50	59	118	50	**50**
Total		**742**	**2,076**	**36**	**731**	**1,950**	**37**	**37**	**436**	**1,239**	**35**	**417**	**1,106**	**38**	**37**
Queens	41	7	103	7	0	93	0	**4**	5	57	9	0	51	0	**5**
	42	7	147	5	6	146	4	**5**	4	93	4	1	74	1	**3**
	43	2	112	2	4	118	3	**3**	1	67	2	2	76	3	**3**
	44	6	97	6	16	82	20	**13**	5	57	9	9	55	16	**13**
Total		**22**	**459**	**5**	**26**	**439**	**6**	**6**	**15**	**274**	**5**	**12**	**256**	**5**	**5**
Richmond	45	7	66	11	1	62	2	**7**	4	44	9	0	34	0	**5**
	46	0	66	0	0	53	0	**0**	0	43	0	0	29	0	**0**
Total		**7**	**132**	**5**	**1**	**115**	**1**	**3**	**4**	**87**	**9**	**0**	**63**	**0**	**5**
Grand Total		**1,842**	**5,500**	**33***	**1,746**	**5,249**	**33**	**33**	**1,040**	**3,187**	**33**	**1,010**	**3,006**	**33***	**33**

*It is a curious coincidence that the proportion of Jews in the total population was found to be the same as the proportion in the school population. This fact argues strongly in favor of the contention that the proportion of school children among Jews is about the same as in the general population of New York. Cf. "The Jewish Population of New York," in the Jewish Communal Register, 1918, p. 81.

TABLE II-A

CORRELATION BETWEEN TWO METHODS OF ASCERTAINING NUMBER OF JEWISH CHILDREN IN NEW YORK CITY

(Holiday Method and Census Method)

District	Deviation X (Holiday Method)	Deviation Y (Census Method)	XY	X^2	Y^2
1	−27.6	−30	+828.0	761.8	900
2	+46:1	+28	+1290.8	2125.2	784
3	+61.4	+69	+4236.6	3779.9	4761
4	+60.8	+50	+3040.0	3696.6	2500
5	+62.2	+67	+4167.4	3868.8	4489
6	+42.3	+30	+1269.0	1789.3	900
7	+45.6	+29	+1322.4	2079.4	841
8	−6.9	−9	+62.1	47.6	81
9	−29.3	−31	+908.3	858.5	961
10	−21.2	−23	+487.6	449.4	529
11	−20.4	−15	+306.0	416.2	225
12	−18.1	−15	+271.5	327.6	225
13	−12.9	−18	+232.2	165.4	324
14	−25.7	−28	+719.6	660.5	784
15	−1.4	−5	+7.0	1.9	25
16	+22.1	+12	+265.2	488.4	144
17	+24.1	+15	+261.5	580.8	225
18	−14.3	−8	+114.4	204.5	64
19	+23.1	+12	+277.2	533.6	144
20	+12.3	+1	+12.3	151.3	1
21	−13.9	−1	+13.9	193.2	1
22	−4.2	+7	−29.4	17.6	49
23	−2.9	−1	+2.9	8.4	1
24	+20.8	+4	+83.2	432.6	16
25	+19.3	+15	+289.5	372.5	225
26	−28.1	−26	+720.6	789.6	676
27	−27.8	−22	+611.6	772.8	484
28	−29.1	−21	+611.1	846.8	462
29	−19.6	−8	+156.8	384.2	64
30	−27.4	−19	+520.6	750.8	361
31	+23.5	+18	+423.0	552.2	324
32	+23.5	+38	+893.0	552.2	1444
33	+39.3	+36	+1414.8	1544.5	1296
34	−23.9	−12	−286.8	571.2	144
35	−6.3	−10	+63.0	39.7	100
36	−21.6	+2	−43.2	466.6	4
37	−13.8	−13	+179.4	190.4	169
38	−22.3	−9	+200.7	497.3	81
39	+54.6	+44	+2402.4	2981.1	1936
40	+19.5	+19	+370.5	380.2	361
41	−32.6	−26	+847.6	1061.7	676
42	−28.9	−28	+801.2	835.2	784
43	−30.1	−28	+842.8	906.0	784
44	−29.2	−18	+525.6	852.6	324
45	−30.7	−26	+798.2	942.5	676
46	−31.7	−31	+982.7	1004.9	961
Total			33,998.4	40,933.5	30,986

$$r = \frac{\Sigma XY}{(\sqrt{\Sigma X^2})\ (\sqrt{\Sigma Y^2})} = \frac{33998.4}{(\sqrt{40,933.5})\ (\sqrt{30,986})} = \frac{33,998.4}{(202.3)\ (176)} = \frac{33,998.4}{35,604.8} = .955$$

TABLE III.

ESTIMATED NUMBER OF JEWISH CHILDREN IN NEW YORK CITY—DISTRIBUTION BY PUBLIC SCHOOL DISTRICTS

	District	Proportion			Average Daily Register		Estimated Number of Jewish Children			
							Estimate on Basis of School Attendance		Corrected Estimate	
		Abnormal Absence on Jewish Holidays	Census Judgments Jewish	Estimated Proportion Jewish	1913–1914	1915–1916	1914	1916	1914	1916
Manhattan	1	9.3	1	**7**	13,278	14,032	1,235	**1,305**	929	**982**
	2	83.0	59	**77**	8,368	8,437	6,945	**7,003**	6,446	**6,506**
	3	98.3	100	**98**	13,048	12,171	12,826	**11,964**	12,787	**11,928**
	4	97.7	81	**94**	16,008	15,961	15,640	**15,594**	15,048	**15,003**
	5	99.1	98	**99**	10,318	9,900	10,225	**9,811**	10,215	**9,801**
	6	79.2	61	**75**	13,359	12,895	10,583	**10,213**	10,019	**9,671**
	7	82.5	60	**77**	18,811	18,632	15,519	**15,371**	14,484	**14,347**
	8	30.0	22	**28**	11,909	12,726	3,573	**3,818**	3,335	**3,563**
	9	7.6	0	**6**	11,566	11,715	879	**890**	694	**703**
	10	15.7	8	**14**	6,278	6,190	986	**972**	878	**867**
	11	16.5	16	**16**	7,658	7,989	1,264	**1,318**	1,225	**1,278**
	12	18.8	16	**18**	9,081	9,506	1,707	**1,787**	1,635	**1,711**
	13	24.0	13	**21**	8,858	8,509	2,126	**2,042**	1,860	**1,787**
	14	11.2	3	**9**	7,641	7,906	856	**885**	688	**712**
	15	35.5	26	**33**	13,339	13,619	4,736	**4,835**	4,402	**4,494**
	16	59.0	43	**55**	13,396	13,568	7,314	**8,015**	6,818	**7,462**
	17	61.0	46	**55**	18,201	19,862	11,103	**12,116**	10,011	**10,924**
	18	22.6	23	**22**	8,660	9,209	1,957	**2,081**	1,905	**2,026**
	19	60.8	43	**57**	15,759	15,582	9,581	**9,474**	8,983	**8,882**
	20	49.2	32	**45**	13,763	15,785	6,771	**7,766**	6,193	**7,101**
	21	23.0	30	**23**	13,049	13,470	3,001	**3,098**	3,001	**3,098**
	22	32.7	38	**32**	14,605	16,751	4,776	**5,478**	4,674	**5,360**
Total		**51.2**	**38**	**48**	**265,953**	**274,925**	**133,603**	**135,836**	**126,230**	**128,206**
Bronx	23	34.0	30	**33**	18,124	18,361	6,162	**6,243**	5,981	**16,059**
	24	57.7	35	**52**	23,570	26,356	13,600	**15,207**	12,256	**13,705**
	25	56.2	46	**54**	30,637	34,153	17,218	**19,194**	16,544	**18,443**
	26	8.8	5	**8**	18,651	20,630	1,641	**1,815**	1,492	**1,650**
Total		**42.3**	**32**	**40**	**90,982**	**99,500**	**38,621**	**42,459**	**36,273**	**39,857**
Brooklyn	27	9.1	9	**9**	13,553	15,945	1,233	**1,451**	1,220	**1,435**
	28	7.8	10	**8**	13,322	14,513	1,039	**1,132**	1,066	**1,161**
	29	17.3	23	**17**	15,605	16,331	2,700	**2,825**	2,653	**2,776**
	30	9.5	12	**9**	19,786	18,910	1,880	**1,796**	1,781	**1,702**
	31	60.4	49	**58**	16,405	18,552	9,909	**11,205**	9,515	**10,760**
	32	60.4	69	**60**	25,575	25,539	15,447	**15,426**	15,345	**15,923**
	33	76.2	67	**74**	16,090	16,046	12,261	**12,227**	11,907	**11,874**
	34	13.0	19	**13**	14,309	15,195	1,860	**2,175**	1,860	**1,975**
	35	30.6	21	**28**	16,261	16,554	4,976	**5,066**	4,553	**4,635**
	36	15.3	33	**16**	16,135	17,811	2,569	**2,725**	2,582	**2,850**
	37	23.1	18	**22**	23,542	25,109	5,438	**5,800**	5,179	**5,524**
	38	14.6	22	**15**	19,338	23,575	2,823	**3,502**	2,901	**3,536**
	39	91.5	75	**88**	26,326	27,332	24,118	**25,009**	23,167	**24,052**
	40	56.4	50	**55**	24,819	27,081	13,998	**15,274**	13,650	**14,895**
Total		**38.0**	**37**	**38**	**261,066**	**279,493**	**100,251**	**105,613**	**97,379**	**103,098**
Queens	41	4.3	5	**5**	9,549	10,341	411	**445**	477	**517**
	42	8.0	3	**7**	15,434	17,142	1,235	**1,371**	1,080	**1,200**
	43	6.8	3	**6**	11,871	13,291	807	**904**	712	**797**
	44	7.7	13	**8**	19,478	21,162	1,500	**1,629**	1,558	**1,693**
Total		**7.3**	**5**	**7**	**65,881**	**61,936**	**3,953**	**4,349**	**3,827**	**4,207**
Richmond	45	6.2	5	**6**	7,889	8,685	489	**538**	473	**511**
	46	5.2	0	4	6,286	6,717	327	**349**	251	**269**
Total		**5.8**	**3**	**5**	**14,175**	**15,402**	**816**	**287**	**724**	**780**
Grand Total		**40.5**	**33**	**38**	**698,059**	**730,756**	**277,244**	**289,144**	**264,433**	**276,148**

TABLE IV

NUMBER OF JEWISH CHILDREN RECEIVING INSTRUCTION IN JEWISH SCHOOLS (EXCLUDING CHEDARIM AND PRIVATE TUITION)

	School District	No. of Schools	No. of Pupils	Proportion of Jewish Children
				%
Manhattan	1	0	0	0
	2	8	2,078	31.7
	3	5	2,682	22.5
	4	7	1,615	10.8
	5	4	800	8.2
	6	4	773	8.0
	7	8	2,559	17.8
	8	4	394	11.1
	9	0	0	0
	10	1	120	13.8
	11	1	180	14.1
	12	4	557	32.6
	13	5	884	49.5
	14	2	317	44.5
	15	2	523	11.7
	16	4	695	9.3
	17	6	2,830	25.9
	18	2	292	14.4
	19	10	2,502	28.4
	20	3	854	12.0
	21	2	225	7.3
	22	6	1,533	28.6
	Total	89	22,413	17.5
Bronx	23	4	755	12.4
	24	12	2,032	14.8
	25	10	2,093	11.3
	26	4	480	29.1
	Total	30	5,360	13.4

	School District	No. of Schools	No. of Pupils	Proportion of Jewish Children
				%
Brooklyn	27	1	140	9.7
	28	1	500	43.0
	29	2	270	9.8
	30	2	355	20.8
	31	4	1,035	9.6
	32	8	1,791	11.2
	33	6	1,290	10.9
	34	1	150	7.6
	35	1	60	1.3
	36	4	865	30.3
	37	3	1,000	18.1
	38	9	1,722	48.9
	39	7	2,319	9.6
	40	6	1,505	10.1
	Total	55	13,002	12.6
Queens	41	0	0	0
	42	2	120	10.0
	43	1	50	6.3
	44	3	408	18.2
	Total	6	578	11.3
Richmond	45	1	50	9.8
	46	0	0	0
	Total	1	50	6.4
	Grand Total	181	41,403	14.9

TABLE V

TYPES OF JEWISH SCHOOL ACCOMMODATION IN NEW YORK CITY

(Including only surveyed schools)

Borough	A. Special School Buildings		B. Institutional Buildings		C. Remodelled Buildings (Dwellings, etc.)		D. Vestries or Other Parts of Synagogue Buildings		E. Rented Rooms		Total	
	Schools	Pupils	Schools	Pupils	Schools	Pupils	Schools	Pupils	Schools	Pupils	Schools	Pupils
Manhattan	7	5,127	13	4,395	15	4,684	35	6,189	14	1,590	84	21,985
Bronx	0	0	0	0	5	1,198	19	3,457	5	645	29	5,300
Brooklyn	3	3,138	3	616	12	3,085	28	5,193	7	995	53	13,027
Queens	0	0	0	0	0	0	3	408	3	180	6	588
Richmond	0	0	0	0	0	0	0	0	1	50	1	50
TOTAL	10	8,265	16	5,011	32	8,967	85	15,247	30	3,460	173*	40,950

*To this number should be added three schools of the Bureau of Education, which have no buildings of their own, and are here included with the schools in which they are situated. Concerning five other schools, information was lacking. Schools situated in remodelled buildings, or occupying the major part of such buildings, even if they do not own them, are classed under type C and not under type E. Besides the children included in this table, there are 14,000 children in the Chedarim (practically all rented rooms) and 10,000 children are taught in their own homes.

TABLE VI

IMMEDIATE ADDITIONAL ACCOMMODATION NEEDED TO PROVIDE FOR ONE-FOURTH OF THE JEWISH CHILDREN

District	One-fourth of the Jewish Children in the District	No. of Children for Whom there is Available Accommodation	No. of Children for Whom Additional Accommodation is Needed Immediately	No. of Rooms Needed 1917	No. and Size of Buildings Needed		
					8-room	12-room	16-room
MANHATTAN							
1	291	.....	291	2	..	..	..
2	1,626	2,078	.....	..	..	..	..
3	2,982	5,391	.....	..	..	..	..
4	3,751	1,855	1,896	16	..	..	..
5	2,450	960	960	10	..	1	..
6	2,418	883	1,535	13	..	1	..
7	3,587	4,014	.....	..	..	..	..
8	890	524	366	3	..	..	..
9	176	.....	176	1	..	..	..
10	217	120	97	1	..	..	..
11	319	180	139	1	..	..	..
12	428	694	.....	..	..	..	..
13	447	1,041	.....	..	..	..	..
14	178	377	.....	..	..	..	..
15	1,124	1,275	.....	..	..	..	..
16	1,865	745	1,120	9	1	..	..
17	2,731	3,898	.....	..	..	..	..
18	506	432	74	..	..	..	..
19	2,220	3,050	.....	..	..	..	..
20	1,175	954	221	2	..	..	..
21	775	225	550	4	..	..	..
22	1,340	1,813	.....	..	..	..	..
TOTAL	32,096	30,594	7,425	62	1	2	..
BRONX							
23	1,515	855	660	5	..	..	..
24	3,426	2,372	1,054	9	1	..	..
25	4,611	2,590	2,021	17	..	..	1
26	412	480	.....	..	..	..	..
TOTAL	9,964	6,297	3,735	31	1	..	1
BROOKLYN							
27	359	140	219	2	..	..	..
28	290	500	.....	..	..	..	..
29	694	270	424	3	..	..	..
30	425	355	70	..	..	..	..
31	2,690	1,325	1,365	12	..	1	..
32	3,981	2,561	1,420	12	..	1	..
33	2,968	1,840	1,128	10	..	1	..
34	494	150	344	3	..	..	..
35	1,159	60	1,099	9	1	..	..
36	712	965	.....	..	..	..	..
37	1,381	1,630	.....	..	..	..	..
38	884	1,722	.....	..	..	..	..
39	6,013	3,009	3,004	25	..	2	..
40	3,724	2,690	1,034	9	..	1	..
TOTAL	25,774	17,217	10,107	84	1	6	..
QUEENS							
41	129	.....	129	1	..	..	..
42	300	120	180	1	..	..	..
43	199	50	149	1	..	..	..
44	423	308	115	1	..	..	..
TOTAL	1,051	478	573	4	..	..	..
45	128	50	78	..	..	..	..
46	67	.....	67	1	..	..	..
TOTAL	195	50	145	1	..	..	..
GRAND TOTAL	69,080	54,636	21,985	182	3	8	1

TABLE VII

COST OF JEWISH SCHOOL BUILDINGS—NEW YORK CITY

(Erected since 1908)

School	Date Built	Cost	No. of Rooms	Cost per Room	Size of Building			Cost per Cubic Foot	Extra Classroom Facilities			
					Grounds	Floors	Cubic Area (Approximate)		Auditorium	Gymnasium	Play Ground	Social Rooms
Salanter Talmud Torah 74 East 118th Street.	1908	$35,000	6	$5,833	20x100	3	104,000	$0.33	1	0	0	0
Uptown Talmud Torah 132 East 111th Street.	1909	190,000	24	7,916	87x100	5	687,700	.27	1	1	2	1
Downtown Talmud Torah 394 East Houston Street.	1911	66,000	12	5,555	40x70	3	145,600	.45	0	0	0	0
Hebrew Free School 400 Stone Avenue.	1912	100,000	20	5,000	75x100	4	487,500	.20	1	1	0	0
Glory of Israel T. T. 363 Pennsylvania Avenue.	1913	50,000	12	4,166	100x100	2	390,000	.12	1	0	0	0
Rabbi Jacob Joseph School 167 Henry Street.	1914	90,000	16	5,625	40x85	5	360,200	.25	1	0	0	0
Talmud Torah Hechodosh 146 Stockton Street.	1914	28,500	9	3,166	40x100	3	144,000	.20	1	0	0	0
Central Jewish Institute 125 East 85th Street.	1916	160,000	12	13,333	57x100	5*	518,700	.31	1	1	2	3
TOTAL		$719,500	111	$6,482				$0.28				

*Basement, almost two stories, contains large gymnasium and balcony.

TABLE VIII

DISTRIBUTION OF JEWISH SCHOOLS BY NUMBER OF PUPILS ENROLLED

Pupils — Schools	Pupils — Schools
1475 — 1	217 — 1
1041 — 1	210 — 1
950 — 1	200 — 11
875 — 1	195 — 1
813 — 1	190 — 1
734 — 1	185 — 1
708 — 1	180 — 2
638 — 1	175 — 2
600 — 3	172 — 1
595 — 1	170 — 4
585 — 1	160 — 5 — Median
562 — 1	155 — 1
528 — 1	153 — 1
525 — 1	150 — 13
508 — 1	147 — 1
500 — 2	145 — 1
488 — 1	140 — 2
463 — 1	138 — 1
448 — 1	135 — 1
430 — 1	130 — 1
400 — 5	125 — 3
378 — 1	120 — 8
375 — 1	115 — 4
360 — 1	110 — 3
355 — 1	101 — 1
350 — 6	100 — 9 — L. Q.
347 — 1	92 — 1
305 — 1	90 — 2
300 — 4	85 — 2
291 — 1	80 — 3
282 — 1 — U. Q.	78 — 1
280 — 2	75 — 4
279 — 1	70 — 2
275 — 1	69 — 1
255 — 1	65 — 1
250 — 4	60 — 10
240 — 1	55 — 3
228 — 1	52 — 1
227 — 1	51 — 1
225 — 2	50 — 7
220 — 1	40 — 1

TABLE IX.

ORGANIZATION OF JEWISH SCHOOLS OF NEW YORK SHOWING DISTRIBUTION BY TYPES OF CONTROL AND TIME SCHEDULES

Type of Control	Borough*	Weekday		Sunday		Parochial		Total	
		Schools	Pupils	Schools	Pupils	Schools	Pupils	Schools	Pupils
Communal	Manhattan	32	11,063	..	.....	3	785	35	11,848
	Bronx	11	2,093	..	.....	..	.....	11	2,093
	Brooklyn	21	6,808	..	.....	1	200	22	7,008
	Queens	2	110	..	.....	..	...	2	110
	TOTAL	67	20,124	..	.....	4	985	71	21,109
Congregational	Manhattan	21	3,200	18	3,656	..	...	39	6,856
	Bronx	13	2,330	5	827	..	...	18	3,157
	Brooklyn	13	2,405	13	2,468	..	...	26	4,873
	Queens	3	188	1	280	..	...	4	468
	TOTAL	50	8,123	37	7,231	..	...	87	15,354
Institutional	Manhattan	8	2,499	2	495	..	...	10	2,994
	Brooklyn	2	491	2	225	..	...	4	716
	TOTAL	10	2,990	4	720	..	...	14	3,710
GRAND TOTAL		127	31,237**	41	7,951	4	985	172***	40,173

*Where boroughs are not given, there is no school of that type.
**To this number should be added the pupils in the Chedarim and children taught at home.
***Not including the nine private schools surveyed.

TABLE X

COST OF JEWISH SUNDAY SCHOOL INSTRUCTION 1916-1917

DISTRIBUTION OF 22 SCHOOLS

	Expenditure	Register	Per Capita Cost
Schools with Volunteer Teaching Staffs	$275	600	$ .45
	60	101	.59
	240	282	.86
	400	300	1.33
	400	250	1.60
	400	250	1.60
	250	150	1.66
	250	125	2.00—Median
	400	200	2.00
	800	375	2.13
	500	200	2.50
	650	217	2.99
	1,000	300	3.33
	475	140	3.39
	600	170	3.52
Schools with Paid Teaching Staffs	1,200	172	6.87
	1,500	200	7.50
	900	100	9.00
	50	355	14.08—Median
	3,700	220	16.81
	3,000	155	26.09
	6,708	227	29.55
Total......	23,758	5,089	

TABLE XI

COST OF JEWISH WEEKDAY INSTRUCTION
1916-1917

DISTRIBUTION OF 34 SCHOOLS

Expenditure	Register	Per Capita Cost
$1,764	225	$7.85
1,560	195	8.00
1,075	125	8.60
3,057	350	8.71
1,400	115	12.19
11,000	875	12.58
2,200	160	13.75
7,000	508	13.78
7,000	500	14.00—L. Q.
6,000	350	17.15
3,500	180	19.44
5,000	250	20.00
3,000	150	20.00
7,000	347	20.18
12,000	585	20.51
3,500	160	21.87
13,550	600	22.59—M.
17,000	738	23.02
3,500	150	23.33
6,500	275	23.63
3,600	150	23.00
12,000	500	24.00
24,438	950	25.78
38,000	1,475	25.79
10,000	378	26.44
4,000	150	26.68—U. Q.
2,700	100	27.00
10,000	350	28.59
12,000	400	30.00
12,000	350	34.28
18,000	500	36.00
4,000	110	36.36
22,000	600	36.66
6,500	150	43.33
Total, 295,844	13,001	22.75 (Average)

TABLE XII

ITEMIZED EXPENDITURE OF TEN JEWISH WEEKDAY SCHOOLS

1916 - 1917

SCHOOLS	A	B	C	D	E	F	G	H	I	J	TOTAL
Amortization of Mortgages	$5,000							$427			$5,427
First and Second Mortgages on Building and Cemetery		$2,344									2,344
Interest on Mortgage	5,996					$1,213					7,209
Mortgage and Interest			$200		$1,295				$5,607		7,102
Interest on Mortgage and Loans				$1,493							1,493
Interest on Loans	348					55					403
Loans Paid		3,393						5			3,398
Loans Paid and Interest									2,012		2,012
Insurance	82	211	160		5	62		12	117		649
Water Tax								5			5
Heat and Light				694		387			1,093		2,174
Heat	1,230										1,230
Light	1,656		283		567						2,506
Coal		54	64		373			54			545
Gas		96						77			173
Electricity		241									241
Commission on Charity Boxes						46					46
House Expenses	1,087	274									1,361
General Expense				169						$574	743
Sundry Expense					172			2			174
Miscellaneous						232			41		273
Expenses on School, House, Light, Rent, Loans, Affairs, Printing, etc							$1,743				1,743
Social Worker	45										45
Relief Fund		21									21
Aid Society		53									53
Passover Fund for Poor		138									138
Donation to Hospital		11									11

TABLE XII—Continued

ITEMIZED EXPENDITURE OF TEN JEWISH WEEKDAY SCHOOLS

1916 - 1917

SCHOOLS	A	B	C	D	E	F	G	H	I	J	TOTAL
Gift to Principal				100							100
Ball Expenses		315						150			465
Theatre Expenses						457					457
Coffee Klatsch						32					32
Holiday Party								10			10
Concert Expenses								21			21
Summer Campaign	70										70
Wood								3			3
Repairs and Improvements	1,630		115	740	248	39		112	434		3,318
Building Expenses		1,347									1,347
Painting Expense			248								248
Plumber					29						29
Blackboards		13									13
Desks		20									20
Fire Extinguisher					14						14
Furniture and Fixtures										1,441	1,441
Books and Supplies						12					12
Books	108			57	362			11		858	1,396
Books and "Jewish Child"		166								783	949
School Expense			115								115
School Apparatus										20	20
Postage, Printing, Books and Stationery									394		394
Postage, Stationery and Printing	1,402			251	181	32				689	2,555
Postage							56	25			81
Printing		71						52			123
Stationery								6			6
Advertisement		100						3			103
Telephone	18	41		45	45	75					224
Salaries							6,078				6,078

TABLE XII—Continued

ITEMIZED EXPENDITURE OF TEN JEWISH WEEKDAY SCHOOLS

1916 - 1917

SCHOOLS	A	B	C	D	E	F	G	H	I	J	TOTAL
Salaries: Teachers, Principal, Secretary and Janitor					7,348						7,348
Salaries: Teachers, Principal and Staff	14,944		2,907					3,970	9,842		31,663
Teachers' Salaries		3,788		5,250		4,075				12,455	25,568
Principal's and Staff's Salaries		1,619									1,619
Monitor Service				100							100
Salaries of Secretary and Staff	2,500	705		1,770				589	1,143		6,707
Auditing				50							50
Office Salaries						1,713					1,713
Clerical Service										649	649
Salaries of Janitor and Staff	5,352	472	319	743				91	1,216		8,193
Cantor and Singers		421							1,349		1,770
Prayer Service				391							391
Synagogue Expenses						69		40	92		201
Cost of Collection	4,068	1,020	214	846	555			316	1,068	1,172	9,259
Collections of Donations		25									25
Collection of Tuition Fees						254					254
Entertainments										253	253
Jewish Community Dues		10							10		20
Delegates to Jewish Congress								5			5
Commission on Sale of Building	400										400
Rent								766			766
Signs								5			5
Signs on Benches		35									35
Cleaning Synagogue		30									30
Window and Electric Service				67							67
Janitor's Expenses						31		4			35
TOTAL	$45,936	$17,034	$4,625	$12,766	$11,194	$8,784	$7,877	$6,761	$24,418	$18,894	$158,289

TABLE XIII

DISTRIBUTION OF EXPENDITURE
in
TEN JEWISH WEEKDAY SCHOOLS
(SUMMARY)

	AMOUNT	PER CENT
A. Debt Service and Fixed Charges..........	$30,067	19.0
1. Amortization and Interest on Mortgage..	23,575	14.8
2. Amortization and Interest on Loans.....	5,813	3.6
3. Insurance	649	.4
4. Other Expenses	30	
B. Expenses of Operation and Maintenance...	24,252	15.3
1. Janitorial Service......................	9,193	5.8
2. Heat and Light........................	6,872	4.3
3. Replacement and Repairs...............	6,470	4.1
4. Other Expenses.........................	1,717	1.1
C. Expenses of Administration..............	14,426	9.1
1. Secretary and Staff....................	9,356	5.9
2. Other Administrative Salaries...........	1,808	1.1
3. Expenses of Secretary's office...........	3,262	2.1
D. Expenses of Instruction and Supervision...	71,869	45.4
1. Salaries: Principal and Staff...........	6,619	4.2
2. Teachers' Salaries.....................	62,758	39.7
3. Books and School Supplies..............	2,377	1.5
4. Other Expenses........................	115	.1
E. Expenses of Collection and Miscellaneous Outlay...........................	17,675	11.2
1. Cost of Collection....................	9,584	6.1
2. Expenses of Charity Entertainments.....	1,055	.7
3. Synagogue Expenses...................	2,362	1.5
4. Donations for Charitable Purposes.......	322	.2
5. Sundry Expenses........................	4,352	2.7
TOTAL...........................	$158,289	

TABLE XIV

ITEMIZED INCOME OF TEN JEWISH WEEKDAY SCHOOLS
1916 - 1917

SCHOOLS	A	B	C	D	E	F	G	H	I	J	TOTAL
Tuition Fees	$9,426	$3,905	$1,565	$5,010	$1,922	$2,784	$4,999	$3,572	$7,722	$6,736	$47,641
Books and "Jewish Child"		89	106		168			31	20		414
Education Fund	962	900							2,875		4,737
Federation Fund				165							165
Membership Dues	12,123	2,000		1,412	2,789	1,974	686	1,972	5,226		27,282
Subscriptions										12,158	12,158
Donations	9,484	118	421	1,724	1,183	2,269	849	967	2,437		19,452
Bequests	100										100
Charity Boxes	372	929	349	44	250	764					2,708
Collections			144		2,696						2,840
Renting Synagogue Seats for the Holidays	4,477	2,394	364			578		231	2,304		10,348
Synagogue Income		759		1,087							1,846
Synagogue Donations						261					261
Rents	5,914				1,675	859		145	462		9,055
Cemetery		568									568
Entertainments and Balls		904		2,347			579				3,830
Raffle		25				482		19			526
Theatre	4,094					995		8			5,097
Coffee Klatsch						77					77
Affairs							703				703
Concert								24			24

TABLE XIV—Continued

ITEMIZED INCOME OF TEN JEWISH WEEKDAY SCHOOLS

1916 - 1917

Schools	A	B	C	D	E	F	G	H	I	J	Total
Ball and Concert									1,962		1,962
Malbish Arumim (Ladies' Auxiliary)				463							463
Relief Fund		43									43
Passover Fund		207									207
Hebrew Aid Society		52									52
Loans		3,379							1,465		4,844
Interest					27						27
Miscellaneous			7		18	84		7	83		199
Loans, Rent, miscellaneous							931				931
Special Tax								59			59
Stamps								63			63
School Benches (sale)									84		84
Telephone Calls									3		3
Total	$46,852	$16,272	$2,956	$12,252	$10,728	$11,127	$8,747	$6,198	$24,643	$18,894	$158,669

TABLE XV

SOURCE OF INCOME
of
TEN JEWISH WEEKDAY SCHOOLS
(SUMMARY)

	Amount	Per Cent.	Corrected Per Cent.*
A. From Pupils................	$48,055	30.4	(32.6%)
1. Tuition Fees..............	47,641	30.1	
2. Books	414	.3	
B. From Synagogue; Building rents; and other property..	21,978	13.8	(10.4%) net*
1. Rental of Seats............	10,348	6.5	
2. Rent of Rooms.............	9,055	5.7	
3. Cemetery	568	.3	
4. Other Items of Income......	2,007	1.3	
C. From Community...........	82,426	51.9	(56.0%)
1. Membership Dues and Subscriptions	39,440	24.8	
2. Donations and Bequests.....	19,552	12.3	
3. From Communal Funds.....	4,902	3.1**	
4. Charity Boxes and Collections	5,548	3.5	
5. Charity Entertainments.....	12,219	7.7	
6. Other Items of Income......	765	.5	
D. Miscellaneous	6,210	3.9	(.9%)*
1. Loans	4,844	3.0	
2. Other Items of Income......	1,366	.9	
Total....................	$158,669	100.0	100.0

* The proportion of 13.8% income from synagogue, etc. (B), is the **gross** income. From this proportion should be deducted the expenses connected with this source of income. It was not possible to do this from the available data (1917). But a detailed examination of the finances of seven schools for the year 1916 showed that about 30% of the sums obtained in this manner are spent upon obtaining this money (salaries, etc.).

The $4,844.00 quoted as "loans" (D1) was also deducted, so that the corrected proportions were calculated on a basis of $147,232.00. The corrected figures are given in parentheses.

** This includes only the subventions of the Education Fund of the Bureau of Jewish Education. Since 1917 this fund has been discontinued and all of the Community Funds (C) are being placed in the hands of the Federation for the Support of Jewish Philanthropic Societies.

TABLE XVI

PROPORTION OF PAYING AND NON-PAYING PUPILS IN EIGHT JEWISH WEEKDAY SCHOOLS

1916 - 1917

Month	Free Pupils			Pay Pupils				Delinquent Pupils			Non-Paying Pupils
	Total Register	No.	%	No.	%	Amount to be Collected	Average Fee	Collected From	% Collected	% Delinquent	% Free and Delinquent
October	4,576	832	18.2	3,744	81.8	$3,883	$1.03	2,423	52.9	29.9	47.1
November	4,748	805	17.0	3,751	79.0	3,725	.99	2,641	55.6	23.4	40.4
December	....	....	....	....	....	....	....	....	....	....	....
January	5,325	1019	19.1	4,254	79.9	4,578	1.07	3,342	62.8	17.1	36.2
February	4,626	905	19.6	3,690	79.8	3,977	1.08	3,150	68.2	11.6	31.2
March	4,610	709	19.3	3,769	80.0	3,930	1.04	3,126	68.5	11.5	30.8
April	4,796	899	18.8	3,893	81.1	4,250	1.09	3,379	70.4	10.7	29.5
May	4,922	954	19.4	3,881	78.8	4,079	1.05	3,238	65.5	13.3	32.7
June	4,816	940	19.5	3,862	80.2	4,245	1.09	3,042	63.2	17.0	36.5
July	4,594	919	20.0	3,662	79.7	4,020	1.09	2,636	57.3	22.4	42.4
August	4,524	888	19.5	3,625	80.0	4,001	1.10	2,392	52.9	27.1	46.6
Average	4,753	907	19.0	3,813	80.0	$4,069	$1.06	2,937	61.7	18.3	37.3

TABLE XVII

NUMBER OF PUPILS PER TEACHER in JEWISH SCHOOLS

Communal Weekday Schools	Congregational Sunday Schools
1—25	1—5
1—30	1—11
1—33	1—14
1—36	4—15
2—37	2—16—L. Q.
1—42	2—17
3—50	1—18
1—52—L. Q.	5—19—Median
2—53	1—20
1—54	2—22
1—57	1—24
1—58	2—25
3—60	2—27—U. Q.
2—61	1—28
1—69	1—29
2—70—Median	1—31
1—73	1—32
2—77	1—39
2—80	2—43
3—83	1—44
1—86	1—56
1—87—U. Q.	
1—97	
1—100	
1—102	
1—106	
1—112	
1—114	
1—117	
1—120	
1—122	
1—128	

TABLE XVIII

PROPORTION OF SEXES AMONG PUPILS in JEWISH SCHOOLS *

1916-1917

Schools		Total Pupils	No. Boys	No. Girls	Proportion Girls
Sunday Schools	Congregational	7,664	3,610	4,054	52.8%
	Institutional	774	197	577	79.5%
	Total	8,438	3,807	4,631	54.8%
Weekday Schools	Communal	15,151	11,591	3,560	23.5%
	Congregational	4,543	3,330	1,213	26.8%
	Institutional	2,344	1,225	1,119	47.5%
	Total	22,038	16,146	5,892	26.7%
Parochial Schools		980	980	0	0
TOTAL		31,456	20,933	10,523	33.4%

* Out of the 181 schools surveyed 112 reported on this item.

TABLE XIX

REGULARITY OF ATTENDANCE
in
SEVEN JEWISH WEEKDAY SCHOOLS

JANUARY TO AUGUST, 1917*

January	86.2%
February	85.4%
March	85.9%
April	86.1%
May	88.7%
June	84.8%
July	73.3%
August	67.0%
Average—(for 8 months)	**82.1%**
Average (excluding summer months)	**86.1%**

* Data for 1916 not taken because it was the year of the epidemic of infantile paralysis in New York. No later data than August, 1917, available at time of writing.

TABLE XX

ELIMINATION STUDIES

A. GRADE POPULATION

	Jewish School			Public School*
	Total	%	% of First Grade	% of First Grade
Year I	1,207	37.5	100.0	100.0
" II	774	24.0	64.1	72.3
" III	533	16.5	44.1	69.2
" IV	368	11.4	30.4	64.0
" V	191	5.9	15.8	55.2
" VI	107	3.3	8.8	46.2
" VII	32	.9	2.6	36.8
Total......	3,212	100.0		

B. AGE POPULATION

	Jewish School			Public School*
	Number	% of Total	% of 10 Year Olds	% of 10 Year Olds
5 Years	4	.1	.7	24
6 "	122	3.8	21.5	77
7 "	379	11.8	66.9	92
8 "	536	16.7	94.6	96
9 "	601	18.8	106.1	98
10 "	566	17.7	100.0	100
11 "	443	13.8	78.2	99
12 "	367	11.4	64.8	96
13 "	142	4.4	25.0	89
14 "	44	1.3	4.2	62
15 "	8	.2	1.2	34
Total......	3,212	100.0		

* According to: Ayres L. P. "Laggards in Our Schools," p. 13.

ELIMINATION STUDIES

C. PROPORTION ELIMINATED IN TEN JEWISH WEEKDAY SCHOOLS
(Five Boys' Schools, Four Girls' Schools and One Mixed School)
JULY 1, 1916 TO JUNE 30, 1918

Months	Initial Register (All Schools)	Admitted		Total Register	Left	
1916—July	6,763	227	3.4%	6,990	482	6.9%
August	6.508	48	.7	6 556	281	4.3
September	6,275	142	2.3	6,417	479	7.5
October	5,938	552	9.3	6,490	799	12.3
November	5,691	636	11.2	6,327	318	5.1
December	6,009	778	13.0	6,787	586	8.6
1917—January	6,201	678	11.0	6,879	655	9.3
February	6,224	581	9.3	6,805	369	5.4
March	6,436	376	5.9	6,812	578	8.5
April	6.234	540	8.7	6,774	548	8.1
May	6,226	1,810	29.2	8,036	619	7.7
June	7.417	487	6.5	7,904	586	7.4
Total 1916-1917	75,922	6.855		82,777	6,300	7.6
1917—July	7,318	255	3.5	7,573	480	6.3%
August	7,093	191	2.7	7,284	691	9.5
September	6,593	303	4.6	6,896	309	4.5
October	6,587	529	8.0	7,116	193	2.7
November	6 923	1,594	23.0	8,517	302	3.5
December	8,215	863	10.5	9,078	374	4.1
1918—January	8,704	575	6.6	9,279	764	8.2
February	8,515	381	4.5	8,896	449	5.0
March	8,447	313	3.7	8,760	515	5.9
April	8.245	1,652	20.1	9,897	357	3.6
May	9.540	798	8.4	10,338	316	3.0
June	10,022	322	3.1	10,344	795	7.9
Total 1917-1918	96,202	7,776		103.978	5,547	5.3
GRAND TOTAL	172,124	14,631		186,755	11,847	6.3

TABLE XXII

ELIMINATION STUDIES

D. PROPORTION ELIMINATED IN TEN WEEKDAY SCHOOLS SHOWING PROPORTION FOR EACH SCHOOL 1917—1918

SCHOOL	AVERAGE MONTHLY REGISTER	AVERAGE MONTHLY ELIMINATION	
		PUPILS	%
Boys' School A.........	518	31	5.9
" " B.........	1,475	49	3.3
" " C.........	646	37	5.7
" " D.........	975	47	4.8
" " E.........	378	17	4.5
Mixed School F.........	1,052	40	3.8
Girls' School G.........	595	46	7.7
" " H.........	869	81	9.3
" " I.........	813	68	8.3
" " J.........	562	45	8.0
Average	7,883	461	5.8

E. LENGTH OF STAY OF CHILDREN IN TEN JEWISH WEEKDAY SCHOOLS

(Five Boys' Schools, Four Girls' Schools and One Mixed School)

1916—1917

Length of stay	Number	Length of stay	Number	Length of stay	Number
1 Month	100	2 Years 4 Months	23	4 Years 7 Months	5
2 "	282	2 " 5 "	22	4 " 8 "	2
3 "	295	2 " 6 "	18	4 " 9 "	3
4 "	234 L.Q.	2 " 7 "	33	4 " 10 "	5
5 "	189	2 " 8 "	20	4 " 11 "	5
6 "	169	2 " 9 "	21	5 " 0 "	3
7 "	131	2 " 10 "	19	5 " 1 "	6
8 "	111 M.	2 " 11 "	15	5 " 2 "	8
9 "	106	3 " 0 "	15	5 " 3 "	2
10 "	87	3 " 1 "	17	5 " 4 "	7
11 "	62	3 " 2 "	11	5 " 5 "	3
1 Year 0 "	61	3 " 3 "	10	5 " 6 "	1
1 " 1 "	57	3 " 4 "	18	5 " 7 "	2
1 " 2 "	57	3 " 5 "	12	5 " 8 "	1
1 " 3 "	49	3 " 6 "	14	5 " 9 "	0
1 " 4 "	48	3 " 7 "	11	5 " 10 "	2
1 " 5 "	53	3 " 8 "	11	5 " 11 "	2
1 " 6 "	43	3 " 9 "	6	6 " 0 "	0
1 " 7 "	40	3 " 10 "	13	6 " 1 "	0
1 " 8 "	38	3 " 11 "	18	6 " 2 "	0
1 " 9 "	42 U.Q.	4 " 0 "	7	6 " 3 "	0
1 " 10 "	33	4 " 1 "	10	6 " 4 "	0
1 " 11 "	31	4 " 2 "	12	6 " 5 "	0
2 " 0 "	29	4 " 3 "	6	6 " 6 "	0
2 " 1 "	34	4 " 4 "	7	6 " 7 "	0
2 " 2 "	18	4 " 5 "	10	6 " 8 "	1
2 " 3 "	20	4 " 6 "	9	6 " 9 "	1
				TOTAL	2,866

SUMMARY

Less than 1 year	1,766 or 61.5%		Less than 4 years	2,746 or 95.7%	
" " 2 years	2,318 " 81.0%		" " 5 "	2,827 " 98.5%	
" " 3 "	2,590 " 80.3%		" " 6 "	2,864 " 99.9%	
			" " 7 "	2,866 " 100%	

TABLE XXIV

ELIMINATION STUDIES

F. CAUSES OF ELIMINATION IN FOUR JEWISH SCHOOLS

(Two Boys' Schools and Two Girls' Schools)

1914—1915

Apparent Cause	Number of Cases	%
1. Inability or unwillingness to pay Tuition Fees	261	22.9
2. Removal without transfer, or school too distant	243	21.4
3. Left temporarily and did not return	185	16.2
4. Lack of progress	61	5.3
5. Dissatisfaction with methods of teaching, or subjects of study	60	5.3
6. Child not interested	51	4.5
7. Child busy with other work, no time for Jewish school	38	3.3
8. Child incorrigible, discharged for disciplinary reasons	36	3.1
9. Frequent absence or truancy	28	2.5
10. Dissatisfaction with class or grade	28	2.5
11. General dissatisfaction	24	2.2
12. Receiving other instruction	24	2.2
13. Parents indifferent	18	1.6
14. Time of instruction inconvenient	18	1.6
15. Child working after school hours	14	1.2
16. Child ill	12	1.1
17. Child too old	11	.9
18. Dissatisfaction with teacher	10	.8
19. Child too young	5	.4
20. Removal with transfer	5	.4
21. Death	5	.4
22. Graduation from Jewish school	3	.2
Total	1,140	100%

TABLE XXV

AGE GRADE TABLE
SHOWING DISTRIBUTION OF PUPILS IN FIVE JEWISH WEEK-DAY SCHOOLS

Age	Year I	II	III	IV	V	VI	VII	Total
5 years	4	...	...	...	...	...	...	4
6 years	118	4	...	...	...	...	...	122
7 years	319	49	10	1	...	...	...	379
8 years	304	178	41	9	2	2	...	536
9 years	225	213	131	24	1	7	...	601
10 years	128	189	140	76	23	8	2	566
11 years	70	93	117	102	33	20	8	443
12 years	29	36	58	120	82	36	6	367
13 years	8	11	26	33	28	25	11	142
14 years	2	1	9	3	17	7	5	44
15 years	....	...	1	...	5	2	...	8
Total	1,207	774	533	368	191	107	32	3,212

TABLE XXVI

PROPORTION OF RETARDATION IN THE JEWISH SCHOOLS

(Year) Grade	Under-Age		Normal		Over-Age		Total	
	Pupils	%	Pupils	%	Pupils	%	Pupils	%
I............	4	.3	741	61.4	462	38.3	1207	100
II............	4	.5	440	56.8	330	42.7	774	100
III............	10	1.8	312	58.6	211	39.6	533	100
IV............	10	2.8	202	54.9	156	42.3	368	100
V............	3	1.5	138	72.3	50	26.2	191	100
VI............	17	15.8	81	75.8	9	8.4	107	100
VII............	10	31.3	22	68.7	...	...	32	100
TOTAL......	58	1.8	1936	60.3	1218	37.9	3212	100

TABLE XXVII

PROPORTION OF THE SEXES IN THE TEACHING STAFFS OF JEWISH SCHOOLS, NEW YORK

(125 SCHOOLS REPORTING OUT OF A TOTAL OF 181)

		No. Schools Reporting	No. of Teachers			Proportion of Women
			Male	Female	Total	
Weekday Schools	Communal	41	200	43	243	17.1%
	Congregational	34	93	44	137	32.1%
	Institutional	7	20	7	27	24.1%
TOTAL		82	313	94	407	23.0%
Sunday Schools	Congregational	34	117	142	259	54.8%
	Institutional	5	15	21	36	58.3%
TOTAL		39	132	163	295	55.2%
Parochial Schools		4	54	0	54	0%
GRAND TOTAL		125	499	257	756	33.9%

TABLE XXVIII

AGE AND SEX OF TEACHERS IN THE JEWISH SCHOOLS OF NEW YORK

Weekday				Sunday				Parochial				Total			
Male		Female		Male		Female		Male		Female		Male		Female	
No.	Age	No.	Age	No.	Age	No.	Age	No.	Age	No.	Age	No.	Age	No.	Age
						1	16							1	16
1	16½											1	16½		
2	17					2	17					2	17	2	17
1	17½											1	17½		
3	18	5	18			3	18					3	18	8	18
3	19	5	19			4	19					3	19	9	19
1	19½											1	19½		
6	20	7	20	1	20	7	20					7	20	14	20
1	20½											1	20½		
7	21	M–5	21	1	21	5	21					8	21	10	21
9	22	5	22	1	22	M-4	22					10	22	M–9	22
6	23	4	23	2	23	4	23					8	23	8	23
M–8	24	7	24	M–3	24	5	24					11–M	24	12	24
3	25	1	25	2	25	2	25					5	25	3	25
5	26	2	26	3	26	2	26					8	26	4	26
4	27					2	27					4	27	2	27
2	28	1	28	1	28	1	28					3	28	2	28
1	29											1	29		
1	30											1	30		
2	31											2	31		
						1	32							1	32
1	33					1	33	1	33			2	33	1	33
3	34					2	34					3	34	2	34
						2	35							2	35
1	36			1	36							2	36		
1	37											1	37		
1	38											1	38		
2	40											2	40		
								1	42			1	42		
2	43											2	43		
2	44											2	44		
1	45											1	45		
1	47											1	47		
1	48							1	48			2	48		
						1	49							1	49
								2	50			2	50		
1	51											1	51		
1	53											1	53		
1	56							1	56			2	56		
1	57											1	57		
1	58											1	58		
1	60											1	60		
1	62											1	62		
TOTAL, 89		42		15		49		6				110		91	

TABLE XXIX

AMOUNT OF WORK DONE BY TEACHERS IN JEWISH WEEKDAY SCHOOLS

1. Hours		2. Classes		3. Pupils	
No. of Teachers	No. Hours Teaching	No. of Teachers	No. of Classes	No. of Schools	No. Pupils Per Teacher
5	5	30	1	1	25
1	6	M—47	2	1	30
2	7	34	3	1	33
8	8	17	4	1	36
1	9	6	5	2	37
10	10	8	6	1	42
1	11	7	8	3	50
3	12	1	9	1	52
7	13			2	53
1	14			1	54
20	15			1	57
9	16			1	58
3	17			3	60
Median— 7	18			2	61
1	19			1	69
Mode—40	20			M—2	70
18	22			1	73
2	25			2	77
2	28			2	80
2	30			3	83
8	32			1	86
				1	87
				1	97
				1	100
				1	102
				1	106
				1	112
				1	114
				1	117
				1	120
				1	122
				1	128
151	17.4 (Av.)	150	2.9 (Av.)	41	76.9 (Av.)

TABLE XXX

SALARIES OF TEACHERS IN JEWISH SCHOOLS
(SHOWING LOWEST AND HIGHEST SALARIES PAID)
1917

Communal Weekday School				Congregational Sunday School			
Lowest		Highest		Lowest		Highest	
No.	Monthly Salary	No.	Monthly Salary	No.	Monthly Salary	No.	Monthly Salary
1	$25	1	$40	3	$4	1	$4
1	30	2	45	2	6	1	5
1	32	1	48	1	7	1	6
1	35	1	50	M—3	8	1	8
1	38	1	56	4	10	4	10
7	40	7	60	1	12	1	12
1	44	1	63	2	15	1	14
2	45	1	64	1	20	2	15
M—15	50	3	65			1	16
1	52	2	68			1	20
1	55	2	70			1	25
8	60	M—2	72			1	30
4	64	11	75			1	35
1	65	4	80				
1	68	3	85				
1	70	3	88				
		1	100				
46	$50 Average	46	$70 Average	17	$ 9 Average	17	$14 Average

45 Communal Weekday Schools reported out of 65. Median range of salaries $600 lowest and $850 highest.

30 Congregational Sunday Schools reported out of 37. Of these 17 have paid staffs and 13 volunteer staffs. Median salary, in schools with paid staffs, $2 per session lowest and $3 highest.

TABLE XXXI

COMPARISON OF SECULAR CURRICULA:

Public Schools and Jewish Parochial Schools

(SHOWING NUMBER OF HOURS ALLOTED TO EACH SUBJECT)

Subjects	Parochial	N. Y. Public Schools		% of Minimum	Average for 20 American Cities	%
		Minimum	Maximum			
Opening Exercises	0	400	400	0	269	0
Physical Training, Recess, Physiology and Hygiene	576	768	1,020	75.0	908	63.5
English	2,260	2,808	3,460	80.6	2,614	86.2
Mathematics	800	847	1,315	94.4	981	81.5
History	250	280	486	89.2	360	69.5
Geography	403	234	360	172.2	474	85.0
Penmanship	391	380	380*	102.8	362	108.1
Nature Study	0	240	360	0	279	0
Science	0	108	160	0		
Drawing	120	468	640	25.6	410	29.3
Constructive Work and Sewing	0	200	200	0	316	0
Shopwork and Cooking	0	108	108	0		
Music	0	216	348	0	366	0
Electives	0	133	133	0	...	...
Miscellaneous	...	...	...	...	397	0
Total	4,800	7,190	9,370	66.7	7,736	64.6

* No maximum stated.

APPENDICES

APPENDIX AA

DIFFERENCES OF SOCIAL ATTITUDE AMONG THE JEWS OF AMERICA

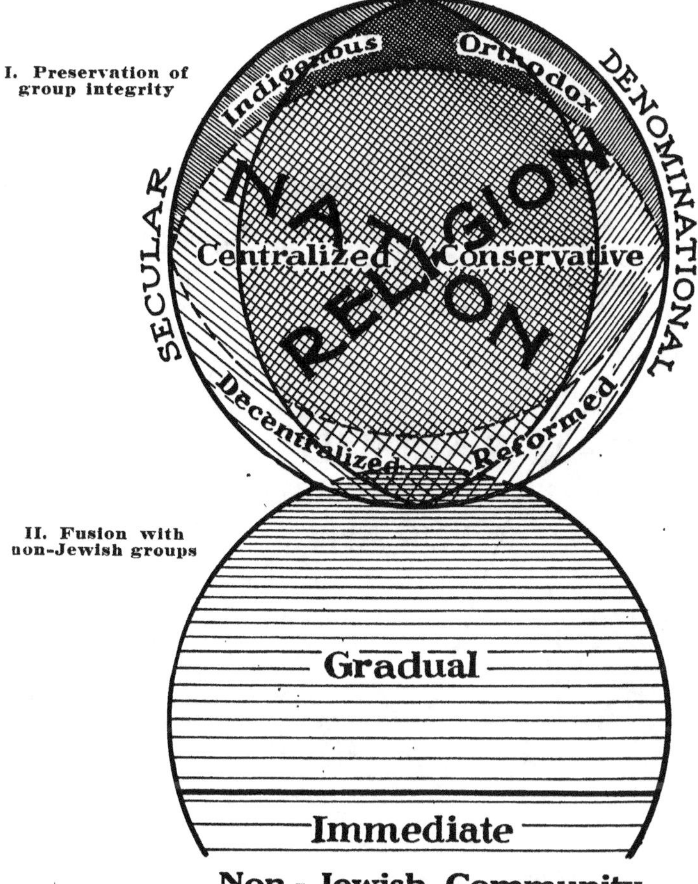

This diagram is in illustration of the discussion of the social bases underlying Jewish education in America: ch. I, particularly pp. 1-16. It shows: (a) the complexity of the composition of the Jewish group; (b) the variety of attitudes prevailing among American Jews; and (c) the large amount of overlapping. Those who believe in preserving the integrity of Jewish life overlap those who believe in fusing, immediately or gradually, with the non-Jewish groups. Those who view the Jews as a religious group (orthodox, conservative or reform) overlap those who consider the Jews a nation, whether their national attitudes be indigenous (Palestine only), centralized, or decentralized. Those who regard the Jews merely as a denominational sect are at the one extreme, and those who have a secular-national attitude toward Jewish life are at the other extreme.

APPENDIX BB

THE VARIETY OF EDUCATIONAL SYSTEMS BASED UPON DIFFERENCES OF JEWISH ATTITUDES

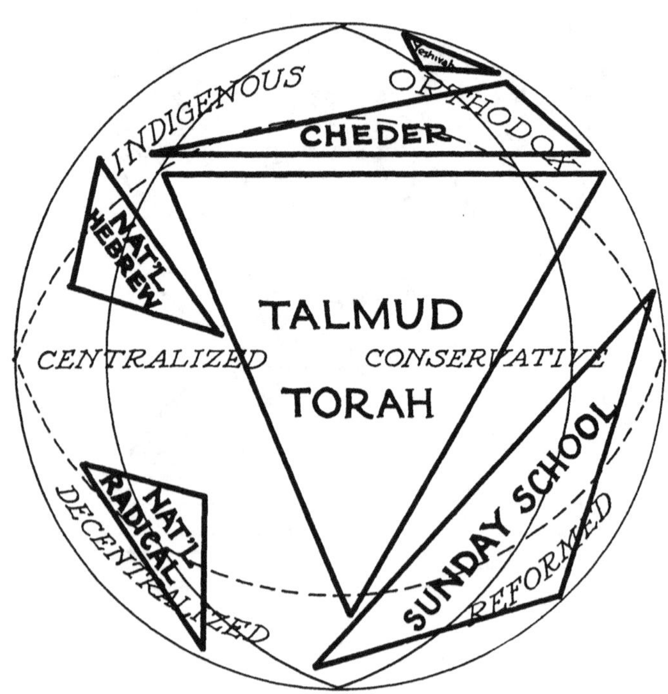

This diagram is in illustration of the discussion of the social bases underlying Jewish education in America: ch. I, pp. 1-16. The triangles indicate the groups that support each of the various school systems in vogue among the Jews of New York.

APPENDIX A

EXTRACTS FROM THE MINUTES OF THE SHEARITH ISRAEL CONGREGATION CONCERNING ITS RELIGIOUS SCHOOL[1]

1731: "On the 21st of Nisan, the 7th day of Pesach, the day of completing the first year of the opening of the synagogue, there was made codez [consecrated] the Yeshibat called Minhat Areb, in the name of the following gentlemen, Mosseh son of Sarah and Jahacob, of Abraham, and of Mosseh Mendez da Costa, for the use of this Congregation Sheerit Israel and as a Beth Hamidras for the pupils, in conformity with the direction to that effect given by Jahacob Mendez da Costa Signior, residing in London, to Messrs. Mordechay and David Gomez of New York. And may God bestow His blessing upon us. Amen."

JANUARY 30, 1737: David Mendes Machado, was elected "to act as hazan or reader to this our K. K. de Seherit Yiseracl. The said Mr. Machado promising and obliges himself to keep a publick school in due form for teaching the Hebrew language, either the whole morning or afternoon as he shall think most proper, and any poor that shall be thought unable to pay for their children's learning they shall be taught gratis."

1744: Joshua Isaacs bequeathed "£50 to our congregation of Jews in New York, the income to be for the support of a Hebrew School to teach poor children the Hebrew tongue."

APRIL 15, 1747: It was agreed that the Hazan "David Mendez Machado shall attend at the Hebra to Teach Children the Hebrew, from Nine to Twelve Each morning and from Two till Five Thursday afternoons, to receive Eight Shillings pr quarter from Each child that comes to said School and one Load wood Yearly from Each child. Also that the parnass or one of the adjuntos shall visit the said school weekly. Also that said Mr. Machado shall Teach such children Gratis that Cant afford Payment."

DECEMBER 7, 1755: It was decided at a Meeting of the Parnasim and Elders of the Congregation "that Twenty Pounds pr annum be added to the Salary of the Hazan on condition that he opens a School at his own house every day in the week (Fryday afternoon, Holy Days and Fast Days Excepted) & teaches such poor children Gratis that shall have an order from the Parnas Presidents, the Hebrew, Spanish, English, writting & Arithmetick. In the Summer from 9 to 12 in the forenoon & from 2 to 5 in the afternoon & that the children may be strictly kept to their learning, the Parnasim and the Elders according to their Seniority to visit sd school monthly to examine the children and judge if the Scholars under the Hazans care advance in their learning; the above additional Salary to commence from last Rosh a Shanah & to continue whilst the Hazan discharges the duty above expressed."

---

[1] I am indebted to Drs. H. Pereira Mendes and David de Sola Pool, rabbis of the Shearith Israel Congregation, for their coöperation in giving me the minutes of the Congregation dealing with the religious school. Dr. Pool has written an interesting account of the early days of the school, in the Jewish Teacher, May, 1917, under the title, "The Earliest Jewish Religious School in America." The extracts in this appendix until 1800, are quoted from this article.

SEPTEMBER 5, 1756: It was voted "that the Hazan be excused from keeping school on Sundays in the afternoon on accot. of his ill state of Health agreeable to what he setts forth in his petition." Hazan Pereira resigned his office shortly afterwards on account of ill health, and it was agreed by the "Parnasim & adjuntos to wright to the Parnasim & Elders of the Portuguese Cong. of London to send us one to whome wee ordred fifty Pounds Starling Salary pr annum to serve as a Hazan & teach the poor children Hebrew, English & Spanish; the letter being dated ye 4th Elul, 5518."

1760: "At a meeting of Parnasim & Elders, was ordered, that the Said Parnasim, should write to Mr. Benjamin Perreyra, to procure a Person, qualified to teach the Children of this Congregation the Hebrew Language, and agree to allow such teacher, Forty Pounds pr Annum: Twenty Pounds of which to be taken out of Hazan's Salary, the other Twenty Pounds to be Paid out of the Sedaka."

APRIL 25, 1762: That "the Parnasim, and Assistants; agreed with Mr. Abraham Is. Abrahams to keep a publick school in the Hebra, to teach the Hebrew Language, and translate the same into English, also to teach English, Reading, Writing and Cyphering. The Congregation to allow him Twenty Pounds per Annum with liberty of having offerings made him in Synagogue. He is to teach all such Children gratis, that can not afford to pay, all others are to be paid for Quarterly, as he may agree with those who send them to school. In case the Hazan should be absent or indisposed, Said Abrahams is to perform in that function, and if the fore-mention'd allowances should happen to fall short of Expectation or his deserts, upon application to the Parnassim and Assistants They are to take it into Consideration."

OCTOBER 21, 1764: It was resolved that all the children in Synagogue "whether Scholars or not, who are seated, on the places, in the Corner, appropriated for them while there, shall be govern'd by the Rabbi, or turnd from thence, on proper application to the Parnassim."

FEBRUARY 1768: The Parnassim & Assistants agree to appoint the Ribbi Mr. Abraham Abrahams to act for the Present in the office of Samas, whereupon the Ribbi, being called, the Parnas Presidente delivered him the Keys & requested as a favor, that he would Serve the office of Samas in every Respect till farther directions, which office the Ribbi, accepted in Complyance with the request aforesaid.

MARCH 6, 1768: It was "resolved that for the future Abraham Abrahams the Ribbi, should have Ten Pounds allowed him, in Consideration of his removing from the House he now lives in belonging to the Synagogue, & that the Hazan (Gershom Mendes Seixas) is to Go into said House the first of May next, after which Time he is to have no Allowance for House Rent. Mr. Abrahams the Ribbi, soliciting for Fifteen Pounds in Place of Ten Pounds, it was agreed That if at the close of the year, any moneys should Remain in the Hands of the Parnas Belonging to the Synegouge, that he should then Pay to the Ribbi, the Sum of Fifteen By him Solicited For."

DECEMBER 26, 1785: "The Cong: then proceeded to the affixg: of a Ribbi and after debating on the same, it was moved & seconded, that Public Notice be given in Synagogue That any person capable of keeping a school, deliver in their proposals in writing to the Parnassim and Adjuntos by this day three weeks, when the Congregation are to meet & the same be laid before them—And that it be understood, the Hebra will be appropriated for the use of the School."

JANUARY 15, 1786: "The Parnas informed the Congregation that no Person has yet offered to serve as Ribbi and it was resolved that the further time of Sixteen Weeks be allow'd and that the Parnassim & Junta exert themselves to procure Terms from some proper Person & then convene the Congregation."

DECEMBER 7, 1793: A memorandum shows us that Seixas was paid £32; 10 per quarter for keeping school, a marked increase in the salary of the teacher. But Seixas seems to have effected a further improvement on his salary; for, from a stray note we learn, that in the following year, 1794, he was conducting a religious school, charging four pounds a year for each child.

SEPTEMBER 20, 1794: A report of Ephraim Hart, Parnas, and Jacob Hart is in existence, in which they declare "that the school children had made very little progress" since their last visit.

MAY 18, 1808:[2] Committee of trustees to write to Mr. Carvalho to learn his terms to teach pupils Hebrew & English for 3 years subject to regulations hereafter to be established. Said letter named salary $700 for 30 to 35 scholars, six hours per day instruction.

MAY 13, 1808: Mr. Carvalho states salary not enough as an assistant would be required by him.

MAY 26, 1808: Rules & Regulations of Polonies T. T. School, submitted by Committee to trustees for adoption and contract with Carvalho as teacher adopted, 100 copies of Rules ordered printed.

MAY 29, 1808: $75 added to the salary of Shames, $30 to salary of Clerk in consequence of additional duties as Clerk to Polonies T. T. School.

1808: Shabuoth two days notice read by the Hazan that the Polonies T. T. School will be opened on Sunday 5th of June, for admission of scholars, 5 free scholarships to be admitted, application for these 5 free scholarships to be made at the school at the same time mentioned.

NOVEMBER 13, 1808: Trustee meeting resolved to notify Mr. Carvalho that the trustees in future cannot furnish scholars with any article of stationery except ink.

MARCH 15, 1809: Letter of Revd. E. Carvalho asking to be relieved from the obligations of his contract as teacher or to have his salary increased $500 the congregation Beth Elohim in Charleston having made to him the offer of his old situation, as Hazan permanently his health had become impaired here, the warm climate would suit him better. Trustees declined his request expecting him to do his duty.

[2] From this point on the extracts are taken from manuscript copy of minutes in possession of the congregation.

JANUARY 3, 1811: Mr. N. Judah presented the draft of a memorial to the legislature received from Mr. Dewitt Clinton which was read as follows:—

To the Honorable the Legislature of the State of New York.

The petition of the trustees of the Congregation of Shearith Israel in the City of New York most respectfully represent:

That from the year 1793 a school has been supported from the funds of the said Congregation for the education of their indigent children. That on the 8th of April, 1801, certain school monies were distributed among seven charity schools of the said city, supported by religious societies. That the free school of the Roman Catholic church and that of your memorialists were overlooked in this benevolent distribution. That on the 21st of March, 1806, a law was passed placing the school of the former on the same footing as the others. That your memorialists also made application to the legislature, but did not succeed owing as they presume to the pressure of business. Your memorialists fully persuaded that the Legislature will look with an equal eye upon all occupations of people who conduct themselves as good and faithful citizens, and conscious that nothing has been omitted on their part to deserve the same countenance and encouragement which has been exhibited to others, do most respectfully pray your Honorable body to extend the same relief to their charity school which has been granted to all others in this city. Ordered that the clerk prepare a copy of the same and hand it to the President of the Board for the signatures of the members thereof, and that when completed, it be delivered to Mr. Dewitt Clinton to be by him presented to the Legislature, with the certificate of the school being supported from the funds of the Congregation attached thereto.

APRIL 3, 1811: Meeting of Trustees. The President produced a plan for the establishment of a school after the 7th day of June next. With a copy of circular to be sent to each congregator which he received from Dr. Hart and Mr. Gomperts. On Motion of Mr. Moses seconded by Mr. Nathan, Resolved that a printed circular signed by the clerk be sent to each congregator, and that Dr. Hart and Mr. Gomperts be a committee to wait on them to procure subscriptions, and that the letter be in the following words.

New York, April 1811.

Sir:—Pursuant to a resolution of the Board of Trustees of the Congregation Shearith Israel, I have to inform you that Mr. G. S. Gomperts and Dr. Joel Hart, are appointed a committee to obtain contributions for the continuance of Polonies Talmud Torah, and that they will wait on you for that purpose. In consequence of Mr. Carvalho's intention to leave the city, the situation of preceptor to the above seminary will become vacant from which circumstance it is deemed expedient to adopt further measures for its support of continuance. Teachers of approved merits and talents will be engaged for the instruction of the scholars in Hebrew, English, and other branches of education. It is contemplated to extend the benefits of this institution by abolishing the present stipulated prices for the admission of scholars, and if hereafter agreed on, to remove the school to a more central situation, to admit all applicants of the Jewish persuasion, above the age of 5 years, and to receive as payment for scholars, whatever remuneration subscribers may deem proper to contribute. It is hoped the generosity of the Congregators will afford every aid towards so laudable an institution.

APRIL 22d, 1811: The Mayor's compliments to the Trustees of the Congregation Shearith Israel and sends the enclosed section of an act which passed the Legislature for their benefit. 19th of April; 1811.

Extract from the act entitled an act of the payment of certain officers of government and for other purposes passed April 9, 1811.

"And be it further enacted that it shall be lawful for the Mayor, Aldermen and commonalty of the City of New York to pay to the trustees of Shearith Israel in the city of New York the like sum as was paid to the other religious congregation respectively by virtue of the act entitled "an act for directing certain monies to be applied for the use of free schools in the City of New York" and the act entitled an "Act respecting the free school of St. Peters Church in the City of New York" the monies so paid to be applied according to the directions of the first mentioned act, and the treasurer of this State is hereby directed to pay to the said Mayor, Aldermen and the Commonalty of the City of New York the sum so paid by them, but of the unappropriated money arising from the duties at on sales at auction in the said city."

Thanks were unanimously passed to the Mayor, Hon. DeWitt Clinton, Memorial drawn up as to payment of money, 24th of April, 1811.

Mr. Carvalho's resignation.

JUNE 16, 1811: *Be it Resolved* that the following notice be given in synagogue on the ensuing Sabbath. The Congregation are hereby notified that the trustees will apply the interest arising on $1565.78, received from the Legislature "for the purpose of instructing poor children in the most useful branches of common education" in conformity to the injunctions contained in an act directing certain monies to be applied for the use of free schools in the City of New York, passed 8th day of April, 1801, and those persons desirous of benefiting thereby will make application in remitting to the Board of Trustees on or before the 28th of April.

FEBRUARY 9th, 1812: Resolved as the opinion of this Board that it is expedient to re-establish the Talmud Torah that the same be opened on the first of May next, and that a Proclamation be made in synagogue on the two succeeding Sabbaths, that one hundred and sixty dollars per annum, the interest arising from the bequest of Myer Polonies, and the money granted by the State, be appropriated for that purpose; the clerk is instructed to write the following letter to the Hazan:

Sir:

Pursuant to a resolution of the Board of Trustees, I am instructed to request, that you will make proclamation in Synagogue on the two succeeding Sabbaths to the following effect; that the trustees have resolved to re-establish the Talmud Torah to go into operation on the first of May next; that one hundred and sixty dollars in equal quarterly instalments will be paid a teacher for the same, and on the following conditions, for the tuition of ten free scholars, in Hebrew and English, from the age of five, until thirteen.

That he shall provide the necessary requisitics, stationery and fuel, and that a school room shall be provided for him. The teacher will have the privilege to increase the number of scholars, not to exceed forty, on such terms as he may be able to agree with their parents, or guardians. Those persons who may be disposed to apply for situation of teacher subject to the above proposals, will signify the same in writing to the Parnas, on or before the first of March ensuing.

MARCH 8th, 1812: Messrs. Judah and Gomez the committee appointed to confer with Mr. Simeon Levy reported as follows:

That Mr. Levy will agree to keep the school for one year from the first of May next, for one hundred and sixty dollars, conformable to the offers made by the trustees proclaimed in synagogue, and teach ten children to read and translate the Hebrew in the usual manner as heretofore taught by a congregational teacher. That he will teach them English, reading, writing and arithmetic; he will also find stationery and fuel; the parents and guardians of the children to provide reading and spelling books.

That he will enter into such regulations as the committee and himself may agree for the government of the school.

New York March 8th, 1812.

(Signed) Benj. Judah
Isaac Gomez.

Resolved that Mr. Simeon Levy be taken up as a teacher of the Talmud Torah on the terms mentioned in the foregoing report for one year. Resolved that the children who are now educated at the expense of the Congregation, are not to continue at their respective places of tuition after the expiration of the present quarter; and that the Hazan notify the Congregation in synagogue that the Polonies Talmud Torah will commence on the first day of May next, and those members of the Congregation who are disposed to send their children will apply to the Board of Trustees in writing on or before the fifteenth of April next.

OCTOBER 27, 1812: Report of Revenue.

$900 devised by Myer Polonies deceased, for the establishment of a free school, called P. T. T.

$1565.78 from Legislature "to aid the funds of the Congregation with the interest arising thereon for the instruction of indigent children belonging to this sceiety."

The interest arising from this last fund and that of Myer Polonies before mentioned together with the appropriation taken from the funds of the congregation to aid the establishment of the Hebrew and English School, under the direction and tuition of Mr. Simeon Levy allowing him for his services at the rate of one hundred and sixty dollars per annum; he procuring pens, ink, and fuel, for one year from the first day of May last the trustees furnishing room and school books for the accommodation of the scholars.

School extended to 20 children from 4 years to 15, the ages particularized by the act for the establishment of common schools in the state of New York, passed 12th day March, 1813.

DECEMBER 28, 1817: The Committee appointed on the subject of the revival of the school of Polonies Talmud Torah as their opinion, that the school should be opened, under the direction of the Trustees, and that Rabbi Pique be engaged to teach the Hebrew therein on the following terms.

That the number of charity children not to exceed twelve at any one period.

That the Rabbi be allowed to receive pay scholars at a rate and terms that he hold them alone responsible for the payment without any responsibility on the part of the trustees.

MAY 24, 1818: Rev. Pique to get a competent assistant for the English department, including writing, arithmetic and geography, to be paid by him.

FEBRUARY 4, 1821: Rabbi Pique has one pay scholar and 5 free scholars, 4 of whom he admitted without permission of the Board. Resolved his services dispensed with.

JULY 2, 1821: Application from Mr. I. Alvarez de Leon to teach Hebrew, Arithmetic, Writing and English Grammar to eight or ten boys in the charitable school; the salary will be just what it has been with the former teachers, neither more nor less; the sum I understand is $300. Some told me it amounts to more, others, somewhat less; day scholars to pay as per schedule.

Should any art, science or language etc. not mentioned in the above statement be desired to be taught to day scholars, a separate distinct agreement will be entered into with the parents or guardians of the boys.

JULY 18, 1821: Mr. Alvarez elected for six months to teach the English language, writing and arithmetic, and the scholars only to be the children of Jews.

SEPTEMBER 21, 1821: Mr. de Leon discharged.

New York, Sept. 21, 1821.

Mr. I. Alvarez de Leon,

Sir:

The trustees finding that no disposition exists on the part of families to send their children under your superintendence, that the objects for which you were engaged are frustrated, are compelled to announce to you that your duties as teacher are terminated; considering however that you may have been disappointed in your expectations, the trustees actuated by friendly feelings towards you, have agreed to appropriate to your order the sum of fifty dollars, I am Sir,

Your humble servant,

H. B. SEIXAS, *Clerk.*

MARCH 21, 1822:

The Parnas and Trustees
of K. K. Shearith Israel.
New York.

As the subscriber intends opening a school for educating the youth of our Congregation in the Hebrew language, and as he has already obtained a number of scholars he would wish to commence as soon as possible. He therefore solicits the permission of the Parnas and Trustees of K. K. Shearith Israel, to occupy the school room in the Esnoga Yard for that purpose during their pleasure.

Resolved that Mr. Rivera be permitted during the pleasure of the trustees to occupy the school room, and to keep the same in good order.

JULY 17, 1822: The trustees to have the right of sending a number of children to the school as they may from time to time think proper, for which they will pay Mr. Morpurgo a quarter in advance, at the rate of $2.50 per quarter for each scholar during the time they shall continue to attend his school, Mr. Morpurgo to keep a list of the scholars sent by the trustees with an account of their attendance.

The scholars shall not be permitted to riot or make a noise in the synagogue yard or about the premises, or in any manner to disturb the neighbors. List of persons who have engaged their children for $2.50 per quarter (3 times per week in afternoons only) which considered for the ordinary time is equal to 10 dollars per quarter.

N. Judah	2 scholars	4 quarters
E. S. Lazarus....................	2 scholars	4 quarters
H. Hendricks.....................	3 scholars	on return from country
Joseph Hart	3 scholars	4 quarters
H. M. Salomon..................	3 scholars	
Mr. Delong	1 scholar	
Mr. Jackson	2 scholars	
Mr. Crommelin	2 scholars	
Mr. Deyong	1 scholar	
I. I. Hart........................	3 scholars	

B. Hart, S. Nathan and Mr. Tobias are expected to send their children after the school is open.

SEPTEMBER 30, 1823: To the President and Members of the Board of Trustees.

Gentlemen:

Encouraged by several of my friends, I contemplate as soon as arrangements can be effected to establish a school in the city, for teaching the Hebrew language, thereby affording the means of acquiring and diffusing a better knowledge of our Holy religion and its divine precepts.

Should this undertaking meet your approval I shall feel grateful for such aid as your liberality may think proper to extend in promoting the object in view for the tuition of those children you may determine to send under the direction and regulation of your Board. In return every effort shall be made on my part in fulfilling the all important duties so as to render general satisfaction.

With fervent prayers for the prosperity of yourself and Congregation, collectively and individually,

I remain, respectfully gentlemen,

Your obedient servant,

(Signed) ABRM. H. COHEN.

And the same being under consideration it was Resolved that the sum of $225 the school fund interest for one year be appropriated to be paid monthly to Mr. Cohen with the use of the school room. Mr. Cohen to teach such free scholars as the trustees may think proper to send and to be under such rules and regulations as shall be agreed on by the trustees and Mr. Cohen. And that Messrs. Noah and Zuntz be a Committee to confer with Mr. Cohen on the subject of the school and to report to the Board.

APRIL 25, 1827: On motion Resolved that the salary hereafter to be paid to Mr. Abraham H. Cohen as the teacher of the school Polonies Talmud Torah shall be confined to the income of the school fund, which at present amounts to two hundred and eighty dollars thirty six cents per annum, to take effect from the 12th day of May next, and that the clerk furnish him with a copy of this resolution.

Rabbi A. H. Cohen's resignation as teacher of the Talmud Torah School accepted.

DECEMBER 13, 1828: The following letter was received from Mr. Joshua Moses.

New York, Dec. 8, 1828.

In behalf and for the "Society for the Education of Poor Children and Relief of Indigent Persons" permission is requested for the use of the synagogue on the 2d Sunday of January next for the delivery of an oration, etc.

(Signed) JOSHUA MOSES, *President.*

To the Parnas & Trustees

of the Cong. of K. K. Shearith Israel.

On motion Resolved that the use of the Congregation be granted for the purpose of delivering an oration and for such other arrangements as shall be approved by the Parnas.

APRIL 29, 1829: On motion Resolved that Messrs. Naphtali Phillips, Joseph L. Joseph and David Hart be a Committee to open the school under the charge of the Rev. Isaac B. Seixas on such terms and conditions as they shall think advisable, provided the sum to be allowed does not exceed the amount annually received as interest on the Polonies Talmud Torah fund, and that the said adopt rules and regulations for the admission of scholars and for the conducting and superintending the said school, the contract to be for one year including free scholars.

JUNE 21, 1829: The Committee appointed at the last meeting to take measures to open the school, reported a contract with the Rev. Isaac B. Seixas which is as follows:

Isaac B. Seixas agreed with the trustees of the Congregation Shearith Israel to open the school of Polonies Talmud Torah under the superintendence and direction of said trustees, they agreeing to pay Mr. Seixas the amount of the interest of the school fund in quarterly payments, Mr. Seixas to teach the Hebrew to such free scholars as shall be admitted by the trustees or their committee and to give to the scholars the necessary instruction in relation to their duties as Yehudim.

This agreement to continue in force for one year if not sooner annulled by three months notice to that effect to be given by either party, and may be extended as to time by a memorandum on this agreement.

New York, May 10, 1829.

(Signed) I. B. SEIXAS.

On motion resolved that the above report be accepted.

JULY 1, 1833: Society for the education of poor children and relief of indigent persons of the Jewish Persuasion.

Resolved that a letter be addressed to the Board of Trustees in relation to the time when the teacher of the Polonies School shall teach the orphans under the care of this society, he having refused to teach them on Sundays unless they attended the other days, when the school was opened, and which they are precluded from doing by their English studies.

Passed at a meeting of the Board of Managers, held June 2, 1833,

(Signed) M. H. CARDOZO, *Sec.*

On motion resolved that the teacher of the Polonies Talmud Torah be directed to teach the three boys alluded to in the foregoing communication on Sundays at the usual school hours.

SEPTEMBER 22, 1834: Resolved that the teacher of Polonies T. T. School be requested to communicate in writing to this Board at its next meeting.

1st. The number and names of free scholars attending said school.

2d. The days on which they attend, the number of hours in said day for which said school is kept open.

3rd. Whether said scholars attend regularly or not, in what branches they are taught, and what progress they have made in the several branches.

4th. Whether or not, any other than free scholars attend this school. The clerk to communicate a copy of the above to the Rev. I. B. Seixas, teacher.

SEPTEMBER 25, 1834: A communication was received from the Rev. I. B. Seixas, teacher of the school of Polonies T. T., as required by a resolution passed at last meeting, to be put on file.

On motion resolved that it is expedient to reorganize the school of P. T. T.

Resolved that the present arrangement with the teacher shall cease and determine three months from 1st Oct. ensuing, and that notice thereof be given by the clerk on the part of the trustees to the teacher of said school.

OCTOBER 29, 1838: A communication was received from the "Lady's Assoc. for the general instruction of children of the Jewish persuasion," asking for the use of a room to hold their meetings in, and for the general objects of the institution. On motion resolved that the President inform the Lady's Assoc., that the congregational meeting room may be used for the purpose required; and with an assurance on the part of this Board, that it views the efforts now making by the association as a most praiseworthy undertaking, and that they have the best wishes of this Board for their success.

DECEMBER 26, 1838: Resolved that it is expedient to reorganize the school of P. T. T. under the competent and suitable teacher; and one qualified to aid the Hazan in his duties as such when required.

Resolved that Messrs. Judah, Gomez and Tobias be a committee to ascertain where a suitable person can be obtained and on what terms, and to report the same to this Board as soon as possible, with such observations as they may deem necessary.

FEBRUARY 7, 1839: The Committee, in relation to the school of P. T. T. reported that they had sent circulars to different places, in relation thereto.

SEPTEMBER 7, 1839: A letter was received from Miss Sophia Tobias, sec'y to the ladies composing the assoc. for the moral and religious instruction of Jewish children requesting permission to allow offerings to be made in synagogue in aid of their funds; the consideration of which was postponed.

''Deemed inexpedient'' at meeting Oct. 15, 1839.

OCTOBER 22, 1839: An invitation to attend to the examination of the children under the charge of the Ladies Assoc. was received and accepted.

DECEMBER 1, 1839: 24 Kislev, 5600. A letter from the Rev. J. J. Lyons, Hazan, was received, stating that he proposes commencing a school for the Hebrew language, as soon as the preliminary arrangements can be made and asking the action of the Board in the premises.

DECEMBER 8, 1839: The Board went into the consideration of the letter received from the Rev. Mr. Lyons at the last meeting, and the following was moved by Mr. Hart.

Resolved that the trustees will pay to the Rev. Jacques J. Lyons at the rate of $3 per quarter for each scholar that they shall place under his charge to be instructed in the Hebrew on such days and hours as shall be agreed on by the teacher and the trustees. The latter receiving the right to withdraw any scholar at any time from the school, when payment for the said scholar shall cease.

The payment to be made from the interest arising from the fund of the P. T. T. S.

A Committee of the Board of Trustees to superintend said school in relation to the scholars sent by them, and to be subject to such regulations as may be agreed on by the teacher and committee.

NOVEMBER 14, 1841: The committee to whom was referred the communication from the society ''For the education of poor children, and relief of indigent persons of the Jewish persuasion.'' Beg leave to report that they had an interview with Messrs. S. I. Joseph, Henry Hendricks and Jacob L. Seixas, the gentlemen composing the Committee on the part of the society, who after stating the wishes and expectations with regard to disposition of the fund in the hands of the trustees, commonly called the Polonies Fund, solicited the yearly interest accruing thereon, to assist it in establishing a school upon an extended scale, which the society appears to have deemed expedient to establish, if the co-operation of the trustees can be obtained. If this cannot be conceded to its full extent, then as a very important auxiliary to a commencement, they asked the amount of one year's interest, so that if the school did not succeed according to the fond anticipations of the society, or to the satisfaction of the trustees, they, the trustees, could if they please, discontinue any further allowance; and as a return for this, the school would educate any number of poor children, that the trustees might see fit to send.

Your committee could not give those gentlemen a definite answer, to either of those propositions, they did not possess power so to do. But they thought themselves authorized to make to them the same offer that had been made to individuals, that is, that the trustees would pay for Hebrew scholars, who would become such under their authority, provided the cost of their tuition did not exceed the interest for the time being.

The evident intention of Mr. Polony in this bequest is plainly discernible in the words of his will. It was to form a fund, the interest of which to be appropriated for the purpose of educating the poor of the congregation Shearith Israel, in the Hebrew, under the authority and at the discretion of the trustees of that Congregation. The residue of the fund being a bequest of Miss Pinto, a sum of money from the state, and free will offerings made in synagogue, the whole of which has been consolidated and has been received by this cong. and always designated by them as the "P. T. T. Fund."

Attempts have frequently been made by the trustees to establish a school which has generally failed. In cases where they have been partially successful for a short time, they have resulted in a very considerable loss to this cong. and for which no charge has even yet been made against the fund, altho it would be perfectly equitable, and the straitened circumstances of the cong. at times, subsequently to the period at which those losses, accrued, would more than have justified such charge.

Your committee deem it proper to state, that they think the trustees would not be justifiable in making any appropriation of that money, other than that above named, and which was offered to the society through their committee. Or in the establishment of a school, to be under their exclusive control. And that any other appropriation would not be carrying out the intention of the testators, nor of the other contributors to that fund, but would render the trustees obnoxious to the charge of a dereliction of duty, and might possibly make the Cong. liable to respond in damages.

(Signed) David Hart.
E. S. Lazarus.

JUNE 22, 1842: A letter from M. M. Noah and Lewis I. Cohen in behalf of themselves and others respecting the establishment of a Hebrew school, was received and the consideration thereof was on motion of Mr. Tobias postponed.

JUNE 30, 1842: Resolved that the application of Mr. M. M. Noah and Lewis I. Cohen relative to the establishment of a Hebrew school be referred to a committee to report thereon; also a plan for establishing a Hebrew school by this Board, and the President appointed Messrs. Phillips, Nathan and Seixas the committee.

JULY 5, 1842: Mr. Phillips from the committee appointed at the last meeting in relation to the establishment of a Hebrew school, presented a report in conformity thereto, accompanied with several resolutions, which were considered and unanimously adopted. And in conformity to the first resolution Messrs. Lazarus, Nathan and Phillips were appointed inspectors in conjunction with Messrs. M. M. Noah, Lewis I. Cohen and Sol. I. Joseph members of the cong. The inspectors to have the power to fill any vacancy that may take place.

REPORT OF THE SCHOOL COMMITTEE

The Committee to whom was referred the communication from Messrs. M. M. Noah and Lewis I. Cohen relative to the establishment of a Hebrew school, with instructions to report a plan for establishing the same, under the direction of the Board of Trustees, beg leave to report, that they have embraced the very earliest opportunity of giving the same the attention that the importance of the matter demanded, and fully impressed with the correctness of the views set forth in the statement of the very respectable members of the cong. referred to above, as to the necessity of devising means for instruction in the Hebrew language. Your committee are however unable to arrive at the conclusion that the Board fund for the purpose of aiding in establishing a school in the manner asked for in their communication.

By the last will and testament of Myer Polonics, a legacy was left our cong. for the express purpose of establishing a Hebrew school, and by 7th article of Constitution, it is made imperatively the duty of the Board of Trustees to form a school under such regulations, as they may deem salutary and proper.

It will therefore be seen that to carry out the views of Messrs. Noah and Cohen in the manner proposed by them, would require on the part of the Board of Trustees at best the assumption of doubtful powers, hence your committee feel bound to report as their opinion, that the trustees would not be justified, however, sound or desirable may be proposition of Messrs. Noah and Cohen in parting with the avails of the school fund according to the plan asked for by them.

Your committee however regard the communication of Messrs. Noah and Cohen as of vast importance and with great satisfaction. It is to them very substantial and positive evidence that the members of the cong. are beginning earnestly to feel the necessity of finding means to perpetuate the holy and beautiful language of our faith, without which its essence and purity would be endangered; and they deem it the duty of the Board promptly to respond to the call, and to send their aid to carry out the wishes of the cong. in the manner in which they have the power.

Indeed any further delay on the part of the trustees to discharge benevolent trust imposed on them by the donors of the school fund, might warrant the belief, that they had lost sight of a most important duty, and were neglectful of a charge of vast importance to the rising generation.

It is therefore indisputable that the expenditure of the school fund interest for the purpose of education can only be allowed by the trustees in accordance with the 7th article of our constitution, which is under their management and control, with the assistance of some suitable teacher or teachers.

Your committee has been informally advised that a society for benevolent purposes, composed principally if not entirely of members of our cong. are disposed to grant annually a portion of the interest of their permanent fund to aid in conducting a school. This accession of means to the interest of the school fund would tend greatly to increase the ability of the Board of Trustees to establish and keep up an effective school for Hebrew instruction; but as the interest of the school fund, together with the aid that might be received from the society alluded to, would still be insufficient to maintain the necessary expenses incidental to a desirable school, an additional source of revenue would be required. This could be accomplished by donations, subscriptions and the receiving of moderate pay from those able to contribute for their education, while at the same time, those unable, could receive instruction without charge.

Your committee feeling therefore the necessity of the Board of Trustees at once moving earnestly in establishing a school, propose the following plan and resolutions.

Resolved that the Board of Trustees will establish a school for instruction in the Hebrew language according to the Portuguese custom or mode of reading, under the name of the "Polonies Talmud Torah" as early as the requisite arrangements can be completed; said school to be held in the room under the synagogue known as the school room.

Resolved that a committee of three members of this Board, who together with a like number, from the cong. appointed in the same manner, shall constitute a board of inspectors to serve for one year from the establishment of the school, whose duties shall be:

FIRST—To give general notice of the formation of the school, and to receive applications for the office of teacher; to decide on the qualifications of the applicants, and to make proper selection and agreement as to compensation, etc.

SECOND—To form a code of rules and regulations for governing and conducting the schools.

THIRD—To visit the school at least once in every month, to observe the progress of the scholars, and to report the same in writing to Board of Trustees once in every six months.

FOURTH—To have the power of admitting and discharging scholars, and to decide all differences that may arise between them and the teacher.

FIFTH—Any difference between the teacher and the inspector shall be reported to the Board of Trustees, who shall decide on the matter in dispute.

SIXTH—The Board of Inspectors may advise such means as may be proper, either by donations, subscriptions, or otherwise, to raise a revenue in addition to the interest of the school fund appropriated by the Board.

SECOND—Resolved that the code of rules and regulations for governing and conducting the school, be submitted to the Board of Trustees for approval, prior to its adoption by the Board of Inspectors.

THIRD—Resolved that the Board of Trustees reserve the right to make, amend, or abolish any rules or regulations governing the school.

FOURTH—Resolved that with a view of carrying the foregoing resolutions into effect, the Board of Trustees do hereby appropriate the interest of the school fund for one year from the commencement of the school.

Your Committee having thus to the best of their ability discharged the trust imposed on them, submit their views to the attention of the Board, in hope that they will be found worthy of consideration and prompt action.

All of which is respectfully submitted:

(Signed) Isaac Phillips)
Benjamin Nathan) *Committee*
Jacob L. Seixas)

JULY 14, 1842: M. M. Noah, President of the Board of Inspectors of the School P. T. T. transmitted the following being the proceedings of the society for the education of poor children, etc.

M. M. NOAH, ESQ.,

Chairman of the Board of Inspectors.

Sir: At a meeting of the society for the education of poor children and relief of indigent persons, etc. held this morning, an application from the inspectors for a portion of the annual income of the society to aid in establishing a school was laid before them and the following resolution adopted:

FIRST—Resolved that the Trustees of the Cong. Shearith Israel be requested to modify their regulations of the contemplated Polonies T. T. School, so as to make it imperative on themselves, always to nominate three inspectors of the school, out of the members of this society, and such inspectors as shall be subject to the approval of the Board of Managers of this society.

SECOND—Resolved that if the trustees modify their regulations as requested, this society appropriate the sum of two hundred and fifty dollars for one year towards the establishment of the Polonies T. T. S. under the rules and regulations as pointed out by the trustees of the Cong. Shearith Israel.

THIRD—Resolved that the Board of Managers are hereby empowered to continue the above appropriation of $250 from year to year, if they see fit, unless otherwise ordered by the society.

FOURTH—Resolved that the sum of $250 appropriated as above by this society be placed at the disposal of the inspectors to be chosen from this society, who are hereby authorized to unite with the inspectors chosen from the trustees, to make such disbursements of the portion of the funds donated by this society, as will accord with the concurrent arrangement of the whole Board of Inspectors; and that the president of this society is hereby directed to draw an order or orders on the treasurer for the amount as required by the Board of Inspectors.

FIFTH—Resolved that the Secretary furnish the trustees annually with a list of the members of this society, to guide them in their annual nomination of inspectors.

SIXTH—Resolved that the three inspectors appointed from the society be requested to report semi-annually the state of the school and all other information on the subject that they may deem necessary.

SEVENTH—Resolved that the secretary communicate the above resolutions to Mr. Noah, Chairman of the Board of Inspectors. Extracts from the minutes 19 July, 1842. M. H. Cardozo, Secretary.

The foregoing communication being under the consideration, the following resolution was offered by Mr. Phillips and adopted.

Resolved that the Board of Trustees will annually select from the society for the education of poor children and relief of indigent persons of the Jewish persuasion, three of its members to unite with the Board of Inspectors appointed by the trustees to conduct the school Polonies T. T. in accordance with the first resolution contained in the foregoing communication.

Messrs. Tobias I. Tobias, Lewis I. Cohen, Solomon I. Joseph were then appointed to represent the society. Who with Messrs. M. M. Noah, E. S. Lazarus, Benjamin Nathan and Mr. Isaac Phillips constitute the Board of Inspectors of the school of Polonies T. T. for one year from the establishment of the school.

MAY 22, 1843: An invitation from the Misses Palaches to the trustees to be present at the examination of their pupils in the basement of the synagogue on the 28th inst. was received and accepted.

JULY 11, 1843: A letter was received from the Rev. J. J. Lyons, stating his intention to open a class for instruction in the Hebrew language, and requesting the use of the school room for the purpose at such times as will not interfere with prior appropriations. The request was complied with, during the pleasure of the Board.

FEBRUARY 6, 1844: A letter from Rev. J. J. Lyons in relation to his establishing a Hebrew school, and "asking the cooperation of the Board to effect his purpose." On motion it was resolved in addition to the use of the school room heretofore granted to him on the 11th July last, the President of the Board allow such fuel as he may deem necessary for the use of the school.

MAY 5, 1845: Mr. Joseph and Mr. Seixas the Committee in relation to the establishment of the Polonies T. T. S. made report thereon, which was accepted accompanied by the following resolutions, which were adopted.

FIRST—Resolved that the sum of two hundred dollars be appropriated for one year for the re-establishment of the P. T. T. S. which sum shall be taken from the annual income of the fund of said school.

SECOND—Resolved that a committee of three members of the Board be appointed, who shall select a competent teacher and report such selection to the Board for their confirmation.

THIRD—Resolved that on the confirmation of such teacher by the board, that a contract shall be entered into with him, and to be approved by the Board, with rules and regulations for the government of the school.

SEPTEMBER 24, 1845: Messrs. Joseph and Phillips the Committee for that purpose, reported a set of rules and regulations for the school of P. T. T. with the draft of a contract with the Rev. J. J. Lyons as teacher, and the same having been agreed to on the part of Mr. Lyons, were now adopted on the part of the Board; the above committee to have the contract executed, and to have one hundred copies of the rules and regulations printed.

Messrs. Joseph and Phillips were appointed the committee to superintend the school until the first of May next.

Rules, etc. children must be six or over and able to read and write English.

Sundays, 9—1. Tuesday and Thursday afternoons.

MAY 25, 1846: A letter from Rev. J. J. Lyons stating "that his health will no longer permit him to retain the office of teacher of the school P. T. T. and that he will be compelled to resign the same at the termination of the present quarter."

Mr. Abrahams offered the following:

Whereas the Rev. J. J. Lyons having rendered his resignation as teacher of the school P. T. T. on account of ill health. Be it resolved that the quarter's salary be paid to Mr. Lyons, and that the school be discontinued until the first of November, and the resignation of Mr. Lyons be laid on the table.

Mr. Phillips moved that the same be amended so as to read as follows after the words of Mr. Lyons. "And that his resignation be accepted, and that the school committee be authorized to receive applications for filling the situation, and report for the consideration of the trustees the names of any applicant for the office."

The amendment was not agreed to, the question recurring on the resolution of Abrahams.

The resolution offered by Mr. Abrahams was not adopted. Mr. Judah offered the following resolution:

Resolved that the school be suspended from the end of the present quarter for three months.

The resolution offered by Mr. Judah was not adopted.

OCTOBER 25, 1846: A letter was received from Rev. J. J. Lyons, stating that his health being re-established, begs leave to recall his resignation tendered in June last as teacher in the school of P. T. T. and reports himself ready to reopen the school.

On motion Mr. Phillips, Resolved that the school of P. T. T. be reopened on the first of Nov. ensuing under the same rules and regulations as heretofore established; and that Mr. Abrahams and Mr. Seixas be the committee to superintend the same. Notice of this resolution to be placed in the vestibule of the synagogue.

OCTOBER 31, 1849: Mr. Abrahams seconded by Mr. Noah moved that a room be allowed for the purpose of teaching adults Hebrew, and for lectures, to assemble three nights in the week, which was declared lost by the following vote.

Ayes—Mr. Noah, Mr. Abrahams, 2. Nays—Mr. Lazarus, Mr. Seixas, Mr. Joseph, Mr. Phillips, 4.

Mr. Phillips one of the school committee made a report in writing of the situation of the school of Polonies Talmud Torah, which was read and ordered on file, and on motion of Mr. Phillips the sum of twenty-five dollars was appropriated for procuring books, etc. for the use of the school, to be expended under the direction of the Committee.

MARCH 6, 1854: Resolved that the president and clerk of this Board be authorized and empowered to apply for and receive the sum of thirteen thousand dollars bequeathed by the late Judah Touro to the Talmud Torah fund attached to this Congregation and to said Congregation, and to give the necessary and legal acquittances and discharges on payment thereof.

OCTOBER 26, 1854: Resolved that it is the wish of the electors of this Congregation that the trustees take measures to invite candidates in order to fill the office of *teacher and lecturer* and submit their names to a special meeting of the electors of the Congregation to be convened for the purpose of taking action thereon.

The President declared the same lost. Mr. Lazarus then moved the consideration of the plan ordered by the committee for extending the usefulness of the school of P. T. T., as ordered to be printed.

MARCH 5, 1855: Resolved that the Rev. J. J. Lyons be and he is hereby appointed Hebrew teacher in the *school of Polonies Talmud Torah* and superintendent of the same at a salary of *$500* for *one year* from the time the school commences.

APRIL 11, 1855: The *school committee* reported the following rules and regulations of the *Polonies Talmud Torah School* which were considered by sections and unanimously agreed to. And that the following persons be appointed as teachers to the school.

Thomas B. Sanford, English teacher, $300 per annum; Miss Harriet Ruden, English teacher, $100 per annum; Mrs. David Phillips, Janitress, $100 per annum.

School from 9—3, or 9½—3½ p. m. according to season daily.

APRIL 7, 1856: The President offered the following resolutions: Resolved that the present organization of Polonies Talmud Torah School as related to instruction both in Hebrew and English be discontinued with the expiration of the present quarter which will occur on the 23d inst., and that the superintendent, teacher and janitress be notified that their services will be dispensed with from that time.

Resolved that the Polonies T. T. School for the instruction (without charge) in Hebrew, of scholars attached to this Congregation be opened under the care and direction of the Rev. J. J. Lyons (and under the supervision of the Committee on the P. T. T. S. from the 1st of May next on every Wednesday afternoon, and every Sunday morning excepting on festivals) and that the Rev. J. J. Lyons be paid for his services at the rate of $250 per annum.

APRIL 19, 1857: On motion of Mr. Hart it was resolved that the balance of the yearly interest arising from the Polonies Talmud Torah fund be transferred to the credit of the Congregation in consideration of the services of the Rev. Dr. Fischel as lecturer and instructor to said school. (Mr. Lazarus in the negative).

MAY 11, 1862: The clerk was directed in making up the annual account for the present year to credit the school fund with as much interest as will balance the amount paid the teacher, and the Rev. Dr. Fischel, late lecturer and instructor for their services.

OCTOBER 11, 1874: A letter was received from the Rev. H. S. Jacobs preacher in reference to organizing a religious school. On motion of Dr. Blumenthal it was Resolved that a committee of three be appointed to confer with the Rev. M. Jacobs with a view to the organization of a system of religious instruction, and that such committee invite the co-operation of the Hebrew synagogues in that important work.

OCTOBER 18, 1874: The Committee appointed at last meeting to confer with the Rev. M. Jacobs with a view to the organization by a system of religious instruction submitted a unanimous report which was accepted and ordered on file, and on motion of Dr. Blumenthal seconded by Mr. G. Nathan it was resolved, that the President appoint a committee of the Polonies T. T. School, and to have charge and direction of the subject of religious instruction, whether in connection with that school or otherwise, and that such committee have full power to make such arrangements and to take such action on behalf of this Board as shall in their judgment be necessary in furtherance of the purposes aforesaid.

DECEMBER 6, 1874: The Committee of Conference with the ministers of the Cong. regarding the organization of a religious Sunday School and English religious meetings—according to resolution adopted by the Board of Trustees, Oct. 11, 5635 (1874) have the honor to report:

That they have held the desired Conferences with the Revd. Gentlemen and that they (the committee) fully believe in the feasibility of the proposed plan for the establishment of a religious Sunday School, as distinguished from the Talmud Torah Hebrew School; also, in the necessity, utility and practicability of the weekly evening meetings for religious instruction for adults; and finally of the readiness of the Revd. Mr. Jacobs to enter upon the latter; and both the minister's willingness to begin the work of the former at once, and furthermore the conviction and recommendation of the committee, that action should be taken, by the Board of trustees and the Congregation *without delay,* in furtherance of said project.

New York, Oct. 18, 5635 (1874).

APPENDIX B

GERMAN-POLISH CONGREGATIONS PRIOR TO 1850

B'nai Jeshurun	1825	Polish-English	Elm Street
Anshe Chesed	1828	German	Henry Street
Ahavath Zedakah	1835	Polish	Center and Elm Sts.
Shaarey Shomayim	1839	German	Attorney Street
Shaarey Zedak	1840	Polish	Henry Street
Bikur Cholim	1842	German	Attorney Street
Beth Israel	1844	Polish	Pike & Center Sts.
Emanu-El	1845	German (reform)	Chrystie St.
Shaarey Tefilla	1848	Polish	Wooster Street
B'nai Israel	1848	Dutch	Chrystie Street
Bikur Cholim	1849	Polish	Pearl & Center Sts.
Shaarey Rachamim	1850	German	Attorney Street

See—Asmonean IX—20 (March 3, 1854).

Also Proceedings of American Jewish Historical Society, Vol. IX—97.

APPENDIX C

"MISSION SCHOOLS IN NEW YORK CITY, 1896"

From the Report of the Religious School Committee, Chairman, Julia Richman, of the National Council of Jewish Women, at their first convention in 1896:

Total No. of congregations, N. Y. C........................ 135

Congregations having Sabbath schools, where religious instruction is in English language.................... 28

Congregations with mission classes.................... 4

Other mission schools as follows:

Of the Council of Jewish Women, having 150 pupils...... 2

Of the Hebrew Free School Assoc., having 4,000 pupils.... 2

Of congregational sisterhoods, having 1,000 pupils........ 6

Of the Hebrew Technical Institute, having 200 pupils.... 1

United Hebrew Charities, having 100 pupils............. 1

Jewish children of Sabbath school age, receiving religious instruction, approximately 8,000

Jewish children of Sabbath school age, without religious instruction, approximately from...................15,000 to 20,000

APPENDIX D

HEBREW SABBATH SCHOOL UNION

SECTION 1.

ORGANIC LAW OF SABBATH SCHOOL UNION

1. The Union was established with the object of advancing a common system, methods and discipline in Jewish Sabbath schools.

2. Every Jewish Sabbath school may become a member of the Union, with the conditions that

a. the government of this Union shall be vested in a Board of Directors, elected bi-annually, by the representatives of the schools;

b. every superintendent and chairman of the school committee shall represent the Board of Directors of the Union in their respective localities.

3. It shall be the duty of the Board of Directors to authorize the publication of a weekly Sabbath School paper, and also all other literature; as well as carry out the object of this Union.

4. It shall be the duty of every superintendent to collect from every pupil the sum of 5c. every two weeks, to be used in defraying the expenses of the Union publications. For this amount each pupil shall be entitled to a Bible, the Union's educational organ, and all such books as will be published under its auspices. Said books to be retained in the Sabbath school library, for the exclusive use of the pupils.

SECTION 2.

SABBATH SCHOOL PUBLICATIONS

6-9 yrs.	1. Primary reader series.
	2. Teachers' Text books for Primary Reader Series.
9 yrs.	3. Adam to Joseph................Pt. 1. of Jr. Bible Stories
10 yrs.	4. Life of Moses..................Pt. 2. of Jr. Bible Stories
11 yrs.	5. Joshua and Judges..............Pt. 3. of Jr. Bible Stories
12 yrs.	6. Saul to the Exiles...............Pt. 4. of Jr. Bible Stories
	7. Teachers' Text book for Saul to the Exile
9-12 yrs.	8. Moral and Religious Themes—Series A of Jr. Supplementary Work.
	9. Tales from the Midrash—Series B of Jr. Supplementary Work.
13 yrs.	10. Stories of the Prophets—A Special Study of the Prophetic Period.
	11. Loose Leaf Binder
	12. Bound volumes of Pictures used in Leaflets (a gift book)

SECTION 3.

CURRICULUM ADOPTED BY SABBATH SCHOOL UNION DURING THE CONVENTION 1886.

That the matter to be taught in Sabbath schools should embrace:

a. Instruction in the principles, doctrines and precepts of Judaism.
b. Reading of the Bible in the vernacular translation.
c. The Hebrew language at least to the extent of understanding Hebrew prayers, and appropriate portions of the Bible.
d. Jewish History covering Biblical and Post-biblical periods.
e. Music, with a view to prepare children to participate in services.

The course of instruction is to be five years, at least three hours a week. Sabbath schools shall also maintain a confirmation class, and a two years' course for post-confirmation classes.

STATISTICAL REPORT OF HEBREW SABBATH SCHOOLS

Proceedings, U. A. H. A. 1889 (p. 2503).

	New York City						Brooklyn
Name	Beth-El S.S.	Sch. Rel. Instruction	Rel. School	Mrs. Louis, D. T. S.S.	Sunday Sch.	H. F. S.	Beth Elohim
Congregation attached	Beth-El	Emanuel	Israel, Harlem	None	Ahavath Chesed	None	Temple Beth Elohim
Supt. or Princ.	Dr. K. Kohler	Gottheil Silverman	Harris	Mrs. M. D. Louis	A. Kohut & S. B. Hamburger	J. C. Noot H. Lustig Miss Hayes	Dr. L. Wintner
Children Enrolled:							
Total	320	279	400	225	445	2,191	129
Boys	176	145	...	...	201	1,028	57
Girls	144	134	...	...	244	1,163	72
Average Attendance	310	250	...	175	350	1,840	90
Number Classes	8	14	14	6	6	43	5
Number Teachers, Total	8	17	20	6	11	20	4
Paid	8	9	...	...	5	20	4
Volunteer	...	8	20	6	6	...	...
Weekly hours Instruction	4	3	4	3	4	5	3
Subjects taught	Heb. Bible; P. B. Hist., Religion	Heb. Bible; P. B. Hist.	Heb. Bible; P. B. Hist., Music	History, Religion	Heb. Bible; History Religion	Heb. Hist.. Religion	Heb. Hist., Catechism
Text Books used	Katzenberg's Primer B. H. Bible (Moses); Kohler's Chron. Tables Magnus, P. B. H. Man. of Religion	Katzenberg's DeSola's textbooks, Dr. Guthrie's Manual	Katzenberg's DeSola's textbooks, Magnus, K. History	Oral Instruction	Katzenberg's reader; Prayer Book; Deutsch, B. H.	Pentateuch Prayer Book; Katzenberg's & Mendes' Catechism	Katzenberg's Primer and History

APPENDIX E

EXTRACTS FROM CONSTITUTION OF THE MACHZIKE TALMUD TORAH—1885

225 East Broadway

ARTICLE I

NAME AND LANGUAGE

SEC. 1. This institution shall always bear the name of Machzike Talmud Torah School.

SEC. 2. All business and transactions at the meetings shall be conducted in the Jewish or in the English language.

SEC. 3. All books of this institution, and especially the minute-book, shall be kept in the Jewish language.

ARTICLE II

OBJECT

SEC. 1. The object of this School shall be to instruct poor Jewish children gratis in the Hebrew language and literature and to give them a religious education.

SEC. 2. The instruction shall be conducted on strictly orthodox principles.

ARTICLE III

INCOME

SEC. 1. The income of the M. T. T. School shall consist: firstly, of dues of members who will pay from $3.00 and upwards per year, or proportionally monthly. Secondly, of donations and charity boxes, as also of other income as the Board of Directors will decide upon.

ARTICLE IV

DUES OF MEMBERS AND THEIR RIGHTS

SEC. 1. Every person of the Jewish faith, man or woman can become a member of the M. T. T. School.

SEC. 2. Every member shall pay (as mentioned in Art. 3) not less than Three ($3) Dollars per year.

SEC. 3. Any person having in his or her house a Box of the M. T. T. School bringing in about $3 a year has the full rights of a regular member.

SEC. 4. Any person who gives the sum of $100 in one payment to the M. T. T. School shall remain a member of the same during his life time, even if he no longer pays his dues. Donators of the sum of $100 for sake that their name be engraved on the tablets in the hall of the M. T. T. School, have to pay their dues extra.

SEC. 5. Each member has the right to sign two (2) applications during the year, every one of which admits one scholar.

SEC. 6. Each member has the right to attend meetings and to submit his propositions for the good and welfare of the M. T. T. School, but has no right to vote for or against a motion except at the election of officers and directors, when every member is entitled to a vote.

SEC. 7. Every member can be elected director.

ARTICLE V

OFFICERS AND DIRECTORS

SEC. 1. The M. T. T. School shall be managed by thirty directors which number is never to be exceeded.

ARTICLE VII

NOMINATION AND ELECTION OF OFFICERS AND DIRECTORS

SEC. 1. At the first meeting in the month of Heshvon a committee of five directors shall be appointed to recommend new directors and at the second meeting of the same month, nominations for the following officers shall take place: President, Vice-Presidents, Treasurer, also nominations for new Directors.

SEC. 6. The 30 Directors shall be divided into three parts, namely: Ten for the term of 3 years, ten for 2 years and ten for 1 year. Those that will have the most votes shall be elected for 3 years, those that have less, shall be elected for 2 years, those that have less, shall be elected for 1 year. Entitled to the election for directorship are those directors that their time expired, and those that were proposed for directors at the election only on the previous year; and those that have the least of votes shall be accounted as Associated Directors.

ARTICLE XIII

DUTIES OF DIRECTORS

SEC. 5. If a Director has any objection to make against the management of the M. T. T. School, he shall by no means speak of this to any person who is not a director, but must declare his objection to the Directors at the meeting.

SEC. 6. If a Director has any objection to make concerning the order of instruction he shall bring it up before the Board of Education which Board shall pass upon it at its meeting. He must however not speak about this to the teacher at time of instruction.

ARTICLE XIV

COMMITTEE AND THEIR DUTIES

SEC. 1. At the first meeting after the election of officers, the President has to appoint out of the Directors the following standing (yearly) committees: *a.* A Finance Committee composed of five Directors; *b.* A committee of two Directors for each day in the week to visit the classes daily; *c.* A Board of Education of nine Directors; *d.* A Propaganda Committee of eleven Directors; *e.* A Committee of five Directors for admission of children; *f*. A Printing Committee of three Directors; *g*. A Repairing Committee of three Directors; *h*. A Committee of five Directors for wills and testaments.

SEC. 3. The Finance Committee shall have the supervision of all financial matters of the M. T. T. School and shall see that the same is in good order. It is the duty of this committee to examine four times a year the account books, also all receipts and accounts of the collectors, and they shall also see that at the election of officers a written report is brought by the Secretary of all the incomes and disbursements of the past year and that the same is read before the Directors and members.

SEC. 5. The Board of Education shall supervise over the order of instruction and shall make out in connection with the principal, the progress of all the classes, and they shall also see that the principal and all teachers fulfill their duties and orders given them by this committee. Furthermore every one of this committee shall visit the M. T. T. School during instruction at least once in every fourteen days.

SEC. 6. At the engagement of a teacher or of a principal, the Board of Education must examine same and in case he satisfactorily passes said examination, the Board of Education shall recommend him to the Directors, who shall decide whether he be accepted or not. At the engagement of a teacher or principal the Board of Education shall inform him in writing of his acceptation, his duties, etc.

SEC. 7. If the Board of Education finds that a teacher or the principal does not fulfill his duties or is no longer fit for his office, said Board shall report this at the next meeting of the Board of Directors, where a committee of five shall be appointed, who shall join the Board of Education and by common decision said teacher or principal shall be dismissed from his office. They must, however, give him one month's prolongation to enable him to find another position.

SEC. 8. The Board of Education cannot decide upon the salary of a teacher or principal. This has to be decided at a meeting of the Directors.

SEC. 10. The vote on motions made by the Board of Education requires a majority of the members present, excepting the vote on engagement of a teacher or principal when a two-thirds vote of the members present is required.

SEC. 11. The minority of the Board of Education cannot protest before the Directors against the decision of the majority.

SEC. 12. The Board of Education has the privilege to enlarge or to lessen the schedule of subjects of every class. It cannot, however, abolish any subject whatever of the programme of instruction. In such a case the Chairman of the Board must bring it before a meeting of the Board of Directors when a special meeting shall be called and the subject decided by a two-thirds vote.

SEC. 13. The Chairman and every member of the Board of Education must be present at every meeting called for improvement of the order of instruction, and assist at the annual and semi-annual examinations.

SEC. 14. The Board of Education shall consist of such members who were active directors for two years and who thoroughly understand the Hebrew language.

SEC. 15. The Board of Education must present at every meeting of the Directors a report about the order of instruction.

SEC. 16. The Committee on Repairing must attend to all repairings of the Talmud Torah School.

SEC. 19. The Propaganda Committee must think of and try to improve the Finances of the Talmud Torah School.

SEC. 20. Furthermore, this committee shall see that good solicitors and collectors be engaged to get new members for the Talmud Torah School and to collect all moneys for same.

SEC. 21. When this committee deems it necessary for the financial welfare of the Talmud Torah School that an extra meeting of the Directors be called, the chairman shall notify the President, who shall see that this request is granted.

SEC. 22. Furthermore, this committee shall endeavor to put charity boxes in all homes of our co-religionists in the City of New York and that Collectors be appointed who shall put on the boxes. The collection of the money from the boxes takes place every three months. The recompense of the collectors and other expenses must be decided at a meeting of the Board of Directors.

SEC. 24. The members of the Visiting Committee shall report of their daily visits in the classes at every meeting of the Directors.

SEC. 25. The Printing Committee shall attend to all printings necessary for the Talmud Torah School.

SEC. 27. The Committee for the Admission of Children must be present at the Talmud Torah School semi-annually, namely, in the intermediary days between the first and last days of the feasts of Passover and Tabernacles to assist the principal in admitting children for tuition and at the same time to investigate if the parents of said children are really poor.

SEC. 28. The Committee on Wills and Testaments must see that all testamentary donations to this school are punctually collected.

ARTICLE XVI

THE PRINCIPAL AND HIS DUTIES

SEC. 1. The Talmud Torah School shall have a principal who shall supervise the programme of instruction and everything concerning tuition.

SEC. 2. The principal must be thoroughly acquainted with the Hebrew Bible, grammar, language and shall also be fluent with the English language.

SEC. 3. The principal, at his engagement, must show satisfactory references.

SEC. 4. No person can be engaged as principal unless he has sufficient experience as a teacher of the Hebrew language.

SEC. 5. The principal must be orthodox in his beliefs.

SEC. 6. The principal shall see that the teachers abide strictly to their programmes, begin their sessions at the correct hour, the children shall not be absent too often and shall not be noisy during instruction.

SEC. 7. It is the duty of the principal to notify the parents of their boy's absence or of disorderly conduct.

SEC. 8. Furthermore, he shall, with assistance of the Board of Education arrange the course of instruction of all classes and hand them to their respective teachers.

SEC. 9. He shall also make the annual and semi-annual examinations and acquaint the Board of Education of the result of said examinations and also enter same in book.

SEC. 10. At every meeting of the Board of Education the principal shall report orally concerning the order of instruction and everything pertaining to tuition.

SEC. 11. The principal shall keep a record book of the number of scholars in which he shall also record the absence and tardiness of the same. He shall also record the time when scholars leave school or are expelled from same.

SEC. 12. Every six months the principal must submit a report of the number of the newly received scholars and also the number of scholars that left during these six months.

SEC. 13. If the Board of Education with the consent of the Directors finds it necessary that the principal shall also teach a class, the principal shall comply with this demand without extra compensation, besides this he must fulfill all other orders of the Board of Education which are for the welfare of the course of tuition.

SEC. 14. The principal shall be engaged for one year. Thirty days before the expiration of his year his salary for the ensuing year shall be determined by the officers and directors at a regular meeting. The directors shall be notified in writing that the salary of the principal will be decided on at this meeting.

ARTICLE XVII

TEACHERS AND THEIR DUTIES

SEC. 1. The teachers must have a thorough knowledge of the Hebrew language and be orthodox Jews.

SEC. 2. It is the duty of the teachers to instruct according to the programmes of the Board of Education and to complete the subject contained therein. Besides this, it is their duty to comply with all orders given them by the principal and by the Board of Education.

SEC. 3. Each teacher shall be in his classroom an hour before the beginning of the day's work.

SEC. 4. Every teacher must present a written weekly report to the principal of the conduct and attendance of his scholars and to send to the principal after tuition hours all disobedient scholars.

SEC. 5. If a teacher is absent from his class a certain amount shall be deducted from his salary, except in case of accident.

SEC. 6. When a teacher has an objection to make against the orders of the principal or of the Board of Education he shall bring this objection before said Board of Education but cannot bring it up at a meeting of the directors.

SEC. 7. Teachers are engaged for one month only.

ARTICLE XVIII

SCHOLARS

SEC. 1. A child can be admitted to school by having two members sign their names to the blank, certifying that said child's parents are really poor.

SEC. 2. A boy can attend school until the age of fifteen only.

SEC. 3. The pupil's class-term is one year, however, if he fails to complete the programme of his class during the year he shall remain another year in the same class. If he does not complete the programme in this year also, the Board of Education or the Principal shall then expel him from school.

SEC. 5. If a boy disobeys his teacher or is disorderly during the class session or is late or absent too often, and notwithstanding the principal punished him several times and notified his parents, he does not improve, the principal shall then expel him and notify his parents thereof.

SEC. 7. Children can be admitted to school twice a year, namely, in the intermediary days between the first and last days of the feasts of Passover and Tabernacles but in necessary cases the principal has the power to admit children at any other time than that above set forth.

ARTICLE XIX

SUBJECTS AND TIME OF INSTRUCTION

SEC. 1. The subjects of instruction are as follows:

a. Reading Hebrew, beginning from a, b, c, up to fluently reading in accordance with the rules of Hebrew grammar.

b. Holy Scriptures and Grammar.

c. Jewish penmanship.

d. Construction of Hebrew sentences.

e. Benedictions and prayers and translation of same.

f. Meanings of holidays.

g. Reading of the portion of the week, the Haphtora according to the accentual marks and notes, also the benedictions pertaining thereto.

h. Shulchan-Or\ch. Orach-Chayyim.

i. Creeds of the Jewish faith and Jewish history.

Sec. 2. If the Board of Education and the Directors find it necessary to teach Talmud also and they have the necessary means thereof, they may open classes for its instruction.

Sec. 3. The time of instruction of evening classes is from 4 o'clock p. m. sharp until 7 p. m., the Board of Education, however, has the power to prolong it to 8 p. m., but the teacher shall receive extra compensation, according to the decision of the directors. The evening classes shall not hold sessions on Friday.

Sec. 4. On Saturday the instruction for the evening classes shall be from 2 p. m. The morning classes shall not hold sessions on Saturday. (Morning classes are for children below public school ages).

Sec. 5. The morning classes shall hold sessions from 9 a. m. to 12 m.

Sec. 6. On days where there are no public school sessions the evening classes shall receive instruction in the morning, namely: from 9 a. m. to 12 m.

Sec. 7. There shall be no instruction on the following days: All holidays, such as Rosh Hashono, Passover, Shevuoth, Sukkoth, Purim and also all the fast days. The morning classes, however, shall receive instruction on fast days.

Sec. 8. During the public school vacations all classes shall receive instruction on Fridays instead of Saturdays.

ARTICLE XX

PROMOTION

Sec. 1. The promotion of the evening classes shall take place once a year: Sukkoth. The promotion of the morning classes shall take place twice a year.

Sec. 2. Every scholar who has completed the programme of his classes and thoroughly knows the subjects thereof shall be promoted to a higher class. If, however, a scholar has good abilities and is fit for the study of higher subjects than are taught in his class the principal can at any time promote him.

Sec. 3. Immediately after promotion, the principal shall post up in the classes the new programmes so that the teachers will be able to teach accordingly.

ARTICLE XXI

MINION IN THE M. T. T. SCHOOL BUILDING

Sec. 1. There shall always be a minion (quorum of worshippers) in the M. T. T. Building to pray on all Saturdays and holidays.

Sec. 3. The income of the Minion, such as from Alioth, Nedorim, etc., and from seats sold for the Yomim-Neroim, shall be delivered in full by the Gabbai to the Treasurer of the M. T. T. School.

Sec. 7. If a scholar reaches his thirteenth year and his parents desire that his Bar Mitzvah festival be celebrated in the M. T. T. School, their desire shall be fulfilled. The Maftir shall then belong to this boy and cannot be given to any director even if it be Yahr-zeit of the death of his parents.

Sec. 8. The rites of the Minion shall be strictly Orthodox.

ARTICLE XXII.

THE JANITOR AND HIS DUTIES

Sec. 6. The janitor shall stand in the hall at the time of entrance and exit of children and see that everything is in order. He shall also keep them in order during recess. Furthermore, he shall attend to all orders given him by the officers and directors, for the welfare of the M. T. T.

ARTICLE XXIII.

BENEFITS OF OFFICERS, DIRECTORS AND MEMBERS

Sec. 1. If an officer or director falls sick a committee of directors shall be appointed the members of which shall take turns in daily visiting him.

Sec. 2. If the sickness be serious the scholars of all the classes shall read the psalms and pray for him.

Sec. 3. If an officer or director dies, a special meeting shall immediately be called to arrange matters regarding the attendance of directors at the ablution of the body and funeral procession. Thirty children under the guidance of a teacher shall also be sent to the house of the deceased for the purpose of reading the Psalms at the ablution of the body and to accompany the funeral. At the death of the director's wife, twenty children shall be sent for the above purposes.

Sec. 4. The M. T. T. School shall furnish two carriages in which the committee shall accompany the funeral to the cemetery in order to give the deceased his last honors.

Sec. 5. In the Shivah a committee of directors shall be appointed, the members of which shall take turns to console the bereaved family.

Sec. 6. During the year of mourning a director shall say Kaddish every Saturday at the minion in the M. T. T. School. Also on the Saturday preceding Yahrzeit, Hazkorath N'Shomoth shall be read for the repose of the soul of deceased.

Sec. 7. Evening, morning and afternoon services shall be held in the M. T. T. School by a quorum of directors on the day of Yahrzeit. Directors shall be reminded in writing by the Secretary of the day of Yahrzeit.

Sec. 8. If a member of the M. T. T. is sick and desires the scholars of the school to read the Psalms for his sake, his wish shall be fulfilled.

Sec. 9. If a member dies and bequeaths the M. T. T. School $100 to $500 and his family desires the pupils of the school to go to the funeral, 25 children shall be sent. If, however, he bequeaths a sum of $500 to $1000 then shall 50 pupils be sent to the funeral. The directors, must, however, be positive that the money is collectible.

APPENDIX F

PART I—EXTRACTS FROM CONSTITUTION OF THE MACHZIKE YESHIBATH ETZ CHAIM

ARTICLE I

NAME AND LANGUAGE

Sec. 1. This Academy shall always bear the name of Machzeki Jeshibath Etz Chaiem.

Sec. 2. All business and transactions shall be made in the Jewish language, especially the Minute Book which shall be in the Hebrew Language (Loshon Hakodosh).

ARTICLE II

Sec. 1. The purpose of this Academy shall be to give free instruction to poor Hebrew Children in the Hebrew language and the Jewish religion—Talmud, Bible, and Shulchan Aruch during the whole day from nine in morning until four in the afternoon.

Also from four in the afternoon, two hours shall be devoted to teach the native language, English, and one hour to teach Hebrew—Loshon Hakodosh, and Jargon to read and write.

Sec. 2. This Academy shall be guided according to the strict Orthodox and Talmudical Law and the custom of Poland and Russia.

ARTICLE III

MEMBERSHIP

Sec. 1. Every Hebrew can become a member of this Academy.

Sec. 2. The dues shall be from three dollars a year and upwards.

Sec. 3. When a member gives to this Academy a hundred dollars at one time, he remains a member during his whole life time.

ARTICLE IV

OFFICERS

Sec. 2. The ten Directors shall be divided into the following committees:—

One committee consisting of four Directors, named Trustees, whose duty it is to superintend the house and money affairs, such as to repaint the house when it is necessary, to make programmes, to appoint Hebrew and English teachers, to buy books and everything which belongs to it, according to the income of the time.

Sec. 3. Another Committee consisting of six members who shall be called Leaders—Mnahalim, shall superintend the course of study in Talmud, Bible and Shulchan Aruch to appoint Hebrew teachers, and also in a position to discharge a Hebrew teacher, if they have sufficient reason for it.

ARTICLE VIII

COLLECTOR

SEC. 1. The Academy shall have a Collector, and give him such a percent of the sum collected as the President and Trustees will decide.

SEC. 2. Every week he shall remit the money collected to the Secretary.

ARTICLE XII

TEACHERS

SEC. 1. It is the duty of the Teachers to teach according to the programme of the Board of Leaders.

SEC. 2. They must be found in the Academy every day in the week in the right time according to the Programme of the Board of Leaders.

ARTICLE XIII

EXAMINATIONS

SEC. 1. The principal examination shall take place on the fifteenth day of Shebat and on the fifteenth day of Ab.

SEC. 2. Ordinary examinations shall be made by the Leaders from time to time according to their opinion.

SEC. 3. Excepting the Leaders and the Officers of the Academy, no one has the right to come in the Academy and examine the children, without the permission of the Superintendent of the Academy.

ARTICLE XIV

BENEFIT

SEC. 1. When an officer becomes sick and this is reported to the Secretary, a Director shall visit him daily.

SEC. 2. When a Director dies, the Secretary shall send notice to all the Officers that they shall pay the last honor to the deceased.

SEC. 3. The Academy shall send a carriage and also a committee of four, to the cemetery.

SEC. 4. Ten children from every class shall attend the funeral and say Psalm.

SEC. 5. When anyone was a Director or any other officer during the three years following the establishment of the Academy, he shall be entitled to all this during his whole life, provided that he obeys the Jewish Law and is interested in the benefit of the Academy.

SEC. 6. The Directors shall assemble in the Academy every morning and evening of the seven days of mourning to pray jointly. Also a chapter of Mishna shall be learned every day, together with the prayer beginning with "Anna" and "Kadish" for the rising of his soul.

SEC. 7. "Hazkoras Nshomos" הזכרת נשמות shall be made every Saturday and Holiday of the first year.

SEC. 8. The same shall be made every "Jahrzeit" day as long as the Academy exists.

SEC. 9. If any man not an officer of the Academy, should have given a Hundred dollars at one time to the Academy, "Hazkoras Nshamos" shall be made every Saturday and Holiday of the first year of his death.

SEC. 10. When any one gave $500 at one time or left that sum to the Academy, "Hazkoras Nshamos" shall be made during the first year, and a "Neir Nishmas" (Candle for his soul), shall be lighted on the "Jahrzeit Day" during the first ten years.

SEC. 11. When any man left $1,000, "Hazkoras Nshamos" shall be made during the first year, and the twenty years following his death, a candle shall be lighted on the "Jahrzeit" day.

SEC. 12. When any man gives more than a $1,000, then all the above things shall be made as long as the Academy exists, the "Jahrzeit" shall be held and a chapter "Mishna" shall be learned on that day.

SEC. 13. When such donations are given to the Academy, the names of the donators shall be inscribed on a tablet of the Academy, to be remembered forever.

PART II

EXTRACTS FROM MINUTES OF MACHZIKE JESHIBATH ETZ CHAIM

קבלו עליהם הוועד הנ"ל באלה ובשבועה שתתקיים לדורות הבאים ולא ישנה אשר כל מנהגי הישיבה תתנהגו (sic) רק על פי כל מנהגי פולין ורוסלאנד כאשר נהגו אבותינו ואבות אבותינו, ואם ח"ו יציע אחד מאנשי הוועד דבר או איזה ענין אשר ימצא בדבריו איזה תרעובות או שמץ מנהו שינוי או תמורה או חליפין אף מנהג קל וקטן ממנהגי פולין הן בשם הן במעשה ואף אם הדבר יוצע ונתיישר בעיני רבים דהוועד מסכימים אנו אנשי הוועד ומקבלים עלינו אשר אחד מהוועד קטן או גדול דל או עשיר יוכל לעכב על זה ועל זה נאמר לא תה' אחרי הרבים לרעות וכו'.... גם קבלו עליהם אנשי הוועד הנ"ל אשר גבאים ומנהלים, ומשגיחים ומלמדים, ונאמנים, יקובלו רק אנשים כשרים ונאמנים יראי ה' לומדי תורה אנשי מעשה אנשים אשר מעולם לא יצא עליהם שם רע בין אדם למקום הן בין אדם לחבירו הן אם הקילו אפילו בדבר קטן מן הקטנים מכל המצות מכל אשר נצטוינו בתורתנו הקדושה הן בכתב והן בע"פ והן אם הקיל אפילו ממנהג קל אשר נהגו אבותינו בכ"ו ופ' אין לו זכות לבוא ולשרת בקודש להיות גבאי או מנהל או משגיח או מלמד או נאמן בהישיבה ואם אחר התמנותו ופקודתו של הגבאי או המנהל או המשגיח או המלמד או הנאמן המצא תמצא בו איזה שמץ דופי אשר עבר על איזה דין תורה על איזה מנהג הנזכר לעיל אזי מחוייבים אנשי הוועד לשאול

את פיו ואם אמת הדבר ואם יתוודע על זה ואם יקבל על עצמו אשר
בל ישוב לכסלה עוד ואם יתן המתלא נכונה על הדבר הזה שהי' אנוס
או איזה סיבה ח"ו גרם לו לעשות כזה ישאר על משמרתו ופקודתו
ואם שתי אלה לא יעשה לו ויצא ממשמרתו ופקודתו כי את קדש ה'
חלל ואין לו זכות לעולם לבוא בקודש—

ואמרת להזהיר גדולים על הקטנים שיתקיימו כל דבר הנ"ל שנת
תרמ"ז אור ליום ב' פרשה אמור פה ניוארק בבית הישיבה 47 איסט
בראדווייא.

The Board decided, by oath and by everlasting pledge, which shall not be altered, that all the directors of the Yeshibah shall conduct themselves, only according to the customs of Poland and Russia, in accordance with the customs of our fathers and our forefathers. And if, God forbid, any one of the directors shall suggest any matter or any subject which shall contain an admixture or inkling of any change or alteration or deviation, even from the smallest and least of the customs of Poland, either nominal or actual, even if the matter which is thus proposed, shall be considered right by the majority of the Board, we, the Board of Directors, hereby agree and accept upon us, that even one member of the Board, whether he be small or great, poor or rich, may prevent such action. Therefore is it written: ''Go not after the many to commit evil, etc.''........ The Board has also decided that as directors and principals and inspectors and teachers and officials, only pious, faithful, God-fearing men, men who are versed in the Torah, and who are observant, men who never had a bad reputation, either in their relations between man and God, or between man and man, even if they had slighted the smallest of all the Commandments, which were commanded to us by our Holy Torah, either in written or oral tradition. If any one slighted the smallest of the customs of our forefathers, etc., he has no right to serve in holy things, to be director, or principal, or inspector, or teacher, or official, in this Yeshibah. And if after the appointment of the director or principal, or inspector or official, there should be found against him the slightest suspicion that he had transgressed upon any law of the Torah, or upon any of the above mentioned customs, then this Board of Directors is in duty bound to question him as to the truth of the matter, and if he shall admit this or shall take upon himself that he shall not again return to folly, or if he should give a sufficient excuse for the matter, that he was compelled, or because some misfortune, God forbid, caused him to act thus, he may remain in his position. But if he should do neither of those two things, then he shall go forth from his position, for he has desecrated the holy things of the Lord, and he has no permission at any time to deal with holy things. And thou shalt warn both great and small that they shall keep the above resolution.

Here in New York, at the House of the Yeshibah, 47 East Broadway, 1908; the second day of the Parsha Emor.

APPENDIX G

CIRCULAR (ca. 1899) of the SHAAREI ZION SCHOOL
The First National Hebrew School in New York

דער וויכטיגסטער אידישער אינסטיטוט היער איז די מוסטער־שולע
פיר די בעסערע יוגענד

„שערי ציון"

וועלכע פראגרעסירט דאָס 6טע יאָהר, און בעשטעהט פון:

1. עלעמענטאַר־שולע (אָנפאַנגס־שולע): א"ב, עברי ע"פ דקדוק, אָנפאַנג חומש.— פון 9 אוהר מאָרגענס ביז 3 (4) נאכמיטאגס.

2. א מיטטעל־שולע: תורה ונביאים ראשונים (התחלת נביאים אחרונים).— פון 3 (4) ביז 7 אוהר.

3. א האָך־שולע (ישיבה): תנ"ך, גמרא, יודישע היסטריע.—פון 4 ביז 7 (8) אוהר.

אויסערדעם אין דער מאָרגען־שולע אויך: ענגליש און רעכנען; אין די אבענד־שולע: דייטש (און יידיש שרייבען), דקדוק, נגינת הטעמים, רש"י צו חומש, ש"ע און נאָך אַנדערעס. אַלעס נאָך דען בעסטען מעטהאָדען — מייסטענס אָריגינאַל.

העברעאיש אין אַלע קלאַססען אַלס א לעבעדיגע שפּראַך: שרייבען און שפּרעכען. 6-7 יעהריגע קינדער שרייבען און שפּרעכען העברעאיש צום בע־וואונדערען.

די שולע האָט אויך א פיינעם לעזע־ביבליאָטהעק פון די בעסטע העברעאישע יוגענד־ביכער, דורך וועלכע די קינדער היער ענטוויקלען זיך אין העברעאיש זעהר שנעל, הויפּטזעכליך ווערען די קינדער היער ענטוויקעלט און ערצויגען, בעזאָנדערע בעאָבאַכטונג אויף זיטטע און זויבערקייט. אם בעסטען ווערען היער קליינע קינדער, אָנפאַנגער גענומען — בעפאָר זיי ווערען פערנאַכלעסיגט, פאַרגרעבט און פאַרדאָרבען.

איינע טעכטער־שולע

פיר העברעאיש (אויך חומש), יידיש און דייטש.—אבענדס צווישען 5 און 7 אוהר.

די גרעסטע מענער: רבנים, גדולים, חכמים, געלעהרטע, פּעדאַגאָגען, האָבען די שולע בעזוכט און זי אַנערקענט אַלס די בעסטע אין גאַנץ אַמעריקאַ.

די עפענטליכע עקזאַמינייישאָנס וועלען פון יעצט אָן געהאַלטען ווערען יעדען חוה"מ פסח און חוה"מ סכות. (דאָס בעסטע קינד פון יעדער קלאַסע בעקומט איין זילבערנעם מעדאַל, און פון דער העכסטען—גמרא—קלאַסע, איין גאָלדענעם מעדאַל.

אַכטונגספאָלל,

ז. ה. נ י י מ א ן,

40 לעאָנאַרד סט., צווישען מק־קיבבען און סיגעל סטס.

APPENDIX H

EXTRACT FROM ACT OF INCORPORATION

Jewish Community (Kehillah) New York

"The objects of said corporation shall be, to stimulate and encourage the instruction of the Jews residing in the City of New York, in the tenets of their religion and in their history, language, literature, institutions and traditions of their people; to conduct, support and maintain schools and classes for that purpose; to publish and distribute text books, maps, charts and illustrations to facilitate such instruction; to conduct lectures and classes in civics and other kindred subjects; to establish an educational bureau to further the foregoing purpose......" (January, 1913).

APPENDIX I

COMPARATIVE SIZE OF POPULATION OF NEW YORK CITY

A. *New York*..1,500,000

B. *Countries of Western Europe and Palestine.*

Total 1,251,933

Germany	615,021
Great Britain	245,000
Holland	106,309
France	100,000
Palestine	100,000
Italy	43,929
Switzerland	19,023
Belgium	15,000
Scandinavian countries	10,000
Spain and Portugal	4,481
Luxemburg	1,270

(Cf. Am. Jewish Year Book, 1915-16, pages 343-344)

C. *Largest Jewish Cities in the World* (Cf. with New York)

Warsaw	298,137
Budapest	203,687
Chicago	200,000
Vienna	175,318
London	160,000
Lodz	150,000
Berlin	142,289
Odessa	138,035
Jerusalem	48,400

(Cf. Anglo-Jewish Year Book, 1917; pp. 173-175.)

APPENDIX J

ESTIMATES OF JEWISH POPULATION (1790-1917)*

YEAR	UNITED STATES	NEW YORK	AUTHORITY
1790	1,243	385 (state)	United States Census Bureau
1812	——	400	Rev. Gershom Mendes, quoted in "History of Jews," 1812; Hannah Adams
1818	3,000	——	Mordecai M. Noah
1824	6,000	——	Solomon Etting
1826	6,000	——	Isaac C. Harby
July 1826	No more than 6,000	950 (state)	S. Gilmen, Article in North American Review
1840	15,000	——	American Almanac
1846	——	10,000	Rev. Isaac Leeser
1848	50,000	12,000 to 13,000 (city)	M. A. Berk, "History of the Jews up to the Present Time"
1877	189,576	——	Census of Board of Delegates of American Israelites, and Union of Hebrew Congregations; William B. Hackenberg, of Philadelphia, in charge.
1880	230,257	60,000	" "
1888	400,000	125,000	Isaac Markens, "The Hebrews in America"
1891	——	225,250	Chas. Frank, Secretary, U. H. C.
Jan. 1892	——	East of Bowery and South of 14th St., 135,000; scattered through the city 40,000 more.	Richard Wheatley, Article on "Jews in New York," Century Magazine.
Feb. 1897	——	250,000	Richard Wheatley in Harper's Magazine
Apr. 9, 1897	——	350,000	Jacob H. Schiff, Address before Anglo Jewish Ass'n in London
1897	937,800	350,000 (state)	David Sulzberger, in American Jewish Historical Society.
1905	1,508,435	672,000	Joseph Jacobs
1907	1,777,185	600,000	Henrietta Szold, American Jewish Year Book
1910	2,043,762	——	American Jewish Year Book, 1910
1910	2,349,754	——	Joseph Jacobs, 1914 Year Book
1910	——	861,980	United States Census Bureau: Yiddish speaking only
1911	——	900,000	Joseph Jacobs, Jewish Communal Directory, 1912
1912	——	975,000	Joseph Jacobs, American Jewish Year Book, 1914-1915
1912	——	1,550,000	Walter Laidlaw, Census of Federation of Churches
July 1913	——	1,330,000	American Journal of Statistics, July, 1913, "Jews in New York City," Prof. Chalmers of Cornell.
1917	——	1,500,000	Jewish Communal Register, New York, 1918, pp. 75-89, "The Jewish Population of New York," by Alexander M. Dushkin.

* The estimates, unless otherwise stated, were obtained from the following sources: American Jewish Hist. Soc., 6:141 and 19:178; Jewish Encyclopedia, Vol. 12; American Jewish Year Book, 1914-1915; American Journal of Statistics, July, 1913.

APPENDIX K

PERCENT. OF SCHOOL CHILDREN HAVING FATHERS OF DESIGNATED RACES—New York City 1910

Race of Father	Manhattan	Brooklyn	Bronx	Queens	Richmond
American White	17.9	31.9	35.3	44.8	48.1
American Negro	1.4	1.0	.7	1.1	1.4
Armenian	.1	—	—	—	—
Bohemian	1.6	.1	.7	1.6	—
Canadian French	.1	.1	—	—	—
Canadian Other	.3	.5	.6	.4	—
Danish	.2	.4	.4	.5	—
Dutch	.1	.2	.2	.3	—
English	1.6	2.6	2.8	3.5	3.9
French	.6	.5	.7	1.0	.8
Finnish	.1	.2	—	—	—
German	8.6	11.4	17.9	25.5	15.5
Greek	.1	—	—	—	—
Hebrew, German	4.8	3.1	4.5	1.2	1.0
Hebrew, Polish	4.7	1.7	1.3	.3	—
Hebrew, Roumanian	2.5	1.6	.9	—	—
Hebrew, Russian	24.3	19.7	10.7	1.4	1.8
Hebrew, Other	9.8	3.8	2.8	.6	—
Irish	5.3	4.5	6.8	6.0	5.9
Italian, North	3.5	2.9	2.7	2.2	3.0
Italian, South	8.8	6.9	5.1	4.4	6.3
Magyar	.8	.3	.5	—	—
Norwegian	.2	1.5	.4	.4	2.5
Polish	.2	.6	.4	1.6	1.3
Roumanian	.1	.1	—	—	—
Russian	.3	.4	.5	.3	—
Scotch	.6	.9	1.2	1.4	1.4
Slovak	.1	.1	—	—	—
Spanish American	.2	.2	—	—	—
Swedish	.6	1.9	1.5	1.0	1.7
Syrian	.1	.1	—	—	—
Welsh	.1	.1	—	—	—
West Indian Negro	.1	—	—	—	—
Lithuanian	—	.1	—	—	—
Spanish	—	.1	—	—	—
Other Races	.3	.4	1.4	1.5	5.5
TOTAL	100.	100.	100.	100.	100.
TOTAL HEBREW	46.1	29.9	20.2	3.5	2.8

APPENDIX L

(Set A—Personal Survey)

SECRETARY'S QUESTIONNAIRE: A.

Name of School..
Address..................................Tel. No..............
President..............Address ....Secretary ....

I. BUILDING AND SITE:

Size of Lot (in feet)...
Size of Bldg.: Frontage........depth........height (floors)........
Assessed Value of Building and Site...............................
Amount of Mortgage: 1st..............interest rate..............
2nd.............. " " ....
Material of Construction: stone.....brick.....cement.....wood.....
Date when built..

II. ACCOMMODATION AND EQUIPMENT:

Number of rooms...........seating capacity of auditorium.........
Size of playground......outdoor......indoor......roof garden......
Size of gymnasium..............use made of gym.................
....
Is building: Fire-proof...............partly fire-proof............
not fire-proof..............
Who are the underwriters.......................................

III. TUITION FEES:

No. pupils on register.......on date of........How many pay......
Range of tuition fees: per week...........per month...........
Are records kept of individual payments.......................
....

IV. STAFF:

No. men teachers.................salary distribution*.............
....
....
No. women teachers.............salary distribution*.............
....
....
No. clerks in secretary's office................................
Salary of: principal ....secretary...............
" " rabbi ....shammas ....
" " cantor and choir.............other officers (not janitors)
....

* State whether per week or per month.

(Set A—Personal Survey)

SECRETARY'S QUESTIONNAIRE: B.

V. Finances:

Expenditure:
Total annual expenditure..................Year ending...........
Mortgage: annual amortization.............Interest...............
Interest on loans.........................Insurance..............
Heat..........light..........repairs and improvements............
Telephone..............furniture and school apparatus..............
Books..................school supplies ....
Postage, stationery and printing.............advertising............
Salaries of teachers............of principal and his staff...........
Salaries of secretary and his staff.........of janitorial staff.........
Salary of superintendent..
Salaries of other officers: specify.................................
....
Cost of collection of: tuition fees........synagogue donations.......
membership dues ....total...........
Cost of Canvassing for: membership.........pupils........total........
" " regulating attendance (attendance officers)....................
Miscellaneous: total ....
(Specify main items)...
....

Income:

From school: tuition fees............endowment funds.............
From synagogue: seat sales.........donations (synagogue).........
Rent for weddings...
Miscellaneous ....
From building: rent of rooms for meetings.......................
Rent of auditorium for meetings, etc..........................
From education fund...
From membership: total..
From less than $5.00 members............................
From $5.00 to $10.00 members............................
From over $10.00 members...............................
From balls ....
" banquets ....
" theatres ....
" raffles ....
....
....
From general donations..
Donations to building fund...

(Set A—Personal Survey)

PRINCIPAL'S QUESTIONNAIRE: A.

Name of school..
Principal ....

I. PUPILS:

Number of boys..........Number of girls..........Total..........
Average daily attendance..
No. of pupils: under 9 yrs. age.......9-13 yrs......over 13 yrs......
Number of clerks in principal's office.............................

II. MANAGEMENT:

Method of collecting tuition fees: frequency.......................
Place ....
Where is bulk collected...
Methods of following up pupils who leave school..................
....
Methods of Dealing with Absentees................................
....
Methods of dealing with tardy pupils..............................
Does principal have definite system for visiting classes..............
Describe ....
....
Are teachers' conferences held...........How frequently..........
Of what nature..
Does principal help teachers: through demonstration lessons..........
" personal criticism.............
" other means: describe..........
....
Are records kept: Pupils' record cards...........................
Class roll book................................
Pupils' monthly reports.........................
Inventory of supplies...........................

III. GRADING:

Length of full course in years.........No. grades per year.........
Actual number of grades in school........on date...............
Number of classes in 1st year.......2nd.......3rd.......4th.......
5th.......6th.......7th.......8th.......9th.......10th.......
Hours of instruction: Weekdays, from..............to............
Saturdays, from..............to............
Sundays, from...............to............
No. of shifts on weekdays......on Saturdays......on Sundays......
No. of hours each class is taught during week......................
No. days per week pupils attend...................................

(Set B—Questionnaire Survey)

PRINCIPAL'S QUESTIONNAIRE: B.

IV. SCHEDULE OF STUDIES:
No. of periods of instruction for entire course................
Length of each period..
No. of periods devoted to:

A. Hebrew: Total..
Mechanics of Hebrew reading (siddur or reader)................
Appreciation of Hebrew reading (Hebrew reader)...............
Grammar ....Conversation ....Writing ....

B. Bible: Total..
Torah..............................Early Prophets ....
Latter prophets and hagiographa...........................

C. Prayer Book: Total......................................
Order of prayers...
Prayers (translation and explanation).......................
Prayers (memorization: Blessings and special prayers)..........

D. Ceremonies: Total.......................................
Oral explanation.................Shulchan Aruch............

E. History: Total..
Biblical ....Post-Biblical ....

F. Talmud: Total..
Agadah ....Halacha ....

G. Post-Talmudic Lit.: Total...............................
Mediaeval ....modern ....

H. Music: Total...
Haftorah and Sedra............synagogue responses...........
Holiday and folk songs.....................................

I. Yiddish ....

V. EXTRA-CURRICULAR ACTIVITIES:
Is there a children's synagogue—On sabbaths............ ....
On holidays...................on week days.................
Are there children's clubs....................................
How many...................of what nature................
Are parents' meetings held....................................
How often...................of what nature................

VI. GENERAL REMARKS:
....
....
....
....
....
....
....

(Set A—Personal Survey)

OBSERVATION QUESTIONNAIRE

A. For Building

Name of school..

I. ACCOMMODATION AND EQUIPMENT:

Condition of building: Appearance..............................
Repairs ....
How many entrances..............How many stairways.............
How many fire escapes............Where situated.................
Sanitary condition of Walls.....................................
Floors ....
Stairways ....
Windows ....
Desks and seats............................
How many toilets: Boys: No. urinals....No. seats...Girls: No. seats...
Where situated ....
Are there drinking fountains.............Where situated...........
If not, what drinking water accommodation: Faucet....Common cup...
Is there special fire apparatus..............What kind.............
Where placed ....
Is there special office for principal................Size.............
Is there special office for secretary................Size.............
Is there a children's library or reading room........Size.............
Is there a teachers' rest room.....................................
Is there a telephone in secretary's office..........................
" " " " " principal's office..........................
" " " " " other rooms..................................
Is there a gong system.........Are there clocks and gongs..........
electrically regulated ....

GENERAL REMARKS:

....
....
....
....
....

(Set A—Personal Survey)

OBSERVATION QUESTIONNAIRE

B. For Classrooms (not in session)

SCHOOL:

Room number..........Situation: floor..........Facing..........
Size of room................Number of partitions................
Light: number of windows..........Size (approximate)............
Kind of artificial light..
Kind of heating system: steam heat......Heated air......Stove......
Ventilation through: windows........Special system........Kind of system ....
Desks and seats: number..........To seat..........Pupils.........
Kind: desks and seats........Armchairs........Chairs........
Benches ....Adjustable ....Movable ....
Condition ....
Is there a teacher's desk..
" " " blackboard ....Condition ....
" " " cloakroom or wardrobe......Where situated.............
....
....
Are there decorations: pictures.................Plants.............
Maps ....Other.............
Condition of books and school supplies..........................
....

C. For Classrooms (in session)

School.......................Room number......................
Light: sufficiency of natural light..............................
" " artificial light ....
Condition of air in room: fresh.............Stagnant.............
Dusty..........Cold ....Warm ....Heavy ....
Is there sufficient clothing accommodation........................
If not, what disposition is made of clothing......................
....
General decorum..
....
....
Entrance and dismissals: order...............Quiet...............
Speed....................Supervision by......................
General remarks ....
....
....
....
....
....

(Set B—Questionnaire Survey)

I.

Name of synagogue or school..

Address ....

Type of school (please indicate by checking)

Sunday school Sabbath school Weekday school

Name of rabbi.........................Address...................

Name of principal.......................Address...................

No. of pupils: Total............Boys............Girls..............

No. of classes...................No. rooms used......................

Location of rooms: Vestry......Adjoining building......Elsewhere......

Days and hours school is taught:

On..........from......to...... On...........from.....to.....

On..........from......to...... On...........from.....to.....

On..........from......to...... On...........from.....to.....

No. of hours of instruction per week given to each class.................

No. of teachers: Men...................Women...................

Management of school by: Rabbi..........School committee...........

Special principal....................Head teacher................

(If by several, please indicate. If special principal, please also state salary: $.............).

Please list the number and kinds of activities carried on in your school, outside of the regular classroom instruction (clubs, auxiliaries, festivities, parents' associations, etc.

....

....

....

....

....

....

....

Do pupils pay tuition fees...

If so; how much: Weekly........Monthly........Annually........

How is it collected, where and by whom.....................

....

What is the average sum collected monthly (approximately)............

How much money does your school spend yearly.......................

Remarks ....

....

....

....

(Set B—Questionnaire Survey)

II.

School ....

COURSE OF STUDY

Subject	No. of Weeks	No. Hours per Week	Text Books Used
	First Year		
	Second Year		
	Third Year		
	Fourth Year		
	Fifth Year		
	Sixth Year		

(Set B—Questionnaire Survey)

TEACHER'S QUESTIONNAIRE

No...............

Sex..................Age ....Salary ....

No. classes teaching............No. hours teaching per week............

SECULAR TRAINING:

School	Years in Attendance	Degree or Diploma
....	....	....
....	....	....
....	....	....
....	....	....
....	....	....

JEWISH TRAINING:

Place or School	Years
....	....
....	....
....	....
....	....
....	....

PEDAGOGIC TRAINING (Course in Pedagogy):

School	Years
....	....
....	....
....	....
....	....
....	....

PEDAGOGIC EXPERIENCE (No. Years Teaching):

Where	Years	Principal or Superintendent in Charge
....	....	....
....	....	....
....	....	....
....	....	....
....	....	....

OTHER OCCUPATIONS BESIDES JEWISH TEACHING:

Remunerative	Voluntary
....	....
....	....
....	....
....	....
....	....

APPENDIX M

JEWISH SCHOOLS IN NEW YORK CITY

Surveyed January-August, 1917

No.	Name	Address	District	Enrollment	Type
1.	Adath Israel Congregation Religious School	551 E. 169th St.	25	185	Congregational Week-day and Sunday School
2.	Adath Israel Temple Religious School	West Fifth St., Coney Island	38	60	Congregational Sunday School
3.	Khal Adath Jeshurun Talmud Torah	1275 Hoe Ave., Bx.	25	115	Congregational Week-day School
4.	Adereth-El Talmud Torah	135 E. 29th St.	12	110	Congregational Week-day School
5.	Agudath Jeshurun Congregation Religious School	113 E. 86th St.	16	85	Congregational Sunday School
6.	Ahavath Chesed Shaar Hashomayim Religious School	55th St. & Lexington Ave.	12	160	Congregational Sunday School
7.	Ahavath Sholom Temple Sunday School	710-712 Quincy St.	32	101	Congregational Sunday School
8.	Ahavath Achim Congregation Sunday School	Ave. R & 16th St., B'klyn	38	100	Congregational Sunday School
9.	Ahavath Israel Congregation Ridgewood T. T.	1372-4 Gates Ave., B'klyn	35	60	Congregational Week-day School
10.	Albert Lucas Sunday School	13-15 Pike St.	2	350	Congregational Sunday School
11.	Ansche Chesed Congregation Hebrew School	1881 Seventh Avenue	19	300	Congregational Week-day School
12.	Ansche Emeth Mt. Sinai Cong. Sunday School	St. Nicholas Ave. & 181st St.	22	55	Congregational Sunday School
13.	Ansche Polen Talmud Torah	169 Suffolk St.	5	100	Communal Week-day School
14.	Ansche Zedek Cong. Talmud Torah	1760 Park Pl., B'klyn	36	240	Congregational Week-day School
15.	Ansche Zitomerer Talmud Torah	337 E. 4th St.	7	585	Communal Week-day School
16.	Atereth Israel Talmud Torah	115 Fountain Ave., B'klyn	40	90	Communal Week-day School
17.	Atereth Israel Cong. Hebrew School	323 E. 82d St.	75	75	Congregational Week-day School
18.	Atereth Tifereth Israel Talmud Torah	479-81 Ashford St., B'klyn	40	150	Communal Week-day School
19.	Augustower Talmud Torah	122 W. 129th St.	21	75	Congregational Week-day School
20.	Austrian Talmudical School	42 Morrel Street	33	175	Communal Week-day School

JEWISH SCHOOLS IN NEW YORK CITY (Continued)

No.	Name	Address	District	Enrollment	Type
21.	Beth Abraham Cong. T. T. and Sunday School	535 East 146th St.	23	400	Congregational Week-day and Sunday School
22.	Beth-El Congregation Sunday School	5th Ave. & 76th St.	13	153	Congregational Sunday School
23.	Beth-El Congregation Religious School	110 Noble Street, Greenpoint	34	150	Congregational Week-day and Sunday School
24.	Beth Elohim Congregation Sunday School	274 Keap Street	31	172	Congregational Sunday School
25.	Beth Elohim Temple Religious School	961 So. Blvd	23	150	Congregational Week-day and Sunday School
26.	Beth Elohim Cong. Sunday School	8th Ave. & Garfield Pl.	30	305	Congregational Sunday School
27.	Beth Emeth Cong. Hebrew School	Church Ave. & Marlboro Road	38	217	Congregational Week-day School
28.	Beth Hamidrosh Hagodol Talmud Torah	829 Forest Ave., Bx.	24	130	Congregational Week-day School
29.	Beth Israel Ansche Emeth Cong. Talmud Torah	236 Harrison St., B'klyn.	28	400	Congregational Week-day and Sunday School
30.	Beth Israel Ansche Galizia and Bukovien Talmud Torah	3886 Park Ave.	25	150	Congregational Week-day School
31.	Beth Israel Bikur Cholim Cong. Religious School	72d St. & Lexington Ave.	13	280	Congregational Week-day and Sunday School
32.	Beth Sefer Ivry	216 Sumner Ave.	32	100	Private Week-day School
33.	Beth Sefer Ivry	91 Seigel St., B'klyn.	33	190	Private Week-day School
34.	Beth Sefer Ivry Hatcheyo	417 New Jersey Ave.	40	115	Private Week-day School
35.	Beth Jehuda Cong. Sunday School	904 Bedford Ave.	29	100	Congregational Sunday School
36.	Beth Sholom Hebrew School	157 Marcy Ave., B'klyn.	31	128	Congregational Week-day School
37.	Beth Sholom People's Bay Temple Religious School	24th St. & Benson Ave., B'klyn.	38	200	Congregational Sunday School
38.	Beth Yavneh Yeshibah	409 Blake Ave., B'klyn.	39	85	Communal Week-day School
39.	Bialestoker Talmud Torah	7-11 Willett Street	3	100	Congregational Week-day School
40.	B'nai Israel Cong. Religious School	535 W. 148th Street	22	60	Congregational Week-day and Sunday School
41.	B'nai Israel Talmud Torah	293 E. 3d Street	7	70	Congregational Week-day School

No.	Name	Address	District	Enrollment	Type
42.	B'nai Israel Ansche Fordham Talmud Torah	2294 Arthur Ave., Bx.	26	70	Congregational Week-day School
43.	B'nai Jacob School Cong. Talmud Torah.	136 Prospect Ave., B'klyn	30	50	Communal Week-day School
44.	B'nai Sholom Temple Sunday School	403 9th Street, B'klyn	38	200	Congregational Sunday School
45.	Bohemian Amer. Israelite Cong. Talmud Torah	310-12 E. 72d Street	13	51	Congregational Week-day School
46.	Brightside Day Nursery and Kindergarten Sabbath School	89 Cannon Street	4	355	Institutional Sunday School
47.	Bronx Talmud Torah	456 E. 166th Street	24	50	Communal Week-day School
48.	Bureau of Ed. School No. 1	132 E. 111th Street	17	595	Communal Week-day School
49.	Bureau of Ed. School No. 2	394 E. Houston Street	7	488	Communal Week-day School
50.	Bureau of Ed. School No. 3	400 Stone Avenue	39	813	Communal Week-day School
51.	Bureau of Ed. School No. 4	31 W. 110th Street	19	562	Communal Week-day School
52.	Bureau of Ed. School No. 5	34 Stuyvesant Street	8	200	Communal Week-day School
53.	Central Jewish Institute	125 E. 85th Street	15	448	Communal Week-day School
54.	Council of Jewish Women School, N. Y. Section Religious School	71 St. Marks Place	6	40	Institutional Week-day and Sunday School
55.	Crippled Children East Side Free School	157 Henry Street	2	210	Institutional Week-day School
56.	Darchey Noim Talmud Torah	78 Second Street	7	228	Communal Week-day School
57.	Derech Emunah Heb. School	Larkin St. & Vernon Ave., Arverne, L. I.	44	50	Congregational Week-day School
58.	Down Town Talmud Torah	394 E. Houston Street	7	638	Communal Week-day School
59.	East New York Talmud Torah	872 Dumont Ave., B'klyn	40	115	Communal Week-day School
60.	Educational Alliance	197 E. Broadway	3	1041	Institutional Week-day School
61.	Emanuel Cong. Sunday School	521 5th Avenue	12	227	Congregational Sunday School
62.	Emanuel Temple Religious School	14th Ave. & 49th St., B'klyn	37	600	Congregational Sunday School
63.	Etz Chaim Cong. of Yorkville Sunday School	107 E. 92d Street	16	120	Congregational Sunday School
64.	Ezra Hebrew School	1745 Washington Avenue	25	508	Communal Week-day School

JEWISH SCHOOLS IN NEW YORK CITY (Continued)

No.	Name	Address	District	Enrollment	Type
65.	Federation Settlement Sunday School	240 E. 105th Street	17	140	Institutional Sunday School
66.	First Van Nest Hebrew Talmud Torah	1712 Garfield Street, Bx	26	80	Communal Week-day School
67.	Flatbush Hebrew School Cong. Shareh Torah	2252 Bedford Ave., B'klyn	38	60	Congregational Week-day School
68.	Free Synagogue Religious School	36 West 68th Street	14	170	Congregational Sunday School
69.	Free Synagogue Religious School	155 Clinton Street	3	282	Congregational Sunday School
70.	Free Synagogue, South Bronx School	142d St. & 3rd Ave., Bx	23	150	Congregational Sunday School
71.	Free Synagogue, Hunt's Point School	161st St. & So. Blvd	24	250	Congregational Sunday School
72.	Free Synagogue, McKinley Sq. School	Auerbach Casino, 169th St. & Boston Road	25	125	Congregational Sunday School
73.	Hagoan Rabbi Elihu Yeshibah	297 Saratoga Ave., B'klyn	36	150	Communal Week-day School
74.	Hebrew Day Nursery and Kindergarten	35 Montgomery Street	4	150	Institutional Week-day School
75.	Hebrew Educational Alliance of Greenpoint	961 Manhattan Avenue	33	200	Institutional Week-day School
76.	Hebrew Educational Institute of So. B'klyn	374 7th Street, B'klyn	38	125	Institutional Week-day School
77.	Heb. Ed. Soc. of B'klyn	564 Hopkinson Ave., B'klyn	39	291	Institutional Week-day and Sunday School
78.	Hebrew Free School	400 Stone Avenue	39	950	Communal Week-day School
79.	Hebrew Free School of Staten Island	386 Jersey Street, S. I.	45	50	Communal Week-day School
80.	Hebrew National Orphan Asylum School	52 St. Marks Place	6	100	Institutional Week-day School
81.	Hebrew Orphan Asylum	136th St. & Amsterdam Ave	22	708	Institutional Week-day School
82.	Hebrew Tabernacle Religious School	218 West 120th Street	19	350	Congregational Sunday School
83.	Hunt's Point T. T.	1019 Garrison Avenue	24	110	Communal Week-day School
84.	Israel Congregation, Sunday School	Bedford & Lafayette Avenues	29	170	Congregational Sunday School
85.	Israel Cong. of Harlem, Sunday School	120th St. & Lenox Ave.	19	220	Congregational Sunday School
86.	Israel Sisterhood Temple School	311 E. 116th Street	20	279	Congregational Sunday School
87.	Israel Temple Sunday School	Roanoke Ave. & State St., Far Rockaway, L. I.	44	280	Congregational Sunday School
88.	Judah Halevi T. T.	166th St. & Morris Ave	24	115	Congregational Week-day School

JEWISH SCHOOLS IN NEW YORK CITY (Continued)

No.	Name	Address	District	Enrollment	Type
89.	Judean Institute Cong. B'nai Israel	4th Ave. & 54th St., B'klyn	37	255	Congregational Week-day and Sunday School
90.	Kehilath Israel Cong., Heb. School	1162 Jackson Ave., Bx	25	150	Congregational Week-day School
91.	Kneseth Israel T. T	205 W. 139th Street	21	150	Communal Week-day School
92.	Kramer, Fein & Fuchs Privato Heb. School	67 Lewis Street	4	125	Private Week-day School
93.	Machzikei T. T	225 East Broadway	3	734	Communal Week-day School
94.	Machzikei T. T	68 E. 7th Street	6	463	Communal Week-day School
95.	Machzikei Talmud T	1319 43d St., B'klyn	38	600	Communal Week-day School
96.	Machzikei Talmud T. Ansche Emes	217 Corona Avenue, L. I	42	60	Congregational Week-day School
97.	Machzikei Ha-dath D'Tharas Hakodosh Talmud Torah	307-9 E. 102d Street	17	60	Communal Week-day School
98.	Middle Village Talmud Torah	10 Hynman St., Middle Village, L. I	42	60	Communal Week-day School
99.	Mishkan Israel Talmud Torah	27 Bendaman Ave., Jamaica, L. I.	43	50	Communal Week-day School
100.	Modern Hebrew School	34 W. 115th Street	19	170	Private Week-day School
101.	Montefiore Cong. Tal. Tor	764 Hewett Place, B'klyn	24	300	Congregational Week-day School
102.	Montefiore Hebrew Free Sch	40 Gouverneur Street	4	347	Communal Week-day School
103.	Mt. Nebo Cong. Rel. School	562 W. 150th Street	22	375	Congregational Sunday School
104.	Mt. Sinai Cong. Sunday School	305 State Street, B'klyn	27	140	Congregational Sunday School
105.	Mt. Zion Cong. Rel. School	37 W. 119th Street	19	300	Congregational Sunday School
106.	National Hebrew School	206 East Broadway	2	528	Communal Week-day School
107.	National Hebrew School	183 McKibben Street, B'klyn	33	225	Communal Week-day School
108.	National Hebrew School	63 Tompkins Avenue, B'klyn	32	350	Communal Week-day School
109.	National Hebrew School	844 DeKalb Avenue, B'klyn	32	120	Communal Week-day School
110.	National Hebrew School	1670 Bathgate Ave., Bronx	25	250	Communal Week-day School
111.	National Radical School	188 Ludlow Street	5	150	Communal Week-day School
112.	National Radical School	46 E. 104th Street	17	200	Communal Week-day School
113a.	Neumann Hebrew School	210 Stockton Street	32	80	Private Week-day School
113.	National Radical School	1701 Pitkin Avenue	39	100	Communal Sunday School

JEWISH SCHOOLS IN NEW YORK CITY (Continued)

No.	Name	Address	District	Enrollment	Type
114.	New Lots Talmud Torah	644 Georgia Avenue	40	160	Communal Week-day School
115.	New Synagogue Sunday School	76th St. & Broadway	18	55	Congregational Sunday School
116.	Ohab Zedek Talmud Torah	18 W. 116th Street	19	175	Congregational Week-day School
117.	Ohab Zedek Hebrew School	630 E. 5th Street	7	80	Institutional Week-day School
118.	Ohel Torah Talmud Torah	802 E. 6th Street	7	350	Communal Week-day School
119.	Orach Chaim Cong. Heb. Sch	92d St. & Lex. Ave. (Y. M. H.A.)	16	400	Congregational Week-day School
120.	Peni-El Cong. Heb. Sch	525 W. 147th Street	22	135	Congregational Week-day School
121.	Petach Tikvah Cong. Hebrew School	Lincoln Pl., cor. Rochester Ave., B'klyn	32	400	Congregational Week-day School
122.	Pincus Elijah Heb. Sch	118 W. 95th Street	18	92	Congregational Week-day School
123.	Rabbinical College	9-11 Montgomery Street	4	160	Communal Parochial School
124.	Rabbenu Mordecai Rosenblatt Yeshibah	98 E. Broadway	2	50	Communal Week-day School
125.	Rabbi Chaim Berlin of Harlem Talmud Torah	227 E. 100th Street	16	90	Communal Week-day School
126.	Rabbi Chayim Berlin Yeshibah	1899 Prospect Place, B'klyn	36	200	Communal Parochial School
127.	Rabbi Israel Salanter Talmud Torah	76 E. 118th Street	20	500	Communal Week-day School
128.	Rabbi Jacob David of Slutzk Talmud Torah	85 Henry Street	2	160	Communal Week-day School
129.	Rabbi Jacob Joseph Yeshibah	167 Henry Street	3	525	Communal Parochial School
130.	Rabbi Joseph Moses Schapiro Yeshibah	108-10 Attorney Street	5	250	Communal Week-day School
131.	Rabbi Shmuel Mohliver Talmud Torah	295 Henry Street	4	100	Congregational Week-day School
132.	Rabbi Sol Kluger Yeshibah	319 Rivington Street	4	378	Communal Week-day School
133.	Rodeph Sholom Congregation	Lexington Ave. & 63d St	13	200	Congregational Sunday School
134.	School of Biblical Instruction	61 Meserole Street, B'klyn	33	350	Communal Week-day School
135.	Shaarei Shomaim Cong	91 Rivington Street	5	300	Congregational Week-day School
136.	Shaaray Tefila Cong	160 W. 82d Street	18	200	Congregational Sunday School
137.	Shaarei Tefila Hebrew School	Central & Nelson Avenues, Far Rockaway	44	78	Congregational Week-day School
138.	Shaarei Tefilah Talmud Torah	8669 Bay 16th Street, B'klyn	37	145	Congregational Week-day School

No.	Name	Address	Dis-trict	Enroll-ment	Type
139.	Shaarei Zedek Cong. Sunday School	Putnam Ave., near Reid Ave., Brooklyn	32	200	Congregational Sunday School
140.	Shaarei Zedek Aram Zovah Chevra Talmud Torah	48-52 Orchard Street	2	120	Congregational Week-day School
141.	Shaarei Zedek Hebrew School	23 W. 118th Street	19	150	Congregational Week-day School
142.	Shaaray Zion Talmud Torah	811 E. 179th Street	26	80	Congregational Week-day School
143.	Shearith B'nai Israel	22 E. 113th Street	20	75	Congregational Sunday School
144.	Shearith Israel Cong	99 Central Park West	14	147	Congregational Sunday and Week-day School
145.	Shearith Israel Cong. Sisterhood Rel. Sch.	73 Allen Street	6	170	Institutional Week-day School
146.	Sholem Aleichem Folks Schule	1387 Washington Avenue	25	150	Communal Week-day School
147.	Shomrim Laboker Chevra Hebrew School	511 E. 136th Street	23	55	Congregational Week-day School
148.	Sinai Cong. of the Bronx	951 Stebbins Ave., Bronx	24	430	Congregational Sunday and Week-day School
149.	Sons of Israel Hebrew School	73 Bay 22d Street	38	160	Congregational Week-day School
150.	Tachkemoni Hebrew School	1378 Prospect Ave., Bronx	25	110	Private Week-day School
151.	Talmudical Institute of Harlem	56 W. 114th Street	19	100	Communal Parochial School
152.	Talmudical School of Brooklyn	57 Graham Ave., B'klyn	33	150	Communal Week-day School
153.	Talmud Torah Congregation	221 E. 51st Street	12	60	Congregational Week-day School
154.	Talmud Torah Hechodosh	146 Stockton Street, B'klyn	32	400	Communal Week-day School
155.	Temple of Peace Religious School	542 W. 162d Street	22	52	Congregational Sunday School
156.	Tifereth Achim Talmud Torah	200 E. 20th Street	8	69	Communal Week-day School
157.	Tifereth Israel Talmud Torah	363 Pennsylvania Ave., B'klyn	40	875	Communal Week-day School
158.	Tifereth Israel Talmud Torah	37-9 Throop Ave., B'klyn	31	225	Communal Week-day School
159.	Tifereth Israel Cong., Talmud Torah	Willoughby & Throop Avenues, Brooklyn	32	120	Congregational Week-day School

JEWISH SCHOOLS IN NEW YORK CITY (Continued)

No.	Name	Address	District	Enrollment	Type
160.	Tifereth Yisroel Talmud Torah	327 E. 13th Street	8	75	Communal Week-day School
161.	Tifereth Israel Talmud Torah	1038 Prospect Avenue	24	65	Communal Week-day School
162.	Tifereth Israel of Kensington Rel. School	West St. & Ditmas Ave., B'klyn	39	120	Congregational Sunday School
163.	Tifereth Jerusalem Talmud Torah	147 East Broadway	2	600	Communal Week-day School
164.	Tifereth Zion Talmud Torah	1887 Prospect Place, B'klyn	36	275	Communal Week-day School
165.	Tomchay Torah Talmud Torah	790 E. 156th Street	24	180	Communal Week-day School
166.	Tomchei Talmud Torah of Yeshibath Walozin	9 Rutgers Street	2	60	Communal Week-day School
167.	Torah Me-Zion School	199 Christopher Ave., B'klyn	39	60	Congregational Sunday and Week-day School
168.	Torath Chaim Yeshibah	105 E. 103d Street	17	360	Communal Week-day School
169.	Torath Chaim Yeshibah	293 E. 3rd Street	7	120	Communal Week-day School
170.	Toras Moshe Talmud Torah	667 Dawson Street	24	195	Communal Week-day School
171.	Tremont Hebrew Free School	484 E. 173rd Street	25	350	Communal Week-day School
172.	Tremont Temple Religious School	2064 Concourse Ave., Bronx	26	250	Congregational Sunday School
173.	Uptown Talmud Torah	132 E. 111th Street	17	1475	Communal Week-day School
174.	Washington Heights Talmud Torah	510 W. 161st Street	22	200	Congregational Week-day School
175.	West Side Talmud Torah	347 W. 35th Street	11	180	Private Week-day School
176.	West Side Private Hebrew School	230 Seventh Avenue	10	120	Private Week-day School
177.	Williamsburg Hebrew School	310 S. First Street	31	500	Communal Week-day School
178.	Zerubbabel Hebrew School	22 W. 114th Street	19	120	Private Week-day School
179.	Zichron Ephraim Congregation	67th St., near 3rd Ave	13	200	Congregational Week-day School
180.	Zion Hebrew Institute	1342 Stebbins Avenue	24	155	Communal Week-day School
181.	Zion Talmud Torah of Manhattan	388 Third Avenue	8	50	Communal Week-day School

APPENDIX N

CENTRAL JEWISH INSTITUTE

125 East 85th Street

SCORE OF BUILDING

	1		2		3	
I—SITE..........	—	—	—	—	125	**85**
A. Location	—	—	55	**45**	—	—
1. Accessibility	25	**15**	—	—	—	—
2. Environment	30	**30**	—	—	—	—
B. Drainage	—	—	30	**20**	—	—
1. Elevation	20	**12**	—	—	—	—
2. Nature of soil...........	10	**8**	—	—	—	—
C. Size and Form.............	40	**20**	40	**20**	—	—
II—BUILDING.....	—	—	—	—	165	**122**
A. Placement	—	—	25	**19**	—	—
1. Orientation	15	**12**	—	—	—	—
2. Position on site.........	10	**7**	—	—	—	—
B. Gross Structure............	—	—	60	**49**	—	—
1. Type	5	**4**	—	—	—	—
2. Material	10	**10**	—	—	—	—
3. Height	5	**2**	—	—	—	—
4. Roof	5	**5**	—	—	—	—
5. Foundations	5	**4**	—	—	—	—
6. Walls	5	**4**	—	—	—	—
7. Entrances	10	**5**	—	—	—	—
8. Aesthetic balance........	5	**5**	—	—	—	—
9. Condition	10	**10**	—	—	—	—
C. Internal Structure...........	—	—	80	**54**	—	—
1. Stairways	35	**25**	—	—	—	—
2. Corridors	20	**12**	—	—	—	—
3. Basement	15	**12**	—	—	—	—
4. Color scheme............	5	**5**	—	—	—	—
5. Attic	5	—	—	—	—	—
III—SERVICE SYSTEMS..	—	—	—	—	280	**182**
A. Heating and Ventilation.....	—	—	70	**5**	—	—
1. Kind	10	**0**	—	—	—	—
2. Installation	10	**0**	—	—	—	—
3. Air supply..............	15	**5**	—	—	—	—

CENTRAL JEWISH INSTITUTE, 125 East 85th Street

SCORE OF BUILDING—(Continued)

	1		2		3	
4. Fans and motors........	10	**0**	—	—	—	—
5. Distribution	10	**0**	—	—	—	—
6. Temperature control.....	10	**0**	—	—	—	—
7. Special provisions.......	5	**0**	—	—	—	—
B. Fire Protection System......	—	—	65	**63**	—	—
1. Apparatus	10	**8**	—	—	—	—
2. Fireproofness	15	**15**	—	—	—	—
3. Escapes	20	**20**	—	—	—	—
4. Electric wiring..........	5	**5**	—	—	—	—
5. Fire doors and partitions	10	**10**	—	—	—	—
6. Exit lights and signs....	5	**5**	—	—	—	—
C. Cleaning System...........	—	—	20	**13**	—	—
1. Kind	5	**3**	—	—	—	—
2. Installation	5	**0**	—	—	—	—
3. Efficiency	10	**10**	—	—	—	—
D. Artificial Lighting System...	—	—	20	**14**	—	—
1. Gas and electricity......	5	**5**	—	—	—	—
2. Outlets and adjustment..	5	**3**	—	—	—	—
3. Illumination	5	**3**	—	—	—	—
4. Method and fixtures.....	5	**3**	—	—	—	—
E. Electric Service System.....	—	—	15	**12**	—	—
1. Clock	5	**2**	—	—	—	—
2. Bell	5	**5**	—	—	—	—
3. Telephone	5	**5**	—	—	—	—
F. Water Supply System.......	—	—	30	**30**	—	—
1. Drinking	10	**10**	—	—	—	—
2. Washing	10	**10**	—	—	—	—
3. Bathing	5	**5**	—	—	—	—
4. Hot and cold...........	5	**5**	—	—	—	—
G. Toilet System..............	—	—	50	**45**	—	—
1. Distribution	10	**9**	—	—	—	—
2. Fixtures	10	**9**	—	—	—	—
3. Adequacy & arrangement	10	**8**	—	—	—	—
4. Seclusion	5	**5**	—	—	—	—
5. Sanitation	15	**14**	—	—	—	—
H. Mechanical Service System...	—	—	10	**0**	—	—
1. Elevator	5	**0**	—	—	—	—
2. Book-lifts	2	**0**	—	—	—	—
3. Waste-chutes	3	**0**	—	—	—	—

CENTRAL JEWISH INSTITUTE, 125 East 85th Street

SCORE OF BUILDING—(Continued)

	1		2		3	
IV—CLASS ROOMS......	—	—	—	—	290	**246**
A. Location and Connection.....	35	**33**	35	**33**	—	—
B. Construction and Finish.....	—	—	95	**71**	—	—
1. Size	25	**22**	—	—	—	—
2. Shape	15	**14**	—	—	—	—
3. Floors	10	**8**	—	—	—	—
4. Walls	10	**8**	—	—	—	—
5. Doors	5	**5**	—	—	—	—
6. Closets	5	**5**	—	—	—	—
7. Blackboards	10	**7**	—	—	—	—
8. Bulletin Board..........	5	**2**	—	—	—	—
9. Color Scheme...........	10	—	—	—	—	—
C. Illumination	—	—	85	**76**	—	—
1. Glass area	45	**42**	—	—	—	—
2. Windows	30	**26**	—	—	—	—
3. Shades	10	**8**	—	—	—	—
D. Cloakrooms and wardrobes...	25	**24**	25	**24**	—	—
E. Equipment	—	—	50	**42**	—	—
1. Seats and desks.........	35	**32**	—	—	—	—
2. Teacher's desk..........	10	**10**	—	—	—	—
3. Other equipment	5	**0**	—	—	—	—
V—SPECIAL ROOMS....	—	—	—	—	140	**52**
A. Large Rooms for General Use	—	—	65	**32**	—	—
1. Playroom	10	**0**	—	—	—	—
2. Auditorium	15	**15**	—	—	—	—
3. Study hall..............	5	—	—	—	—	—
4. Library	10	**10**	—	—	—	—
5. Gymnasium	10	**7**	—	—	—	—
6. Swimming pool.........	5	**0**	—	—	—	—
7. Lunch room............	10	—	—	—	—	—
B. Rooms for School Officials...	—	—	35	**15**	—	—
1. Officers	10	**10**	—	—	—	—
2. Teachers' room.........	10	**0**	—	—	—	—
3. Nurses' room...........	10	—	—	—	—	—
4. Janitor's room..........	5	**5**	—	—	—	—
C. Other Special Service Rooms..	—	—	40	**5**	—	—
1. Laboratories	20	—	—	—	—	—
2. Lecture rooms..........	10	—	—	—	—	—
3. Store rooms............	5	**5**	—	—	—	—
4. Studios	5	—	—	—	—	—
Totals..............	925	**688**	1000	**743**	1000	**743**

SALANTER TALMUD TORAH

74 East 85th Street

SCORE OF BUILDING

	1		2		3	
I—SITE............	—	—	—	—	125	**67**
A. Location	—	—	55	**47**	—	—
1. Accessibility	25	**25**	—	—	—	—
2. Environment	30	**22**	—	—	—	—
B. Drainage	—	—	30	—	—	—
1. Elevation	20	—	—	—	—	—
2. Nature of soil..........	10	—	—	—	—	—
C. Size and Form..............	40	**20**	40	**20**	—	—
II—BUILDING........	—	—	—	—	165	**71**
A. Placement	—	—	25	**12**	—	—
1. Orientation	15	**8**	—	—	—	—
2. Position on site.........	10	**4**	—	—	—	—
B. Gross Structure............	—	—	60	**31**	—	—
1. Type	5	**2**	—	—	—	—
2. Material	10	**8**	—	—	—	—
3. Height	5	**5**	—	—	—	—
4. Roof	5	**3**	—	—	—	—
5. Foundations	5	—	—	—	—	—
6. Walls	5	**2**	—	—	—	—
7. Entrances	10	**3**	—	—	—	—
8. Aesthetic balance........	5	**2**	—	—	—	—
9. Condition	10	**6**	—	—	—	—
C. Internal Structure..........	—	—	80	**28**	—	—
1. Stairways	35	**18**	—	—	—	—
2. Corridors	20	**8**	—	—	—	—
3. Basement	15	**0**	—	—	—	—
4. Color scheme............	5	**2**	—	—	—	—
5. Attic	5	—	—	—	—	—
III—SERVICE SYSTEMS..	—	—	—	—	280	**98**
A. Heating and Ventilation.....	—	—	70	**6**	—	—
1. Kind	10	**0**	—	—	—	—
2. Installation	10	**0**	—	—	—	—
3. Air supply..............	15	**6**	—	—	—	—
4. Fans and motors........	10	**0**	—	—	—	—
5. Distribution	10	**0**	—	—	—	—
6. Temperature control.....	10	**0**	—	—	—	—
7. Special provisions.......	5	**0**	—	—	—	—

SALANTER TALMUD TORAH, 74 East 85th Street

SCORE OF BUILDING—(Continued)

	1		2		3	
B. Fire Protection System......	—	—	65	**45**	—	—
1. Apparatus	10	**7**	—	—	—	—
2. Fireproofness	15	**10**	—	—	—	—
3. Escapes	20	**18**	—	—	—	—
4. Electric wiring..........	5	—	—	—	—	—
5. Fire doors and partitions.	10	**7**	—	—	—	—
6. Exit lights and signs....	5	**3**	—	—	—	—
C. Cleaning System............	—	—	20	**7**	—	—
1. Kind	5	**2**	—	—	—	—
2. Installation	5	**0**	—	—	—	—
3. Efficiency	10	**5**	—	—	—	—
D. Artificial Lighting System....	—	—	20	**9**	—	—
1. Gas and electricity......	5	**5**	—	—	—	—
2. Outlets and adjustment..	5	—	—	—	—	—
3. Illumination	5	**2**	—	—	—	—
4. Method and fixtures.....	5	**2**	—	—	—	—
E. Electric Service System......	—	—	15	**5**	—	—
1. Clock	5	**0**	—	—	—	—
2. Bell	5	**2**	—	—	—	—
3. Telephone	5	**3**	—	—	—	—
F. Water Supply System........	—	—	30	**3**	—	—
1. Drinking	10	**0**	—	—	—	—
2. Washing	10	**3**	—	—	—	—
3. Bathing	5	**0**	—	—	—	—
4. Hot and cold...........	5	**0**	—	—	—	—
G. Toilet System..............	—	—	50	**23**	—	—
1. Distribution	10	**4**	—	—	—	—
2. Fixtures	10	**6**	—	—	—	—
3. Adequacy and arrangement	10	**2**	—	—	—	—
4. Seclusion	5	**4**	—	—	—	—
5. Sanitation	15	**7**	—	—	—	—
H. Mechanical Service System..	—	—	10	—	—	—
1. Elevator	5	—	—	—	—	—
2. Book-lifts	2	—	—	—	—	—
3. Waste-chutes	3	—	—	—	—	—
IV—CLASS ROOMS......	—	—	—	—	290	**114**
A. Location and Connection.....	35	**30**	35	**30**	—	—
B. Construction and Finish.....	—	—	95	**38**	—	—
1. Size	25	**15**	—	—	—	—
2. Shape	15	**6**	—	—	—	—
3. Floors	10	**7**	—	—	—	—

SALANTER TALMUD TORAH, 74 East 85th Street

SCORE OF BUILDING—(Continued)

	1		2		3	
4. Walls	10	**4**	—	—	—	—
5. Doors	5	**4**	—	—	—	—
6. Closets	5	0	—	—	—	—
7. Blackboards	10	**2**	—	—	—	—
8. Bulletin Board	5	**0**	—	—	—	—
9. Color Scheme	10	**0**	—	—	—	—
C. Illumination	—	—	85	**25**	—	—
1. Glass area	45	**10**	—	—	—	—
2. Windows	30	**15**	—	—	—	—
3. Shades	10	**0**	—	—	—	—
D. Cloakrooms and wardrobes	25	**0**	25	**0**	—	—
E. Equipment	—	—	50	**21**	—	—
1. Seats and desks	35	**15**	—	—	—	—
2. Teacher's desk	10	**6**	—	—	—	—
3. Other equipment	5	**0**	—	—	—	—
V—SPECIAL ROOMS	—	—	—	—	140	**12**
A. Large Rooms for General Use	—	—	65	**6**	—	—
1. Playroom	10	**0**	—	—	—	—
2. Auditorium	15	**6**	—	—	—	—
3. Study hall	5	—	—	—	—	—
4. Library	10	**0**	—	—	—	—
5. Gymnasium	10	**0**	—	—	—	—
6. Swimming pool	5	**0**	—	—	—	—
7. Lunch room	10	—	—	—	—	—
B. Rooms for School Officials	—	—	35	**6**	—	—
1. Officers	10	**4**	—	—	—	—
2. Teachers' room	10	**0**	—	—	—	—
3. Nurses' room	10	—	—	—	—	—
4. Janitor's room	5	**2**	—	—	—	—
C. Other Special Service Rooms	—	—	40	—	—	—
1. Laboratories	20	—	—	—	—	—
2. Lecture rooms	10	—	—	—	—	—
3. Store rooms	5	—	—	—	—	—
4. Studios	5	—	—	—	—	—
Totals	875	**362**	1000	**413**	1000	**413**

APPENDIX O

FINANCIAL ACCOUNTING IN JEWISH SCHOOLS[1]

An examination of the unpublished financial statements[2] presented annually by the Boards of Directors, reveals the following shortcomings in the fiscal accounting of Jewish schools, shortcomings which are to be expected in the present unco-ordinated status of Jewish education in New York:

1. The items of expense, as well as those of income, are "lumped," so that it is often impossible to make use of them. For example, such an item as "Expense for school: heat, light, rent, loan, printing, etc."[3] is valueless for the purpose of cost accounting, or of comparison with the records of other schools. Nor are items like "Salaries," or "General expense," or "Donations" any better.

2. The terminology used by the various schools is often not the same, so that items are sometimes included under one heading and sometimes under another. For instance, "Supplies" are sometimes listed as "Printing, stationery, etc.," sometimes as "School expense," and sometimes as "Office expense."

3. Many of the schools do not audit their books regularly, and only the largest of them call in the services of a public accountant for this purpose.

4. Since the records are not supervised either by the principal or by any one else who is interested in the educational phases of the school work, the system of accounting is organized not for educational, but for business purposes. No study of *units of cost* per pupil, per classroom, per activity, etc., is possible from such records.

SUGGESTIONS FOR REORGANIZING FINANCIAL ACCOUNTING

A number of concrete suggestions may be made aiming toward the reorganization of financial accounting:

(1) The *principal must be trained* so that he can himself supervise this phase of the work. It seems hardly possible for the Jewish schools to make real progress (especially under conditions of increased costs), as long as the classroom work is in the hands of one who does not understand and cannot control the financial aspects of his school.

(2) An *annual Budget* should be prepared by the principal, with the approval of the Board of Directors, at the beginning of each year. This budget should be itemized in as great detail as possible, and should be

---

[1] The entire question of financial accounting in the Jewish schools is discussed by the author at greater length, in a paper entitled: "Financial Accounting in Jewish Religious Schools," submitted in partial fulfillment of the requirements for the Ph. D. degree, in the Department of Educational Administration, Teachers' College, Columbia, August, 1917. (On file in that department, also in Bureau of Jewish Education.)

[2] Twelve schools co-operated with the writer to the extent of giving him a financial statement of the income and expenditure of the fiscal year 1916. Some of these statements are presented in Appendix O.

[3] Cf. School G. below; p. 520.

based upon the amount spent upon each item during the previous year, increased by such additional outlay for the coming year as may be deemed necessary.[4] The principal as well as the Board of Directors should compare every month the expenses of the school with the budget allowance, so as to guard against unexpected and unpleasant deficits at the end of the year.

(3) *Reports* should be published regularly by the Jewish schools, annually or bi-annually. These reports should be regarded in the nature of "self-surveys," both by the Board of Directors and by the principal of the school. The annual reports should contain statistical information concerning enrollment and attendance, "retardation and elimination," grading of pupils, time schedules, courses of study, salaries of the teaching staff, etc. They should also give a detailed presentation of the financial conditions of the school, showing itemized expenditure and income. This information should be properly interpreted and graphically presented, so as to focus the attention of the public upon the more important needs of the school. The annual report, if properly compiled and judiciously distributed, can perform an important function in bringing the activities and the needs of the school before the Jewish public.

(4) The system of financial recording should be organized on the basis of *educational units of cost.* It is blind imitation to copy the methods of business accounting without copying also its spirit, which consists in accurate accounting for units of cost. The units of cost which hold true in business affairs are not applicable to the control of educational policies, no more than the cost accounting of a department store would satisfy the conditions obtained in the running of a railroad. The Jewish schools must determine their *own* units of cost to meet their peculiar needs, and must conduct their accounts accordingly.

(5) Lastly, it is suggested that whatever financial reports and reports are used, should as far as possible be *uniform* among all the Jewish schools, or at least among the communal weekday schools. Unless the systems of accounting are uniform, it will not be possible to compare the cost of one school with that of another, nor to obtain any financial information concerning Jewish education in general.

UNITS OF COSTS AND PLAN OF UNIFORM ACCOUNTING

The following units of cost are proposed for Jewish schools, on the basis of the standards suggested in public education:[7]

1. Cost and net income *per department* or activity.
   (School; Synagogue; Social Center, etc.)
2. *Per pupil* cost for each function of expenditure.

[4] Thus, the budgetary allowance for "Teacher's Salary" should be based upon the **actual salary** schedule in vogue, plus contemplated **increases in salary** of present teachers, plus salaries of new teachers who may be needed for additional work.

[7] Hutchinson: "School Costs and School Accounting."

(Administration; Instruction; Operation; Maintenance; Auxiliary Agencies, and Sundry activities; Fixed charges; Debt service; and Capital outlay.)

3. *Per classroom* cost of building and capital outlay.

4. *Per dollar cost of collecting* income from each source.
   (Pupils; Synagogue, building rents and other property; Community; etc.)

A simple system of accounting such as is here outlined[8] would make it possible for all Jewish schools to keep uniform records which would enable them to determine the cost of each of these units. The essentials of such a system are: (1) an ordinary *Voucher Book,* all payments being made by vouchers; (2) a *Cash Book* for recording daily receipts and expenditures;[9] and (3) a set of *Ledger Sheets,* kept by Departments (School, Social Center, etc.) and by Functions of Expenditure (Instruction, General Control, Capital Outlay, etc.).[10] A *Cumulative Monthly Report* should be compiled every month,[11] which would show at a glance the financial status of the school to date. A few of the larger Jewish educational institutions have already reorganized their records on this basis, and find it very satisfactory. This system should be regularly audited by an accredited accountant, who understands the specific purposes of Jewish financial records.

(Model Forms for financial accounting in the Jewish schools will be found on the following pages: 514-517).

[8] These record forms are based upon the standard forms found in: (1) the "Report of the N. E. A. Committee on Uniform Records and Reports" (Bulletin 3, U. S. Bureau of Education, 1912); (2) "Handbook of Instruction for Recording Disbursements for School Purposes," with accompanying voucher register and ledger sheets, compiled by the Statistical Division of the New York State Education Department, 1916; and (3) Hutchinson: "School Costs and School Accounting."

[9] Cf. Cash Book Form.

[10] Cf. Ledger Sheets (Forms I to VI).

[11] Cf. Cumulative Monthly Report (Form M).

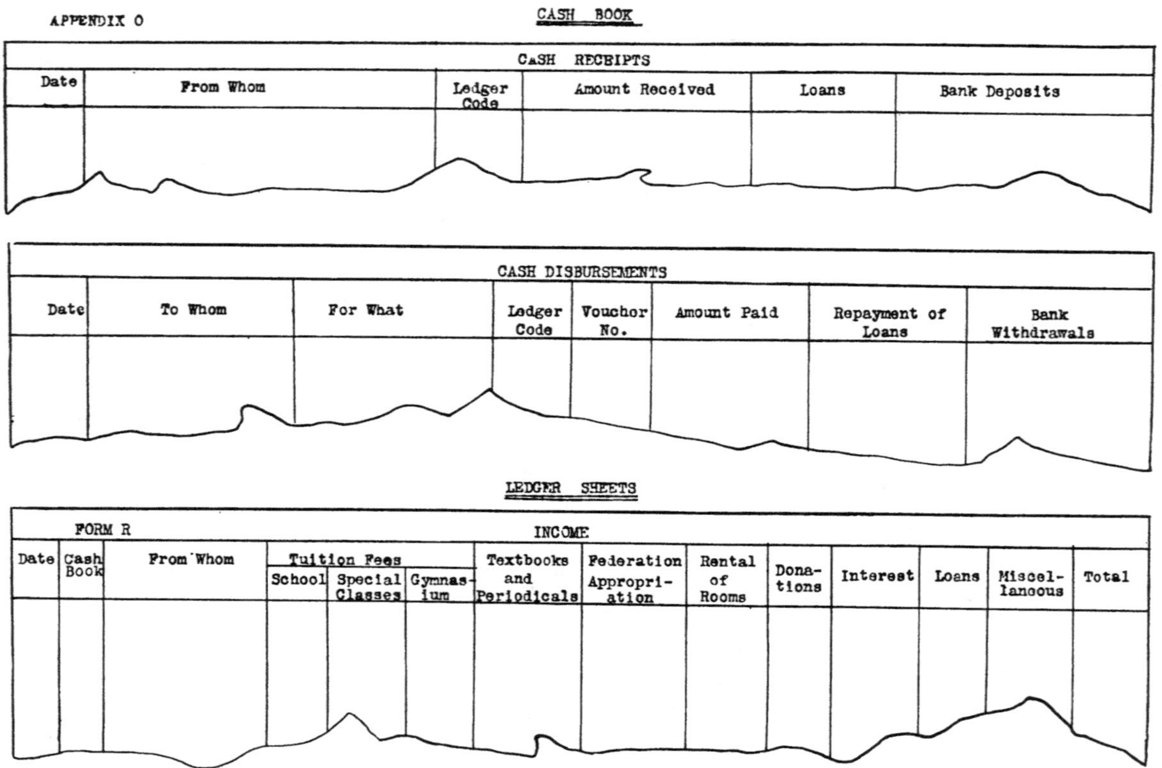

APPENDIX O

CASH BOOK

CASH RECEIPTS					
Date	From Whom	Ledger Code	Amount Received	Loans	Bank Deposits

CASH DISBURSEMENTS							
Date	To Whom	For What	Ledger Code	Voucher No.	Amount Paid	Repayment of Loans	Bank Withdrawals

LEDGER SHEETS

FORM R

INCOME														
Date	Cash Book	From Whom	Tuition Fees			Textbooks and Periodicals	Federation Appropri-ation	Rental of Rooms	Dona-tions	Interest	Loans	Miscel-laneous	Total
			School	Special Classes	Gymnas-ium								

LEDGER SHEETS (DISBURSEMENTS)

FORM I

CAPITAL OUTLAY, DEBT SERVICE AND FIXED CHARGES																
Date	Voucher No.	Cash Book	To Whom	For What	Capital Outlay				Debt Service		Fixed Charges				Miscellaneous	Total
					New furniture	Alterations and Improvements		Other Outlay	Interest on Mortgage	Interest on Loans	Amortization of Mortgage	Insurance	Taxes and Dues	Other Fixed Charges		
						Of Building	Of Grounds									

FORM II

PHYSICAL MAINTENANCE AND OPERATION														
Date	Voucher No.	Cash Book	To Whom	For What	Repairs and Replacements				Janitor Service			Light	Fuel	Total
					Building	Heating Lighting and Plumbing Systems	Furniture and Equipment	Other Expense	Salaries	Supplies	Other Service			

FORM III

GENERAL CONTROL - CENTRAL OFFICE (Administration)																
Date	Voucher No.	Cash Book	To Whom	For What	Salaries				Supplies		Printing	Advertising	Telephone Service	Miscellaneous	Total
					Executive Director	Secretaries and Clerks	Evening Assistant	Other Salaries	Stationery	Postage					

LEDGER SHEETS (DISBURSEMENTS

FORM IV A					INSTITUTIONAL OPERATION - SCHOOL										
					Supervision				and	Instruction					
					Salaries		Supplies Office			Salaries		Supplies (classroom)			
Date	Voucher No.	Cash Book	To Whom	For What	School Principal	School Clerks and Assistants	Stationery and Printing	Postage	Collection, Investigation and Canvassing	Regular Teachers	Special Teachers	Text-Books	Stationery and other Institutional Supplies	Periodicals, Bulletins	Total Cost of Supervision and Instruction
			SIMILAR		SHEETS		FOR	ALL	OTHER		DEPARTMENTS				

FORM IV B					INSTITUTIONAL OPERATION - SCHOOL (Social Activities and Miscellaneous)									
					Entertainment and Festivals				Library					
Date	Voucher No.	Cash Book	To Whom	For What	Printing and Postage	Salaries	Supplies	Other Expenses	Salaries	Books and Periodicals	Supplies	Other Expenses	Sundries	Total Cost of Social Activities and Miscellaneous
			SIMILAR		SHEETS		FOR	ALL	OTHER		DEPARTMENTS			

FORM V					INSTITUTIONAL OPERATION - MISCELLANEOUS								
					Parents' Association		Special Classes			General Social and Communal Activities			
Date	Voucher No.	Cash Book	To Whom	For What	Stationery and	Other Expenses	Salaries of Teachers	Supplies	Other Expenses	Professional Services	Stationery and Postage	Other Expenses	Total
			SIMILAR		SHEETS	FOR	ALL	OTHER		DEPARTMENTS			

APPENDIX O

FORM M

CUMULATIVE MONTHLY EXPENDITURE AND BALANCE SHEET

Month of....................191..

Ledger Code	APPROPRIATION	OFFICE					SCHOOL					OTHER DEPARTMENTS (Each kept separately)					TOTAL				
		Expend. for Month	Expend. to Date	Allot. to Date	Surplus	Deficit	Expend. for Month	Expend. to Date	Allot. to Date	Surplus	Deficit	Expend. for Month	Expend. to Date	Allot. to Date	Surplus	Deficit	Expend. for Month	Expend. to Date	Allot. to Date	Surplus	Deficit
	A.Physical Maintenance																				
	1.Repairs and replac. Bldg.																				
	2. " Steam,Light,Plumbing																				
	3. " Furniture.																				
	B.Physical Operation of Plant																				
	1.Janitor Salaries																				
	2.Janitor Supplies																				
	3.Other Janitorial Service																				
	4.Light																				
	5.Fuel																				
	C.Inst.Operation-General Control																				
	1.Salaries																				
	a.Executive and Supervision																				
	b.Clerical																				
	c.Other Assistants																				
	2.Supplies																				
	a.Stationery and forms																				
	b. Postage																				
	3.Other Administrative Exp.																				
	4.Telephone																				
	D.Inst. Operation-Instruction																				
	1.Salaries																				
	a.Regular Teachers																				
	b.Special Teachers																				
	2.Supplies																				
	a.Text Books																				
	b.Periodicals, etc.																				
	c.Other Supplies																				
	E.Auxiliary Agencies																				
	1.Entertainments																				
	2.Library																				
	3.Propaganda																				
	F.Sundries																				
	Total Current Expense																				
	No. of Pupils																				
	Per Capita Cost																				
	G. Permanent Outlay																				
	1. Capital Outlay																				
	2. Debt Service																				
	3. Fixed Charges																				
	G R A N D T O T A L																				

ANNUAL STATEMENTS
OF INCOME AND EXPENDITURE

SCHOOL A

INCOME:	*Year Ending October 31, 1916*	
Tuition Fees	$9,426.25	
Seat Sales	4,476.90	
Rents	5,914.00	
Education Fund	962.50	
Membership Dues	12,123.85	
Theatres	4,094.00	
Charity Boxes	372.35	
Requests	100.00	
Classroom Tablets	1,700.00	
General Donations	9,484.26	
TOTAL		$49,154.11

EXPENDITURE:		
Annual Amortization	$5,000.00	
Interest	5,996.02	
Interest on Loans	348.30	
Insurance	82.30	
Heat	1,230.00	
Light	1,656.13	
Repairs and Improvements	1,630.00	
Telephone	18.07	
Books	108.23	
Postage, Stationery, Printing and Advertising	1,401.98	
Salaries of Teachers, Principal and Staff	14,944.03	
Salaries of Secretary and Staff	2,500.00	
Salaries of Janitorial Staff	5,352.38	
Cost of Collection	4,068.65	
Principal paid off mortgage		
House Expenses	1,086.76	
Social Workers	45.00	
Summer Campaign	70.00	
Commission on Sale of Branch	400.00	
TOTAL		$45,946.85

SCHOOL B

INCOME	*Year Ending March 31, 1917*
Balance	$104.94
Tuition Fees	3,904.60
Books and "Jewish Child"	88.66
Education Fund	900.00
Membership Dues	2,000.00

Donations	118.27	
Charity Boxes	929.11	
Seats	2,393.90	
Megile Geld	37.85	
Sefer Torah	185.00	
Cemetery	567.70	
Entertainment and Ball	904.40	
Hebrew Aid Society	52.00	
Relief Fund	42.87	
Bar Mitzvah	115.50	
Kaddish	420.84	
Moyes Chitim	207.13	
Raffle	25.20	
Loans and Exchange Checks	3,378.99	
TOTAL		$16,376.96

EXPENDITURE:

Teachers' Salaries	$3,788.00	
Principal's Salary	1,619.14	
Secretary's Salary	704.84	
Collectors' Salaries	1,020.11	
Books and "Jewish Child"	166.05	
Coal	53.50	
Gas	95.58	
Electricity	241.25	
Telephone	41.43	
House Expenses	274.29	
Janitor	472.83	
Building Expenses	1,346.98	
Insurance	210.86	
Printing	70.87	
Advertisements	100.33	
Black Board	13.42	
Desks	20.00	
Cantor and Singers	420.50	
Signs on Benches	34.75	
Cleaning Synagogue	30.41	
Collection of Donations	25.00	
Ball Expenses	314.91	
1st and 2nd mortgage, Cemetery and Funeral Exp.	2,343.76	
Loans Paid	3,393.00	
Relief Fund	20.64	
Jewish Community	10.00	
Aid Society	52.75	
Moyes Chitim	138.48	
Denver and Beth David Hospital	10.92	
TOTAL		$17,034.60

SCHOOL E

INCOME:	*Year Ending November 1, 1916*	
Balance	$2,232.49	
Dues Collected	2,788.55	
Collections	2,632.00	
Charity Boxes	250.21	
Donations	1,182.80	
Weekly from Pupils	1,922.39	
Books	167.65	
Plate Money	63.54	
Daily Interest at Bank	26.87	
Leases	1,675.00	
Returns on Insurance	18.00	
TOTAL		$10,727.01
EXPENDITURE:		
Teachers, Principal, Secretary and Janitor	$7,347.55	
Lights	566.50	
Coal	373.00	
Repairs	248.04	
Stationery and Postage	180.54	
Telephone	45.15	
Mortgage Expense and Interest	1,295.00	
Plumber	28.50	
Books	362.15	
Extra Insurance	5.01	
Fire Extinguisher	13.50	
Sundry Expenses	146.94	
Collections	554.81	
Return Exp. Werner	25.00	
TOTAL		$11,191.69

SCHOOL G

INCOME:	*Year Ending December, 1916*	
Dues	$686.00	
Pupils' Fees	4,999.43	
Affairs	703.35	
Loans, Rent, Miscellaneous	930.78	
Donations	849.17	
TOTAL		$8,168.73
Salaries	$6,078.00	
EXPENDITURE:		
Postage	55.72	
Expenses for School House, Light, Rent, Loans, Affairs, Printing	1,743.31	
TOTAL		$7,877.03

APPENDIX P

FORMS OF SCHOOL RECORDS FOR THE USE OF JEWISH SCHOOLS

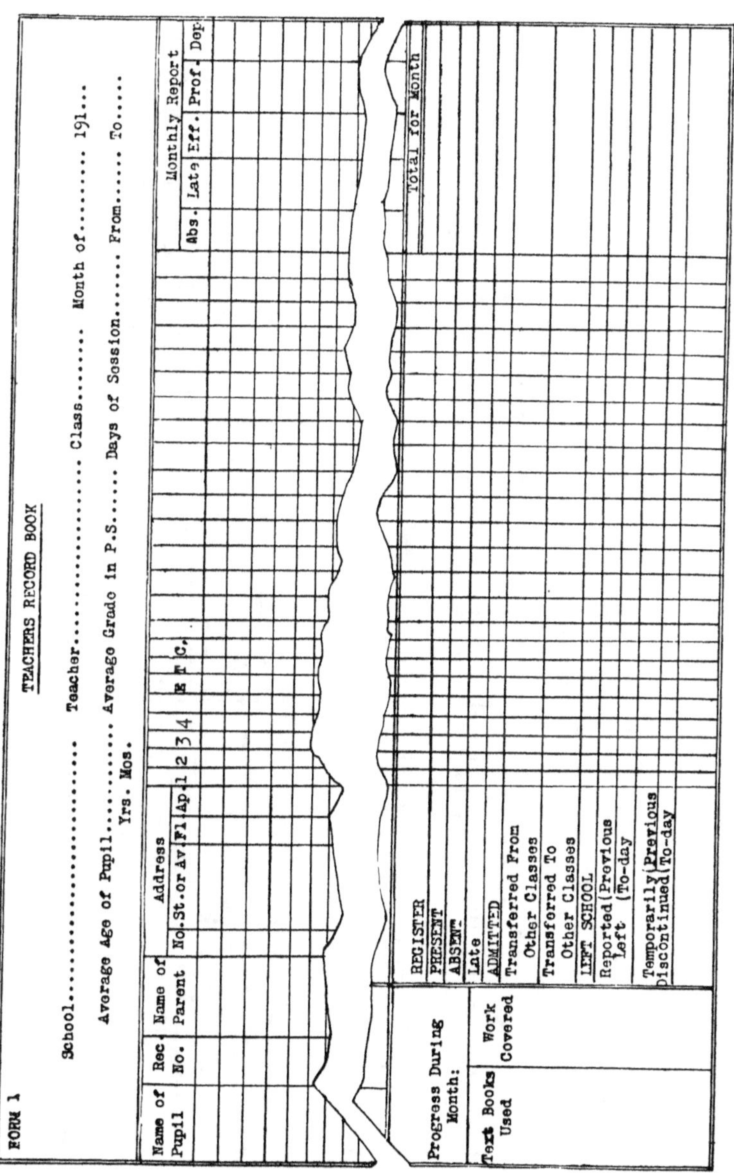

FORM 1

TEACHERS RECORD BOOK

School.......................... Teacher.................... Class........ Month of.......... 191...

Average Age of Pupil............. Average Grade in P.S...... Days of Session....... From...... To.....

Yrs. Mos.

Name of Pupil	Rec. No.	Name of Parent	Address: No.	St. or Av.	Fl.	Ap.	1	2	3	4	E T C.	Monthly Report: Abs.	Late	Eff.	Prof.	Dep.

Progress During Month:	
Text Books Used	Work Covered

	Total for Month
REGISTER	
PRESENT	
ABSENT	
Late	
ADMITTED	
Transferred From Other Classes	
Transferred To Other Classes	
LEFT SCHOOL	
Reported Left (Previous	
(To-day	
Temporarily Discontinued (Previous	
(To-day	

APPENDIX P

FORM 2

TEACHER'S MONTHLY CLASS REPORT

School........................ Teacher..................... Class.......... Term: From......... To........... 191...

Average Age of Pupil............ Average Grade in P.S........ Days of Session.......... From........ To........

Name of Pupil	Record No.	Name of Parent	Address				Age		Grade	September					(Same for Six Months)					Term Total						Admitted to Class		Left Schl	Promot. Demot or Transf.	
			No.	St. or Av.	Fl.	Ap.	Yrs.	Mos.	In P.S.	Eff.	Prof.	Dep.	Abs.	Late	Eff.	Prof.	Dep.	Abs.	Late	Eff.	Prof.	Dep.	Pres.	Abs.	Late	From	Date	Date	Class	Date

No. Sessions a Week ______

No " During Term ______

Text Books used	Work Covered

REGISTER (Initial)

ADMITTED

Trans. From other Classes

Trans. To other Classes

LEFT SCHOOL

Reported Left

Temporarily Discontinued

REGISTER (Final)

No. Pupils Promoted ______ Not Promoted ______

APPENDIX F, FORM 6

CUMULATIVE PUPIL'S RECORD CARD

Name of Pupil ____ Family ____ Given ____ Born ____ Mo Yr. ____ in ____ country ____ Arrived in U.S. ____ Mo. Yr.

Date of Admission ____ Class in P.S. ____ Class in H.S. ____ Record No. ____

No.	Street	Fl.	Rm.	No.	Street	Fl.	Rm.	No.	Street	Fl.	Rm.	No.	Street	Fl.	Room

Name of Father or Guardian ____ Name of Mother ____

Parent's Occupation ____ Business Address ____

PREVIOUS HEBREW EDUCATION OF PUPIL

Name of School	Years Spent	Subjects Studied	Accomplishment	Date of Leaving	Reason for Leaving

In marking accomplishment the principal will please use the letters A,B,C and D: A = Excellent; B = Good; C = Fair; D = Poor.

RECORD OF PUPIL'S LEAVING AND READMISSION

	Date	Reason	Date	Reason
Left				
Readmitted				
Left				
Readmitted				

REVERSE SIDE

Date Pupil Was Admit.	Date Pupil Left Class	To Class	No. of Sessions a Week	No. of Hours a Week	Class in P.S.	Age	Attendance: Times Present	Attendance: Times Absent	Standing: E	Standing: P	Standing: D	Subjects in which Pupil Excels	Subjects in which Pupil Deficient	Extra-class-room Activities

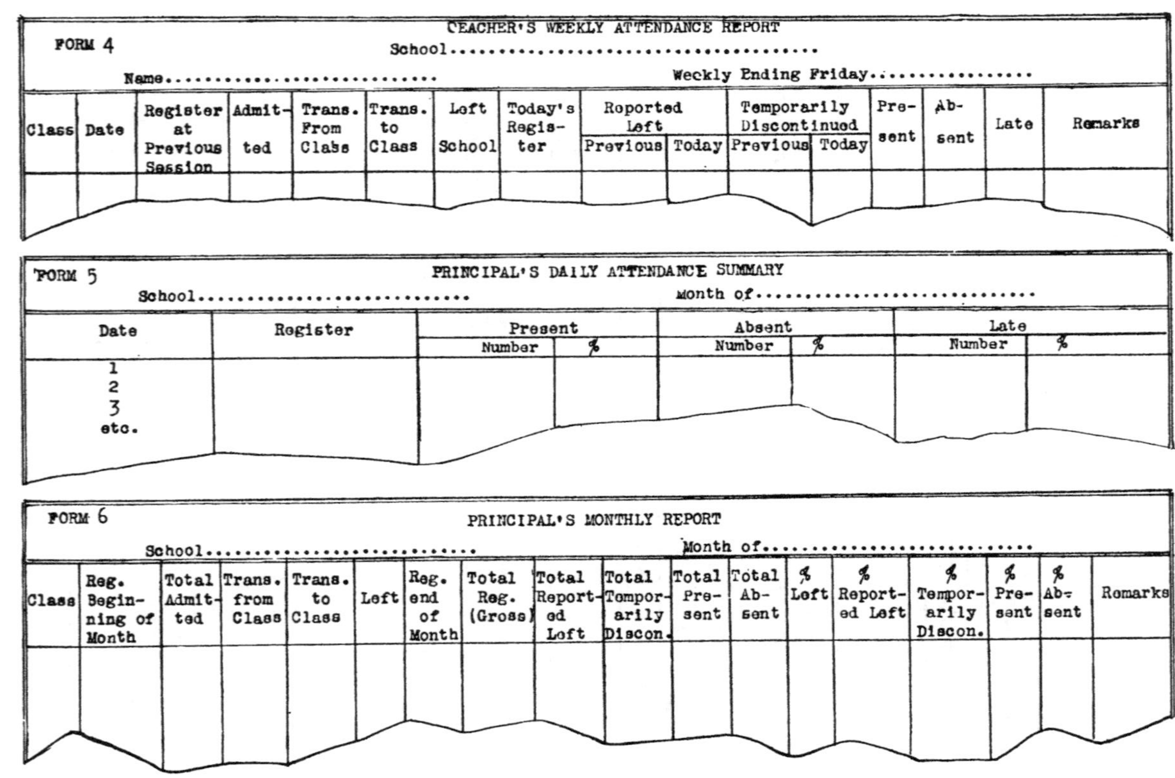

FORM 4

TEACHER'S WEEKLY ATTENDANCE REPORT

School....................................

Name.......................... Weekly Ending Friday................

Class	Date	Register at Previous Session	Admit-ted	Trans. From Class	Trans. to Class	Left School	Today's Regis-ter	Reported Left		Temporarily Discontinued		Pre-sent	Ab-sent	Late	Remarks
								Previous	Today	Previous	Today				

FORM 5

PRINCIPAL'S DAILY ATTENDANCE SUMMARY

School.......................... Month of..........................

Date	Register	Present		Absent		Late	
		Number	%	Number	%	Number	%
1 2 3 etc.							

FORM 6

PRINCIPAL'S MONTHLY REPORT

School.......................... Month of..........................

Class	Reg. Begin-ning of Month	Total Admit-ted	Trans. from Class	Trans. to Class	Left	Reg. end of Month	Total Reg. (Gross)	Total Report-ed Left	Total Tempor-arily Discon.	Total Pre-sent	Total Ab-sent	% Left	% Report-ed Left	% Tempor-arily Discon.	% Pre-sent	% Ab-sent	Remarks

APPENDIX Q

DATA ON THE PROFESSIONAL EQUIPMENT OF JEWISH TEACHERS

From the Teachers' Questionnaires sent to the teachers in the Jewish Schools of New York (See Appendix L, p. 494), some data were obtained with reference to the secular, pedagogic, and Jewish training of the teachers. No conclusions can be derived from these data; first, because the number of cases studied is not sufficient; and second, because these teachers are not typical, representing most probably the best Jewish weekday schools in the city.

Out of the 134 Jewish weekday school teachers who answered our questionnaires, *76 received more than a high school education,* as follows:

13 received from 1 to 2 years' training above the high school
24 received from 2 to 3 years' training above the high school
13 received from 3 to 4 years' training above the high school
18 received from 4 to 5 years' training above the high school
3 received from 5 to 6 years' training above the high school
3 received from 6 to 7 years' training above the high school
2 received from 7 to 8 years' training above the high school

Among the 134 teachers, *84 degrees or diplomas* were reported:

46 high school diplomas or equivalents
3 teachers' diplomas — 2 LL. B.
28 B. A. or B. S. — 5 M. A.

Most of these teachers received their general education in New York schools, reporting the following places as the schools of their instruction:

36 The College of the City of New York
13 Hunter College
14 Columbia University
5 New York University
3 New York Training School for Teachers
2 Brooklyn Polytechnic Institute
1 Barnard College
2 Pennsylvania University
1 Brown University
1 Baltimore City College
5 Russian Gymnasia
3 Gymnasium at Jaffa, Palestine
1 Teachers' Seminary, Jerusalem

An attempt was also made to obtain some information concerning the *pedagogic training* received by Jewish weekday teachers. Of the 134 teachers above mentioned, the following reported as having received some pedagogic training, in the form of courses in education, psychology, etc.:

In General Schools:

20 The College of the City of New York
8 Columbia University
8 Hunter College

3 New York Training School for Teachers
2 Brown University
2 New York University

In Jewish Schools:

15 The Teachers' Institute of the Jewish Theological Seminary, N. Y.
2 Gratz College, Philadelphia
4 Training School, Russia
1 Teachers' Institute, Galicia
1 Gymnasium at Jaffa, Palestine
2 Teachers' Seminary, Jerusalem
7 National Hebrew School, New York (Graduate Course)

The following give the number of years of their pedagogic training:

3 less than 1 year	7 from 3 to 4 years
20 from 1 to 2 years	2 from 4 to 5 years
23 from 2 to 3 years	1 from 5 to 6 years

The validity of these figures is dubious, both in point of accuracy of report and in point of value of training. While a good many of the Jewish teachers, especially in the better weekday schools, receive specific training in pedagogy, this training is not valuable, consisting as it does of a few courses in general psychology and in the principles of education. As yet there are no definite requirements made upon Jewish teachers for pedagogic training.

With regard to the *Jewish knowledge* of teachers, the information gathered is even more difficult to evaluate. It would, of course, be absurd to measure their knowledge in terms of the number of years of instruction which they received: one year's training in a Yeshibah in Russia, or in a school of Palestine, is, from the viewpoint of acquiring Jewish knowledge, worth much more than one year of Jewish schooling in American Talmud Torahs; and similarly, one year in a Talmud Torah or Hebrew school is worth several years of Sunday school work. The following places are reported as the source of Jewish education among the weekday teachers who answered the questionnaires:

American Schools:

38 American Hebrew Schools and Talmud Torahs
3 American Yeshibahs
40 Teachers' Institute of the Jewish Theological Seminary, N. Y.
2 Gratz College, Philadelphia
1 Hebrew Union College, Cincinnati

Foreign Schools:

40 Yeshibahs in Russia
12 Other Eastern European Schools
1 Hebrew School in England
6 Hebrew Schools in Palestine
6 Privately taught

APPENDIX R

DERIVATION AND USE OF SCORE CARD FOR JEWISH TEACHERS

The method of deriving the Teachers' Score Card was as follows: The factors which go to make up the ideal teacher were analyzed in detail,[1] and grouped under five large headings: (1) personality, (2) training, (3) teaching ability, (4) classroom management, and (5) service. These large divisions, together with the chief sub-divisions, (such as physique, character, etc.) were then judged as to the relative value which each would have on the basis of 1,000 points for all of the items. Forty judges were asked to give their estimates of the respective worth of these items. These judges consisted of: (1) Jewish teachers and principals, (2) workers in the Bureau of Jewish Education, and (3) a class of graduate students (non-Jews) in Teachers' College, Columbia University. The median of these judgments was taken as the value used in the score card. Thus "personality" was given by the 40 judges 175 points out of the total of 1,000; "teaching ability," 325 points; "discipline," 70 points; "volunteer service," 30 points, etc.

For the purpose of actual scoring, however, these items were considered too general. They were therefore analyzed further into their elements: such as, appearance, voice, etc. (cf. score card). It would have been desirable to obtain judgments as to the relative worth of these subdivisions also; but the additional probable accuracy to be derived from this further sub-valuation, was not considered worth the labor involved. Instead, the scheme of marking these items was worked out in accordance with the laws underlying the frequency of distribution of merit. From a wide study of the distribution of teachers' marks, Prof. Cattell[2] found that of any group of objects to be evaluated, 10% will be very poor; 20% poor; 40% medium, 20% good, and 10% excellent. We have, therefore, provided ten columns for the practical purposes of scoring: one for "very poor"; two for "poor"; four for "medium," two for good"; and one for "excellent." Thus from 0-10 "very poor," from 10-30 is "poor," from 30-70 is "medium," from 70-90 is "good," and from 90-100 "excellent." If a teacher is to be rated as "poor—almost-medium," the mark should be placed in the 20-30 column; if "medium—almost-good," it is to be placed in the 60-70 column, etc.

In scoring any teacher, therefore, the score card should be used together with the evaluations of the larger items, and the standing of the teacher in each sub-item is to be indicated by an X in the particular column estimated. The scores of the sub-items under each head should then be averaged, in order to obtain the rating of the teacher in that particular factor of his work. Thus, if it is desired to find out the efficiency of the

---

[1] See below pp. 526-535. In the score card (see Part II, Chapter 9, opposite p. 300) the arrangement of items differs slightly from that used in the standards.

[2] J. McK. Cattell: "Examinations, Grades and Credits," Popular Science Monthly: LXVI; 367.

teacher in the ''technique of teaching'' (item III-B of Score Card), it is necessary to average the marks given for: ''skill in motivation; the use of apperceptive mass; organization of lesson; provision for use of knowledge; variation in use of teaching types; and skill in the use of questioning, narration, recitation, review and examination, assignment and study,'' (cf. score card). In the particular illustration used in the score card,[3] the teacher obtained an average of ''medium—almost good,'' 60-70% of the full 90 points allotted for perfect work in the ''technique of teaching.'' In other words, that teacher is credited with 58.5 points for that item. Similarly all the other items can be marked.

It is possible to *diagram* this analysis of the efficiency of the teacher.[4] We shall call the diagram which is here suggested a ''*Valugram,*'' because it shows the worth of the teacher in each factor of his work. The accompanying chart indicates how this may be done. If we make any horizontal line stand for the total value of the teacher, we can indicate the particular factors (personality, training, etc.) by perpendicular lines of proportionate length. If then we make these lines horizontal in turn, we can again subdivide them in the same way for each of their sub-headings. By placing alongside of these standard lines thinner ones indicating the value of the teacher in each of the items, his particular strength and weakness can be seen at a glance. In this manner it is possible to diagram the work not only of one teacher, but of the staff of an entire school, for comparative purposes.

Accompanying the score card there should be a *written definition* of the terms and an explanation of the *standards* for each item. For practical purposes it may be best for each school principal to set up his *own* standards in co-operation with his teachers. Only for marking teachers of several schools need a central set of standards be used. Such a set of standards for judging the efficiency and merit of teachers in Jewish weekday schools is here suggested. It is only tentative and needs much elaboration and improvement. In scoring teachers it must, of course, be borne in mind that for most of the qualifications suggested there is a *minimum*, below which no teacher should fall no matter how high his attainments in other qualifications; for example, a teacher must have a minimum amount of knowledge no matter how nice a person he may be otherwise.

I. PERSONALITY

Ref: Palmer: ''The Ideal Teacher''; White: ''School Management,'' pp. 17-48; Fitch: ''Lectures on Teaching,'' ch. I; Seely: ''New School Management,'' ch. I and II; Milner: ''The Teacher,'' chaps. IV-VIII.

A. PHYSIQUE

1. Appearance:

[3] Cf. Score Card, opp. p. 300. This illustration is an actual case, representing the estimate of a Jewish school principal of one of his best teachers.

[4] For comparison with other schemes of diagramming scores, cf. School and Society, Dec. 29th, 1917.

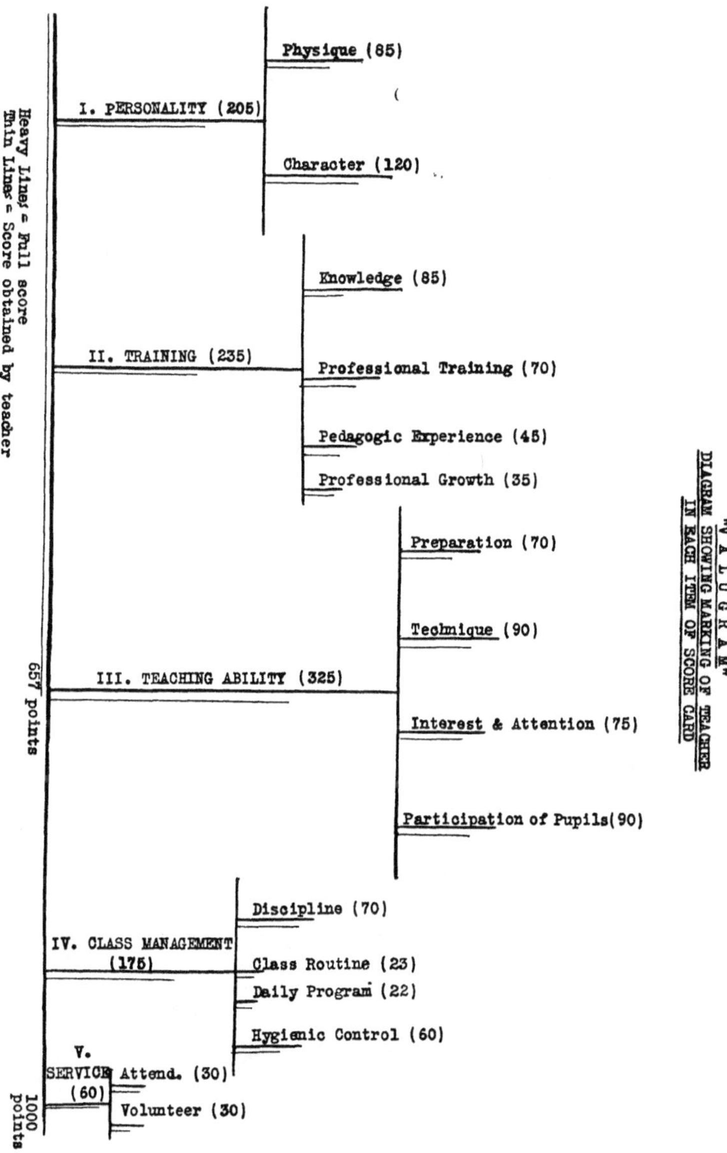
"V A L U G R A M"
DIAGRAM SHOWING MARKING OF TEACHER
IN EACH ITEM OF SCORE CARD
Heavy Lines = Full score
Thin Lines = Score obtained by teacher
I. PERSONALITY (205)
Physique (85)
Character (120)
II. TRAINING (235)
Knowledge (85)
Professional Training (70)
Pedagogic Experience (45)
Professional Growth (35)
III. TEACHING ABILITY (325)
Preparation (70)
Technique (90)
Interest & Attention (75)
Participation of Pupils(90)
657 points
IV. CLASS MANAGEMENT (175)
Discipline (70)
Class Routine (23)
Daily Program (22)
Hygienic Control (60)
V. SERVICE (60)
Attend. (30)
Volunteer (30)
1000 points

- *a* Features: pleasing, expressive, adaptable.
- *b* Stature: normal.
- *c* Dress: neat and well kept.

2. Voice and Speech:
   - *a* Quality: soft, low pitched and well modulated.
   - *b* Force: clear, distinct, sufficiently loud to be heard by all pupils in room.

3. Sight and Hearing:
   - *a* Normal eyesight and hearing.
   - *b* Sense alertness; eye should have "governing power."

4. Health:
   - *a* General well-being: vigor, buoyancy, strength, endurance.
   - *b* Sound constitution: absence of organic defects or chronic maladies.
   - *c* Freedom from nervousness, and frequent headaches.

B. Character

1. Temperament:
   - *a* Reverence
   - *b* Loyalty and love for the Jewish people, its ideals and culture.
   - *c* Optimism and cheerfulness.
   - *d* Persistence.
   - *e* Self-control.
   - *f* Sense of humor.

2. Bearing: (manner)
   - *a* Dignity, refinement.
   - *b* Confidence.
   - *c* Enthusiasm.

3. Relation to Principal:
   - *a* Co-operation, friendliness.
   - *b* Frankness, Courage.

4 Relation to Pupils:
   - *a* Love, sympathy with child life.
   - *b* Patience.
   - *c* Tact.
   - *d* Sense of justice, fairness.
   - *e* Understanding of individual pupils; (knowledge of home conditions, especially of weaker pupils).

5. Relation to Work:
   - *a* Devotion, sincerity.
   - *b* Reliability, punctuality, responsibility.
   - *c* Initiative, progressiveness.
   - *d* Thoroughness, industry.
   - *e* System, neatness.
   - *f* Professional attitude (profession vs. job), attitude of "student."

II. Training

Ref: Colgrove: "The Teacher and the School," chaps. I-IV; Ruediger: "Agencies for Improving Teachers in Service"; Milner: "The Teacher," chap. III.

A. Knowledge

1. Secular: High School Diploma or Equivalent (minimum).
2. Jewish:

a Specific: Adequate knowledge of the particular subjects which teaches.

b General:

1 Literature

a Bible

1 Knowledge in original
2 Some knowledge of theories of modern Bible criticism.

b Post-Biblical Literature: acquaintance with Apocrypha, Mishna and Talmud, Spanish philosophers and poets, Commentators, Shulchan Aruch, and Modern Hebrew Literature.

2 History

a Knowledge of Jewish political and social history.
b Definite point of view in the interpretation of Jewish history.
c Sympathetic understanding of the social psychology of the Jewish people.

3 Religion:

a Jewish Philosophy and Ethics.

1 Knowledge of general principles and historic significance of ethical and philosophic personalities and movements in Judaism.
2 Point of view in Jewish life.

b Ceremonies and Institutions:

1 Sympathetic knowledge of origin, history and observance.
2 Definite point of view and attitude.

4 Jewish music: Knowledge of better-known folk songs and liturgic responses and chants.

B. Professional Training:

1. Should hold teacher's diploma or certificate; or its equivalent in courses of Psychology, Principles of Education, Methods and Class Management.

C. Pedagogic Experience:

1. Length: two years of class teaching.
2. Kind: under supervision and closely related to present work.

D. Professional Growth:

1. Study:

a Should pursue definite line of study, while in service.
b Should keep in touch with educational thought and activity.
c Should keep in touch with current Jewish life; conditions, thought, and activities.

2. Extra-school Interests:

a Should be affiliated actively with some Jewish work or organization.
b Should be affiliated with some civic work or organization.

III. Teaching Ability

Ref: McMurry: ''Elementary School Standards,'' chaps. I, IV, VII, VIII, XI, and XII; Strayer: ''Brief Course in the Teaching Process;'' Strayer and Norsworthy: ''How to Teach.''

A. Preparation.

1. Subject Matter.

a Should have adequate knowledge of facts presented.
b Should possess rich background of knowledge; confidence.

2. Plan:

a Should keep plan book, (full form for beginners, wider planning for more experienced teachers).

Full form suggested: (not for all lessons or subjects).

1 Purpose of lesson.
2 Outline of subject matter.
3 Method of treatment.
4 Development: leading or pivotal questions.
5 Provision for drill, summaries, reviews and assignment.
6 References and illustrative material to be employed.

3. Illustrative Material:

a Should be sufficient to make lesson as concrete as possible.
b Should be attractive and interesting in form.

B. Technique:

1. Presentation of New Work: (whether fact, problem or model).

a Use of apperceptive mass.
b Organization of lesson.

1 Central aim clearly brought out.
2 Clear sequence and development.

c Proper emphasis of important and difficult points.
d Provision for use by pupils of knowledge presented.

2. Motivation: Should vitalize the lesson by relating it to actual needs and interests of child both in its school and in its out-of-school life.

3. Adherence to Plan:

a Sufficient adherence to plan for proper development of central aim of lesson.

b Adaptability to new situations raised by pupils' questions or changed conditions.

4. Skill in Teaching Process: (Ref: Earhart: "Types of Teaching," chapters V-XV: Thorndike: "Education," Chapters IX-X).

a Variety in Use of Teaching Types: No single teaching type should be rigidly adhered to; all of the following types should be employed wherever necessary:

1 Narration, exposition or description.
2 Questioning.
3 Drill and practice.
4 Recitation.
5 Review and examination.
6 Assignment and study.

b Skill in Use of Teaching Types:

The following are suggested standards in the various types of teaching:

1 Questioning: (Ref: Fitch: "Art of Questioning"; Betts: "The Recitation," chap. III; De Garmo: "Interest and Education," chap. XIV).

Quality:

a Should stimulate thought on part of child, rather than memory or yes-and-no answers.

b Should be definite, and pertinent to lesson.

c Should provoke questions on part of child.

Form:

a Should be clearly and correctly worded.

b Should not be leading or suggestive of answer.

c Should be few in number, rather than many rapid-fire questions.

d Should be striking, interesting in form.

e Should not be repeated, as a rule, except for emphasis.

Distribution:

a Should question all children, not bright ones alone.

b Should be put to whole class, rather than to individual previously named.

Skill with Answers:

a When possible should utilize child's answer.

b Should criticize wrong answers constructively, making child realize wherein these are false.

c Should not repeat verbatim pupil's answers.

2 Narration; Exposition or Description:

a Should proceed clearly and smoothly.
b Should be vivid; proper use of details.
c Should be delivered with enthusiasm and conviction.
d Language should be carefully chosen.

3 Recitation: (Ref. Betts: "The Recitation," chaps. I, II, IV).

Quality:

a Should not be mere hearing of lesson; should supplement and illustrate.
b Where lesson permits, should test thought and power of pupil rather than text.
c Care should be taken that pupils' recitation is accurate in content and adequate in form.

Form:

a Recitation should not be meant for individual reciting only; whole class should be made to feel responsibility.
b No regular order of calling upon to recite should be followed.

5 Drill and Practice:

a Drill should be motivated, so that pupils can see its necessity.
b Pupils should have correct idea of thing to be done.
c Maximum attention should be obtained throughout repetition.
d Special emphasis should be laid on difficult parts or forms.
e Aim should be first accuracy, then facility and rapidity.
f Form should be varied so as not to become monotonous.
g Should not be prolonged to the point of fatigue.
h Drill should be repeated from time to time with gradually lengthened intervals between drills.

5 Review and Examination:

a Should be new view or new relationship of known facts, rather than mere recall.
b Should have definite purpose, which should be clear to the pupils as well as to the teacher.
c Should be used frequently; either as part of lesson or as separate lesson.
d Results of review or test should be analyzed by teacher for discovering weakness in teaching.

6 Assignment and Study: (Ref. McMurry: "How to Study," chap. II; Earhart: "Training Children to Study," chap. VIII; Betts: "The Recitation," chap. V).

a Teacher should, wherever possible, aim to give pupils power to study for themselves.

b Definite time should be set aside for assignment and for study.

c Teacher should give specific purpose for studying.

d Teacher should prepare for obstacles likely to be met.

e When necessary teacher should suggest method of working and collateral sources and references.

f Assignment by pages alone should not be employed.

C. Interest and Attention.

Ref. Dewey: "Interest and Effort"; De Garmo: "Interest and Education," chaps. I-VIII; Thorndike: "Principles of Teaching, chap. V: Colvin: "Learning Process," XVII and XIX.

1. Amount: Should be continuous and concentrated.

2. Kind:

a Interest should be active *i.e.*, the stimulus should be some compelling vital motive.

Grades of Interest:

1 Active: with stimulus in motivation.

2 Passive: with stimulus in teacher's personality.

3 Artificial: with stimulus in marks, prizes, etc.

b Attention should be spontaneous and not forced, involuntary rather than voluntary.

D. Participation of Pupils.

Ref. Dewey: "School and Society," chap. II; "Moral Principles of Education," chap. III.

a Expression: As much opportunity should be given to the pupils to express themselves as possible. Children should do most of the talking.

b Initiative: Pupils should be encouraged to suggest, to question, and to do independent work.

c Co-operation: Pupils should be encouraged to question and to help each other in their work.

IV. Class Management

Ref. Bagley: "Class Management."

A. Discipline.

Ref. Bagley: "School Discipline," Morehouse: "Discipline of the School;" Seely: "New School Management," chap. VIII; Perry: "Discipline as a School Problem."

1. Class Spirit:

a Condition in the room should be that of orderly, quiet, busy work.

b Attitude of pupils should be respectful, pleasant, and cooperative.

c Seating arrangement should be such that most of the pupils can see each other.

2. Corrective Discipline:

a Attitude of the teacher in matters of discipline should be: Persistent, courageous, tactful.
b Authority of the teacher in cases of discipline should be secure.
c Punishments should conform to following standards:

1 Should be reformative and corrective rather than punitive.

2 Should involve the pupil's knowledge of the offense and whenever possible the need for readjustment between the teacher and himself.

3 Where possible, should be closely associated with the offense in time and in kind.

4 Should reach individual rather than group.

5 Should interfere as little as possible with work of pupils and class.

6 Should be the least that is sufficient to accomplish the desired end.

Punishment in rank of merit and severity are:

a Reproof and reprimand.
b Consulting parents.
c Deprivation: demerit, detention, isolation.
d Suspension: private.
e Public reprimand or suspension.
f Corporal punishment.
g Expulsion

B. Class Routine.

1. Movements in classroom: (lines going to blackboard, dismissals, etc.)

a Order, system, speed.
b As much freedom as is compatible with good order.

2. Passing of books, clothing, etc. should be mechanized.

C. Daily Program.

1. Scope: Daily program should provide explicitly and systematically for instruction in all subjects required by curriculum.

2. Arrangement: There should be equitable balance between habit-forming and inspirational subjects.

3. Periods: There should be frequent change of periods.

Standard: Length of periods generally adopted:

Children 7 to 10 years old—15-20 minutes.
" 11 " 12 " " 25 "
" 12 " 13 " " 30 "

4. Recess: Program should provide for recess or setting-up exercise. (Medical Standard for two-hour session is: recess of 10 minutes; where session shorter than two hours, three-minute setting up exercise with open windows should be provided at change of periods.)

D. Control of Hygienic Conditions.

Ref. Hoag: "Health Index of Children;" Shaw: "School Hygiene," chaps. VIII-XII; Dresslar: "School Hygiene," chaps. X-XXI; Terman: "Hygiene of the School Child;" Rapeer: "Health Supervision in the Schools."

1. Posture:
   a General: Teacher should insure normal erect posture of pupils, body firmly supported, head and shoulders erect.
   b Writing: Child should sit with weight equally distributed, shoulders parallel to edge of desk, back erect.
2. Eye and Ear strain:
   a Paper and books should be held at least 12 inches away from eyes.
   b Shades should be manipulated so that at no time does glare fall upon blackboard or upon objects handled by teacher.
   c Seating arrangement should be such that each child can easily see and hear everything that is taking place, without strain. For this purpose the teacher should test pupils upon entrance into class by whisper ear test, and by any simple eye test.
   d Children should not be required to look closely at books or writing for more than 20-25 minutes. Change of tension should be provided.
3. Ventilation.
   a Teacher should control windows where there is no artificial ventilation, so as to get complete change of air every 20-25 minutes. Some part of window should be open constantly.
   b Short breathing exercises should be provided in which all windows should be opened for a few minutes.
4. Temperature:
   a The temperature of the room should be kept at 67° F.
   b Variation never more than 2 degrees.
5. Sanitation:
   a Clean blackboards, desks and floors.
   b Provision for pencil sharpening, waste paper, etc.
   c Regular habits should be insisted on.

V. Service

A. Attendance.

1. Should not be absent more than 2.5% of sessions.
2. Should be regularly in his room 20 minutes before beginning of session.

B. Volunteer Service.

Teacher should participate during the school year in at least one volunteer activity of any of the following classes:

I. Administrative: Lines, special clerical work.

2. Educative: Volunteer classes, clubs, synagogue service, library.

3. Social: Playground, entertainment and plays, home visiting.

APPENDIX S

MEASURING THE ACHIEVEMENT OF PUPILS IN THE JEWISH SCHOOLS

To what extent are the subjects of study in the curricula of the various schools learned by the pupils? How much do the graduates of the Jewish schools really know of Hebrew, History, Jewish Literature, etc.? The answers to these questions cannot be forthcoming at present, because of the fact that there are as yet no means of objectively measuring the knowledge and the achievement of Jewish school children. It is useless to say that the child "knows Hebrew," or "is familiar with Jewish institutions," or "has a knowledge of the Bible," etc. These phrases do not mean the same to all. Our judgments must necessarily be subjective, depending upon our standards of knowledge. It is no more instructive to say that the pupils "went through the Bible," or "are up to the modern period of Jewish history," or "can read easy Hebrew prose," etc. These phrases are general "blanket terms," capable of covering a multitude of pedagogic shortcomings. Objective tests and standards are needed, whereby it may be possible to know exactly how much of a particular study has been acquired by a particular child, or by a class of children.

In general education, one of the most important educational movements during the last decade has been in this direction of measuring educational products scientifically. A number of objective tests or "scales" have been devised for measuring the achievement of children in such subjects as handwriting, composition, arithmetic, spelling, reading, and other school subjects.[1] Educators are now at work on similar scales in history, literature and the other branches of the public school curriculum. Because of these scales, schoolmen are now no longer confined to such general statements as that a pupil "writes poorly or well," or "is proficient in arithmetic." A pupil's achievement is "measured" by saying that he writes as well as, let us say, quality 14 on the *Thorndike Handwriting Scale*, or that he can perform correctly so many arithmetical operations

---

[1] For a practical summary of the scales so far developed, see Chapman and Rush: "Scientific Measurement of Classroom Products."

and examples of the *Curtis Arithmetic Tests* or of the *Woody Scale in Arithmetic.* These are but the mere beginnings of the scientific measurement of educational achievement of pupils. Some of the more important school subjects, and particularly the more elusive educational products in terms of character, such as initiative, sense of proportion, grasp, etc., still evade the measuring rod of educators. But strong efforts are being made to bring these also within the focus of scientific measurement.

In Jewish education this movement has scarcely made itself felt. The transition from the mediaeval stages of educational management to modern pedagogic treatment has been very rapid; but as yet the struggle is in terms of the more crude and fundamental issues of organization and management. It can hardly be expected that Jewish educational students, of whom there are but a handful in the entire country, should have had the opportunity to turn their attention in this direction. One such attempt has been made, however, and in spite of its evident shortcomings, it is presented here as an indication of what may be done in this field by Jewish educators.

In 1916, Mr. Meir Isaacs, at that time principal of one of the schools conducted by the Bureau of Jewish Education, undertook to test objectively the relative merits of two methods of teaching the mechanics of Hebrew reading. As opposed to the ordinary alphabetical method, whereby the children are first taught the letters of the alphabet, and then proceed to the reading of syllables and words mechanically, Mr. Isaacs proposed what he called the "liturgic" method, or "singing" method. This consists of first teaching the children by rote some very simple and familiar synagogue melody, such as the "En Kelohenu" or the "Sh'ma Yisroel," and then instructing them in reading the words of that song phonetically. The schools of the Bureau of Jewish Education undertook to experiment with this method for some time, and Mr. Isaacs felt that an objective means was needed for measuring the relative achievement of pupils in the mechanics of Hebrew reading by both methods.

For this purpose he used a passage from the regular prayer book of the pupils, which he printed on special sheets. Together with an assistant, he selected at random ten pupils from every class in four of the Intermediate Schools for Jewish girls, and in four of the Hebrew Preparatory Schools. Each child read for him this passage individually, from its own prayer book, while the examiner marked on the special sheet the reading elements (letters and vowels) which the child misread. At the end of two minutes, the child was told to stop. The number of letters and vowels read was counted, and deductions were made for errors. The following table shows the average scores for the various grades of the Intermediate Schools, and of the Preparatory Schools:[2]

[2] It should be borne in mind that the pupils in the Preparatory Schools are specially selected girls who are given intensive training, with the ultimate purpose of preparing them to enter the Training School for Jewish teachers.

GRADES	Reading Elements (Letters, Vowels, Etc.) Correctly read by average pupil in 2 minutes	
	Intermediate Schools	Preparatory Schools
1-A	128	241
1-B	255	402
2-A	324	497
2-B	443	756
3-A	563	714
3-B	570	812

The number of cases studied here does not warrant generalization. But the method used is interesting. It is evident that crude as this study is, it offers the *beginning* of an objective means of measuring the ability of children to read Hebrew. Thus, if we take the preparatory grades as nearer to the situation which obtains in the boys' schools of the city,[3] it may be said that a child who reads less than 240 letters and vowels correctly in two minutes, does as well as the average student of the 1-A grade; a child who can read 402 letters and vowels correctly in two minutes, does as well as the average student of the 1-B grade, etc. In testing a school, therefore, the results need not be stated in statements like "the pupils know how to read well," or "fairly well," or "poorly," but it can actually be said that in that school the average 2-A child reads so many letters and vowels correctly per minute; the average 3-B pupil so many letters and vowels, etc. Thus, if we take three of the Preparatory Schools tested, the results may be stated as follows:

GRADE	SCHOOLS			AVERAGE
	A	B	C	
1-A	260	233	134	209
1-B	392	411	...	402
2-A	513	490	471	491
2-B	756	714	550	673
3-A	...	808	620	714
3-B	801	898	812	837
Average	544	592	513	554

It is seen that Schools A and B have done the best work in this subject, whereas School C is a good deal below the average. Moreover, as regards

[3] Most of the Talmud Torahs give more hours of instruction per class than do the Preparatory Schools.

the lower grades, School A seems to be doing better work than School B, which would imply that the work in Hebrew reading in that school has been improving markedly.

Again, let it be repeated, that it is not the intention to generalize from these results. The study merely indicates the method of approach in scientific measurement. What is needed to make the particular table, recorded above, into a *scale* for the mechanics of Hebrew reading, is to test many thousands of cases with many passages of Hebrew, so as to be able to establish a "norm" or a standard for the various schools. Very much more difficult will it be to develop similar objective tests in Appreciative Reading, Hebrew Literature, History, Jewish Music and Religion. For adequate testing of each of these branches, many objective tests would be needed, each dealing with one element of the subject.

APPENDIX T

PROGRAM OF THE CENTRAL JEWISH INSTITUTE

The following program of activities for the month of December, 1917, (when this was written), illustrates the general scope of the Community School Center. While to be sure some of the activities mentioned do not recur every month, and other activities are peculiar to this institution, nevertheless, the program does indicate the lines along which the modern Jewish school centers are trying to develop:

I. Classes of the Central Jewish Institute

A. Talmud Torah

Register—507 pupils. 15 graded classes.

Boys' Classes: Afternoons: Monday, Tuesday, Wednesday and Thursday.
Girls' Classes: Sunday mornings, Tuesday and Thursday afternoons.

B. Special Classes

Advanced Hebrew and History—High School Boys and Girls.
Elementary Hebrew and History—High School Girls.
Discussion Group in Jewish Questions—High School Boys.
Jewish Ceremonies and Bible for Young Women—Monday evenings.
Classes in Piano at nominal rates—Monday and Tuesday afternoons.
Special Bar Mitzvah Class—Every evening but Friday.

II. Classes Conducted by Educational Agencies of the Community

A. The Jewish Communal School (Lectures)

Religious Education ....Monday afternoon
Correctional Work ....Tuesday afternoon
Administration of Communal Institutions ....Tuesday afternoon
Work of the Y. M. H. and Kindred Associations....Wednesday afternoon

The Social Care of the Sick......................Wednesday afternoon
Principles of Relief Work.......................Thursday afternoon
Extension Education ....Thursday afternoon

B. The Board of Education (public schools)

Illustrated Public Lectures.......................Wednesday evening
English to Foreigners.........Monday, Tuesday and Wednesday evening

C. The Institute of Musical Art.

Piano Classes...................Monday, Thursday and Friday evening

D. The Guild for the Jewish Blind.

Religious Class.....................................Sunday mornings

III. The League of the Jewish Youth

Local Council ....1st and 3rd Sundays
General Council..............................Last Sunday of Month
Organizers' Training Camp..................................Tuesday
Camp Meetings (Girls and Boys):

1. Juniors ....Wednesdays or Sundays
2. Intermediates ....Wednesdays or Sundays
3. Seniors ....Wednesdays

Festival Clubs (Girls and Boys):

1. Choir, Senior ....Tuesday
2. Art (all ranks)..................................Wednesday
3. Institute Players, Senior...........................Sunday
4. Dramatic, Senior and Intermediate.......................Sunday
5. Dancing, Intermediate and Junior.....................Thursday

IV. The Circle of Jewish Children

A. Festival Clubs (Girls and Boys):

Choir: 1. Junior ....Sunday
2. Intermediate ....Sunday
Dramatic: 1. Junior ....Monday
2. Senior ....Wednesday
Dancing (Girls): 1. Junior ....Wednesday
2. Intermediate ....Wednesday

B. Hadassah Club ....Wednesday

C. Bezalel Clubs ....Sunday

V. Club Events

Tableau and Dance...............................Topaz Social Club
Menorah Smoker...........................N. Y. University Students
Entertainment and Dance.........................Daughters of Israel
Convention ....Young Judea

Dance ....Young Judea
Entertainment and Dance...........................All C. J. I. Clubs

VI. Jewish Communal Organizations Meeting Regularly at the Central Jewish Institute

City Council of the League of the Jewish Youth
Collegiate Zionist League
Jewish Teachers' Association
Hamizpah
Jewish Welfare Board

VII. Chanukah Celebrations

Hadassah Chanukah Evening
The Circle of Jewish Children
Children of the Talmud Torah
Collegiate Zionist League
Parents' Mass Meeting
League of the Jewish Youth

VIII. Religious Services

Children's Services.........................Friday evening at Sundown
Children's Services.....................Sabbath Afternoon at 3 o'clock
Adult Services.............Daily and Sabbaths, mornings, afternoons and evenings (in the adjoining synagogue building)

IX. Governing and Auxiliary Bodies

Board of Directors
Women's Auxiliary
Co-workers' League

BIBLIOGRAPHY

BIBLIOGRAPHY*

I. SOURCES FOR THE STUDY OF JEWISH EDUCATION IN NEW YORK CITY

A. Educational Works

1. PUBLICATIONS OF INSTITUTIONS AND PERIODICALS:

Bureau of Jewish Education. Director, S. Benderly. Publications:

——Bulletin No. 1, October, 1910.

——The problem of Jewish education in New York, 1911.

——A Survey of the financial status of the Jewish religious schools of New York City; with full data of the eight largest Talmud Torahs. 1911.

——Aims and activities of the Bureau of Education. 1912.

——A brief survey of thirty-one conferences held by Talmud Torah principals in New York, 1912. Reported by Israel Konowitz.
Hebrew and English.

——The Gary plan and Jewish education. Report. (Jewish Teacher, vol. 1, pp. 41-47, 1916.)

——Annual reports, 1910 to date, incorporated in the annual reports of the Kehillah; see Section B.

Downtown Talmud Torah. Annual report, 1912.

Educational Alliance. Souvenir book of fair. 1895.

——Fair Journal. 1895.

——Annual reports, 1896—date.

Emanu-El, Temple, Religious School. Stern, Myer: The rise and progress of Reform Judaism, embracing a history of Temple Emanu-El. 1895.
Passim.

Etz Chaim, Yeshibath. Minutes, 1887-1915.
Hebrew Ms. at the Rabbinical College.

Federation for the Support of Jewish Philanthropic Societies. Report of Special Committee of Seven. May 1917.
On the proposal to admit the Jewish religious schools.

Harlem Hebrew Educational Institute of the Uptown Talmud Torah.

——Annual reports, 1910-1915.

* The place of publication is New York, except when otherwise stated.

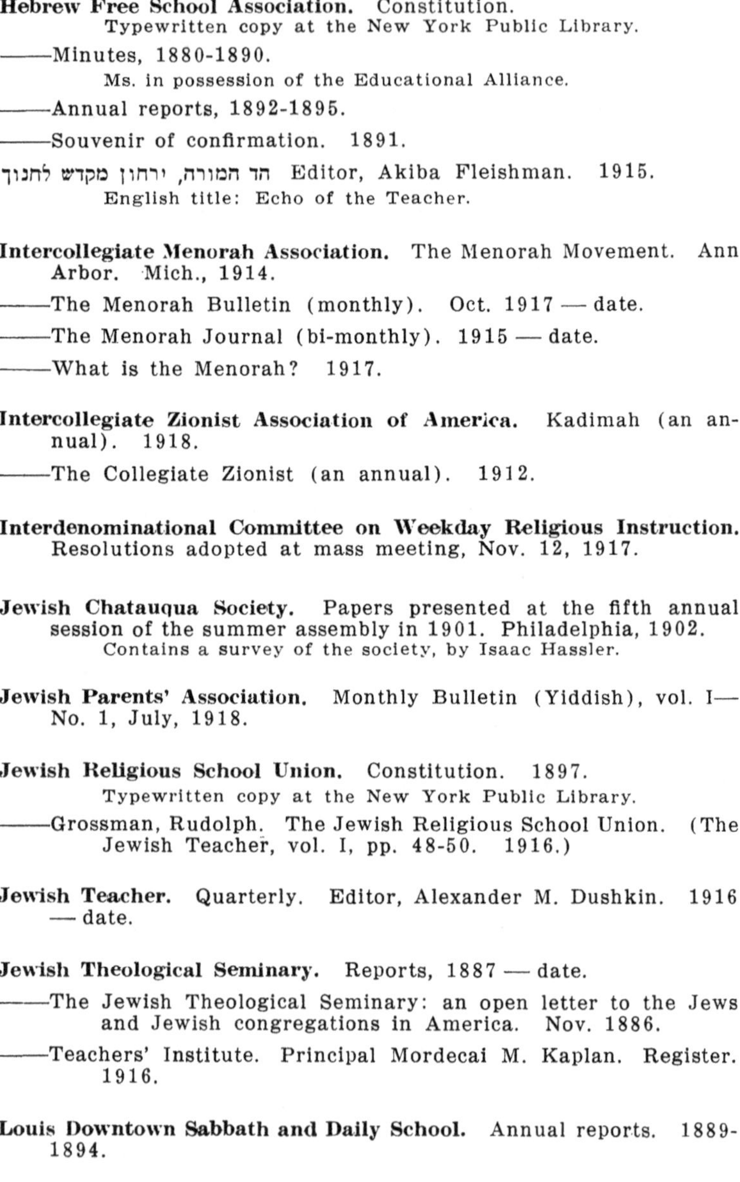

Hebrew Free School Association. Constitution.
Typewritten copy at the New York Public Library.

——Minutes, 1880-1890.
Ms. in possession of the Educational Alliance.

——Annual reports, 1892-1895.

——Souvenir of confirmation. 1891.

הד המורה, ירחון מקדש לחנוך Editor, Akiba Fleishman. 1915.
English title: Echo of the Teacher.

Intercollegiate Menorah Association. The Menorah Movement. Ann Arbor. Mich., 1914.

——The Menorah Bulletin (monthly). Oct. 1917 — date.

——The Menorah Journal (bi-monthly). 1915 — date.

——What is the Menorah? 1917.

Intercollegiate Zionist Association of America. Kadimah (an annual). 1918.

——The Collegiate Zionist (an annual). 1912.

Interdenominational Committee on Weekday Religious Instruction. Resolutions adopted at mass meeting, Nov. 12, 1917.

Jewish Chatauqua Society. Papers presented at the fifth annual session of the summer assembly in 1901. Philadelphia, 1902.
Contains a survey of the society, by Isaac Hassler.

Jewish Parents' Association. Monthly Bulletin (Yiddish), vol. I— No. 1, July, 1918.

Jewish Religious School Union. Constitution. 1897.
Typewritten copy at the New York Public Library.

——Grossman, Rudolph. The Jewish Religious School Union. (The Jewish Teacher, vol. I, pp. 48-50. 1916.)

Jewish Teacher. Quarterly. Editor, Alexander M. Dushkin. 1916 — date.

Jewish Theological Seminary. Reports, 1887 — date.

——The Jewish Theological Seminary: an open letter to the Jews and Jewish congregations in America. Nov. 1886.

——Teachers' Institute. Principal Mordecai M. Kaplan. Register. 1916.

Louis Downtown Sabbath and Daily School. Annual reports. 1889-1894.

Machzike Talmud Torah. Constitution. 1887.

——Minutes, 1883-1918.
Yiddish Ms.

Mizrachi Teachers' Institute. Principal Meyer Waxman. Register. 1918/1919. Hebrew and English.

——Waxman, Meyer. The Mizrachi Teachers' Institute. (Jewish Teacher, vol. I. pp. 241-244. 1917)

Montefiore Talmud Torah. Souvenir and membership book. 1905.

National Hebrew School. School Journal. 1910-1912.

Rabbi Jacob Joseph School. פנקס 1901-1904.
Hebrew Ms.

——Constitution; ca. 1907.

——Rabbi Jacob Joseph School: its high aims and ideals; ca. 1909.

School for Jewish Communal Work. Announcement. 1916-1917.

Shearith Israel, Congregation, Schools. Minutes of the congregation. 1730-1854. American Jewish Historical Society. Publications, vol. 21: The Lyons Collection vol. 1. 1913.

(The second volume of this collection is in process of publication. Extracts from the minutes concerning the religious school will also be found supra, appendix A.)

——Pool, David de Sola. The earliest Jewish religious school in America. (Jewish Teacher, vol. 1, pp. 161-166. 1917.)

Union of American Hebrew Congregations. Department of Synagog and School Extension. Survey of Jewish education in the Bronx, 1916.

Young Judea. Annual. 1917.

——Leaders' Bulletins. 1916-1918.

2. WRITINGS OF INDIVIDUAL AUTHORS:

Benderly, S. Present status of Jewish religious education in New York. (Jewish Communal Register. 1917/1918, pp. 349-365.)
See also Bureau of Education publications in Section I-A.

Berkson, Isaac B. A system of Jewish education for girls. (Jewish Teacher, vol. 1, pp. 95-112. 1917.)

Dushkin, Alexander M. Notes on Jewish educational agencies in New York. (Jewish Communal Register, 1917/1918. pp. 367-463.)

Friedlaender, Israel. The problem of Jewish education in America and the Bureau of Education of the Jewish Community of New York City. (U. S. Commissioner of Education. Report for the year ended June 30, 1913, vol. 1, pp. 365-393. Washington, 1914.)

Greenstone, Julius, H. Jewish education in America. (American Jewish Year Book, 5675. 1914/1915, pp. 90-127. 1914.)

——The Talmud Torah in America. (Jewish Teacher, vol. 1, pp. 28-34. 1916)

Hurwitz, Solomon T. H. The Jewish parochial school. (Jewish Teacher, vol. 1, pp. 211-215. 1917.)

Kohler, Max J. and Sulzberger, Cyrus L. New York (Jewish Encyclopedia, vol. 9, pp. 259-289. 1905.)

Konowitz, Israel. מצב החנוך העברי באמריקה.
(לוח אחיעבר) vol. 1, pp. 39-62. 1918.)
See also Bureau of Education publications in Section I-A.

Lehmann, Eugene H. Jewish religious education. (Encyclopedia of Sunday schools and religious education, vol. 2, p. 587. 1915.)

Lieberman, H. די אידישע ערציהונג אין אַמעריקאַ
Zweite geänderte Auflage, 1916.
——די אידישע רעליגיאָן אין דער נאַציאָנאַל־ראַדיקאַלער ערציהונג. 1915.

Philipson, David. The reform movement in Judaism. 1907.

——Max Lilienthal. 1915.

Richman, Julia. The Jewish sunday school movement in the United States. (Jewish Quarterly Review, vol. 12, pp. 563-601. 1900.)

B. General Works

American Hebrew. Weekly. 1879 — date.

American Jewish Historical Society. Publications. 1893-1918.
Especially vols. 2, 3, 6, 9, 11, 18 and 21.

American Jewish Year Book. 1899 — date.
Especially the years 5661 and 5668, containing a directory of national and local organizations in the United States.

Asmonean. Weekly, 1849-1858.

Central Conference of American Rabbis. Year books. 1890 — date.

Council of Jewish Women. Proceedings. 1893 — date.

האביב Juvenile magazine. 1915.

התרן Monthly and afterwards weekly. 1913 — date.

Hebrew Standard. Weekly. 1882 — date.

Helpful Thoughts. Juvenile magazine. Edited by Julia Richman. 1894-1906.

Jewish Daily News. Yiddish. 1885 — date.

Jewish Messenger. Weekly. 1857-1902.

Jewish Morning Journal. Yiddish. 1906 — date.

Kehillah (Jewish Community). Annual reports. 1909 — date.

——Jewish communal register. Second edition. 1917/1918.

——The Jewish Community. J. L. Magnes, Address delivered before constituent convention. 1909.

New York City. Department of Health. Weekly bulletin, vol. IV, no. 16. April 17, 1915.

Report on Chedarim.

New York State. Laws. 34th session, vol. VI, pp. 333-334. April 9, 1811.

Subsidy granted to the Polonies Talmud Torah.

Occident. Monthly. Phila., 1843-1869.

Union of American Hebrew Congregations. Proceedings. 1873 — date. Cincinnati, Ohio.

Union League Club. Report. Committee on political reform. Sectarian appropriations of public money and property. Feb. 22, 1872.

Weinberger, Moses. היהודים והיהדות בנויורק 1887

English title: The Jews and Judaism in New York.

Young Israel. An illustrated monthly magazine for young people. Edited by Louis Schnabel. 1871-1876.

II. EDUCATIONAL AND OTHER WORKS REFERRED TO IN THE TEXT *

Achad Ha'am (Asher Ginzberg). על פרשת דרכים 4 vols. Berlin, 1903-1913.

——Selected Essays. Translation by L. Simon. Phila., 1912.

Adler, Felix. Moral instruction of children. 1905.

——A vision of New York as the democratic metropolis. 1916.

Athearn, C. W. Religious education and American democracy. Boston, 1917.

Ayres, L. P. Laggards in our schools. 1913.

——The Cleveland school survey. School buildings and Equipment Cleveland, 1916.

——The Cleveland school survey. Summary volume. Cleveland, 1917.

Bagley, W. Classroom management. 1907.

Bard, H. E. The city school district. 1909.

Benderly, S. The fundamental elements in the solution of the problem of Jewish education, (Jewish Teacher, vol. 1, pp. 17-27. 1916.)

——Can a system of Jewish education in America be self-supporting? (ibid. pp. 204-219. 1917.)

Berkson, Isaac B. The community school center. (Jewish Teacher, vol. 1, pp. 224-234. 1917.)

Boyce, A. C. Methods of measuring teacher's efficiency. 14th year book of the National Society for the Study of Education. Part I. Chicago, 1915.

Brill, A. A. Mental adjustment in Jews. (Jewish Teacher, vol. 1, pp. 141-150, 1917.)

Brown, M. C. Sunday school movement in the United States. 1912.

Bruce, Wm. G. School architecture; a handy manual for use of architects and school authorities. Milwaukee, 1910.

Bourgin, Herz. די געשיכטע פון דער אידישער ארבייטער בעוועגונג 1915.

Bourne, R. S. Trans-national America. Atlantic Monthly. July, 1916.

* The place of publication is New York, except when otherwise stated.

Burns, James A. The Catholic school system in the United States: Its principles, origin and establishment. 1908.

——Growth and development of the Catholic school system in the United States. 1912.

Carnegie Foundation for the Advancement of Teaching. Seventh annual report, 1912.

——Ninth annual report. 1914.

——Twelfth annual report. 1917.

Chalmers, W. The Jews of New York. American Journal of Statistics. July, 1913.

Chapman, J. C. and Rush, G. P. Scientific measurement of classroom products. Boston, 1917.

Coit, Stanton. The soul of America. 1914.

Collier John and Barrows, Edward M. The city where crime is play. 1914.

Cubberley, E. P. Changing conceptions of education. Boston, 1909.

——Public school administration. 1916.

——Educational administration and supervision. 1918.

Daly, C. P. The settlement of Jews in North America. 1893.

Dewey, John. School and society. Chicago, 1900.

——The child and the curriculum. Chicago, 1906.

——Moral principles in education. Boston, 1909.

——Interest and effort in education. 1913.

——Democracy and education. 1916.

——Principles of nationality. Menorah Journal, Sept. 1917.

Dresslar, F. American school houses. Washington, 1911. U. S. Bureau of Education. Bulletin 1910, no. 5.

Dubnow, S. Die grundlagen des national judenthums. Translation, by I. Friedlaender, Berlin, 1905.

Dushkin, Alexander M. The profession of Jewish education. (Menorah Journal, April and June 1917). Also reprint.

Dutton, S. T. and Snedden, D. S. Administration of public education in United States. 1912.

Friedlaender, I. Dunbow's theory of Jewish nationalism. 1905.

Giddings, F. H. Principles of sociology. 1896.

Goodnow, F. J. and Howe, F. C. Report. The organization, status and procedure of the Department of Education of New York City, 1911-1913.

Gould, F. J. Children's book of moral lessons. 4 vols. London, 1905.

——Conduct stories for the moral instruction of children. London, 1910.

——Moral instruction, its theory and practice. London, 1913.

——Syllabus of moral and civic instruction for the elementary schools. London, 1914.

Guthrie, W. N. Uncle Sam and old world conquerors. 1915.

Hanus, P. H. School efficiency a constructive study applied to New York City, 1913.

Herzl, Theodore. Der Judenstaat. Leipzig, 1896.

——The Jewish state. English translation. London, 1896.

Hutchinson, J. H. School costs and school accounting. 1914.

Jewish Year Book. London, 1917.

Joseph, Samuel. Jewish immigration to the United States. 1914.

Kallen, H. M. Democracy vs. the melting pot. The Nation. Feb. 1915.

Kayserling, M. Christopher Columbus and the participation of the Jews in Spanish and Portuguese discoveries. 1894.

Keyes, C. H. Progress through the grades of the city schools. 1911.

Koos, L. V. The fruits of school surveys. School and Society, Jan. 13, 1917.

Laidlaw, Walter. Statistical sources for demographic studies of Greater New York. 1910.

Levin, S. אין מלחמה צייטען 1915.

Linder, Leo J. Jewish students in New York City High Schools. Jewish Daily News. (Tageblatt). Feb. 12, 1918.

Löwe, H. Der Schulchan Aruch. Berlin, 1896.

Morais, H. S. The Jews of Philadelphia. Phila., 1894.

Morehouse, F. M. The discipline of the school. Boston, 1914.

National Education Association. Report of committee on uniform records and reports. U. S. Bureau of Education Bulletin, 1912 no. 3. Washington, 1912.

National Society for the Study of Education. The city school as the community center. Tenth year book. Chicago, 1911.

——Minimum essentials in elementary school subjects. Fourteenth year book. Part I. Chicago, 1911.

——Methods of measuring teacher's efficiency. Fourteenth year book. Part II. Chicago, 1915.

——The measurement of educational products. Seventeenth year book. Bloomington, Ill. 1918.

New York City. Superintendent of schools. Annual reports 1912-1916.

——Director of Bureau of Attendance. Report 1914-1915.

——Elementary school circular No. 1. 1913-1914, issued June 25, 1915.

——Budget of the Board of Education, 1917-1918.

New York State. Laws. Chapter 786 — art. 33A. Sections 865-868. June 8, 1917.

Reorganization of the Department of Education.

Oppenheim, Samuel. The early history of the Jews in New York, 1654-1664. 1909.

Palmer, A. The New York public school. 1905.

Peoples' Institute. Twentieth anniversary year book. 1918.

Perry, A. C. Discipline as a school problem. 1915.

——Management of a city school. 1914.

Prosser, C. A. The teacher and old age. 1913.

Revolutionary Russia. דאָס רעוואָלוציאָנערע רוסלאַנד Jewish Socialist Federation of America. 1917.

Ruediger, W. C. Agencies for improvement of teachers in service. U. S. Bureau of Education. Bulletin 1911, no. 3. Washington. 1911.

Spaulding, F. E. The application of the principles of scientific management. Proceedings National Education Association. 1913.

Strayer, G. D. Age and grade census of schools and colleges. A study of retardation and elimination. U. S. Bureau of Education. Bulletin 1911, no. 5. Washington, 1911.

———Score card for school buildings. (Teachers College bulletin 7th ser. no. 12). 1916.

Theisen, W. W. The city superintendent and the board of education. 1917.

Thorndike, E. L. Elimination of pupils from school. U. S. Bureau of Education Bulletin no. 4. Washington, 1907.

Van Denburg, J. K. Causes of the elimination of students in public secondary schools of New York City. 1911.

Van Sickle, J. H. Provision for exceptional children in public schools. U. S. Bureau of Education. Bulletin 1911, No. 14. Washington, 1911.

Ward, E. J. The social center. 1913.

Webster, Wm. C. Recent centralizing tendencies in state educational administration. 1897.

Wenner, Geo. U. Religious education and the public school; an American problem. 1907.

United States Immigration Commission. Abstract of report on the children of immigrants in schools. Washington, 1911.

United States Federal Census of 1910. Vol. III. Population. Washington, 1911.

Zhitlowsky, Ch. געזאַמעלטע שריפטען (seven volumes). 1912-1917.

III. SELECTED LIST OF TEXT BOOKS *

Current in the Jewish Schools of New York

A. Bible

Bialik, Ch. N. ספורי המקרא Five books. Odessa, 1906-1908.

Bureau of Jewish Education. ספר התלמיד Years 3-4. 1913-1918.

——Bible folders. 1913.

Department of Synagog and School Extension. Union of American Hebrew Congregations. Junior bible stories.

——Primary bible pictures.

Kohn, Eugene. Manual for teaching biblical history. 1917.

Lehman-Kent. Junior bible for Jewish children.

Magilnitzky, J. חומש לבתי ספר ולעם Phila. 1906.

Malachowsky, H. ספורי החומש 1909.

Schneider, M. B. בית הספר (American edition). 1907.

B. Hebrew

Bercus, S. H. and Bregman, H. P. שפת ילדים Odessa, 1911.

Bureau of Jewish Education. ספר התלמיד Years 1-2. 1912-1918.

—— אוצרי Series of pamphlets for home reading. 1918.

——שחרות Juvenile magazine. Monthly. 1916 to date.

Fichman, J. פרקים ראשונים Wilna, 1913.

Fischman, P. L. and Lieberman, M. M. שפה חיה Riga, 1910.

Goldin, H. הזמן 1918.

* The place of publication is New York, except when otherwise stated.

Goldin, H. and Silk, B. עברית (שנה ראשונה שניה ושלישית) 1910.

Krauskopf, J. and Berkowitz, H. The Union Hebrew Readers, (designed for Sabbath schools). Cincinnati, 1897.

Krynski, M. הדבור העברי Warsaw. 1905-1906.

—— ראשית דעת Warsaw, 1906.

—— הסגנון העברי Warsaw. 1909-1912.

Levi, Gerson, B. Beginners' Hebrew Course. Jewish Chautauqua Society. Philadelphia, 1903. (Chautauqua system of Jewish education).

Scharfstein, Z. בן ישראל 1918.

Tawjew, I. H. המכין Warsaw, 1903. American edition, 1905.

C. History

Dubnow, S. קורות העברים (three parts). Warsaw, 1908.

Friedman, D. A. תולדות ישורון 1894.

Harris, M. H. The people of the book; (three parts). 1896.

——A thousand years of Jewish history. 1904.

——History of mediaeval Jews. 1907.

——Modern Jewish history. 1910.

Jawitz, W. דברי הימים לעם ישראל Warsaw, 1892.

Magnus, Lady K. Outline of Jewish history. Philadelphia, 1890.

Rabinowitz, A. S. תולדות עם ישראל Warsaw, 1913.

Scharfstein, Z. הסטוריה לילדים 1916.

D. Music

Goldfarb, S. and I. Friday Evening Melodies. 1918.

——The Jewish Songster. 1917.

Idelson, A. H. ספר השירים Berlin and Jerusalem. 1911.

Pines, N. הזמיר Warsaw, 1905.

E. Religion

Greenstone, J. H. Religion of Israel. Philadelphia, 1902.

——Methods of teaching the Jewish religion. Philadelphia, 1915.

Guttmacher, A. Sabbath School companion.

Joseph, M. Judaism as creed and life. London, 1903.

Mendes, H. P. The Jewish religion ethically presented. 1915.

F. Talmud and Aggadah

Baruch, I. L. אוצר ספרות ישראל Wiena, 1913.

Bialik, Ch. N. and Rawnitzky, I. H. ספר האגדה Odessa, 1912.

Goldman, J. גמרא למתחילים 1917.

Lerner, I. B. כל אגדות ישראל Warsaw and Piotrkow, 1902-1905.

Levin, N. מבוא התלמיד Wiena, 1908.

G. Yiddish

Elbe, Leon. די אידישע שפראך 1914.

Enteen, J. and Elbe, L. פון דעם אידישען קוואל 1916.

Levin, J. די נייע אידישע שול 1916.

H. Current Events

The Ark. Monthly. 1911 —

Jewish Child. Weekly. Published by the Bureau of Jewish Education. 1912 —

Young Judean. Monthly. Published by the Zionist Organization of America. 1909—